# Management and Conservation of Small Populations

Proceedings of a conference
held in Melbourne, Australia
September 26-27, 1989

Edited by Tim W. Clark
and John H. Seebeck

# Contents

# Preface

This volume describes the proceedings of a Conference on the Management and Conservation of Small Populations held at The Royal Melbourne Zoological Gardens, September 26 and 27, 1989. The Conference co-sponsors—the Department of Conservation, Forests and Lands, Victoria, the Zoological Board of Victoria and the Chicago Zoological Society—seek to highlight both the susceptibility to extinction of small populations and the management measures they urgently require. The Conference introduces key concepts and applied tools to manage and restore small populations to viable levels. The extinction process and the host of systematic and random factors and forces that comprise this process are described. This provides a background to understand the concept of population viability, *i.e.* populations of sufficient size, distribution and other characteristics to have a high probability of withstanding foreseeable extinction pressures for at least 100 years. The information needed for reliable scientific understanding of small populations is outlined, including quantitative life history data, population ecology and genetics.

The definition of a 'small' population depends on the life history characteristics of the species, its dispersion properties, and the nature and stability of its habitat. Thus, there is no precise definition of the number at which a species becomes endangered. Tales persist of species 'successfully' restored from the last few individuals, and some people think conservationists have a habit of 'crying wolf'. Nevertheless, we consider that any vertebrate population of 2,000 or less should be considered small and extremely vulnerable. As Conference participant Bob Lacy said, 'Small is bigger than a lot of people think.'

The Conference uses eight cases to illustrate these concepts and tools. The case of the eastern barred bandicoot, *Perameles gunnii*, is covered in depth. Not only does it represent the host of extinction factors and processes facing taxa worldwide, but it also demonstrates the workings of an ongoing, multidisciplinary, cooperative program that aims to conserve this species on mainland Australia. This program draws on knowledge from biogeography, taxonomy, paleontology, field ecology, population dynamics, behaviour, veterinary medicine and genetics. Although much remains to be learned about bandicoot biology, adequate data exist to permit simulation modelling to estimate the viability of the bandicoot population. Recovery targets of numbers of individuals and populations are then established and used in decision analysis—a group forum using both objective and subjective scientific and management information—to explore and define management options. Management measures are then scheduled and implemented. The other case studies represent special conservation challenges and a range of ideas, problems, considerations and techniques not covered by the bandicoot case.

This volume seeks to promote the essential contribution of population viability analysis, decision analysis and adaptive management in the management and conservation of all small populations. It hopes to demonstrate the benefits of cooperation in the planning, funding and implementing of research and management. There is expertise and commitment in many diverse but pertinent fields, and the urgency and seriousness of the problem demand all the best efforts. This volume also emphasises that, because endangered populations and species are components of ecosystems, it is essential ultimately to manage for ecosystem integrity in both structure and process.

Although we do not want to foster the notion that species conservation can be a 'cookbook' process (and we certainly have no recipes), we believe strongly that success in restoring endangered species demands a valid conceptual framework, knowledge from multidisciplinary sources and the use of certain techniques, *e.g.* modelling population behavior, employing decision analysis, setting targets, establishing and scheduling objectives, assigning accountability, monitoring and managing adaptively. We are also not suggesting that applying these tools will ensure species conservation. On the contrary, building up low species numbers to secure sizes and protecting and expanding habitats are agonizingly complex, uncertain, costly and slow biological challenges. But a concomitant challenge requires conservationists to establish well-designed and managed programs to achieve the goals.

This book of proceedings is designed for several audiences. Firstly, we hope management and conservation professionals currently working on small populations in land and wildlife agencies, zoos and non-governmental conservation organizations will find this volume valuable. An understanding of the concepts and applied tools described here can improve the management of each small population under their stewardship. Secondly, it is targeted for university students at both the graduate and post-graduate levels. These materials can serve as a good introduction to conservation biology and how it is being applied. But not only biology students should find this interesting. Because conservation is not simply a biological problem but an issue reflecting societal goals and involving the full range of government, public and private interests, students of public policy can learn from the development and outcomes of the programs described in these case studies. Thirdly, this volume is targeted for laymen and governmental administrators with little formal grounding in the biological sciences

or 'hands-on' experience, but who have a keen interest in the conservation of biodiversity. The introductory readings, the discussions and conclusions of each paper, the findings of the workshops and the summary are understandable and informative.

The core philosophy of conservation biology, in view of the unprecedented number of life-forms currently threatened with extinction and the many forces threatening them, was advanced by Frankel and Soulé in *Conservation and Evolution* (1981, Cambridge University Press, pp. 78-79,97):

Our goal is to provide a scientifically defensible basis for certain management decisions. In effect, this usually means employing a rough approximation of some critical parameter instead of waiting for the precise theory or information that may never arrive. Such an approach really needs no defense. Conservationists cannot afford the luxury of methodological elegance. We are soldiers in a war and soldiers must be pragmatists. Thus our tenet that crude initiatives based on rough guidelines are better than the paralysis of procrastination induced in some scientists by the fear of inadequate data. To delay the implementation of conservation and management programs until we have a definitive understanding of all complexities of the evolutionary process is analogous to allowing cancer to go untreated until we can prevent it.

Conservationists cannot afford the luxury and excitement of adversary science. The weakness of this parochial style of intellectual progress is that years or decades may pass before a clear resolution is reached and before timid technocrats or politicians decide that action will not bring a storm of criticism. By the turn of the century most options will be closed. It behooves us, therefore, to give serious and humble attention to all points of view and to be willing to compromise.

We agree fervently with this sentiment, that the need is immediate, that—like witnesses to any human catastrophe—we must unleash all our faculties, our skills, and our prerogatives to preserve our planet's biodiversity.

Many people deserve special recognition for their direct assistance in the production of this volume. Denise Casey, Karin Nelson, Elizabeth Fitzgerald, Diane Cavalieri, Cathy Pawlowski, Carol Ann Lauer, and Susan Stokely Rice all laboriously edited the manuscripts and produced the final volume. Brier Gough and Tracey Wylie prepared the cover illustration. Session chairmen Graeme Phipps, Tony Lee, Angus Martin and Bob Warneke provided able management of the various sessions. For their help in facilitating or arranging the Conference, we especially appreciate the assistance and support of Rod Gowans of the Department of Conservation, Forests and Lands; Pat Feilman, Gerry Griffin, Gaye Hamilton and Peter Myroniuk of the Zoological Board of Victoria; and Pam Parker and George Rabb of the Chicago Zoological Society. A special thank you to Cathy Patrick for supporting Denise Casey's editorial assistance and for her continuing interest in conservation of Australian fauna. And to all the other people, too numerous to mention by name, who assisted directly or indirectly, we sincerely thank you.

Finally, we note with gratitude that the Chicago Zoological Society was enabled to publish these proceedings through its Chicago Board of Trade Endangered Species Fund. Thanks to all the donors to this fund.

Editors
*Tim W. Clark*
*John H. Seebeck*

# Opening Speech

*The Honorable Kay Setches, Minister for Conservation, Forests and Lands*

Thank you for your invitation to formally open this conference. A wide variety of wildlife researchers and managers from Australia, the United States of America, and New Zealand have been brought together for this conference to encourage the development of a unified framework for endangered species management and conservation. It is my pleasure to welcome you here today for this important work.

The origin of most of the problems of survival confronting wildlife today rest in the increase in human population. For many species, this has resulted in a change from a large, continuous population to a number of smaller and fragmented populations. As a species becomes more and more fragmented, its chances of survival are lessened. Ultimately, it faces extinction.

The worldwide problem of managing such endangered species is being addressed by many wildlife biologists; the problems certainly are not restricted to one country or continent. New concepts, new technologies, and new tools are being developed for use in concert with traditional methods.

In Australia, we have abundant examples of the destructive process I have outlined, and consequently a large number of wildlife species that are endangered. The eastern barred bandicoot experiences most of the problems confronted by an endangered species and is being used as a model to demonstrate the application of techniques being used to develop a comprehensive conservation strategy.

Following an introductory paper on the causes and consequences of species endangerment, there will be a series of papers concentrating on the eastern barred bandicoot. A review of past and recent studies of the field ecology of the eastern barred bandicoot will demonstrate why population and habitat characteristics need to be known before management of populations or habitat can be carried out. Similarly, without an understanding of the species' behaviour it is not possible to properly plan for the distribution and dispersion of habitat. Genetic research and the derived genetic management are recognised as being of major importance for conservation planning, and the implications, especially for captive breeding, will be discussed. Finally, the veterinary aspects of wild and captive animals are an essential component of any management strategy. Parasites, pesticides and pathogens will affect the potential survival of the bandicoot.

The conference will then examine how this and other information and techniques can be used to coordinate the eastern barred bandicoot recovery strategy being carried out by the Department of Conservation, Forests and Lands. A Statewide strategy has been prepared which includes the establishment of satellite colonies away from Hamilton, and plans for the stabilisation and size increase of the local population.

The procedures used for conservation of the eastern barred bandicoot can be used to support the conservation of endangered species generally. How these and other species can be managed using the suite of techniques available to conservation biologists and wildlife managers will also be discussed to show how the range of techniques now available can be used for small population management. The button wrinklewort (a grassland daisy), the giant Gippsland earthworm, the Eltham copper butterfly, the Australian damselfly, our helmeted honeyeater, the orange-bellied parrot, and Leadbeater's possum are all species that exist as small, fragmented populations.

The contributed papers and the results of the workshops which will follow will be published, and I believe these will form a valuable reference for the future.

Conservation and management of endangered species is a major government commitment under the Flora and Fauna Guarantee and the State Conservation Strategy. The government has already committed substantial funds to research and management of many of the species to be discussed at the conference.

The *Flora and Fauna Guarantee Act* provides a framework for the legal protection of our native species and for a major program of state government and community action. The aim is to ensure that Victoria's native flora and fauna survive, flourish and retain their potential for evolutionary development.

The *Act* provides for native species or biological communities which have been identified as being threatened to be listed. It also allows for the listing of threatening processes that may affect the long-term survival and evolutionary development of plants and animals. When a listing occurs, an action statement must be prepared which details measures for the management of the listed species or biological community or potentially threatening process.

My government has allocated approximately $10 million for flora and fauna work for 1989-1990, with an additional sum of over $5 million for wetlands and associated wildlife. In addition, initiatives and new expenditures on activities clearly aimed at conservation of flora and fauna in this financial year bring the total to over $20 million. This includes allocations for the helmeted honeyeater ($250,000), Leadbeater's possum ($200,000) and funds to complete the purchase of Greens Bush ($8.8 million).

Finally, I would like to acknowledge that the conference is jointly and generously sponsored by the Zoological Board of Victoria and the Chicago Zoological Society together with my Department.

I wish you an interesting and enlightening conference on the conservation and management of small populations.

# Opening Remarks from the Zoological Board
of Victoria

*Patricia Feilman, Zoological Board of Victoria*

It is always exciting to attend a conference that aspires to break new ground or to bring together groups of people with common goals who have not previously had an opportunity to exchange ideas and techniques. I believe this conference meets these criteria very well. Its subject material is, as I understand it, the first attempt in Australia to explore in depth the management of small populations. It certainly has brought together many strata of people involved with the preservation or conservation of wildlife. All have a great deal to contribute and I am sure that this will become apparent over the next two days. We may find that we need to confront the reality of changes we must make culturally and individually in our daily lives to maintain a significant portion of this integral part of our cultures, our biological heritage. As this will be the first time that a number of you will have interacted with zoo personnel, I think it is appropriate if I attempt to define the role which I believe zoos are capable of performing in the wide area of conservation strategy. My remarks apply to our own institution but I believe they also reflect the commitment of other Australasian zoos.

The long-held view of this Board until recently was that a zoo cannot make a direct contribution to conservation. It cannot replace the natural habitat and therefore can only be involved in preservation—the successful breeding of animals. It was considered that the role of the Board rested on its education program, both for children and the general public, by providing the props so that conservation could be understood, and by providing recreational pleasure and enjoyment, and I quote from the former Chairman: 'that the breeding of animals, no matter how successful, in the absence of suitable available natural habitat is not in itself conservation. It is preservation and it may go no further than ensuring the continuation of the species in captivity, removed from its habitat, and therefore precluded from making its potential contribution to evolution which is substantially the basis of conservation.' Many would still agree with these sentiments which, if taken to their ultimate conclusion, suggest that there is virtually no role for zoos in the subjects we are to discuss over the next two days. However, sentiment is changing and changing fast, due to the recognition of the wholesale destruction of natural habitats and the resultant loss of species going on all over the world. Australia is no exception. Many who would have agreed with the earlier view are now deeply concerned that the rapid loss of natural habitats means that if vigorous attempts are not made to put in place captive breeding programs with a view first to preservation, and further down the track to posssible habitat restoration and reintroduction, then there is no hope for an ever-growing number of species. This is the premise from which the Zoological Board of Victoria has substantially upgraded its contribution to conservation issues over the last two years and is committed to further enhancement of its programs in future years within the limits of its restricted financial resources.

Many of you will be familiar with the IUCN Policy Statement on Captive Breeding as adopted in September 1987. As it so succinctly embraces the underlying principle from which the ZBV has developed its stance, I think it is worth quoting:

> 'Summary: Habitat protection alone is not sufficient if the expressed goal of the World Conservation Strategy, the maintenance of biotic diversity, is to be achieved. Establishment of self-sustaining captive populations and other supportive intervention will be needed to avoid the loss of many species, especially those at high risk in greatly reduced, highly fragmented and disturbed habitats. Captive breeding programs need to be established before species are reduced to critically low numbers, and thereafter need to be coordinated internationally according to sound biological principles, with a view to the maintaining or re-establishment of viable populations in the wild.'

There have been international meetings addressing the conservation issues in recent months. The IUCN Species Survival Commission, of which Dr. George Rabb, Director of Brookfield Zoo, is now Chairman, met in Rome this August. The Theriological Congress met there as well. The Captive Breeding Specialists Groups also met. The International Union of Directors of Zoological Gardens has just met. CITES will meet in a couple of weeks. Agendas of all of these meetings have focussed on conservation. Efforts have increased. Consciousness has increased. Yet numbers of species needing recovery of their populations have increased virtually everywhere. Elephants and rhinos are continuing to disappear as we sit here, despite the efforts of the International Ivory Trade Review, major campaigns of key conservation organisations, and new programs and resources devoted to the preservation of these species by governments. Something is not working.

That something is not directly related to the effort and dollar resources devoted to conservation problems. Perhaps we are on the threshold of finding that biological knowledge in its traditional academic forms is not sufficient to address the forces that lead to losses of species. Perhaps the interplay of biological science from a wide variety of related disciplines interwoven with understanding possible through the analysis of economic, political, cultural and historical factors is essential. This synthesis of many approaches to conservation is more complex and probably more central to the solutions of conservation issues than our established perceptions of wildlife problems have allowed us to recognise.

This audience knows only too well the difference between rhetoric and performance, so it now is necessary to discuss the special qualifications that zoos can offer to play their part in what must inevitably be a cooperative thrust. Firstly, we are a member of the worldwide community of zoos which since the early 1970s has worked strenuously to develop the Species Management Programs aimed at the cooperative management of species at risk, taking account of demographic security and genetic diversity. In Australia this allows us to be involved in worldwide programs covering both exotic and Australian species, and ensures that scarce resources can be deployed in the most effective manner. We are therefore able to enter this field with excellent scientific backup and access to highly developed technical skills.

Secondly, and this, I believe, is our strongest and unique qualification—we have an animal management staff superbly equipped to handle almost any challenge presented to us both in captive breeding and also in understanding animal behaviour, health and welfare. Not to harness this talent is a squandering of scarce human resources. The ZBV believes that there is a great opportunity for these skills to be used in conservation programs. This has happened in the past but in a fairly unfocussed fashion. The very fact that we are here today and contributing to this program shows that our staff skills are now being recognised as a significant element in the race against time.

Thirdly, we are an institution which has a somewhat unique standing in the community:

1. we are not a government department;
2. we are not a profit-driven organisation;
3. we are by-and-large apolitical;
4. we are an old and respected institution—Melbourne is one of the oldest zoos in the world (132 years);
5. we have a high community profile—1.5 million visitors per year at our three properties;
6. we have a great capacity to educate and to influence people's perceptions of animals;
7. we can act as a shop window for conservation issues by effective displays, driving home whatever messages are appropriate;
8. because of our independence, we can act as coordinators to bring together parties with differing agendas. The joint Brookfield/Zoological Board of Victoria program for the eastern barred bandicoot is a classic example of this role being successfully implemented. This communication expertise can sometimes bridge gaps between separate government departments as well as the private sector;
9. we are able to attract funds from the private sector which are mostly not freely offered to government departments; and
10. because of the quite diverse nature of our operations, our external relationships tap into a wide range of expert skills—medical, scientific, educational, marketing, media, and so on, all of which at some stage can be very valuable in conservation strategies.

These are what I perceive to be our skills.

Over the last nine months we have been undergoing a very comprehensive review of our operations at all properties of our staffing structures, and out of this I expect will come a commitment to greatly improve our scientific expertise.

We are vastly indebted to the Chicago Zoological Society and Brookfield Zoo staff members for their input into our joint research program—their experience in this area is so greatly superior to ours that we have been very much the novice partner, but we have learnt a great deal and I believe we are now poised to play an important part in collaborative programs with a number of the organisations represented here today. I would like to think ours could be a catalytic role as well as a contributing and supporting one. The helmeted honeyeater project may prove to be the forerunner of many other programs.

Wildlife managers have the specific knowledge of the biology of the ecosystems in the parks and reserves under their protection. Researchers from academic institutions have the specialised backgrounds in fields essential to generating knowledge necessary to an understanding of factors relevant to the survival of species. Zoological parks have the specialised facilities and the long-standing experience of managing wildlife in captivity. The private conservation organisations are a critical link with public awareness, as well as resources of personnel and commitment.

These are the tools for successful species recovery. The strength of the linkages among these resources can provide for increased numbers of populations of targeted species in parks and reserves. Increased security for those populations is attained through increased understanding of factors threatening them. It may also be further augmented and secured through the insurance role provided by captive breeding at zoos and similar facilities. And a corollary of each of these components is their individually unique opportunities to communicate with their individual audiences, the visitors to parks, the students, memberships in organisations, and visitors to the zoos.

Together we have an opportunity to try some new approaches to achieving common goals in conservation. I hope that the efforts here will be taken up in parallel elsewhere in the world. Effective stewardship of our wildlife resources calls for far more successes than have made up the global records of species survival during the past decade.

Thank you for giving me this opportunity to project the Zoo Board's position and I hope that the next two days' discussions will be educational and inspirational.

# Opening Remarks from the Department of Conservation, Forests and Lands

*Don Saunders, Director of National Parks and Wildlife*

The direction taken by wildlife research in Victoria has changed greatly in recent years. Until that change, we concentrated on survey work, which, although fundamental to protecting our fauna, provided only a small part of what we needed to know.

A few years ago our position could be summarised as follows:

1. Although we had a lot of valuable information on the distribution of species, our efforts had been concentrated on mammals and birds. We knew a lot less about reptiles and amphibians, and almost nothing about invertebrates.

2. We had a list of those species which, to the best of our knowledge, were rare, endangered or threatened, but in most cases we did not know why they were in that position or how rapidly they were declining.

3. Even if we did know something of the reasons behind the decline of a species, we usually did not have management plans, the rehabilitation or recovery techniques, the funds required for recovery programs or the overview of all species on a Statewide basis to enable realistic priorities to be set.

We have certainly moved a long way towards filling the gaps in our knowledge in the last few years, but we still have a very long way to go.

To a large extent, the change in direction came about with production of the State Conservation Strategy in 1987, at least insofar as community-wide recognition of the needs. This was followed by the Flora and Fauna Guarantee, which is certainly the strongest statement in Australia, if not the world, on conservation of species. The Guarantee provides us with an enormous challenge, but how do we achieve it?

In the past, there was a tendency to say 'protect the habitat and the species will survive.' For the majority of species that still holds. But for most other species it is not as simple as that. In some cases, most of the habitat has been lost, in others there are changes taking place in the habitat which are threatening the survival of species, such as introduced predators, competitive species which are favoured by human activities, and climatic change.

Some of the papers at this Conference will be dealing with these threatening factors in detail, so I will not pursue that issue, other than to point out that the helmeted honeyeater is a classic example. We have spent a lot of money buying land and protecting habitat for the helmeted honeyeater, but the population continues to decline. It is now obvious that there are very complex issues involved.

From a funding point of view, it is very encouraging that both the Victorian and the Commonwealth Governments are supporting conservation of threatened species with policies and with funds. The Department of Conservation, Forests and Lands has excellent research and planning staff and a very strong field operation. We are now working on management plans or strategies for some 20 species of fauna.

We are currently in the position where we have the desire, the Government support, and, to some extent, the resources to make a solid start on conserving our small faunal populations, but in many cases we don't have the methods.

This brings me to the importance of the Conference. We need to explore new techniques and to make contact with people working in similar areas. There are tremendous advantages in getting together, sharing ideas and pooling resources.

Because of this, I welcome the involvement of the Zoological Board of Victoria, not only at this Conference, but also in some of our endangered species programs. It was always something of a mystery to me why our zoo was not more actively involved in the conservation of Victoria's native animals in the past, but I am pleased that this has now changed.

The involvement of the Chicago Zoological Society is also most welcome, bringing not only an international flavour, but also expertise in wildlife biology and conservation, along with experience in public relations. In particular, I wish to pay tribute to the work of Pamela Parker and Tim Clark, who have shown such a keen interest in helping with our wildlife programs in Victoria.

Finally, the Department of Conservation, Forests and Lands had great pleasure in co-hosting this Conference and we look forward to an outcome that will help us meet the challenges ahead.

# Opening Remarks from the Chicago Zoological Society

*Peter B. Freeman, Trustee, Chicago Zoological Society*

The guiding force of conservation and its social framework are not new. The essential interdependence of the diverse forms of life, including mankind, can be traced to the earliest stages of human history. For example, almost two thousand years ago the Roman poet Lucretius wrote in *De Rerum Natura* that 'we hold the earth in usufruct,' borrowing a term of art from Roman law meaning the right to enjoyment of the fruits of land belonging to another without impairing the land itself. As the earth shrinks and both the land and its fruits disappear, this concept is undergoing a belated resurgence.

There are, however, two new developments of great moment: (1) the recent intervention of governments, such as the State of Victoria, in the conservation of biota, and (2) the emergence of the scientific expertise essential to the effective use of governmental power in that endeavour. It is the intersection of these developments that brings the sponsoring institutions and all of the participants together and should be kept in mind.

The advent of governmental intervention in the arena of conservation biology is embodied in the *Flora and Fauna Guarantee Act* of 1988. Like other legislation in this area, that Act reflects the product of changing social values and a consensus among competing political interests. It is a well-crafted product of considerable cooperative efforts among the scientific, legal and political communities.

The vision expressed in the *Flora and Fauna Guarantee Act* must now be realized in its implementation. Too often, the feast of legislative pronouncements chokes on the gristle of reality.

In order to accomplish the objectives of the Act, an even closer and more durable cooperation among the diverse disciplines of conservation biology and government must be cultivated. Because of the nature of the problem addressed by the Act, effective governmental action is essential to the attainment of the goals of conservation of the biota. Because of the nature of the government, effective administration of the Act will depend on help from the scientific community and supportive institutions whose expertise is essential to shape the priorities and methods of administration and to support the enforcement of the government's provisions. This, indeed, is an interdependence that will challenge the wisdom and wit of all involved.

It is not necessary for all scientists to become lawyers and politicians, nor for all government officers to become scientists. What is needed, however, is the appreciation of the nature of the mutual endeavor, the issues that must be addressed, the roles of each participant in the processes of government, and the resolution of political and legal disputes that will surely arise in the lifetime of the legislation. Any sensible implementation of the Act must deal with certain hard realities of the present and future, including limited economic, human and political resources, the need for priority and focus in the use of those resources and the important contribution that needs to be made by other non-governmental parts of the community.

From a legal standpoint, the implementation of the Act will turn on the concept of 'discretion', expressed in the statute in the use of terms such as 'reasonable' and 'may'. The exercise of discretion involves a judgment which considers the diverse factors delineated in the law and in society as a whole. From the consideration of these factors, a balance of the competing interests emerges, guided by the legislative purpose and statutory language. In short, we are engaged in the process of deciding when and what to do for which species and ecosystems and how to do that.

This sounds simple, but in practice it requires some serious appreciation of the basic principles and values expressed in the Act and their application to all of the ways in which human activities can conflict with the conservation of biota. Again, from a legal standpoint, the statute's explicit language, its stated purpose and its legislative history can be considered in deciding upon the approximate governmental action. The purpose of the Act is described as 'a legal and administrative structure to enable and promote the conservation of Victoria's native flora and fauna and to provide for a choice of procedures . . . for conservation, management or control of flora and fauna . . .' (Section 1). Like the legislation's title, the avowed purpose imbues the entire Act with the interests of conservation and gives the protection of flora and fauna a special legal value.

The succeeding provisions of the Act elaborate and emphasize specific concerns and attributes of species needing protection. For example, Section 4 lists a series of objectives:

> (a) to guarantee that all taxa of Victoria's flora and fauna . . . can survive, flourish and retain their potential for evolutionary development in the wild; and
> (b) to conserve Victoria's communities of flora and fauna; and
> (c) to manage potentially threatening processes; and
> (d) to ensure that any use of flora or fauna by humans is sustainable; and
> (e) to ensure that the genetic diversity of flora and fauna is maintained; and
> (f) to provide programs—
> > (i) of community education in the conservation of flora and fauna; and

> > (ii) to encourage cooperative management of flora and fauna through, amongst other things, the entering into of land management cooperative agreements; and
> > (iii) of assisting and giving incentives to people, including landholders, to enable flora and fauna to be conserved; and
> (g) to encourage the conserving of flora and fauna through cooperative community endeavours.

Other sections refer to 'a demonstrable state of decline which is likely to result in extinction or . . . is significantly prone to future threats [of extinction], as well as those which are below the level of subspecies . . . [a] narrowly defined because of its taxonomic composition, environmental condition or geography . . . [where] there is a special need to conserve it' (Section 11; emphasis added).

These provisions contain considerable technical content to scientists, but they have a lot of room for interpretation in the halls of government, and many of the words are meaningless to the public. Governmental enforcement of the Act depends on the meaning of some very different terms with less precise definitions—at least to scientists— but with great significance to the outcome of the analysis. Thus, Section 19(3)(b), relating to the preparation of action statements, requires consideration of 'any other relevant nature conservation, social and economic matters,' and the provision guiding the actual making of an interim conservation order are even more cryptic.

'In making an order the Minister must consider—

> (a) any nature conservation matters; and
> (b) the social and economic consequences of making the order; and
> (c) any other relevant matters'

(Section 26(5)).

Obviously, all of this will entail a lot of hard slogging with concrete problems involving specific species and subspecies in different social and economic circumstances. It will necessarily involve a combination of talents in order to obtain a consensus on at least the following crucial issues:

1. the identification and evaluation of the species or subspecies from taxonomic, evolutionary, ecological and societal standpoints;

2. the assessment of the threat to the species, and its ecological impact, as well as the condition and future of the ecosystems involved;

3. the determination of the actions necessary to conserve the species and its ecosystem and an evaluation of effective long-term management;

4. the identification and evaluation of competing individual, economic and societal interests, including an assessment of the impact of species protection on those interests;

5. the identification and evaluation of alternative methods of balancing the conservation of the species' ecosystem with other socially important interests; and

6. the determination of the extent and manner in which resources should be expended in this process.

In this process, the reliability of the basic scientific data and the availability of expertise are essential not only to the factual predicate of government actions but also to the very process of balancing the competing interests and to developing practical solutions to the problems. Numerous scientific and other disciplines may be needed to assess the status, significance and survival of threatened species and to evaluate the potential success of various alternative courses of action.

The interplay between the scientific community and the government should not end there, nor does the supportive framework of other institutions of society, such as zoos, museums and educational institutions. Underlying the dry verbiage of the legislators is a fundamental value which the society has placed on the conservation of species. The various expressions of this value need to be explored, articulated, and, when necessary, advocated. A species may have a recognized or potential economic value, or it may impact on the health or welfare of human beings. A species may have special significance as a 'keystone' or 'bellwether' of the health of an ecosystem. Some species have special symbolic significance, as a political emblem or a source of entertainment. Other species are so much a part of the consciousness of the people that it is difficult to conceive of a world without them. Some have great appeal for their beauty. Many species have a special evolutionary significance or are important from a purely scientific standpoint. Under the Act, every species has a unique value recognized by virtue of what it is.

Embedded in each and all of these expressions and in the fabric of this Act can be an expression of a new integration of the human species and its society, on the one hand, and the earth's biological richness. The threat to species needs to be understood, and the capability for species management needs to be worked out. Creative solutions to many dilemmas need to be developed in order to accommodate the interests of conservation with other interests of society. Many of these solutions may depend on the active participation of zoos and other institutions in order to be accomplished.

We at the Chicago Zoological Society have been privileged to co-sponsor this conference and to lend our support to this step in the implementation of the *Flora and Fauna Guarantee Act*. We hope that we can look forward to a continued and constructive role in supporting cooperation among the groups and individuals who attended the conference in their future efforts.

# Management and Conservation of Small Populations

*Tim W. Clark[1], Robert M. Warneke[2], and Graeme G. George[3]*

## Abstract

Loss of biodiversity—the variety and variability among living organisms and ecological processes—has serious implications for this and future generations. To prevent widespread extinctions, we must understand the extinction process as a largely population-level phenomenon. Population viability assessment is described, including five approaches to determining population size and area requirements. Management of small populations requires certain information—life history, population ecology, genetics, and modelling. Also, appreciation of the large temporal and sometimes spatial scales and complexity of the task, and understanding that uncertainty is present in ecological systems are essential. Biological diversity can be maintained through onsite and offsite management; zoos, for instance, are leaders in offsite captive breeding management and techniques. The status of Australia's flora and fauna and natural ecosystems is reviewed. We call for development of more effective programs based on a useful model of extinction, compilation of all relevant data from diverse scientific fields, appropriate and timely management both onsite and offsite, adaptive management, and close working relationships between researchers, managers, zoos, universities, governments and non-governmental groups.

## Introduction

Concern for the quality of the environment is growing worldwide, and for several reasons, it often centres on small dwindling populations of plants and animals. First, nothing so clearly illustrates the substantive problems of environmental decay as much as the endangerment and extinction of species. It is often asked, if the world is being made unlivable for millions of other life-forms, what are we doing to the livability of our own environment? Second, as species and populations are destroyed, the ecosystems they compose are degraded or destroyed, and vital ecological processes and services may be lost, such as cycling of essential nutrients and gases. Such losses have serious implications for the welfare of humans. In growing recognition of the species extinction crisis and its implications, national and international policies and programs are being discussed or implemented to protect species and ecosystems. Conservation science and management are also mobilising to meet this accelerating challenge (Ginsberg 1987, Soulé 1985, 1986, 1987, Soulé and Wilcox 1980, Soulé and Simberloff 1986). But redressing the unprecedented loss of global biological diversity is not a priority in all countries. This is unfortunate, because the losses undermine all societies' capabilities to respond to future needs and opportunities.

Biological diversity, defined most simply, is the variety and variability among living organisms and the ecological processes in which they occur (Office of Technology Assessment 1987). Usually measured in terms of genes, populations, species and ecosystems, this living diversity is the

[1] Department of Conservation Biology, Chicago Zoological Society, Brookfield, Illinois 60513, U.S.A.
[2] National Parks and Wildlife Division, Department of Conservation, Forests and Lands. Arthur Rylah Institute for Environmental Research, 123 Brown Street, Heidelberg, Victoria 3084, Australia.
[3] Zoological Board of Victoria, P.O. Box 72, Parkville, Victoria 3052, Australia.

basis of evolutionary adaptation, and is fundamental to all ecological processes (Interagency Task Force 1985). Living diversity has many utilitarian, as well as aesthetic, educational, research, recreational, cultural heritage, and tourist benefits.

Before the massive environmental alterations caused by humans in recent decades, nearly all living organisms survived without any human intervention. But in recent times, many species have been reduced to small, fragmented populations which are highly susceptible to extinction. Now further human intervention is needed to prevent extinctions. We must learn about the extinction process and develop appropriate management strategies.

This conference focusses on single species approaches to management and conservation. It emphasises maintenance of viable wild populations, but also discusses management of small, captive, supporting populations. For wild populations, management must be able to predict and control the types of environmental changes that threaten species and populations. This, of course, requires extensive knowledge about the ecology of individuals and populations. Thus population biology, field studies of demographics, life-history, habitat relationships, behaviour, physiology, and construction of mathematical models of population behaviour are all essential ingredients to successful conservation and management. Fundamental to all this are reliable scientific knowledge (Romesberg 1981), rapid, sound decision making (Maguire 1986), appropriately organised and managed programs (Clark *et al.* 1989), and progress in the face of uncertainty using the principles of 'adaptive management' (Holling 1973, 1978).

This conference will examine basic concepts and applied tools of conservation biology (see Mlot 1989). The concepts of population viability assessment, decision analysis, and adaptive management will be illustrated, as well as important tools including computer modelling, conservation genetics, captive breeding, reintroduction and monitoring. These concepts and tools are currently being used to develop a model program to conserve the eastern barred bandicoot (*Perameles gunnii*) in Victoria, but are applicable to other species recovery efforts, too. The bandicoot program and several other cases—including a plant, invertebrates, birds, and another mammal—will illustrate application of the various concepts and tools.

The conference material is not a cookbook for conservation, but it can help develop a common framework for successful, cooperative management applicable to many plant and animal species.

## A General Model of Extinction

Extinction is the irrevocable loss of a biological element, and is basically a population-level process (Gilpin and Soulé 1986), although four levels of biological diversity are recognised (Table 1). The loss of a community type occurs because of the cumulative loss of all the patches of that community type. In turn, each patch is lost because the populations that make it up are lost. The loss of a species occurs because of the cumulative loss of all the separate populations over its range. And lastly, the loss of genetic diversity occurs because of the extinction of populations (Brussard 1985). It is obvious, then, that the population is the basic ecological and evolutionary unit, and that the loss of diversity at all four levels results from the extinction of populations. Fortunately, many conservation efforts focus on populations.

In many instances, endangered species do not occur in just one population, but in several small habitat patches that may exchange individuals regularly, irregularly, or not at all. Most populations of plants and animals are distributed this way. These few populations can be collectively thought of as a population of populations, or a 'metapopulation'. Each population in the metapopulation, depending on whether it communicates with other populations, shows varying probabilities of survival (Wilcox 1986). This idea was

*Table 1.*—Four levels of biological diversity.

| Level of Biological Diversity | Biological Element | Example |
| --- | --- | --- |
| Molecular | Genes | Genes for salinity tolerance |
| Populational | Populations | Eastern barred bandicoot (*Perameles gunnii*) on mainland |
| Species | Species | Numbat (*Myrmecobius fasciatus*) |
| Ecosystem | Community | Rain forest |

first described by Andrewartha and Birch (1954), though Levins (1970) more fully conceptualised the notion.

Our discussion now allows us to outline a general model of extinction (Fig. 1). First, a population becomes reduced in size and simplified in structure largely because of deterministic factors, probably habitat loss, fragmentation and isolation. Once the population is diminished, its susceptibility to chance factors increases. Finally, one or more chance factors depress the population to a threshold below which it cannot grow, and given enough time, the remaining individuals perish.

In reality, there are many demographic, behavioural, genetic, environmental, and catastrophic variables in this model, as well as a host of extrabiological variables that can affect the survivorship of small populations, among them socioeconomic, policy, and program considerations (Fig. 2) (see Clark 1986, Clark and Harvey 1988).

## The Concept of Population Viability

Attempts to understand why small populations are endangered have led to the science of population viability assessment (PVA; Simberloff 1988). Determining the 'minimum viable population' size of a species and its area requirements allows scientists and managers to establish and manage

habitat preserves to help ensure survival of the population. Even though the concept of population viability is several decades old (see reviews in Simberloff 1986 and Simberloff 1988), Mark Shaffer (1981) first succinctly formulated it and applied it to grizzly bear (*Ursus arctos*) management in the Yellowstone National Park region (Shaffer 1978). He described the pressing need for biologists to understand the relationship between a population's size and the probability of extinction. It is well known that the smaller a population, the greater the risk of extinction, but the question Shaffer (1981) and others asked was 'how large a population and habitat base is large enough?' His classic paper examined conservation at the population level, discussed various procedures available to determine viable population sizes and their area requirements, and related these to an overall conservation strategy.

Populations are regulated by two classes of factors—systematic and stochastic. Unravelling cause and effect relationships in the extinction process illustrates these two classes of factors. Habitat loss is an example of a systematic factor; its effects on a population are generally predictable. Storms are an example of a chance or stochastic factor; their effects on a population are generally unpredictable.

Four sources of chance events or uncertainty were identified by Shaffer (1981). First are demographic chance events. Chance plays a role in

# The Extinction Process

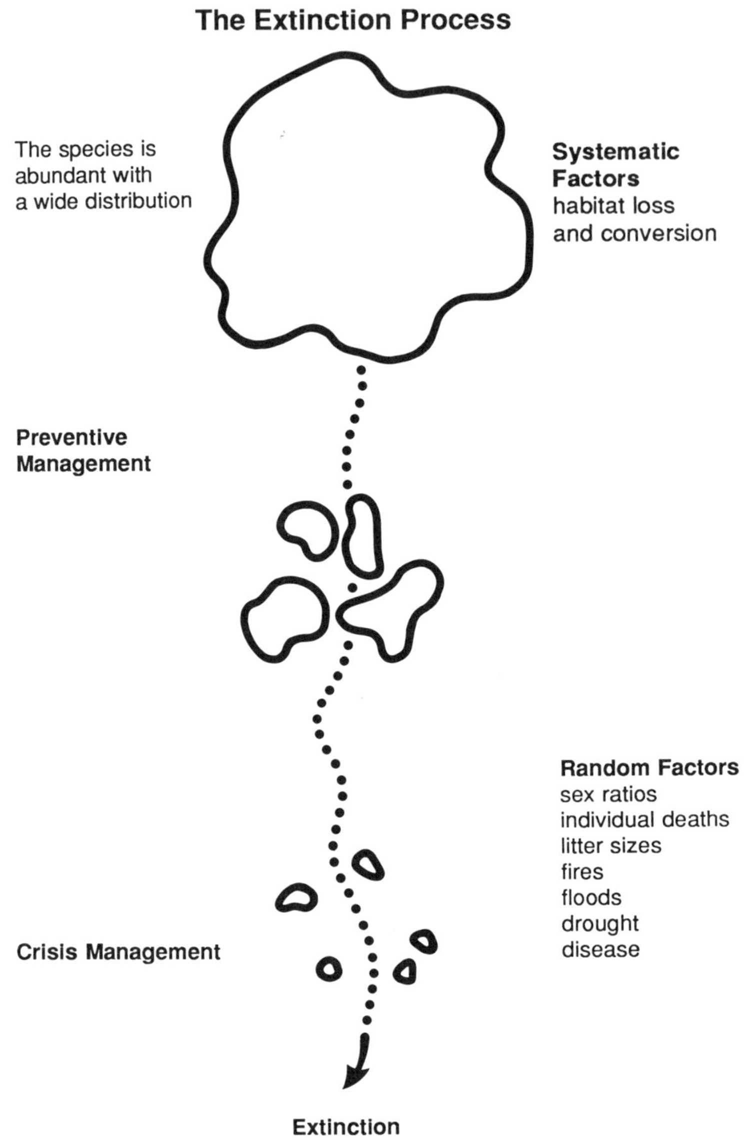


*Figure 1.*—A general extinction model illustrating the fragmentation of a population's distribution into smaller and more isolated patches and the role of systematic and random factors in this process.

survivorship of individuals, which individuals mate with one another, and sex of offspring. Second are environmental chance events. Chance plays a role in habitat occupancy and in variations in weather. Third are natural catastrophes. Fires, droughts and floods may occur randomly over time and space. And fourth are genetic chance events. Chance plays a role in changes in gene frequencies due to inbreeding and genetic drift. Shaffer (1981) argued that if a target population could be kept above a certain size, it would have a high resistance to extinction. He called this the 'minimal viable population' (MVP) size and stated that 'A minimum viable population for any given species in any given area is the smallest isolated population having a 99% chance of remaining extant for 1,000 years despite the foreseeable effects of demographic, environmental, and genetic stochasticity [chance] and natural catastrophes' (p. 132). Since then, viability has often been defined as a 95+% or 99% chance of a population surviving for 100 years. Such definitions have been used in several endangered species recovery plans (*e.g.* black-footed ferret, *Mustela nigripes*; Harris *et al.* 1989; Lacy and Clark 1989; Brussard and Gilpin 1989).

Shaffer then outlined five possible approaches to determining MVP size and area requirements: experiments, biogeographic patterns, theoretical models, simulation models, or genetic considerations. Although no single method is perfect, all can contribute to better understanding of population size, survival probabilities, and size of area needed; for some populations, several approaches can be used simultaneously. Experiments are the most straightforward approach. A manager simply creates or finds populations of various sizes and observes whether they survive or not. Of course, for species that are already endangered, experiments are not possible. Second, biogeographic patterns allow scientists to study distribution patterns in patchy or insular habitats and get an estimate of the size of populations that persist and their area requirements. Despite some drawbacks of analysis, it is one of the key means of determin-

ing population and area requirements. Third, several theoretical models predict the probability that a small population will go extinct and the time it will take. Fourth, simulation models, because they are not subject to many of the constraints of theoretical (analytic) models, provide a highly useful approach. These computer models depend on actual data derived from the population under consideration; without good field data, their utility is limited. Finally, genetic considerations and their implications for population viability are usually based on avoiding inbreeding or other problems.

Since Shaffer's paper, many advances have been made in estimating population viability and area requirements, especially with theoretical and simulation models and genetic considerations. A thorough review is given by Simberloff (1988). It is clear that the concept of population viability is an invaluable one, which will receive increased management use and scientific refinement (Conner 1988).


*Management Considerations*

The International Union for Conservation of Nature and Natural Resources (IUCN) (1987:2) noted that 'The vulnerability of small populations has been consistently underestimated.... Management to best reduce the risk of extinction requires [actions] when the wild population is still in the thousands.' They emphasised that 'Vertebrate taxa with a current census below one thousand individuals in the wild require close and swift [management] cooperation.'

*Information Needs*

Managing small populations requires understanding key life-history features, population dynamics and genetics, evolutionary concerns, and incorporating this knowledge into exploratory, predictive models (National Research Council 1986). All have direct management implications.

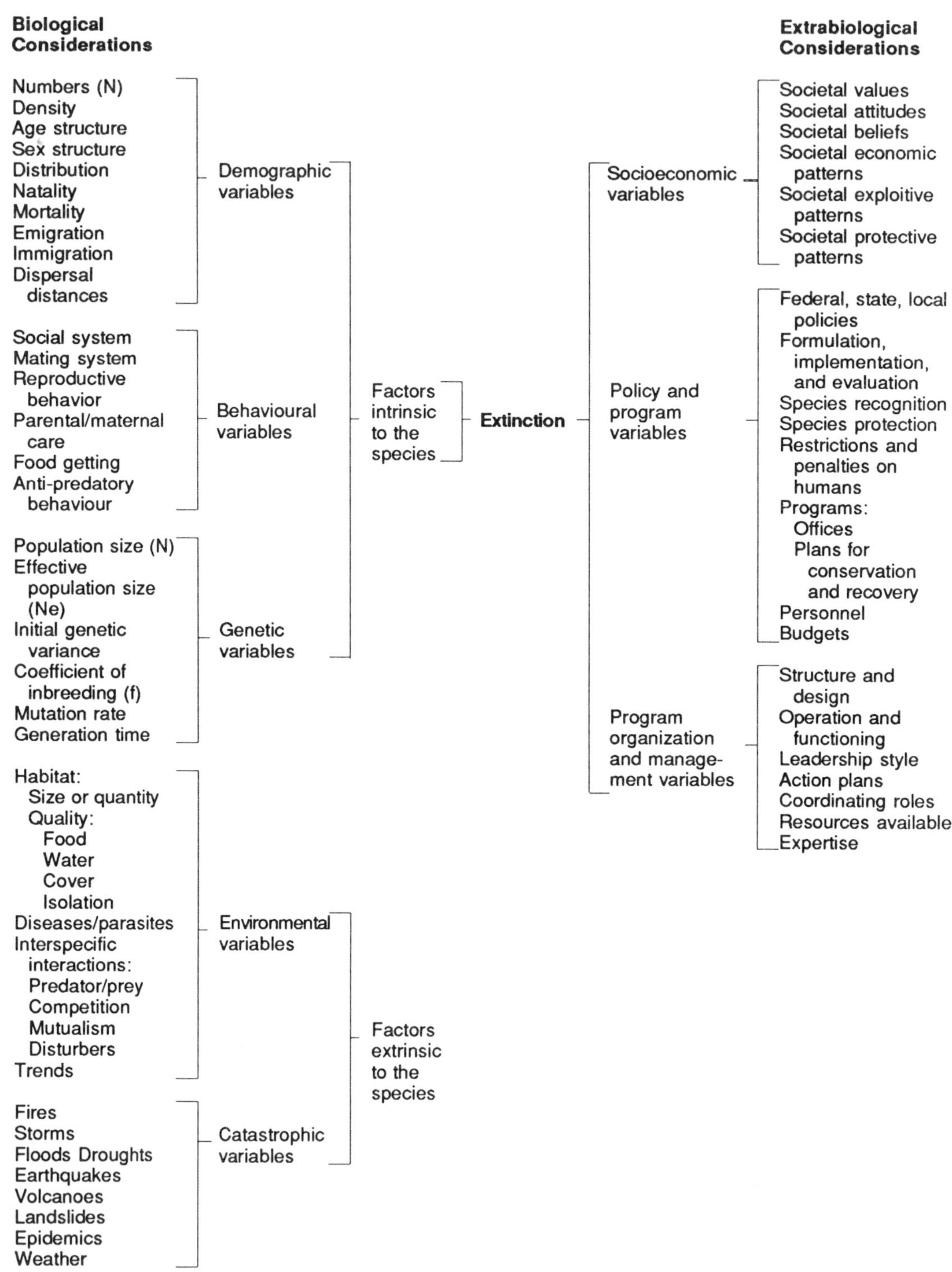


*Figure 2.*—An extinction map showing both biological and extrabiological factors that can cause species extinctions (Clark 1989).

First, life-history studies include investigations of individuals, comparative studies and theoretical studies of life-history patterns. Understanding individual behaviour requires specific knowledge about the species and population and how individual behavioural 'decisions' are made. This has been emphasised by Simberloff (1986) and Zimmerman and Bierregaard (1986), who noted that sound conservation science must be founded on autecological studies of individual systems. The key aspects of a species' behavioural ecology are habitat selection, mating systems, and social interactions (National Research Council 1986). Habitat quality and distribution are also key features; management of endangered species often depends on habitat management. If habitat diminishes in quality or extent, individuals and populations are threatened. Species and populations also vary in their dispersion patterns in space (clumped, random, or even) and in their density, dispersal, and migratory behavior (National Research Council 1986). Management of endangered species must consider the implications of these patterns. Some habitats may shrink in size during certain seasons, and these 'bottleneck' periods must be considered. Some species migrate between habitat patches of various sizes and so both habitats must be carefully managed. Small populations of plants and animals clumped in dense pockets of isolated habitat are highly susceptible to catastrophic reductions from chance events (*e.g.* floods, fires, droughts, disease). Even though life-history information is essential to successful management, it yields only partial understanding of the causes and effects of changes in a population's numbers, density, and composition, for example.

Second, population dynamics demonstrate the complex interaction of changing population attributes, such as numbers, density, reproduction, mortality and gene frequencies. Populations are regulated in two fundamental ways—density-dependent and density-independent. Species have different intrinsic rates of increases; some can recover more quickly from population lows than others. Managers need this kind of knowledge to determine how a population will respond if mortality is reduced by improved habitat management, for example.

Third, in small isolated populations confined to habitat patches or islands, there are several genetic and evolutionary concerns. Genetic deterioration can lead to extinction, already well documented in small captive populations (Lacy 1987), through deleterious effects of inbreeding which result in loss of genetic variation (Frankel and Soulé 1981; Schonewald-Cox *et al.* 1983; Soulé and Wilcox 1980; and others). To measure whether a population is susceptible to genetic erosion factors, an estimate of its 'effective' size is necessary.

Fourth, models of population dynamics and genetics can be used for understanding the behavior of populations and for exploring the implications of various management interventions. Many of these models estimate the viability or probability of persistence of populations of various sizes and dynamics. These abstract constructions and simplifications do not, of course, duplicate reality (Horton and Becak 1987), but they do capture essential conceptual information without complicating details. The more complex models incorporate not only growth, death, and birth rates, but also dispersal, breeding structure, chance events like catastrophes or other types of environmental variation, and inbreeding and genetic drift.

*Time and Space Scales*

The scales and complexity of these many management tasks need attention. For example, when we alter natural habitats and communities, we alter the size and distribution of wild populations, *i.e.* the spatial scale of the population's dynamics. Environmental changes also alter temporal scales. Changes that are inconsequential to a large population (*e.g.* a lengthy, severe drought) can be catastrophic to a small one. Managers must appreciate the appropriate scales in analyzing and manipulating population and habitat processes to conserve small populations (National Resource Council 1986).

Unfortunately, this is not a straightforward exercise. Most management must proceed in the face of considerable uncertainty about the population or ecological system under management. This is why the adaptive management approach is so useful (Holling 1973, 1978). Some degree of uncertainty will always be present, but the sources and consequences of the uncertainty can and must be identified. This is often the most important and useful information a scientist can give a manager (National Resource Council 1986).

*Uncertainty in Ecological Systems*

The behaviour of small populations and other ecological systems is not well understood in many cases. Data necessary for accurate predictions are often absent, especially when temporal and spatial scales of the ecological system are themselves changing. Nevertheless, some main sources of uncertainty in ecological systems can be identified: complexity, natural variability, random variability, errors of estimation, and lack of knowledge (National Research Council 1986). First, relationships among individuals, populations and their environments are complex; changes in one can have direct or indirect effects on others. Cumulative effects may occur from combinations of factors. Second, ecological systems show natural variability in time and space because of both intrinsic and extrinsic processes which may or may not be known or measurable. Third, populations behave in probabilistic rather than deterministic ways because of the many forces acting on them. Thus, appropriate responses to these probabilistic perturbations can never be predicted precisely. Fourth, because it is difficult or impossible to measure these random forces, measurement errors are likely. It is common for errors of estimation to combine with natural variability to make detection of cause-and-effect relationships

a real challenge. And fifth, we simply often lack basic knowledge about populations or other ecological systems as a basis for making predictions and management decisions.

*Onsite and Offsite Management*

There are two general approaches to maintain biological diversity, often closely linked (Table 2; Office of Technology Assessment 1987). Onsite management focusses on species and populations *in situ,* but it can also address entire communities and ecosystems. Offsite management (removing entities to protected locations), focusses on populations, organisms, tissues, ova, sperm, seeds, or embryos. Leadbeater's possum (*Gymnobelideus leadbeateri*), for instance, is currently managed in both wild and captive populations.

Maintaining genetic, population, species, or ecosystem diversity onsite in natural environments is the most effective way to conserve the maximum biodiversity over the long term (Office of Technology Assessment 1987). Traditionally, management strategies for onsite conservation have focussed on preservation in parks, refuges, or natural areas, but more recently, efforts have included integrating conservation with development (*e.g.* World Conservation Strategy; IUCN 1980). Principles have been proposed for refuge design (Fig. 3 after IUCN 1980; Wilson and Willis 1975). But often, refuge design and strategies for integrating biodiversity with development are determined more by socioeconomic and political factors than by conservation science. Techniques for reintroducing species to the wild and restoring communities are costly, slow, and not well-developed (Kleinman 1989; Griffith *et al.* 1989).

Offsite management of biodiversity often includes captive breeding of wild populations or some other activity, *e.g.* maintaining genetic diversity via cryopreservation. In all cases, captive breed-

*Table 2.*—Examples of management systems to maintain biological diversity (Office of Technology Assessment 1987:6).

| Onsite | | Offsite | |
| --- | --- | --- | --- |
| **Ecosystem mgmt.** | **Species mgmt.** | **Living collections** | **Germplasm storage** |
| National parks | Agroecosystems | Zoological parks | Seed and pollen banks |
| Research natural areas | Wildlife refuges | Botanic gardens | Semen, ova, and embryo banks |
| Marine sanctuaries | *In situ* gene-banks | Field collections | Microbial culture collections |
| Resource development planning | Game parks and reserves | Captive breeding programs | Tissue culture collections |
| <————————Increasing emphasis on natural processes | | Increasing human intervention————————> | |

ing programs should reinforce maintenance of onsite conservation management, not replace it.

There is a growing number of instances of offsite management. In the United States, the entire world population of two highly endangered taxa, the black-footed ferret and the California condor (*Gymnogyps californianus*), have been taken into captivity for breeding as the only viable alternative to their total extinction. In both cases, the object is to restore populations to viable levels in the wild. In Australia, captive breeding is an integral part of current recovery efforts for the numbat and the western quoll (*Dasyurus geoffroii*) in Western Australia, the greater bilby (*Macrotis lagotis*) and western hare-wallaby (*Lagorchestes hirsutus*) in the Northern Territory, the orange-bellied parrot (*Neophema chrysogaster*) in Tasmania, and the mallee-fowl (*Leipoa ocellata*) in New South Wales.

Further examples include a wide range of species. Recovery of the Lord Howe Island woodhen (*Tricholimnus sylvestris*) was aided by rapid expansion of the population through captive-breeding. Captive populations of brush-tailed bettong (*Bettongia penicillata*) and Leadbeater's possum have been utilised for trial releases to the wild in South Australia and Victoria respectively, and plans are currently underway for captive breeding of the helmeted honeyeater (*Lichenostomus melanops cassidix*) in Victoria. Other species, such as the long-footed potoroo (*Potorous longipes*) in Victoria, are being established in captivity as potential support for threatened wild populations. Zoos play an important role in many of these programs.

Zoos worldwide have increasingly focussed their captive-breeding efforts on species whose wild populations are threatened with extinction in the hope that such captive-bred populations could be used to support or restore the wild populations. Pedigree information recorded in studbooks has long been utilised to assist in the establishment and management of captive populations. The first international studbook for a zoo animal was established in 1932 for the European bison (*Bison bonasus*), a species all but extinct in the wild. Pere David's deer (*Elaphurus davidianus*), Asian wild horse (*Equus caballus przewalskii*), Arabian oryx (*Oryx leucoryx*) and scimitar-horned oryx (*O. dammah*) are other ungulates, extinct or virtually extinct in the wild, whose captive populations have been used for recent attempts at re-establishment in parts of their historic range. These were also subjects of early studbook management.

Studbook data sets have proven to be invaluable when used with modern techniques for genetic and demographic analysis, which use computer programs to analyse a population's performance. These determine coefficients of inbreeding, survival of founder alleles in descendent populations, reproductive and mortality rates, and population projections (George 1988).

Population genetics theory is now applied to captive breeding programs. The goal is to maintain evolutionary potential in captive populations through maintenance of 90% of the initial genetic (allelic) diversity over 200 years.

The need for close coordination of breeding programs to achieve genetic goals has resulted in the establishment of several regional species management schemes (George 1986). The first to be organised were the Species Survival Plans (SSP) of the American Association of Zoological Parks and Aquariums (AAZPA), which began in 1979. The Association of Zoo Directors of Australia and New Zealand (AZDANZ) commenced local studbooks in 1976 and expanded this program into the Australasian Species Management Scheme in 1984 (George 1987, Baker and George 1988). Within the National Federation of Zoo-

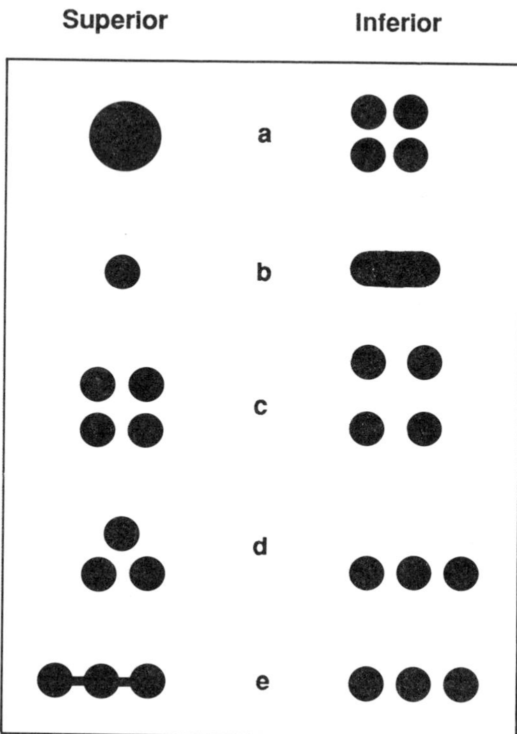


*Figure 3.*—Suggested refuge design principles (after Wilson and Willis 1975).

logical Gardens of Great Britain and Ireland, the Joint Management of Species Group and the Anthropoid Ape Advisory Panel foreshadowed more extensive programs in the late 1980s. More recently, the European zoos have developed the Europäisches Erhaltungstucht Programm (EEP), the Japanese Zoo Association has developed a Species Survival Committee, and the Dutch Zoo Federation has established a National Foundation for Research to promote diversity through captive breeding and to support conservation of wild populations in natural habitats. Studbook data sets are the cornerstone of these programs. International coordination of regional programs is achieved through the International Studbook system supervised by the International Union of Directors of Zoological Gardens (IUDZG) and the Captive Breeding Specialist Group (CBSG), Species Survival Commission, IUCN.

Several zoo-based research facilities worldwide (*e.g.* Institute of Zoology, London; National Zoo, Washington; Center for Reproduction of Endangered Species, San Diego) are leading the investigation of new technologies for genetic conservation (*e.g.* artifical insemination, cryopreservation of germplasm and embryo transfer to surrogates) to assist standard captive breeding efforts. These will become essential techniques in the near future as zoos do not have the space or resources to maintain adequate populations of all the species that will need *ex situ* support to ensure their long-term conservation.

## Australia and Extinctions

A comprehensive review of the distribution and status of the Australian biota is not possible, as many areas and ecosystems await survey and many taxonomic groups are poorly known. An overview by Richardson (1987) of the orders of the kingdom Animalia represented in Australia reveals that more than 75% of the estimated terrestrial and aquatic vertebrate fauna has now been described. By comparison, the invertebrates have received scant attention, except for the phylum Arthropoda, of which possibly half the estimated fauna is known. The Australian flora is also far from being adequately known. As recently as 1978 only 37 of 222 families of flowering plants were being actively studied by herbaria (Ride and McCusker 1978). Estimates vary, but there is little doubt that the entire flora will eventually be shown to comprise over 25,000 species (George 1981). We limit our discussion to the vascular flora and terrestrial vertebrates, as these are relatively well-documented and efforts

to conserve and manage species can occur within a well-established framework of legislation and government policy.

## *Modification and Destruction of Natural Ecosystems*

None of the major ecosystems of continental Australia remains unaffected by human activity, and most have undergone phenomenal changes in the 200 years since European settlement. The rapid expansion of the pastoral industry grossly altered the more open and accessible foothill forests, woodlands, mallee, shrublands, and tussock grasslands of the semi-arid inland. The consequent deleterious effects on the flora and fauna were later exacerbated by the introduction and rapid spread of rabbits and other exotics, and the complete conversion of whole land systems to wheat growing and improved pastures in areas of more reliable rainfall, including large areas of mallee. Much of the dense eucalypt and subtropical rain forests of the Eastern Divide and coastal plains and the jarrah forests of southwestern Western Australia have been cleared for more intensive forms of agriculture, or for an expanding urban population and industrial developments. Most of the remaining forests have been extensively modified by cutting for sawlogs and other forest products. Natural hydrological systems have also been eliminated or grossly modified by the draining of wetlands and the damming of rivers to service irrigation and the urban and industrial centres. These developments have tended to concentrate adjacent to rivers, estuaries, and at favored locations on the coast, causing increasing problems of pollution. Dryland salting resulting from injudicious clearing of native vegetation and improper irrigation practices is now affecting huge areas of once-fertile land.

The situation in Victoria has been characterised in statistical terms as follows (Frood and Calder 1987): over 60% of natural vegetation in the State has been cleared, 95% of privately owned lands have been cleared, more than 35% of the swamps and wetlands have been drained, close to 80% of rivers and wetlands have been substantially modified, 95% of grassland communities have been eliminated or modified by pasture improvement, 50% of native forests have been eliminated and 70% of remaining forests have been modified by forestry and other practices.

*Assessment of the Problems of Flora and Conservation*

An awareness and concern for Australia's flora and fauna developed within the scientific and general communities as species declined or disappeared and the scale and intensity of changes to ecosystems become obvious. This concern was focussed, and became a stimulus to action during the mid-1970s as the result of two important developments: the initiative of the International Biological Program (IBP) in relation to the conservation of terrestrial communities, and promotion of the plight of endangered species by IUCN, first of birds and mammals, then of plants and other animal groups. In association with the IBP, the Australian Academy of Science sponsored a national assessment of the status of plant communities. The major findings of this project (Specht *et al.* 1974), which addressed the representation of plant communities in national parks and reserves, led directly to proposals for a national system of ecological reserves in Australia (Fenner 1975). Specht (see Fenner 1975) also listed data on rare and endangered species supplied by State herbaria. Assessments of status varied between States, emphasising the need for a national list based on uniform criteria. Subsequent Australian lists for both plants and animals are based on and generally compatible with criteria established by the IUCN, and recognise the following categories: extinct (X), endangered (E), vulnerable (V), rare (R), and poorly known (K).

A recent national review of rare or threatened plants (Leigh *et al.* 1981) identified 150 families and 654 genera with one or more vulnerable or threatened taxa, totalling 2,206 species. Of this total, 78 were presumed to be extinct, 200 endangered, 612 vulnerable, 852 rare and 464 poorly known. The 1,742 species in the first four categories (X+E+V+R) comprise 8.7% of the estimated total vascular flora (20,000 species), and with the inclusion of those poorly known, the proportion rises to 11.0%. Of the 2,206 species of national concern, 158 are recorded for Victoria in 95 genera and 47 families, representing 5% of the total of 3,162 species native to the State.

According to recent reviews of the four classes of terrestrial vertebrates, the fauna of Australia consists of about 600 species of birds (Blakers *et al.* 1984; omitting the infrequent or irregular visitors, oceanic seabirds and vagrants), 245 mammals (Strahan 1983), 650 reptiles (excluding the sea snakes)(see Wilson and Knowles 1988) and 200 amphibians, totalling approximately 1,700 species.

The national list of endangered vertebrates endorsed by the Council of Nature Conservation Ministers (CONCOM) currently stands at 97 taxa, including 11 birds endemic to oceanic islands under Australian jurisdiction (Cocos-Keeling, Christmas, Norfolk, Lord Howe, and Macquarie Islands), three marine mammals, one marine turtle and four freshwater fish. The list includes all but two of the continental species presumed to be extinct (Table 3), those being *Notomys amplus* and *Pseudomys gouldi* (see Strahan 1983). If these two rodents are included, precisely half of the 80 endangered taxa are mammals, although representatives of that class comprise only 14% of the total terrestrial fauna. Furthermore, all but one of the 19 presumed extinctions have been of mammals, predominantly small to medium-sized marsupials and rodents of the arid and semi-arid inland.

*Legal Responsibilities for Conserving Flora and Fauna*

Under the Australian Constitution, responsibility for conserving and managing flora and fauna lies primarily with the States. Apart from the few and limited areas of federal lands, the role of the

*Table 3.*—Endangered terrestrial fauna of Australia (CONCOM 1988).

| Class | Total Australian species | Endangered species, including extinctions | Total Victorian species | Endangered species in Victoria on CONCOM list |
|---|---|---|---|---|
| Mammals | 245 | 38 (16)[1] | 119 | 10 |
| Birds | 605 | 26 (1) | 360 | 10 |
| Reptiles | 650 | 8 (0) | 109 | 0 |
| Amphibians | 200 | 6 (0) | 33 | 1 |
| | 1700 | 78 (17) | 621 | 21 |

[1]Does not include *Notomys amplus* and *Pseudomys gouldi*, also presumed extinct (Strahan 1983; Watts and Aslin 1981).

Commonwealth is limited to matters such as export and international treaties such as the 'Agreement between the Government of Japan for the Protection of Migratory Birds and Birds in Danger of Extinction and their Environment' (see list of treaties in Wilson and Knowles 1988). However, since the creation of the Australian National Parks and Wildlife Service (ANPWS) in 1974, the Commonwealth government has actively encouraged the development of national policies in cooperation with the States. More recently the Commonwealth has extended its authority by using a variety of powers, including its role in relation to the 'Convention Concerning the Protection of the World Cultural and Natural Heritage' to influence developments within States that affect ecosystems (Wilson and Knowles 1988).

For many years, Victorian legislation protecting flora and fauna (birds and mammals) focussed on the protection of species by preventing killing, disturbance, taking from the wild, and possession and trade, except under license. Some State fauna legislation now includes amphibians and reptiles by a 'catch-all' definition of wildlife, rather than listing by name each protected species or groups of species in a schedule to the relevant Act.

Native fish are protected under fisheries legislation primarily designed to manage stocks for sport and commercial fishing.

Some protection of habitats has been achieved by reservation of ecologically significant and substantial areas as national parks and nature reserves. However, the location of nature reserves in excess of 10,000 ha throughout Australia, as mapped by Leigh *et al.* (1981), graphically illustrates the problems of representation, insularity and distance. Additional and important reserves have since been created, *e.g.* Kakadu National Park in Arnhem Land, but many ecosystems remain poorly or wholly unrepresented. Therefore, despite the intention that these large reserves and the many smaller ones will protect ecosystems and sustain ecological processes, a major limitation is the lack of a legal means to protect the habitats of species outside reserve boundaries and to link them with effective habitat corridors.

The first significant step in the direction is the Victorian *Flora and Fauna Guarantee Act* 1988, which breaks new ground by not only protecting all native species of plants and animals, including invertebrates, but by recognising and providing for the protection of critical habitats of species,

*Table 4.*—Victorian studies of significant taxa undertaken for management.

| Species | Contributors | | | | | |
|---|---|---|---|---|---|---|
| | CFL[1] | Other States | ANPWS[2] | National Estate | WWF[3] | Universities |
| **Mammals** | | | | | | |
| Mountain pygmy possum | x | x | | | x | |
| Leadbeater's possum | x | | | | | x |
| Long-footed potoroo | x | x | x | | | x |
| Brush-tailed rock-wallaby | x | | | | | |
| Koala | x | | x | | x | x |
| Eastern barred bandicoot | x | | | | x | x |
| **Birds** | | | | | | |
| Ground parrot | x | | | | | |
| Orange-bellied parrot | x | x | x | | | |
| Superb parrot | x | | | | | |
| Long-billed corella | x | x | | | | |
| Red-tailed black cockatoo | x | | | x | | |
| Helmeted honeyeater | x | | | | | x |
| Black-eared miner | x | | | | | |
| Regent honeyeater | x | | x | | | |
| Little tern | x | x | x | | | |
| **Reptiles** | | | | | | |
| *Delma impar* | x | | | x | | x |
| *Aprasia aurita* | x | | | x | | |
| **Amphibians** | | | | | | |
| Spotted tree frog | x | | | x | | |
| Baw Baw frog | x | | | | | |
| **Invertebrates** | | | | | | |
| Eltham copper butterfly | x | | | | | |
| Altona skipper butterfly | x | | | x | | |

[1]Department of Conservation, Forests and Lands
[2]Australian National Parks and Wildlife Service
[3]World Wildlife Fund Australia

threatened communities and countering threatening processes (Dept. of Conservation, Forests and Lands 1987, Victorian Government 1988). In its simplest terms, the guarantee is intended to ensure that native species survive, flourish, and maintain their potential for evolutionary development in the wild. Thus, the Act codifies an ecological ethic, which is unique in the history of Australian conservation legislation.

*Conservation and Management*

During the past two decades, the output of biological and ecological research in Australia has increased dramatically. One clear measure of this is the number, variety, and quality of studies reported in the major Australian journals serving the broad disciplines of botany, zoology, wildlife, and ecology, as well as the more specialised journals catering to limnology, herpetology, ornithology, and mammalogy.

Field surveys of flora and fauna have been an area of increased endeavour during the period, but the results have not been adequately reported. Natural resource agencies have given strong support to these inventory studies because they provide important baseline data on species distribution and status, which are being increasingly used by land-use planners and managers. Substantial computerised databases are being developed in some states, in resource agencies, museums and herbaria.

The Victorian Department of Conservation, Forest and Lands flora and fauna databases are probably the most comprehensive, in terms of coverage and detail (*e.g.* the *Atlas of Victorian Wildlife* contains more than 25,000 locality records of amphibians and reptiles, 800,000 of birds and nearly 60,000 of mammals). The bird data are a subset of the Royal Australasian Ornithologists Union's *Atlas of Australian Birds* (Blakers *et al.* 1984), augmented by the results of field studies and a program of fauna surveys conducted throughout Victoria from 1970 to the present.

A great deal of biological information is now available on a wide variety of species as a result of research by natural resource agencies, museums, herbaria, the Commonwealth Science and Industrial Research Organisation, universities and other tertiary institutions, and skilled field naturalists. However, literature reviews and the consolidation of published data are rarely sufficient to prepare management guidelines. In recent times, an encouraging number of field studies has been undertaken with the specific aim of providing information for managing populations of species and subspecies believed to be at risk. In Victoria, the status, biology and habitat requirements of more than 20 taxa have been investigated because they were believed to be at risk and required active management (Table 4).

For managers responsible for small populations of endangered species, there are many concepts and tools directly useful to them. These new technologies, coupled with an expanding store of biological and ecological information about Australia's flora and fauna, offer unprecedented opportunities for effectively managing populations and ecosystems. This challenge will, we hope, receive wide support and recognition through the recently formed Australasian Wildlife Management Society, and other management organisations.

*Conclusions*

In conclusion, the work before conservation biologists and others is vitally important. We are the last generation that can prevent the extinction of large numbers of plants and animals. If we fail over the next few years and into the next few decades, there will likely be relatively little biodiversity left to conserve.

As we strive to develop more effective science, management programs and policies, we need to do several things. First, we need to make sure that we bring all the relevant data to bear on the task, including results of rigorously designed and conducted field studies on life histories, population dynamics and genetics, as well as information from all the relevant disciplines—botany, ecology, behaviour, physiology, veterinary medicine, genetics. We need to construct models where appropriate. We need to foster a cooperative, open problem-solving climate. Second, we need to make sure that we use a model of the extinction process which recognises both systematic and stochastic factors to guide scientists, managers and policy specialists. And lastly, we need to make sure conservation science and management employ the appropriate and timely mix of onsite and offsite techniques. This will require advances in field procedures and zoo research. And it will require a much closer, productive working relationship between field biologists and managers, zoos, universities, and government and nongovernment organisations. A philosophy of adaptive management should guide these cooperative conservation efforts.


## Acknowledgments

Denise Casey provided critical advice on this manuscript.


## References


Andrewartha, H.G., and Birch, L.C. 1954. *The Distribution and Abundance of Animals*. Univ. of Chicago Press: Chicago.

Baker, R.M., and George, G.G. 1988. Species management programmes in Australia and New Zealand. *Int. Zoo Yearb.* **27**:19-26.

Blakers, M., Davies, S.J.J.F., and Reilly, P.N. 1984. *The Atlas of Australian Birds*. RAOU and Melbourne Univ. Press: Melbourne.

Brussard, P.F. 1985. Minimum viable populations: how many are too few? *Restoration and Management Notes* **3**:21-25.

Brussard, P.F., and Gilpin, M.E. 1989. Demographic and genetic problems associated with small population size, with special reference to the black-footed ferret *Mustela nigripes*. In *Proceedings of the Workshop on Reproductive Biology of Black-Footed Ferrets and Small Population Biology as They Relate to Conservation,* eds U.S. Seal, S.H. Anderson, M. Bogan, and E.T. Thorne. Yale Univ. Press: New Haven.

Clark, T.W. 1986. Case studies in wildlife policy education. *Renewable Resources Journal* **4**:111-16.

Clark, T.W. 1989. *Conservation Biology of the Endangered Black-Footed Ferret*. Special Scientific Report No. 2. Wildlife Preservation Trust International: Philadelphia.

Clark, T.W., and Harvey, A.H. 1988. Implementing endangered species recovery policy: learning as we go? *Endangered Species Update* **5**(10):35-42.

Clark, T.W., Crete, R., and Cada, J. 1989. Designing and managing successful endangered species recovery programs. *Environ. Manage.* **13**:159-170.

CONCOM (Council of Nature Conservation Ministers). 1988. List of Endangered Vertebrate Fauna, as amended April 1988. Issued by the Australian National Parks and Wildlife Service, Canberra.

Connner, R.N. 1988. Wildlife populations: minimally viable or ecologically functional? *Wildl. Soc. Bull.* **16**:80-84.

Department of Conservation, Forests and Lands, Victoria. 1987. *Questions and answers on proposed legislation for a Flora and Fauna Guarantee Act 1987*. Govt. Printer: Melbourne.

Fenner, F. 1975. *A National System of Ecological Reserves in Australia*. Australian Academy of Science Rep. No. 19.

Frankel, O.H., and Soulé, M.E. 1981. *Conservation and Evolution*. Cambridge Univ. Press: Cambridge.

Frood, D., and Calder, M. 1987. *Nature Conservation in Victoria*. 2 vols. Victorian National Parks Association, Melbourne.

George, A.S. 1981. The background to the Flora of Australia. In *Flora of Australia,* vol. 1. Bureau of Flora and Fauna: Canberra.

George, G.G. 1986. A strategy for the co-operative management of species required for display in the zoos of Australia and New Zealand. *Bull. Zoo Manage.* **24**:21-25.

George, G.G. 1987. The Australian Species Management Scheme—three down the track. *Bull. Zoo Manage.* **25**:38-43.

George, G.G. 1988. Conservation genetics and the management of species in captivity. In *Australian Wildlife, The John Keep Refresher Course for Veterinarians, Proc. 104,* ed. D. I. Bryden. Pp. 945-52. Post-grad. Comm. Veter. Sci., Univ. Sydney.

Gilpin, M.E., and Soulé, M.E. 1986. Minimum viable populations: processes of species extinction. In *Conservation Biology,* ed. M. E. Soulé. Pp. 19-34. Sinauer Associates: Sunderland, Massachusetts.

Ginsberg, J.R. 1987. What is conservation biology? *Trends in Ecology and Evol.* 2:262-264.

Griffith, B., Scott, J.M., Carpernter, J.W., and Reed, C. 1989. Translocation as a species conservation tool: status and strategy. *Science* 245:477-480.

Harris, R., Clark, T.W., and Shaffer, M. 1989. Estimating extinction probabilities for the black-footed ferret. In *Reproductive Biology of Black-Footed Ferrets and Small Population Biology as They Relate to Conservation,* eds U.S. Seal, S.H. Anderson, M. Bogan and E.T. Thorne. Yale Univ. Press: New Haven.

Holling, C.S. 1973. Resilience and stability of ecological systems. *Ann. Rev. Ecol. Systematics* 4:1-23.

Holling, C.S. (ed). 1978. *Adaptive environmental assessment and management.* Intl. Ser. on Applied Systems Analysis 3, International Institute for Applied Systems Analysis. John Wiley and Sons: Toronto.

Horton, J.C., and Becak, C.J. 1987. Modeling for biologists. *BioScience* 37:808-809.

Interagency Task Force. 1985. *U.S. Strategy on the Conservation of Biological Diversity.* An Interagency task force report to Congress. Govt. Print. Off.: Washington.

International Union for Conservation of Nature and Natural Resources. 1980. *World Conservation Strategy.* IUCN: Gland.

International Union for Conservation of Nature and Natural Resources. 1987. *The IUCN Policy Statement on Captive Breeding.* IUCN: Gland.

Lacy, R.C. 1987. Loss of genetic diversity from managed populations: interacting effects of drift, mutation, immigration, selection, and population subdivision. *Conserv. Biol.* 1:143-158.

Lacy, R.C., and Clark, T.W. 1989. Genetic variability in black-footed ferret populations: past, present, and future. In *Proc. Workshop on Reproductive Biology of Black-Footed Ferrets and Small Population Biology as They Relate to Conservation,* eds U.S. Seal, S.H. Anderson, M. Bogan, and E.T. Thorne. Pp. 83-103. Yale Univ. Press: New Haven.

Leigh, J., Briggs, J., and Hartley, W. 1981. Rare or threatened Australian plants. Aust. Nat. Parks. Wildl. Serv. Special Publ. No. 7.

Levins, R. 1970. Extinction. In *Some Mathematical Questions in Biology,* vol. 2, ed. M. Gerstenhabaer. Pp. 77-107. Amer. Math. Soc.: Providence, Rhode Island.

Kleiman, D.G. 1989. Reintroduction of captive mammals for conservation. *BioScience* 39:152-161.

Maguire, L.A. 1986. Using decision analysis to manage endangered species populations. *J. Environ. Manage.* 22:345-360.

Mlot, C. 1989. The science of saving endangered species. *BioScience* 39:68-69.

National Research Council. 1986. Ecological knowledge and environmental problem-solving: concepts and case studies. Committee on the Applications of Ecological Theory to Environmental Problems. National Academy of Science Press: Washington.

Office of Technology Assessment. 1987. *Technologies to Maintain Biological Diversity.* U. S. Congress OTA-F-330. Govt. Print. Off.: Washington.

Richardson, B.J. 1987. The Animal Kingdom in Australia. In *Fauna of Australia,* vol. 1A. Bureau of Flora and Fauna: Canberra.

Ride, W.D.L., and McCusker, A. 1978. The extent and nature of programs in biological survey conducted primarily by State museums and herbaria. In *Australian Biological Resources Study 1973-1978.* Aust. Govt. Publ. Serv.: Canberra.

Romesberg, H.C. 1981. Wildlife science: gaining reliable knowledge. *J. Wildl. Manage.* 45:293-313.

Samson, F.B. 1986. Minimum viable populations—a review. *Natural Areas J.* 3:15-23.

Schonewald-Cox, C.M., Chambers, S.M., MacBryde, B., and Thomas, L. 1983. *Genetics and Conservation: a Reference for Managing Wild Animal and Plant Populations.* Benjamin/ Cummings Publ. Co., Advanced Book Program: Sydney.

Shaffer, M.L. 1978. Determining minimum viable population sizes: a case study of the grizzly bear (*Ursus arctos* L.). Ph.D. Thesis, Duke University, Durham, North Carolina.

Shaffer, M.L. 1981. Minimum population sizes for species conservation. *BioScience* 31:131-134.

Simberloff, D. 1986. The proximate causes of extinction. In *Patterns and Processes in the History of Life,* eds D.M. Raup and D. Jablonski. Pp. 259-276. Springer-Verlag: Berlin.

Simberloff, D. 1988. The contribution of population and community biology to conservation science. *Ann. Rev. Evol. and Systematics* 19:473-511.

Soulé, M.E. 1985. What is conservation biology? *BioScience* 35:727-734.

Soulé, M.E. (ed.) 1986. *Conservation Biology: the Science of Scarcity and Diversity.* Sinauer Associates: Sunderland, Massachusetts.

Soulé, M.E. 1987. *Viable Populations for Conservation.* Cambridge University Press: Sydney.

Soulé, M.E., and Wilcox, B.A. (eds.) 1980. *Conservation Biology: an Evolutionary-Ecological Perspective.* Sinauer Associates: Sunderland, Massachusetts.

Soulé, M.E., and Simberloff, D. 1986. What do genetics and ecology tell us about the design of nature reserves? *Biol. Conserv.* **35**:19-40.

Strahan, R. (ed.) 1983. *The Australian Museum Complete Book of Australian Mammmals.* Angus and Robertson: Sydney.

Specht, R.L., Roe, E.M., and Boughton, V.H. 1974. Conservation of major plant communities in Australia and Papua New Guinea. *Aust. J. Botany,* Suppl. No. 7.

Victorian Government. 1988. *Acts 1988 No. 47, Flora and Fauna Guarantee Act 1988.* Vic. Govt. Publ. Off.: Melbourne.

Watts, C.H.S. and Aslin, H.J. 1981. *The Rodents of Australia.* Angus and Robertson, Sydney.

Wilcox, B.A. 1986. Extinction models and conservation. *Tree* **1**:46-47.

Wilson, S.K., and Knowles, D.G. 1988. *Australian Reptiles. A Photgraphic Reference of the Terrestrial Reptiles of Australia.* Collins: Sydney.

Wilson, E.O., and Willis, E.O. 1975. Applied biogeography. In *Ecology and Evolution of Communities,* eds. J. L. Cody and J. M. Diamond. Pp. 523-534. Harvard University Press: Cambridge.

Zimmerman, B.L., and Bierregaard, R.O. 1986. Relevance of the equilibrium theory of island biogeography and species-area relations to conservation with a case from Amazonia. *J. Biogeog.* **13**:133-143.

# Eastern Barred Bandicoot Case

The eastern barred bandicoot (*Perameles gunnii*) exists today on the Australian mainland in one small population near Hamilton, Victoria. It formerly occupied a much wider range and occurred in much larger numbers. The eastern barred bandicoot was chosen as a 'representative' case to explore in detail in the Conference because 1) it is threatened with extinction by a host of factors and processes and 2) an ongoing program to restore the species in Victoria, involving many organizations and drawing data from various scientific disciplines, has used concepts and techniques which we feel can be valuable for many other species.

The bandicoot is a small to medium-sized marsupial that in many ways demonstrates problems faced by many similar-sized marsupials in Australia. It is still represented in the fauna of Tasmania, but its taxonomic relationship to the mainland form is ill-defined and its status in Tasmania may be declining. Many characteristics of its biology and its location make it well-suited to a multidisciplinary conservation approach. Adequate data exist to employ a population viability assessment to set recovery targets and a decision analysis to find optimal management strategies. These objectives have been met because of these approaches and the information presented and synthesised in this section. Management actions can now be scheduled and executed in a timely manner and guided by a philosophy of adaptive management. Increased management of the wild population, captive breeding and accurate monitoring are all needed to secure a future for the species on the mainland.

# Status, Distribution and Biogeography of the Eastern Barred Bandicoot, *Perameles gunnii,* in Victoria

*John H. Seebeck[1], Andrew F. Bennett[1], and Anthony C. Dufty[2]*

## Abstract

Before European settlement, the eastern barred bandicoot, *Perameles gunnii,* was abundantly distributed across the western volcanic plains of Victoria in grassland and open woodland habitats. The species persisted widely over a large region despite climatic fluctuations, fire, predation by dingoes and hunting by Aboriginals. Population reduction began subsequent to settlement of the plains in the 1840s. Factors involved in this change of status include a host of systematic and stochastic processes: habitat alteration by the introduction of domestic stock and its effects on soil structure; pasture establishment; changing fire regimes; addition of fertilizers; rabbits; and closer settlement. Direct losses caused by rabbit trapping, predation by introduced carnivores, poisons, pesticides and motor vehicles have combined with habitat changes to reduce the range and numbers of bandicoots to one population at Hamilton. The species follows the typical pattern of endangerment. This population is critically small and unstable, and management of the continuing factors that have brought about this situation is essential for conservation of the species.

## Introduction

There is rarely a single cause or event leading to the endangerment and, ultimately, to the extinction of native animals. Single processes can have dramatic effects, as witness the extinction of the dodo, Steller's sea cow, passenger pigeon and the near-extinction of the bison, mainly by hunting. Usually, however, endangerment stems from a combination of numerous factors. Major processes, such as habitat alteration and deliberate persecution by humans, can be the primary contributors to the fragmentation of large populations into smaller and more vulnerable populations. These small populations are then particularly sensitive to chance variation in demographic processes, loss of genetic diversity, environmental fluctuations and a variety of catastrophes (*e.g.* Petterson 1985; Simberloff 1988, Clark *et al.*, this volume).

The reduction from a large continuous population to a series of small, disjunct populations, the classic portrayal of the extinction process, has been repeated many times within the Australian mammal fauna since European settlement. Perhaps the most dramatic illustrations come from species of the arid or semi-arid zone. For example, the burrowing bettong (*Bettongia lesueur*) was formerly distributed across almost two-thirds of the continent, but is now only found on three islands off the Western Australian coast (Seebeck *et al.* 1989). Similarly, the numbat (*Myrmecobius fasciatus*) was formerly widespread across semi-arid southern Australia, but now is known only from several woodland blocks in south-western Western Australia (Friend and Kinnear 1983).

On mainland Australia, the eastern barred bandicoot (*Perameles gunnii*) is a notable example of a species that has experienced a dramatic decline in both distribution and status. Seebeck (1979) has discussed the decline of this species in Victoria and has suggested that a series of events was instrumental in the reduction of

[1]National Parks and Wildlife Division, Department of Conservation, Forests and Lands, Victoria. Arthur Rylah Insitute for Environmental Research, 123 Brown Street, Heidelberg, Victoria 3084, Australia.
[2]Department of Zoology, The University of Melbourne, Parkville, Victoria 3052, Australia.

*P. gunnii* in that State. In this paper we document the changing status of the eastern barred bandicoot, discuss the contribution of various processes to that changed status, and examine the lessons that may be learned for future management of this and other declining species. Attention is focussed primarily on the western volcanic plains of Victoria, where the eastern barred bandicoot has declined to a single, small and endangered population.

The eastern barred bandicoot is a small (about 700g) terrestrial marsupial. It is grizzled, yellowish-brown above and slaty grey below, with three or four pale bars on the hindquarters. The tail and feet are white on the upper surface. The forefeet are armed with long claws, and the hindfeet are characteristically syndactylous (Seebeck 1983) (Fig. 1).


*Distribution at the Time of*
*European Settlement*

At the time of European settlement in Australia, *P. gunnii* was widespread across the plains of southwestern Victoria, was probably widely distributed in northern and eastern Tasmania (Hocking, in press) and occurred in the southeastern corner of South Australia (Kemper, in press) (Fig. 2). In Tasmania, the historical distribution of *P. gunnii* was probably associated with natural grasslands and grassy woodlands (Hocking, in press). Certainly, its present distribution is strongly associated with open grassland, although it occurs on a variety of soil types. Heinsohn (1966) found that, in northwestern Tasmania, *P. gunnii* used open paddocks most and open forest least from the range of habitats that were available.

The former distribution of *P. gunnii* in southeastern South Australia is poorly known, but the species does not appear to have been widespread or abundant. In contrast to its primary use of grassland habitats in Victoria and Tasmania, it apparently occurred in a rather different environment in southeastern South Australia (Kemper, in press) in a habitat of open forest, banksia and mallee shrubland on sandy soils. It is probable that it utilized grassy areas within the scrub and woodland.

In Victoria, the eastern barred bandicoot was virtually confined to the western volcanic plains that extend from Melbourne almost to the South Australian border, covering an area of some 23,000 km². These plains are mostly gently undulating terrain, dissected by shallow drainage lines, dotted with swamps and lakes, and pierced by the emergent cones of extinct volcanoes. Willis (1964, 1984) has described in detail the vegetation of the plains, and recognised three major formations: the drier stony basalt plains in the east; the weathered basalt plains, with higher rainfall, towards the west; and the basalt barriers (or stony rises) that occur between Colac and Camperdown and elsewhere, and result from the most recent volcanic activity. The drier plains supported open tussock grassland generally devoid of trees except for scattered, stunted river red gum (*Eucalyptus camaldulensis*) and swamp gum (*E. ovata*) adjacent to wetlands. Grasses and daisies dominated the flora, with many species of wallaby-grasses (*Danthonia* spp.), spear-grasses (*Stipa* spp.), kangaroo grass (*Themeda triandra*) and daisies of the genus *Brachycome* being widespread and abundant. The growth form of isolated tufts separated by bare ground provided not only cover, but foraging areas for the bandicoots.

With increasing rainfall from east to west there was a change in grass species, with *Poa labillardieri* replacing *Themeda* and *Stipa* as the dominant species on moister sites. Tree growth became more widespread, and a savannah woodland of *E. camaldulensis* associated with silver banksia (*Banksia marginata*), blackwood (*Acacia melanoxylon*), black wattle (*A. mearnsii*) and sweet bursaria (*Bursaria spinosa*) developed in the west.

The stoney rises support woodlands of manna gum (*E. viminalis*) and blackwood, with tree everlasting (*Helichrysum dendroideum*) and bracken (*Pteridium esculentum*) as common understorey species among the rocky barriers. Grasslands are poorly developed in this formation.

*Figure 1.*—The eastern barred bandicoot, *Perameles gunnii*.

## *Status in Western Victoria at the Time of European Settlement.*

The nature of the distribution of the bandicoots across the plains can never be known, but it is probable that the extensive area of native grassland and grassy woodlands enabled *P. gunnii* to occupy this region as a large, essentially continuous population. The wide geographic spread of known localities supports this contention (Fig. 3). If modern assessments of density (Dufty 1988; Minta *et al.*, this volume) can be translated to the undisturbed state, then the species must have been abundant. Three factors, climate, fire and predation, are believed to have been the major controlling influences on the status of the eastern barred bandicoot in western Victoria prior to European settlement.

### *Climate*

Through its effect on food supply, climatic variation can exert a major influence on the carrying capacity of the environment. Thus, seasonal fluctuations in rainfall and temperature regimes, particularly extreme fluctuations resulting in droughts or flooding, must certainly have affected local abundance both on a seasonal and longer term basis. Evidence from recent studies at Hamilton suggests that population numbers decline and reproduction ceases during severe drought (Brown 1985). Seebeck (1979) reported that at Hamilton a contraction of the population distribution towards drainage lines had been observed during times of low rainfall, presumably related to the greater accessibility of food in moister soils than in dry hard soils. Conversely, flooding probably causes a retreat to higher ground, with concomitant crowding and perhaps aggressive social interaction, in addition to the death of nestling young by drowning.

### *Fire*

Fire, either from lightning strikes or aboriginal burning, was a natural component of the grassland ecology of the volcanic plains. William Buckley (in Morgan 1852) described fires deliberately lit by Aboriginals in southwestern Victoria, and Robinson (1841) also noted recently burned areas during his travels across the plains. In dry conditions, wildfires may have been extensive and could have killed large numbers of bandicoots. However, the high reproductive potential of the species enables populations so devastated by natural catastrophic events to recover rapidly. Fires also promote successional change in vegetation communities, and could

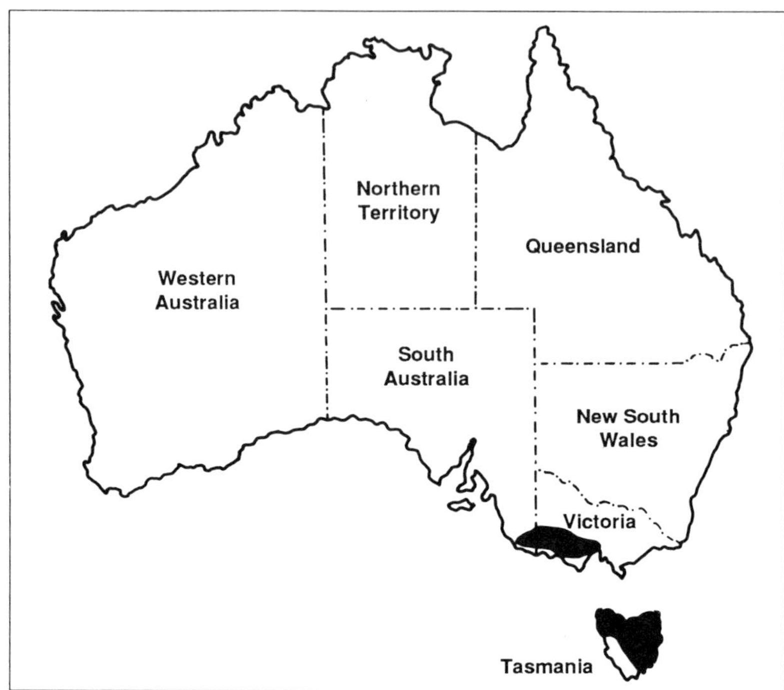



*Figure 2.*—Pre-European distribution of *Perameles gunnii* in southeastern Australia.

therefore influence the availability and spatial pattern of grassland communities, as well as micro-habitat features such as dense tussocks for shelter.

*Predation*

*P. gunnii* was well-known to the Aboriginal inhabitants of western Victoria, and was included amongst the mammals hunted for food (Smyth 1878). Dawson (1881) recorded three language-group names for 'banded bandicoot', and anthropological deposits containing the remains of *P. gunnii* are known from several western Victorian sites (Coutts *et al.* 1976). However, although the hunting impact on local populations may have been dramatic, it is unlikely that the effects would have been permanent. Robinson (1841, p. 73), for example, commenting on the local impact of an Aboriginal camp, remarked 'Desolations met with where there are natives long resident—all trees are denuded and die. . .animals are destroyed, ground broken. . .'

Other potential predators of adult or juvenile bandicoots included the dingo (*Canis familiaris dingo*), tiger quoll (*Dasyurus maculatus*), eastern quoll (*D. viverrinus*), nocturnal and diurnal birds of prey, and perhaps snakes (*e.g.* tiger snake, *Notechis scutatus*).

*Status after European Settlement*

The status of *P. gunnii* following European settlement in southern Australia has differed dramatically between Tasmania and the mainland states. In Tasmania, the species has thrived despite intensive agricultural settlement, and it now occurs in large numbers in rural areas (Hocking, in press). Its abundance may have increased since settlement (Seebeck 1983), perhaps due to its ability to utilise agricultural pastures and other developed rural habitats. However, in South Australia, the species is presumed extinct, with the last recorded specimen from near Mt Gambier in 1893 (Aitken 1983); while in Victoria, the

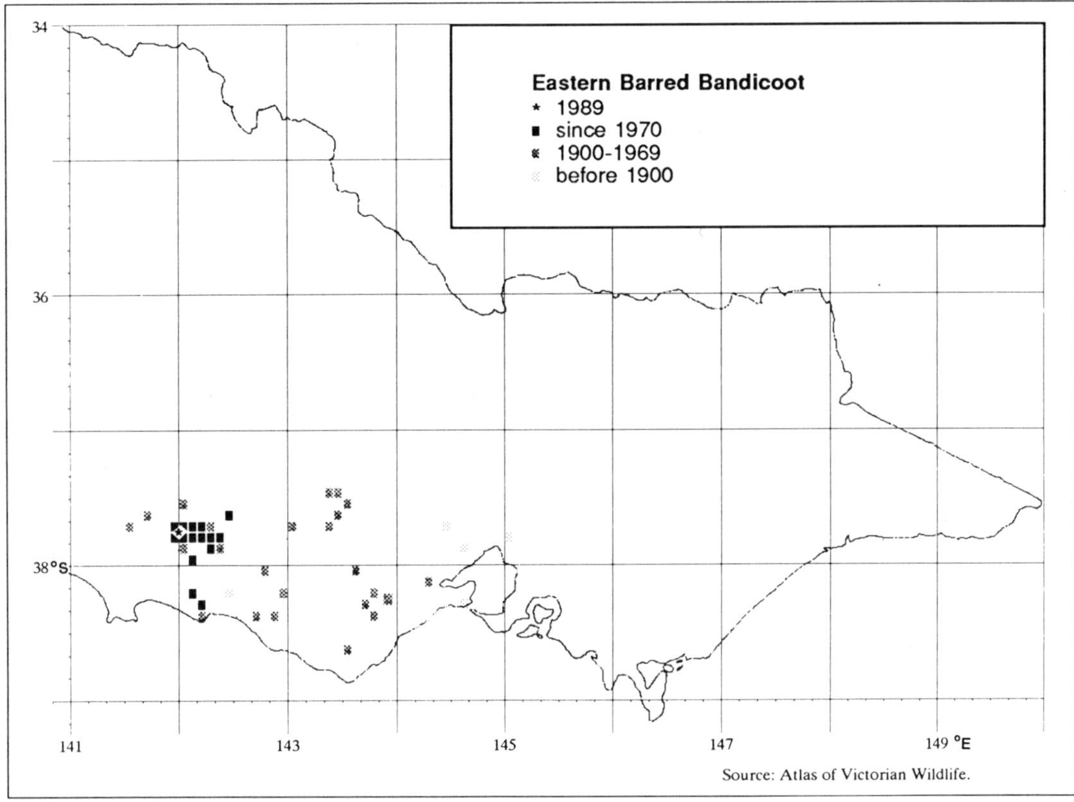


*Figure 3.*—Distribution of *Perameles gunnii* in Victoria, 1840-1989.

formerly extensive population has contracted in distribution to a small remnant centred on the urgan fringe of Hamilton (Seebeck 1979; Moon 1984; Dufty 1988; Brown 1989). We discuss below the suite of factors potentially contributing to the decline of the eastern barred bandicoot in western Victoria.

*Changing Status in Western Victoria*

Settlement of the western plains of Victoria began in the 1830s, but the occurrence of *P. gunnii* among the wealth of wildlife surrounding them was seldom recorded by the earliest European settlers. The earliest specimen in the Museum of Victoria is dated 1867, and its origin is not known with certainty. Gould (1863) suggested that *P. gunnii* occurred at Port Phillip and specimens from Port Phillip were in Gould's collection (Thomas 1888). Dawson (1881) listed Aboriginal names for 'banded bandicoot' collected since his arrival in the western district in 1844. No doubt he had collected specimens of bandicoots, as he was a 'fine amateur taxidermist [who] built up a large natural history collection' (Critchett 1981), but the whereabouts of those specimens, formerly in the Camperdown Museum, is not known. Brown (1989) listed specimens held in the Museum of Victoria that were collected between 1881 and 1929 which illustrate the distribution across the plains, and he pointed out that after 1930, specimens were rarely collected, and those that were came from a much less widespread area.

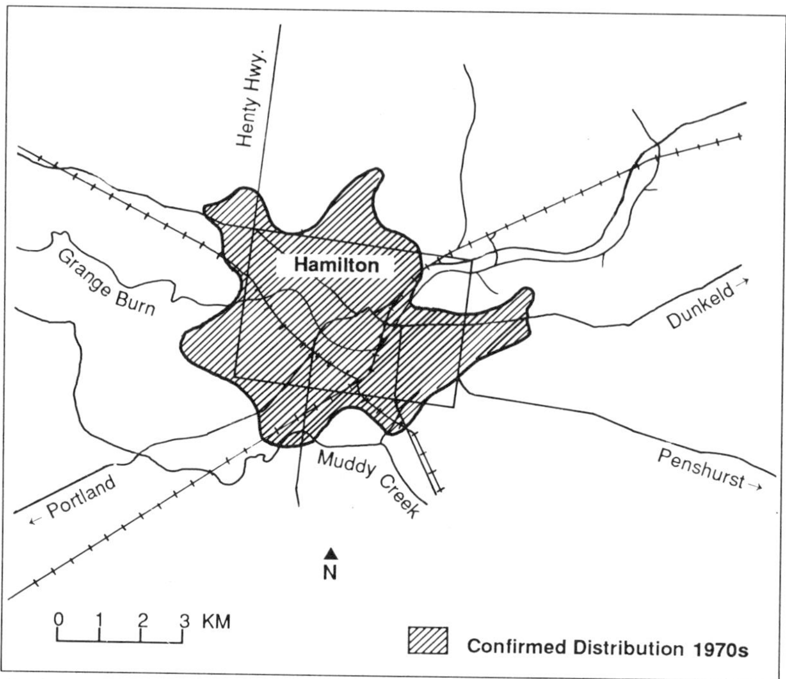


*Figure 4a.*—Distribution of *Perameles gunnii* at Hamilton, 1970s.

Despite this wide distribution of specimen records, there is little information describing the chronological change in status. Seebeck (1979) reported the decline of a population from abundance to extinction at Mt Gellibrand near Colac between 1903 and the 1950s; and in the Hamilton district, from 1960 to the present, we have witnessed a contraction of range and a marked decline in numbers (Seebeck 1979; Dufty 1988; Brown 1989) (Fig. 4, a, b, c). The population decline at Hamilton has accelerated dramatically in the last decade. During 1983-1985 the geographic range of the population was estimated to be some 1,400 ha (Sherwin and Brown, in press), but by 1988 it was estimated to be only about 600 ha (Dufty 1988). An associated decrease in population size has occurred, with the population in late 1988 estimated to be only about 220 animals (Dufty 1988), and about 180 by Minta *et al.* (this volume). Lacy and Clark (this volume) have modelled this decline.

What has caused this change to the status of *P. gunnii?* Seebeck (1979) and Brown (1989) have listed a number of factors that can be grouped into two main categories: habitat alteration, and introduced predators and competitors.

*Habitat Changes*

Habitat loss through agricultural development in western Victoria is difficult to quantify, especially as there is some evidence that despite conversion of the natural environment to grazing properties, the bandicoots initially continued to thrive. The very fact that they were able to maintain populations around Hamilton until recently supports this view. But the early modification of the native vegetation by clearing, grazing and ploughing was accompanied and succeeded by a further series of changes, all of which have combined to create an alien landscape.

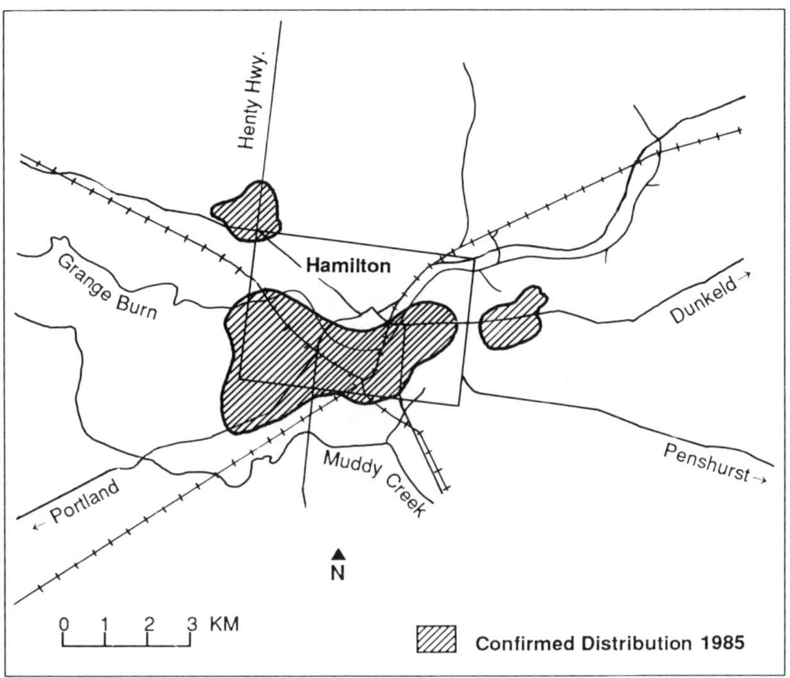



*Figure 4b.*—Distribution of *Perameles gunnii* at Hamilton, 1985.

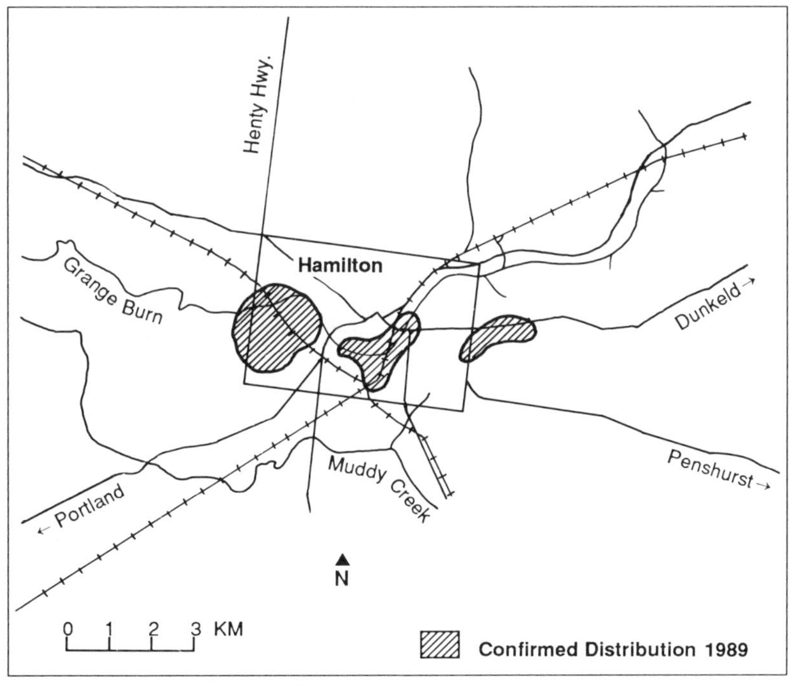



*Figure 4c.*—Distribution of *Perameles gunnii* at Hamilton, 1989.

Changes to the composition and diversity of grasslands were brought about by the introduction (from the 1860s onwards) of exotic pasture grasses and legumes; by the selective grazing of stock; and, in the years following World War I, by an increasing use of fertilizers. Native grasses (*e.g. Themeda, Danthonia, Stipa, Poa*) are virtually absent from developed farmland on the plains of western Victoria, and now persist only as small remnants in areas such as roadside and railway reserves, cemetaries, and several small nature reserves. These factors have also resulted in changes to the physical structure of grasslands; from patchy cover of tussocks to a continuous sward of reduced height. These changes are presumed to have altered the availability of dense cover used by *P. gunnii* for diurnal shelter and predator avoidance, and also to have influenced the composition, diversity and abundance of the invertebrate food resources available to the bandicoots.

Soil structure and associated soil invertebrate fauna in farmland environments has also changed, largely due to the impact of stock. Brown (1989) summarised recent research on the effects of different stocking rates on pasture composition and on changes to the invertebrate fauna of the soil. High stocking rates can result in soil compaction, a diminished species diversity of both plants and invertebrates, and a reduction in the body weight and numbers of earthworms, an important bandicoot food item. Observations at Hamilton suggest that bandicoots selectively feed in less-trampled areas, such as along fence lines and within fenced-off areas.

*Introduced Animals*

The introduction of the European rabbit (*Oryctolagus cuniculus*) and its subsequent impact on the landscape has been well documented (Rolls 1969). Brown (1989) has examined the role that rabbits may have played in the changing status of bandicoots, and concluded that it was a complex one, incorporating a) destruction and change to the vegetation, b) direct deaths due to rabbit trapping and c) an increase in the fox (*Vulpes vulpes*)

population. Millions of rabbits were trapped in western Victoria between 1868 and 1914 (Hebb 1888; Rolls 1969; Garden 1984; Brown 1989) and large numbers of bandicoots also must have been killed. Rabbit control measures after 1945, including trapping, poisoning and warren destruction further increased pressure on the bandicoots. The introduction of myxomatosis and 1080 poison in the 1950s, which produced a rapid decline in rabbit numbers, made predation by foxes more likely as they turned to secondary prey species (Brown 1989).

Foxes arrived in the Hamilton region between about 1906 and the beginning of World War I and had an immediate and dramatic affect on bandicoots (G.J. Milligan in Seebeck 1979). The present abundance of *P. gunnii* in Tasmania where foxes are absent supports the belief that this introduced predator was a significant contributor to the decline of the bandicoots on the mainland. Foxes may still be an important predator of bandicoots at Hamilton, and at sites where re-introduction programs are underway or planned, the control of foxes is a major problem.

Predation of *P. gunnii* by domestic and feral cats (*Felis catus*) in the Hamilton area, particularly of juvenile bandicoots by domestic cats, is believed to be a major factor in preventing the stabilization and increase of the local population (Brown 1989). Cats may also be involved in the decline through transmission of disease, particularly Toxoplasmosis. Brown (1989), Obendorf and Munday (in press) and Lenghaus *et al.* (this volume) have described the detrimental effects on bandicoots of infection by the toxoplasma organism. Domestic dogs have hunted and killed bandicoots throughout the period of settlement, and still kill small numbers of animals at Hamilton.

*Other Factors*

Natural catastrophes, such as wildfires and floods, have occurred both prior to and since European settlement. However, their impact on *P. gunnii* is likely to have been greater since settlement due to the increased isolation and disjunction of populations, and the reduced opportunity for re-colonisation from nearby populations. For example, the local disappearance of bandicoots in the Woolsthorpe district coincided with a major flood in 1946 (Bennett 1982); and in recent times the extensive fires of February 1977 may have eliminated an outlying population at Carranballac.

Recent preliminary studies on pesticide levels in *P. gunnii* (C. Lenghaus, personal communication 1989) suggest that there may be a link between levels of organochlorines accumulated by bandicoots and their health, reproductive capacity, and the survivorship of young. This may be a further stress factor on the population.

At Hamilton, closer settlement and changing living demands have resulted in an alteration and reduction of habitat within township boundaries and on the perimeter, as paddocks and small rural properties have been converted to high-standard residential areas.

Road kills of bandicoots are now believed to have a significant impact on the declining Hamilton population (Brown 1989). This effect is exacerbated by the location of the remnant population within and on the fringe of an urban area, where vehicular traffic is constantly high.

## Discussion

Charting the decline of *P. gunnii* on the mainland demonstrates just how easy it has been to 'lose' a species, even one with a high reproductive rate and an apparently strong capacity to survive in an almost alien environment. Although a large number of factors have clearly contributed to the demise of *P. gunnii*, we suggest that there have been two major phases in this decline. Firstly, via a complex sequence of events, habitat alteration reduced the availability, quality, and abundance of important resources such as thick vegetation cover for shelter and invertebrate foods. This phase began with the introduction of sheep in the 1840s, and later was intensified by the introduc-

tion and population explosion of rabbits, the clearing of vegetation, pasture improvement, altered fire regimes, and increasing intensification of farming practices. At the same time as these habitat changes were taking place, additional pressures were imposed by the introduction of foxes as predators, sustained at high population levels by the availability of rabbits as a major prey item. The combined results of these processes were the reduction and fragmentation of the formerly extensive (and continuous) range of *P. gunnii* in western Victoria to smaller, distinct populations. Thus, by the 1940s, the species still occurred at a number of localities across the plains (*e.g.* Orford, Hamilton, Woolsthorpe, Mt Gellibrand), but these were becoming increasingly isolated.

A second phase in the decline of *P. gunnii* has been the decline and local extinction of most of the smaller and isolated populations. In addition to continued modification of habitat and predation by introduced predators, small populations became increasingly vulnerable to a complex of additional factors to which a larger population may be resilient. Natural catastrophes such as fires, floods and drought; destruction during rabbit control operations; predation by farm dogs; and the loss of genetic diversity through population bottlenecks and inbreeding are examples of additional pressures that together may have eliminated most of the remaining small populations. The remnant population at Hamilton is the last of these small fragmented populations of the plains to have survived. Predation of bandicoots by domestic cats, road kills, disease, loss of genetic diversity, and perhaps pesticide contamination are the additional stresses superimposed on declining habitat quality for this local population. Figure 5 graphically illustrates the sequence and continuing effects of factors affecting the status of *P. gunnii* in Victoria since European settlement.

Having recognized the complex factors that have contributed to the historical decline of *P. gunnii*, how does this guide us in 'turning around' this

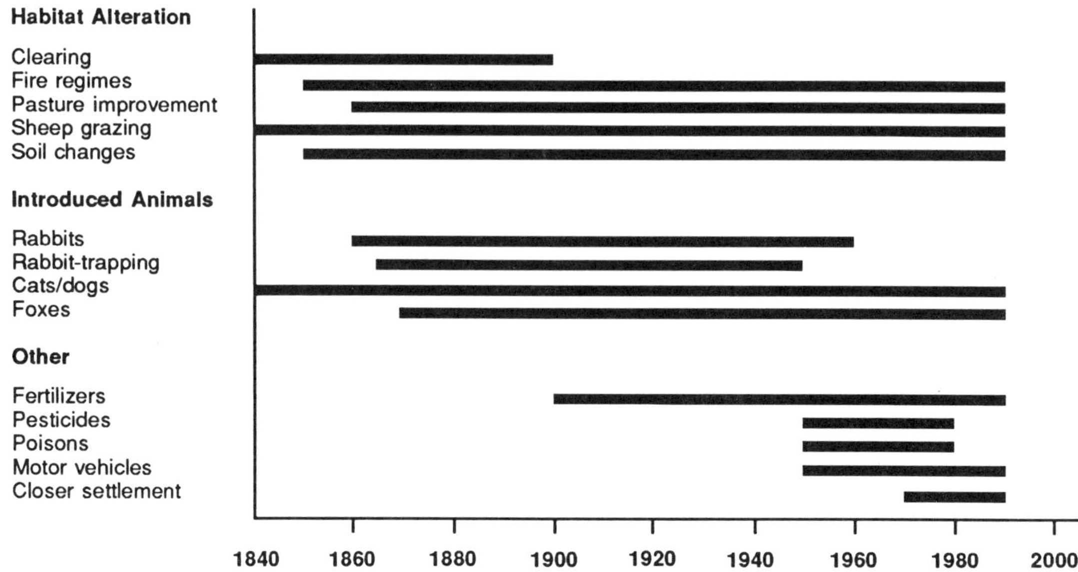



*Figure 5.*—Factors affecting the status of *Perameles gunnii* in western Victoria since European settlement.

process of decline? The most important point is to recognize that the process of decline is due almost entirely to factors initiated by humans, and that most of these factors are amenable to manipulation by wildlife managers.

It will not be feasible or practical to prevent all further changes in private land use that will affect habitat quality for bandicoots. However, it is possible, through encouragement and incentives on private land, and careful management of public lands, to enhance and expand the area of suitable habitat available to bandicoots. Arnold *et al.* (this volume) describe the strategies that are being followed at Hamilton to meet this goal. Valuable insights may also be gained by investigating the quality of habitat in rural areas in Tasmania where populations of *P. gunnii* have persisted in stable numbers.

Predation of bandicoots by introduced predators is a major challenge to management. The reduction or prevention of cat predation, a serious problem at Hamilton, can be addressed. Existing legislative powers under the *Local Government Act* can be used to limit or control the numbers of cats kept as pets, and forthcoming legislation under the proposed *Companion Animals Act* will provide significant powers to local Government for cat and dog control. The question is not *how* cat control can be achieved, but *when* it can be achieved, and whether or not the bandicoot population survives that long.

Fox predation in reintroduction areas for bandicoots continues to be a management concern, and combinations of existing and novel control techniques need to be applied at such sites. If these techniques prove successful and economic to apply, the implications for a wide range of wildlife species are enormous. Recent experience with small macropods has demonstrated the dramatic effects that foxes, even in small numbers, can have on small populations (Giles 1988; Kinnear *et al.* 1988; Kinnear 1989; K.A. Johnson personal communication), and the rapid popula-

30

tion recovery that can occur in the absence of foxes. Not only could protection of many wildlife species that live or nest near to, and on, the ground be much easier to undertake, but the potential for reintroduction would be greatly enhanced. Species such as the Tasmanian bettong (*Bettongia gaimardi*), red-bellied pademelon (*Thylogale billardierii*) and eastern quoll (*Dasyurus viverrinus*), now extinct in Victoria but still extant in Tasmania, are prime contenders for such a future program.

Recent legislation in Victoria has banned the use of organochlorines as insecticides, and this should limit potential pesticide pollution (see Lenghaus *et al.*, this volume). Reduction of road kills as a source of wildlife mortality can be addressed through effective speed reduction, the installation of tunnels and underpasses, education and driver awareness, and techniques to prevent animals from coming to the road edge (see Arnold *et al.*, this volume).

The loss of genetic diversity in small populations, recently investigated for the Hamilton population of *P. gunnii* (Sherwin and Brown, in press), can be addressed by intensive management strategies, including the establishment of captive populations and judicious exchange of individuals between populations (see Robinson *et al.*, this volume).

*P. gunnii* is one of many species of wildlife in Australia that have experienced a dramatic decline in distribution and status. This species, like others such as the brush-tailed bettong (*Bettongia penicillata*), rufous hare-wallaby (*Lagorchestes hirsutus*), and red-tailed phascogale (*Phascogale calura*), survives on the mainland as small remnant populations. Others, such as the eastern quoll, burrowing bettong and stick-nest rat (*Leporillus conditor*) are no longer present on the mainland and survive only as island populations. Documentation of the decline in status of such species and identification of the factors contributing to that changed status is an important step in the effort to preserve and conserve these species. The biggest challenge, however, is to use this information constructively to develop effective strategies and tactics for the recovery and growth of these species' populations.

## Acknowledgments

Our thanks to all those people over the years who have helped to document the story of the eastern barred bandicoot in Victoria. Many of them have been acknowledged in previous papers, but special mention must go to Lionel Elmore, late of Hamilton, a bandicoot recorder for many years; Joan Dixon (Museum of Victoria), for access to records held in that institution; Peter Brown, Victoria College, Rusden Campus; and Peter Rawlinson, LaTrobe University.

Tim Clark and Denise Casey offered constructive comment on earlier versions of this paper.

## References

Aitken, P.F. 1983. Mammals. In *Natural History of the South East,* eds M.J. Tyler, C.R. Twidale, J.K. Ling and J.W. Holmes. Pp. 127-133. Royal Society of South Australia: Adelaide.

Bennett, A.F. 1982. The mammals of the Woolsthorpe area, western Victoria: and the changes that have occurred since European settlement. *Victorian Nat.* **99**:229-240.

Brown, P.R. 1985. A preliminary report on investigations into the ecology and conservation of the mainland population of the Eastern Barred Bandicoot *Perameles gunnii:* March 1983-June 1985. Unpubl. Rept. to World Wildlife Fund Australia for Project 55, 26 pp.

Brown, P.R. 1989. Management Plan for the Conservation of the Eastern Barred Bandicoot, *Perameles gunnii,* in Victoria. National Parks and Wildlife Division, Victoria. *Arthur Rylah Institute for Environmental Research Tech. Rep. Ser.* No. 63. Department of Conservation, Forests and Lands: Melbourne.

Coutts, P.J.F., Witter, D. McIlwraith, M. and Frank, R. 1976. The Mound People of western Victoria. A preliminary statement. *Rec. Victorian Arch. Surv.* **1**:1-54 + tables.

Critchett, J. 1981. Introduction to facsimile edition (1981) of Dawson, J. (1881) *Australian Aborigines. The Languages and Customs of Several Tribes in the Western District of Victoria, Australia.* Australian Institute of Aboriginal Studies: Canberra.

Dawson, J. 1881. *Australian Aborigines. The Languages and Customs of Several Tribes of Aborigines in the Western District of Victoria, Australia.* George Robertson: Melbourne.

Dufty, A.C. 1988. The distribution, population abundance, status, movement and activity of the Eastern Barred Bandicoot, *Perameles gunnii,* at Hamilton. B.Sc. (Honours) Thesis, La Trobe University, Bundoora, Victoria.

Friend, J.A. and Kinnear, J.E. 1983. Numbat *Myrmecobius fasciatus* In *Complete Book of Australian Mammals.* ed. R. Strahan. Pp. 85-86. Angus and Robertson: Sydney.

Garden, D. 1984. *Hamilton: A Western District History.* Hargreen: Melbourne.

Giles, J. 1988. Progress Report-Parma Wallaby Project. Unpubl. rept. to Australian National Parks and Wildlife Service. 7 pp.

Gould, J. 1863. *The Mammals of Australia.* The Author: London.

Hebb, I. 1888. *The History of Colac and District.* Colac Herald, Colac. New edition 1970 by The Hawthorn Press, Melbourne.

Heinsohn, G.E. 1966. Ecology and reproduction of the Tasmanian bandicoots (*Perameles gunni* and *Isoodon obesulus*). *Univ. Calif. Publ. Zool.* **80**:1-96.

Hocking, G.J. In press. The status of bandicoots in Tasmania. In *Bandicoots and Bilbies,* eds J.H. Seebeck, P.R. Brown, R.L. Wallis and C.M. Kemper. Surrey Beatty and Sons: Sydney.

Kemper, C. In press. The status of Peramelidae and Thylacomyidae in South Australia. In *Bandicoots and Bilbies,* eds J.H. Seebeck, P.R. Brown, R.L. Wallis and C.M. Kemper. Surrey Beatty and Sons, Sydney.

Kinnear, J.E. 1989. Foxes and wallabies: evidence for multiple population domains. *Abstr. 35th Scien. Mtg. Aust. Mammal Soc.,* Apr. 1989, p. 22.

Kinnear, J.E., Onus, M.L. and Bromilow, R.N. 1988. Fox control and rock-wallaby population dynamics. *Aust. Wildl. Res.* **15**:435-450.

Moon, B.R. 1984. Current Distribution of the Eastern Barred Bandicoot, *Perameles gunnii* in Victoria. Fisheries and Wildlife Service, Victoria. *Arthur Rylah Institute for Environmental Research Tech. Rep. Ser.* No. 5. Department of Conservation, Forests and Lands: Melbourne.

Morgan, J. 1852. *The Life and Adventures of William Buckley.* New edition 1980, Australian National University Press: Canberra.

Obendorf, D.L., and Munday, B.L. In press. Toxoplasmosis in wild Eastern Barred Bandicoots, *Perameles gunnii.* In *Bandicoots and Bilbies,* eds J.H. Seebeck, P.R. Brown, R.L. Wallis and C.M. Kemper. Surrey Beatty and Sons: Sydney.

Petterson, B. 1985. Extinction of an isolated population of the Middle spotted woodpecker *Dendrocopos medius* (L.) in Sweden and its relation to general theories on extinction. *Biol. Conserv.* **32**:335-53.

Robinson, G.A. 1841. Journal, May to August 1841. Ed. G. Presland, 1980. *Rec. Victorian Arch. Surv.* **11**:1-202.

Rolls, E. 1969. *They All Ran Wild.* Angus and Robertson: Sydney.

Seebeck, J.H. 1979. Status of the Barred Bandicoot, *Perameles gunnii,* in Victoria: with a note on husbandry of a captive colony. *Aust. Wildl. Res.* **6**:255-264.

Seebeck, J.H. 1983. Eastern Barred Bandicoot *Perameles gunnii.* In *Complete Book of Australian Mammals,* ed. R. Strahan. p. 100. Angus and Robertson: Sydney.

Seebeck, J.H., Bennett, A.F. and Scotts, D.J. 1989. Ecology of the Potoroidae—a Review. In *Kangaroos, Wallabies and Rat-Kangaroos,* eds G. Grigg, P. Jarman and I. Hume. Pp. 67-88. Surrey Beatty and Sons: Sydney.

Sherwin, W.B. and Brown, P.R. In press. Problems in the estimation of the effective size of a population of the Eastern Barred Bandicoot, *Perameles gunnii* in Hamilton, Victoria. In *Bandicoots and Bilbies,* eds J.H. Seebeck, P.R. Brown, R.L. Wallis and C.M. Kemper. Surrey Beatty and Sons: Sydney.

Simberloff, D.S. 1988. The contribution of population and community biology to conservation science. *Ann. Rev. Ecol. Syst.* **19**:473-511.

Smyth, R. Brough 1878. *The Aborigines of Victoria.* John Ferres, Government Printer: Melbourne.

Thomas, O. 1888. *Catalogue of the Marsupialia and Monotremata in the Collection of the British Museum (Natural History).* British Museum (Natural History): London.

Willis, J.H. 1964. Vegetation of the Basalt Plains in western Victoria. *Proc. R. Soc. Victoria* **77**:397-418.

Willis, J.H. 1984. Plant life of the western plains. In *The Western Plains—A Natural and Social History,* eds D. Conley and C. Dennis. Pp. 27-38. Australian Institute of Agricultural Science: Melbourne.

# The Taxonomy and Palaeontology of the Eastern Barred Bandicoot: Their Bearing on Management of the Victorian Population

*Graeme G. George[1], Joan Dixon[2], Graeme Challis[2] and Robert C. Lacy[3]*


## Abstract

The eastern barred bandicoot (*Perameles gunnii*) is one of four modern species in the genus *Perameles*, only three of which are extant. *P. gunnii* occurs in two populations—one in Tasmania and one in western Victoria. The Victorian population has been intermittently confused with the eastern subspecies of the western barred bandicoot, *P. bougainville fasciata*. Tasmania has been separated from mainland Australia for most of the Tertiary. Land bridges across Bass Strait during the Pleistocene glaciations allowed southeastern Australian species to spread into Tasmania. Periodic isolation of Tasmanian populations during interglacial rises in sea level has resulted in subspeciation of many terrestrial mammals. The degree of differentiation of the two populations of *P. gunnii* has some bearing on the management options for the Victorian population. Skull morphometrics of modern Victorian and Tasmanian material and sub-fossil material from western Victorian caves are compared to see if differences are significant, to support genetic studies that are currently being undertaken elsewhere. Observed differences, combined with minor differences in habitat and reproductive biology, suggest that some evolutionary differentiation of the two populations has occurred over the last 8,000-10,000 years. Conservation and recovery of the Victorian population should proceed independently of the Tasmanian population, while prospects for recovery remain good, but introduction of Tasmanian genes remains a future option.


## Introduction

The maintenance of biodiversity is now the major goal of conservation. Biological diversity is present at the level of ecosystems, species, populations and genes (Clark *et al.*, this volume). At the species level, the degree of uniqueness is likely to have an effect on the priorities given to conservation efforts, but at the population level the degree of adaptation to habitat and the role of species as integral parts of unique ecosystems are just as important. It is important that, prior to the implementation of conservation programs, the taxonomic status of the population in question is determined.

The eastern barred bandicoot (*P. gunnii*) is one of three extant species of the genus *Perameles*, the others being the long-nosed bandicoot (*P. nasuta*) of eastern Australian forests and the western barred bandicoot (*P. bougainville*), formerly widespread across the semi-arid zone of southern Australia, but now limited to the islands of Shark Bay in Western Australia. A fourth species, the desert bandicoot (*P. eremiana*), of central Australia, is apparently extinct. *P. gunnii* occurs in two discrete populations, one in eastern and northern Tasmania, and a second on the basalt plains of western Victoria (Fig. 1). Despite their geographical separation by the marine barrier of Bass Strait, they have not been distinguished taxonomically. The taxonomic issue as it relates to the conservation of *P. gunnii* in Victoria is twofold: (1) Do the Victorian barred bandicoots differ biologically


[1]Zoological Board of Victoria, P.O. Box 72, Parkville, Victoria 3052, Australia.
[2]Museum of Victoria, 328 Swanston Street, Melbourne, Victoria 3000, Australia.
[3]Chicago Zoological Society, Brookfield, Illinois 60513, U.S.A.

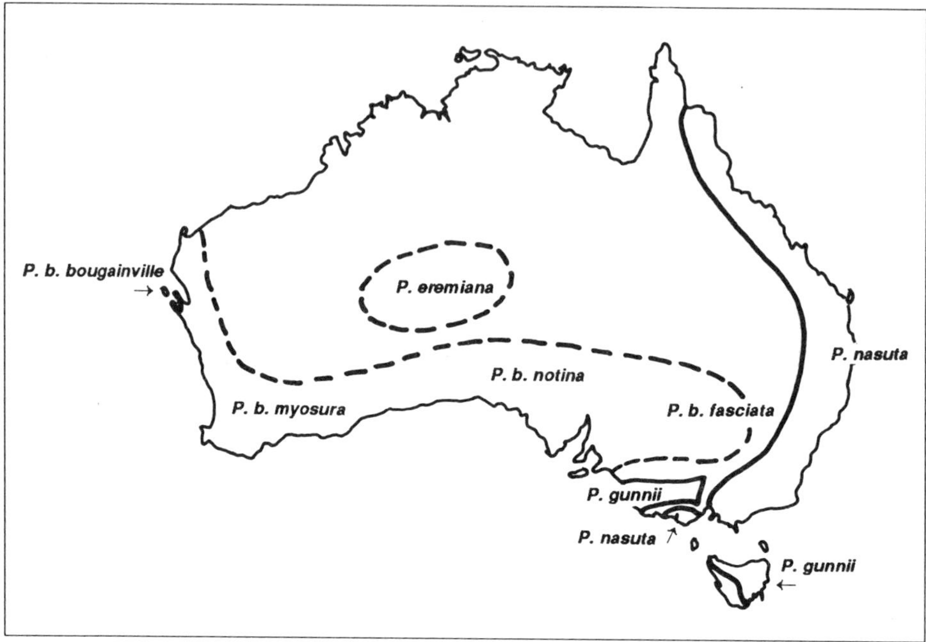



*Figure 1.*—Historical range of the four species of *Perameles* (after Strahan 1983).

from those in Tasmania? and (2) How should the two populations be treated in conservation efforts?

Australian wildlife legislation deals primarily with species. In the United States of America, the wording of the *Endangered Species Act* and related legislation protects all biologically divergent forms regardless of formal taxonomic status, but the legal interpretation is often that a Latin name equates with meaningful biological divergence. In Australia, in theory, it should not matter whether the Victorian and Tasmanian populations differ. The eastern barred bandicoot should be protected in Victoria as part of the State's fauna whether or not it exists also in Tasmania; legally, of course, it must be protected under both the *Wildlife Act* and the *Flora and Fauna Guarantee Act.*

While we usually deal with species as the units of evolution, ecological processes and even many evolutionary processes are really population phenomena. Selection occurs at the level of populations (*i.e.* the level of relatively common interchange of genes), thus adaptation is to environmental conditions at the scale of the range of local, discrete populations. Demographically, isolated populations are independent entities, so extinction is also a population phenomenon (Clark *et al.,* this volume). Of course, migrants can reintroduce genetic variants into local populations, and can re-colonise vacant habitat after local extinction.

The biological tragedy of our modern world is that populations that were formerly widespread have become so fragmented and isolated that genetic and demographic interchange between reduced local populations is largely impossible. Under these conditions, the occasional extinction of local populations (an entirely natural and quite common process) eventually results in global extinction. As theoretical models and unfortunate experiences make all too clear, no single isolated population is likely to persist for great periods of time. Large isolated populations survive much longer than do small ones, but they all go sooner or later (Lacy and Clark, this volume). For these reasons, the emphasis of conservation must shift from species to populations. Obviously, the more divergent a population is, the more we ought to avoid exterminating it, but all discrete populations form parts of ecological communities and ecosystems, and constitute part of the natural (and often cultural) heritage of at least the local community of people. We should not wait until there is only one population in some remote site before conservation measures are taken. Unfortunately, this has happened with the eastern barred bandicoot in Victoria, which is now represented by a single remaining population near the City of Hamilton.

The degree of taxonomic divergence between related forms may be a critical determinant of the intensity and nature of effort that goes into the conservation of populations. The decision has already been made in Victoria to attempt to conserve the remnant population of the eastern barred bandicoot and to establish new populations in areas of the animal's former range (Brown 1989; Seebeck, this volume). The desirability of supplementing these populations with animals from Tasmania has been raised, but action has been deferred because of uncertainty about the degree of evolutionary divergence between the two populations. Accordingly, we undertook to review the taxonomic status and fossil history of *P. gunnii* to assist the consideration of options for management of the gene pool during conservation of the species in Victoria.


*The Modern History of* P. gunnii
*in Victoria*

The species was described by Gray (1838) from a specimen collected in Tasmania by Ronald Gunn and lodged in the British Museum (Natural History). The discovery of another small barred bandicoot on the Liverpool Plains of New South Wales by Sir George Grey during his expeditions of 1837-1839 resulted in the description of *Perameles fasciata* (Gray 1841). The two species were compared by Waterhouse (1846) and differences described. The Blandowski Expedition of 1857 subsequently collected numbers of *P. fasciata* around the junction of the Murray and Darling Rivers (Krefft 1866).

Gould (1863) commented that *P. gunnii* appeared to be more common in the northern than in the southern parts of Tasmania and 'if I mistake not, inhabits the islands in Bass's Straits, and even the southern portions of the continent of Australia'. Referring to Gould's comments, Thomas (1888) felt that the occurrence of the species in Victoria was 'by no means improbable, considering the number of Tasmanian species recently discovered in that colony.'

The Museum of Victoria has several early records of *P. gunnii*, some of which are still present as specimens in the collections. An early record by John Leadbeater is from Werribee in 1882, and others from Bacchus Marsh were registered around this time.

Despite the foregoing, all barred bandicoots in Victoria were assumed to be *P. fasciata* for much of the 20th century. The checklist of Iredale and Troughton (1934) gave the distribution of *P. gunnii* as 'Tasmania' and of *P. fasciata* as 'New South Wales, Victoria'. Troughton (1941) repeated this view. In his review of the family, Tate (1948) did not mention the possibility of *P. gunnii* occurring in Victoria. He also incorrectly cited the type specimens in the British Museum, and in his account of *P. fasciata* he misquoted Waterhouse (1846). Charles Brazenor collected specimens in 1949 at Mount Gellibrand near Colac and registered these at the National Museum of Victoria as *P. fasciata*. In his Handbook, Brazenor (1950) described *P. nasuta* as 'usually found at higher elevations away from the coast' and *P. fasciata* as 'now confined to the plains of the Western District'. By that time the population of

*P. fasciata* along the Murray had disappeared, and all remaining Victorian barred *Perameles* were presumably *P. gunnii.*

Lyne (1951) compared Tasmanian and Victorian specimens of barred bandicoot and concluded that the Western District animal was conspecific with *P. gunnii*. Troughton (1954) referred to Brazenor's specimens of *P. gunnii* in the Museum of Victoria from Mount Gellibrand, but the museum records were not corrected until Joan Dixon was appointed curator in 1965. In 1961 and 1968 Dixon searched for *P. gunnii* in the Mount Gellibrand district but was unable to find any evidence of their continued occurrence in that area.

Wakefield (1963a,b,c) examined cave deposits of sub-fossil material, including both *P. gunnii* and *P. fasciata*, and concluded that the small animal of the Murray-Darling basin was an eastern representative of *P. bougainville*. He listed the form as a subspecies *P. b. fasciata* as per Thomas (1888).

Heinsohn (1966) carried out a live-trapping study from February 1961 to May 1962 in northwestern Tasmania. He observed and trapped *P. gunnii* mainly in open areas, which it used extensively, in contrast to *Isoodon obesulus* which preferred a taller vegetation cover. These findings are very much in line with the situation which pertains in western Victoria. Heinsohn (1966) established that the breeding season occurred from late May to the following December, and could even extend as long as March if an adequate food supply were available. At Hamilton, breeding occurs year-round (reviewed in Lacy and Clark, this volume).

Freedman (1967), and Freedman and Joffe (1967), reviewed the genus *Perameles*. Morphological differences between the Tasmanian and Victorian populations of *P. gunnii* were found but it was concluded that the differences were not significant enough to warrant separation as subspecies.

Seebeck (1979) reviewed the status of *P. gunnii* in Victoria, documenting the original distribution within the State and the drastic decline over recent decades. Recent field workers have felt that the two populations were visibly different (P.R. Brown, personal communication) but no further attempts have been made to distinguish the Victorian animals nomenclatorially. Sherwin, in an Appendix to the Management Plan for the remnant population (see Brown 1989), discussed the lack of genetic variability found among either population in an electrophoretic study of protein enzyme systems.

*Fossil History*

The eastern barred bandicoot is one of many species which have populations both sides of Bass Strait. The geology of the strait is summarised by Sutherland (1973). It covers a structural depression, the Bass Basin (Jennings 1959), which developed in the mid-Mesozoic (Griffith 1971) prior to the Cretaceous separation of Australia from Antarctica. For much of the Tertiary, the Bass Basin was under water with long periods of vulcanism during the late Eocene to early Oligocene and the Miocene to Pliocene.

The extent of faunal interchange between Tasmania and mainland Australia during the Tertiary is unknown, as the fossil record is poor. A late Oligocene deposit at Geilston Bay near Hobart has yielded fragmentary material of four higher-level taxa—Families Dasyurida, Phalangeridae and Burramyidae, and Superfamily Diprotodontoidea (Tedford *et al.* 1975). No fossils of similar age have yet been found on the mainland. At Fossil Bluff near Wynyard on the northwestern coast, the unique *Wynyardia bassiana* is known from an early Miocene sandstone (Spencer 1900). South Australian fossils have been referred to the family Wynyardiidae but these are only tentatively assigned (Rich 1982).

The oldest bandicoots yet known from southeastern Australia have been found in middle Miocene

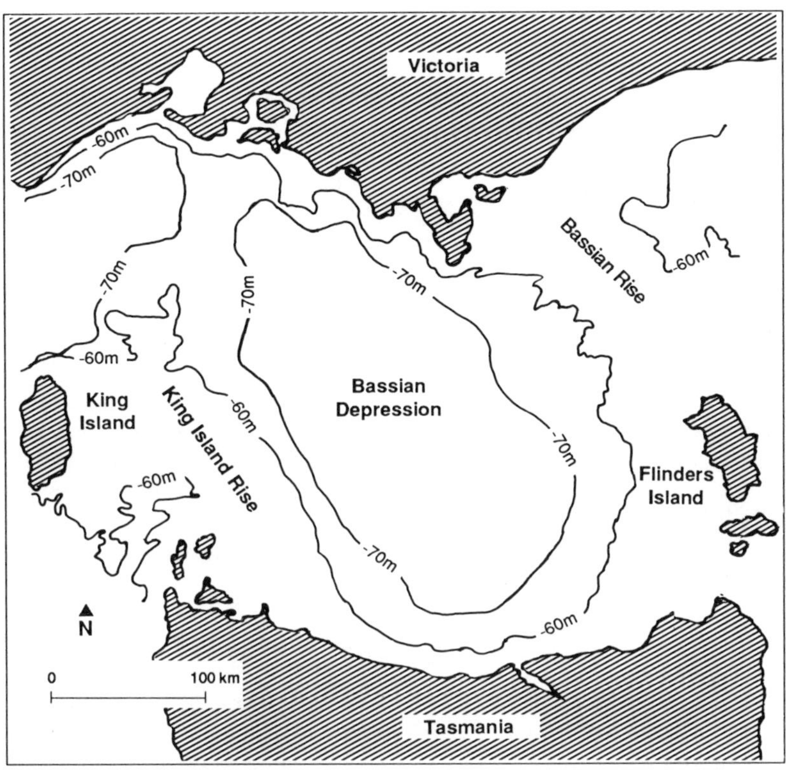



*Figure 2.*—The topography of Bass Strait showing the −60m and −70m submarine contours (after Blom 1988).

deposits in northeastern South Australia. These have not yet been identified to genus or species (T. Rich, personal communication). Bandicoots proliferated on the Australian mainland during the Miocene (Archer 1984). The Riversleigh deposits in Queensland contain a rich and diverse bandicoot fauna, including antechinus-sized forms which may represent an entirely new family (M. Archer, personal communication). The oldest bandicoots known from Victoria are, coincidentally, from near Hamilton, along the Grange Burn creek, in sub-basaltic fossil soils of early Pliocene age (Turnbull and Lundelius 1970). This material has affinities with *Peroryctes* and *Echymipera*, genera which are today restricted to the tropical rain forests of Cape York and New Guinea. Other elements of the Pliocene Hamilton fauna also suggest a rain-forest environment at that time. A possibly contemporaneous fauna occuring near

Bow in eastern New South Wales contains both *Isoodon* and *Perameles* (Skilbeck 1980), genera which are today found primarily in sclerophyll forests, woodlands and grasslands.

Quaternary deposits from northern Tasmania and the Bass Strait islands contain modern species, typical of Tasmania today, along with extinct species which were widespread across southern Australia during the Pleistocene (Hope 1973).

During glacial periods of the Pleistocene, marine regressions exposed land bridges across the King Island and Bassian (Flinders Island) Rises, connecting Tasmania with the Mornington Peninsula and Wilson's Promontory of southern Victoria (Fig. 2; Sutherland 1973). Hope (1969) suggested that the thylacine (*Thylacinus cynocephalus*) entered Tasmania during this period. The lack of endemism at the species level among the marsupials and rodents suggests that the whole modern terrestrial mammal fauna of Tasmania was established during these periods of lowered sea level.

The oldest fossil records of *P. gunnii* in the region are from Pleistocene levels in Cave Bay Cave on Hunter Island, off north-western Tasmania, where the species has been found in layers up to 19,000 years old (Bowdler 1984). *P. gunnii* has also been identified from Prime Seal Island in the Furneaux Group, off north-eastern Tasmania, in Pleistocene deposits ranging from 8,000 to 17,000 years of age (B. Marshall, personal communication).

Wakefield (1963a,b,c; 1964a,b; 1967) identified *P. gunnii* in several sub-fossil cave deposits of Holocene age in western Victoria, together with the smaller *P. bougainville*, a species which has not been recorded from the basalt plains in historical times. He found *P. nasuta* but not *P. gunnii* in Pleistocene layers in McEachern's Cave in western Victoria (Wakefield 1967). *P. gunnii* has also been recorded from cave deposits at Naracoorte in south-eastern South Australia (Tideman 1967). Hope (1973) recorded the presence of *P. gunnii* in Ranga Cave on Flinders Island. The top levels of the Ranga Cave deposit are about 8,000 years old, but the bandicoot specimen may be older than this date (B. Marshall, personal communication).

Thus the fossil evidence shows *P. gunnii* to have had a range from southeastern South Australia to the Bassian Basin during the late Pleistocene-early Holocene. Despite the comments of Gould (1845-1863), there is no evidence of *P. gunnii* occurring on Bass Strait Islands in historic times. However, *P. gunnii* persisted in south-eastern South Australia until the 1890s when specimens in the South Australian Museum were collected in low rainfall areas with sandy soils (Kemper in press).

Pollen analysis of soil cores has confirmed that Bass Strait land bridges were occupied by grasslands at the height of the Pleistocene glaciations, the area being rather arid until 9,000 years ago (Hope 1978; Colhoun *et al.* 1982). These open grassland habitats provided the opportunity for *P. gunnii* to spread from western Victoria during the last glacial period. Recent archeological evidence suggests that aboriginal man reached Tasmania over 30,000 years ago (Cosgrove 1989). However, no bandicoots have been found among extremely rich mammal deposits in caves in southwestern Tasmania (B. Marshall, personal communication). Their presence on the King Island and Bassian rises in the Pleistocene may be explained by more favourable, open habitats across the Bass Basin than occurred in south-western Tasmania during the last glacial period. The timing of the spread of *P. gunnii* into favourable open habitats in northern and eastern Tasmania has yet to be determined.


*Speciation Across Bass Strait*

The terrestrial mammals which form part of the modern Tasmanian fauna are differentiated from their mainland counterparts at several levels: 1) very distinct subspecies, sometimes regarded as full species, *e.g.* common ringtail possum (*Pseudocheirus peregrinus*), common wombat (*Vombatus ursinus*), long-nosed potoroo (*Potorous tridactylus*); 2) distinct subspecies in Victoria and Tasmania, with questionably distinct forms on the Bass Strait Islands in some cases, *e.g.* red-necked wallaby (*Macropus rufogriseus*); 3) weakly differentiated subspecies of questionable status, *e.g.* southern brown bandicoot (*Isoodon obesulus*); 4) species where no subspecies have been described, *e.g.* tiger quoll (*Dasyurus maculatus*), eastern quoll (*D. viverrinus*). The monotypic eastern barred bandicoot falls into the last category.

These varied levels of differentiation may be due in part to different rates of evolution. They may also reflect the length of time that species have been in Tasmania and the frequency and timing of their isolation from mainland populations during marine transgressions of Bass Strait.

The two populations of *P. gunnii* may have been in contact until the inundation of the Bassian Rise about 8,000 years ago, which is the most recent estimate of final separation based on analysis of sea-floor sediments (Blom 1988). Many Holarctic species have been fragmented into North American and Eurasian populations from about 12,000 to 16,000 years ago by the same rises in sea level, and taxonomists have debated whether such taxa (*e.g.* wolf (*Canis lupus*); North American moose (*Alces alces americanus*) and European elk (*Alces a. alces*); North American elk (*Cervus canadensis*) and Eurasian red deer (*Cervus elaphus*); black-footed ferret (*Mustela nigripes*) and Siberian polecat (*Mustela eversmanni*); red fox (*Vulpes vulpes*)) should be considered subspecies, full species, or just geographic populations. Mayr (1963) gave a few specific examples for which the times since divergence are well known. The English Channel submerged 8,000 years ago, and the British red deer is considered distinct from the continental form at the subspecies level. Newfoundland, Canada became habitable for mammals about 12,000 years ago and 10 of its 14 native mammals are considered to have evolved into well-defined subspecies (a few distinct almost at the species level). Evolution can be much faster, as evidenced by distinctive subspecies on relatively recent islands (*e.g. Peromyscus polionotus*, the beach mouse, has an endemic, well-differentiated subspecies on many of the dune islands along the Gulf Coast of the United States) and by morphological divergence in introduced animals around the world.

As neither the Victorian nor Tasmanian populations of *P. gunnii* have occupied extensive geographical ranges, their populations, once separated, could be expected to diverge at a faster-than-average rate due to genetic drift in small populations and some degree of selection for differences in habitat.

## Morphometric Comparison of Populations

Morphology is often a sensitive indicator of adaptive divergence and is the primary basis on which subspecies are based. To assist in the resolution of the taxonomic ranking of the Victorian population of *P. gunnii*, a study of the morphometrics of the skull was undertaken by J. Dixon and G. Challis to supplement the genetic work of our colleagues at La Trobe University (Robinson *et al.*, this volume).

Modern Victorian and Tasmanian specimens of *P. gunnii* were examined from the collections of the Museum of Victoria, Queen Victoria Museum and Art Gallery, Launceston, and the Tasmanian Museum and Art Gallery, Hobart. Skins of specimens from the Museum of Victoria were measured for the following parameters; total length, tail length, pes length, ear length and weight (Jones 1923-25). All linear measurements are in millimetres and weights in grams. Measurements of Tasmanian skins were obtained from the card records of the Tasmanian Museum and Art Gallery. Individuals with body measurements more than two standard deviations below the mean were excluded from the analysis as they were not fully adult. Skulls from all three museums were examined and immature specimens (those where the last molar was not fully erupted) were deleted. Ten parameters were measured, one was calculated. Cranial measurements were based on those of Thomas (1888) as indicated in Figure 3. The facial index is the ratio of the basi-facial axis to the basi-cranial axis, expressed as a percentage.

Fossil material from western Victoria held in the Museum of Victoria was also examined. It consisted mainly of mandibles, and lacked teeth for the most part. The length of the molar row was measured medially from the anterior limit of the first molar socket to the posterior limit of the fourth molar socket. A selection of modern Victorian and Tasmanian mandibles was measured similarly. The data were analysed using Statview SE version 1.03 on a Macintosh computer.

The means and standard deviations of each measurement are shown in Table 1. The results of the mandibular measurements comparing Victorian,

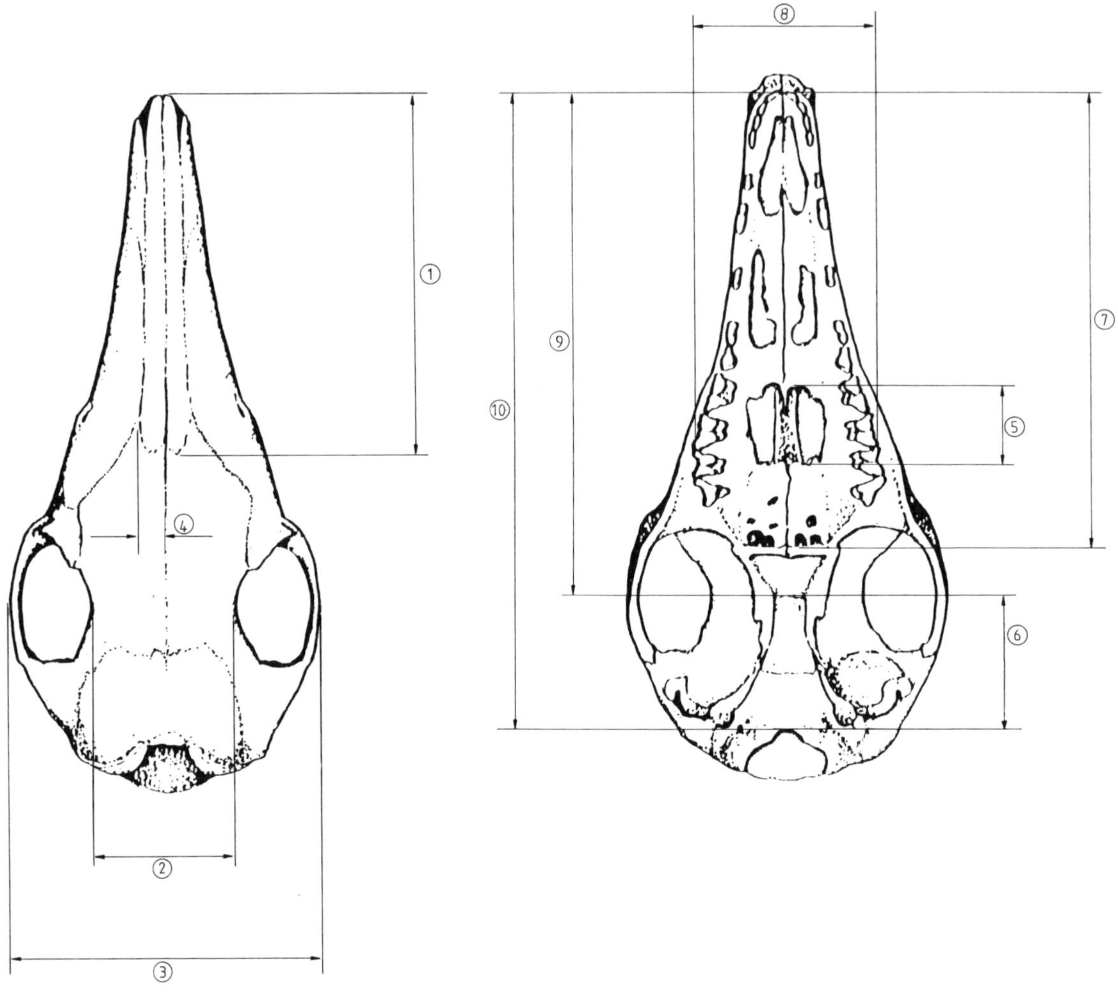


*Figure 3.*—Eastern barred bandicoot skull measurements. 1. Nasal length. 2. Interorbital width. 3. Width. 4. Nasal width. 5. Palatal foramen. 6. Basi-cranial axis. 7. Palate length. 8. Width at M3. 9. Basi-facial axis. 10. Basal length.

Tasmanian and fossil Victorian samples are shown in Table 2. Each modern population, Victorian and Tasmanian, was separately analysed for sexual dimorphism for each character measured, using t-tests. The results are shown in Table 3.

The Tasmanian specimens show significant differences in four of the skull measurements: basal and nasal length and the basi-cranial axis and basi-facial axis measurements, in all of which males are larger than females. These measurements were not found to be significantly different in the Victorian specimens, but female nasal width and facial index were found to be significantly larger than male measurements, and among the body measurements male pes length was larger. Most characters do not show any significant sex differences, but those that do are sufficiently numerous to require a comparison between Victoria and Tasmania to be made for each sex. Details of the results of t-tests, comparing Tasmanian males and females against Victorian males and females are shown in Table 4.

*Table 1.*—Comparison of body and skull measurements between Victorian and Tasmanian eastern barred bandicoots.

| Variable | Female Mean | N | SD | Min. | Max. | Male Mean | N | SD | Min. | Max. |
|---|---|---|---|---|---|---|---|---|---|---|
| **Victoria** | | | | | | | | | | |
| Skull measurements | | | | | | | | | | |
| Basal length | 66.8 | 7 | 1.889 | 64.5 | 70.2 | 67.4 | 15 | 2.997 | 63.5 | 72.1 |
| Width | 30.6 | 7 | 0.682 | 29.3 | 31.4 | 30.9 | 15 | 1.423 | 28.4 | 33.6 |
| Nasal length | 33.3 | 9 | 1.184 | 31.1 | 35 | 33.5 | 17 | 1.838 | 30.3 | 37.3 |
| Nasal width | 6.5 | 9 | 0.383 | 6 | 7.1 | 6 | 18 | 0.416 | 5.4 | 6.9 |
| Interorbital width | 14.6 | 9 | 0.491 | 13.9 | 15.3 | 14.5 | 17 | 0.543 | 13.4 | 15.4 |
| Palate length | 45.9 | 7 | 0.899 | 45.1 | 47.7 | 46.3 | 16 | 1.911 | 43.8 | 50.1 |
| Width at M3 | 19.3 | 8 | 0.604 | 18.6 | 20.2 | 19.5 | 17 | 0.859 | 18 | 21.2 |
| Palatal foramen | 9.7 | 8 | 0.811 | 8.7 | 11.1 | 9.2 | 17 | 0.716 | 8.2 | 10.4 |
| Basi-cranial axis | 17.2 | 7 | 0.475 | 16.6 | 17.9 | 17.7 | 15 | 0.966 | 15.9 | 19.3 |
| Basi-facial axis | 51.1 | 7 | 1.557 | 49.2 | 53.9 | 51.2 | 15 | 2.159 | 47.8 | 54.3 |
| Facial Index | 297.5 | 7 | 7.297 | 289.4 | 310.8 | 289.5 | 15 | 8.508 | 274.7 | 304.4 |
| Body measurements | | | | | | | | | | |
| Total length | 407 | 16 | 34.73 | 345 | 488 | 416.1 | 25 | 25.82 | 380 | 477 |
| Head-body | 320.4 | 19 | 27.13 | 270 | 398 | 331.6 | 27 | 26.75 | 294 | 400 |
| Tail length | 87.32 | 17 | 9.989 | 68 | 96 | 87 | 25 | 11.82 | 63 | 108 |
| Head length | - | - | - | - | - | - | - | - | - | - |
| Ear length | 39.01 | 19 | 5.403 | 30 | 46 | 40.41 | 28 | 5.506 | 31.9 | 48 |
| Pes length | 69.47 | 19 | 3.795 | 61 | 78 | 72.13 | 28 | 4.426 | 63 | 80 |
| Weight | 721.4 | 6 | 123.6 | 594.5 | 881 | 723 | 14 | 138.5 | 466 | 910 |
| **Tasmania** | | | | | | | | | | |
| Skull measurements | | | | | | | | | | |
| Basal length | 70.8 | 14 | 2.182 | 67 | 74 | 73 | 17 | 3.316 | 67.3 | 79.4 |
| Width | 32.5 | 11 | 1.309 | 30 | 34 | 33 | 17 | 1.325 | 30.8 | 35.6 |
| Nasal length | 36.5 | 15 | 1.502 | 33.2 | 38.8 | 37.7 | 17 | 1.851 | 35.2 | 41.6 |
| Nasal width | 6.8 | 15 | 0.689 | 5.5 | 8.1 | 7.1 | 17 | 0.76 | 5.8 | 8.5 |
| Interorbital width | 15.7 | 15 | 0.703 | 14.6 | 17.4 | 15.7 | 18 | 0.807 | 14.5 | 18.2 |
| Palate length | 49.5 | 14 | 1.75 | 46.5 | 52.2 | 50.8 | 17 | 2.153 | 47.2 | 55.2 |
| Width at M3 | 20.4 | 14 | 0.873 | 19.2 | 21.9 | 20.3 | 18 | 0.648 | 18.9 | 21.6 |
| Palatal foramen | 10 | 12 | 1.197 | 7.9 | 11.6 | 9.8 | 17 | 0.902 | 8.5 | 11.6 |
| Basi-cranial axis | 17.5 | 14 | 0.921 | 15.7 | 18.8 | 18.3 | 18 | 0.754 | 17.3 | 20 |
| Basi-facial axis | 54.9 | 14 | 1.859 | 51.7 | 57.6 | 56.5 | 17 | 2.402 | 52.4 | 61.4 |
| Facial Index | 313.6 | 14 | 12.13 | 293.8 | 331.2 | 305.9 | 17 | 18.18 | 243.5 | 328.5 |
| Body measurements | | | | | | | | | | |
| Total length | 415.4 | 20 | 28.38 | 367 | 470 | 425.2 | 31 | 39.47 | 320 | 510 |
| Head-body length | 325.7 | 19 | 26.63 | 290 | 379 | 335.2 | 30 | 31.84 | 253 | 412 |
| Tail length | 90.21 | 21 | 6.443 | 76 | 100 | 87.13 | 30 | 13.57 | 58 | 105 |
| Head length | 96.45 | 11 | 5.751 | 89 | 104 | 93.44 | 16 | 6.229 | 76 | 102 |
| Ear length | 47.53 | 19 | 2.871 | 39.7 | 50 | 47.24 | 21 | 3.375 | 41 | 52 |
| Pes length | 72.93 | 18 | 5.616 | 65 | 83.5 | 73.57 | 21 | 4.742 | 66 | 82.5 |
| Weight | 1025 | 22 | 289 | 600 | 1800 | 965.8 | 33 | 260.7 | 433 | 1750 |

*Table 2.*—Comparison of molar row lengths of eastern barred bandicoots from Victorian, Tasmanian and fossil samples.

| Statistic | Victoria | Fossil | Tasmania | t-test | Probability |
|---|---|---|---|---|---|
| Mean | 154.8 | 149.4 | 162.1 | Victoria > Fossil | 0.0074 |
| N | 9 | 9 | 10 | Tasmania > Victoria | 0.0002 |
| SD | 2.68 | 4.48 | 3.87 | Tasmania > Fossil | 0.0001 |
| Min. | 150 | 142 | 156 | | |
| Max. | 159 | 155 | 168 | | |

*Table 3.*—Morphometric and statistical comparison of sexual dimorphism in eastern barred bandicoots from Tasmania and Victoria.

| Variable | Tasmania | Probability[1] | Victoria | Probability |
|---|---|---|---|---|
| Skull measurements | | | | |
| Basal length | M > F | 0.0449 | M > F | ns |
| Width | M > F | ns | M > F | ns |
| Nasal length | M > F | 0.0449 | M > F | ns |
| Nasal width | M > F | ns | F > M | 0.0149 |
| Interorbital width | M > F | ns | F > M | ns |
| Palate length | M > F | ns | M > F | ns |
| M3 width | F > M | ns | M > F | ns |
| Palatal foramen | F > M | ns | F > M | ns |
| Basi-cranial axis | M > F | 0.0096 | M > F | ns |
| Basi-facial axis | M > F | 0.0476 | M > F | ns |
| Facial index | F > M | ns | F > M | 0.0457 |
| Body measurements | | | | |
| Total length | M > F | ns | M > F | ns |
| Head-body length | M > F | ns | M > F | ns |
| Tail length | F > M | ns | F > M | ns |
| Head length | F > M | ns | — | — |
| Ear length | F > M | ns | M > F | ns |
| Pes length | M > F | ns | M > F | 0.0379 |
| Weight | F > M | ns | M > F | ns |

[1]ns = Not Significant.

It can be seen that for all parameters measured, the Tasmanian specimens are larger, though not always significantly so. The Tasmanian males are significantly larger than their Victorian counterparts for all skull measurements at the 5% level at least, and often at the 0.1% level. For females, the Tasmanian population is again the larger, although three of eleven skull measurements were not found to be significantly different at the 5% level between the two populations, and only the ear, pes length and weight were significantly different for the body measurements.

*Table 4.*—Statistical comparison of female and male morphometrics in Tasmanian and Victorian eastern barred bandicoots.

| Variable | Females | Probability | CD | Males | Probability | CD |
|---|---|---|---|---|---|---|
| **Skull measurements** | | | | | | |
| Basal length | Tas > Vic | *** | 0.982 | Tas > Vic | **** | 0.887 |
| Width | Tas > Vic | ** | 0.954 | Tas > Vic | **** | 0.764 |
| Nasal length | Tas > Vic | **** | 1.191 | Tas > Vic | **** | 1.138 |
| Inter-orbital width | Tas > Vic | *** | 0.921 | Tas > Vic | **** | 0.889 |
| Palate length | Tas > Vic | **** | 1.359 | Tas > Vic | **** | 1.107 |
| Width at M3 | Tas > Vic | ** | 0.745 | Tas > Vic | ** | 0.531 |
| Palatal foramen | Tas > Vic | ns | 0.149 | Tas > Vic | * | 0.371 |
| Basi-cranial axis | Tas > Vic | ns | 0.215 | Tas > Vic | * | 0.349 |
| Basi-facial axis | Tas > Vic | *** | 1.112 | Tas > Vic | **** | 1.162 |
| Nasal width | Tas > Vic | ns | 0.280 | Tas > Vic | **** | 0.935 |
| Facial Index | Tas > Vic | ** | 0.829 | Tas > Vic | **** | 0.614 |
| **Body measurements** | | | | | | |
| Total length | Tas > Vic | ns | 0.133 | Tas > Vic | ns | 0.139 |
| Head-body length | Tas > Vic | ns | 0.098 | Tas > Vic | ns | 0.061 |
| Tail length | Tas > Vic | ns | 0.176 | Tas > Vic | ns | 0.005 |
| Ear length | Tas > Vic | **** | 1.030 | Tas > Vic | **** | 0.769 |
| Pes length | Tas > Vic | * | 0.368 | Tas > Vic | ns | 0.157 |
| Weight | Tas > Vic | * | 0.736 | Tas > Vic | *** | 0.608 |

[1]ns = Not Significant
*p ≤ 0.05
**p ≤ 0.01
***p ≤ 0.001
****p ≤ 0.0001
CD = Coefficient of Difference.

Although many measurements were found to differ significantly, the differences between the two populations are not large enough to justify subspecific distinction under the 'seventy-five percent' rule of Mayr (1969). The measure by which two populations are deemed to be sufficiently different to be termed subspecies is the coefficient of difference (CD): the ratio of the difference of the means to the sum of the standard deviations. A CD value of 1.28 or more is conventionally required to justify subspecific distinction. In the case of Victorian and Tasmanian populations, the CD value for all measurements, with the exception of female palate length, is less than 1.28. Thus the morphometric data, although demonstrating morphological divergence, does not support subspecific differentiation on traditional grounds.

## Genetic Consequences of Management Options

The introduction of Tasmanian animals into the Victorian population, to boost numbers or to increase average heterozygosity, has been considered (Brown 1989), but was rejected because of uncertainty about the degree of divergence between the two populations and the effects that such an introduction might have on the remnant Victorian population. The two populations of *P. gunnii* have been separated from each other by the marine barrier of Bass Strait for at least 8,000 years. There is no evidence that gene flow was interrupted at any earlier date. Genetic studies of the Victorian and Tasmanian populations (Sherwin 1989; Sherwin and Brown in press; Robinson *et al.*, this volume) have not demonstrated any genetic distance between them, as no polymorphic loci have been found by electrophoresis of isoenzymes from either population. Gene frequency differences at polymorphic loci are usually considerable after 16,000 years, especially in small populations (such as the Victorian eastern barred bandicoot) which are subject to rapid genetic drift. The expected rate of allele substitution (the replacement of the fixed allele at a monomorphic locus with another allele) is too slow, however, to lead one to expect to find any fixed differences between these bandicoots or any other mammal subspecies pair. Electrophoretically detectable amino acid replacements in enzymatic proteins occur at rates of about 0.1 to 1.6/site/$10^9$ years, or about 0.2 to 10/protein/$10^7$ years (Nei 1987). Thus, no amino acid replacements would be expected between subspecies that diverged 16,000 years ago in a typical sample of 20 to 50 enzymes analysed by electrophoresis. Even the highest observed replacement rate, 9/site/$10^9$ years for the non-enzymatic (and perhaps non-functional) fibrinopeptides, amounts to only about one change per million years in the peptide. Fixation of new mutations (whether due to selection or drift) is too slow a process to allow the use of monomorphic loci for subspecies level taxonomy (Nei 1987). Thus the genetic evidence to date does not refute the morphological evidence that divergence has not reached the level usually required for subspecific differentiation.

Schmitt (1978) studied electrophoretic variation in island populations of the bush rat (*Rattus fuscipes*) separated from the South Australian mainland for 8,000-10,000 years by the postglacial rise in sea-levels. Schmitt found that loci which were polymorphic on the mainland were monomorphic on the islands due to genetic drift.

It is possible that Victorian *P. gunnii* were originally more genetically variable than they are at present. The observed lack of variability may indicate past genetic bottlenecks before the two modern populations were separated by Bass Strait, or drift due to small population size after separation. If the latter were the case, one might have expected to find fixed allelic differences between the two populations.

The cheetah (*Acinonyx jubatus*) is known to be depauperate in genetic variability, attributed to past population bottlenecks (O'Brien *et al.* 1983). Increasing the fitness of the captive breeding zoo population of cheetahs has been advocated by crossing the South African subspecies (*A. j. jubatus*) with East African animals (*A. j. raineyi*) to introduce some additional heterozygosity (O'Brien *et al.* 1985).

Supplementing the gene pool of the Victorian population *P. gunnii* by introduction of animals from the Tasmanian population is not expected to increase average heterozygosity greatly, if at all, as measurable by electrophoresis of blood proteins. It would also seem unlikely that genetic incompatibility would be a problem if the populations were crossed. There remains the possibility, however, that each population has developed coadapted gene complexes through selection for each environment and that any artificial migration of genes might place hybrid individuals at a disadvantage. This could be tested by a trial cross of Tasmanian and Victorian animals at a reintroduction site remote from the existing population or proposed satellite populations. The results of such a trial cross would demonstrate the likely outcome of such genetic admixture if needed on a larger scale, in the event that current recovery strategies do not succeed in arresting the continued decline of the existing population. This scenario presupposes that recovery is dependent on an increase in genetic variability to enable the population to resist environmental pressures. It is likely that factors other than genetic ones are primarily responsible for the continued decline of the species in Victoria (Seebeck *et al.*, this volume).

*Conclusion*

Although no electrophoretically detectable variation in proteins has been observed between Victorian and Tasmanian bandicoots, minor differences in the habitats occupied by the two populations and differences in reproductive patterns (Heinsohn 1966; Lacy and Clark, this volume), combined with the demonstrated morphological divergence, indicate that some genetic differentiation has occurred. The extent of this divergence is yet to be confirmed. Results of DNA analysis may assist in defining the degree of divergence. In the meantime, it would seem prudent to continue to manage the Victorian population without genetic input from the Tasmanian populations while prospects for recovery are good (Maguire *et al.;* Seebeck; Arnold *et al.,* this volume). If in the future it becomes necessary to boost the Victorian populations with an infusion of Tasmanian genes, the genetic risks and consequences may be better understood.

## Acknowledgments

Thanks are extended to Dr. R. Green, Zoologist, Queen Victoria Museum and Art Gallery, Launceston; and Mr. A. P. Andrews, Curator of Vertebrates, Tasmanian Museum and Art Gallery Hobart, for loan of *Perameles gunnii* specimens. The Design Department of the Museum of Victoria prepared the diagrams. Dr. T. Clark examined material in Tasmanian museums and copied records for our use. Dr. R. Cosgrove and Mr. B. Marshall of the Archaeology Department, La Trobe University, provided information on cave deposits and palaeoclimates and assisted with references. Dr. T. Rich, Museum of Victoria, provided information on Tertiary fossils.

## References

Archer, M. 1984. The Australian marsupial radiation. In *Vertebrate Zoogeography and Evolution in Australasia,* eds M. Archer and G. Clayton. p. 650. Hesperian Press, Carlisle: Western Australia.

Blom, W. M. 1988. Late quaternary sediments and sea-levels in Bass Basin, southeastern Australia—a preliminary report. *Search* **19**:94-96.

Bowdler, S. 1984. Hunter Hill, Hunter Island: archaeological investigations of a prehistoric Tasmanian site. *Terra Australis.* **8**:1-148.

Brazenor, C. W. 1950. *The Mammals of Victoria.* Handbook No. 1, Museum of Victoria. Brown, Prior, Anderson: Melbourne.

Brown, P. R. 1989. Management Plan for the Conservation of the Eastern Barred Bandicoot, *Perameles gunnii* in Victoria. National Parks and Wildlife Division, Victoria. *Arthur Rylah Institute for Environmental Research Tech. Rep. Ser.* No. **63**. Department of Conservation, Forests and Lands: Melbourne.

Colhoun, E. A., van de Geer, G, and Mook, W. G. 1982. Stratigraphy, pollen analysis, and palaeoclimatic interpretation of Pulbeena Swamp, Northwestern Tasmania. *Quaternary Research* **18**:108-126.

Cosgrove, R. 1989. Thirty thousand years of human colonization in Tasmania: new Pleistocene dates. *Science* **243**:1706-1708.

Freedman, L. 1967. Skull and tooth variation in the genus *Perameles,* Part 1—Anatomical features. *Rec. Aust. Mus.* **27**:147-165.

Freedman, L. and Joffe, A. D. 1967. Skull and tooth variation in the genus *Perameles,* Part 3—Metrical features of *P. gunnii* and *P. bougainville. Rec. Aust. Mus.* **27**:197-212.

Gould, J. 1845-1863. *The Mammals of Australia.* The Author: London.

Gray, J. E. 1838. Notices accompanying a collection of quadrupeds and fish from Van Diemen's Land. *Ann. Nat. Hist.* **1**:101-111.

Gray, J. E. 1841. Appendix C in G. Grey. *Journals of Two Expeditions of Discovery in Northwest and Western Australia.* Vol. 2, p. 407. T. and W. Boone: London.

Griffith, J. R. 1971. Continental margin tectonics and the evolution of south east Australia. *J. Austral. Petrol. Expl. Assoc.* **11**:75-79.

Heinsohn, G. E. 1966. Ecology and reproduction of the Tasmanian bandicoots (*Perameles gunni* and *Isoodon obesulus*). *Univ. Calif. Publ. Zool.* **80**:1-107.

Hope, G. S. 1978. The late Pleistocene and Holocene vegetational history of Hunter Island, northwestern Tasmania. *Aust. J. of Botany* **26**:493-514.

Hope, J. H. 1969. Wildlife of Bass Strait. In *Bass Strait: Australia's Last Frontier.* Australian Broadcasting Corporation: Sydney.

Hope, J. H. 1973. Mammals of the Bass Strait Islands. *Proc. R. Soc. Vict.* **85**:163-196.

Iredale, T. and Troughton, E. Le G. 1934. A check-list of the mammals recorded from Australia. *Mem. Aust. Mus.* **6**:1-122.

Jennings, J. N. 1959. The submarine topography of Bass Strait. *Proc. Roy. Roc. Vict.* **71**:49-72.

Jones, F. Wood 1923-25. *The Mammals of South Australia.* Govt. Printer: Adelaide.

Kemper, C. In press. The status of *Peramelidae* and *Thylacomyidae* in South Australia. In *Bandicoots and Bilbies,* eds J. H. Seebeck, P. R. Brown, R. J. Wallis and C.M. Kemper. Surrey Beatty and Sons: Sydney.

Krefft G. 1866. On the vertebrata of the lower Murray and Darling; their habits, economy, and geographical distribution. *Trans. Phil. Soc. N.S.W.* 1866 Pp. 1-33.

Lyne, A. G. 1951. Notes on external characters of the barred bandicoot (*Perameles gunnii* Gray) with special reference to the pouch young. *Proc. Zool. Soc.* 121:587-598.

Mayr, E. 1963. *Animal Species and Evolution.* Harvard University Press: Cambridge, Massachusetts.

Mayr, E. 1969. *Principles of Systematic Zoology.* McGraw-Hill: New York.

Nei, M. 1987. *Molecular Evolutionary Genetics.* Columbia University Press: New York.

O'Brien, S. J., Wildt, D. E., Goldman, D., Merril, C. R. and Bush, M. 1983. The cheetah is depauperate in genetic variation. *Science* 221:459-462.

O'Brien, S. J., Roelke, M. E., Marker, L., Newman, A., Wrinkler, C. A., Meltzer, D., Colly, L., Evermann, J. F., Bush, M. and Wildt, D. E. 1985. Genetic basis for species vulnerability in the cheetah. *Science* 227:1428-1434.

Rich, T. H. 1982. Monotremes, placentals and marsupials, their record in Australia and its biases. In *The Fossil Vertebrate Record of Australasia,* eds P. V. Rich and E. M. Thompson. Pp. 386-572. Monash University: Clayton, Victoria.

Schmitt, L. H. 1978. Genetic variation in isolated populations of the Australian bush-rat *Rattus fuscipes. Evolution* 32:1-14.

Seebeck, J. H. 1979. Status of the Barred Bandicoot, *Perameles gunnii,* in Victoria, with a note on husbandry of a captive colony. *Aust. Wildl. Res.* 6: 255-264.

Sherwin, W. B. 1989. Conservation genetics and taxonomy of *Perameles gunnii.* In *Management Plan for the Conservation of the Eastern Barred Bandicoot,* Parameles gunnii, *in Victoria.* P.R. Brown. Pp. 60-63. National Parks and Wildlife Division, Victoria. *Arthur Rylah Institute for Environmental Research Tech. Rep. Ser.* No. 63. Department of Conservation, Forests and Lands: Melbourne.

Sherwin, W. B., and Brown, P. R. In press. Problems in the estimation of the effective size of a population of the Eastern Barred Bandicoot, *Perameles gunnii* at Hamilton, Victoria. In *Bandicoots and Bilbies,* eds J. H. Seebeck, P. R. Brown, R. L. Wallis and C.M. Kemper. Surrey Beatty and Sons: Sydney.

Skilbeck, C. G. 1980. A preliminary report on the late Cainozoic geology and fossil fauna of Bow, New South Wales. *Proc. Linn. Soc. N.S.W.* 104:171-181.

Spencer, B. 1900. A description of *Wynyardia bassiania,* a fossil marsupial from the Tertiary beds of Table Cape, Tasmania. *Proc. Zool. Soc. London.* Pp. 776-795.

Strahan, R. (ed.) 1983. *The Australian Museum Complete Book of Australian Mammals.* Angus and Robertson: Sydney.

Sutherland, F. L. 1973. The geological development of the southern shores and islands of Bass Strait. *Proc. R. Soc. Vict.* 85:133-144.

Tate, G. H. H. 1948. Results of the Archbold expeditions. No. 60. Studies in the *Peramelidae* (Marsupialia). *Bull. Amer. Mus. Nat. Hist.* 92:317-346.

Tedford, R.H., Bank, M.R., Kemp, J.R., McDougall, I., and Sutherland, F.L. 1975. Recognition of the oldest known fossil marsupials from Australia. *Nature* 255:141-142.

Thomas, O. 1888. *Catalogue of the Marsupialia and Monotremata in the Collection of the British Museum (Natural History).* British Museum (Natural History): London.

Tideman, C. R. 1967. Some mammal remains in cave deposits in the southeast of South Australia. *S. Aust. Nat.* 42:21-27.

Troughton, E. Le G. 1941. *Furred Animals of Australia.* First edition. Angus and Robertson: Sydney.

Troughton, E. Le G. 1954. *Furred Animals of Australia.* Fifth edition. Angus and Robertson: Sydney.

Turnbull, W. D., and Lundelius, E. L. 1970. The Hamilton fauna, a late Pliocene mammalian fauna from the Grange Burn, Victoria. *Fieldiana, Geology* 19:1-163.

Wakefield, N. A. 1963a. Sub-fossils from Mount Hamilton, Victoria. *Victorian Nat.* 79:323-330.

Wakefield, N. A. 1963b. Mammal sub-fossils from near Portland, Victoria. *Victorian Nat.* 80:39-45.

Wakefield, N. A. 1963c. Mammal remains from the Grampians, Victoria. *Victorian Nat.* 80:130-133.

Wakefield, N. A. 1964a. Recent mammalian sub-fossils of the basalt plains of Victoria. *Proc. R. Soc. Vict.* 77:19-25.

Wakefield, N. A. 1964b. Mammal sub-fossils from basalt caves in southwest Victoria. *Victorian Nat.* 80:274-278.

Wakefield, N. A. 1967. Preliminary report on McEachern's Cave, southwest Victoria. *Victorian Nat.* 84:363-383.

Waterhouse, G. R. 1846. *A Natural History of the Mammalia* Vol. 1. Hippolyte Balliere: London. p. 380.

# Population Estimates and Characteristics of the Eastern Barred Bandicoot in Victoria, with Recommendations for Population Monitoring

*Steven C. Minta[1,2], Tim W. Clark[1,3] and Peter Goldstraw[4]*

## Abstract

The eastern barred bandicoot, *Perameles gunnii,* was formerly distributed throughout the Western Victoria Plains and is now restricted to a single population in and around the City of Hamilton in western Victoria. Accurate data on its status is essential, as is an established means to assess its condition annually. We used prior population assessments by Moon (1984), Dufty (1988), and Brown (1989) to establish six live-trapping grids to investigate some population characteristics. The standard grid contained 100 traps spaced at 25 m intervals and covered 5 ha. Grids were placed mostly in areas of moderate to high bandicoot density and trapped for 8 days between late November 1988 and early March 1989. We used the comprehensive mark-recapture program CAPTURE for analysis of population numbers and density. Trap success was very high and trap response in the population was highly variable. Animals tended to exhibit a behavioural response (*i.e.* 'trap happy'), an individual response (heterogeneity of capture probabilities due to age, sex or individual differences), or a combination of both. Overall, individuals had a high recapture rate: 147 different individuals were captured a total of 482 times; 118 were adults and 29 were juveniles (<500 g). The adult sex ratio was male-biased (p=0.01) and the juvenile sex ratio was female-biased (p=0.09). We captured 62 animals marked by Dufty (1988) earlier in the year. Extent of movements within grids was greater for adults than juveniles. The mean capture rate was 0.456 with females greater than males, depending on the grid. Habitat analysis was complicated by the pattern of vegetation and human structures. Generally, edge habitat and habitat with nearby cover accounted for highest trap success. Density estimation was difficult due to larger-than-expected home ranges and lack of population closure. After qualifications, bandicoot densities on the five main grids were probably 1-1.5 bandicoots per ha. We analyse factors affecting population and density estimation of eastern barred bandicoots and conclude with possible study designs for long-term population monitoring.

## Introduction

There is a pressing need for accurate data on Hamilton's wild eastern barred bandicoot population, on other populations as they are established at captive breeding sites, and eventually on populations reintroduced into areas of the species' former range. For the next few years, annually updated information on distribution and density of the Hamilton population is the essential minimum. Data on age and sex structure, reproductive rates, and age and sex specific survivorship rates would also be invaluable. Understanding the population's habitat relationships is also important.

These data are essential for managing recovery in several ways (see Romesburg 1981). First, the population monitoring in late 1988 and early 1989 reported in this paper serves as a baseline against which future monitoring results can be compared. Second, monitoring results can be used to derive even more effective monitoring procedures as described in this paper. Third, the data can be used in demographic and genetic

---

[1] Northern Rockies Conservation Cooperative, Box 2705, Jackson, Wyoming 83001, U.S.A.

[2] Division of Biological Sciences, University of Montana, Missoula, Montana 59812, U.S.A.

[3] Department of Conservation Biology, Chicago Zoological Society, Brookfield, Illinois 60513, U.S.A.

[4] Department of Conservation, Forests and Lands, Portland Region, 214 Koroit Street, Warrnambool, Victoria 3280, Australia.

models to estimate population sizes needed for long-term survival, estimates that can then be used to set management targets. These models and targets can be updated annually with growing information about the population's behaviour. Fourth, as habitat management over the next few years is undertaken in Hamilton to increase bandicoot distribution and density to meet population targets, annual population monitoring can measure progress. Depending on the population's response, management can be tailored in an adaptive manner (see Holling 1978). Towards these ends, this paper describes some population characteristics of the eastern barred bandicoot population in late 1988 and early 1989 and makes some recommendations for an annual monitoring program.

The eastern barred bandicoot was distributed historically throughout the Western Victoria Plains (Seebeck 1979, Brown 1989), but today is found only in and near the city of Hamilton. Hamilton (2150 ha, 186 m above sea level) has a population of about 10,500 and lies near the western margin of the Plains. The Plains are characterized by an undulating topography, with low rounded hills, valleys, swampy water courses, and broken patches of lava outcrops. Basaltic soils of recent origin dominate. Mean annual rainfall (1869-1976) is 691 mm and an annual mean of 166 rain days results in a Mediterranean climate of cool wet winters and warm dry summers. Mean minimum temperature (July) is 4.7° C and mean maximum (January) is 26.4° C. Floods, droughts, and fires are common.

Pre-settlement (1840s) vegetation was a perennial tussock grassland and some savannah. Dominant species were wallaby grasses (*Danthonia* spp.), spear grasses (*Stipa* spp.), tussock grass (*Poa labillardieri*) and kangaroo grass (*Thereda australis* Willis 1974). Savannah woodlands were dominated by river red gum (*Eucalyptus camaldudensis*). Now, sheep and cattle production dominate land uses and have drastically altered native biotic communities. Seebeck (1979) and Moon (1984) note that the eastern barred bandicoot decline is due to replacement of its original habitat with crops and sown pastures and introduction of livestock and other species.

## Methods

### Trapping and Handling

Field methods followed Seebeck (1979), Dufty (1988) and Brown (1989). Eastern barred bandicoots were live-trap sampled in five square grids, each containing approximately 100 traps spaced at 25 m, and one rectangular grid of 105 traps (35 station of 3 traps) spaced at 100 m (see Table 1, Fig. 1). Grids were operated for 4 days, closed for 4 to 8 days, and operated for another 4 days. Each 8-day grid sample yielded about 800 trap-nights (one trap set for one night = one trap night). Spring-loaded cage traps (350 mm long, 300 mm wide, and 160 mm tall, made of 10 mm wire mesh) were baited with a mixture of peanut butter, honey and rolled oats, and set before 1900 hrs daily. Traps were closed and animals processed during early morning. Traps were moved nightly a distance approximately 10% of the intertrap spacing to randomize samples from each trap station.

On first capture, animals were weighed, measured (standard measurements), sexed, condition and external parasites checked, distinguishing features noted, ear tattooed, and for females, pouches examined and pouch young measured and sexed. All bandicoots were processed and released at the capture site, often in less than three minutes. On subsequent captures, animals were weighed, tattoo numbers recorded, pouches checked in selected cases, and released. Bandicoots were transferred from traps to pillow slip-sized bags for processing. On release, the bandicoots ran to cover, and the destination site and the route of travel were mapped where possible.

The first four grids were located in areas thought to contain the greatest *P. gunnii* densities based on work by Dufty (1988), Brown (1989) and

*Table 1.*—Grid dimensions and trapping dates for grids and sessions, City of Hamilton area, 1988-1989. General description of weather during trapping was typical for the season and area.

| Grid and Session | | Dates Operated | Weather Description | | | Grid Description[1] | | |
|---|---|---|---|---|---|---|---|---|
| | | | Temp. (°C) | Wind | Moisture | Dimensions in Traps @ 25 m | Area (ha) | Trap Stations |
| Chatsworth Rd. | I | Nov. 25 - Nov.28 | 11-17 | windy | rainy | [2]10x11 | 4.95 | 94 |
| | II | Dec. 4 - Dec. 7 | 11-18 | breezy | damp | | | |
| Hamilton Tip | I | Nov. 30 - Dec. 3 | 11-20 | breezy | damp | 10x10 | 5.06 | 100 |
| | II | Dec. 13 - Dec. 16 | 16-25 | calm | dry | | | |
| Grange Street | I | Dec. 9 - Dec. 12 | 11-24 | calm | dry | 10x10 | 5.06 | 100 |
| | II | Dec. 17 - Dec. 20 | 11-17 | calm | dry | | | |
| Kennedy Oval | I | Jan. 3- Jan. 6 | cool | calm | damp | 10x10 | 5.06 | 100 |
| | II | Jan. 10 - Jan. 13 | cool | windy | rainy | | | |
| Adelaide | I | Feb. 26 - Mar. 2 | hot | calm | dry | 10x10 | 5.06 | 100 |
| | II | Mar. 7 - Mar. 10 | warm | calm | damp | | | |
| City | All | Mar. 3 - Mar. 6 | hot | calm | dry | 5x7 | 24.00 | 35 |

[1]Grids had 25 m trap station spacing with one trap per station, except City grid which had 100 m trap station spacing with three traps per station, totalling 105 traps.
[2]One end of grid was not square.

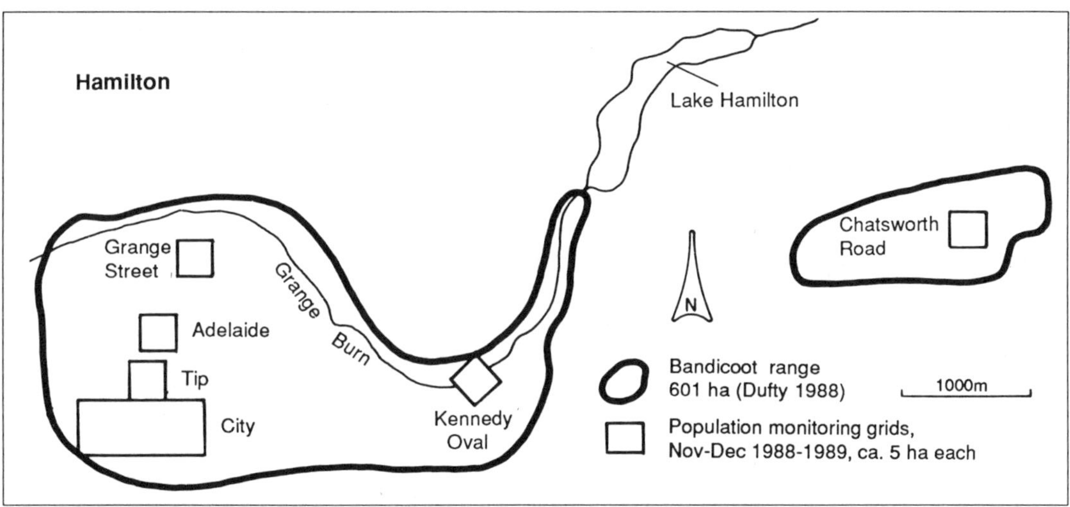


*Figure 1.*—Map of study area containing boundary of the City of Hamilton, current range of *P. gunnii* and locations of the six mark-recapture grids.

Seebeck (personal communication). The fifth grid (Adelaide) was located mid-distance between two of these grids. The sixth grid (City) contained an area thought to include a steep population gradient. Bandicoot densities were correlated with patterns of vegetation and human structures. To examine habitat selection, we classified the vegetation within a circle of 5 m radius around each trap. Vegetative type was categorized as 1) mixed grass/forbs $\leq$ 10 cm (slashed or grazed), 2) mixed grass/forbs 11-50 cm, 3) mixed grass/forbs > 50 cm, 4) low-canopy woody vegetation in contact with ground surface or herbaceous layer and 5) high-canopy woody vegetation not in contact with surface or herbaceous layer. Because the habitat formed a fine-resolution mosaic, we used two habitat variables: primary habitat type was the majority vegetative element and secondary habitat type was the minority element. We also noted the nearest man-made structures for each trap station, such as houses, log piles, sheds, car bodies, roads, stacked brush piles, etc. The collinearity of human structures with vegetation, the large number of discrete categories, and the small sample size precluded a statistical analysis of habitat selection that included human structures. We chose the method of Neu *et al.* (1974) for habitat analysis of vegetative categories based on the evaluation of resource selection methods in Alldredge and Ratti (1986).

*Population Estimation*

*Assumptions.* There are three critical considerations in constructing mark-recapture models: what population size N means (this relates to geographic closure), whether the model should be demographically closed or open, and how to model capture probabilities (White *et al.* 1982; see Appendix). We estimated N, density (D), and other parameters with Program CAPTURE (Otis *et al.* 1978; March 1982 version) using a DEC-2065 minicomputer. Program CAPTURE focusses on mark-recapture and capture removal methods for trapping studies in which a population is assumed to be closed. It allows comprehensive, state-of-the-art model building, rigorous statistical treatment, and exact maximum likelihood estimators of model parameters. Readers who are not familiar with mark-recapture methods should refer to general reviews such as Overton and Davis (1969), Caughley (1977), and Seber (1982, 1986). White *et al.* (1982) is an excellent discussion of mark-recapture models with a large emphasis on Program CAPTURE. The description in the Appendix, as well as data analysis, relies extensively on Otis *et al.* (1978) and White *et al.* (1982).

*Monte Carlo Method of Population Estimation.* In general, two or more independent population estimates should be calculated (Smith *et al.* 1975, Skalski and Robson 1982, Seber 1982). This is particularly true with the present *P. gunnii* data sets, where numbers of animals captured is low and estimators from Program CAPTURE may be inefficient. To aid in examination of closure and effective grid size, we split the trapping occasions for each grid into two 4-day periods which were separated by 4-8 days. This separation also facilitated the application of a second population estimation method based on Monte Carlo simulation (Minta and Mangel 1989). Monte Carlo simulation can lead to a full probability distribution for the population. From this probability distribution, one can compute maximum likelihood estimates and a 95% likelihood interval on the population. The shape and asymmetry of the distribution and width of likelihood intervals are determined by sampling heterogeneity and sample size. The method is especially applicable to small data sets and situations in which non-random catchability is likely after the initial capture. With this technique, all animals are marked and then later recaptured (or preferably resighted). The first 4-day period was considered the initial marking period while the second 4-day period was considered the period of recapture; newly captured animals need not be marked. Thus, any new animals captured during the second period are considered as 'unknown,' and those captures are simply pooled and totalled. This unknown seg-

*Table 2.*—Summary of sex and reproductive data for mark-recapture grids, City of Hamilton area.

| Grid | All Captures[1] | | All Captures | | Adult Captures[4] | | Juv. Captures | | Litter |
| | Indiv. | Total | Ratio[2] | Prob.[3] | Ratio | Prob. | Ratio | Prob. | Size[5] |
|---|---|---|---|---|---|---|---|---|---|
| Chatsworth | 36 | 126 | 22:14 | 0.18 | 18:11 | 0.19 | 4:3 | 0.71 | 2.25 (8) |
| Hamilton Tip | 29 | 105 | 15:14 | 0.85 | 11:8 | 0.49 | 4:6 | 0.52 | 1.78 (9) |
| Grange Street | 23 | 85 | 15:8 | 0.14 | 15:7 | 0.09 | 0:1 | - | 2.00 (7) |
| Kennedy Oval | 18 | 78 | 10:8 | 0.64 | 10:3 | 0.05 | 0:5 | 0.03 | 1.33 (3) |
| Adelaide | 20 | 51 | 10:10 | 1.00 | 10:8 | 0.64 | 0:2 | - | - |
| City | 21 | 37 | 11:10 | 0.83 | 9:8 | 0.81 | 2:2 | - | - |
| Total | 147 | 482 | 83:64 | 0.12 | 73:45 | 0.01 | 10:19 | 0.09 | - |

[1]For both sessions combined: different individuals captured and total of captures and recaptures.
[2]Male:Female ratio of different individuals captured.
[3]Observed probability of sex ratio. $H_o$ : $\mu$=p=0.5. Two-tailed test, normal approximation.
[4]Adults weigh 500 g or more, juveniles are less than 500 g.
[5]Mean litter size with number of litters in parentheses.

ment of the population is then simulated to come from the exact distribution of recapture frequencies of the marked (known) population segment. Computations were performed on an IBM-PC clone.

### Other Statistical Analyses

Analysis of variance (ANOVA), contingency table analysis, and regression analysis follow Winer (1971). ANOVA analyses should be viewed as illustrating trends and are not intended for exact statistical inference. Angular transformation and Bartlett's test of homogeneity follow Steel and Torrie (1980). Small-sample t-test and examination of normality (kurtosis and skewness) follow Mendenhall and Scheaffer (1973). Tests of ratios and proportions follow Fleiss (1981) and Steel and Torrie (1980). All chi-square and z-score tests were corrected for continuity where possible and should be viewed as conservative. All pairwise tests are two-tailed unless otherwise stated. Statistical tests are reported as standard observed probabilities. One standard error (SE) is used in text description and in all figures. Computations were performed on a Macintosh SE microcomputer using Excel, MacSpin, and StatView software.

### Results

### General

Dates of trapping sessions and a qualitative description of weather during each session are summarized in Table 1. The main sampling effort was concentrated within a 7-week period for the first four grids. Adelaide and City grids were operated some six weeks later.

The sex ratio of adults for all grids is significantly male biased; however, there is considerable variation from grid to grid (Table 2). Four times more adults than juveniles were captured, and the total juvenile sex ratio was biased toward females. Because two individuals on the Chatsworth grid (an adult female and a juvenile male) escaped before they were ear tattooed, they will be excluded from remaining analyses.

Numerous factors affect trappability of eastern barred bandicoots, and this, in turn modifies assumptions and strongly shapes the analysis of population attributes. Internal variables that determine individual trappability are difficult to measure, but can be correlated with subpopulation components, such as age and sex. External

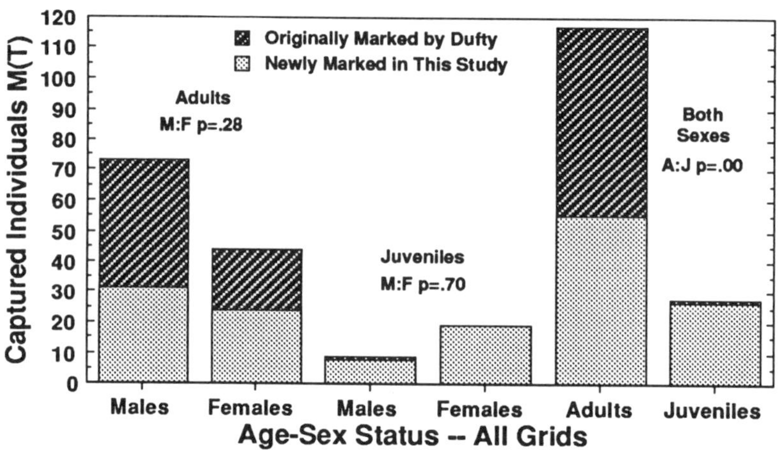


*Figure 2.*—Proportions of age-sex categories ear-tattooed by A. Dufty (1988) prior to this study. Data from all grids are combined. Chi-square (2x2) probability that one age-sex category is more likely to be marked originally by Dufty. Thus, for adults, more males were marked by Dufty than were females (p=0.28) relative to their proportion in the sampled population.

variables, such as habitat, can explain some of the spatial variation in trappability. Habitat patterns cannot elucidate differential trappability *per se*, but do help interpret population closure and the meaning of density estimates. When multiple grids are sequentially sampled, there are two scales involved: within grid and among grids. Before presenting results of population estimation, we examine movement and capture rates by age and sex, both within and among grids. We then analyse habitat selection within grids.

*Movement*

*Among Studies and Among Grids.* In addition to our ear-tattooing on the six grids in the present study, Dufty (1988) ear-tattooed 106 eastern barred bandicoots in the area of the City of Hamilton between May 5 and September 13, 1988. Our grids were placed in areas previously trapped by Dufty, and of the 145 animals captured on our grids, 62 (42.8%) had been marked earlier by Dufty. Of these inter-grid captures, five bandicoots (4.1%; four males, one female) were also captured once each on other grids during this study: Adelaide accounted for two (from Grange Street and Hamilton Tip), and City accounted for three (all from Hamilton Tip). Only one inter-grid capture occurred within this study: one female was captured on the City, Adelaide, and Hamilton Tip grids.

Recaptures, or animals captured on more than one grid or during more than one study, were confined to adults (Fig. 2). The exceptional juvenile was a recapture from Dufty's study, a male averaging 499 g in seven captures on the Hamilton Tip grid. Adult males were more likely to be recaptured than were adult females. Figure 3 shows the number of recaptures, relative to animals captured once, for each grid. Among grids there was little variation in the ratio of recaptures to animals captured once (p=0.98, df=5). Chatsworth Road and Hamilton Tip had more recaptured males than females, Chatsworth Road significantly so.

*Movement Within Grids.* Maximum travel, or the maximum distance moved by an animal among trap stations (all occasions), is an indicator of general movement. There were 107 animals recaptured at least once within single grids. The mean distance moved was 104.2 m (SE = 5.72, range = 0-230). Overall, adults ($\bar{x}$=110.2 m) moved further than juveniles ($\bar{x}$=78.8 m, df=106,

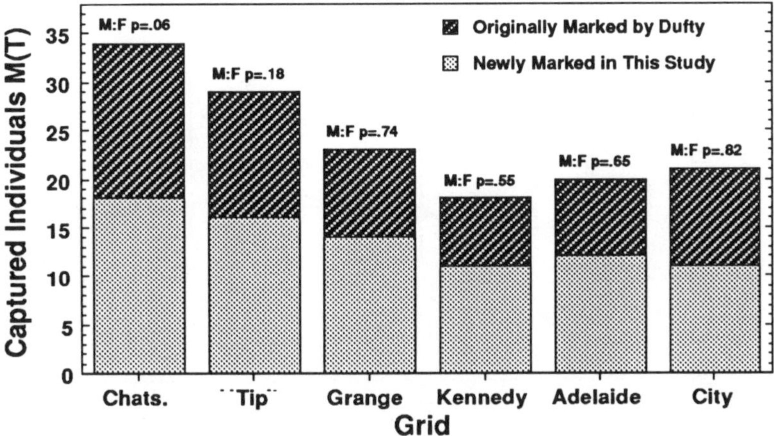

*Figure 3.*—Male-female ratio of captured individuals, M(T), for each grid. Data sorted by grid and sex. Chi-square probability calculated from test of two proportions.

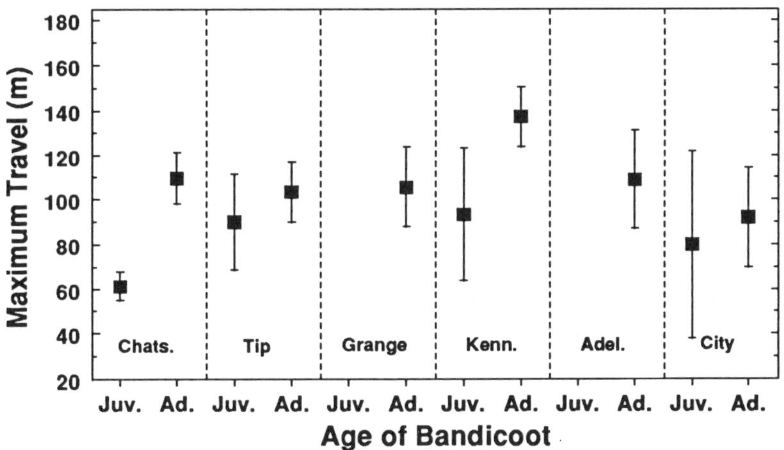

*Figure 4.*—Maximum distance travelled on grid by individuals who were trapped ≥2 times. Data sorted by grid and age. Ad.=Adults. Juv.=Juveniles. Grange Street grid had one juvenile capture.

p=0.03). Figure 4 shows the age variation in movement for each grid. Adult males ($\bar{x}$=111.0 m) did not differ from adult females ($\bar{x}$=108.5 m, df=86, p=0.87) and similarly, juvenile males ($\bar{x}$=78.3 m) did not differ from juvenile females ($\bar{x}$=78.9 m, df=19, p=0.98). Figure 5 shows the adult sex variation in movement for each grid.

Two-way ANOVA (sex and grid) indicates that sex does not influence maximum travel (p=0.74), grids do not influence maximum travel (p=0.48), and there is no interaction between sex and grid (p=0.57). Two-way ANOVA (sex and age) indicates that sex does not influence maximum travel (p=0.96), but age has considerable influence upon

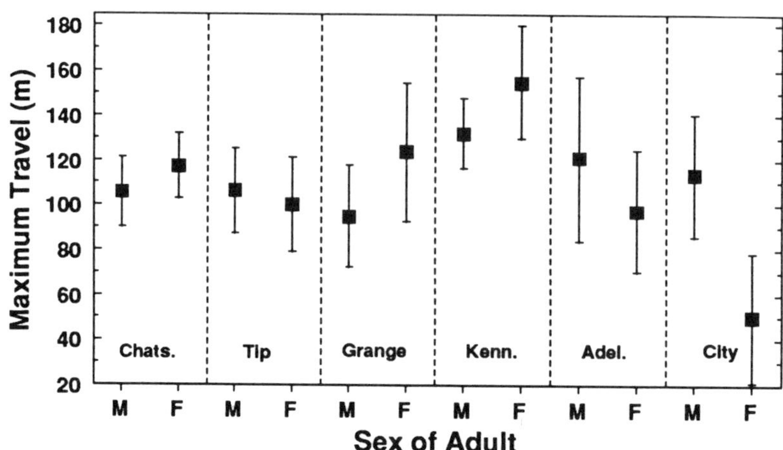



*Figure 5.*—Maximum distance travelled on grid by individuals who were trapped ≥2 times. Data sorted by grid and sex. M=Males. F=Females.

maximum travel (p=0.05), and there is no interaction between sex and age on maximum travel (p=0.93). Two-way ANOVA (age and grid) indicates that age has significant influence upon maximum travel (p=0.04), grid does not influence maximum travel (p=0.84), and there is no interaction between age and grid on maximum travel (p=0.94).

Inferences about maximum travel should be viewed with caution since maximum travel is correlated with the number of captures, or capture rate, and is confounded by grid size relative to home range size, home range overlap with grid, and prior occupancy of a trap. For example, there is a reliable correlation between maximum travel and the capture rates of individuals (Spearman Rho = 0.44; Pearson r=0.45). Polynomial regression (quadratic) depicts maximum travel increasing with number of captures up to 5-6 captures, at which point there is no further increase with increased number of captures to a maximum of 8 (SE of beta coefficient: $x=14.6$, $x^2=1.5$; overall p<0.0001).

*Capture Rates*

Mark-recapture population estimation is based on the analysis of variation in individual capture frequencies. Parameter estimation of meaningful subpopulation components (age and sex) requires very large sample sizes. When separate grids are used for characterising a population, it is useful to examine patterns of capture variation that might be affecting population and density estimation. The capture rate of an individual is the proportion of times it was captured within the number of possible trapping occasions (eight except four for City grid). Because the distribution of rates is truncated at both ends, we used the angular transformation to normalize the data (due to assymmetry). We back-transformed means but not error terms (due to assymmetry).

The mean capture rate for the 145 captures on all grids was 0.456 (SE=0.023). Adults had a slightly higher overall capture rate ($\bar{x}=0.469$, n=117) than juveniles ($\bar{x}=0.407$, n=28, p=0.38). Figure 6

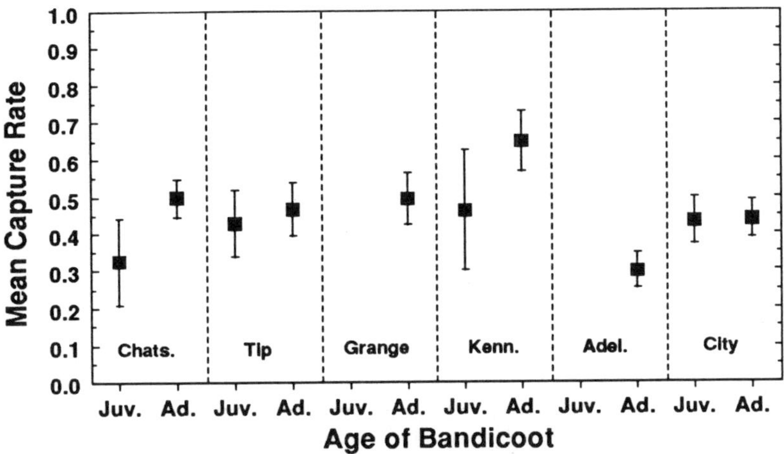



*Figure 6.*—Mean capture rates and SEs of eastern barred bandicoots by grid and age for all data. Capture rates computed for each individual by dividing the number of captures by the total possible (number of trap occasions). These proportions were then normalized with angular transform for analysis (see Methods) and means were back-transformed for presentation in this figure.

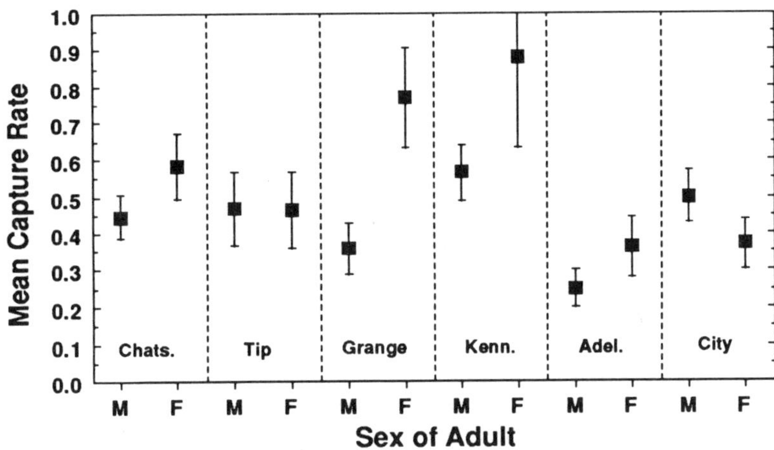



*Figure 7.*—Mean capture rates and SEs of eastern barred bandicoots by grid and sex for adults. Capture rates computed for each individual by dividing the number of captures by the total possible (number of trap occasions). These proportions were then normalized with angular transform for analysis (see Methods) and means were back-transformed for presentation in this figure.

shows the age variation in capture rate for each grid. Adult females had a higher overall capture rate ($\bar{x}=0.549$) than males ($\bar{x}=0.427$, $p=0.09$, $df=116$) but juvenile females ($\bar{x}=0.383$) had an insignificantly lower overall capture rate than juvenile males ($\bar{x}=0.457$, $p=0.56$, $df=27$). Figure 7 shows the high degree of sexual variation in adult capture rates for each grid. Although sample size is small, the elevated capture rates for the Grange Street and Kennedy Oval grids are due substantially to the extremely high female capture rates.

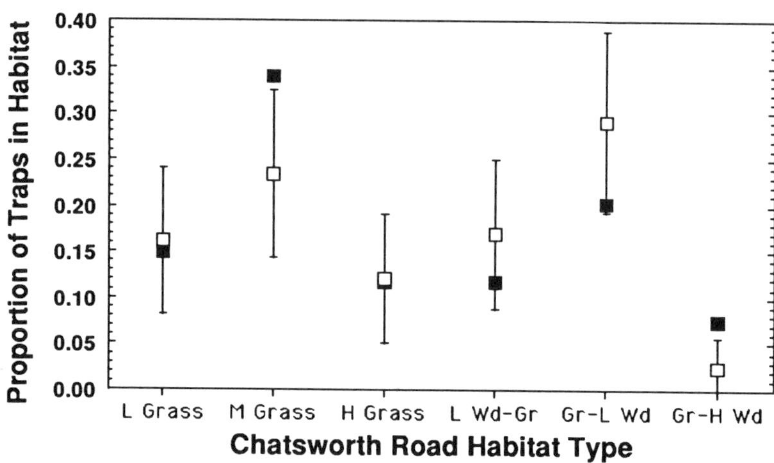


*Figure 8.*—Summary of habitat analysis for Chatsworth Road grid. L=low, M=medium, H=high, Wd=woody, Gr=grass (see Methods for definitions). Filled squares represent habitat availability (expected proportion of habitat use) on grid by the proportion of traps on the grid that are located in that habitat type (category). Unfilled squares represent actual proportion of habitat types used by eastern barred bandicoots based on trap success. The greater the difference between expected habitat use and actual habitat use, the more that habitat is selected for or avoided. Thus, Medium Grass category was avoided while Low Woody vegetation mixed with grasses was preferred. Interval estimates are based on Bonferoni normal statistics (alpha=0.1).

Three-way ANOVA (sex, age, and grid) was nonsignificant, but incidence tables indicated that capture rate was influenced by complex interaction among the three factors. Because the design was highly non-orthogonal, the hypothesis of sex and grid effects was based on the largest fraction of the total data. Two-way ANOVA (sex and grid) reveals that sex influences capture rate (p=0.02), grids influence capture rate (p=0.02), and there is a small amount of interaction between sex and grid (p=0.22).

*Habitat Analysis*

The vegetative component of the habitat was partitioned into no more than six discrete categories due to sample size restrictions. Consequently, categories varied from grid to grid and could not be combined. Human structures were another component of the bandicoot habitat that clearly determined fine-grained densities, but could not be readily quantified because of their structural diversity and complexity. Although some structures may confound the relationship between capture rate and vegetative habitat selection, other structures were highly correlated. For example, in some cases roadways and fence rows modified vegetation favorably from the bandicoots' standpoint. As a result of this variability, as well as the relative availability of other vegetative categories existing on a particular grid, vegetative types on some grids may be highly preferred, while in others the same vegetative type may be avoided.

Grasses were the primary vegetation type in all categories on Grange Street, Hamilton Tip and Kennedy Oval grids (Figs. 9-11). The dominant vegetative types on the Chatsworth Road grid were medium height grasses and grass associated with woody types (Fig. 8). At that location, bandicoots preferred trap stations in grasses if mixed with low wood, and definitively avoided traps in the predominant medium grasses as well as grasses in high wood. In sharp contrast, medium grasses were a minority habitat on the Grange Street grid but were highly preferred, so much so that other grasses tended to be avoided, especially low grasses (Fig. 10). On the Hamilton Tip grid

56

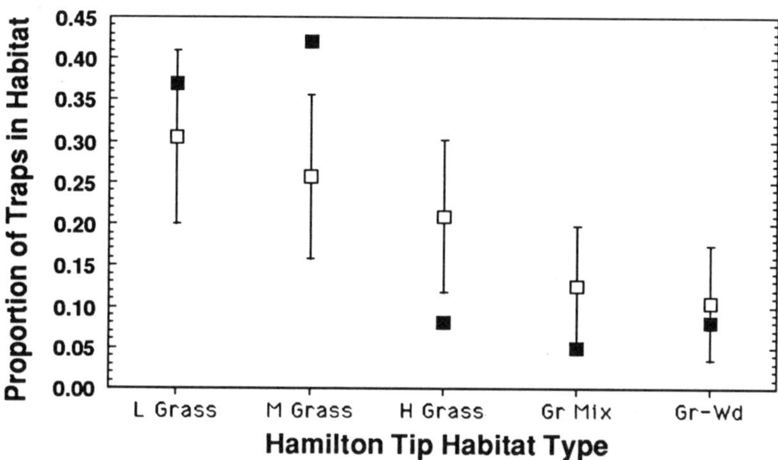



*Figure 9.*—Summary of habitat analysis for Hamilton Tip grid.  See legend of Figure 8 for description.

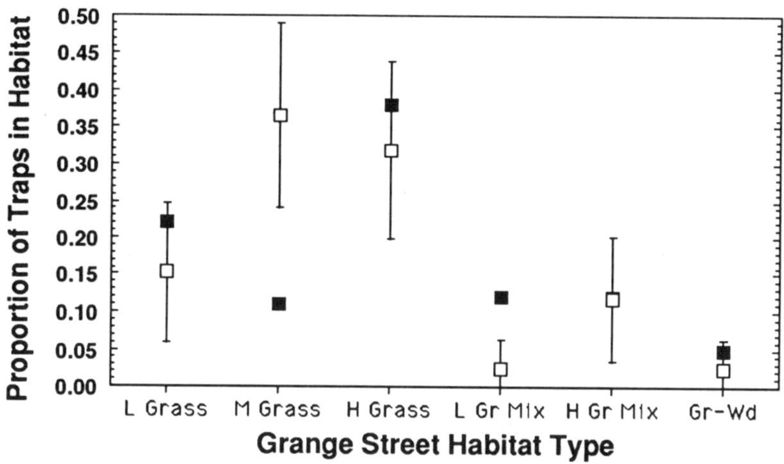



*Figure 10.*—Summary of habitat analysis for Grange Street grid.  See legend of Figure 8 for description.

(Fig. 9), bandicoots preferred high grass and grass mixes while avoiding pure low and medium grass categories.  Similarly, on the Kennedy Oval grid (Fig. 11), avoidance of low and medium grass was offset by preference for  high grass.

Grasses made up almost all vegetative classifications on the Adelaide and City grids.  Medium grasses were avoided and high grasses preferred on the Adelaide grid (Fig. 12).  The City grid was exceptional in that three traps accounted for 16 (43%) of all captures during the single 4-day trap session.  Those three traps were in low grass, but they were also closest to bandicoot shelters.  To illustrate the importance of structural (cover) components of the habitat, we separated the three

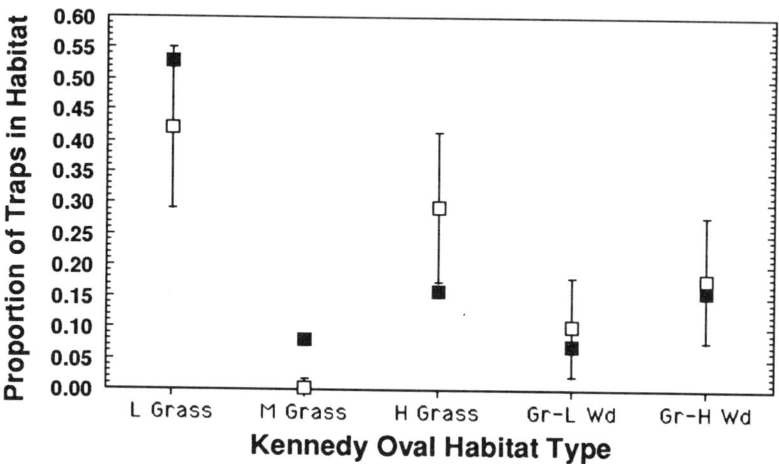


*Figure 11.*—Summary of habitat analysis for Kennedy Oval grid.  See legend of Figure 8 for description.

trap stations into a unique category (Fig. 13). The classification results in a strong avoidance of low grasses in the absence of shelter, but a strong attraction to low grasses in the presence of shelters.

### Population Estimation

*Summary Statistics and Model Selection.*  More than a dozen different estimates of population size can be computed from one of four basic summary statistics: N(J), the number of captures each day; U(J), the number of unmarked animals caught on day J; M(J), the number of marked animals in the population just after the Jth capture occasion; F(J), the number of individuals captured exactly J times [calculated at the end of the study] such that J=1,2, ... T, where T is the last trap occasion.  In our data T=4 for each session and T=8 for both sessions.  Inspection of these statistics provides insights into the type of differential trappability, population closure, the selection of models for estimation, and the interpretation of statistical results.  Keep in mind that the interval between trap occasions is one day except between occasions 4 and 5, for which the interval is 4-8 days.

In general, we might expect individual responses (heterogeneity in capture probabilities) when there are differences arising from age and sex, as we have shown to be true in the previous section.  In good mark-recapture data, the average capture rate should be at least 0.3 for the small data sets generated by the bandicoot grids.  Very few new animals should be caught by the last few occasions.  Similarly, the capture frequency data should show many animals caught 2,3,4, or more times and there should not be a strong spike at F(1) (captured once only).  The plot of N(J) is representative of variation in capture probabilities over time and, therefore, temporal response; the more variable, the more likely $M_t$ will be selected—all else being equal (see Appendix).  Unfortunately, sample sizes were too small to compute goodness of fit tests for $M_t$ except as an alternate hypothesis to $M_o$, which may have contributed to its lack of selection in our data, even when it may have been the most appropriate model.

The best clue for detecting individual response arises from irregularities in the frequencies of captures.  Trap response can be detected from the steady increase or decline in N(J) and a large

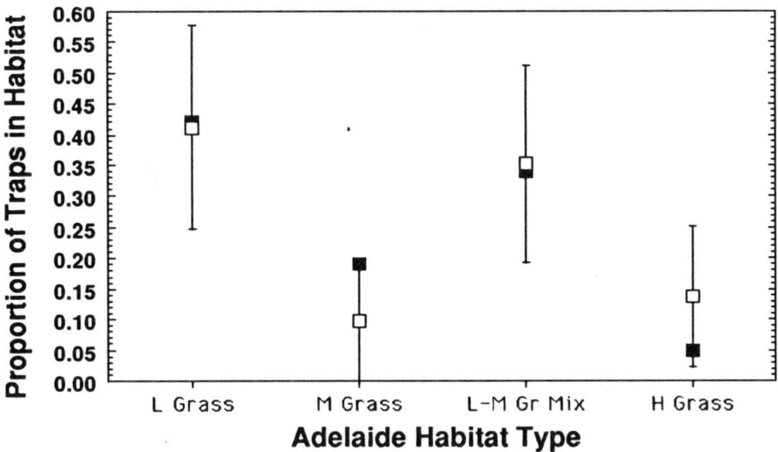


*Figure 12.*—Summary of habitat analysis for Adelaide grid.  See legend of Figure 8 for description.

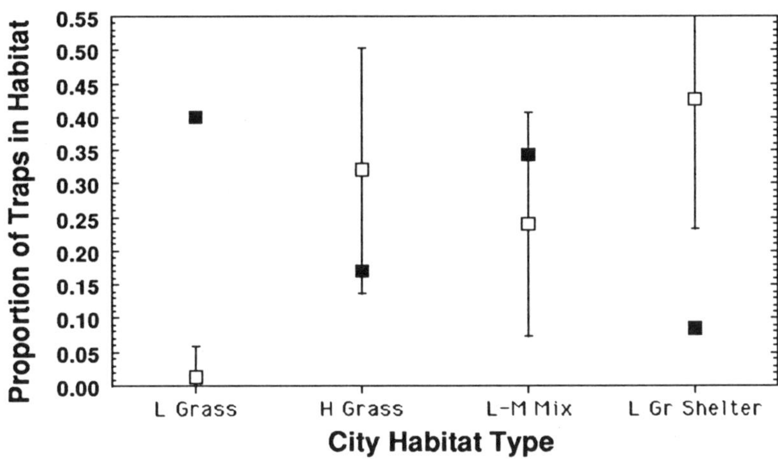


*Figure 13.*—Summary of habitat analysis for City grid.  See legend of Figure 8 for description.

difference in probability of first capture versus recapture.  These are rough generalizations and each source of differential trappability interacts with other sources present in diverse and complicated ways. Consequently, the model selection of Program CAPTURE may or may not match our visual assessment of the summary statistics.

The accumulation of marked animals, M(J), over all trapping occasions for each grid is plotted in Figure 14. The total of captured individuals at the end of the study, M(T), is the minimum population size.  Ideally, the curve of M(J) should climb and level off if there is no immigration and the animal's home range size is small relative to the size of the grid. Figures 15-20 plot the other summary statistics for each grid.  Chatsworth Road had an unusual increase U(J) on day 3, also manifested by the increase in N(J) (Fig. 15). Among the many reasons for this spike are:

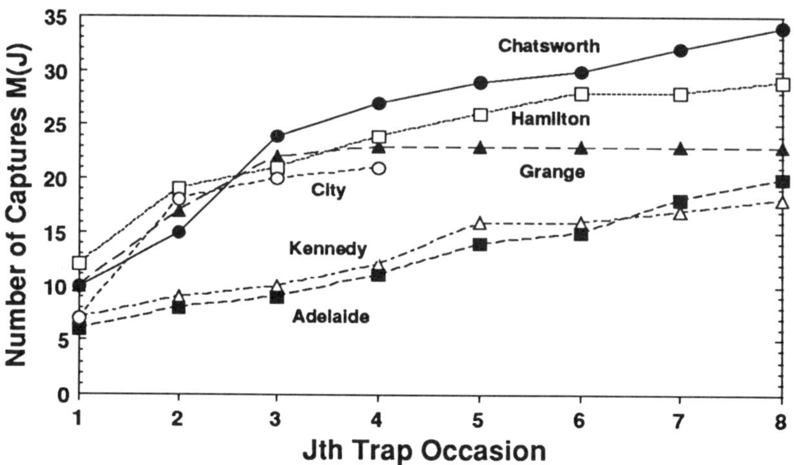


*Figure 14.*—Accumulation of total captures at each occasion M(J) for all six grids.

1) untrapped individuals may have suddenly become attracted to the traps, 2) there may have been an influx of individuals onto the grid, or 3) heavily occupied traps in favored areas may have become available. Note also from F(J) that 44% of the individuals were captured $\leq 2$ times, whereas 50% were captured $\geq 4$ times. More specifically, an animal's probability of capture changed after initial capture, from 0.28 to 0.54—a strong case for 'trap happiness'. From the evidence, there is a trap response with the possibility of an individual response. The best selection, model $M_b$, and the very high selection value of 0.96 for the alternative $M_{bh}$, tells us there is little reason to choose one model over the other (Table 3). Indeed, when model $M_b$ is true, individual response after day 1 will cause difficulty in selecting the correct model.

The relatively smooth decline in U(J) for Hamilton Tip (Fig. 16), in conjunction with the spikes in capture frequencies, indicates individual response and model $M_h$ is selected for all occasions and both sessions (Table 3). The terminal drop in N(J) may contribute to the model selection. Grange Street (Fig. 17) also has a very smooth decline in U(J) but exhibits a distinctive split in both the F(J) and N(J) patterns. The patterns show a dichotomy which corresponds with the split in trapping ses-

sions (days 1-4 and 5-8); thus, the model selections are sensible: overall, $M_h$ is best, but the null model, $M_o$, is the best model for the individual sessions with $M_h$ being second choice for both, due in part to the pattern of N(J).

Kennedy Oval (Fig. 18) displays a peak in U(J) on day 5 (beginning of the second session) and a generally increasing N(J), promoting selection of model $M_b$ for all occasions but model $M_o$ for the separated 4-day sessions. Adelaide (Fig. 19) is more complex. The distribution of F(J) points to a relatively low capture and recapture rate; N(J) and U(J) are erratic. Apparently trap, temporal, and individual responses are interacting in a way that is difficult to visualize from these summary statistics. The temporal response may be gleaned by comparing the large increase in total animals captured beginning on day 5 to the small increase in new animals. $M_{bh}$ is the selected model with $M_{tbh}$ a close second. City grid (Fig. 20) demonstrates the merit of the rule, never trap less than 5 occasions. Sample sizes are too small for good estimation and selection procedures. There are simply too few data to support rejection of the null model and $M_h$ is an inadequate alternative; Otis *et al.* (1978) caution against using models with selection values less than 0.75.

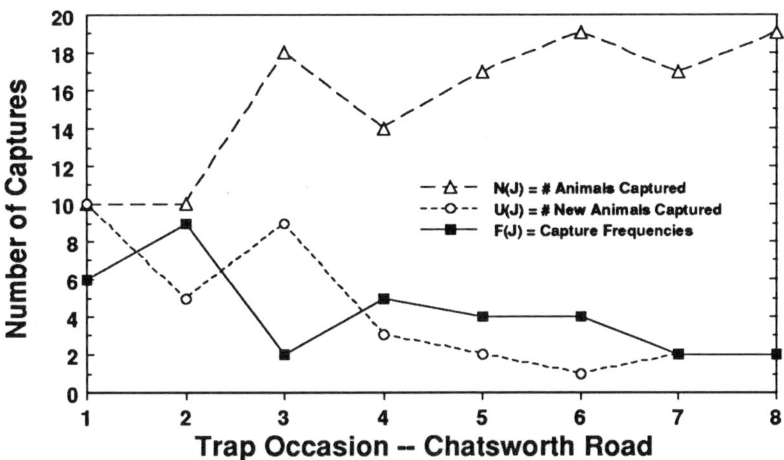


*Figure 15.*—Plot of summary statistics for Chatsworth Road grid. See text for explanation of variables. Note that F(J) refers to number of individuals captured exactly J times. Therefore, six individuals were captured once while nine individuals were captured twice.

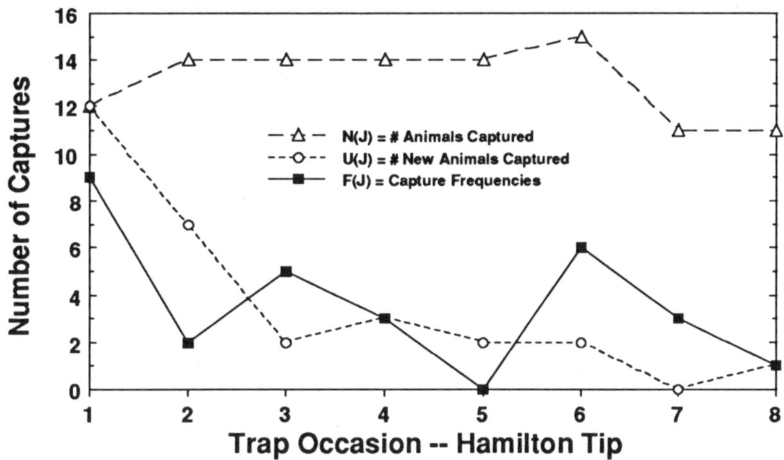


*Figure 16.*—Plot of summary statistics for Hamilton Tip grid. See Figure 15 for description.

*Closure.* Closure is more likely to be true for shorter sampling intervals. Table 3 lists the closure tests for each grid and grid session. As expected, there are far more rejections of closure for combined 8-day periods (extended over a 12-16 day sampling interval) than for single 4-day sessions. We would also expect to see more temporal response $(M_t)$ as well as jumps in U(J) for 8-day periods than 4-day sessions. Those jumps occurred only on the Kennedy Oval grid and, to a minor extent, on the Adelaide grid. A second indication of closure is given by the 'ring' test (Table 3), which examines for any apparent attraction of animals by the grid; it is significant for all 8-day periods, indicating that some immigration may have occurred. However, the test

61

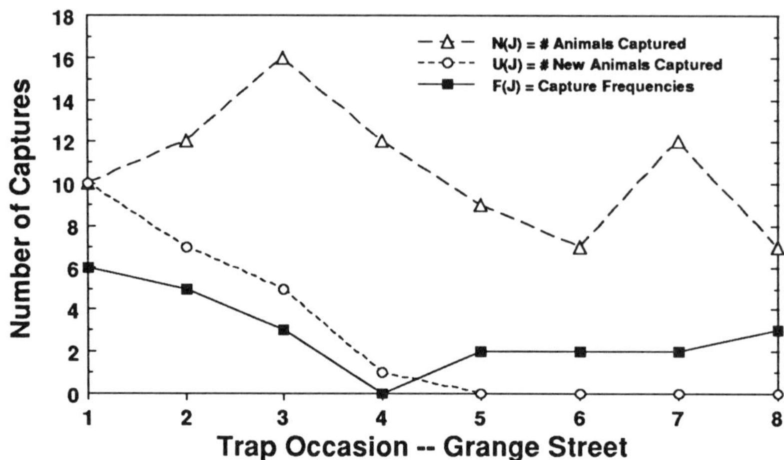


*Figure 17.*—Plot of summary statistics for Grange Street grid. See Figure 15 for description.

may be indicating that the grid is small relative to home ranges, therefore animals with home ranges that overlap the grid have an increased chance of capture over a longer period of time. This would still be a type of 'immigration' and thus reason to reject closure. This phenomenon would also be made more apparent if grids were laid out so that edges of the grid corresponded to attractive habitat.

We fail to reject closure for Chatsworth Road. The test cannot be trusted since trap responses are extremely difficult to untangle from true failures of closure, and there is no truly unbiased test whenever there is strong behavioral variation. Because the trap response is positive, we accept closure tentatively, despite the spike in F(J) on day 3. Significant trap responses on the Kennedy Oval and Adelaide grids also make closure tests suspicious. Since the spike in U(J) is followed by a continuous low until day 8, we believe the population was not closed for the 8-day period, but closed for the individual 4-day sessions. Overall, we expect that population and density estimates will be inflated to some degree for all grids because of the bias introduced by lack of closure.

*Estimates of P. gunnii Numbers.* Population estimates, $\hat{N}$, with 95% confidence intervals (CIs) appear in Figure 21. We include M(T), the total number of captured individuals on a grid, as the minimum population estimate. If the lower CI limit is less than that number, then M(T) should replace the lower CI limit. The larger M(T) is relative to the lower CI limit, the more likely the population estimate is inadequate due to poor experimental results such as small-sample bias. A large average capture probability is another gauge of trustworthy estimation. Reliability of estimation results is also expressed in $CV(\hat{N})$, the coefficient of variation ($SE(\hat{N})/\hat{N}$) expressed as a percent). Table 3 reports the $CV(\hat{N})$s for all estimates. Reliable scientific studies require $CV(\hat{N})$s of no more than 20% and investigators should try for less than 10% (White *et al.* 1982). Small $CV(\hat{N})$s suggest that population estimates are precise but if the model is incorrectly specified or the experimental results are poor, then the estimate may not be accurate.

Comparison of lower estimates for each 4-day session and the higher estimates for all data suggest that failure of closure may have inflated the

*Table 3*. Model description for all grids and trapping sessions from Program CAPTURE. Values of parameters and tests apply to 'best' model or the alternative models.

| Grid and Sessions | Model Selection[1] | | Closure Test[2] (Prob.) | Avg. Capture Rate[3] | CV of $\hat{N}$[4] % | Strip Test[5] (Prob.) | Uniformity Test of Density[6] (Prob.) | | |
|---|---|---|---|---|---|---|---|---|---|
| | Best | Alternative | | | | | Row | Col. | Ring |
| Chatsworth Rd.  All | $M_b$ | $M_{bh}$ (.96) | 0.10 | 0.28 | 7.5 | 0.12 | 0.00 | 0.01 | 0.01 |
| Days 1-4 | $M_h$ | $M_o$ (.96) | 0.19 | 0.34 | 12.7 | 0.03 | 0.32 | 0.02 | 0.21 |
| Days 5-8 | $M_h$ | $M_o$ (.89) | 0.32 | 0.62 | 6.0 | 0.15 | 0.08 | 0.09 | 0.01 |
| Hamilton Tip  All | $M_h$ | $M_o$ (.83) | 0.03 | 0.25 | 19.4 | 0.01 | 0.00 | 0.00 | 0.03 |
| Days 1-4 | $M_h$ | $M_o$ (.91) | 0.61 | 0.42 | 12.4 | 0.00 | 0.00 | 0.03 | 0.30 |
| Days 5-8 | $M_h$ | $M_o$ (.92) | 0.08 | 0.49 | 10.9 | 0.01 | 0.00 | 0.02 | 0.01 |
| Grange Street  All | $M_h$ | $M_o$ (.96) | 0.07 | 0.41 | 7.4 | 0.00 | 0.00 | 0.03 | 0.00 |
| Days 1-4 | $M_o$ | $M_h$ (.87) | 0.04 | 0.53 | 5.3 | 0.00 | 0.07 | 0.14 | 0.00 |
| Days 5-8 | $M_o$ | $M_h$ (.73) | 0.42 | 0.58 | 5.0 | 0.00 | 0.04 | 0.28 | 0.64 |
| Kennedy Oval  All | $M_b$ | $M_{bh}$ (.93) | 0.03 | 0.28 | 9.6 | 0.00 | 0.00 | 0.00 | 0.02 |
| Days 1-4 | $M_o$ | $M_h$ (.85) | 0.27 | 0.65 | 11.6 | 0.50 | 0.06 | 0.00 | 0.14 |
| Days 5-8 | $M_o$ | $M_h$ (.83) | 0.39 | 0.69 | 4.8 | 0.15 | 0.05 | 0.01 | 0.17 |
| Adelaide  All | $M_{bh}$ | $M_{tbh}$ (.94)* | 0.81 | 0.28 | 8.3 | 0.00 | 0.00 | 0.00 | 0.00 |
| Days 1-4 | $M_{th}$ | $M_h$ (.55) | 0.70 | — | 15.0 | — | 0.30 | 0.00 | 0.18 |
| Days 5-8 | $M_o$ | $M_h$ (.77) | 0.66 | 0.37 | 11.0 | 0.50 | 0.00 | 0.00 | 0.00 |
| City  All | $M_o$ | $M_h$ (.70) | 0.72 | 0.39 | 10.9 | 0.00 | 0.00 | 0.18 | — |

[1]Best or most appropriate model from CAPTURE's selection procedure is normalized to a value of 1.00. Alternative model is the second most appropriate model with relative value in parentheses.

[2]Population closure for grid. Probability is significance level for $H_o$ : Population is closed. The lower the probability, the more likely we would reject the hypothesis.

[3]Depending on model, this is average or expected probability of capture for population.

[4]Coefficient of variation for population estimate.

[5]A test of whether $\hat{W}$, the estimated width of the boundary strip, is different from zero. The lower the probability, the more likely $\hat{D}$, the estimate of density using $\hat{W}$, is better than the naive estimate which is based on the actual grid area.

[6]Tests uniformity of density on the grid by examining gradients of differential trap success across rows, across columns, and from concentric rings of traps (beginning at edge of grid).

*Serious failure criteria for $M_{tbh}$ and third alternative, $M_b$ (.91). There is no estimator for $M_{tbh}$. The next best alternative for which there is an estimator was $M_h$ (.77).

8-day estimates (Fig. 21). Keep in mind the very small sample sizes for 4-day sessions do not make them as reliable, especially if they are accompanied by suspiciously narrow CIs. The Monte Carlo simulation results, which use data from the second session and are much more robust to small-sample biases, corroborate upwardly biased 8-day estimates. For Chatsworth Road, $\hat{N}$=33 with 95% likelihood intervals of $31 \leq N \leq 38$ (Fig. 22), supporting the possibility that M(T) is likely to be higher than the true population size. The spike in U(J) is not as influential in the second session and trap response is diminished. The pattern of large spikes in the F(J) distribution for Hamilton Tip may have contributed to the large $\hat{N}$ and large CV($\hat{N}$). The 4-day sessions as well as the Monte Carlo simulation ($\hat{N}$=29, $27 \leq N \leq 34$) point to a more likely estimate corresponding to the number of individuals captured (29), especially given the tight likelihood interval (Fig. 22).

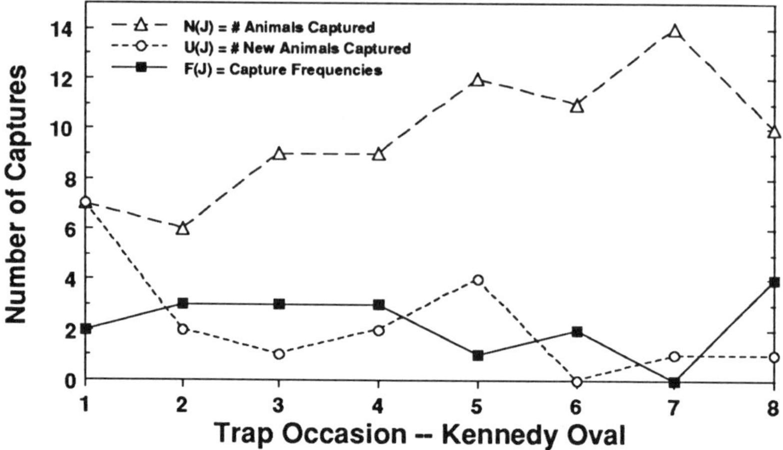



*Figure 18.*—Plot of summary statistics for Kennedy Oval grid. See Figure 15 for description.

The Grange Street estimate seems reasonable. We would neglect the estimate for the second session because of very low sample sizes, particularly regarding N(J). Monte Carlo could not and need not be calculated since there were no new individuals captured in the second session, in which case M(T) is the default estimate. Kennedy Oval is a good example of lack of closure: the spike in U(J) conjoined with trap response leads us to conclude that the 8-day and second session estimates are too high. Failure of closure similarly influences the Monte Carlo estimation ($\hat{N}$=17, 16≤N≤20) because it is based on second session data (Fig. 22). We think the first session is probably closer to the actual population number.

Adelaide is difficult to interpret. The small number of total captures and their variation from occasion to occasion, the low recapture rate, the continual appearance of unmarked individuals throughout the sampling interval, and our inability to assess closure are the major factors which confound our evaluation of the estimate results. We conclude that the temporal response in trappability is correlated with weather. During the first session, temperatures were very high and the humidity very low. The weather shifted to cooler and damper conditions for the second session. Thus, new individuals were trapped and more animals were captured, probably individuals that were in the vicinity of the grid during the first session. This makes the very strong rejection of closure more sensible for both sessions. These conclusions suggest that the second session is likely to be the best estimate. This is supported by the Monte Carlo estimate, which gave a population estimate of 19 (17≤N≤22), very close to the second-session CAPTURE estimate (Fig. 22). The single estimate available for the City grid is based on such small sample sizes, particularly for recaptures, that we consider the population estimate to be tentative at best. The purpose of the City grid was more for the examination of a gradient in population density which is discussed below.

*Density Estimation.* A uniform density of animals over the grid is assumed in the derivation of the estimation method and, therefore, we do not wish to see a rejection of the uniformity hypotheses. There are three tests for uniform density: across columns, down rows, and for concentric rings of traps (see Appendix). Table 3 lists the test results. There is a severe lack of uniformity on the grids which is determined by the complex and

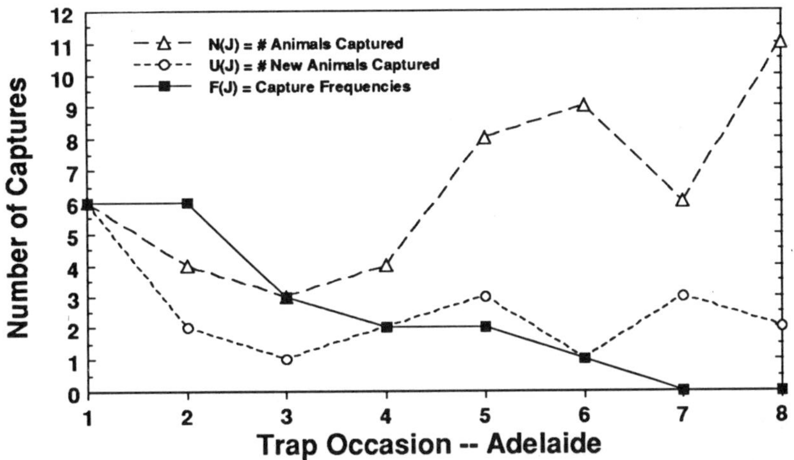



*Figure 19.*—Plot of summary statistics for Adelaide grid. See Figure 15 for description.

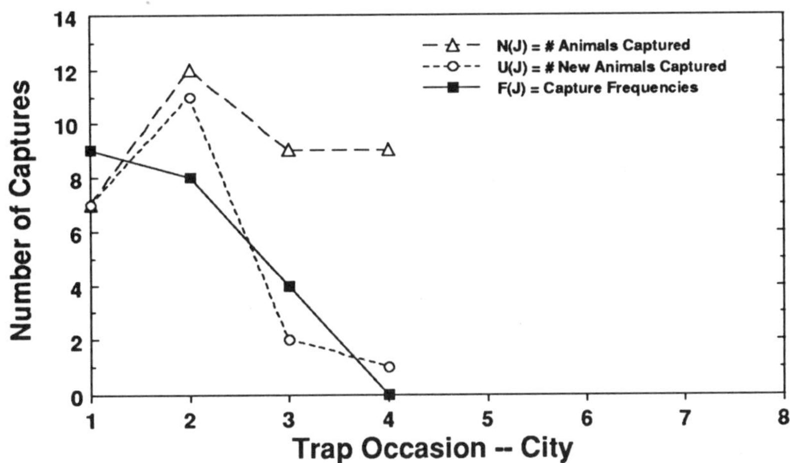



*Figure 20.*—Plot of summary statistics for City grid. See Figure 15 for description.

extreme heterogeneity of the eastern barred bandicoots' environment. The size of the grids and, thus, the trap spacing, are too small to effectively 'smooth' the heterogeneity and reduce its magnitude. In other words, the resolution of the spatial unit (grid) is too fine-grained relative to the coarse-grained density gradients exhibited by the bandicoots. When sampling with quadrats (grids), the outcome of mismatching the sampling scale of an experimental design with the biological scale of the animal is a large variance over space. (This may have been similarly manifested for population estimation by not matching the grid size to home range size.)

We give several visual examples of nonuniformity in captures in Figures 23-25. The areas of high capture success on the Hamilton Tip grid (Fig. 23) are highly correlated with cover and edge habitat produced by concentrations of fence rows, other man-made features, and associated diversity of vegetation. Grange Street grid (Fig. 24) contained an old railway along the diagonal of the grid with residential structures and gardens next to it on one side. Areas of lowest capture success are heavily grazed fields. The City grid was deliberately placed with one edge along the fence row edge of a large section of land known to be very poor bandicoot habitat. In contrast, the habitat on the other side of the fence row (Hamilton Tip grid) contained fair numbers of bandicoots (Fig. 1). The capture success graphed in Figure 25 was expected for City grid, especially considering the three shelters near the fence row.

If density is not uniform across a grid, defining the concept of parameter D becomes difficult. White *et al.* (1982) are not sure how severely the estimation method is affected if the uniform density condition is not met, but they assume safely that accuracy is decreased. We are justifiably cautious about the density estimates reported in Figure 26. The associated strip widths used in calculating the density estimates are shown in Figure 27. Refer to Table 3 for strip tests which reveal that the addition of the strip widths are necessary for estimating the densities in most cases.

The large SEs for density estimates and for strip widths allow us to see that precision of the estimators is very low. Coupled with the unknown accuracy of the estimators due to nonuniformity, we can only conclude that densities may be in the neighborhood of 1.5 eastern barred bandicoots per ha.

*Body Weights*

Eastern barred bandicoots were weighed at each capture and recapture. There was considerable individual variation in weights by occasion, but individuals tended to lose weight each time they were captured, and lost weight as a function of the number of captures (range = 2-8). Sample sizes and data structure precluded a thorough analysis of weight loss, though regressions of weight loss for each individual over the eight trap occasions reveal a trend. Of the 19 individuals for which there was adequate data on the Chatsworth grid, 17 showed weight loss (negative regression slope), 10 significantly so (at p<0.1); 2 showed weight gain (positive regression slope). Similar figures for the Grange Street grid reveal: 8 showed weight loss, 6 significantly so; 3 showed weight gain. For Hamilton Tip grid: 10 showed weight loss, 1 significantly so; 7 showed weight gain, 1 significantly so. For Kennedy Oval grid: 12 showed weight loss, 5 significantly so; 1 showed weight gain. We did not analyse Adelaide and City grids.

*Discussion*

Few population studies have been conducted on *P. gunnii*. Brown (1985, 1989) and Dufty (1988) collected mark-recapture data from the City of Hamilton population. Dufty (1988) supplemented these data with short-term telemetry work. Heinsohn (1966) collected diverse data, including Petersen mark-recapture, near the northwest tip of Tasmania. We will compare our results with these studies and refer to them without citing the dates.

We found a male-biased adult sex ratio, female-biased juvenile sex ratio, and adult-biased age ratio. Brown and Dufty classified eastern barred bandicoots weighing less than 500 g as juveniles, but Heinsohn used a different age classification system and his results are not comparable to ours. Heinsohn live-trapped from May 1961 to February 1962 and found an adult (sexually mature) sex ratio of 50.6% males (n=85) and a pouch-young sex ratio of 46.0% males (n=76). Brown live-trapped between March 1983 and June 1985 and, of all weaned bandicoots, captured 53.3% males (n=90). From a total of 106 captures, Dufty found an adult sex ratio of 65.9% males (n=88), a juvenile sex ratio of 69% males (n=18), and an even sex ratio for pouch young (n=35 litters). We captured 80.3% (n=147) adults relative to juveniles which is comparable to the adult-biased results of Dufty (83.0%, n=106) and Brown (70%, n=90). The differences between sex and age may

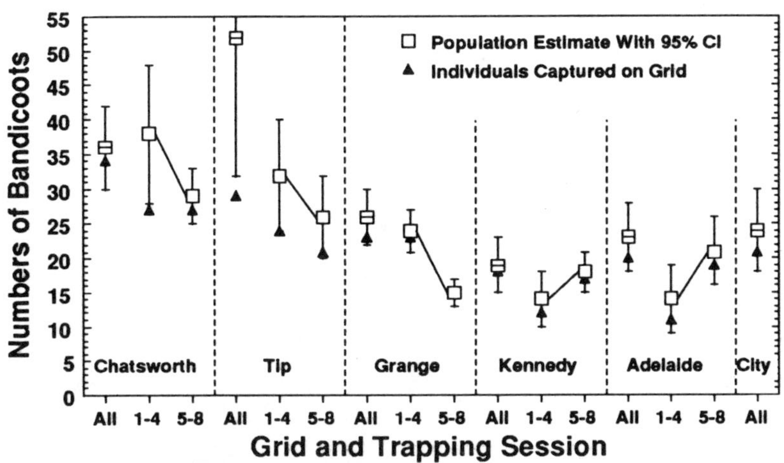


*Figure 21.*—Population estimates from Program CAPTURE for each grid and session (days). 'All' refers to both sessions combined, days 1-8. M(T), the total number of individuals captured on a grid during a sampling period, is represented by filled triangles. M(T) replaces the lower population limit if greater than the lower 95% confidence interval limit.

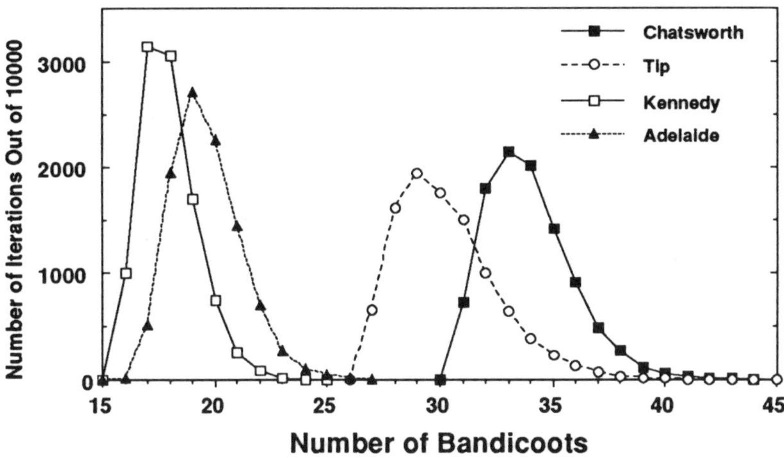


*Figure 22.*—Probability distribution population estimate of Chatsworth Road, Hamilton Tip, Kennedy Oval, and Adelaide grids using Monte Carlo simulation. Maximum likelihood estimator is largest value of iterations. See text for explanation.

be real or related to trapping susceptibility. The analysis of among-grid movements, within-grid movements, capture rates, and high degree of individual response (heterogeneity) leads us to conclude that the calculated (apparent) sex and age ratios may be influenced by interacting trap biases due to age and sex. Of course, all data are from animals that have been captured at least once, and we do not have access to the uncatchable portion of the population, if it exists. Even though we cannot accurately discriminate apparent age and sex ratios from real ratios, our assessment of the sources of biases is that the trend or direction of the ratios is real and can be used to

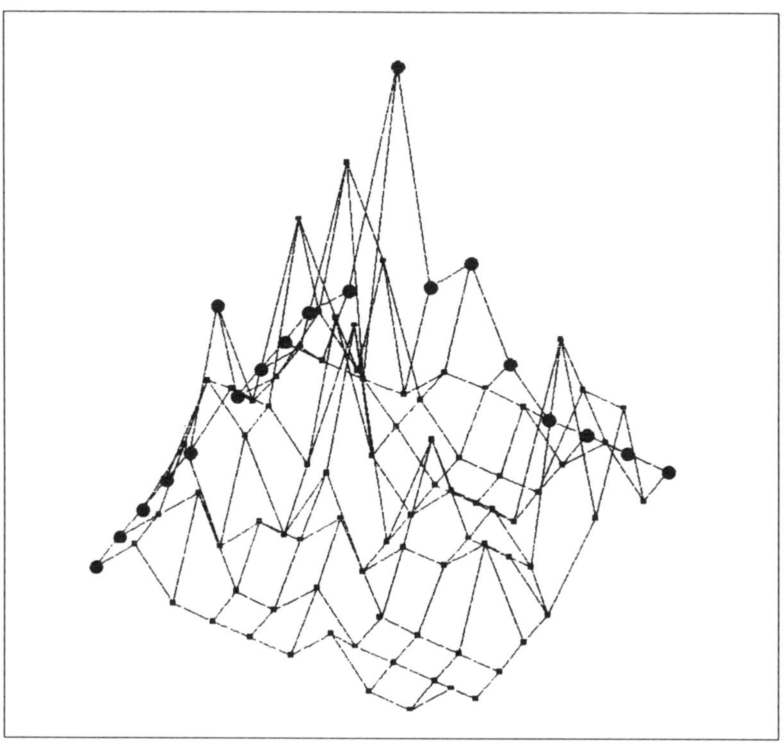

*Figure 23.*—Three dimensional representation of capture success at each trap station on the Hamilton Tip grid. X and Y axes are spatial coordinates of grid; Z axis is number of captures. Filled circles are the rear edges of the grid in the view.

track among-year differences within a study area at the same time of year. Dufty and Brown found that age and sex ratios derived from trapping data fluctuated on a monthly basis. Thus, comparisons of seasonal studies with studies carried out over a year or more are tenuous. For possible interpretations of ratios, we refer the reader to discussions of sex allocation under food deprivation and population stress (*e.g.* Cockburn 1988).

Little can be determined about *P. gunnii* population turnover. To some extent, among-study captures of eastern barred bandicoots are an indication. Dufty captured none of Brown's marked bandicoots after three years had elapsed, but in the present study we captured 58.5% of the ban-

dicoots originally marked by Dufty. The time interval between these captures ranged from 2.5 months to 10 months. Unfortunately, we do not know which animals were marked on which of Dufty's trapping areas, and therefore we have no idea about site fidelity. Considering the close proximity of three of the grids in this study, the absence of intergrid movement implies little dispersal and wide-ranging movement, at least at this time of year.

Vegetation alone is not an adequate indicator of habitat preference. Examination of trap success overlaid upon land-use maps reveals the importance of cover offered by human structures and other human alterations. The interaction of vege-

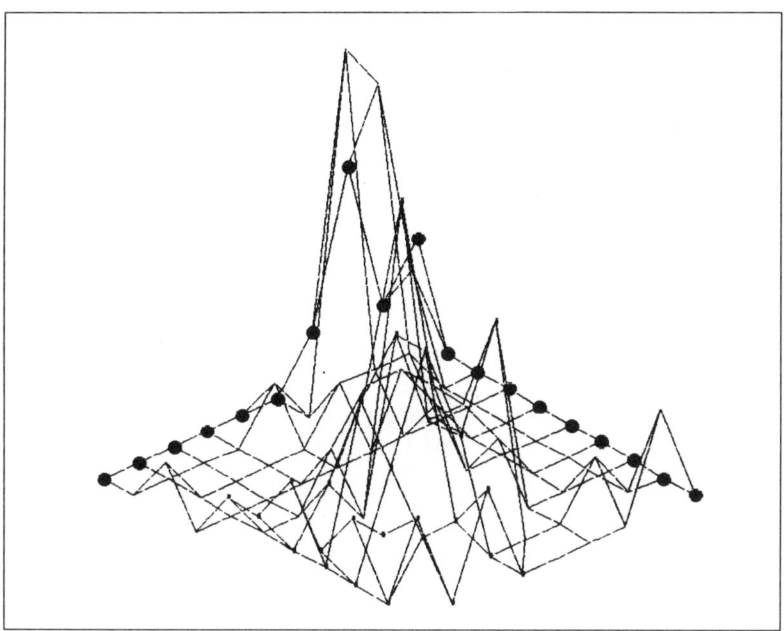

*Figure 24.*—Three dimensional representation of capture success at each trap station on the Grange Street grid. X and Y axes are spatial coordinates of grid; Z axis is number of captures. Filled circles are the rear edges of the grid in the view.

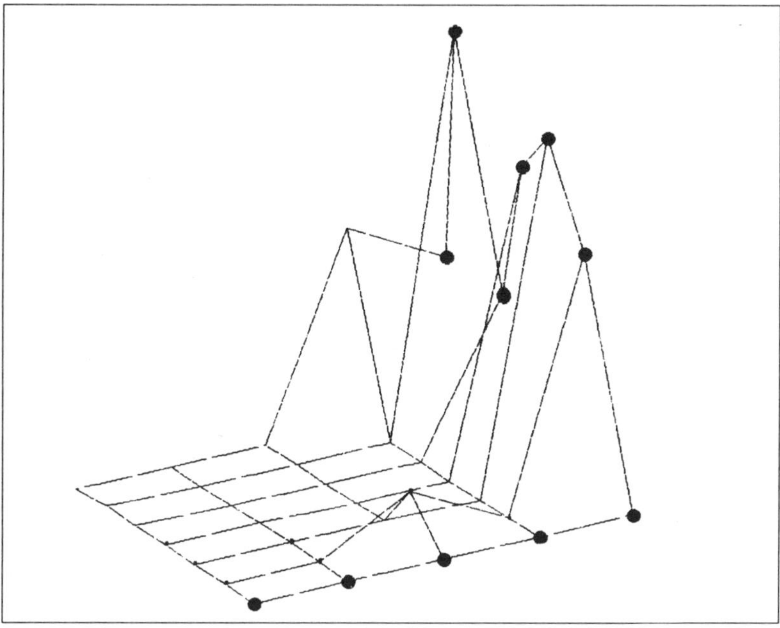

*Figure 25.*—Three dimensional representation of capture success at each trap station on the City grid. X and Y axes are spatial coordinates of grid; Z axis is number of captures. Filled circles are two edges of the grid.

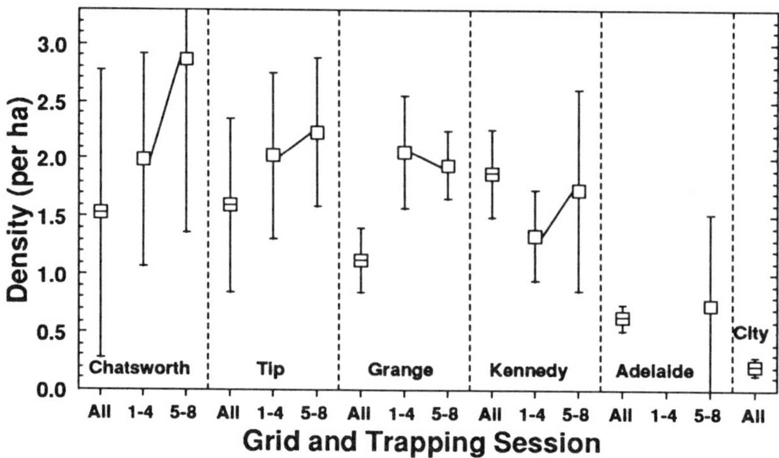



*Figure 26.*—Density estimates from Program CAPTURE for each grid and session (days). 'All' refers to both sessions combined, days 1-8. Confidence intervals are 95%.

tation with human structures produces an extremely complex environment, which leads to highly non-uniform capture success. Although the relationship between vegetation and human structures is collinear and is difficult to separate and quantify, its conspicuousness to the observer should allow adjustment of differential trap rates (and therefore avoidance of trap saturation) by varying the number of traps per station in future population work. Heinsohn found highest mean capture per 100 trap nights (n=2,265) in open paddocks (40), followed by paddock edge (32), low ground cover (32), scrub adjoining paddock (23), and forest/heath/burned scrub (31). Even though open paddocks were the most preferred single category, Heinsohn noted that eastern barred bandicoots relied mainly on the cover provided by the dense, thorny hedgerows for nest sites and for refuge from danger. Thus, more animals were captured in edge habitat or habitat with a cover component. Domestic cats are numerous in the City of Hamilton and the danger may encourage bandicoots to forage and travel closer to cover than they do in other areas (*i.e.* Heinsohn's study area).

Population estimates of eastern barred bandicoots are comparable only as densities since the use and sizes of grids or 'trapping areas' varied from study to study. Densities obtained from grids can be used for extrapolating to other areas within a geographic region if the grids are randomly or systematically placed within that region. Our study is the only relatively large-scale grid trapping for the Hamilton bandicoots. For the purposes of Dufty, Brown, and this study, trapping was done in areas thought to have moderate to high densities. Dufty's 6-ha Kennedy Oval trapping area produced a naive density estimate of 2.5 eastern barred bandicoots per ha, his 12-ha Chatsworth Road trapping area produced an estimate of 5.25 per ha, and his 102-ha Municipal Tip trapping area produced an estimate of 1.49 per ha. The Municipal Tip area included much of the area containing our Grange Street, Adelaide, and Hamilton Tip grids. Brown found that the number of animals known to be alive (M(T), a conservative estimate) varied monthly from 11 to 21 on a 36-ha trapping area over a period of 2+ years. The average naive density estimator was 0.44 eastern barred bandicoots per ha. Heinsohn also found monthly fluctuations of bandicoots (13-43) on a 29.6 ha trapping area, giving an average naive density of 0.85 per ha. Whether or not a grid is used and the size of the grid dramatically affects the naive density estimator: the larger

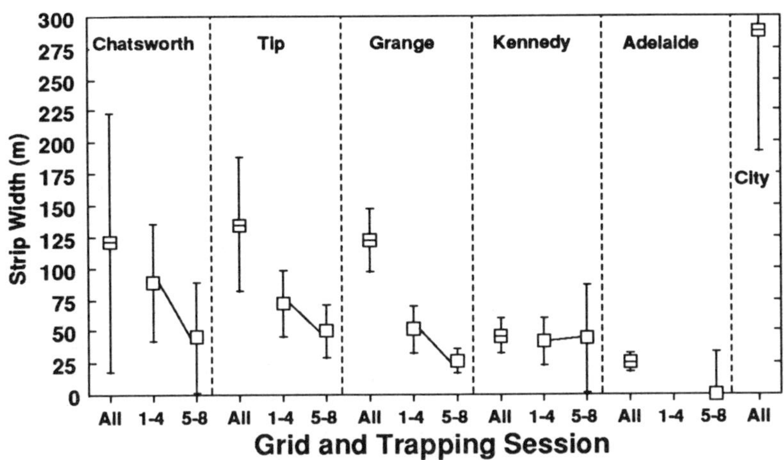


*Figure 27.*—Strip-width estimates from Program CAPTURE for each grid and session (days). 'All' refers to both sessions combined, days 1-8. Confidence intervals are 95%. For exact probabilities on strip hypothesis, see Table 3.

the grid, the smaller the estimate because of decreased edge effect. Naive densities are always larger than densities calculated with a strip width.

Strip widths effectively compensate for edge effects within reasonable limits of grid size. Grids that are too small relative to home ranges will give unreliable population estimates and introduce large error terms into density estimation. Heinsohn calculated home ranges from live-trapping data using all grids and trap lines in his study area. The mean home range of nine females that were caught over a period of 9-13 months was 3.24 ha (range 0.93-11.4). Four males, caught during an 11-13 month period had a mean home range size of 25.6 ha (range 18.7-39.7). Heinsohn suggests that males may not have discrete home ranges over the time interval he sampled. Females covered a mean linear distance of 134 m (between two points) within 24 hours (n=38 observations); males covered a mean linear distance of 259 m within 24 hours (n=91 observations). Dufty calculated home range estimates of five males (me-

dian = 5.6 ha) and two females (1.0 and 3.8 ha) from telemetry data spanning periods up to 17 days. Unfortunately, immediate post-release telemetry data has been determined to be unreliable for most animals. Dufty believes home ranges for males to be between 10-20 ha and for females about 3.5 ha (Dufty, personal communication).

The variation among studies and, more importantly, the tremendous variation within studies (among grids and trapping areas and among months) influences the variables used for population estimation. As a result, estimation becomes highly problematic. The most important variable, capture rate, varies by individual, age, sex, time, and location. Immigration, transience, movement rates, grid attraction (e.g. to baits), and home range size contribute to the problems of reliable and repeatable estimation of eastern barred bandicoot numbers and densities. Overlaid upon these types of variation is the complex and extremely heterogeneous habitat.

*Recommended Population
Monitoring Procedures*

There is no escaping the fact that population monitoring of eastern barred bandicoots will demand a large investment of resources and effort. Depending on the goals of population monitoring, design considerations can reduce the variability to varying degrees. We will now evaluate some of these considerations in light of the variables we have discussed, along with logistical and practical factors.

The best monitoring program for annual population assessment would use grids for density estimation and be repeated yearly at the same time and locations. Trapping should be done in cool weather, avoiding hot and dry weather. Trapping should be conducted at the time of year when individual movement, especially dispersal, is least. Trap spacing should be 100 m with 11x11 grids for 1 square km. It is better to have one large grid than many small ones for bandicoots: closure will be better satisfied, edge effect will be reduced, better habitat analysis can be accomplished, and there is a higher likelihood of stratifying population by age and sex to adjust for heterogeneous trap response. Place at least one trap per station, adding one or two traps per station depending on suspected rate of trap success based on vegetation and cover in immediate area. Traps can be shifted in the first few days to refine initial assessments of trap success. Place the edges of grids so they are not exactly coincidental with natural habitat edges where density is likely to be higher. This is particularly important if the grid is to be placed upon a suspected population gradient. Trap for four days, check traps twice daily with traps shut down between the two occasions spanning the heat of the day. For example, open traps at 1700; check traps at the following 0100, leaving them open; check again at daylight and close traps until 1700. The shorter 4-day period will increase probability of closure, and because animals tended to lose weight from first to last capture on all grids, decrease stress on the bandicoots. Lack of

closure may be due to the trapping procedure itself (grid attraction); thus, the two checks per day will keep trap occasions high enough for reasonable density estimation. Data can be later analyzed as two 4-day sessions (evening vs. early morning) to inspect trap response and for the existence of activity periods. The grid can be moved to another area to obtain a second estimation within a short period of time.

The disadvantages of using a large grid are the large initial investment of traps and the intensive use of manpower for grid processing. Petersen's or Bailey's triple-catch estimators (Seber 1982) do not require the numerous trapping occasions, but do require a grid for density estimation with resulting density estimation weaker due to fewer trapping occasions. Thus, the cost of traps and the effort of grid layout are still necessary and with small additional effort a full multiple mark-recapture density estimate can be achieved. Another alternative for density estimation is the line assessment method (Smith *et al.* 1971, 1975, O'Farrell *et al.* 1977, O'Farrell and Austin 1978). The method can be quite complex and is heavily dependent on the trap layout, study design, and knowledge of the animal. We do not recommend it but encourage readers to consult the original sources as well as Seber (1982).

If density estimation is not a goal, then population numbers can be compared from year to year and area to area. The exact timing, spacing, and configuration of trap design must be precisely replicable. Recaptures can be obtained from retrapping or resighting. An independent form of 'recapture,' such as resighting, is superior, but likely to be biased by habitat conditions and practical considerations in residential areas, and therefore, we cannot recommend it. The minimal design would use trap transects of equal length systematically placed throughout the target area for a Petersen or triple-catch estimate (Seber 1982). The estimate would have no relation to actual numbers of bandicoots, but its consistency would allow relative comparisons among areas and years. If trap response varies as it did in this study, the response cannot be detected and even relative comparisons will be biased. Line transects could be placed to assess population gradients throughout the bandicoots' present range and in anticipation of monitoring range expansion. This strategy should be instigated regardless of the primary method of population or density estimation.

The most economical assessment is a rough index of annual change or trend monitoring in the population within an area, but it gives the least information about the population. If trend is the goal, then we need only detect changes from year to year. Because population numbers and densities are of no concern, we are not constrained by many of the mark-recapture assumptions regarding spatial design and trap distribution. Traps may be placed in high-density areas (*e.g.* short transects along edge rows) as long as the procedure is identically repeated in following years. The sampling area must include typical high-density areas on the species' range periphery, even though eastern barred bandicoots may be extremely low density. The distribution of traps should systematically sample the entire present distribution of *P. gunnii*. Enough traps should be placed at each station along the transect to ensure all eastern barred bandicoots have the opportunity of entering a vacant trap. Traps should be open an entire 24-hour cycle to accommodate variations in activity cycles. Transects should be far enough apart so as not to capture the same individual twice within the same year. We assume there are no major habitat shifts from year to year in the sampled area. Design details can be refined via statistical consultation.

We have outlined several options for a monitoring program for the Hamilton area. The scientific and management goals of population monitoring are important, but in reality, budgets determine goals and therefore methods of a monitoring program. For further discussion of study design, see references we have cited.

*Acknowledgments*

This project is a cooperative effort between the Zoological Board of Victoria, Department of Conservation, Forests and Lands, and the Chicago Zoological Society (U.S.A.). Additional support was provided via the Northern Rockies Conservation Cooperative. The primary field team comprised John Seebeck, Denise Casey, Ann Harvey, Cathy Patrick, Peter Goonan, Andrew Mann, Elizabeth Fenton, Peter Goldstraw, Charlie Dunn, and Tim Clark. Many people aided the field work directly and through advice, including John Seebeck, Barry Wright, Peter Brown, Anthony Dufty, Bill Sherwin, Helen Daley, Judith Tomlin, Peter Myroniuk, Sandi Smith, John Arlidge, Leslie Muirhead, and Gert Skipper. The Royal Zoological Society of South Australia under the direction of Robert Baker supported Peter Goonan and Andrew Mann. The manuscript was critically reviewed by Denise Casey, Bill Sherwin, Ian Mansergh, Peter Goonan, John Seebeck, and Anthony Dufty.

*Appendix*

*Models.* Variation in capture probabilities (differential catchability) dramatically influences the reliability of population estimators. Program CAPTURE attempts to identify the source of this variation and apply the most appropriate model for parameter estimation. (1) Model $M_o$ is the simplest model and assumes the same capture probability p on every capture occasion; that is, all members of the population are equally at risk to capture on every trapping occasion. Moreover, the occasions themselves do not affect capture probabilities. The appropriate estimator is referred to as the null estimator. (2) Model $M_t$, the most common model, allows capture probabilities to vary only by time (trapping occasion). The same capture probability is assumed to apply to all N animals in the population on each occasion (*e.g.* due to weather conditions). The exact maximum likelihood of the Darroch (1958) and Schnabel (1938) approximations is computed. (3) When animals exhibit a behavioral response to capture, especially to first capture, then Model $M_b$ is used. If probability of recapture, c, is lower than first-capture probability, the animals are exhibiting trap avoidance (trap shy). If c is relatively higher, then animals are 'trap happy', or attracted to traps. The appropriate estimator is based on methods applied to removal data and is referred to as a Zippin estimator (Zippin 1956). Variation by time (external reasons; population level), $M_t$, has no relation to behavioral response (internal response to trap; individual level), $M_b$, yet we may find it difficult to distinguish between the two causes of variation. (4) Model $M_h$ allows capture probabilities to vary by animal due to sex, age, social dominance, home range size or innate level of activity. In other words, the model accounts for innate heterogeneity, *i.e.* variations among individuals in capture probabilities. The method of estimation is referred to as the jackknife estimator. We will refer to variation in capture probability 1) with time (model $M_t$) as 'temporal response', 2) with behavior (model $M_b$) as 'trap response', and 3) with individual heterogeneity as 'individual response'.

In addition to the four basic models discussed above, there are four other combinations produced when sources of variation interact. They are $M_{tb}$, $M_{th}$, $M_{bh}$, and $M_{tbh}$. Because of the increased complexity, $M_{bh}$ is the only one for which an estimator has been derived (generalized removal). Program CAPTURE uses goodness-of-fit tests with an automated procedure (multivariate discriminant function analysis) to suggest the simplest, best-fitting model for any given set of capture-recapture data. If the selected model has no estimator, then the next best alternative may be used. We used alternative estimators if the 'best' model failed in certain criteria essential to parameter optimization or estimation. Our choices of final models for each grid and session were based on interpretation of error terms and intermediate statistical outputs of Program CAPTURE. We feel our interpretations were not influenced by outcome (population number and density) of potential model choices. The final selection of model alternatives gave lower estimates in every case due to the pervasive problem of closure and heterogeneity.

*Closure.* Geographic closure limits or contains the population by a boundary. Demographic closure is the absence of birth, immigration, death, and emmigration. All models assume both kinds of closure. Unfortunately, a statistical test for closure is impossible: no valid test can be constructed on the basis of only the capture-recapture data. The problem is that true failure of closure cannot be distinguished from trap response or from certain patterns of temporal response. Program CAPTURE however, computes a closure test assuming Model $M_h$ is the null hypothesis. The test is not valid if closure is true and a different model holds, although it can be used as an indicator with additional information, such as tests of uniformity of captures on the grid and examination of capture probabilities over time.

*Density Estimation.* The problem of density estimation is finding the area to which the population estimate applies. Merely dividing the population estimate, $\hat{N}$, by the area enclosed by the trapping grid (referred to as the naive density estimate) leads to severe overestimation as a result of what has been called 'edge effect', *i.e.* not all animals have their entire home range within the trapping grid, but may still be caught because some traps near the grid boundary are within their home range. Thus, the effective area trapped is somewhat larger than the grid and is a function of the grid size relative to the ranging characteristics of the animal. Otis *et al.* (1978) looked at three possible approaches to solve this problem, the first two relying on the concept of a boundary strip about the grid such that the effective trapping area is the grid area plus this boundary strip area of width W. The first approach estimates home range size from capture locations and W becomes some function of home range (*e.g.* one-half home range diameter; Dice 1938, Stickel 1954). However, Otis *et al.* (1978) believe estimation of W based on movement data remains unsatisfactory. A second approach involves the use of assessment lines (Smith *et al.* 1971, 1975, O'Farrell *et al.* 1977, O'Farrell and Austin 1978). This approach has produced good results but the method can become quite complex and is heavily dependent on the design of the trap layout. The third approach, used by Program CAPTURE, jointly estimates density and the parameter W (with a generalized nonlinear least-squares method) by using data drawn from selected subgrids. The estimated boundary strip area is added to the grid area for estimating D. If uniformity of captures (density) by grid row, column, or ring does not hold, then defining the concept of parameter D becomes difficult.

## References


Alldredge, J. R., and Ratti, J. T. 1986. Comparison of some statistical techniques for analysis of resource selection. *J. Wildl. Manage.* **50**:157-165.

Brown, P.R. 1985. A preliminary report on investigations into the ecology and conservation of the mainland population of the Eastern Barred Bandicoot *Perameles gunnii*: March 1983-June 1985. Unpubl. rept. to World Wildlife Fund Australia for Project 55, 26 pp.

Brown, P. R. 1989. Management Plan for the Conservation of the Eastern Barred Bandicoot, *Perameles gunnii*, in Victoria. National Parks and Wildlife Division, Victoria. *Arthur Rylah Institute for Environmental Research Tech. Rep. Ser.* No. 63. Department of Conservation, Forests and Lands: Melbourne.

Caughley, G. 1977. *Analysis of Vertebrate Populations.* John Wiley and Sons: New York.

Cockburn, A. 1988. *Social Behaviour in Fluctuating Populations.* Croom Helm: Sydney.

Darroch, J. N. 1958. The multiple recapture census: I. Estimation of a closed population. *Biometrika* 45:343-359.

Dice, L. R. 1938. Some census methods for mammals. *J. Wildl. Manage.* 2:119-398-407.

Dufty, A. C. 1988. The distribution, population abundance, status, movements and activities of the Eastern Barred Bandicoot, *Perameles gunnii*, at Hamilton. B. Sc. (Honours) Thesis, La Trobe University, Bundoora, Victoria.

Fleiss, J. L. 1981. *Statistical Methods for Rates and Proportions.* 2nd Edition. John Wiley and Sons: New York.

Heinsohn, G. E. 1966. Ecology and reproduction of the Tasmanian bandicoots (*Perameles gunni* and *Isoodon obesulus*). *Univ. Calif. Publ. Zool.* 80:1-107.

Holling, C. S. (ed.) 1978. *Adaptive environmental assessment and management.* Intl. Ser. on Applied Systems Analysis 3, International Institute for Applied Systems Analysis. John Wiley and Sons: Toronto.

Mendenhall, W. and Scheaffer, R. L. 1973. *Mathematical Statistics with Applications.* Duxbury Press: North Scituate, MA.

Minta, S. C., and Mangel, M. 1989. A simple population estimate based on simulation for capture-recapture and capture-resight data. *Ecology* 70:1738-1751.

Moon, B. R. 1984. Current distribution of the Eastern Barred Bandicoot, *Perameles gunnii*, in Victoria. Fisheries and Wildlife Division, Victoria. *Arthur Rylah Institute for Environmental Research Tech. Rep. Ser.* No. 5. Department of Conservation, Forests and Lands: Melbourne.

Neu, C. W., Byers, C. R. and Peek, J. M. 1974. A technique for analysis of utilization-availability data. *J. Wildl. Manage.* 38:541-545.

O'Farrell, M. J., and Austin, G. T. 1978. A comparison of different trapping configurations with the assessment line technique for density estimations. *J. Mamm.* 59:866-868.

O'Farrell, M. J., Kaufman, D. W., and Lundahl D. W. 1977. Use of live-trapping with the assessment line method for density estimation. *J. Mamm.* 58:575-582.

Otis, D. L., Burnham, K. P., White, G. C., and Anderson D. R. 1978. Statistical inference from capture data on closed animal populations. *Wildl. Monogr.* 62:1-135.

Overton, W. S., and Davis D. E. 1969. Estimating the number of animals in wildlife populations. In *Wildlife Management Techniques*, ed. R. H. Giles, Jr. Pp. 403-455. 3rd Edition. The Wildlife Society: Washington, D.C.

Romesburg, H. C. 1981. Wildlife science: gaining reliable knowledge. *J. Wildl. Manage.* 45:293-313.

Schnabel, Z. E. 1938. The estimation of the total fish population of a lake. *Amer. Math. Mon.* 45:348-352.

Seber, G.A.F. 1982. *The Estimation of Animal Abundance and Related Parameters.* 2nd Edition. Charles Griffin: London.

Seber, G.A.F. 1986. A review of estimating animal abundance. *Biometrics* 42:267-292.

Seebeck, J. H. 1979. Status of the Barred Bandicoot, *Perameles gunnii*, in Victoria: with a note on husbandry of a captive colony. *Aust. Wildl. Res.* 6:225-264.

Skalski, J. R., and Robson, D. S. 1982. A mark and removal field procedure for estimating population abundance. *J. Wildl. Manage.* 46:741-751.

Smith, M. H., Blessing, R., Chelton, J. G., Gentry, J. B., Golley, F. B., and McGinnis, J. T. 1971. Determining density of small mammal populations using a grid and assessment lines. *Acta Theriol.* 16:105-125.

Smith, M. H., Gardner, R. H., Gentry, J. B., Kaufman, D. W., and O'Farrell, M. J. 1975. Density estimation of small animal populations. In *Small Mammals: Their Production and Population Dynamics,* eds F. B. Golley, K. Petrusewicz, and L. Ruszkowski. Pp. 25-53. *Internatl. Biol. Prog. 5.* Cambridge University Press: London.

Steel, R. G. D., and Torrie, J. H. 1980. *Principles and Procedures of Statistics.* Second Edition. McGraw-Hill Book Company: New York.

Stickel, L. F. 1954. A comparison of certain methods of measuring ranges of small mammals. *J. Mammal.* 35:1-15.

White, G. C., Anderson, D. R., Burnham, K. P., and Otis, D. L. 1982. *Capture-recapture and Removal Methods for Sampling Closed Populations.* Los Alamos Nat'l. Lab.: Los Alamos, NM.

Winer, B. J. 1971. *Statistical Principles in Experimental Design.* 2nd Edition. McGraw-Hill: New York.

Zippin, C. 1956. An evaluation of the removal method of estimating animal populations. *Biometrics* 12:163-189.

# Applied Behaviour: Its Role in Conservation Biology of the Eastern Barred Bandicoot

*Graeme Coulson*[1]

## Abstract

Behaviour studies are an integral part of the management of human-animal conflicts. Such conflicts arise in domestic animal production, parasite and pathogen control, pest animal management, and wildlife conservation. The study of animal behaviour is concerned with four levels of analysis, each tending to focus on different aspects of behaviour: biochemical and neural mechanisms, ontogenetic development, adaptive significance, and evolution. Each level of behavioural analysis can provide insight into the conservation biology of species with small populations, as is illustrated by the eastern barred bandicoot, *Perameles gunnii*. There have been some studies of the behaviour of this species, mainly using captive Tasmanian animals, and a behavioural repertoire, while probably incomplete, can be compiled from the literature. The eastern barred bandicoot is strictly nocturnal, devoting much of its active time budget to foraging for predominantly invertebrate prey in open habitats. Olfaction appears to be the main sensory modality used in prey detection and social interaction. The eastern barred bandicoot is essentially solitary, and most interactions are limited to mutual avoidance, but males are the more aggressive sex and can inflict fatal injuries in captivity. Males also occupy larger home ranges which overlap the ranges of several females, consistent with a polygynous mating system. Several avenues for further applied research emerge from this review: the significance of scent-marking in the establishment and maintenance of home range, the influence of home range size on the lifetime reproductive success of males and the effect of disturbance and temporal changes in food availability on time budgets.

## Introduction

In a recent review paper entitled 'Applied Ethology', Monaghan (1984) argued that the theory and methods of ethology can be applied to 'the problems we face with animals.' Such problems arise when the interests of animals and humans conflict in some way. Monaghan identified three areas of potential conflict:

1. *Domestic animals.* The behaviour of domestic animals has been the subject of much ethological research aimed at maximising the yield of animal products (*e.g.* Kiley-Worthington 1977; Craig 1981). More recently, increasing concern about animal welfare has stimulated considerable ethological research into the issue of stress and suffering in captive animals (*e.g.* Broom 1988; Dawkins 1988).

2. *Parasites and pathogens.* The life-cycle of parasitic and pathogenic organisms often has essential behavioural components. Ticks (Ixodides), for example, climb to the top of shrubs and adopt a 'sit and wait' strategy until a suitable host comes within range (Noble and Noble 1976). Studies have also shown the significance of the behaviour of animal vectors that are involved in the transmission of parasites and pathogens. For example, the tendency of herring gulls, *Larus*

[1]Institute of Education, University of Melbourne, Parkville 3052, Australia.

*argentatus,* to feed at rubbish tips and sewage outfalls, and to roost at reservoirs, has been linked to the introduction of *Salmonella* to water supplies (Duncan 1981).

3. *Competitors.* Species that compete successfully with humans are generally labelled as pests, while those that are unsuccessful may become threatened with extinction. Many methods of pest control rely on understanding and manipulating the behaviour of the pest species. Numerous methods have been used, usually with the aim of excluding the pest from disputed areas such as crops: playback of alarm or distress calls (*e.g.* Boudreau 1968; Slater 1980), visual 'scarers' (*e.g.* Thomas 1972; Inglis 1980), electric fencing (*e.g.* McCutchan 1980; McKillop and Sibley 1988), habitat modification (*e.g.* Thomas 1972; van Tets *et al.* 1977), and chemical repellents (*e.g.* Wright 1980; Conover 1984).

Monaghan (1984) focussed on the application of behaviour studies to the management of pest species, whereas applications to the management of small populations were not discussed. The aim of this review is to redress that imbalance by emphasising the integral role of behaviour studies in the conservation biology of species at risk. The contribution of behaviour studies will be illustrated by reference to the eastern barred bandicoot, *Perameles gunnii.* This species, once widespread on the native grasslands of the basalt plains of Victoria, is now reduced to a small population restricted to the City of Hamilton, western Victoria (Brown 1989). The current knowledge of its behaviour will be reviewed, concentrating on those aspects of behaviour that are particularly relevant to its conservation and where further behavioural research would be of value.

## *Studying Animal Behaviour*

Tinbergen (1963) distinguished four types of questions that may be asked in animal behaviour studies:

1. *Mechanism.* The internal and external factors that are involved in the performance of behaviour, usually considered in the short term.

2. *Ontogeny.* The interaction between genetics and experience in the development of behaviour in the lifetime of an individual.

3. *Function.* The current adaptive value of behaviour in terms of survival and reproductive success.

4. *Evolution.* The origin of behaviour in the phylogenetic history of the species.

These questions about behaviour operate as separate levels of analysis. While logically distinct, the levels are not mutually exclusive. Instead, as Martin and Bateson (1986) and Sherman (1988) have stressed, the four levels offer complementary explanations for the same behaviour. The first two approaches, often referred to as proximate causes, are generally the domain of neurobiology and comparative psychology, whereas the second two approaches, which search for the 'ultimate' cause of behaviour, characterise the disciplines of classical ethology and behavioural ecology.

Studying behaviour is not merely a matter of observing some individuals and recording anything that occurs. The techniques used in the sampling of behaviour must be appropriate to the level of analysis required and to the biology of the target species. While a general, qualitative familiarity with the behaviour of the species is an advantage, most behaviour studies depend on precise quantification of behaviour. Sampling methods used to quantify behaviour have been discussed by Altmann (1974) and Martin and Bateson (1986).

## *Behavioural Repertoire*

The basis of any behavioural analysis is a catalogue, often termed an ethogram, of the full range of behaviours performed by the species under study. As Fagen and Goldman (1977) have shown, the number of unique acts observed in a study is a function of the total occurrence of all acts. This relationship is usually logarithmic, so new acts in the catalogue are accumulated rapidly at first but become decreasingly frequent, and the rarest acts may not be detected without considerable effort.

The effort devoted to observation of the behaviour of the eastern barred bandicoot has been comparatively small. Heinsohn (1966) made observations of captive and free-ranging animals but did not specify the time involved. The only systematic observations have been by Moloney (1982) and Clunie (1987) who, respectively, carried out 165 and 65 animal hours (no. of animals x no. of hours) of observation on captive animals. It is probable that this effort was insufficient to yield a complete repertoire for the species. In addition, the captive situation, while offering advantages in terms of reliable proximity to the animals, is likely to alter the frequency of occurrence of some acts (Burghardt 1975; Leuthold 1977), further limiting the completeness of the repertoire.

Comparative data are available from studies of other species of the Peramelidae by Heinsohn (1966), Stodart (1966), Buchmann and Grecian (1974), Day *et al.* (1974), Gordon (1974), Lyne (1974, 1981), Johnson and Johnson (1983), Moloney (1982) and Clunie (1987), and the behaviour of peramelids has been reviewed by Stodart (1977), Russell (1982, 1984) and Gordon and Hulbert (1989).

*Individual Behaviour*

A total of 24 distinct acts has been compiled from the descriptions given by Moloney (1982) and Clunie (1987). The nomenclature used by these authors has been retained except where changes were necessary to avoid ambiguity. These acts are summarised in Table 1, and some are illustrated in Figure 1.

When stationary, eastern barred bandicoots adopted one of several stances in which the body was horizontal to the substrate ('quadrupedal', 'sit', 'crouch', 'huddle' and 'tripedal'). Moloney (1982) concluded that two, the 'crouch' and 'tripedal' stances, were associated with disturbance. The 'tripedal' stance was the only one in which one fore-limb was raised from the substrate and retracted towards the body (see cover illustration of Brown, 1989), and was interpreted by Moloney (1982) as an 'indecision-alert' stance. This posture has also been recorded in the southern brown bandicoot, *Isoodon obesulus*, by Moloney (1982) and Clunie (1987). It is of interest at the evolutionary level of analysis since a similar posture occurs in many of the Dasyuridae (Croft 1982), with which the bandicoots are grouped in the Polyprotodonta, whereas the posture has not been reported in the Diprotodonta (Biggins 1984; Coulson 1989).

Locomotion in eastern barred bandicoots involved four different gaits. The 'walk' and 'run' were used mainly when foraging, and the 'gallop' and 'leap' were used when the animals were disturbed. Leaping consisted of sudden vertical jumps, up to 1.5 m, and on landing the bandicoot would gallop off in a different direction to that taken before the leap. These actions were often accompanied by 'honk' vocalisations. Moloney (1982) argued, at the functional level, that such erratic movements may be a means of escaping attack by predators.

Three upright stances ('bipedal', 'rear' and 'full-stretch') were associated with exploratory behaviour. The responses of eastern barred bandicoots to novel stimuli (other than prey) have not been systematically investigated, although there has been some research on other peramelids (Russell and Pearce 1971; Day *et al.* 1974).

Comfort acts ('scratch', 'wipe', and 'lick') were generally carried out when stationary, but the 'stretch' was usually performed on emergence

*Table 1.*—A summary of acts recorded in individual behaviour of the eastern barred bandicoot, after Moloney (1982) and Clunie (1987).

| Act | Description |
| --- | --- |
| Quadrupedal | Four limbs on substrate, body elevated but parallel with substrate. |
| Sit | As for quadrupedal, but hind-quarters lowered to contact substrate. |
| Crouch | Four limbs on substrate, body in contact with substrate. |
| Huddle | As for crouch, but head extended and in contact with substrate. |
| Bipedal | Hind-limbs and tail in contact with substrate, head parallel with substrate. |
| Tripedal | Similar to sitting, but one fore-paw raised and retracted towards body. |
| Rear | As for bipedal, but head extended vertically. |
| Full-stretch | Only hind digits and tail tip on substrate, body and head extended vertically. |
| Climb | Climbing wire mesh of enclosure. |
| Walk | Slow quadrupedal locomotion. |
| Run | Faster quadrupedal locomotion. |
| Gallop | Rapid locomotion, powerful simultaneous thrusts by the hind-feet. |
| Leap | Vertical springing (up to 1.5 m), change of direction on landing. |
| Honk | Loud honking vocalisation, 130 ms in duration, up to three honks given. |
| Nose | Lateral movement of snout across the substrate, with audible sniffing. |
| Dig | Excavating substrate with fore-limbs and inserting snout in holes. |
| Drink | Lapping water, in quadrupedal posture. |
| Feed | Ingesting food, larger items held on substrate with fore-paws, usually in quadrupedal posture. |
| Scrape | Pulling nesting materials backwards with fore-limbs. |
| Scratch | Raking movements of hind feet to groom fur on most of the body (except rump and belly). |
| Wipe | Rubbing the snout with licked fore-paws. |
| Lick | Licking and chewing of fur on most of the body (except head and neck). |
| Shake | Vigorous shaking of body, often when moving. |
| Stretch | Fore-paws under head, body elongated, back arched downwards, accompanied by yawning. |

from the nest and the 'shake', which dislodged water from the fur, often occurred while bandicoots were mobile. Clunie (1987), but not Moloney (1982), observed pouch cleaning in the eastern barred bandicoot, as has been reported in the long-nosed bandicoot, *P. nasuta,* (Stodart 1966). Nest construction was similar to that described in the long-nosed bandicoot (Stodart 1966); nesting material was pulled back towards and under the body ('scrape') while the hind-limbs were spaced widely apart.

*Figure 1.*—Some acts recorded in individual behaviour of the eastern barred bandicoot, after Moloney (1982): (a) quadrupedal, (b) crouch, (c) tripedal, (d) lick.

Foraging movements were accompanied by energetic sniffing of the substrate ('nose'), punctuated by digging the characteristic conical pits in the soil ('dig') and inserting the snout to extract and ingest food items ('feed'). Heinsohn (1966) and Moloney (1982) proposed that olfaction was the major sensory modality used in locating food, and experiments by Quin (1985) supported that view. In addition, Moloney (1982) tested the ability of eastern barred bandicoots to kill small vertebrate prey, finding that skinks, *Leiolopisma metallica,* were readily attacked and killed, but that attacks on laboratory mice, *Mus musculus,* and infant chickens, *Gallus domesticus,* were generally unsuccessful.

## Social Behaviour

Heinsohn (1966) noted that interactions between free-ranging eastern barred bandicoots were rarely observed. Mutual avoidance is the predominant pattern of social behaviour in this species, as has been found in other bandicoots studied (Stodart 1977; Russell 1984), and the species can be regarded as essentially solitary.

Moloney (1982) and Clunie (1987) used contrived dyadic encounters to investigate social interactions in captive eastern barred bandicoots. This procedure has the advantage of increasing the rate of interactions for the purpose of analysis,

*Table 2*.—A summary of acts recorded in social behaviour of the eastern barred bandicoot, after Moloney (1982) and Clunie (1987).

| Act | Description |
| --- | --- |
| Cloaca | Nosing cloaca of conspecific. |
| Arched | As for quadrupedal, but head slightly lowered and back arched. |
| Gape | Mouth gaping |
| Pounce | Rearing above and falling onto the back of conspecific. |
| Strike | Striking conspecific, usually on the back, with fore-paws. |
| Chase | Chasing retreating conspecific. |
| Prance | Springing upwards and landing simultaneously on digits of all limbs. |
| Follow | Persistent following of female by male. |
| Mount | Male rearing on hind-limbs and inclining body forwards over female. |
| Thrust | Pelvic thrusting during mounting. |
| Under | Female positioning her head under the body of male. |
| Bite | Male bites female. |
| Snort | Snorting vocalisation given by male. |
| Spit | Spitting vocalisation given by female. |
| Sneeze | Sneezing vocalisation given when retreating. |
| Sniff | Sniffing vocalisation given in nest when disturbed. |

but introduces the likelihood of artifacts of captivity due to the inability of individuals to avoid each other. A total of 16 social acts was compiled from descriptions given by Moloney (1982) and Clunie (1987), and again the nomenclature has been kept as faithful as possible to theirs. The acts are summarised in Table 2, and some are illustrated in Figure 2.

Encounters between males always involved agonistic behaviour. They approached each other, often retreating a number of times, but eventually nosing the cloaca of each other ('cloaca'). One individual then adopted the 'arch' stance with its mouth open ('gape'), usually from behind the opponent. When close together, the aggressor reared up ('rear'), still gaping, then struck the back of the opponent with the fore-paws ('strike'). The subordinate animal then usually fled, giving the 'sneeze' vocalisation, with the aggressor in pursuit ('chase'). The sequence was repeated until the experimenters intervened. This persistent aggression, which is typical of bandicoots (Stodart 1977), would otherwise result in the death of one of the males (Moloncy 1982). By contrast, agonistic interactions between females were quite subdued. They consisted of mutual avoidance, or occasional approaches with a gaping mouth.

Interactions between sexes were similarly restrained, except when sexual behaviour was observed. After tentative approaches, the male sniffed the female's cloaca; the female moved

*Figure 2.*—Some acts recorded in social behaviour of the eastern barred bandicoot, after Moloney (1982): (a) gape, (b) pounce, (c) cloaca, (d) mount.

away and the male followed persistently ('follow'). When cornered, the female attempted to position her head beneath the male's body ('under'), then she moved away with a stiff prancing gait ('prance') and emitted a 'spit' vocalisation as the male followed. Eventually the male mounted the female ('mount') and pelvic thrusts were observed ('thrust'). This was followed by the female making repeated attempts to crawl under the male, which were rebuffed by the male's bites ('bite') and 'snort' vocalisations.

Heinsohn (1966) has made the most detailed observations of parental care and the development of young in the eastern barred bandicoot.

Parturition has not been observed in the eastern barred bandicoot, but is likely to be similar to process described for the northern brown bandicoot, *Isoodon macrourus*, by Lyne (1974): the female lay on one side with one hind-limb elevated and, bracing herself with her fore-limbs, turned her head to lick the urinogenital opening before the young emerged and to lick around them as they crawled towards the pouch. Young eastern barred bandicoots were first recorded out of the pouch at 48-53 days of age, when they either accompanied the mother or remained in the nest in her absence, although as Russell (1985) noted, the young may have left the pouch earlier while still in the nest. The female adopted a modified quadrupedal stance, with the rump elevated, to allow the young to regain the pouch. This brief period of interim pouch life continued up to 58 days, after which the young did not return to the pouch or remain in the nest. The young accompanied the mother, foraging and suckling until 59-61 days, and were independent of her by about 70 days. This rapid development is typical of peramelids (Russell 1985).

## Temporal and Spatial Organisation

The compilation of a behavioural repertoire yields a summary of the behaviours that a species can potentially exhibit. The second stage in a comprehensive behavioural analysis is to determine the way in which behaviour patterns are exhibited in the dimensions of time and space. Less research has been undertaken on this aspect of behaviour in the eastern barred bandicoot, and much of it is based on data derived from captive animals. A comprehensive field study has yet to be conducted.

### Temporal Patterns

The eastern barred bandicoot is strictly nocturnal. Heinsohn (1966), Moloney (1982) and Clunie (1987) found that both captive and free-ranging animals spent the day in the nest and emerged after sunset. In the field, Heinsohn noted that individuals were frequently observed moving in the twilight after sunset. In Moloney's captive study, conducted during autumn and winter in a spacious outdoors enclosure, the mean emergence time was 2.8 hours after sunset, and the mean duration of the active period was 7.6 hours.

Heinsohn's (1966) observations of animals in nest boxes indicated that sleeping and grooming are the main behaviours during the daylight hours. When out of the nest, the eastern barred bandicoot spends most of the time actively foraging. Heinsohn's observations (of an individual in the field for 55 minutes) showed that 92% of the time was devoted to foraging (ingesting at least 18 food items), and the remaining time was spent grooming. Dufty (1988) found a similar pattern in three free-ranging individuals: time spent foraging ranged from 68-80%, and grooming occupied 0-6% of the time. Moloney (1982) and Clunie (1987) recorded detailed activity data in captivity, but because their analysis focussed on interspecific comparison with the southern brown bandicoot, a time budget could not be compiled for the eastern barred bandicoot from their data. Nonetheless, it is probable that a time budget derived in captivity would be unrepresentative of free-ranging animals, as indicated by Moloney's (1982) finding that the proportion of time spent digging was three times greater when food was withheld (17%) than when it was provided.

The activity pattern of the eastern barred bandicoot is similar to the patterns reported in the northern brown bandicoot and long-nosed bandicoot by Stodart (1966), Gordon (1974), and Lyne (1974). Lyne's (1974) wheel-running experiments suggested that the mechanism governing the activity pattern was an endogenous circadian oscillator that was entrained to photoperiod.

### Spatial Patterns

The habitat preferences of the eastern barred bandicoot are fairly well understood: it requires dense ground cover in which to construct nests and open grassland in which to forage (Seebeck 1979; Brown 1989). This spatial pattern of habitat partitioning is related to the temporal pattern referred to above. An adaptive explanation for these patterns, as suggested by Clunie (1987), would be that a bandicoot foraging in the open, and thus exposed to the greatest risk of predation, should maximise its foraging efficiency, then return to the relative security of the nest to rest and groom.

Movements of free-ranging eastern barred bandicoots have been investigated in trapping studies by Heinsohn (1966) and Moloney (1982) and in a trapping and radio-tracking study by Dufty (1988). Some data are available on dispersal: the longest movement (measured in a straight line between locations) recorded in Tasmania was 1.4 km

(Heinsohn 1966) and one animal at Hamilton travelled 2.3 km (Dufty 1988). Moloney (1982) did not trap any females, but Heinsohn (1966) and Dufty (1988) found that the home ranges of males were larger than those of females, and also overlapped several female ranges. A similar pattern has been found in the southern brown bandicoot (Heinsohn 1966; Sampson 1971; Moloney 1982; Clunie 1987) but was less marked in the northern brown bandicoot (Gordon 1974).

## Directions for Behaviour Research

Several avenues for further research into the behaviour of the eastern barred bandicoot have emerged from this review. In part these are aimed at answering 'pure' questions about the species, but they also have clear application to the management of the small population in the City of Hamilton. A significant constraint to any research on a small population is that it has to be compatible with management of the population, and it must be acknowledged that some procedures, which might yield potentially valuable behavioural data, may be inappropriate to the situation. The ongoing trapping program at Hamilton and the existence of captive colonies provide opportunities for integrated research into the behaviour of the eastern barred bandicoot.

The sensory modalities used in mutual avoidance and maintenance of home range are unclear, although Russell (1985) argued that olfaction is the mechanism involved, as it is in foraging. Stoddart (1980) reported that male and female eastern barred bandicoots possess a subauricular gland which produces a pungent odour and is most active in males during the breeding season. He postulated that the odour has a calming effect on both sexes, allowing mating to take place. This hypothesis has not been tested, but there is no evidence of marking behaviour using the subauricular gland. However, Day *et al.* (1974) suggested that urine and faeces may function as territorial markers. The observations of Heinsohn (1966), Moloney (1982) and Clunie (1987) indicate that cloacal odours are important in rec-

ognition of the sex of bandicoots at close range, and that several vocalisations are also involved in agonistic and sexual interactions. A better understanding of the role of odours in the behaviour of the eastern barred bandicoot is needed. Their secretions may prove useful in manipulating behaviour, particularly if they act as either attractants or repellents.

Heinsohn (1966) and Dufty (1988) estimated the size of home ranges using the convex polygon method, which has since been shown to be extremely sensitive to sample size (Macdonald *et al.* 1980). Heinsohn's (1966) data clearly showed bias due to the number of recaptures of individuals. Comparisons between individuals and between sexes should be made using non-parametric analyses that are not subject to bias by sample size (Dixon and Chapman 1980; Anderson 1982) The preliminary work by Dufty (1988) suggests that a full-scale radio-tracking study, using reliable, long-range transmitters, would yield valuable data on home range size, nocturnal and diurnal habitat utilisation, dispersal and mortality.

The question of difference between the sexes in their home range size should be resolved, since larger home ranges in males, together with the aggression observed between males and sexual dimorphism in body size, suggest that the eastern barred bandicoot has a polygynous mating system. The occurrence of polygyny has to be taken into account in estimates of effective population size (Lande and Barrowclough 1987). Individual variation in reproductive success is generally higher in polygynous species than in monogamous species (Wade and Arnold 1980), causing the effective population size to be lower than estimated when mating is assumed to be random. Sherwin and Brown (in press) assumed random mating in their estimate for effective population size of the eastern barred bandicoot at Hamilton.

Finally, foraging behaviour in the eastern barred bandicoot warrants further research. At present, there are no data available on the effects on foraging success of factors such as sex or experience of the bandicoot, disturbance or predation of bandicoots, or the effects of season and the associated changes in photoperiod, prey abundance, soil hardness, and vegetation cover. Observational studies, ideally of marked or radio-collared individuals, could be undertaken within the framework of the current monitoring program. Acoustic telemetry (Alkon *et al.* 1989) is a new technique that has potential for measuring the foraging behaviour of the eastern barred bandicoot. Using this technique, a small microphone and transmitter would be fitted to bandicoots to record the clearly audible sounds of nosing, digging, and feeding, as well as the vocalisations used in social interactions.

## Acknowledgments

I am grateful to a number of people for their assistance in the preparation of this review. Damien Moloney and Pam Clunie gave permission to quote extensively from their unpublished honours theses. Peter Brown and Anthony Dufty were sources of additional unpublished information. John Seebeck provided access to reference material. Members of the animal behaviour discussion group (Department of Zoology, University of Melbourne) gave valuable feedback. Ruth Coulson typed the manuscript diligently. Denise Casey produced the illustrations.

## References


Alkon, P. U., Cohen, Y., and Jordan, P. A. 1989. Towards an acoustic biotelemetry system for animal behaviour studies. *J. Wildl. Manage.* **53**:658-662.

Altmann, J. 1974. Observational study of behaviour: sampling methods. *Behaviour* **49**:227-267.

Anderson, D. J. 1982. The home range: a new nonparametric estimation technique. *Ecology* **63**:103-112.

Biggins, J. G. 1984. Communication in possums: a review. In *Possums and Gliders,* eds A. Smith and I. Hume. Pp. 35-57. Surrey Beatty and Sons: Sydney.

Boudreau, G. W. 1968. Alarm sounds and responses of birds and their application in controlling problem species. *Living Bird* **7**:27-46.

Broom, D. M. 1988. The scientific assessment of animal welfare. *Appl. Anim. Behav. Sci.* **20**:5-19.

Brown, P. R. 1989. Management Plan for the Conservation of the Eastern Barred Bandicoot, *Perameles gunnii,* in Victoria. National Parks and Wildlife Division, Victoria. *Arthur Rylah Institute for Environmental Research Tech. Rep. Ser.* No. 63. Department of Conservation, Forests and Lands: Melbourne.

Buchmann, O. L. K., and Grecian, E. A. 1974. Discrimination-reversal learning in the marsupial *Isoodon obesulus* (Marsupialia, Peramelidae). *Anim. Behav.* **22**:975-981.

Burghardt, G. M. 1975. Behavioral study in zoos and wildlife parks. In *Animal Behavior in Laboratory and Field,* eds E. O. Price and A. W. Stokes. Pp. 9-12. W. H. Freeman: San Francisco.

Clunie, P. 1987. Aspects of the ecology and behaviour of *Isoodon obesulus* (Shaw and Nodder 1797) and *Perameles gunnii* (Gray 1838). B. Sc. (Honours) Thesis, University of Tasmania, Hobart.

Conover, M. R. 1984. Effectiveness of repellents in reducing deer damage in nurseries. *Wildl. Soc. Bull.* **12**:399-404.

Coulson, G. 1989. Repertoires of social behaviour in the Macropodoidea. In *Kangaroos, Wallabies and Rat-kangaroos,* eds G. Grigg, P. Jarman and I. Hume. Pp. 457-473. Surrey Beatty and Sons: Sydney.

Craig, J. V. 1981. *Domestic Animal Behaviour.* Prentice Hall: Hemel Hempstead.

Croft, D. B. 1982. Communication in the Dasyuridae (Marsupialia): a review. In *Carnivorous Marsupials,* ed. M. Archer. Pp. 291-309. Royal Zoological Society of New South Wales: Sydney.

Day, B., Kirkby, R., and Stenhouse, D. 1974. The behaviour of marsupials III. The shortnosed bandicoot, *Isoodon macourus,* (Peramelidae) in the open field. *Aust. Mammal.* **1**:255-259.

Dawkins, M. S. 1988. Behavioural deprivation: a central problem in animal welfare. *Appl. Anim. Behav. Sci.* **20**:209-225.

Dixon, K. R., and Chapman, J. A. 1980. Harmonic mean measure of animal activity areas. *Ecology* **61**:1040-1044.

Dufty, A. C. 1988. The distribution, population abundance, status, movement and activity of the Eastern Barred Bandicoot, *Perameles gunnii,* at Hamilton. B. Sc. (Honours) Thesis, La Trobe University, Bundoora, Victoria.

Duncan, N. 1981. The Abbeystead and Mallowdale gull colony before control. *Bird Study* **28**:133-138.

Fagen, R. M., and Goldman, R. N. 1977. Behavioural catalogue analysis methods. *Anim. Behav.* **25**:261-274.

Gordon, G. 1974. Movements and activity of the Shortnosed Bandicoot *Isoodon macrourus* Gould (Marsupialia). *Mammalia* **38**:405-31.

Gordon, G., and Hulbert, A. J. 1989. Peramelidae. In *Fauna of Australia. Mammalia.* eds D. W. Walton and B. J. Richardson. Pp. 603-624. Australian Government Publishing Service: Canberra.

Heinsohn, G. E. 1966. Ecology and reproduction of the Tasmanian bandicoots (*Perameles gunni* and *Isoodon obesulus*). *Univ. Calif. Publ. Zool.* **80**:1-107.

Inglis, I. R. 1980. Visual bird scarers: an ethological approach. In *Bird Problems in Agriculture,* ed. E. N. Wright. Pp. 121-143. British Crop Protection Publications: Croydon.

Johnson, C. N., and Johnson, K. A. 1983. Behaviour of the bilby, *Macrotis lagotis* (Reid), (Marsupialia: Thylacomyidae) in captivity. *Aust. Wildl. Res.* **10**:77-87.

Kiley-Worthington, M. 1977. *Behavioural Problems of Farm Animals.* Oriel Press: London.

Lande, R. and Barrowclough, G. F. 1987. Effective population size, genetic variation, and their use in population management. In *Viable Populations for Conservation,* ed. M. E. Soulé. Pp. 87-123. Cambridge University Press, Cambridge.

Leuthold, W. 1977. *African Ungulates. A Comparative Review of their Ethology and Behavioural Ecology.* Springer-Verlag: Berlin.

Lyne, A. G. 1974. Gestation period and birth in the marsupial *Isoodon macrourus. Aust. J. Zool.* **22**:303-309.

Lyne, A. G. 1981. Activity rhythms in the marsupials *Isoodon macrourus* and *Perameles nasuta* in captivity. *Aust. J. Zool.* **29**:821-838.

Macdonald, D. W., Ball, F. G., and Hough, N. G. 1980. In *A Handbook on Biotelemetry and Radio Tracking,* eds C. J. Amlaner and D. W. Macdonald. Pp. 405-423. Pergamon Pres: Oxford.

Martin, P., and Bateson, P. 1986. *Measuring Behaviour. An Introductory Guide.* Cambridge University Press: Cambridge.

McCutchan, J. C. 1980. *Electric Fence Design and Principles.* University of Melbourne: Melbourne.

McKillop, I. G., and Sibley, R. M. 1988. Animal behaviour at electric fences and the implications for management. *Mammal Rev.* **18**:91-103.

Moloney, D. J. 1982. A comparison of the behaviour and ecology of the Tasmanian bandicoots, *Perameles gunnii* (Gray 1838) and *Isoodon obesulus* (Shaw and Nodder 1797). B. Sc. (Honours) Thesis, University of Tasmania, Hobart.

Monaghan, P. 1984. Applied ethology. *Anim. Behav.* **32**:908-915.

Noble, E. R., and Noble, G. A. 1976. *Parasitology. The Biology of Animal Parasites.* Lea and Febiger: Philadelphia.

Quin, D. G. 1985. Aspects of the feeding ecology of the bandicoots, *Perameles gunnii* (Gray 1838) and *Isoodon obesulus* (Shaw and Nodder 1797) (Marsupialia: Peramelidae) in southern Tasmania. B. Sc. (Honours) Thesis, University of Tasmania, Hobart.

Russell, E. M. 1982. Patterns of parental care and parental investment in marsupials. *Biol. Rev.* **57**:423-486.

Russell, E. M. 1984. Social behaviour and social organization of marsupials. *Mammal Rev.* **14**:101-154.

Russell, E. M. 1985. The metatherians: order Marsupialia. In *Social Odours in Mammals,* eds D. Macdonald and R. E. Brown. Pp. 45-104. Oxford University Press: Oxford.

Russell, E. M., and Pearce, G. A. 1971. Exploration of novel objects by marsupials. *Behaviour* **40**:313-322.

Sampson, J. C. 1971. The biology of *Bettongia penicillata* (Gray 1837). Ph. D. Thesis, University of Western Australia.

Seebeck, J. H. 1979. Status of the barred bandicoot, *Perameles gunnii,* in Victoria: with a note on husbandry of a captive colony. *Aust. Wildl. Res.* **6**:255-264.

Sherman, P. W. 1988. The levels of analysis. *Anim. Behav.* **36**:616-619.

Sherwin, W. B., and Brown P. R. (In press) Problems in the estimation of the effective population size of the Eastern Barred Bandicoot, *Perameles gunnii,* at Hamilton in Victoria. In *Bandicoots and Bilbies,* eds J. H. Seebeck, P. R. Brown, R. L. Wallis and C.M. Kemper. Surrey Beatty and Sons: Sydney.

Slater, P. J. B. 1980. Bird behaviour and scaring by sounds. In *Bird Problems in Agriculture,* ed. E. N. Wright. Pp. 105-144. British Crop Protection Publications: Croydon.

Stodart, E. 1966. Management and behaviour of breeding groups of the marsupial *Perameles nasuta* Geoffroy in captivity. *Aust. J. Zool.* **14**:611-623.

Stodart, E. 1977. Breeding and behaviour of Australian bandicoots. In *The Biology of Marsupials,* eds B. Stonehouse and D. P. Gilmore. Pp. 179-191. Macmillan: London.

Stoddart, D. M. 1980. Observations on the structure and function of cephalic skin glands in bandicoots (Marsupialia: Peramelidae). *Aust. J. Zool.* **28**:33-41.

Thomas, G. J. 1972. A review of gull damage and management methods at nature reserves. *Biol. Cons.* **4**:117-127.

Tinbergen, N. 1963. On aims and methods of ethology. *Z. Tierpsychol.* **20**:410-433.

van Tets, G. F., Vestjens, W. J. M., D'Andria, A. H., and Barker, R. 1977. *Guide to the Recognition and Reduction of Aerodrome Bird Hazards.* Australian Government Publishing Service: Canberra.

Wade, M. J., and Arnold, S. J. 1980. The intensity of sexual selection in relation to male sexual behaviour, female choice, and sperm precedence. *Anim. Behav.* **28**:446-461.

Wright, E. N. 1980. Chemical bird repellents—a review. In *Bird Problems in Agriculture,* ed. E.N. Wright. Pp. 164-172. British Crop Protection Publications: Croydon.

# Veterinary Aspects of *Perameles gunnii* Biology with Special Reference to Species Conservation


*Cornelis Lenghaus[1], David L. Obendorf[2] and Frank H. Wright[3]*



## Abstract

A critically small population of the eastern barred bandicoot (*Perameles gunnii*) is located at Hamilton, western Victoria. During 1988-1989, a detailed post-mortem examination was made on 52 bandicoots, most of which were submitted either as road kills or cat kills, in an attempt to ascertain whether there were any predisposing factors which could have contributed to these mortalities. Less complete data were also available from 82 bandicoots collected from 1982-1988 and kept deep frozen until examined in 1989. These 134 specimens were compared with data on small numbers of bandicoots kept in captivity in Victoria and from Tasmania. Cause of death was determined for 96 of the 134 bandicoots in the Hamilton population. Road trauma accounted for 55 (57%) bandicoot deaths, of which 39 (41%) were adult males, 12 (12%) were adult females and four (4%) were juvenile males. Predation by cats, dogs or foxes contributed to the deaths of six (6%) adult *P. gunnii*, and 17 (18%) juveniles were killed by cats. Five (5%) adult and 13 (13%) pouch young were found dead in live-traps. Significant disease was not found in pouch young. Severe parasitic disease was common in intact juvenile and adult *P. gunnii* examined soon after death, and included heavy infestations of ticks (*Ixodes tasmani*), fleas (*Pygiopsylla zethi*), mites (*Haemolaelaps marsupialis*) and lice (unidentified sp.), as well as internal roundworms (*Capillaria* sp., *Physaloptera* sp., *Strongyloides/Parastrongyloides* sp., and *Moniliformis* (*Australiformis*) *semoni*). Potentially fatal, generalized infections with the protozoan *Toxoplasma gondii* were present in more than 10% of bandicoots, often in association with the above parasitism. The diseases seen in the Hamilton and Tasmanian populations of *P. gunnii* were similar. These data have implications for species conservation. The impact of any diseases will probably be magnified in captive colonies of *P. gunnii*, and other infectious or stress-related diseases not presently important in the wild population at Hamilton could also become serious problems under restricted conditions. Detailed management strategies and ongoing monitoring of the health of these bandicoots will be necessary to avoid potentially severe losses. For wild bandicoots, the control of domestic and feral cats would be beneficial, by reducing the incidence of toxoplasmosis and predation on juveniles. However, by itself this action may not be enough to save this population. Preliminary investigations indicated that wild bandicoots were commonly exposed to chemicals (*e.g.* dieldrin) used in pest control in urban and farming areas.


## Introduction

The eastern barred bandicoot (*Perameles gunnii*) was once widely distributed across the basalt plains of western Victoria. However, today only a remnant population survives in and around Hamilton, an inland town of 10,500 people situated nearly 300 km west of Melbourne (Seebeck *et al.* this volume). This population is currently declining at about 25% per year due to habitat loss, cat predation, motor vehicle deaths and other causes (Lacy and Clark, this volume). While there has been a Regional Veterinary Laboratory (RVL) in Hamilton since 1971 servicing extensive sheep and cattle industries, it was not until heightened public awareness of the plight of the bandicoot surfaced during 1986-1987 that numbers of these animals became available for post-mortem examinations. Typically, people who brought bandicoots to the laboratory reported that


[1]Department of Agriculture and Rural Affairs, Regional Veterinary Laboratory, Hamilton, Victoria 3300, Australia.
[2]Tasmanian Department of Primary Industry, Mt. Pleasant Laboratories, Launceston, Tasmania 7249, Australia.
[3]Royal Melbourne Zoological Gardens, Parkville, Victoria 3052, Australia.

they had found them dead on highways on the outskirts of Hamilton or on local streets, or that their domestic cat had brought a partly-devoured specimen home. Most of the former were considered 'mature' *P. gunnii,* in excess of 500 g body weight. Many of the latter were 'juveniles' of 120-250 g. Pouch young up to 50 g were sometimes submitted separately or with dead female bandicoots.

It became fashionable to regard the major causes of *P. gunnii* loss as either road kills or cat kills, although the seemingly large numbers presented for examination suggested that there could have been serious pre-existing diseases which caused debility or disorientation, so that bandicoots became more readily the victims of cars or cats. In an attempt to ascertain whether there were predisposing factors contributing to *P. gunnii* mortalities, 52 animals submitted to the RVL during 1988-1989 were subjected to a detailed post-mortem examination. Similar studies were conducted on 82 bandicoots presented to the Arthur Rylah Institute for Environmental Research (ARI) in Melbourne from 1982-1988 and kept frozen at -20°C from that time. Data obtained from small colonies kept in captivity at various times at Healesville Sanctuary and Serendip Wildlife Research Station, both in Victoria, were reviewed. Comparative data were available from *P. gunnii* in Tasmania, although it should be noted that the two populations have been separated for at least 8,000 years (George *et al.* this volume), since the land bridge between Tasmania and the rest of Australia was inundated by the sea after the last Ice Age. It was anticipated that all the information so gathered would prove useful in assessing the disease pressures present on *P. gunnii* in the wild, and possibly predict which diseases might become important in translocated *P. gunnii* kept in colonies under semi-captive conditions. This information is directly relevant to the management and conservation of this species, and especially important to recovery of the mainland population.

## Materials and Methods

Bandicoots were examined as soon as possible after submission to the RVL. Those from ARI were thawed and examined in batches. A standard post-mortem protocol was followed as closely as the poor state of preservation of many of the animals would allow. Bandicoots were weighed and sexed and the following measurements taken: overall body length, length of pes (from hock to beginning of the nail on the main toe), tail, head and ear. The combined circumference of the testes in the scrotum was measured in males, and in females the presence or absence of pouch young and whether teats showed evidence of suckling were recorded. Any tattoo numbers in ears were recorded and the location of previous capture and release was compared with the site where the animal had died. Before any dissection, representative numbers of external parasites (ticks, fleas, lice, mites) were collected and any major external abnormalities such as skin ulceration or signs of trauma noted. Animals were generally autopsied in dorsal recumbency. The legs were reflected laterally by sectioning through the chest and shoulder muscles and through the pelvic joints. A midline skin incision was made from the mandible to the pelvis. The skin was also reflected laterally. The abdomen was opened in the midline and abdominal musculature reflected as for the skin. The ribs were transected with sharp scissors or bone forceps and the rib cage removed to allow easy access to the heart and lungs.

Organs were inspected *in situ* before removal and any significant findings photographed. The tongue, trachea, oesophagus, thymus, heart and lungs were removed together, as were the stomach, intestines to the rectum, spleen and pancreas. Bones of the pelvic arch were transected to allow removal of the urinary bladder, reproductive tract and terminal rectum to the cloaca. Liver, adrenals and kidneys were removed as required. An eye was dissected from its orbit and the brain was

*Table 1.*—Causes of death of 52 eastern barred bandicoots examined during 1988-1989.

| Cause | Adult | | Juvenile | | Pouch Young |
| --- | --- | --- | --- | --- | --- |
| | M | F | M | F | |
| Road Trauma | 15 | 5 | 2 | - | - |
| Predation (Cat, Dog, Fox) | 2 | 2 | 3 | 3 | - |
| Trap Death | 1 | 1 | - | - | 8 |
| Ectoparasitism[1] | - | 2 | - | 2 | - |
| Toxoplasmosis | - | 1 | - | - | - |
| Bacterial Infections | - | 1 | - | 1 | - |

Cause not determined in 1 adult and 2 juveniles (macerated)

[1]Endoparasitism was considered to have contributed to some deaths - see text.

removed after cutting through the calvarium. Representative tissues were taken from all organ systems as available and preserved in 10% formol-saline. Preserved tissues were embedded in paraffin, sectioned at 5 μm and routinely stained with haematoxylin and eosin using standard histological techniques.

Swabs from sites of suspected infectious disease were cultured on sheep blood agar at 37° C and significant bacteria identified using standard bacteriological techniques. Alimentary tract contents were examined macroscopically and microscopically for internal parasites, and representative numbers of any worms found were preserved in 90% ethyl alcohol to which was added 5% glycerol. Sporadically 1% pepsin in 2% HCl was used to digest fresh tissues for 1-3 hours at 37°C, to release worms from the epithelium of the tongue and oesophagus and the lung parenchyma. A minimum of 2 ml of solution was used per gram of tissue. Stomach and intestinal contents were stored frozen at -20° C for subsequent dietary analyses. Liver, kidney, fatty tissue, mammary glands and brain from selected bandicoots were stored at -20° C for organochlorine and organophosphate pesticide residue analyses by gas-liquid chromatography (GLC) techniques.

## Results

### Pathology

*Victorian Bandicoots.* The causes of death of the 52 *P. gunnii* examined at the RVL during 1988-1989 and of the 82 *P. gunnii* collected at the ARI from 1982-1988 are summarized in Tables 1 and 2, respectively. Most bandicoots died of road trauma (41% of 134 specimens).

Histology was only possible on a variable number of tissues from 32 RVL bandicoots and 31 ARI bandicoots. Generalized, active toxoplasmosis was considered to have been the primary cause of death of three adult bandicoots and associated with the deaths of seven other adults (five road kills, one trap death and one from predation). In these bandicoots, there were numerous foci of necrosis and mononuclear inflammatory cells associated with *Toxoplasma gondii* pseudocysts containing bradyzoites. Such focal areas of inflammation and degeneration were most common in the brain, heart, and skeletal muscles, but were also seen in lung, liver and kidneys. Similar foci of inflammation and occasional pseudocysts were sporadically seen in the tissues of many adult and some juvenile bandicoots. It was assumed that these animals were infected, but that

*Table 2.*—Causes of death of 82 eastern barred bandicoots collected between 1982-1988.

| Cause | Adult | | Juvenile | | Pouch Young |
| --- | --- | --- | --- | --- | --- |
| | M | F | M | F | |
| Road Trauma | 24 | 7 | 2 | - | - |
| Predation (Cat, Dog, Fox) | 1 | 1 | 5 | 6 | - |
| Trap Death | 2 | 1 | - | - | 5 |
| Other Trauma (Mower, Earthmover) | 3 | 2 | 1 | 1 | - |
| Toxoplasmosis | 1 | 1 | - | - | - |
| Bronchopneumonia | 1 | - | - | - | - |

Cause not determined/not recorded in 18 bandicoots.

the toxoplasmosis was quiescent at the time of examination. There was no histological evidence for toxoplasmosis in pouch young.

There was little evidence of significant bacterial infections. One adult female had severe cellulitis and mastitis from which *Fusobacterium* sp. bacteria were cultured. A juvenile female had histological evidence of septicaemia associated with a Gram positive bacillus, and an adult male had a severe bronchopneumonia histologically associated with a mixed bacterial infection.

Ectoparasites (ticks, mites, fleas and lice) were present only on bandicoots presented freshly dead, or associated with the wrappings used to transport a freshly dead bandicoot to the laboratory (Fig. 1). Ectoparasites seemingly migrated from their host within hours of death. The only gross evidence then for their ever having been there was the presence of 'blood meals' left by fleas, most readily apparent in the light coloured, finer belly fur. More than 100 fleas and 1,000 larval ticks were counted in one adult female which was thin and had a pale, anaemic carcase. In the absence of other disease or injury, these were considered to be significant as a cause of death. Three other bandicoots (with numerous flea 'blood meals') in a similar body condition were also considered to have died primarily from ectoparasitism. Histo-

logically, severe ectoparasitism was associated with a moderate, diffuse infiltration of lymphocytes and eosinophils in the dermis. Fleas were identified as *Pygiopsylla zethi*, ticks as *Ixodes tasmani*, mites as *Haemolaelaps marsupialis* and the lice were a new species, yet to be described and named.

Nematode parasites were commonly found in the alimentary tract of adult *P. gunnii* (Fig. 2). *Physaloptera* sp. and *Moniliformis/Australiformis semoni* (Schmidt and Edmonds 1989) were readily apparent grossly, in the stomach, though occasionally *M. semoni* was found in the proximal small intestine. Both parasites had their anterior ends deeply embedded in the mucosa. Numbers were usually small, never more than five *M. semoni* were found in one bandicoot, and usually fewer than 10 *Physaloptera*. However, 20-50 *Physaloptera* were present in five bandicoots submitted as road kills, and histologically these had a severe, ulcerative, granulomatous gastritis. The severity of this lesion was considered to have caused serious debility in these animals and may have contributed to their demise. *Capillaria* sp. were found in sieved stomach and intestinal contents, often in scores, occasionally more than 100. They were also seen histologically embedded in the superficial stratified squamous epithelium of the tongue and oesopha-

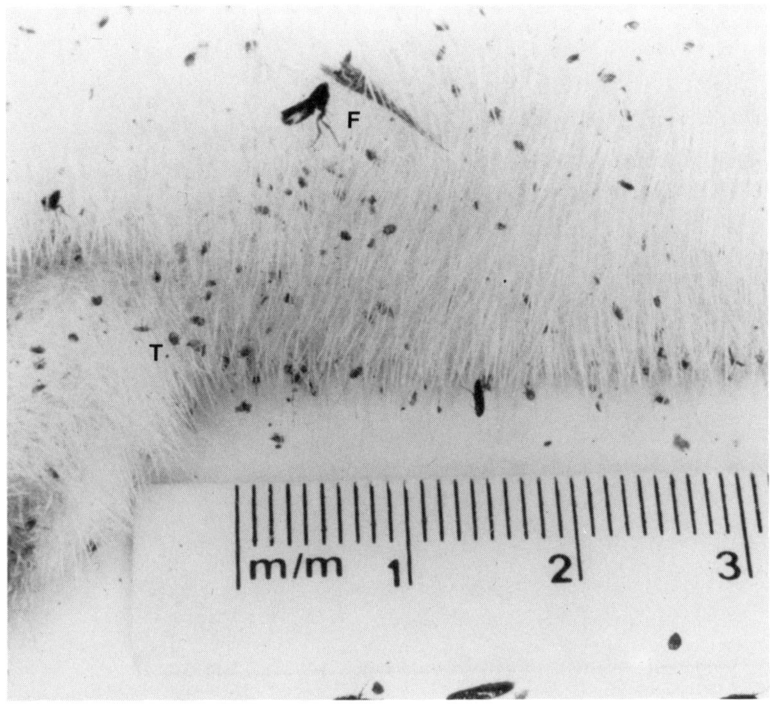

*Figure 1.*—Fleas (F) and larval ticks (T) found on the abdomen of an eastern barred bandicoot.

gus, where their presence provoked a minimal inflammatory response. Individual *Capillaria* nematodes were recovered by blunt dissection under a stereomicroscope, or by gentle digestion of tongue and oesophageal tissues with pepsin solution to release them.

One juvenile bandicoot considered to have died from the effects of ectoparasitism had numerous pinpoint foci of consolidation scattered throughout its lungs. Histologically such foci usually contained single larval nematodes embedded in a nidus of atelectasis and inflammation. Similar larval nematodes were found embedded in the mucosa of the small intestine. They were considered to be migrating *Strongyloides/Parastrongyloides* sp., although intact specimens were not recovered from tissue digests to confirm this suggestion.

Many *P. gunnii* (juveniles and adults) had focal granulomas in the lungs, containing dust particles. Such pneumoconiosis appeared to become progressively more severe in older bandicoots and seemingly reflected the animal's exposure to soil while digging for prey. It was rarely considered severe enough to impair respiratory function seriously.

Three adult bandicoots had kidneys with numerous 1-2 μm diameter developmental stages of a protozoan in endothelial cells of glomerular tufts, and with seemingly completed stages as cysts in renal tubular epithelium. The smaller organisms in the glomeruli stained poorly with Schiff's reagent and were Gram negative (in contrast to *Toxoplasma* bradyzoites which stained strongly with Schiff's reagent and were partly Gram positive). This renal protozoan was considered to be

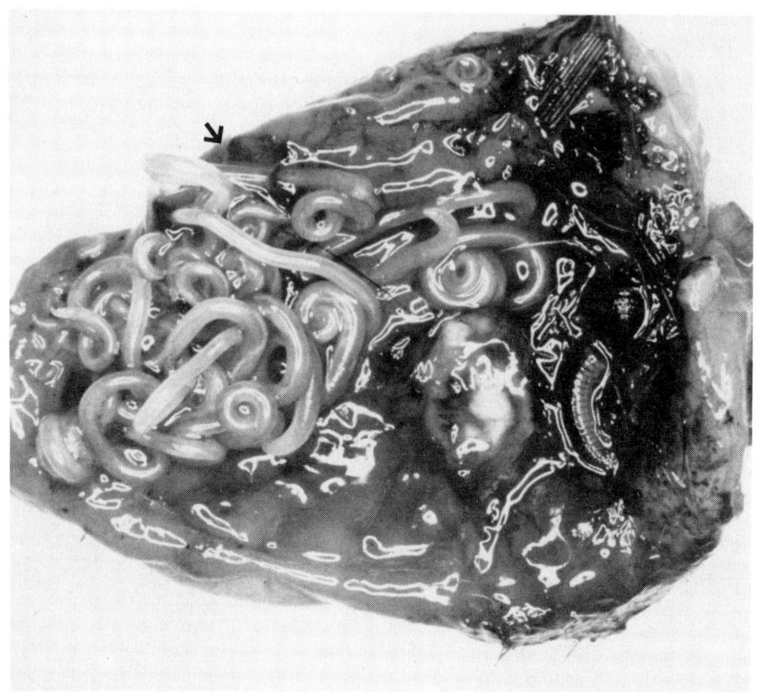

*Figure 2.—Physaloptera* sp. nematode parasites (arrow) present in the opened stomach of an eastern barred bandicoot with a small quantity of ingesta (I) present.

a *Klossiella* sp., (Barker *et al.* 1975) with schizonts in glomeruli and gamonts in renal tubules. They did not appear to be very pathogenic in the animals examined.

Six bandicoots chosen at random had the following liver, kidney, or fat levels for the organochlorine compound dieldrin: positive (no value given), 1.29, 1.30, 1.99, 3.65 and 6.52 ppm.

*Tasmanian Bandicoots.* Toxoplasmosis was also present in wild *P. gunnii* examined in Tasmania. Affected animals were seen during daylight hours displaying signs of incoordination, blindness and erratic staggering movements. As well as encephalitis, there was pneumonitis and myocarditis. Infections with *Capillaria, Moniliformis, Physaloptera* and *Parastrongyloides* sp. of

nematodes were also recorded. *Klossiella* sp. of protozoa were recognized in kidneys.

Severe periodontal disease was seen in emaciated adult *P. gunnii*, characterized by the accumulation of pale plaque material on the sides of teeth and retracted tooth-gum margins, with loose and missing teeth. Severe bronchopneumonia and pleurisy were also seen, probably as a secondary infection, in one bandicoot with periodontal disease. *Actinobacillus* sp. bacteria were isolated from the lung lesions.

A severe, subacute, interstitial nephritis with accumulations of lymphocytes and plasma cells mainly in the interstitium of the renal cortex was seen in one adult *P. gunnii*. There were proteinaceous and cellular casts in tubular lumens. Leptospirosis was considered a diagnostic possibility but could not be confirmed by Levaditi (silver) staining of kidney sections nor by attempted transmission experiments in guinea pigs.

*Captive Bandicoots.* Toxoplasmosis was the commonest cause of death in captive juveniles and young adults. Lesions were as already described but also included a severe pancreatitis and localized peritonitis. Three cases of sudden death with grossly distended urinary bladders were recorded in hand-reared juveniles, which may have resulted from a primary failure to stimulate micturition resulting in 180° bladder torsion, hydronephrosis and uraemia. *Capillaria* sp. and *Parastrongyloides australis* nematodes were considered the cause of diarrhoea and enteritis in several bandicoots from Serendip, in which 4,600 *Parastrongyloides australis* and 700 *Capillaria* sp. were recovered from the intestines of one animal. Large numbers of nematodes were seen in histological section, burrowing through the intestinal mucosa, which had stimulated an infiltration of globule leucocytes and mononuclear inflammatory cells.

A severe exudative dermatitis, otitis externa, conjunctivitis and pouch infection occurred in one adult *P. gunnii* within 3 months of capture and confinement to a cage. Opportunistic bacterial pathogens including *Escherichia coli, Staphylococcus aureus* plus *Corynebacterium, Enterobacter* and *Streptococcus* sp. were isolated at post-mortem. Fight injury and stress-related infections caused bacterial polyserositis (pericarditis, pleuritis and peritonitis) in four juvenile bandicoots kept in an enclosure and unable to disperse away from their parents after weaning. *E. coli, Staphylococcus aureus* and *Aeromonas* sp. were isolated from pus-filled thoracic cavities in these animals (Presidente 1978).

Fungal infection due to *Candida albicans* occurred in a hand-reared juvenile, with thick white plaques coating the tongue, gums, palate, oropharynx, larynx and extending down the oesophagus. Removal of plaque revealed extensive bleeding ulcers. Histologically the lesion was characterized by tissue necrosis and fluid exudation without a significant inflammatory response. Diet or management stress had apparently compromised this animal's immune system.

Many captive bandicoots, both adult and juvenile, showed evidence of gastric haemorrhage from numerous superficial bleeding points in the stomach. Histologically, these bleeding foci were areas of acute necrosis of the mucosa and damage to capillaries. The nature of the necrosis was suggestive of auto-digestion of the mucosa by acid-pepsin activity. Atrophy of the lymphoreticular system was another histopathology feature suggestive of stress and impaired immune competence. The lymphoid follicles in the spleen and lymph nodes showed marked depletion of lymphocytes, while the centres of follicles contained degenerate and necrotic cells or were partially replaced by epithelioid cells and fibrous tissue.

*Anatomy and Histology*

The state of preservation of the bandicoots examined made a detailed systematic examination of any one animal impossible. What follows is therefore a composite picture obtained from many of them. Overall, the observations made were very similar to those described by Tedman (in press) for the northern brown bandicoot (*Isoodon macrourus*).

Teeth were modified for a largely insectivorous diet, with conical or pyramidal crowns set in a narrow, sharply-pointed jaw. The tongue was long, narrow, thick and pointed. Paired, lobed, sub-maxillary salivary glands were located subcutaneously ventro-caudal to the mandible, with a smaller parotid salivary gland at the base of each ear. The oesophagus led to a simple, oval, glandular stomach covered by a large triangular spleen. A rather diffuse pancreas was embedded in mesentery attached to the duodenum. The intestinal tract was of approximately uniform diameter throughout the small and large intestines to the

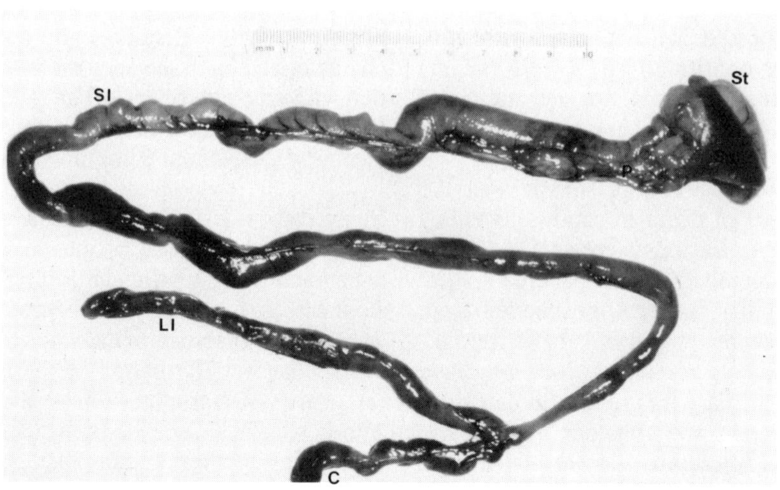

*Figure 3.*—Unopened stomach (St), small intestine (SI), large intestine (LI) and caecum (C) of an eastern barred bandicoot. The stomach is covered by a triangular shaped spleen (Sp). The pancreas (P) is embedded in mesentery attached to the duodenum.

rectum, and included a short tubular caecum at approximately two-thirds the distance from the stomach to the cloaca (Fig. 3). Paired oval rectal glands were attached to the rectal wall near its termination.

Younger animals had a well developed intrathoracic thymus, at the thoracic inlet. The heart was globular with comparatively thick walls, lying within a pericardial sac which was firmly anchored to the sternum. The left lung was unlobed, but the right lung had four lobes, including a small caudal lobe lying transversely along the diaphragm to the left side (Fig. 4).

The liver had four main lobes with the gall bladder lying recessed in the largest, middle lobe. An elongated caudate lobe partly enveloped the right kidney and adrenal. The kidneys were ovoid and indented at the central point of exit of the ureters. The brain was lissencephalic, without obvious sulci or gyri of the cerebral cortex. The cerebellum likewise had a smooth outer surface; however, a sagittal section revealed the more typical mammalian foliar structure. The smooth outer surface of the cerebellum was due to an expanded outer caudal folium essentially enveloping the whole organ (Fig. 5).

With respect to the skeleton, *P. gunnii* did not have clavicles, but did have patellas, and prominent, long, thin epipubic bones embedded in the musculature of the ventral abdomen. In the front feet, the first and fifth digits were vestigial and without claws, the second and third digits were of equal size and carried long curved claws, while the fourth digit was smaller with a short straight claw. In the hind feet, the first digit was again vestigial. The second and third digits were small and syndactylous with only the top joints and small claws independent. The fourth digit was greatly enlarged, with a strong straight claw present. The fifth digit was similar in size to the fourth digit of the front foot, and also carried a short straight claw (Fig. 6).

*Figure 4.*—Ventral view *in situ* of exposed heart (H), lungs, liver (L), stomach (St) and duodenum (D) of an eastern barred bandicoot. The right lung has four lobes (labelled 1, 2, 3, 4) with the fourth lobe lying transversely across to the left side. The left lung (LL) is unlobed. The gall bladder lies recessed in the middle lobe of the liver (arrow).

There was little variation in the mature size of the male's testes, prostate and accessory sex glands carried subcutaneously and immediately craniad of the cloaca, which suggested that breeding was not restricted by season. The testes were carried externally at the level of the anterior pubis, and were only very loosely attached to the epididymides in the scrotum. Each ductus deferens passed from the tail of the epididymis through the inguinal canal lateral to the origin of the epipubic bones, and entered at the head of the urethra. Prominent lymph nodes lying subcutaneously in loose fascia on either side of the ventro- lateral abdominal wall also drained through the inguinal canal.

The prostate was roughly spherical and similar in size to the unopened scrotum. It had a conspicuous wedge of pale tissue ventrally, which narrowed and merged with the bulk of the prostatic tissue as it inserted into the urethra (Fig. 7). The thick-walled urethra passed caudally through the pelvic canal attached to the ventral wall of the rectum and entered the 'S'-shaped penis at the bulbous crus. The penis ended in a bifurcated, spinous glans. The bulky accessory sex glands readily 'shelled out' of their subcutaneous site *en masse;* however, detailed dissection and visualization of the dual pairs of bulbo urethra glands, crus penis and paired urethral bulbs were made difficult because of the large amount of muscle

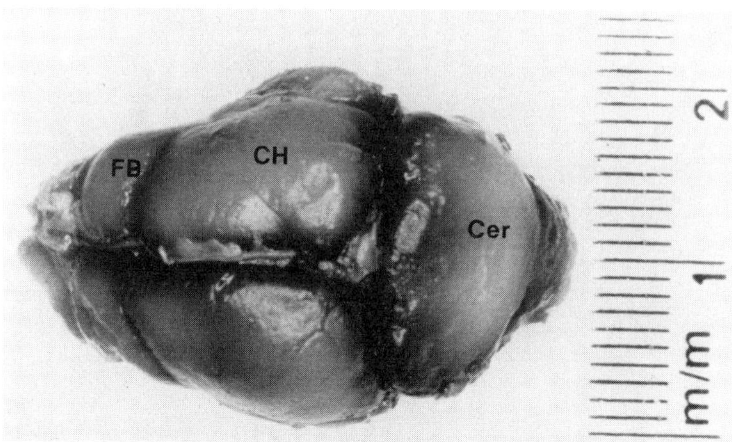

*Figure 5a.*—Dorsal view of eastern barred bandicoot brain, showing smooth surfaced forebrain (FB), cerebral hemisphere (CH) and cerebellum (Cer).

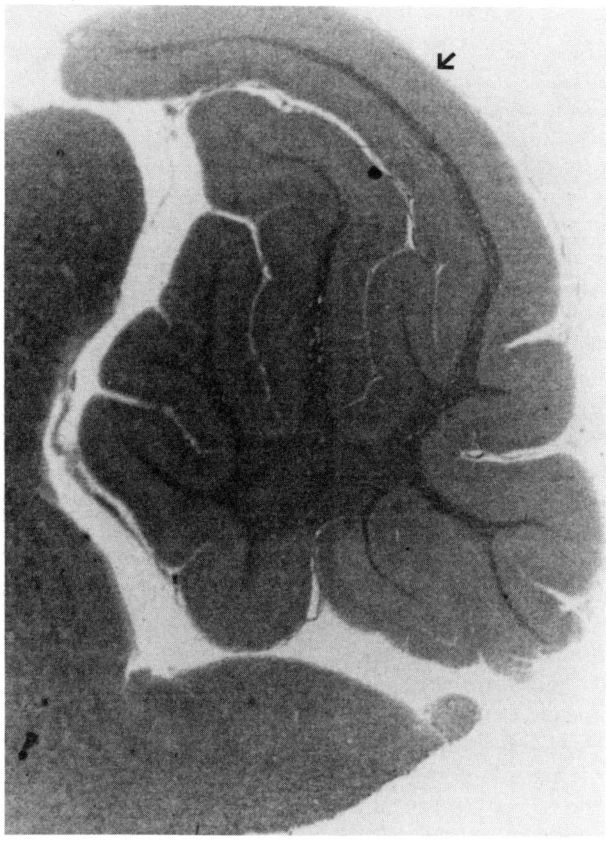

*Figure 5b.*—Sagittal section of cerebellum, showing outer folium, which essentially envelops the whole organ (arrow). Luxol fast blue/cresyl violet stain.  Original magnification x 1.

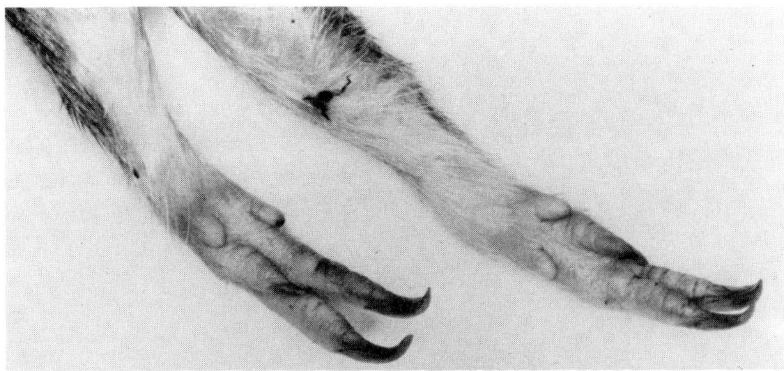

*Figure 6a.*—Volar aspect of eastern barred bandicoot's lower forelimbs, showing vestigial first and fifth digits without claws; strong, curved claws on the second and third digits; a short straight claw on a small fourth digit.

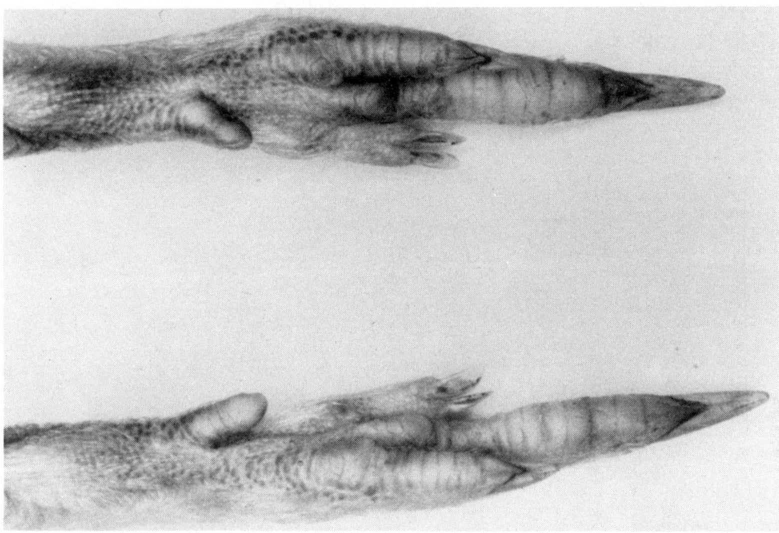

*Figure 6b.*—Volar aspect of eastern barred bandicoot's lower hind limbs, showing a vestigial first digit without a claw; small syndactylous second and third digits with small claws; large fourth digit and small fifth digit with straight claws.

and dense connective tissue uniting these structures (Fig. 8).

Female bandicoots had the pouch opening posteriorly, with four nipples on either side of the ventral midline. Nipples increased in size at least ten-fold as the attached young developed (Fig. 9). Nipples seemingly then regressed in size when not in use.

Adult pregnant (presumably pluriparous) females had hemispherical uterine horns joined in the midline by connective tissue. The ovaries were attached laterally to each uterine horn. Prominent lymph nodes were present at the ends of short peritoneal folds attached to the body of each uterine horn. Ventrally the uterus was covered by two voluminous, thin-walled vaginal caeca, fused in the midline to form an apparently bilobed

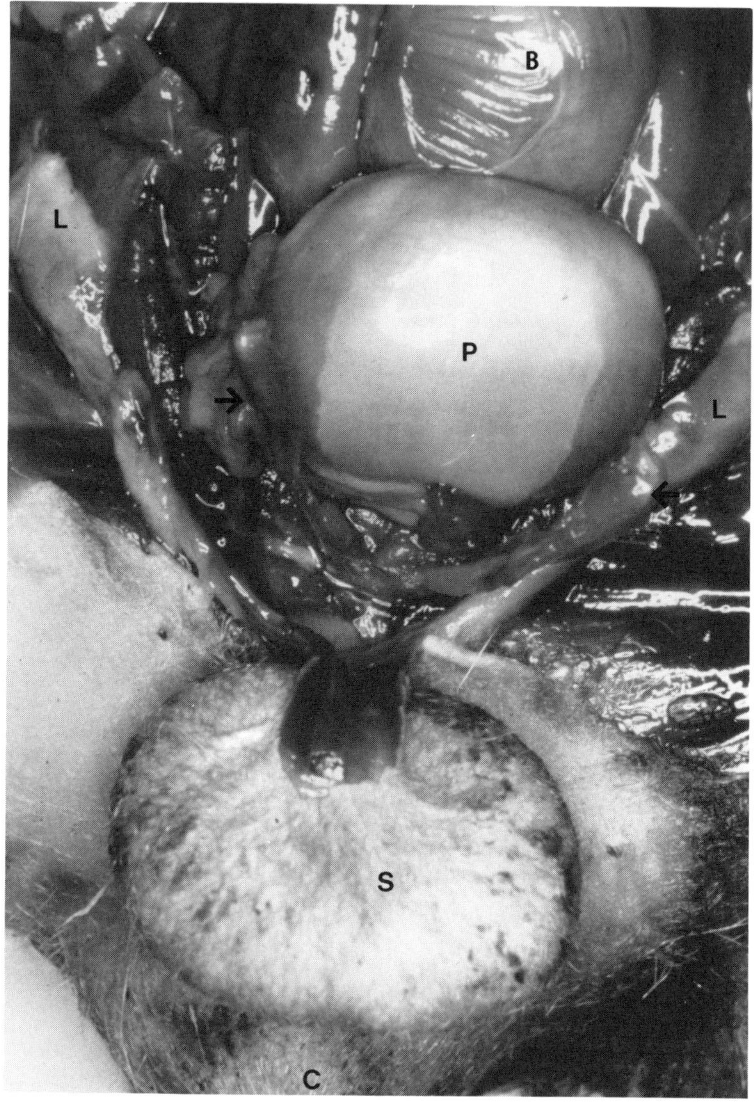



*Figure 7.*—Ventral view of the male eastern barred bandicoot's urogenital system, showing urinary bladder (B), prostate (P), lymph nodes (L) and epipubic bones (arrows). Unopened scrotum (S) obscures the normally prominent subcutaneous bulge of the accessory sex glands, craniad to the cloaca (C).

structure. The bladder was ventral to the vaginal caeca and received the two ureters almost at the neck (Fig. 10). A narrow urethra was attached to the ventral rectal wall and was flanked by two narrow lateral vaginae through the pelvic canal, where the urethra and vaginae entered a short, common urogenital sinus which opened into the cloaca. Even at a stage considered close to parturition, there was seemingly no single birth canal considered large enough to allow simple passage of the perinatal bandicoot.

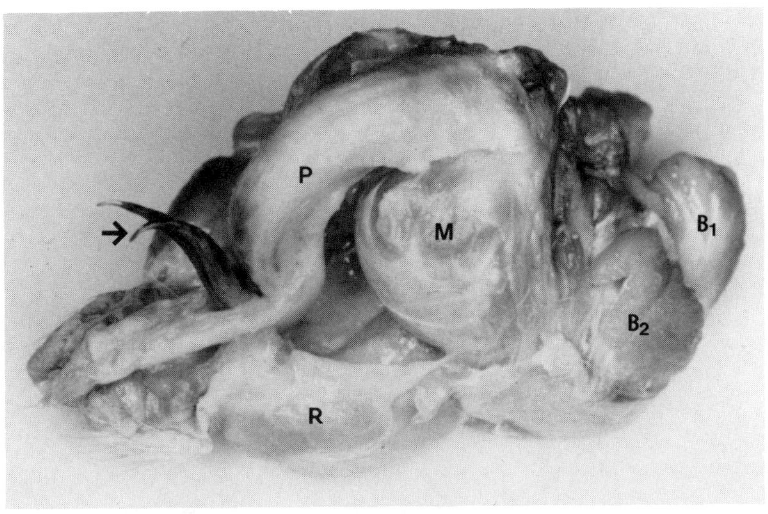

*Figure 8.*—Lateral oblique view of accessory sex glands, and rectal gland (R) in a male eastern barred bandicoot. Paired bulbourethral glands (B₁ & B₂) are partly exposed, while the urethral bulbs are buried in a mass of skeletal muscle (M). The penis (P) ends in a spinous, bifurcated glans (arrow). The cloaca has been partly resected and the prepuce opened.

Histologically all tissues were recognizably mammalian and comparable with even common domestic animals. The only significant exceptions were the more specialized reproductive tracts and the organization of the rectum and urogenital tracts at the cloaca.

It was noted that the enveloping folium of the cerebellum, already described grossly, did contain the molecular layer, Purkinje cell layer and internal granular cell layer as in other species. Bone marrow seemingly carried all the recognized primordia for erythroid, myeloid and lymphoid cells. Megakaryocytes had few lobes. In acute inflammatory reactions provoked by bacteria, a higher proportion of polymorphonuclear leucocytes appeared to be eosinophils rather than neutrophils. While the hepatic architecture was unremarkable, many hepatocytes were binucleate, with occasional trinucleate cells present. As well as the parotid salivary gland at the base of the ear, there was also a small discrete sebaceous gland, with a broad band of sebaceous tissue circling the base of the pinna at the entrance to the auricular canal.

The small intestine was not simply divisible into duodenum, jejunum and ileum. At the entrance to the small intestine, there was a discrete submucosal gland which may have functioned similarly to the more diffuse submucosal Brunner's glands seen in the duodenum of other mammalian species. The large intestine remained essentially unchanged to the rectum. Rectal glands contained little that was recognizable as glandular structures histologically, but were filled with desquamated epithelial cells. The terminal alimentary and urogenital tracts were lined by stratified squamous epithelium, which continued into the cloaca. As well as the rectal glands noted above, there were numerous microscopic circumanal glands present in the wall of the terminal rectum and cloaca. Deep, epithelium-covered invaginations in the wall of the cloaca were intimately surrounded by lymphoid tissue and may have been important in antigen recognition and immunity.

In males, the bulk of the single mass incorporating the accessory sex glands consisted of striated (voluntary) skeletal muscle surrounding in par-

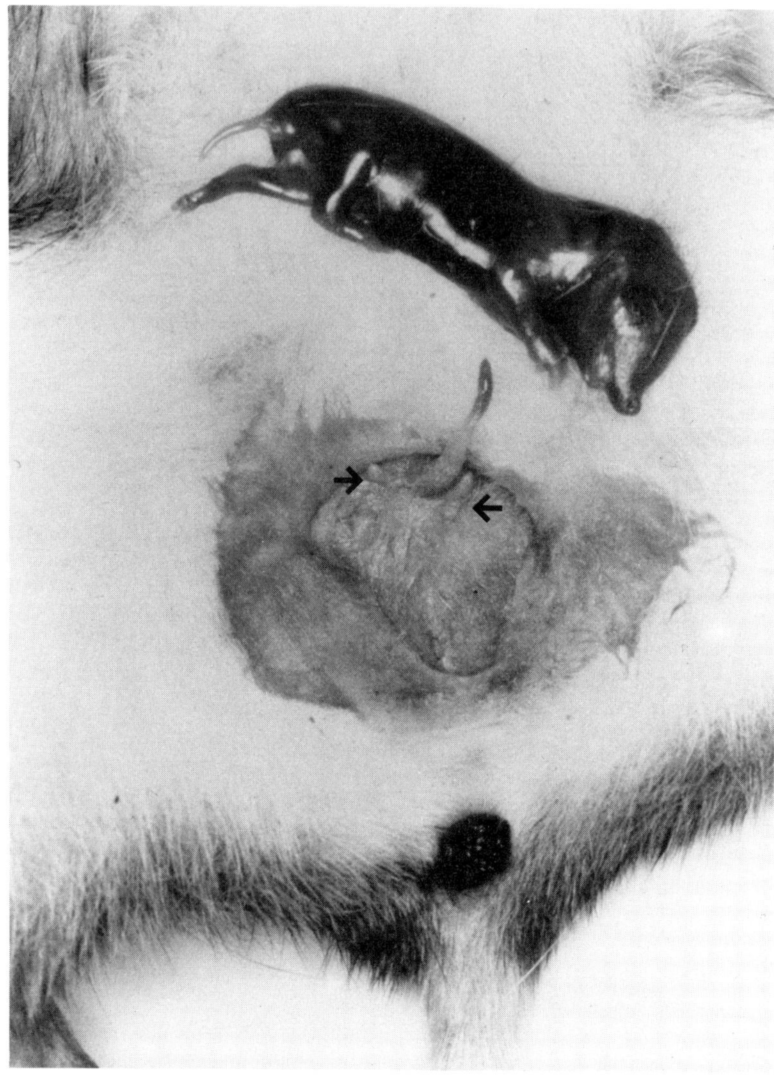

*Figure 9.*—Partly opened pouch in female eastern barred bandicoot showing an enlarged nipple, to which the hairless young bandicoot had been attached. Note comparative size of unutilized nipples (arrows).

ticular the urethral bulbs and crus penis. It was considered that the muscle mass was required to supply the considerable effort (force) that could be required to eject seminal fluids through the tiny orifices in the glans penis. The urethra in the penis was surrounded by cavernous tissue, which presumably became engorged with blood to maintain erection.

The two distinct glandular tissues in the prostate apparently had differing secretions, appearing more colloidal at the periphery and clear in the central wedge, by conventional staining. Both epithelial cell populations had a high mitotic index, particularly the central one. Spermatozoa in seminiferous tubules and epididymides had long, thick, straight tails without any obvious

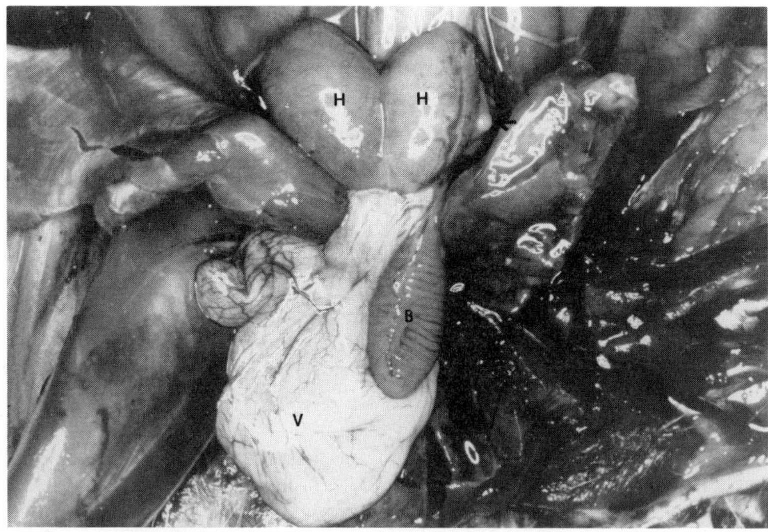

*Figure 10.*—Ventral view of pregnant uterus in an eastern barred bandicoot showing joined uterine horns (H) and ovary (arrow). The vaginal caeca (V) and urinary bladder (B) have been retracted caudally.

further differentiation. Chromatin in the sperm head was attached in a sharply angular 'arrowhead' arrangement.

In females, the narrow elongated lateral vaginae and urethra had a thin wall of smooth muscle and were lined by pseudo-stratified columnar and transitional epithelium respectively. The vaginal caeca contained proteinaceous secretions and were lined by pseudo-stratified columnar epithelium, surrounded by a thin rim of dense connective tissue.

In the pregnant uterus there was a well-developed chorio-allantoic placenta with the trophoblast composed of syncytial cells. The glandular endometrium was well developed and numerous villi of trophoblast cells were intimately associated with maternal capillaries/blood spaces, in which non-nucleated maternal erythrocytes could be readily distinguished from the nucleated foetal blood. Where there were two foetuses in the same uterine horn, they were separated by thin membranes of essentially connective tissue. The foetuses themselves showed a precocious cephalad development. Those examined histologically had a well-developed head, a complement of body somites, forelimb buds and recognizable heart, lungs, liver, kidneys and rudimentary alimentary tract. The corpus luteum of pregnancy comprised the major tissue component in the ovary of the pregnant bandicoot. Longitudinal section of enlarged nipples showed they had at least two teat canals.

## Discussion

This study is based mainly on the dead *P. gunnii* found and submitted for veterinary examination by the general public. The real impetus for the study arose from a general awareness and concern at the ongoing serious decline in bandicoot numbers at Hamilton, assumed to be due to the high incidence of road kills in adults and a failure to augment the breeding population because of predation on juveniles, particularly by cats (Brown 1989). Detailed post-mortem examinations were conducted to ascertain whether particular diseases might have predisposed the animals to the seemingly high mortalities observed.

103

Because of the public interest shown, it can be assumed that a large proportion of the total road kills were submitted. However, many animals which died in less conspicuous areas would certainly have been missed, as would the ones which were eaten by predators or scavengers. In this context nothing is known about the losses due to birds of prey, particularly owls, hunting at night when bandicoots are active. While the emphasis was on disease investigation, the opportunity was also taken to accumulate some overview data on *P. gunnii* anatomy and histology, given the almost total lack of published information.

It was considered that the available data on *P. gunnii* deaths reported from Healesville Sanctuary and Serendip Wildlife Research Station would be important, given the likely need to manage at least some of the Hamilton bandicoot population in semi-captive conditions to safeguard against total extinction from a single catastrophic event such as drought, flood, fire or disease.

Collectively there were less than 50 veterinary reports on *P. gunnii* prior to our study. Although the majority of diseases or pathological conditions reported are not peculiar to the species, they are likely to have a bearing on captive breeding and maintenance. Toxoplasmosis, gastrointestinal parasitism, trauma-related bacterial infections, and some stress-related conditions were considered the most significant pathological entities of *P. gunnii*. Where the factors contributing to the occurrence of disease are known or suspected, an attempt has been made to provide some options for prevention or control.

The protozoan parasite *T. gondii* is a well-recognized cause of disease and mortality in Australian marsupials (Barker *et al.* 1963; Attwood *et al.* 1975; Arundel *et al.* 1977). All the major groups of marsupials, whether they are herbivorous, carnivorous or omnivorous, have been infected with this organism. In Australia, *Toxoplasma* is a parasite of the introduced cat, which is the only definitive host. However, a wide range of mammals and birds are capable of acting as intermediate hosts. These intermediate hosts may acquire infection by 1) the ingestion of the infective oocysts of *T. gondii* which are shed in cats faeces, 2) the ingestion of arthropods or annelids which contain oocysts of *T. gondii* within their digestive tracts, 3) the ingestion of infective *T. gondii* cysts present in the tissues of infected mammals or birds or, 4) transplacental infection when a pregnant female becomes infected during gestation.

For omnivorous and insectivorous marsupials such as *P. gunnii*, a probable source of infection is from eating the arthropods, earthworms and other invertebrates containing *Toxoplasma* oocysts which pass through their alimentary tracts. Such transport hosts acquire oocysts through coprophagia or by ingesting soil or plant material contaminated by cat faeces (Markus 1973; Ruiz and Frenkel 1980). In captivity, bandicoots fed on diets containing fresh meat are also prone to infection. Certain carnivorous marsupials have acquired fatal *Toxoplasma* infections by consuming rations made from fresh sheep meats (Attwood *et al.* 1975). *Toxoplasma* infection in association with interstitial pancreatitis was also reported from these carnivorous marsupials (Attwood and Woolley 1980). In the case of one captive *P. gunnii*, fresh mutton mince was thought to be the major source of *Toxoplasma* infection.

Toxoplasmosis commonly develops in man and domestic or free-ranging animals as a result of lowered immunity (immunosuppressive factors), stress-related conditions (environmental, physiological or population-based stressors), debility, senility or intercurrent disease. *Toxoplasma* infection may remain clinically inapparent, but under the circumstances mentioned above such latent infections may become clinically overt as the parasite undergoes rapid tissue multiplication, dissemination throughout the body and subsequent infection of other host cells. The inflammatory response of the host to the parasite coupled with the tissue damage caused by the parasite are responsible for the clinical disease and the pathology seen at post-mortem.

It is our contention that *Toxoplasma gondii* is capable of exerting a considerable effect on small populations of *P. gunnii*. In captivity, marsupials show a pronounced susceptibility to *Toxoplasma* infection and subsequently may go on to express clinical and often fatal disease. Inappropriate management of captive populations can lead to a lowering of immunological competence which appears to enhance this susceptibility. A wide range of potential stressors can bring this about. Such captive situations in which toxoplasmosis is a major disease risk can be directly compared with small free-ranging populations existing in significantly altered habitats, which arguably could be considered peripheral rather than preferred environments in which to exist. The preferred habitat of *P. gunnii* may be relatively restricted and discrete. Since European settlement, both the quantity and quality of such native grasslands across the bandicoots' range have been adversely affected. The introduction of efficient predators such as cats, dogs and foxes has also had a major effect on the small population at Hamilton (Seebeck 1979).

The two locations in Tasmania where toxoplasmosis was reported bear some similarity with Hamilton in Victoria. Both Tasmanian sites are considerably altered by human agricultural and/ or urban activity to the extent where they would be considered peripheral bandicoot habitat. Defaecation by cats in and around areas frequented by bandicoots was thought to be the principle source of *T. gondii* infection at these locations. Both feral and domestic (pet) cats from adjacent urban areas and/or farms could provide such contamination. Habitat contraction and alteration coupled with unfavourable climate and food availability may be sufficient to allow toxoplasmosis to occur.

Preventive measures for captive populations of *P. gunnii* include cat, dog and fox-proof external enclosures. Food storage areas which encourage rodents also encourage cats. Commercial dry food rations need to be kept in a secure area in sealable bins or hoppers. Fresh meat rations should be avoided, as they are a ready source of *Toxoplasma* infection (particularly sheep meats) and are nutritionally unbalanced. Canned meat-based foods prepared for pet animals are preferable. Soft, sticky foods should be avoided to prevent periodontal disease.

*Physaloptera* sp., *Parastrongyloides* sp. and *Capillaria* sp. parasites, through their burrowing activity cause stomach and intestinal damage leading to fluid, electrolyte and protein loss. The life cycles of these nematodes are not known. It is likely that infective *Parastrongyloides* larvae penetrate the skin, entering the vascular system to pass to the lungs. The larvae migrate into the airways, passing up the trachea to be swallowed. (Larval nematodes have been located in the alveoli of *P. gunnii* infected with *Parastrongyloides*.) In the intestines, the larvae mature to adult males and females. The characteristic thin-shelled eggs containing first-stage larvae are passed in the faeces.

Several species of *Capillaria* occur in *P. gunnii*. Sites of parasitism include the epithelia of the tongue, lips and oesophagus, and the mucosa of the stomach and small intestine. The presence of the typical ovoid bipolar plugged eggs of *Capillaria* sp. in faeces may indicate infections in any or all of these sites. No pathogenicity has been attributed to the *Capillaria* sp. in the upper alimentary tract. The life cycle of the intestinal *Capillaria* sp. may involve insect or annelid intermediate hosts. The life cycle of *Physaloptera* sp. is also likely to be indirect, involving arthropods or insects.

Naturally parasitized animals brought in from wild populations may have clinically inapparent infections of these worms. Continuous faecal contamination of outside enclosures could lead to heavy parasite burdens developing. In these circumstances, a program of treatment on arrival at the holding facility is recommended with routine checks of faeces for the presence of parasitic ova. It is recommended that outside enclosures be situated in well-drained locations. Faeces should be removed from enclosures where possible and overcrowding should be avoided. No anthelmintic treatments have been attempted in *P. gunnii*. Some of the benzimidazole carbamates such as fenbendazole, albendazole and oxfendazole are likely to be safe and effective against *Parastrongyloides* sp. for quarantine and curative treatments. Control of intestinal *Capillaria* sp. may also be successful with these drugs and with pyrantel pamoate. Further research into parasite life cycles, pathogenicity and preventive options is necessary.

Fungal infections such as candidiasis are a common finding in orphaned, hand-reared marsupials (Munday 1988). It is most frequently seen in pouch-dependent macropodids reared on milk diets. It is generally considered that *C. albicans* only causes illness and mortalities when the host's immune system is significantly compromised. This compromise may take the form of inappropriate management, leading to environmental, physiological, or possibly diet-related stress factors. Prolonged administration of antibiotics in these animals may also lead to *Candida* infections (Obendorf 1978). Pouch-dependent and juvenile marsupials have incompletely developed immune systems, which are highly susceptible to challenge by the vast array of potential disease-causing micro-organisms. Impaired cell-mediated immunity, predominantly T (thymus) - cell dependent, is known to favour fungal infections. This is consistent with the pattern seen in cases of candidiasis in macropodid pouch young (Obendorf 1979). The thymus of inappropriately reared pouch young rapidly shrinks in size due to lymphocyte depletion (Speare 1988). Further work is necessary to examine the immune system of marsupials in general. Nothing has been specifically published in relation to *P. gunnii*.

Captive bandicoots are likely to be susceptible to the same infectious diseases as other captive marsupials. *Salmonella* infection is one such possibility. Some free-living species of marsupials harbour *Salmonella* without showing signs of diarrhoea or ill-health. Wild-caught animals may introduce *Salmonella* into a captive colony, and, with appropriate stressors operating, clinical disease can be expressed. Rodent pest control is also important to minimise the possibility of *Salmonella* infection from them.

Herpes viruses have been the cause of multiple mortalities among several species of captive marsupials (Finnie *et al.* 1976; Finnie 1980; Munday 1988). Although no outbreak of herpes virus disease has been reported in bandicoots, two genera in the family Peramelidae do show antibodies to herpes viruses (Finnie 1980). Such viruses are typically present in a latent form, and are activated by stresses such as captivity, overcrowding, nutritional deficiencies, inadequate shelter, intercurrent infections, and inter- or intraspecific aggression. They can then cause clinical, often fatal, disease.

Intestinal coccidiosis caused by *Eimeria* sp. protozoa has been reported to cause deaths in macropodids, particularly captive animals (Munday 1988). While coccidia have not been found in *P. gunnii*, the first indication for their presence would likely be seen as an outbreak of diarrhoea, dysentery and death in animals kept under crowded conditions.

The presence of dieldrin in bandicoots is of concern, but reflects past usage of organochlorine compounds and soil residues, so should rapidly diminish given that all such compounds are now banned in agriculture. However, a large range of chemicals, particularly organophosphates, is still regularly used for control of insects and arthropods, many of which form part of the bandicoot diet. There is a need to test a larger sample from tissues still available, to try and ascertain the impact that broad acre chemical use had on bandicoot numbers in the past, and the need for ongoing monitoring to ascertain whether exposure to organophosphates and other compounds is currently of significance. While long-term soil residues are not of concern, there could be rapid death of bandicoots consuming large numbers of dead and dying invertebrates which had just been poisoned.

This study investigated disease factors which might have contributed to the large numbers of *P. gunnii* reported as road kills and cat kills. The investigations also highlighted some of the problems perceived in keeping bandicoots in semi-captive conditions. The status of bandicoots at Hamilton remains precarious, whether in the wild or captive. It is unlikely that this situation can be easily remedied. Attempting to maintain a stable wild population of bandicoots will require efforts in whole ecosystem management. Approaches concentrating solely on cat control are palliative and unlikely to be effective long-term on their own. The emphasis for small populations of endangered animals must be on improved habitat size and suitability (Clark *et al.*; Maguire *et al.*, this volume). It will be difficult to re-establish *P. gunnii* in parts of its former mainland Australian range because so much of it has been permanently altered for agriculture. Human activities and feral animal introductions have affected their whole ecosystem and place bandicoots, as well as their own unique ecto- and endo-parasites and microbial life forms at risk.

## Acknowledgments

We acknowledge the help of several people and institutions. John Seebeck and others at the Arthur Rylah Institute for Environmental Research provided specimens for examination. Ruth Mitchell and Jan Povey of the Regional Veterinary Laboratory at Hamilton prepared tissues for histological examinations. Denise Casey and Tim Clark reviewed the manuscript.

## References


Arundel, J.H., Barker, I.K., and Beveridge, I. 1977. Diseases of Marsupials. In *The Biology of Marsupials,* eds B. Stonehouse and D. Gilmore. University Park Press: Baltimore, U.S.A. Pp. 141-154.

Attwood, H.D., and Woolley, P.A. 1980. Pancreatic pathology in dasyurid marsupials. *J. Wildl. Dis.* **16**: 245-49.

Attwood, H.D., Woolley, P.A., and Rickard, M.D. 1975. Toxoplasmosis in dasyurid marsupials. *J. Wildl. Dis.* **11**:543-551.

Barker, I.K., Munday, B.L., and Harrigan, K.E. 1975. *Klossiella* sp. infection in the kidneys of peramelid, petaurid and macropodid marsupials. *Z. Parasitenkd.* **46**:35-41.

Barker, S., Calaby, J.M., and Sharman, G.B. 1963. Diseases in Australian laboratory animals. *Vet. Bull.* **33**:539-544.

Brown, P.R. 1989. Management Plan for the Conservation of the Eastern Barred Bandicoot, *Perameles gunnii*, in Victoria. National Parks and Wildlife Division, Victoria. *Arthur Rylah Institute for Environmental Research Tech. Rep. Ser.* No. 63. Department of Conservation, Forests and Lands: Melbourne.

Finnie, E.P. 1980. A marsupial herpesvirus. In *The Comparative Pathology of Zoo animals,* eds R.J. Montali and G. Migaki. The Symposia of the National Zoological Park, Smithsonian Institute, Washington. Pp. 179-182.

Finnie, E.P., Littlejohns, I.R., and Acland, H.M. 1976. Mortalities in parma wallabies (*Macropus parma*) associated with probable herpesvirus. *Aust. Vet. J.* **52**:294.

Markus, M.B. 1973. Earthworms and coccidian oocysts. *Ann. Trop. Med. Parasit.* **68**:247-248.

Munday, B.L. 1988. Marsupial diseases. In *Australian Wildlife: The John Keep Refresher Course for Veterinarians.* Proc. No. 104:299-365. Postgraduate Foundation in Veterinary Science, University of Sydney, Sydney.

Obendorf, D.L. 1978. Candidiasis in young hand-reared kangaroos. *J. Wildl. Dis.* **16**:135-140.

Obendorf, D.L. 1979. Candidiasis in hand-reared kangaroo joeys. *Vic. Vet. Proc.* **37**:44-45.

Presidente, P.J.A. 1978. Diseases seen in free-ranging marsupials and those held in captivity. In *Fauna Part B. Course for Veterinarians. Proceedings* No. 36: 457-471. Post-graduate Foundation in Veterinary Science, University of Sydney, Sydney.

Ruiz, A., and Frenkel, J.K. 1980. Intermediate and transport hosts of *Toxoplasma gondii* in Costa Rica. *Am. J. Trop. Med. Hyg.* **29**:1161-1166.

Schmidt, G.D. and Edmonds, S.J. 1989. *Australiformis semoni* (Linstow, 1898) n. gen., n. comb. (Acanthocephala, Moniliformidae) from marsupials of Australia and New Guinea. *J. Parisitol.* 75: 215-217.

Seebeck, J.H. 1979. Status of the barred bandicoot, *Perameles gunnii* in Victoria, with a note on husbandry of a captive colony. *Aust. Wildl. Res.* 6:255-264.

Speare, R. 1988. Clinical assessment, diseases and management of the orphaned macropod joey. In *Australian Wildlife: The John Keep Refresher Course for Veterinarians.* Proceedings No. 104:211-296. Post-graduate Foundation in Veterinary Science, University of Sydney, Sydney.

Tedman, R.A. In press. Some observations on the visceral anatomy of the bandicoot *Isoodon macrourus* (Marsupialia: Peramelidae). In *Bandicoots and Bilbies,* eds J.H. Seebeck, P.R. Brown, R.L. Walllis, and C.M. Kemper. Surrey Beatty and Sons: Sydney.

# Applications of Conservation Genetics to the Eastern Barred Bandicoot, *Perameles gunnii*


*Nicholas A. Robinson, William B. Sherwin, Neil D. Murray, and Jennifer A.M. Graves[1]*



## Abstract

Conservation genetics deals with the genetic problems of populations that are forced to a low effective population size ($N_e$). Effective size is usually much lower than census size, since it depends, essentially, on the number of parents making approximately equal contributions to subsequent generations. Even with high census size, a low effective size can increase both short-term and long-term chances of extinction, because of inbreeding and loss of genetic variation. Determination of effective size is best achieved by coordination of ecological and genetic studies.

To determine the effective population size of the eastern barred bandicoot, *Perameles gunnii* at Hamilton, Victoria, we re-examine a number of studies. The results ($N_e$=31-135) suggest that the population may face a 50% or more loss of variation in 22 years and a corresponding increase in inbreeding unless management keeps the variation between reproductive output of individual females very low. Other important requirements are a fast, sustained recovery, and prevention of subdivision between subpopulations. The present rate of replacement appears to be far below two weaned offspring from each parent.

Monitoring of genetic variation using protein data have shown no variation within the Hamilton population of bandicoots; however, no variation was detected in the more secure Tasmanian population either. Current studies of DNA variants may determine whether the Hamilton isolate is losing variation.

If the captive colony at Gellibrand Hill Park is managed appropriately in the early generations, it should become large enough to have few genetic or demographic problems. If the mean and variance of lifetime reproductive output of individual parents are the same at Gellibrand as at Hamilton, models demonstrate the necessity to transfer a large number of individuals (64 per generation of 13.4 months) simply to maintain the numbers, and only one half of the current (Hamilton) genetic variation will be represented at Gellibrand Hill after 30 generations. Mean and variance of reproductive output at Gellibrand Hill should improve through management of predators, etc., and equalization of founder representation in early generations. The latter task requires pedigrees, which can be constructed using DNA data. If reproductive parameters are improved, optimal retention of heterozygosity may be achieved with much lower levels of transfer (as few as twelve per generation in the most optimistic model).


## Introduction

If a population is forced to a small size through various factors (*e.g.* habitat destruction) it becomes susceptible to further endangerment through chance, or stochastic, factors such as fires, demographic collapse (Goodman in Soulé and Wilcox 1980), and genetic problems (Frankel 1970; Berry 1971; Tyndale-Biscoe and Calaby 1975; Franklin 1980, Frankel and Soulé 1981; Lande and Barrowclough 1987). However, it should be noted that in terms of their effects on the survival of individuals and populations, many genetic effects do not give the appearance of chance. Suppose, for example, that during a given period there is a 5% chance that a certain population will be subjected to fire, there will quite likely be no fire. However, if there is a 5% chance that each genetic locus (gene) will experience some change such as inbreeding, then approximately 5,000 of the 100,000 or so genes *will* be affected by this change. The exact effect on mortality,


[1]Department of Genetics and Human Variation, La Trobe University, Bundoora, Victoria 3083, Australia.

fertility, etc., will depend on which genes were among the 5% affected, but, unlike the case of the fires, it would be quite incorrect for a manager to hope that no genetic change will occur.

Possible genetic problems of small populations include increased homozygosity of individuals caused by inbreeding, loss of allelic variation caused by random genetic drift, and subdivision, which can intensify these problems. These factors can feed back to produce continuing reductions of census size, in some cases without additional external threats (Fig. 1). Increased homozygosity of individuals can lead to inbreeding depression, with effects such as lowered fertility or viability (Ralls *et al.* 1979; Ralls and Ballou 1982, 1983). Decreased allelic variation can lower the chance that a population will contain individuals which can survive a novel selective force. For example, the vulnerability of the highly genetically uniform cheetah (*Acinonyx jubatus*) to infectious disease has been highlighted by O'Brien *et al.* (1985). Another example of the importance of genetic variation within or between individuals is the reduced reproductive performance of individuals that are homozygous, or share alleles with potential mates, at particular loci. Examples of such loci are the incompatibility loci of plants, and MHC loci of vertebrates. MHC homozygosity has been found to have a major deleterious influence on successful mating and reproduction in mice, cattle, pigs, horses and chickens (Briles and Allen 1961; Warner 1986; Warner *et al.* 1987). Therefore, genetic changes in small populations can have important and harmful effects on demographic parameters.

For genetic purposes, population size is defined in terms of effective size ($N_e$), which has a major effect on both rate of inbreeding and maintenance of genetic variation. Effective population size is, broadly speaking, the number of individuals that make approximately equal contributions to the next generation. This figure is often much less than the census size, because some individuals make small (or zero) contributions compared to other parents.

There have been attempts to specify effective sizes that are adequate to avoid inbreeding and loss of genetic variation. Franklin (1980) suggested that $N_e > 50$ would suffice to prevent problems caused by inbreeding, while Falconer (1960) and Franklin (1980) estimated that $N_e$ should be greater than 500 to avoid loss of variation; for an effective size of 500, census will usually have to be several times larger, so it is advisable to calculate the effective size of each managed or threatened population well before they become critically endangered.

There is disagreement over the exact effective sizes necessary to avoid inbreeding and loss of variation; also, there are good reasons to believe that the same figures would not be applicable to all species (Sherwin and Murray in press). Work on wild populations is required to determine the range of effective sizes that are suitable for conservation and to document the effects of loss of variation or inbreeding. This involves first determining the effective size of particular populations, and then determining whether or not they are losing variation at the predicted rate.

*Determination of Effective Size*

Measurement of the effective number of parents making approximately equal genetic contributions to following generations requires data that are often regarded as the province of the ecologist: density, dispersal, demography, and social systems (Crow and Kimura 1970; Emigh and Pollak 1979; Frankel and Soulé 1981; Lande and Barrowclough 1987). Table 1 lists ways in which genetic, ecological, and other studies of endangered populations can interact productively. For measurement of effective size, the ideal information will include items a, b, c, g, and h in Table 1. If these detailed data cannot be obtained, a less accurate estimate of effective size can be made

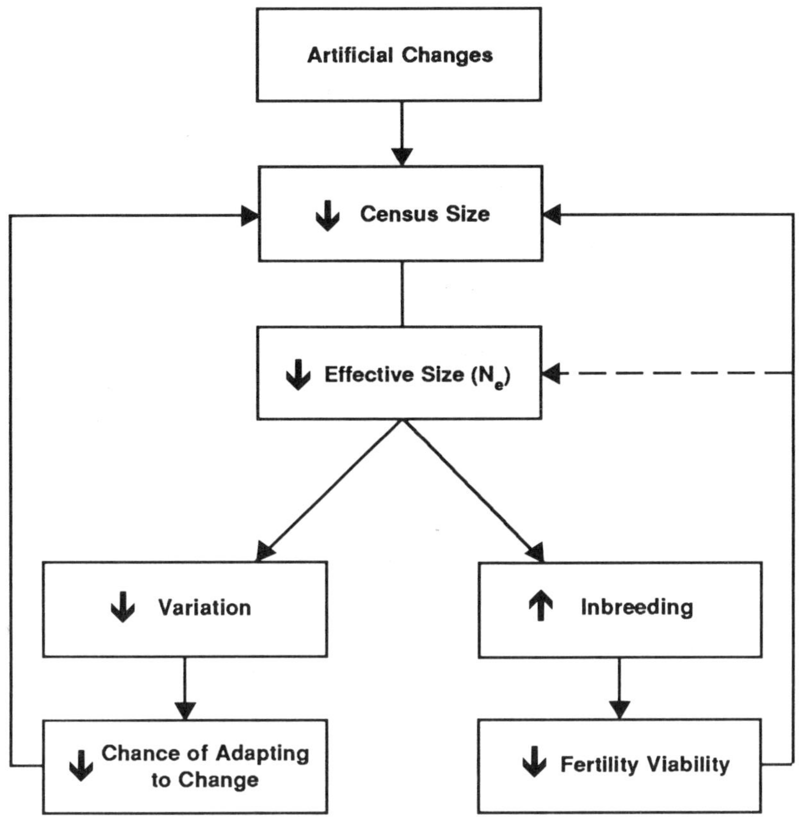


*Figure 1.*—Summary of conservation genetics. Artificial changes which reduce the size of a wild population can trigger one or both of the negative feedback loops shown, which may lead to a continued reduction of census size, even if the initial changes progress no further.

from a knowledge of the census size, sex ratio and the variation between individuals' life histories, *e.g.* variation in lifespan and lifetime reproductive output (Sherwin *et al.* in press a). Whichever method is used to determine effective size, some factors, such as dispersal, and lifetime reproductive output of males, can be more easily measured by genetic analyses than by conventional ecological means (Sherwin and Murray in press).

Using data collected between 1983 and 1985, Sherwin and Brown (in press) calculated the effective population size of the Hamilton population of the eastern barred bandicoot (*P. gunnii*).

Steps in the calculation can be summarised as follows:

| | | |
|---|---|---|
| Census size | | 633±24 |
| Number of new weanlings per generation: | male | 153 |
| | female | 340 |
| Corrected for variation between the lifetime reproductive outputs of individuals: | male | 24 |
| | female | 54 |
| Effective size | | 67 |

*Table 1.*—Data sources and uses for endangered populations. The table is divided along traditional lines of ecological and genetic considerations ($N_e$ = effective population size).

| | Ecological Data | Genetic Sources | Ecological Sources | Genetic Uses | Uses |
|---|---|---|---|---|---|
| a. | Total area inhabited | + | - | Census size | $N_e$ |
| b. | Density, and its fluctuations over generations | + | - | | |
| c. | Lifetime dispersal (Mean Square) | Radio-tracking, tagging | From allele frequencies | Chance of recolonisation | $N_e$, chance of replacement information |
| d. | Generation length (average age of breeding individuals) | Long-term studies, age indices | Not yet possible | Demographic analysis | $N_e$, monitoring inbreeding depression |
| e. | Mean and variance of lifetime reproductive output for each sex | Long-term studies, age indices | Fingerprint, Y-linked and mitochondrial DNA analysis | | |
| f. | Sex ratio | + | Chromosomal study, and c | | |
| g. | Life table (age-specific birth and death rates for both sexes) | A superior alternative to d, e, and f, when extensive coordinated studies are possible | | | |
| h. | Social systems | Direct observation | Fingerprint Y-linked, + mitochondrial DNA analysis | Demographic analysis, captive breeding | $N_e$ |
| i. | Morphometrics | | | | |
| | - unilateral | + | + | Taxonomy | Taxonomy, quantitative genetic variation |
| | - partial family (*e.g.* mother & offspring) | Not usually included in ecological studies, but could easily be done | + | - | |
| | - bilateral (*e.g.* left and right pes length) | | + | Asymmetry (indicator of genetic problems or environmental stress) | |
| j. | DNA and protein variants | Collection of appropriately preserved tissue | + | Taxonomy and see c,e, f,g,h above | Taxonomy, monitoring variation, and see above |

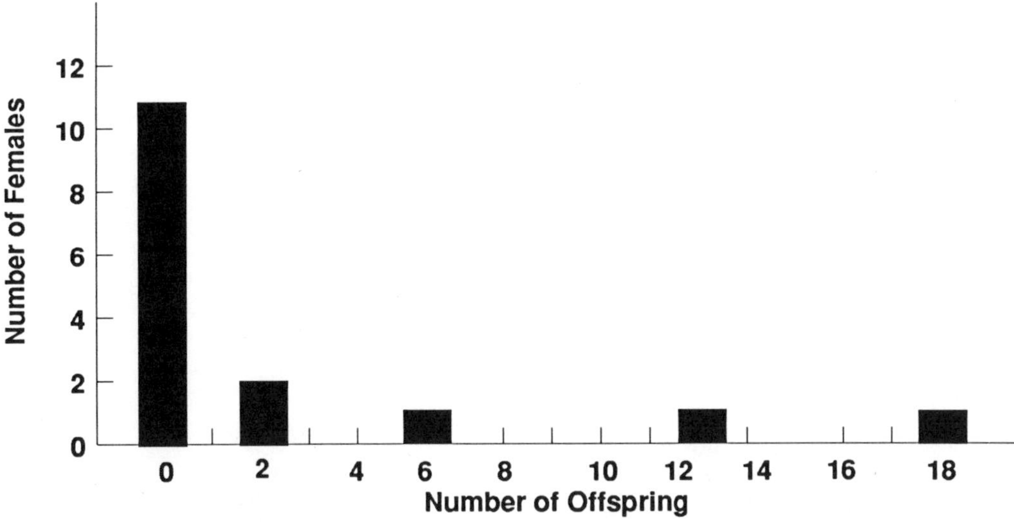



*Figure 2.*—Lifetime production of pouch young by individual female eastern barred bandicoots at Hamilton, Victoria. From Sherwin and Murray (in press).

The effective size was estimated to be 67 (approximately one-tenth of the census size), identifying this as a population which is at risk of losing genetic variation or encountering inbreeding problems. Specific management recommendations resulted from this study; the most important factor depressing effective size below census size is that individual mothers show very high variation in both their production of pouch young (Fig. 2), and the survival of their young to an independent stage. Management that reduces disturbance or predation of young may decrease the variance of reproductive output, and thus increase effective size, even though habitat limitations will restrict census size for some time.

However, Sherwin and Brown (in press) identified a number of areas where more information was needed, especially the census size of the population, its fluctuations between generations, and the variance of male reproductive output. In a small population, such as Hamilton, variation in mitochondrial, Y-linked, and 'fingerprint' regions of DNA, which are used to identify genetically related individuals in humans and other species (Jeffreys *et al.* 1985; Lynch 1988; Burke 1989), may be used to identify the offspring from particular males (and females), to assess their lifetime reproductive output, and its variance between individuals. We have already commenced these studies to assist management of a captive colony of bandicoots (below), and we may be able to use the techniques to improve our estimate of the effective size at Hamilton.

Subsequent studies (Dufty 1988; Minta *et al.*, this volume) have provided data on variation in numbers of litters or pouch young at a given time. These data are comparable to the corresponding parts of the data used by Sherwin and Brown (in press), but lack the long-term or age-specific information necessary to determine mean lifetime reproductive output of females, or its variance, unless many assumptions are made. The one phenomenon which drastically increased the variance of lifetime reproductive output (and therefore depressed $N_e$ considerably) was the number of females who produced no young in their lifetime, whether because of premature death, sterility, or other reasons (Fig. 2). The frequency of such females was 0.69 (n = 16 females followed for their whole apparent lifespan). The frequency of females with no pouch young in the Minta *et al.* study of three areas (Chatsworth Road, Hamilton Tip, Grange Street) was 0.47 (n=36). Presumably some of these females bred before or after this short study, which would lower this figure, but on the other hand, the data give no indication of the number of females who may have had zero reproduction because of premature death, so it is difficult to use this information to adjust the variance of lifetime reproductive output.

Although the variance cannot be checked, the mean of lifetime reproductive output can be estimated from data or changes in census size. Brown (1989) gave a maximum estimate of the census size as 633 individuals, in the period 1983-1985. Dufty estimated the 1988 census size to be 230, with an upper 95% confidence limit of 330, indicating a 50% decline in the population if the two maxima can be compared. Sherwin and Brown (in press) estimated that the mean reproductive output of individuals (k) was 0.43, well below the two offspring per parent that is necessary for a stable population size, although they expressed some doubt as to the accuracy of their estimate. This figure can be recalculated using the known rate of decline (50%) in the 4 years between midpoints of Brown's and Dufty's studies. Four years is approximately 3.6 generations of 13.4 months, where a generation is defined as the average time from conception to fertilisation (all fertilisations averaged, not simply the first fertilisation; Sherwin and Brown in press). This decline suggests a mean reproductive rate of k=0.82, which is higher than the previous estimate, but still well below two.

Sex ratio also affects effective size. The ratio in weanlings (0.45 males to 1 female in Sherwin and Brown's calculations) was found to be 0.53:1 (n=29) by Minta *et al.* (this volume) and 1.1:1 by Dufty (1988). The difference may be partly due to seasonal differences in weight since the weanling category is defined by weight, and the sex ratio changes with age.

We are now in a position to calculate the 1988 effective size of the Hamilton population, using these modifications to the data. Two calculations are carried out—one pessimistic and one optimistic. The values assumed, and the minimum and maximum estimates of $N_e$ are shown below:

|  | Pessimistic | Optimistic |
| --- | --- | --- |
| Census size | 230 | 330 |
| Sex ratio (Weanling) | 0.45:1 | 1:1 |
| Mean reproductive output (k) | 0.43 | 0.82 |
| Male V/k | 11.6 | 2 |
| Female V/k | 11.6 | 5.8 |
| Effective size estimate | 31.2 | 134.5 |

V/k is the ratio of the variance of lifetime reproductive output (V) to its mean (k). Since no values for V in males are available, the pessimistic calculation assumes V/k is the same in both sexes (as did Sherwin and Brown in press). The optimistic approach assumes that V/k in females is only half the value that has been estimated, while V/k in males is extraordinarily low (2); a value of unity would require that each weanling male made an approximately equal contribution to the next generation, which is most unlikely.

Although there is a large difference between the two $N_e$ estimates, both suggest that the population is currently losing variation (Franklin 1980; Lande and Barrowclough 1987). Genetic problems may be worsened by subdivision of the population, if there is no exchange between the Chatsworth Road population and the other areas. Dufty (1988) estimated that 27.3% of the population is at Chatsworth Road, while the data of Minta *et al.* (this volume) suggest a figure of 24.5%. If there is complete genetic isolation of Chatsworth Road from other areas, the effective size estimates must be revised, giving minimum values of 7.8 and 23.4 for the two subpopulations (Chatsworth Road *vs.* other sites), or maxima of 33.6 and 100.1. These figures suggest that one or both of the subpopulations may be becoming inbred at a rate which is expected to significantly affect reproduction, survival, etc. (Franklin 1980). The effects of inbreeding on these parameters have been documented in a number of species (Ralls *et al.* 1988; Warner *et al.* 1987).

Many of the uncertainties in the calculation of $N_e$ could be cleared up by the use of data collected in the course of other ecological and genetic work, if the studies are appropriately designed (Table 1). The methods shown for each factor are often complementary; for example, genetic methods of estimating dispersal between subpopulations are sensitive to much lower levels of exchange than ecological methods.

*Models of Genetic Change at Hamilton*

How the low effective size will influence the rates of inbreeding and loss of variation by genetic drift will depend upon the future trends in the factors affecting it (Table 1, a-h). Note that we cannot assume that any of the listed factors will remain constant, since inbreeding can adversely affect sex ratio (Senner 1980), reproductive performance, and mortality (Ralls *et al.* 1988; Warner *et al.* 1987).

To estimate possible loss of genetic variation (expressed as average heterozygosity), we ran three series of models, using population projections shown in Figure 3. In the first case, we assumed that the population's decline in numbers would be arrested at its present level (e). The second scenario assumes that the population will be returned to its 1983-1985 level relatively quickly, after which it will remain stable (b). A final possibility is that the recent decline is part of a cyclic pattern, which will be repeated indefinitely, so that after recovery, the present situation will return regularly (d). Table 2 shows projections of genetic loss over the next 20 generations (22 years), using various values for the sex ratio and the variation of lifetime reproductive output (measured by V/k, as above). The value of k, mean reproductive output, changes as the population cycles, crashes, or recovers, but its major influence on $N_e$ at any generation is through the value of V/k, which is tabulated.

The results in Table 2 show a wide range of genetic loss, from very moderate to very severe, depending on the conditions modelled. In planning management and further research, it is useful to note the factors which did or did not have a major effect on loss of genetic variation. First, the loss of genetic variation is not greatly affected by a twofold difference in sex ratio (the maximum discrepancy between various studies). However, the variation of reproductive output is more significant: a twofold change in V/k has a marked effect (over twice as much genetic variation is lost in some cases), confirming the suggestion of Sherwin and Brown (in press) that management should aim to minimise the variation between individuals' reproductive outputs. The importance of V/k also emphasizes the need for more data on the variation of lifetime reproductive contributions of individuals (Table 1).

In Table 1, detailed results are not presented for Model a—all genetic variation is lost at extinction. Fast recovery (Model b) is the most optimistic scenario; Model c, slow recovery, is perhaps more realistic, but results in genetic losses which are almost as great as in model d, fluctuations. Fluctuations, although they may be a natural feature of the biology of the species, are extremely dangerous to a small population that has no contact with other populations to replace lost variation. Indeed, genetic losses under Models c and d are not a great deal better than Model e—no recovery, which gives severe loss of variations for all but the most favourable (and unrealistic) combinations of the other variables. Therefore, an increase of census size is necessary, and future fluctuations should be damped by management intervention, if possible.

Subdivision of the population would markedly increase loss of variation, especially at Chatsworth Road. It may be necessary to consider artificial migration in the short term, and corridors of habitat in the long term, to correct inhabited areas. These factors should also be considered in the establishment of new areas of habitat. Varvio *et al.* (1986) discuss subdivision in conservation

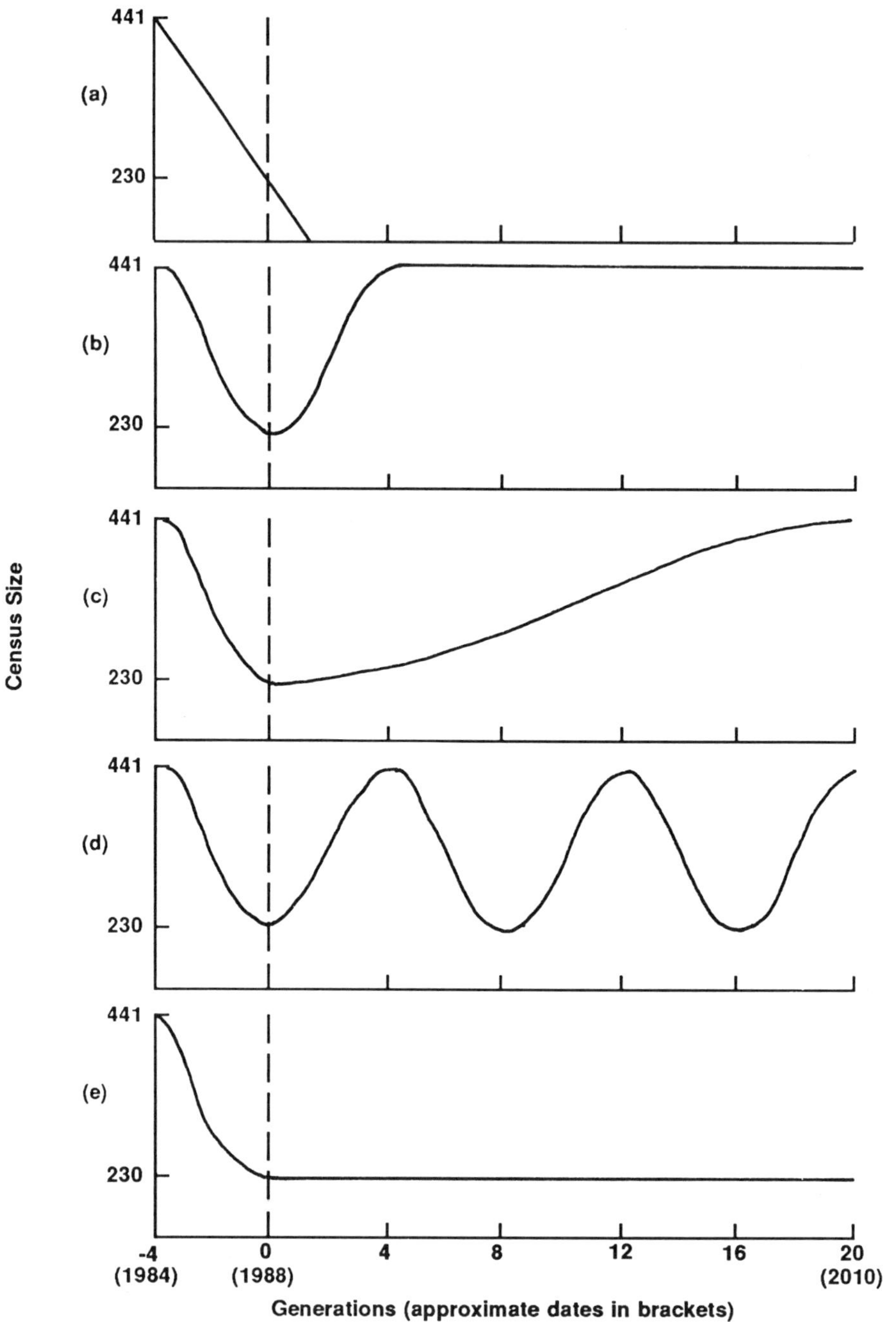


*Figure 3.*—Models of trends in the census size of eastern barred bandicoots at Hamilton. The maximum (1983-1985) census size is corrected from 633 to 441, using Dufty's (1988) estimate of the relative size of the expectation (230) and upper 95% confidence limit (330) of census size.

116

genetics, and conclude that its effects can be minimised with quite small rates of gene flow.

The measure of variation considered, average heterozygosity, does not cover all aspects of genetic variation. Rare alleles, which may be important in such things as disease resistance, will be lost much faster. Additive genetic variance (Table 1, i), which includes the genetic component of many important characteristics such as temperature tolerance and weight and size, is likely to be lost at the same rate as heterozygosity.

It should be emphasised that the simulations are all based on very optimistic assumptions in one important sense: they do not include any effect of inbreeding on survival or reproductive characteristics. Inbreeding is expected to increase at the same rate that average heterozygosity is lost. In the cases where more substantial rates of inbreeding occur, inbreeding depression may well be seen as decreased fertility or viability. This, in turn, would alter V/k and k, causing more severe demographic and genetic problems. For example, Ralls *et al.* (1988), in a study of 38 species of mammals found that mortality was 33% higher, on average, for progeny of parent-offspring or full-sibling matings, than for progeny of unrelated parents. From Table 2, the relatively optimistic demographic circumstances that produce a decline in heterozygosity of 32.7% (c (iii), 1:1, v/k=5.8) produce a population inbreeding coefficient (Falconer 1960) of 0.327. If the average value estimated by Ralls *et al.* (1988) for the effect of inbreeding on juvenile survival applies to the eastern barred bandicoot, this amount of inbreeding would correspond to a juvenile survival rate of only 47% of the existing one.

*Monitoring Genetic Variation at Hamilton*

We have already stated that there are reasons to believe that measuring effective size is not a perfect way of predicting loss of genetic variation—if possible, it is best to monitor this loss. In fact, the distribution of *P. gunnii* allows us to test one of the assertions of conservation genet-ics—that small isolates lose heterozygosity at a rate determined only by genetic drift (Franklin 1980). While the Tasmanian population of this species has remained relatively dense and widespread, the Hamilton population was cut off from other Victorian populations some time between 1937 and 1960. According to conservation genetics theories, which ignore factors other than drift and mutation, the Hamilton population should be losing heterozygosity. Using their estimate of the effective size of the population, Sherwin and Brown (in press) calculated that 15 to 28% of average heterozygosity should have been lost in the Hamilton population. If levels of genetic variation within the Victorian and Tasmanian populations were similar early this century, then there should now be a detectable difference of heterozygosity between them, if the theory advanced above is correct.

A study of 27 loci that code for blood proteins revealed no genetic variation within the Hamilton population (Sherwin *et al.* in press b). However, analysis of samples from two Tasmanian populations (Mole Creek and Huonville) showed no detectable genetic variation either within or between the three populations (two Tasmanian and one Victorian). Therefore, the lack of variation at Hamilton is not due to the decline in numbers this century. In fact, the species may have survived since the last separation of Victoria and Tasmania (c. 10,000 years B.P.), without detectable variation at these 27 loci. This result shows that detection of low levels of variation in endangered populations must be interpreted very cautiously, unless a satisfactory control population has been studied. Also, before reliable conclusions about levels of heterozygosity can be drawn, more than 27 loci must be analysed. We are currently repeating this study using DNA techniques, which allow analysis of many more genes from a small blood sample; also, genes that are more variable can be studied, which eases the statistical problems associated with this work (Archie 1985). The use of DNA techniques will also allow more detailed analysis of reproductive output for $N_e$ studies (Table 1, e).

*Table 2.*—Loss of average heterozygosity by the year 2010 with different models of population decline and recovery. The five basic models (a-e) correspond to those shown in Figure 2. The loss of average heterozygosity is calculated in two ways: for the whole population as a single unit, and as two isolated subpopulations, Chatsworth Road and the other areas, called the 'Major Subpopulation' here. The maximum and minimum population sizes are the same in all cases.

| Sex Ratio m:f | V/k (both sexes) | Change in average heterozygosity (%) | | |
| --- | --- | --- | --- | --- |
| | | Whole Population | Major Subpopulation | Chatsworth Road |
| **(a) Fast decline continues** | | | | |
| - | - | 100% | - | - |
| **(b) Single decline, fast recovery** | | | | |
| 1:2 | 11.6 | -47.2 | -57.7 | -93.9 |
| 1:1 | 11.6 | -43.2 | -53.3 | -91.3 |
| 1:1 | 5.8 | -24.2 | -31.1 | -68.8 |
| 1:2 | 2 | -9.7 | -12.8 | -34.6 |
| 1:2 | 1 | -4.6 | -6.1 | -17.7 |
| 1:1 | 1 | -4.1 | -5.4 | -15.7 |
| **(c) Single decline, slow recovery** | | | | |
| 1:2 | 11.6 | -60.6 | -71.7 | -98.6 |
| 1:1 | 11.6 | -55.2 | -67.1 | -97.5 |
| 1:1 | 5.8 | -32.7 | -41.3 | -81.7 |
| 1:2 | 2 | -12.7 | -16.8 | -44.0 |
| 1:2 | 1 | -5.4 | -7.2 | -20.8 |
| 1:1 | 1 | -4.8 | -6.4 | -18.5 |
| **(d) Regular fluctuations** | | | | |
| 1:2 | 11.6 | -60.1 | -71.2 | -98.5 |
| 1:1 | 11.6 | -55.6 | -66.6 | -97.3 |
| 1:1 | 5.8 | -32.4 | -40.9 | -81.3 |
| 1:2 | 2 | -12.7 | -16.6 | -43.6 |
| 1:2 | 1 | -5.4 | -7.2 | -20.8 |
| 1:1 | 1 | -4.8 | -6.4 | -18.5 |
| **(e) Single decline** | | | | |
| 1:2 | 11.6 | -75.4 | -85.3 | -99.9 |
| 1:1 | 11.6 | -71.0 | -81.4 | -99.7 |
| 1:1 | 5.8 | -44.2 | -54.6 | -92.2 |
| 1:2 | 2 | -17.2 | -22.4 | -55.7 |
| 1:2 | 1 | -6.3 | -8.4 | -24.5 |
| 1:1 | 1 | -5.6 | -7.5 | -21.7 |

When considering the apparently low heterozygosity of eastern barred bandicoots, or some other species, it is often tempting to point to relict populations, such as the western barred bandicoot (*Perameles bougainville*) on Bernier and Dorre Islands, Western Australia, which have been isolated for extremely long periods. The gene pool of such a population has presumably been altered by prolonged mild inbreeding and loss of variation, and the population has adapted to this situation. Before we assume that the recent Hamilton isolate of *P. gunnii* is likely to adapt in the same way, it is worth considering that there are other islands within the former range of barred bandicoots. The absence of the bandicoots from these islands (and parallels in other species) suggests that adaptation to isolation and small population size is uncommon or precarious. Such populations are likely to have low genetic variation, and therefore a poor chance of surviving an event such as the arrival of a new disease.

*Captive Populations*

Whether captive populations will contribute significantly to the conservation of a species will depend greatly on the care with which they are managed to avoid genetic problems, particularly inbreeding, unequal genetic representation of founders, artificial selection, and crossing of distantly related taxa (Frankel and Soulé 1981). Although population sizes must be very small, the opportunities to manipulate the breeding structure enable managers to maintain equal founder representation, and either to reduce inbreeding itself (Senner 1980; Foose *et al.* 1986) or to reduce the inbreeding depression of inbred lines (Templeton and Read 1983). As a general rule, artificial selection should be avoided in captive populations, but they should be subjected to one form of selection: the removal of individuals known to carry deleterious genes (Frankham *et al.* 1986). Depending upon the objectives, some other selection may be appropriate. Frankham *et al.* (1986) discussed appropriate management for four categories of captive populations with different objectives: (1) common species for display,

(2) endangered species for long-term conservation, (3) rare species being multiplied for immediate release back into the wild, or (4) rare species not yet capable of self-sustaining reproduction in captivity. Populations in category 4 may require selection for captive breeding success until they attain self-sustaining status, after which they should be managed as under category 2 (minimal selection). Populations of category 1 can obviously be selected for adaptation to captive breeding, ease of handling, and for classic species phenotype. In the management of category 3 populations there is more emphasis on the maintenance of variation through rapid expansion of the population rather than through equalization of contributions by different founders.

The Gellibrand Hill Park (GHP) colony of eastern barred bandicoots is being established with the aim of producing a backup population for the Hamilton colony. This population, in a semi-wild state, can potentially be large enough to avoid severe problems of inbreeding, loss of genetic variation, or demographic stochasticity. The reasonably natural habitat will avoid many of the problems associated with unintentional artificial selection in captivity. In short, the colony will be a model for captive propagation if it succeeds. However, success will not be achieved if there is considerable loss of variation or inbreeding in the founding or early generations. Steps must be taken to avoid flooding the colony with genes from one or a few founders (see, for example, the range of reproductive outputs in Fig. 2). From the preceding sections, it is clear that genetic problems will be substantial if family sizes are not equalised.

Brown and Seebeck (1989) have outlined the management plan for GHP (Fig. 4). Each Hamilton founder contributes to the production of approximately two litters while in pens at GHP, before relocation to Hamilton. The weanlings produced are released into GHP while reproductively immature, to reduce inbreeding amongst closely related individuals, and new founders from Hamilton are released into the pens to continue the process. The colony located at the

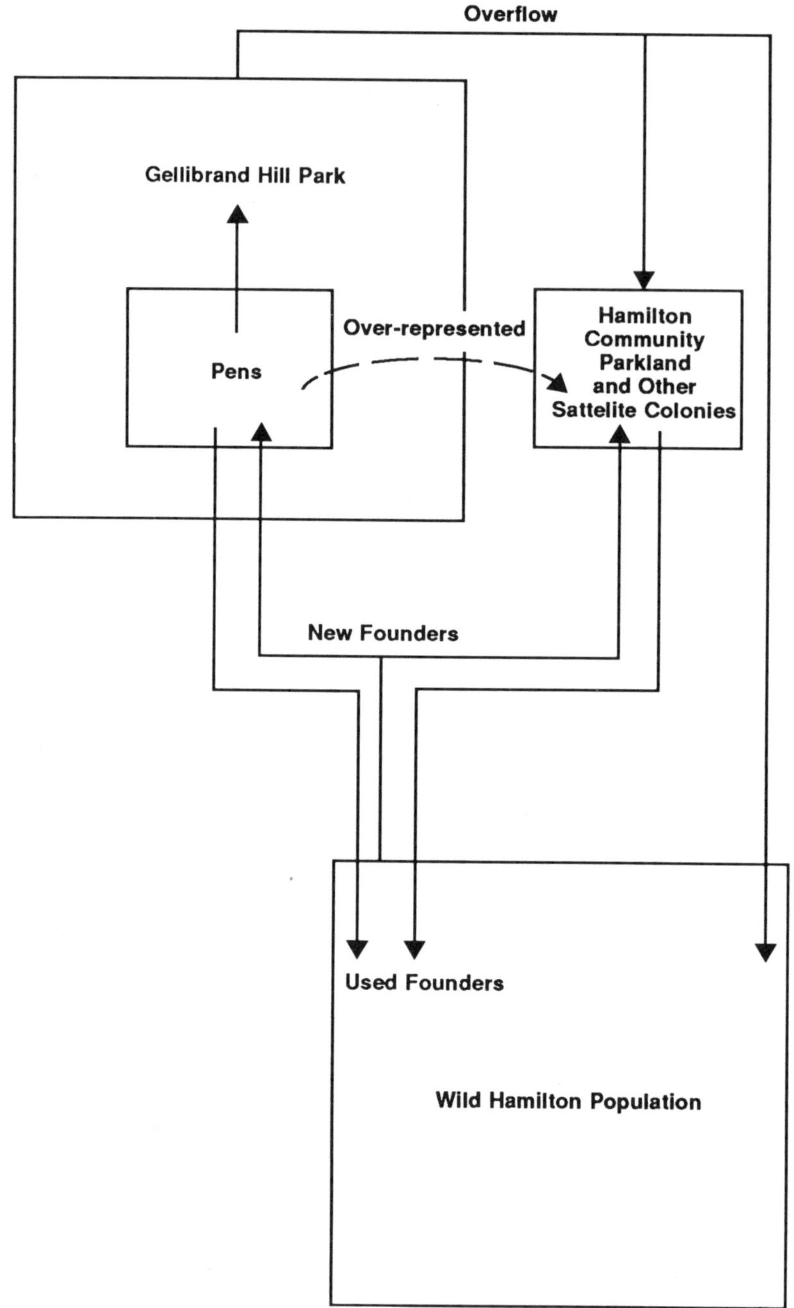



*Figure 4.*—Planned movements of eastern barred bandicoots among the wild Hamilton population, Gellibrand Hill Park and satellite colonies.   Arrows indicate the flow of animals.

Hamilton Community Parklands (HCP) (Seebeck, this volume) and other satellite colonies will have a lower carrying capacity, and be less intensively managed (Maguire *et. al.*, this volume). Genetically, the aim for the colony at GHP is to maximise effective population size ($N_e$) in order to minimize inbreeding depression. This aim can be achieved in the colony by (1) maintaining a ratio of males to females of 1:1 (i.e. transfer excess males and females to other colonies or introduce more individuals to the colony to make up the difference); (2) maximizing the number of unrelated Hamilton individuals contributing offspring to the colony; (3) minimizing variance in family size, especially in the early generations. Ideally, each founder should contribute 5-6 breeding-age offspring in the colony before being returned to Hamilton. Protection from predators and the provision of adequate resources may help to equalize genetic contributions in the second and subsequent generations, but the effectiveness of these strategies will not be known without pedigrees. Also, if accurate pedigree information is available, family size can be equalised by moving offspring to other populations.

In pens, pedigrees can be relatively easily constructed, but outside the pens, genetic data is necessary to establish familial relationships in the early generations. DNA fragments, called probes, that detect multiple patterns of bands when bound to eastern barred bandicoot DNA, can be derived either from eastern barred bandicoots or any other species. In some species (*e.g.* humans) the probes available detect a pattern of bands which are essentially unique for any particular individual, and are therefore known as 'DNA fingerprints' (Jeffreys *et al.* 1985). DNA fingerprints are a useful means of identifying individuals, and, because every fingerprint band is derived from at least one parent, it is possible to determine parentage and estimate degrees of relatedness (first cousins, second cousins, etc.) by determining the degree of similarity between banding patterns (Wetton *et al.* 1987; Lynch 1988). Mitochondrial and Y-linked DNA variants are also useful here (Table 1). We have already found variants for 'fingerprint' patterns in bandicoots (Fig. 5), and

we will examine the inheritance of these patterns, to determine systems that are useful for constructing pedigrees.

We therefore have the potential to assist management decisions at two levels. At the broader level, we can model the retention of genetic variation and the build-up of inbreeding, with different inputs of founders. The aim is to maximise the transfer of genetic information from Hamilton to GHP, while minimising the interference to the Hamilton population. At a more detailed level, we can construct pedigrees in the semi-wild population, and advise on manipulations of the reproductive output of individual parents to maximise the effective size in the early generations. Finally, we will be able to monitor the success of genetic management by the analysis of autosomal DNA variants.

We have written a deterministic computer program which models various management regimes and demographic parameters and predicts the change in average heterozygosity and inbreeding coefficient in the GHP colony. The computer program is designed to accept the following information about wild and captive populations, allowing the calculation of effective population size ($N_e$) every generation:

Demographic Input
- Hamilton census size (held constant at 300 in all cases below, although this may be unduly optimistic)
- mean production of (K), and variance in the production of (V) reproductively mature offspring, at Hamilton and GHP
- sex ratio
- carrying capacity at release site
- average reproductive life

Management Regime Details
- number of animals/pen (assumed to be one breeding pair in all cases below—any departure from this creates genetic problems)
- number of pens
- frequency of relocations
- total number of generations for consideration in captivity.

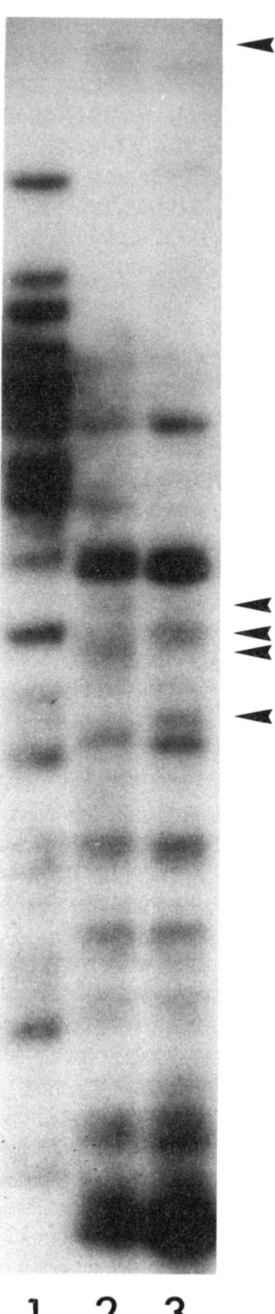



*Figure 5.*—DNA fingerprints of *P. gunnii*. Lane 1 shows a Hamilton individual. Lanes 2 and 3 represent individuals from Mole Creek, Tasmania. Differences in the patterns of animals in the same population (arrowed) allow identification of individuals and their progeny.

The output consists of the inbreeding coefficient (F) and the average amount of heterozygosity (H) that is retained, relative to that found in the Hamilton population at the outset.

Demographic input was based on data for Hamilton *P. gunnii* derived from Sherwin and Brown (in press), and the new estimates described above. For the calculation made here, three scenarios for GHP were considered.

Case A. No improvement in the mean (K) but improvement in the variance (V) of production of reproductively mature offspring,

$$K_{HAMILTON} = 0.85 \qquad K_{GHP} = K_{HCP} = 0.85$$
$$V/K_{HAMILTON} = 11 \qquad V/K_{GHP} = V/K_{HCP} = 5.5$$

Case B. Vast improvement in K, improved V/K,

$$K_{HAMILTON} = 0.85 \qquad K_{GHP} = K_{HCP} = 2$$
$$V/K_{HAMILTON} = 11 \qquad V/K_{GHP} = V/K_{HCP} = 5.5$$

Case C. Lower $K_{HAM}$, slight improvement in K, improved V/K

$$K_{HAMILTON} = 0.42 \qquad K_{GHP} = K_{HCP} = 0.85$$
$$V/K_{HAMILTON} = 11 \qquad V/K_{GHP} = V/K_{HCP} = 5.5$$

Many of the influences affecting the survival of *P. gunnii* in Hamilton may be altered in GHP with appropriate management practices (predator elimination, supplementary food, etc.). Highly successful management practices would result in improved production of reproductively mature offspring in GHP (scenario B). Scenarios C and A represent small and no improvements, respectively, in the production of reproductively mature offspring at GHP.

The output from each scenario is shown in Figures 6 and 7. Consider scenario B in which the average production, and variance in the production of reproductively mature offspring, is improved at GHP relative to Hamilton. The percent of heterozygosity retained in Hamilton is expected to decrease markedly over 30 generations (Fig. 6). Initially, the percentage of heterozygosity at GHP drops below levels retained in Hamilton and in the pens if GHP management uses only two pens (one breeding pair in each) with four

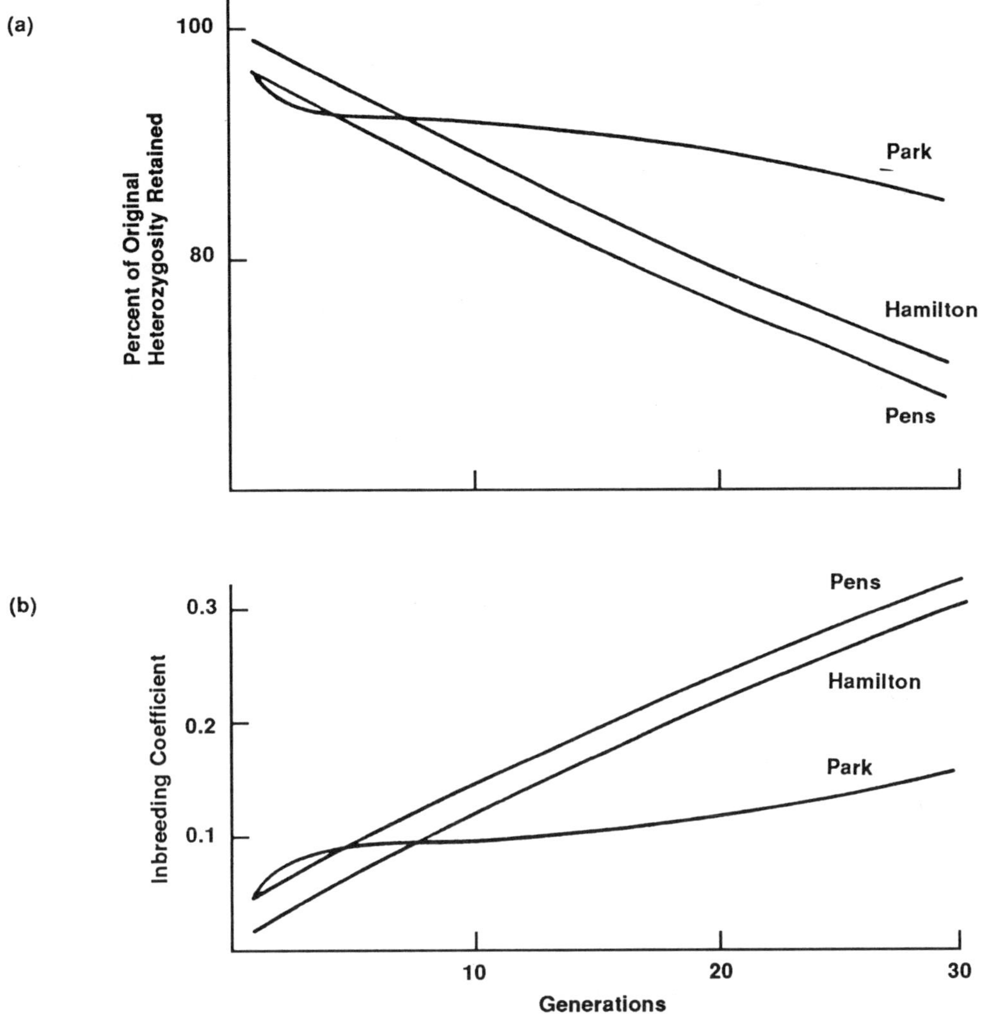


*Figure 6.*—Comparison of genetic changes at Hamilton and Gellibrand Hill Park. Results are shown separately for the pens at GHP and the larger enclosure ('Park'). The percentage of original heterozygosity retained (a) and the inbreeding coefficient (b) are plotted over 30 generations, assuming case B, 2 pens, 4 transfers per generation, and GHP carrying capacity 1,500.

transfers per generation. After five generations of the breeding program, numbers increase in the park, and little park heterozygosity will be lost relative to loss in Hamilton (Fig. 6).

After the carrying capacity of the GHP is reached (assumed to be 1,500 *P. gunnii* for GHP), further release of large numbers of founder offspring (containing relatively low average heterozygosi-

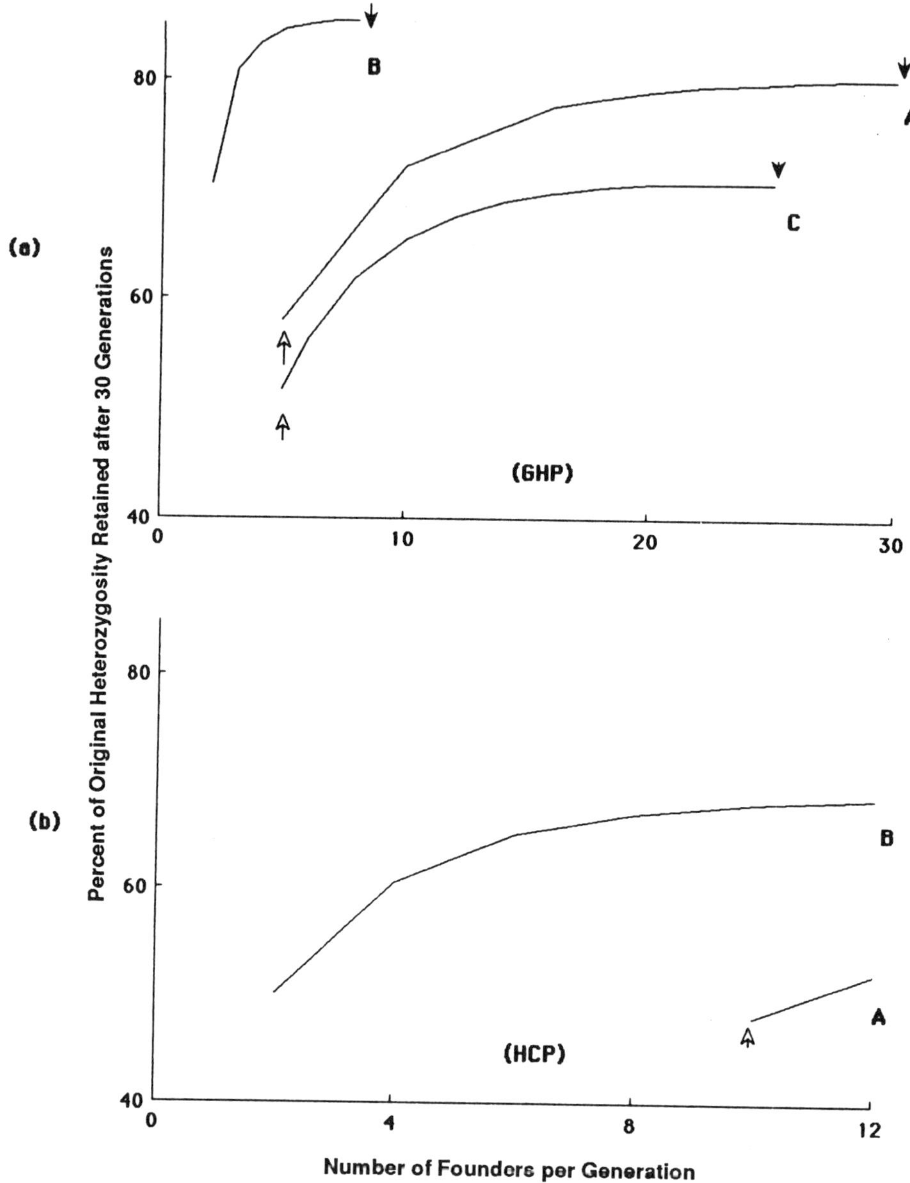



*Figure 7.*—The percentage of original heterozygosity which remains after 30 generations with various numbers of founders per generation for (a) the GHP population, and, (b) the Hamilton Community Parklands population (HCP). Carrying capacities were assumed to be 1,500 (GHP) and 100 (HCP). The open arrows indicate the number of founders required merely to sustain the park population; closed arrows indicate the number of founders required to maximise retention of heterozygosity. Scenario A represents no improvement in the production of reproductively mature offspring, Scenario B represents a large improvement, and Scenario C represents a small improvement.

ties) has a detrimental effect on overall GHP percentage of heterozygosity (Fig. 6). The percentage of heterozygosity at GHP now shows the same rate of decline as in Hamilton (after 30 generations). In reality, this effect is unlikely to be seen, since demographic parameters which result in great loss of heterozygosity from the wild population are likely to lead to its numerical decline to a point where founders cannot be obtained, after ten generations or less.

To maximise long-term retention of genetic variation in GHP, large numbers of pens and frequent transfers from Hamilton to GHP will initially promote the retention of heterozygosity by rapidly bringing GHP up to carrying capacity (maximising $N_e$) (Fig. 7a).

In Table 3, we summarise the minimum number of founders per generation (number of pens x number of transfers) required to maximise heterozygosity and minimise inbreeding, or merely to sustain the numbers of GHP populations. For the most optimistic scenario (case B), few pens (two if one transfer per generation, one if four transfers per generation) are needed to sustain the colonies (Fig. 7a). In this case eight founders per generation could be used to optimise the retention of heterozygosity (Table 3).

If the reproductive success of *P. gunnii* is not improved in GHP but its variance is halved (case A), few pens (>five if one transfer per generation, >two if four transfers per generation) would be required merely to sustain the population. However, many more pens (>28 if one transfer per generation, >eight if four transfers per generation) should be used to optimise the retention of heterozygosity in this case.

If we use values similar to the reproductive output estimates of Sherwin and Brown (in press) ($K_{HAM}=K_{GHP}=0.43$, $V/K_{HAM}=V/K_{GHP}=11$), large numbers of pens (16) and transfers per generation (4) would be needed merely to sustain the GHP population. Even with this many pens and transfers, only 45% of heterozygosity will be retained after 30 generations.

Colonies with low carrying capacity and few breeding pens such as HCP will retain less heterozygosity, even if frequent transfers are made from the surrounding Hamilton population (Fig. 7b). It would be very difficult to make such colonies genetically or demographically self-sufficient. In the case of HCP, a reasonable aim is to provide sufficient transfers to prevent it from losing heterozygosity faster than the general Hamilton population, in the hope that it may be physically reunited with the Hamilton population in the future; in this case, it will constitute an extension of the Hamilton population's area of habitat. For HCP, transfer of four breeding pairs per generation (13.4 months) to each of the two pens gives approximately the same retention of heterozygosity after 30 generations as in the Hamilton population, if scenario B is the case. However, many more transfers will be required (a minimum of five per generation just to sustain the population) if there is no improvement in reproductive success at HCP relative to Hamilton. Clearly, satellite colonies such as HCP will require intensive and continuing demographic support. On the other hand, the continued input of founders to a small population (if achievable) removes the need for careful manipulation of family size each generation. Decisions to establish additional satellites should therefore be made with this in mind.

The retention of rare alleles needs to be considered in future stochastic computer models. For instance, there is only a 45% chance of retaining an allele of frequency 0.01 in a population of $N_e = 200$ over five generations. The impacts of inbreeding depression on demographic parameters need to be known as well. The simulations described here do not include such impacts, so they are unrealistically optimistic. A more complex computer model, incorporating a feedback between inbreeding and demographic variables should therefore be developed. Relevant biological data on inbreeding depression will be available from the GHP colony in cases where relationships of mating individuals are determined by DNA fingerprinting.

*Table 3.*—Management required at GHP to sustain numbers and maximise retention of heterozygosity (minimise inbreeding). Summarised from Figures 7(a) and (b).

| Reproductive output relative to Hamilton | Minimum number of founders per generation | |
|---|---|---|
| | To numerically sustain the GHP population | To maximise retention of heterozygosity at GHP |
| No improvement in K & improvement in V/K | 8 | 28 |
| Vastly improved K & improved V/K | 4 | 8 |
| Pessimistic $K_{HAM}$ estimate with no improvement in K or V/K | 33 | 70 |

Pedigrees for the GHP population are currently being constructed with the aid of DNA fingerprint probes. Other DNA probes will be used to highlight changes in the genetic variation within the GHP colony. Retention of heterozygosity and rare alleles can be monitored by using a panel of DNA probes. Therefore, it will be possible to monitor the outcome of management at GHP and to test computer predictions. Because the success of the colony's management can be monitored in this way, the results of the captive breeding program will hold enormous relevance and importance to the management of this and other endangered populations.

## Conclusions

In 1988, the effective population size of *P. gunnii* at Hamilton appeared to be between 31 and 135. Low effective population size, as well as the apparent division of the population into two isolates, is almost certainly resulting in the loss of some genetic variation. Over 25 generations, this loss could translate into a 53% reduction in juvenile survival, further reducing effective population size and compounding the likelihood of population extinction.

To arrest the loss of genetic variation from Hamilton *P. gunnii*, intensive management is necessary, including the following action.

1. Habitat should be improved and direct eastern barred bandicoot mortality reduced to allow a rapid and steady increase in census size and decrease in the variation of family size, thereby improving effective population size.

2. Habitat corridors should be created and artificial migration carried out (in the short-term) between the two sub-populations at Hamilton.

3. Genetic, ecological and veterinary studies should be coordinated to measure accurately the components of the effective size and the results of inbreeding and loss of variation.

4. Genetic variation should be monitored using DNA technology to test the success of management strategies.

5. Genetic and ecological studies of Tasmanian *P. gunnii* are required to determine their taxonomic and conservation status, and to test the applicability of conservation genetics theories to *P. gunnii*, by comparison of genetic variation in the two states.

At least one intensively-managed colony is essential to reduce the loss of genetic variability from Victorian *P. gunnii*. With intensive management in early generations, large colonies of *P. gunnii* such as GHP could eventually be self-sufficient genetically and demographically, and therefore relatively cheap to manage. They could also act as reservoirs of genetic information which could be used to replenish other populations. However, intensive management at GHP and the creation of additional *P. gunnii* habitat in Victoria would be required to achieve this goal. The Hamilton population's ability to supply founders for such colonies must be assessed very carefully, and the effects monitored (Lacy and Clark, this volume; Maguire *et al.*, this volume). The impact of removals can be minimised if founders are rapidly returned to Hamilton after contributing to the colony.

Maximising the genetic variation of larger colonies (*e.g.* GHP) requires the following action.

1. Founders should be selected from the entire Hamilton range.

2. Many founders should be relocated per generation, to increase numbers in the colonies' initial generations rapidly.

3. Pedigrees should be constructed in the early semi-wild generations, using DNA technology, to help managers avoid the over-representation of founders. Progeny of over-represented founders should be relocated to other colonies or to Hamilton.

4. Numbers of mature males and females should be maintained approximately equally by relocations in early generations.

5. Genetic variation and reproductive parameters should be monitored as a test of management strategies.

The success of GHP depends on the reproductive parameters: mean and variance of lifetime reproductive output. If our most pessimistic estimates for Hamilton are correct, and the management steps outlined for GHP are not successful, very large numbers of relocated individuals will be required per generation simply to maintain numbers, and considerable variation will be lost. If conditions at GHP result in improved reproductive success, then 12 founders per generation would be sufficient for the retention of more than 80% of the original heterozygosity in Hamilton after 30 generations.

Small colonies (*e.g.* HCP) should be managed through continual exchange with a larger population, making them an extension of the larger population. Therefore, less intensive management will be required for such colonies.

The combination of genetic and demographic studies, using both field and computer modelling approaches seems to be essential to the proper management of the eastern barred bandicoot (Clark *et al.*, this volume). We are confident that the management of other small populations will benefit from a similar approach.

## *References*


Archie, J.W. 1985. Statistical analysis of heterozygosity data; independent sample comparisons. *Evolution* **39**:623-637.

Berry, R.J. 1971. Conservation aspects of the genetical constitution of populations. In *The Scientific Management of Animal and Plant Communities for Conservation,* eds E. Duffy and A.S. Watt. *Symp. Brit. Eco. Soc. II.* Pp. 177-206. Blackwell Scientific Publications, Oxford: London.

Briles, W.E., and Allen, C.P. 1961. The B blood group system of chickens. II. The effects of genotype on livability and egg production in seven commercial inbred lines. *Genetics* **46**:1273-1293.

Brown, P.R. 1989. Management Plan for the Conservation of the Eastern Barred Bandicoot, *Perameles gunnii,* in Victoria. National Parks and Wildlife Division, Victoria. *Arthur Rylah Institute for Environmental Research Tech. Rep. Ser.* No. 63. Department of Conservation, Forests and Lands: Melbourne.

Brown, P., and Seebeck, J.H. 1989. Protocol for establishment of a captive breeding colony of *Perameles gunnii* at Gellibrand Hill Park. Appendix 2 in *Management Plan for the Conservation of the Eastern Barred Bandicoot,* Perameles gunnii, *in Victoria.* (P.R. Brown 1989)

Burke, T. 1989. DNA fingerprinting and other methods for the study of mating success. *Trends in Ecol. and Evol.* 4:139-144.

Crow, J.F., and Kimura, M. 1970. *An Introduction to Population Genetics Theory.* Harper and Rowe: New York.

Dufty, A. 1988. The Distribution, Population Abundance, Status, Movement and Activity of the Eastern Barred Bandicoot, *Perameles gunnii,* at Hamilton. B.Sc. (Honours) Thesis. La Trobe University, Bundoora, Victoria.

Emigh, T.H., and Pollak, E. 1979. Fixation probabilities and effective population numbers in diploid populations with overlapping generations. *Theoret. Pop. Biol.* 15:86-107.

Falconer, D.S. 1960. *Introduction to Quantitative Genetics.* Longman: London.

Foose, T.J., Lande, R., Flesness, N.R., Rabb, G., and Read, B. 1986. Propagation plans. *Zoo. Biol.* 5:139-146.

Frankel, O.H. 1970. Variation the essence of life. Sir William Macleay Memorial Lecture. *Proc. Linn. Soc.* 95:158-169.

Frankel, O.H., and Soulé, M.E. 1981. *Conservation and Evolution.* Cambridge University Press: Cambridge.

Frankham, R., Hemmer, H., Ryder, O.A., Cothran, E.G., Soulé, M.E., Murray, N.D., and Snyder, M. 1986. Selection in captive populations. *Zoo. Biol.* 5:127-138.

Franklin, I.R. 1980. Evolutionary change in small populations. In *Conservation Biology,* eds M.E. Soulé and B.A. Wilcox. Pp. 135-150. Sinauer Associates: Sunderland, Mass.

Jeffreys, A.J., Wilson, V., and Thein, S.L. 1985. Individual specific 'fingerprints' of human DNA. *Nature* 316:76-79.

Lande, R., and Barrowclough, G.F. 1987. Effective population size, genetic variation and their use in population management. In *Viable Populations for Conservation,* ed. M.E. Soulé. Pp. 87-124. Cambridge University Press: Cambridge.

Lynch, M. 1988. Estimation of relatedness by DNA fingerprinting. *Mol. Biol. Evol.* 5:584-599.

O'Brien, S.J., Roelke, M.E., Marker, L., Newman, A., Wrinkler, C.A., Meltzer, D., Colly, L., Everman, J.F., Bush, M., and Wildt, D.E. 1985. Genetic basis for species vulnerability in the cheetah. *Science* 227:1428-1434.

Ralls, K., and Ballou, J. 1982. Effects of inbreeding in juvenile mortality in captive primates. *Int. J. Primatology* 3:491-505.

Ralls, K., and Ballou, J. 1983. Extinction: lessons from zoos. In *Genetics and Conservation,* eds C.M. Schonewald-Cox, S.M. Chambers, B. MacBryde and L. Thomas. Pp. 164-184. Benjamin/Cummings: Menlo Park, California.

Ralls, K., Ballou, J.D., and Templeton, A. 1988. Estimates of lethal equivalents and the cost of inbreeding in mammals. *Conserv. Biol.* 2:185-193.

Ralls, K., Brugger, K., and Ballou, J. 1979. Inbreeding and juvenile mortality in small populations of ungulates. *Science* 206:1101-1103.

Senner, J.W. 1980. Inbreeding depression and the survival of zoo populations. In *Conservation Biology: an Evolutionary-Ecological Perspective,* eds M.E. Soulé and B.A. Wilcox. Pp. 209-225. Sinauer Associates: Sunderland, Mass.

Sherwin, W.B., and Brown, P.R. In press. Problems in the estimation of the effective size of a population of the Eastern Barred Bandicoot, *Perameles gunnii* at Hamilton, Victoria. In *Bandicoots and Bilbies,* eds J.H. Seebeck, P.R. Brown, R.L. Wallis, and C.M. Kemper. Surrey Beat y and Sons: Sydney.

Sherwin, W.B., and Murray, N.D. In press. Population and conservation genetics of marsupials. *Aust. J. Zool.*

Sherwin, W.B., Murray, N.D., Graves, J.A.M., and Brown, P.R. In press a. Minimum research on conservation genetics of wild populations. In *Proceedings of the IUCN National Conference on the Conservation of Threatened Species and Their Habitats.* ACIUCN Occasional Paper No. 2, eds P. Eiser and M. Hicks. ACIUCN Sydney.

Sherwin, W.B., Murray, N.D., Graves, J.A.M., and Brown, P.R. In press b. Measurement of genetic variation in endangered populations: bandicoots (Marsupialia: Peramelidae) as an example. *Conserv. Biol.*

Soulé, M.E., and Wilcox, B.A. 1980. *Conservation Biology. An Evolutionary-Ecological Perspective.* Sinauer Associates: Sunderland, Mass.

Templeton, A.R., and Read, B. 1983. The elimination of inbreeding depression in a captive herd of Spekes gazelle. In *Genetics and Conservation, a Reference for Managing Wild Animal and Plant Populations,* eds C.M. Schonewald-Cox, S.M. Chambers, B. MacBryde and L. Thomas. Benjamin/Cummings: Menlo Park, California.

Tyndale-Biscoe, C.H., and Calaby, J.H. 1975. Eucalypt forests as refuges for wildlife. *Aust. For.* **38**:117-133.

Varvio, S.L., Chakraborty, R., and Nei, M. 1986. Genetic variation in subdivided populations and conservation genetics. *Heredity* **57**:189-198.

Warner, C.M. 1986. Genetic manipulation of the major histocompatibility complex. *J. Anim. Sci.* **63**:279-287.

Warner, C.M., Meeker, D.L., and Rothschild, M.F. 1987. Genetic control of immune responsiveness: a review of its use as a tool for selection of disease resistance. *J. Anim. Sci.* **64**:394-406.

Wetton, J.H., Carter, R.E., Parkin, D.T., and Walters, D. 1987. Demographic study of a wild house sparrow population by DNA fingerprinting. *Nature* **327**:147-149.

# Population Viability Assessment of the Eastern Barred Bandicoot in Victoria

*Robert C. Lacy[1] and Tim W. Clark[1,2]*

## Abstract

Small populations are subject to large fluctuations arising from random processes at a variety of levels (genetic, demographic, environmental, and catastrophic), and such variation can place a population at high risk of extinction. We used a computer simulation model to project the likely fate of the remnant population of eastern barred bandicoots (*Perameles gunnii*) in Victoria. With population parameters estimated from available field data, the simulation predicts that the species is almost certain to go extinct in Victoria within 25 years, with a mean extinction time of just 10.6 years. Assuming a greater or lesser frequency of catastrophic floods and droughts alters mean persistence time by only about one year. Increasing the estimated carrying capacity of the habitat has little effect, because the declining population would have no opportunity to exploit a greater carrying capacity. A decrease in available habitat (or a fragmentation of habitat into independent isolates) would accelerate extinction. Even if mortality were decreased to the extent necessary to balance the birth rate, the expected fluctuations around the 'stable' population are sufficient to cause a 19% probability of extinction within 25 years. Greatly reduced mortality, a considerable increase in habitat, and protection from catastrophic events would all be necessary to make the population viable over a moderate time span.

## Introduction

Humans are radically altering the environment: clearing vegetation, replacing diverse, natural ecosystems with agricultural monocultures, eliminating native predators and introducing novel ones, killing native herbivores and placing high densities of grazing livestock on the lands, and spreading disease vectors globally. As a result, many populations of animals that were once large, widely distributed and diverse are in rapid decline, becoming small, fragmented isolates in remaining natural areas, managed nature preserves, or even zoos. Clearly, the eastern barred bandicoot is one of many species that could soon disappear because novel causes of mortality exceed potential reproductive output. Traditionally, wildlife managers have focussed on mean, age-specific determinations of birth and death rates, using life table analyses to determine, for example, whether a population could sustain culling or harvest, or whether it requires increased protection or even supplementation. Recent population estimates show that the eastern barred bandicoot population around Hamilton, Victoria, is not presently self-sustaining; yet in this paper we focus our analyses on processes that put small populations at risk of extinction whether or not the average birth rate exceeds the average death rate.

## Risks of Being Small

When a population is small and isolated from any and all other conspecifics, chance events such as the occurrence, timing, and extent of disease outbreaks, floods and fires, random fluctuations in the sex ratio, and even the randomness of Mendelian transmission of genes can become more important than whether the population has

[1]Department of Conservation Biology, Chicago Zoological Society, Brookfield, Illinois 60513 U.S.A.
[2]Northern Rockies Conservation Cooperative, Box 2705, Jackson, Wyoming 83001 U.S.A.

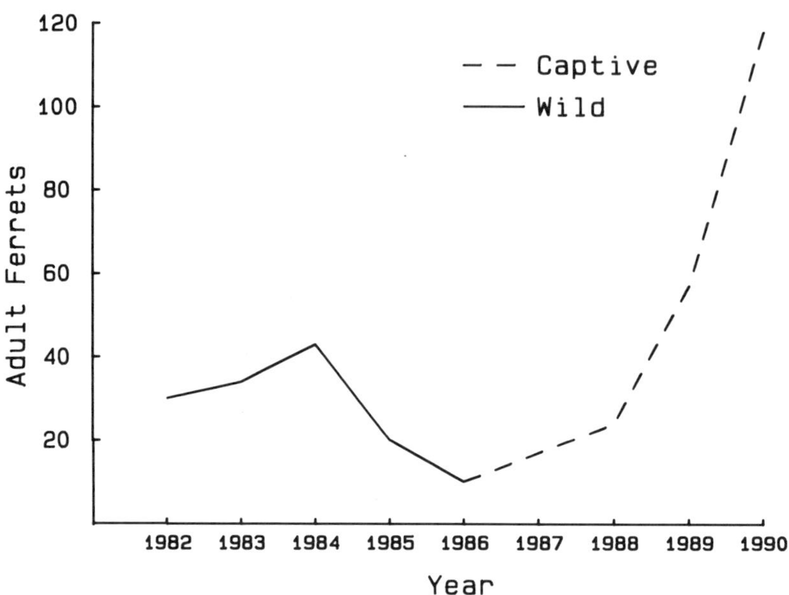



*Figure 1.*—Numbers of adult black-footed ferrets in the only remaining wild population at Meeteetse, Wyoming, and then in captivity from the time that the Meeteetse population was discovered until 1990. Data from Forrest *et al.* (1988) and B. Miller (personal communication).

sufficient habitat to persist, is well adapted to that habitat and has a mean birth rate that exceeds the mean death rate. Populations neither stay constant in size nor follow perfectly linear decline or growth. When numbers are few, fluctuations of a few tens of animals due to the vagaries of reproduction and mortality can lead to large relative changes in overall population size. Figures 1 and 2 show the fluctuations in two remnant populations, black-footed ferrets (*Mustela nigripes*) and Puerto Rican parrots (*Amazona vittata*), during recent years. Both populations were intensively studied and managed; yet the fluctuation in numbers is striking, even for the very long-lived parrot. The primary danger to a small population is simply that with such fluctuations the population size is likely to hit zero before long. Although the underlying causes of extinction may be predictable factors such as habitat destruction, increased predation, or over-hunting, the final extinction event is more likely to result from 'bad luck' that strikes a population that had been reduced previously to such low numbers that it has little buffering from the vissicitudes of the physical, biotic and human environments, and little capacity to recover from short-term perturbations.

## Demographic Stochasticity

Many events in the life of an organism have a random, or stochastic, component, but it is often useful to categorise the stochasticity in the fate of a population into four types (Shaffer 1981). *Demographic* or individual stochasticity is the fluctuation in population size that results from individual reproductive or mortality events being relatively independent outcomes 'sampled' from the mean population parameters. For example, the probability of an individual being killed by a predator may be 25% per year, but somewhat more or less than 25% will be killed in any given year. If predation is random and at a constant probability, p, we would expect the proportion killed to

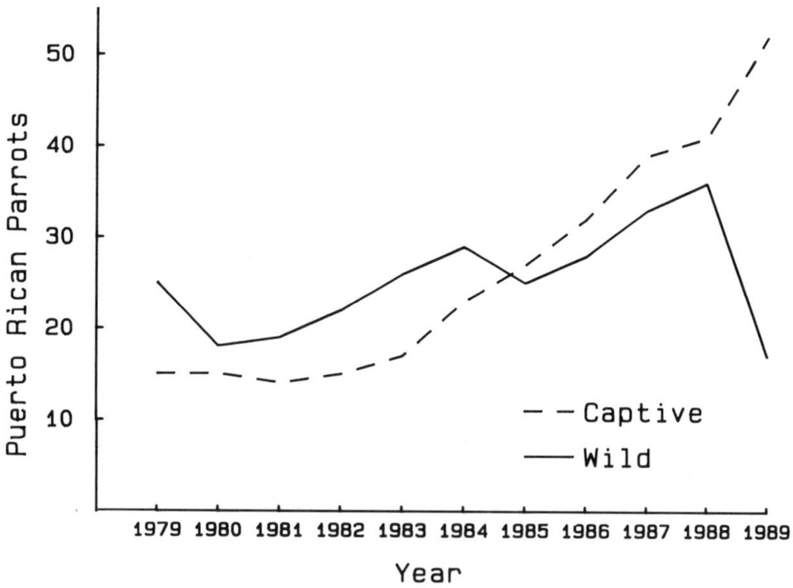



*Figure 2.*—Numbers of Puerto Rican parrots in the wild and in captivity during the past decade. The wild population was decimated in 1989 by a hurricane. Data from Snyder *et al.* (1987), G. Lee and M. Wilson (personal communication).

follow a binomial distribution, with variance $p * (1 - p) / N$. Other causes of mortality and reproduction are similarly probabilistic, for example, the (binomial) probability distribution of finding a mate, and the (multinomial) probability distribution of producing litters of various sizes. Such demographic stochasticity is unimportant if numbers are on the order of 100 or more, but can cause the final extinction of a very small population. By chance, the last five dusky seaside sparrows (*Ammodramus maritimus nigrescens*) were males.

### Environmental Stochasticity

*Environmental* stochasticity is the variation in population birth and death mean rates caused by random fluctuations of the environment. Rainfall, temperature, and local abundance of prey and predators are just a few of many aspects of the environment that can fluctuate more or less randomly, often following normal distributions.

### Catastrophic Events

The third level of stochasticity, *catastrophic* events, are the extreme of environmental variation, but are examined and modelled separately because occasional catastrophes often fall outside the normal range of environmental variation (*e.g.* a hurricane is not just a more extreme storm), because the effects on a population may be much greater than the effects extrapolated from more typical variation (*e.g.* a year-long drought could be much more than four times as damaging as a 3-month drought), and because some catastrophes (*e.g.* fires) are not simply extremes of typical environmental variation. Moreover, rare disasters are often the final insult that drives a small, but otherwise healthy, population extinct. A hurricane decimated one of the two extant populations of whooping cranes (*Grus americana*) in the 1940s. The only remaining wild population of black-footed ferrets was destroyed by an epidemic of sylvatic plague among their prairie dog prey, followed by an epidemic of canine distemper among the ferrets themselves (Seal *et al.* 1989, Clark 1989). Recently, a hurricane decimated the only wild population of Puerto Rican parrots, apparently killing about half of the birds, and leaving the remainder extremely vulnerable to starvation and predation in a defoliated forest.

*Genetic Stochasticity*

A fourth source of stochasticity affecting small populations is random *genetic* change. In sexually reproducing, diploid organisms, progeny are not perfect genetic replicas of their parents, but rather a random draw of one (quite possibly recombined) chromosome of each homologous pair from each parent. As allele frequencies change at random each generation ('genetic drift'), genetic variance is depleted and genetic variants are successively lost from the population. The resulting increased homozygosity (a form of inbreeding) typically reduces fecundity and viability, and the loss of genetic variants reduces the opportunity for natural selection to adapt the population to changing environments (Lacy 1987; Robinson *et al.*, this volume).

*Population Viability Analysis*

Unfortunately, each of the diverse risks faced by a small, isolated population is likely to cause further decline (at least temporarily) in the population size, in turn exacerbating each of the other stochastic factors. The population can be pushed by the cumulative impacts of random events ever more rapidly toward extinction (Gilpin and Soulé 1986), a process described as an 'extinction vortex'. The process of modelling and analysing the various deterministic and stochastic forces determining the fate of a population is termed *Population Viability Analysis* (PVA; Soulé 1987). The result of a PVA is an estimate, based on available information, of the probability that a population will persist over time scales of interest. PVA is a very recent approach, but has already been applied to several species (*e.g.* Parker and Smith

1988; Seal *et al.* 1989; Seal and Lacy 1989; Lacy *et al.* 1989).

Why bother with a PVA, rather than (or in addition to) putting efforts into protecting and recovering an endangered population, regardless of whether it has a 1% or 50% or 99% probability of going extinct within a decade? First, many species need protection, but resources for conservation are limited. We need to know whether a species is in a crisis—literally on the verge of extinction. Will the population be likely to recover if left on its own, or will it require aggressive management to pull it away from the extinction vortex? Secondly, we need to identify those factors that are the primary sources of risk for the population. A recent PVA has suggested that Florida panthers (*Felis concolor coryi*, the only remaining subspecies of mountain lion in the eastern United States) are disappearing because 25% are killed by cars annually, because mercury contamination of the Everglades ecosystem has reached lethal levels for top carnivores, and because deer hunting by humans in southern Florida keeps prey sufficiently scarce to prevent successful reproduction by panthers over much of the habitat. A PVA of the Puerto Rican parrot, on the other hand, demonstrated that species recovery was sufficiently steady to minimise the risk of extinction, unless a hurricane were to strike the island and devastate the Luquillo forest that is home to the 40 or so wild and 40 or so captive parrots. The primary recommendation arising from the parrot PVA was that it was urgent that a subpopulation of captive parrots be moved off the island to provide insurance against the possibility of a catastrophic storm. As evidence that PVAs can be valuable predictors of the future, and that ignoring available information can be disastrous, a severe hurricane did strike Puerto Rico just months after the PVA and before any birds were removed from the Luquillo forest. Similarly, the extreme risk to the one wild population of black-footed ferrets of a canine distemper disease outbreak was identified several years before a distemper epidemic largely exterminated the wild population in 1985 (Clark 1989). Fortunately, 12 ferrets were brought into captivity during the course of the epidemic; even then, six of those died from distemper.

PVA can and should also be used to assess the improved probability of survival that would result from each possible management action. For example, a PVA on the ferrets in 1986 suggested that captive breeding was the only strategy that increased the probability of species survival substantially above zero (Harris *et al.* 1989).

Before presenting our PVA of eastern barred bandicoots, we will stress that the models we use are all still crude. We do not assess all risks in the models, nor do we adequately incorporate the feedback among demographic and genetic components. As a result, our projections of extinction probabilities are almost certainly *under*estimates. Fortunately, our expertise with PVAs evolves and improves with each species considered.

*Simulation Modelling*

Our approach to population viability analysis involves simulation modelling. It is in theory possible to derive equations for the needed probability distribution, but no one has yet proceeded beyond very simplistic analytical treatments. Goodman (1987) has provided equations for estimating the probability of extinction over time from the maximum population size sustainable in the habitat (carrying capacity, K), the mean population growth rate (r), and the variance in r. For bandicoots, we know neither r nor the variance in r across years. To model the Hamilton bandicoot population, we used a computer program (SIM-POP), written by one of us (Robert C. Lacy) in the C programming language. Many of the algorithms in SIMPOP were taken from a simulation program, SPGPC, written in BASIC by James W. Grier of North Dakota State University (Grier 1980a,b; Grier and Barclay 1988). Grier makes his program freely available to anyone with a use for it, and we similarly will provide the source code and provide compiled versions (for use on

microcomputers using the MS-DOS operating system) of SIMPOP. The open flow of information among biologists concerned with conservation has been essential to the very rapid spread of concepts, tools and data needed by many.

SIMPOP models population processes as discrete, sequential events, with probabilistic outcomes determined by a pseudo-random number generator. (For example, a typical random number generator uses the number of seconds elapsed since the year 1900, divides that by the largest single precision number the computer can store in its memory, and then uses the fractional remainder of that division to generate a random number between zero and one. If a number so determined is greater than the probability of an event, that event is deemed to have occurred in the simulation.) The SIMPOP model simulates the birth and death processes of a population by generating random numbers to determine whether each animal lives or dies, and whether each adult female produces broods of size 0, or 1, or 2, or 3, or ... during each year. Mortality and reproduction probabilities are assumed to be the same for each sex, and fecundity is assumed to be independent of age (after an animal reaches reproductive age). Mortality rates are specified for each pre-reproductive age class and for reproductive-age animals. Each simulation is started with a specified number of males and females of each pre-reproductive age class, and a specified number of males and females of breeding age. The computer program simulates and tracks the fate of each population, and outputs summary statistics on the probability of population extinction over a specified time span and the mean time to extinction of those simulated populations that went extinct. A population carrying capacity is imposed by truncation of each age class if the population size after breeding exceeds the specified carrying capacity. Each year in the simulation, the number of animals surviving, as well as the number reproducing, would be expected to follow binomial distributions with means equal to the specified probabilities. Environmental variation in reproduction, survival and the carrying capacity is incorporated into the model by increasing the binomial or Poisson variances in these parameters by an amount specified by the user. These variances are functions of the starting population size, so the effect of doubling the variance in survival, for example, depends on the initial population size (smaller N yields larger binomial variance).

In SIMPOP, catastrophes affecting mortality and breeding are independent. The frequencies and severities of breeding catastrophes and survival catastrophes are specified by the user. A catastrophe is determined to occur if a randomly generated number between 0 and 1 is less than the probability of occurrence (*i.e.* a binomial process is simulated). If a breeding catastrophe occurs, the probability of breeding is multiplied by a severity factor that is drawn from a binomial distribution with mean equal to the severity specified by the user. Similarly, if a survival catastrophe occurs, the probability of surviving each age class is multiplied by a severity factor that is drawn from a binomial distribution with the mean equal to the severity specified by the user. Thus, not all catastrophes are of equal magnitude; rather, they are distributed around a mean specified by the user, with variances set relative to initial population sizes (as for environmental variation). SIMPOP also allows the user to supplement or harvest the population for any number of years in each simulation (see Maguire *et al.* this volume).

Overall, the computer program simulates many of the complex levels of stochasticity that can affect a population. Some of its artificialities are the absence of trends across years (*e.g.* no long-term changes in the environment, and no multi-year environmental perturbations or catastrophes), the independence of environmental variation in birth and death rates, and the lack of density dependence of birth and death rates except when the population exceeds the carrying capacity. The first two of these simplifications are likely to lead to underestimates of extinction rates, while the third may cause underestimation or overestimation of extinction.

## Population Biology Parameters—Eastern Barred Bandicoot

Accurate estimates of both means and variances of population parameters are essential to population viability analysis. Extensive field research is therefore a prerequisite to all population modelling and management. Our data were obtained from reports by Brown (1989), Dufty (1988), and Minta *et al.* (this volume), and from work on eastern barred bandicoots in Tasmania by Heinsohn (1966). We are indebted to the many field researchers who contributed to collection of these data, and we hope that the shortcomings of our analyses will encourage further field work so that future analyses can be more accurate and more useful in directing the recovery and management of the species in Victoria.

### Population Size and Growth Rate

Based on the number of hectares occupied by bandicoots and the presumed density of bandicoots per hectare, it was estimated that about 1,750 eastern barred bandicoots existed when Moon (1984) surveyed the habitat in 1982-1983, a maximum of 633 in 1985 (Brown 1989), and an estimated 229 (maximum of about 300) in 1988 (Dufty 1988). Although these estimates are based on varied field techniques and areas sampled, it is obvious that the Victorian population of eastern barred bandicoots is in rapid decline. Regression analysis of the above data indicates that the population has declined about 25% per year during the 1980s. This is a slower rate of decline than would be projected from the replacement rate (0.48 female offspring per female) estimated by Robinson *et al.* (this volume).

An optimistic estimate of the present population size (in mid-1989) would be 300 bandicoots; a more conservative estimate would be 150. This remnant population is divided between two relatively discrete areas of habitat, a population centered around the Hamilton Municipal Tip, a few other areas in and near the city of Hamilton, and a secondary (though perhaps more healthy) population of about 60 animals in the Chatsworth Road area a short distance east of Hamilton. It is not known whether bandicoots move between these two centres with any regularity. To assess the viability of the Victorian eastern barred bandicoot population as a whole, and the viability of subpopulations such as that in the Chatsworth Road area, we have analysed simulations started with 60, 150 and 300 bandicoots.

*Population Carrying Capacity*

The steady and rapid rate of decline of eastern barred bandicoots in Victoria suggests that the habitat in Hamilton is unable to support more bandicoots than are presently there. It is entirely possible that the population currently exceeds the sustainable carrying capacity. We simulated populations with carrying capacities of 60, 150, and 300 bandicoots. A greater capacity, if available, would have little effect on the simulation results because the negative growth rate of the population makes it unlikely that the Hamilton population would exceed 300 animals (unless causes of mortality are reduced and the present decline reversed; see Maguire *et al.*, this volume).

*Fecundity*

Bandicoots have among the highest reproductive potential of any mammal of their size (Hennemann 1983), with a 12-day gestation (the shortest known for any mammal), weaning at 60 days of age, first breeding at about 4.5 months of age or less, and interbirth intervals of 70-90 days. Studies by Heinsohn (1966) in Tasmania, Dufty (1988), Brown (1989), and Minta *et al.* (this volume) indicate that most females over 500 g were carrying pouch young or were clearly lactating (suggesting that a litter was in a nest) when trapped. The few adult females not observed to be lactating could be the fraction of the adult females expected to be gestating (12/72) if breeding occurs immediately after each litter is weaned. Thus it appears that eastern barred bandicoots in Victo-

ria breed almost continuously after reaching about 500 g (4.5 months). Data from Brown (1989), Dufty (1988), and Minta *et al.* (this volume) all suggest that the mean litter size (after early non-observed mortality) is about 2.20, distributed as about 17% litters of one, 50% litters of two, 29% litters of three and 4% litters of four.

Although it requires 2 to 3 months for a female to raise a litter to independence, the computer simulation assumes that breeding is instantaneous. To model the bandicoot population, we considered the bandicoot life cycle to consist of events occurring at 3-month intervals. We therefore assumed that bandicoots first breed at 6 months of age (about the mid-point in the first breeding cycle), and that they produce subsequent litters every 3 months until they die. Three months is slightly longer than the mean observed interbirth interval, thus allowing for a small fraction of females not breeding at any given time or delaying a breeding episode briefly.

*Mortality*

Unless a large number of marked individuals can be followed over time (by radio-tracking, or by repeated and frequent recaptures), it is very difficult to estimate accurately the age-specific mortality of any natural population. Mortality data on the bandicoots will present a biased view of the causes and frequency of deaths (Lenghaus *et al.* this volume), because most carcasses are never recovered, especially those taken by natural predators. Minta *et al.* did recapture 62 of 106 bandicoots that had been marked 3 to 10 months earlier by Dufty (1988) (and also captured 83 bandicoots not so marked). If Minta *et al.*'s trapping effectively sampled the area used by the bandicoots marked by Dufty, these data would suggest that about 58% of adult eastern barred bandicoots survive 6 months, or about 75% survive each 3-month interval of the simulated population. Given the high mortality rate, it is unlikely that many bandicoots survive long enough to become senescent or even to decline in fertility.

Juvenile mortality is even harder to assess than adult mortality, but is likely to be much greater. The mortality estimates used in our simulations are simply plausible guesses that would result in the observed mean population decline of about 25% per year (given the observed reproductive rate). We assume that mortality from birth to 3 months of age (primarily pre-weaning mortality) would be 50%, that juvenile mortality (3 months to 4.5 months) would be 50% (the period just after independence from the mother being likely to be the time of greatest mortality), and that mortality of young adults entering reproductive condition (4.5 months to 6 months) would be 37% (intermediate between juvenile and adult mortality). (The combined 3 to 6 month mortality would then be 68.75%.) For the purposes of demographic analysis and projection of population growth, it does not matter how pre-reproductive mortality is distributed among infant, juvenile and sub-adult age classes (although effective management of the population may require knowledge of the causes and stages of greatest mortality). Nor will it change demographic trends if litters are initially larger than assumed, but reduced to the observed sizes by undocumented mortality that occurs early in life. The population growth rate will be determined solely by the number of progeny per female that reach reproductive age. Recognizing the uncertainty in these mortality estimates, we also simulated populations with 15% lower mortality at each post-weaning age class, thereby modelling a population with no mean increase or decrease ($\lambda$=1.00) in years without catastrophes.

*Sex Ratio*

Because male and female bandicoots probably utilise differently sized home ranges (Dufty 1988; Minta *et al.* this volume) and have different patterns of activity, it is difficult to assess the population sex ratio from trapping data. Brown (1989) reported a ratio of 69 males: 74 females among trapped adults, Dufty (1988) trapped 73 males and 33 females, and Minta *et al.* (this volume) trapped 52 males and 36 females. Although there is perhaps an excess of males in the population (it is more likely that males range more widely and

are therefore more readily trapped), we conservatively assumed in our analyses that there is a 1:1 sex ratio at birth and that mortality affects both sexes equally.

*Environmental Variability*

The Australian climate is highly variable. Rainfall, temperature and population dynamics of other species (both floral and faunal) probably affect bandicoot survival. Although eastern barred bandicoots appear to breed year-round in Victoria, it is likely that there is some seasonal and annual variation in reproduction. Unfortunately, no study of the Hamilton population of bandicoots has extended long enough to provide data on annual variation in reproduction and mortality. For the purposes of this preliminary PVA, we have conservatively assumed that breeding is continual (a litter every 3 months beginning at age 6 months) and therefore without seasonal and annual variation, and that variation in the mean mortality rate and carrying capacity of the population is approximately comparable to the variation expected to occur due to the random demographic stochasticity. With 25% mortality of adults per 3 months, the binomial variance in mortality expected if mortality is wholly random among individuals is $V = pq/N = 0.00125$ for a population of 150. Thus, we assumed an additional environmental variation in mortality of 0.00125, so that the adult mortality rate every 3 months was drawn from a distribution with mean 0.25 and standard deviation 0.035. Similarly, the environmental variation in carrying capacity was assumed to mirror random (Poisson) variation, so that K varied seasonally around a mean with variance equal to that mean (SD = 12.2, when mean K = 150).

*Catastrophes*

Droughts, floods, and fires are all likely to affect bandicoot populations. Seebeck (1979; Seebeck *et al.* this volume) reported anecdotal evidence that the bandicoots declined markedly during droughts in 1916 and 1966-1968, Heinsohn (1966) reported that drought caused an early termination of the 1961-1962 breeding season in Tasmanian eastern barred bandicoots, and Brown (1989) reported that reproduction ceased during the 1982-1983 drought. Floods and fires could kill bandicoots (often indirectly by forcing them to areas lacking adequate cover to avoid predators), but would be more localised in effect than would droughts. Based on little more than intuition, we estimated that a drought would cause a cessation of breeding for a year but with minimal effect on survival, while a fire or flood would cause an immediate mortality of about 25%, but have little effect on breeding for the year. Historical records indicate that the Hamilton area has had three severe and prolonged droughts this century (1916, 1966-1967, and 1982-1983), four floods (1909, 1946, 1970, and 1983), and one large fire. Thus we estimate the probability of a year-long drought at 3.4% (3/88 years), and the probability of fire or flood at 1.4% per 3-month interval (five occurrences/88 years). Lesser droughts and very local perturbations of the habitat (*e.g.* slashing) undoubtably cause some mortality and reproductive failures, but could be considered under the category of environmental variation (above) rather than catastrophe. Recognising the considerable uncertainty in these estimates of the severity and frequency of catastrophes, we also examined scenarios with either no catastrophes or double the above frequencies.

*Time Scale of Population Projection*

The goals of managing any endangered species should include (minimally) recovery of a self-sustaining population at numbers that make further interventive management unnecessary. A self-sustaining population must be defined in terms of an acceptably low probability of extinction over an acceptably long period of time. (No population is assured of persistence over any time scale, of course, and every population is certain to go extinct eventually.) Shaffer (1981) suggested that a viable population of grizzly bears (*Ursus arctos horribilis*) be defined as one with a 99% probability of persistence for 1,000 years. In the case of the eastern barred bandicoot, a linear projection of the present 25% annual decline

suggests that the Hamilton population will decline to extinction within 20 years. Management must reverse this decline within a few years if the species is to persist in Victoria, and we therefore have confined this preliminary PVA to a 25-year time frame. Once it is believed that population stability has been achieved, it will be important to reassess population viability with the new population parameters in order to determine whether the population is sufficiently robust to survive the various identifiable sources of stochasticity well into the future.

*Results*

Table 1 summarises the population biology parameters that represent our best estimate of the current conditions at Hamilton, the 'Basic scenario', as described above. Figure 3 shows the fates of 10 simulated eastern barred bandicoot populations under this basic scenario. The figure clearly shows the rapid decline projected from the past decade, but also shows moderate variation among runs, including some periods of apparent population stability and short-term increases. Figures 4 and 5 show the frequency distribution and cumulative frequency distribution of times to extinction from 10,000 simulations using the basic parameters. In the majority of simulations, the Hamilton bandicoot population was extinct by the year 2000.

Table 2 shows the results generated from 1,000 computer simulations of the Hamilton population of bandicoots, under several plausible scenarios describing the present population dynamics. For the basic scenario, the SIMPOP program projects that the Hamilton bandicoot population is virtually certain to go extinct within 25 years, with a mean time to extinction of just 10.6 years.

Table 2 also shows scenarios in which we altered several of the parameters for which we have few data. If catastrophes such as fires, droughts and floods have little or no impact on the eastern barred bandicoot population, the simulation still projects that the Hamilton population is likely to

*Table 1.*—Population parameters estimated for the current conditions in the Hamilton population of eastern barred bandicoots; basic scenario used for computer simulations. Deterministic calculations of mean population growth rate and generation time also given.

First age of reproduction: 6 months (approximate mid-point of first breeding cycle)

Litter size distribution:
   0 % females produce litters of size 0
   17 % females produce litters of size 1
   50 % females produce litters of size 2
   29 % females produce litters of size 3
   4 % females produce litters of size 4

Mortality:
   50 % percent mortality between 0 and 3 months of age
   50 % mortality between 3 and 4.5 months of age
   37 % mortality between 4.5 and 6 months of age
   25 % 3-month mortality of adults (> 6 months of age)

Carrying capacity of 150

Environmental stochasticity in mortality and carrying capacity assumed to match demographic variance of the starting population of 150. No environmental variance assumed in reproduction (all adult females assumed to breed every 3 months).

Frequency and severity of catastrophes:
   0.034 probability of drought, causing total reproductive failure
   0.056 annual probability of flood or fire, causing 25% mortality

Initial population size:
   24 male, 24 female juveniles (3 months old)
   51 male, 51 female adults (age $\geq$ 6 months)

Annual population growth rate:
   in absence of catastrophes, $\lambda = 0.75$
   including catastrophes, $\lambda = 0.69$

Generation time = 13.5 months

go extinct, with a mean time to extinction just a year longer than in the basic scenario. Doubling the frequency of catastrophes decreases the mean time to extinction by about one year. A greater carrying capacity (300 vs. 150) has virtually no impact on the population viability, because the declining population would be unable to expand into additional available habitat. If the carrying capacity is only 60, extinction is accelerated considerably. This scenario (#5 in Table 2) also represents the expected fate of the smaller Chatsworth Road population, if it is demographi-cally isolated from the rest of the Hamilton-area bandicoots and if the basic population biology parameters used in the modelling describe accurately the Chatsworth Road sub-population.

The mortality rates used in the basic scenario were chosen so that the population declined at an average rate of 25% per year in the absence of catastrophes. It could be argued, however, that, although the Hamilton bandicoot population has been declining at such a rate through the 1980s, the population is now relatively stable. (This is

*Table 2.*—Results from 1,000 computer simulations of the Victorian population of eastern barred bandicoots. Probability of extinction is given at 5-year intervals, with the mean time to extinction of those simulated populations that became extinct within 25 years.

| Scenario[1] | | Probability of extinction | | | | Mean no. years |
|---|---|---|---|---|---|---|
| | 5 yr | 10 yr | 15 yr | 20 yr | 25 yr | to extinction |
| 1. Basic[2] | 0.01 | 0.48 | 0.91 | 0.99 | 1.00 | 10.6 |
| 2. No catastrophes | 0.01 | 0.35 | 0.81 | 0.97 | 0.99 | 11.9 |
| 3. 2X catastrophes | 0.04 | 0.68 | 0.95 | 0.99 | 1.00 | 9.3 |
| 4. K = 300 | 0.00 | 0.48 | 0.90 | 0.98 | 1.00 | 10.8 |
| 5. K = 60 | 0.18 | 0.81 | 0.98 | 1.00 | 1.00 | 7.8 |
| 6. Zero population growth[3] (ZPG) | 0.00 | 0.01 | 0.04 | 0.11 | 0.19 | 19.0 |
| 7. ZPG + no catastrophes | 0.00 | 0.00 | 0.01 | 0.03 | 0.05 | 19.3 |
| 8. ZPG + 2X catastrophes | 0.00 | 0.03 | 0.14 | 0.31 | 0.47 | 17.7 |
| 9. ZPG + K = 300 | 0.00 | 0.00 | 0.02 | 0.07 | 0.13 | 19.4 |
| 10. ZPG + K = 60 | 0.01 | 0.15 | 0.34 | 0.51 | 0.63 | 14.8 |
| 11. ZPG + no catastrophes + K = 300 | 0.00 | 0.00 | 0.00 | 0.01 | 0.02 | 20.6 |

[1]Population parameters as in the basic scenario, with changes as indicated.
[2]Population parameters estimated for current conditions in the Hamilton population, as described in text and Table 1.
[3]Achieved by a 15% reduction in mortality.

perhaps the most optimistic scenario that is at all plausible; it could not be argued logically that the population is experiencing population growth.) Scenario #6 projects that the Hamilton population has a 19% probability of extinction, if the mean growth rate is zero in those years not affected by a catastrophe. Even if the population growth rate approximates zero and no catastrophes occur (scenario #7), there is a modest probability (5%) that the eastern barred bandicoot will go extinct in Victoria within 25 years. Assuming a carrying capacity of 300 and zero population growth, but with catastrophes (scenario #9), improves the prospects for population survival (13% extinction vs. 19%), but not by much. A small eastern barred bandicoot population, such as that at Chatsworth Road, has a high probability of extinction even if mean birth and death rates are equal (scenario #10).

## Discussion

The simulation results presented here do not tell us what will happen to the Hamilton population of eastern barred bandicoots; rather, they project what is most likely to occur given the mean population parameters estimated from field data and the sources of stochasticity identified in the population. The current population may have birth rates higher or death rates lower than estimated, and other parameters may be more favorable than determined from available data. Thus, even in the absence of amelioration of circumstances, the eastern barred bandicoot may have longer to survive than we have projected—if just because of luck (*e.g.* 21 of 10,000 simulations of the basic scenario survived the 25 years; the Hamilton population could be lucky as well). It is perhaps more likely, however, that we have ne-

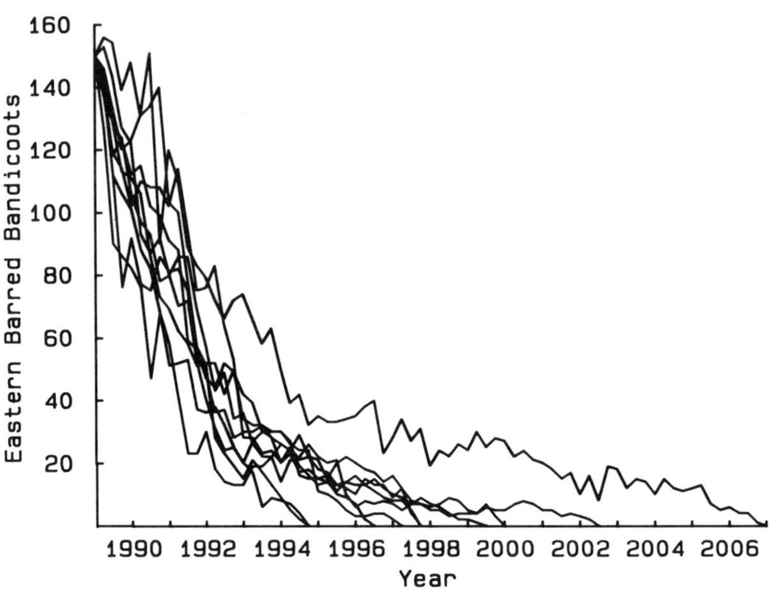



*Figure 3.*—Fates of ten simulated populations of the eastern barred bandicoots, with population biology parameters as described in the text and Table 1 (basic scenario).

glected some sources of population instability (*e.g.* inbreeding effects) in our models, and that the Hamilton population is more at risk than indicated in Table 2 and Figures 4 and 5.

Based on our current best estimate of the population biology of the species, the size of the present population, and the habitat available, we project that the eastern barred bandicoot will be extinct in Victoria in about a decade, and almost certainly within two decades, unless actions are taken to reverse the decline. Alternative, plausible estimates of the current population size, growth rate, and frequency of catastrophe often project greater probability of survival, but in none of the cases examined do we project that the eastern barred bandicoots are secure from extinction in the next few decades.

These results, in accord with PVAs of other species mentioned previously, demonstrate that random fluctuations in population size, caused by easily identifiable sources of stochasticity, make populations as small as the bandicoots in Victoria sufficiently unstable so as to be inviable over modest time scales. Even in the absence of further habitat decay, increased predation, or other causes of population decline, apparently healthy populations of small size have limited expected duration. In widely distributed species, local populations often do go extinct, but are readily recolonised from adjacent populations. A single or a few remnant populations isolated from any possible source of supplementation and recolonisation will not survive indefinitely and perhaps not even for long. Thus, it is not sufficient to protect a remnant population, such as the Hamilton eastern barred

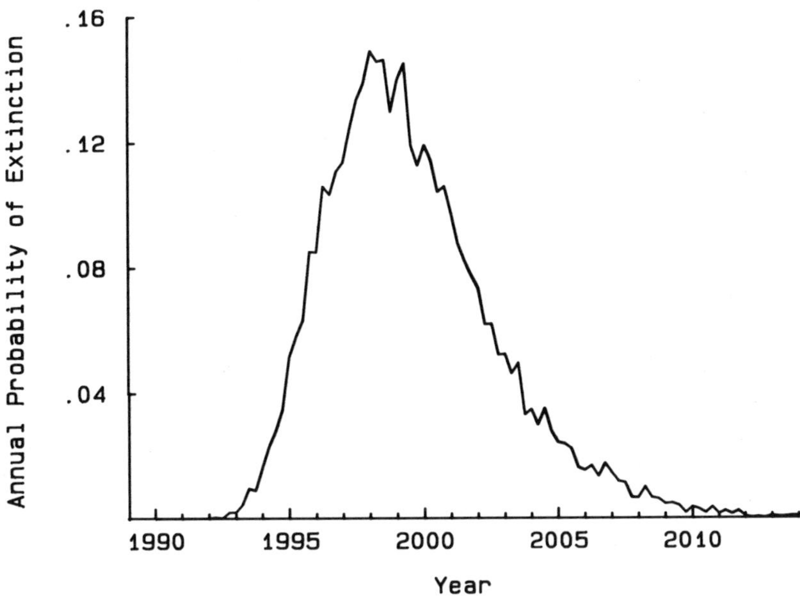


*Figure 4.*—Frequency distribution of times to extinction of the Hamilton population of the eastern barred bandicoot from 10,000 computer simulations, using population parameters as described in the text and Table 1 (basic scenario).

bandicoots, from those causes of decline that eliminated other populations of the species; aggressive action must be taken quickly to increase the numbers of the population and to establish or re-establish additional populations. The goal of recovery must be to pull a population out of the extinction vortex, by returning it to numbers, range and diversity such that normal population dynamics (including temporary local extinctions) do not lead to irreversible regional or global extinction of a taxon.

Population viability assessment is a tool, not a conclusion. It allows quantification of the compound impact of a number of forces impinging upon a population, often when intuition and subjective synthesis are incapable of perceiving the magnitude of extinction risks. By understanding the risks faced by a population, we can determine the urgency of action to change those parameters. Perhaps some of the parameters utilised in the modelling of eastern barred bandicoots in Victoria are wrong—certainly many are based on few data. One consequence of a PVA is that critical aspects of the biology of a species can be identified, indicating where further field work may substantially increase our ability to predict the fate of a population and where management actions to change population dynamics might be especially effective. From Table 2, it can be seen that the bandicoot carrying capacity of the Hamilton area is of little relevance if high mortality continues to cause population decline. Maguire *et al.* (this volume) explore further the efficacy of possible management actions in reducing the probability of extinction of the eastern barred bandicoot in Victoria.

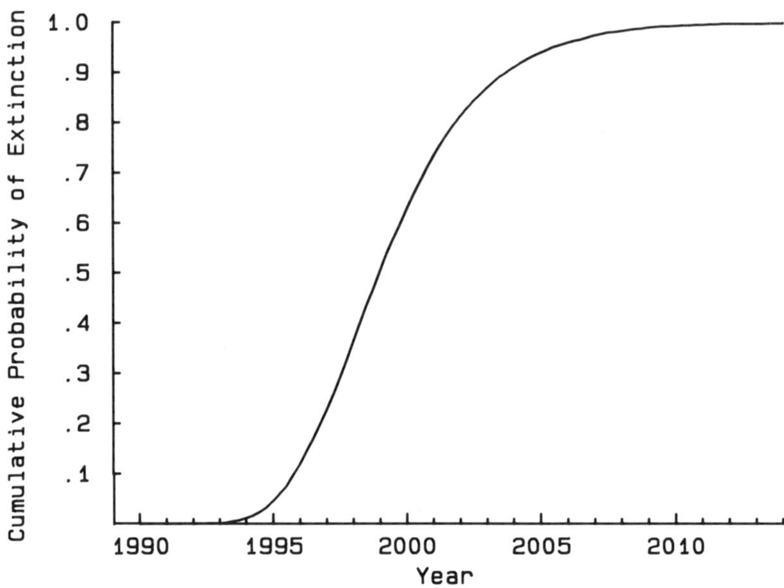


*Figure 5.*—Cumulative frequency distribution of times to extinction of the Hamilton population of the eastern barred bandicoot from 10,000 computer simulations, using population parameters estimated from data on the present Hamilton population, as described in the text and Table 1 (basic scenario).

PVA is a new tool for population management and conservation. We need refinements of the models (incorporating, for example, feedback between demographic fluctuations and random genetic changes), we need more precise data to feed into the models, and we need to monitor populations to confirm the predictive power of the PVAs. As the use of PVA has revealed the critical importance of random variation—in demographic events, in the environment, and in genetic processes—to the final extinction of many populations, it has become apparent that we lack an empirical understanding of the magnitude of such variation in natural systems. We do not know, for example, how reproductive rates and mortality rates vary seasonally and annually for the eastern barred bandicoot, nor do we know the extent of fluctuations in population numbers and density. The PVA of the Victoria population of the eastern barred bandicoot should be repeated, as additional data improve our understanding of the dynamics of the population and, more importantly, as management actions change those factors affecting the probability of population persistence.

## Acknowledgments

James W. Grier graciously made his computer simulation programs available for our use and modification. Many biologists, volunteers, and townspeople have contributed to the data collection around Hamilton; without their efforts neither this analysis nor the recovery of the eastern barred bandicoot would be possible. This research was supported by the Zoological Board of Victoria and the Chicago Zoological Society, in a cooperative program of research and conservation.

## References

Brown, P. R. 1989. Management plan for the conservation of the Eastern Barred Bandicoot, *Perameles gunnii*, in Victoria. National Parks and Wildlife Division, Victoria. *Arthur Rylah Institute for Environmental Research Tech. Rep. Ser.* No. 63. Department of Conservation, Forests and Lands: Melbourne.

Clark, T. W. 1989. *Conservation Biology of the Black-footed Ferret.* Special Scientific Report. Wildlife Preservation Trust International: Philadelphia.

Dufty, A. C. 1988. The distribution, population abundance, status, movements and activities of the Eastern Barred Bandicoot, *Perameles gunnii*, at Hamilton. B. Sc. (Honours) Thesis, La Trobe University, Bundoora, Victoria.

Forrest, S.C., Biggins, D.E., Richardson, L., Clark, T.W., Campbell, T.M. III, Fagerstone, K.A. and Thorne, E.T. 1988. Population attributes for the black-footed ferret (*Mustela nigripes*) at Meeteetse, Wyoming, 1981-1985. *J. Mamm.* **69**:261-273.

Gilpin, M.E., and Soulé, M.E. 1986. Minimum viable populations: processes of species extinction. In *Conservation Biology: The Science of Scarcity and Diversity,* ed. M.E. Soulé. Pp.19-34. Sinauer Associates: Sunderland, Massachusetts.

Goodman, D. 1987. The demography of chance extinction. In *Viable Populations for Conservation,* ed. M. E. Soulé. Pp. 11-34. (Cambridge University Press: Cambridge, Massachusetts.

Grier, J.W. 1980a. Ecology: A simulation model for small populations of animals. *Creative Computing* **6**:116-121.

Grier, J.W. 1980b. Modeling approaches to bald eagle population dynamics. *Wildlife Society Bulletin* **8**:316-322.

Grier, J.W., and Barclay, J.H. 1988. Dynamics of founder populations established by reintroduction. In *Peregrine Falcon Populations,* eds T.J. Cade, J.H. Enderson, C.G. Thelander and C.M. White. Pp. 698-700. The Peregrine Fund: Boise, Idaho.

Harris, R., Clark, T. W., and Shaffer, M. L. 1989. Estimating extinction probabilities for the black-footed ferret. In *Conservation Biology and the Black-Footed Ferret,* eds U. S. Seal, E. T. Thorne, M. A. Bogan and S. H. Anderson. Pp. 69-82. Yale University Press: New Haven, Connecticut.

Heinsohn, G.E. 1966. Ecology and reproduction of the Tasmanian bandicoots (*Perameles gunni* and *Isoodon obesulus*). *Univ. Calif. Publ. Zool.* **80**:1-107.

Hennemann, W.W. 1983. Relationship among body mass, metabolic rate and intrinsic rate of natural increase in mammals. *Oecologia* **56**:104-108.

Lacy, R.C. 1987. Loss of genetic diversity from managed populations: Interacting effects of drift, mutation, immigration, selection, and population subdivision. *Conserv. Biol.* **1**:143-158.

Lacy, R.C, Flesness, N.R., and Seal, U.S. 1989. Puerto Rican parrot population viability analysis. Report to the U.S. Fish and Wildlife Service. Captive Breeding Specialist Group, Species Survival Commission, IUCN, Apple Valley, Minnesota.

Moon, B. R. 1984. Current distribution of the Eastern Barred Bandicoot, *Perameles gunnii* in Victoria. Fisheries and Wildlife Division, Victoria. *Arthur Rylah Institute for Environmental Research Tech. Rep. Ser.* No. 5. Department of Conservation, Forests and Lands: Melbourne.

Parker, W., and Smith, R. 1988. Draft United States Fish and Wildlife Service Recovery Plan/Species Survival Plan (SSP) Masterplan for Red Wolf. US Fish and Wildlife Service, Atlanta, Georgia.

Seal, U.S., and Lacy, R.C. 1989. Florida Panther (*Felis concolor coryi*) Viability Analysis and Species Survival Plan. Report to the U.S. Fish and Wildlife Service. Captive Breeding Special Group, Species Survival Commission, IUCN, Apple Valley, Minnesota.

Seal, U.S., Thorne, E.T., Bogan, M.A., and Anderson, S.H. (eds) 1989. *Conservation Biology and the Black-Footed Ferret.* Yale University Press: New Haven, Connecticut.

Seebeck, J. H. 1979. Status of the Eastern Barred Bandicoot, *Perameles gunnii*, in Victoria: with a note on husbandry of a captive colony. *Aust. Wildl. Res.* **6**:225-264.

Shaffer, M. 1981. Minimum population sizes for species conservation. *Bioscience* **31**:131-134.

Snyder, N.F.R., Wiley, J.W., and Kepler, C.B. 1987. *The Parrots of Luquillo: Natural History and Conservation of the Puerto Rican Parrot.* Western Foundation of Vertebrate Zoology: Los Angeles.

Soulé, M.E. (ed.) 1987. *Viable Populations for Conservation.* Cambridge University Press: Cambridge, Massachusetts.

# An Analysis of Alternative Strategies for Recovering the Eastern Barred Bandicoot in Victoria

*Lynn A. Maguire[1], Robert C. Lacy[2], Robert J. Begg[3] and Tim W. Clark[2]*

## Abstract

The tools of stochastic simulation modelling and decision theory were used to analyse alternatives for recovering the eastern barred bandicoot (*Perameles gunnii*) in Victoria. The first stages of this work are reported here, including a description of the problem and solicitation of subjective information from a knowledgeable group of researchers and managers. The results to date are discussed for management options for the Hamilton population and a framework suggested for evaluating management of the species throughout Victoria—both in the wild and in captivity. The Hamilton population has apparently declined at a rate of about 25% per year over the last 10 years. Mortality factors operating on the eastern barred bandicoot were analysed and modelled. Extinction is virtually inevitable within 25 years unless energetic population management can reverse this downward trend. We conclude that: 1) unless mortality rates at Hamilton are reduced greatly, the population will not expand into new habitat being created by management; 2) removals from the Hamilton population for captive breeding and reintroduction may accelerate its decline towards extinction; 3) an hierarchical program of aggressive management must focus on removal for captive breeding, drastic reductions in mortality at Hamilton, and habitat improvement at Hamilton and elsewhere.

## Introduction

Mainland populations of the eastern barred bandicoot have been reduced to a remnant of only about 150 to 300 individuals at Hamilton, Victoria. This population has apparently declined at a rate of about 25% per year over the past 10 years (Seebeck 1979; Moon 1984; Dufty 1988; Brown 1989; Minta *et al.* this volume). Extinction is virtually inevitable within 25 years unless energetic population management can reverse this downward trend (Lacy and Clark, this volume).

Numerous alternatives for recovering the species through habitat management, predator control and reintroduction have been suggested. Some options, such as double fencing and planting cover plants, are directed toward improving the status of the Hamilton population. Other options, such as captive breeding and establishment of additional fenced and unfenced populations, are aimed at securing the species elsewhere in Victoria.

Careful evaluation of management alternatives is essential because biological and socioeconomic resources for recovering eastern barred bandicoots are limited. Removing animals from the Hamilton population may further jeopardise that population's survival, but animals are needed for both captive and reintroduced populations. Financial resources for habitat improvement and population manipulation are limited, and efforts to change human behaviour regarding cat management, pesticide use and automobile speed will cost both money and good will.

Several features of bandicoot management make such evaluation difficult. The situation is critical: poor choices or inaction now may preclude sur-

[1]School of Forestry and Environmental Studies, Duke University, Durham, North Carolina 27706, U.S.A.
[2]Department of Conservation Biology, Chicago Zoological Society, Brookfield, Illinois 60513, U.S.A.
[3]National Parks and Wildlife Division, Department of Conservation, Forests and Lands, Arthur Rylah Institute for Environmental Research, 123 Brown Street, Heidelberg, Victoria 3084, Australia.

vival of the population. Many features of eastern barred bandicoot population dynamics are uncertain, yet management decisions must be made without waiting for the results of further research. Much of the information on which these decisions must be based is subjective, consisting of the judgment of those with experience in bandicoot biology and management. Some of the uncertainties could be resolved by additional study, *e.g.* the importance of different causes of mortality; some are inherently unpredictable, such as the occurrence of catastrophic fire or flood. The multiple objectives of maintaining the wild population at Hamilton, enhancing survival of the species statewide (in the wild and in captivity), and minimising financial and political costs may not be fully compatible.

Other endangered species programs that share these difficulties have benefited from the application of analytical procedures combining stochastic simulation modelling and decision theory (*e.g.* Maguire 1986; black-footed ferret (*Mustela nigripes*): Maguire 1989, Maguire *et al.* 1988, Harris *et al.* 1989, Lacy and Clark 1989; Sumatran rhino (*Dicerorhinus sumatrensis*): Maguire *et al.* 1987). We used these methods to analyse alternatives for recovering the eastern barred bandicoot. In this paper, we report the first stages of our work, emphasising description of the problem and solicitation of subjective information. The results on management of the Hamilton population are discussed and a framework suggested for evaluating management of the species throughout Victoria, in the wild and in captivity.

## Goals for Bandicoot Recovery

In this analysis, we have assumed that the overall goal for eastern barred bandicoot management is to restore populations in the wild to viable levels. More specifically, the authors and other wildlife managers want to maximise the probability that the Hamilton population will survive the next 25 years, maximise the probability that the species survives in Victoria the next 25 years (including captive and reintroduced populations, as well as the Hamilton population), and do so at minimum financial cost. Five criteria are suggested here to measure the success of alternative management strategies for achieving these goals: 1) the probability of survival for the Hamilton population over the next 25 years; 2) the mean and variance of the Hamilton population size over the next 25 years (for a given mean, minimising the variance will minimise the probability of extinction); 3) the combined probabilities of survival of captive and wild populations over 25 years; 4) the area of habitat available to eastern barred bandicoots in Hamilton; and 5) dollar cost. There are other issues, such as public support for bandicoot recovery, that will be discussed below in the section on implementation.

## Bandicoot Management at Hamilton

### Causes of Mortality

Evidence from trapped animals suggests that reproductive rates in the Hamilton population are high, but that excessive mortality is reducing the population at a rate of nearly 25% per year (Minta *et al.*, Lacy and Clark, both in this volume). Nearly every adult female in the Hamilton population breeds regularly (Brown 1989; Dufty 1988; Minta *et al.* this volume) and litter sizes are the same as those observed in a Tasmanian population of eastern barred bandicoots (Heinsohn 1966), so it is unlikely that population recovery can be achieved through enhanced reproduction. The focus of this analysis, therefore, is on mortality factors at Hamilton and management actions that might decrease them.

Among the presumed causes of mortality are 1) predation by domestic and feral cats; 2) predation by other animals, such as foxes; 3) road kills; 4) diseases and parasites; 5) acute and chronic pesticide poisoning; 6) limitations on food and water; 7) fire and flood; 8) drought; and 9) habitat destruction through slashing and burning. Factors 1 to 6 probably operate more or less continuously in the population, whereas factors 7 to 9 are more sporadic (Fig. 1).

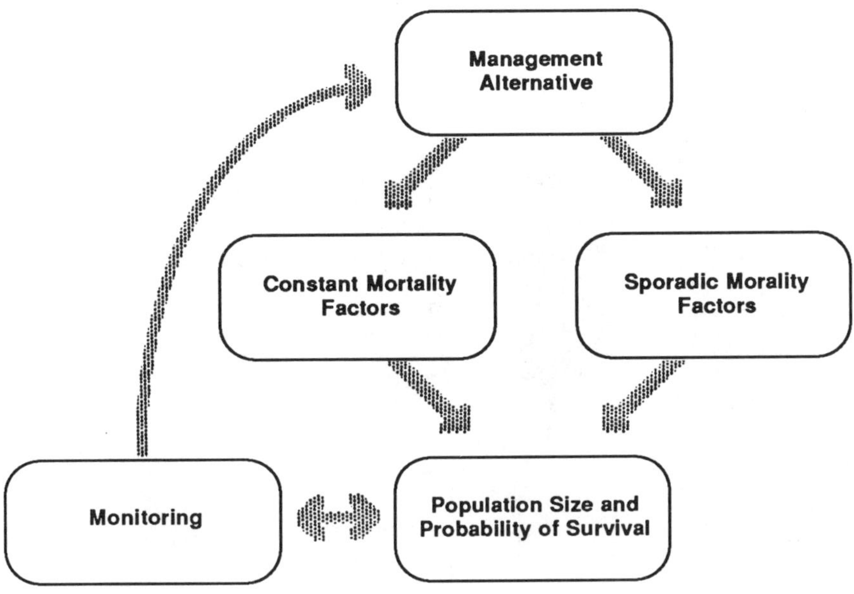


*Figure 1.*—Relationships among mortality factors operating on the Hamilton eastern barred bandicoot population and management and monitoring alternatives.

The relative importance of each factor as a cause of mortality in different segments of the Hamilton population is unknown, and information on the absolute impact of each cause on the Hamilton population is scant. Nevertheless, in order to allocate resources among alternative management actions, we needed to estimate how much each action might reduce mortality and increase population size and probability of survival (Fig. 1). We solicited both objective and subjective information on mortality in the Hamilton population from a group of biologists and wildlife managers familiar with eastern barred bandicoots and constructed histograms of mortality attributable to different causes (Fig. 2; see Appendix I for participants). Appendix II summarises the objective information on which the histograms were based. In some cases, subjective information was used to modify estimates based on objective data. For example, we recognised that estimates from post-mortem examinations were biased, because road kills and domestic cat kills are the most likely sources of carcasses for necropsy. The histograms were done separately for juveniles (<500 g) and for adult males and adult females because these groups differ in vulnerability to different causes of mortality. For example, juveniles appear to be more vulnerable to cat predation. We also made separate estimates for three segments of the population in different areas of Hamilton, because risks of mortality from different causes differ among these areas. For example, the Kennedy Oval area has relatively low mortality due to road kills. In constructing the histograms, we chose to attribute a given death to only one cause, although certainly many of these mortality factors interact (*e.g.* bandicoots weakened by pesticide poisoning or parasites may be especially vulnerable to predators or drought stress).

*Management Actions: Benefits and Costs*

The management actions that are being considered (and implemented) for recovering the Hamilton population to a safer level are aimed at

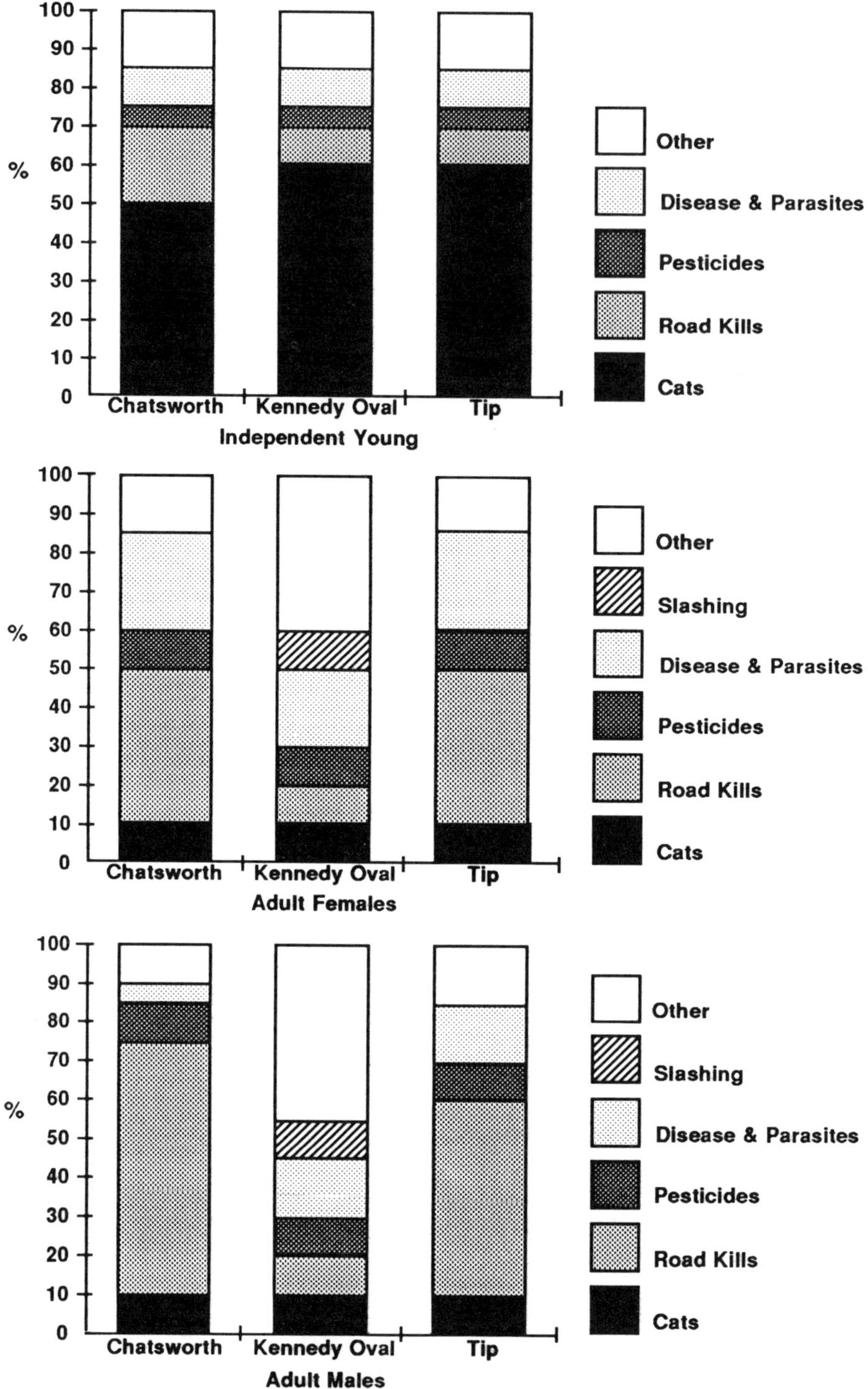



*Figure 2.*—Mortality histograms for various age and sex subpopulations of the Hamilton eastern barred bandicoots.

*Table 1.*—Some management actions and their expected benefits to the Hamilton eastern barred bandicoot population and its habitat. Estimated cost for each management action is given.

| Management actions | Benefits | | | Cost |
| | Mortality | | Habitat | |
| | Source | % Reduction[1] | increase | |
| --- | --- | --- | --- | --- |
| Double fencing and planting | cat | 30% in modified habitat | 40-100 ha/km | $2,700/km |
| Cat control Maximum level | cat | year 1: 10% year 2: 20% years 3+: 50% | —— | $40,000/yr |
| Cat control Minimum level | cat | year 1: 0% year 2: 0% years 3+: 20% | —— | $5,000/yr |
| Road reflectors and reduced speed | road | 20% | —— | $1,100+[2] |

[1] As provided by a panel of experts; see Figure 2. Percent mortality reductions assumed to be the same for adults and juveniles and for both sexes.

[2] A minimum estimate; does not include enforcement cost.

decreasing specific sources of mortality and otherwise improving habitat quality. Using the frequencies of varied causes of mortality estimated by the biologists and wildlife managers (Fig. 2), the next stage of our analysis was to estimate how much each action would benefit the Hamilton population and how much each would cost to implement. We solicited this information from the group listed in Appendix I. Their responses are summarised in Table 1.

*Habitat Improvement: Double Fencing, Planting, Shelters.* Double fencing, particularly with planting of shrubs between the fencelines, provides cover and foraging habitat for bandicoots. Constructing 'hard' shelters of railway sleepers (ties) and sheet metal provides additional refuge from predators. Eastern barred bandicoots appear to range up to 200 to 500 m from cover, so each kilometre of fencing could provide 40 to 100 ha of additional bandicoot habitat (A. Arnold and P. Goldstraw, personal communication), supporting an estimated density of 1.5 bandicoots per ha (Minta *et al.* this volume). Within this improved habitat, the availability of cover may reduce predation by cats by about 30% of current levels in the areas of fencing (Table 1). Costs of double fencing and planting range from $0.20 to $4.70 per metre, depending on what type of planting is done and what materials and labour are supplied by the landowner. The Department of Conservation, Forests and Lands can provide planting materials and drive posts, at a cost of $2.70 per metre. Landowners perceive other benefits from double fencing and planting (*e.g.* windbreaks, conservation of other fauna and flora) besides bandicoot habitat improvement, so the costs of these activities should not be allocated entirely to eastern barred bandicoot recovery.

*Cat Control.* Reducing domestic and feral cat predation on eastern barred bandicoots has been hampered by public sentiment and lack of supportive regulations. However, several actions seem feasible and have at least partial support from local government (C. Lenghaus, personal communication): trapping feral cats (particularly at the Tip); facilitating disposal of unwanted pets;

subsidising neutering of pets; and imposing a curfew on pets. Effective cat control is difficult and will require continuing effort and expenditure. Benefits will not be felt immediately, because reduction in the cat population will take time, and amount of benefit will depend on the level of effort and money expended. We assumed that cat controls will take 3 years to reach full effectiveness, and we examined two levels of effort (Table 1). As with habitat improvement, the benefits of cat control are broader than bandicoot recovery alone, and the costs should be distributed among these other goals as well.

*Road Modifications.* Many of the actions that would be most effective in reducing road kills of eastern barred bandicoots may not be practical or locally accepted (*e.g.* speed humps, culverts, drift fences). The use of reflectors to discourage bandicoots from crossing when vehicles approach is currently being tested (Arnold *et al.* this volume). Reduced speed limits are also possible, particularly because Hamilton residents have requested them already out of concern for children's safety.

The costs and benefits of some other actions that might be undertaken to aid bandicoot recovery were not considered in any detail. These include veterinary treatment to reduce disease incidence and parasite load and reduction in pesticide use (Lenghaus *et al.* this volume). Any attempt to assess the cost of reducing pesticide use should separate urban and rural uses and should account for both possible reductions in yield and reductions in expenditures on pesticides. Reducing pesticide use could have other benefits besides bandicoot recovery (*e.g.* reduced killing of other vertebrates and beneficial invertebrates) and cost should be apportioned among these goals as well.

*Management Strategies for Hamilton Bandicoot Recovery*

To guide choices among the actions that might be taken currently to recover bandicoots at Hamilton, we proposed several specific management strategies and assessed their benefits and costs

(Table 2). 'Status quo' (alternative 1) refers to conditions before 9 km of double fencing were installed in 1989 in the Chatsworth Road and Tip areas (alternative 2). Alternative 1 is the 'Basic scenario' modelled by Lacy and Clark (this volume). Alternatives 3 and 4 illustrate two rates of installing additional double fencing in the Chatsworth and Tip areas. Expected carrying capacities in alternatives 2, 3, and 4 were calculated by assuming that improved habitat would average 1.5 eastern barred bandicoots per ha. For example, an estimated 540 to 1350 additional bandicoots could exploit the 360 to 900 ha of habitat created by 9 km of fencing.

The reductions in mortality rates due to decreased cat predation for the fencing alternatives were calculated by multiplying the expected reduction in cat predation (30%, from Table 1) by the proportion of the Hamilton area bandicoot population expected to occupy this new habitat (using midpoints of ranges: *e.g.* an estimated 945 eastern barred bandicoots would occupy the improved habitat created by 9 km of fencing; thus 945/1095 = 86% of the bandicoots would be subjected to 30% lower mortality due to cats in alternative 2) and then by the percentage of mortality attributable to cat predation in the Chatsworth and Tip areas (*e.g.* a mean of 55% for juveniles, from Figure 2). In alternatives 3 and 4, the bulk of the eastern barred bandicoot population will be in improved habitat, with reduced mortality due to cat predation. Thus, the additional fencing has little impact on the overall levels of mortality. These calculations assume that the eastern barred bandicoots immediately redistribute to occupy the modified habitats in proportion to the ultimate carrying capacities of those areas and that fencing would be equally divided between the Chatsworth and the Tip areas. If bandicoots are slow to move into new habitat, then mortality reductions would be delayed. If bandicoots preferentially move into areas with fencing, or increase in density there because of higher survival without compensating dispersal, then the proportions of the population protected may be greater than assumed and the reductions reported in Table 2 may be slight underestimates. It is uncertain how fast eastern

*Table 2.*—Costs and benefits of some possible management strategies for recovering the Hamilton population of eastern barred bandicoots.

| Recovery strategy | Benefits | | Cost |
|---|---|---|---|
| | % Mortality reduction (Juv/Adult F/Adult M) | Carrying capacity in Hamilton area | |
| 1. Status quo | —— | 150 | —— |
| 2. Fencing and planting 9 km in 1989 in Chatsworth and Tip areas | 14/3/3 | 690-1500 | $24K |
| 3. #2 plus 3 km/yr for 5 years in Chatsworth and Tip areas | year 1: 15/3/3<br>year 3: 15/3/3<br>years 5+: 16/3/3 | 870-1950<br>1230-2850<br>1590-3750 | $65K over 5 yrs |
| 4. #2 plus 9 km/yr for 5 years in Chatsworth and Tip areas | year 1: 15/3/3<br>year 3: 16/3/3<br>years 5+: 16/3/3 | 1230-2850<br>2310-5550<br>3390-8250 | $146K over 5 yrs |
| 5. #2 plus cat control at minimum level in all areas | year 1: 14/3/3<br>year 2: 14/3/3<br>years 3+: 22/4/4 | 690-1500<br>690-1500<br>690-1500 | $29K<br>$5K<br>$5K/yr |
| 6. #2 plus cat control at maximum level in all areas | year 1: 18/3/3<br>year 2: 22/4/4<br>years 3+: 35/6/6 | 690-1500<br>690-1500<br>690-1500 | $64K<br>$40K<br>$40K/yr |
| 7. #2 plus speed limits and reflectors in Chatsworth and Tip areas | 17/10/14 | 690-1500 | $24K +<br>>$1K/yr |
| 8. #2 plus speed limits and reflectors in Chatsworth and Tip areas plus cat control | year 1: 21/11/14<br>year 2: 25/12/15<br>years 3+: 38/14/17 | 690-1500<br>690-1500<br>690-1500 | $65K +<br>$41K +<br>>$41K/yr |

barred bandicoots will expand into habitat provided by double fencing; monitoring this process will be a high priority for the next several years.

Alternatives 5 and 6 add cat control, at two levels, in all three areas to the 9 km double fencing installed in 1989. Since both double fencing and cat control reduce predation, the combined effects of these two actions in habitat created by fencing in the Chatsworth and Tip areas were calculated as above, using a compounded reduction (*e.g.* 65% in the third year for maximum cat control) due to fencing (30%, Table 1) and cat control (50% in the third year). This mortality reduction in the newly created habitat was then averaged with the mortality reduction in original habitat, weighted by the proportion of eastern barred bandicoots occupying new and original habitat (*i.e.* 86% of eastern barred bandicoots in new habitat, 14% in original habitat).

Alternative 7 adds reduced speed limits and reflectors to the 9 km fencing; the road modifications affect only the Chatsworth and Tip areas.

Since road modifications and fencing affect different sources of mortality (road kills and cat predation, respectively) that are likely independent, the reductions in mortality from these two actions were taken to be additive. The reductions due to road modifications in the Chatsworth and Tip areas were calculated by multiplying the percent reduction (20%) by the proportion of eastern barred bandicoots expected in the Chatsworth and Tip areas (1045/1095 = 95%) and then by the mean proportion of mortality attributable to road kills in the Chatsworth and Tip areas. These estimates were then added to the reductions in mortality due to fencing (from alternative 2). To estimate the cost of alternative 7, we assumed that about $1K per year would be spent on maintenance and enforcement, which is surely an underestimate of the cost of effective enforcement. Alternative 8 combines 6 and 7, again assuming additive reductions in mortality due to road kills and cat predation.

Table 2 lists, for each of the eight management strategies, the benefits in terms of reduced mortality and increased habitat available to bandicoots around Hamilton, and the costs in terms of dollars. The benefits can be analysed by population viability assessment (PVA; Lacy and Clark, this volume and below), translating percent reductions in mortality and additional hectares of habitat into additional bandicoots and reduced probability of extinction. Within the framework of decision analysis, relative values could be placed on these biological benefits and financial costs (Maguire 1986), allowing ranking of the eight alternatives in Table 2 by net value, as perceived by wildlife managers, the local populace and/or a broader community (Statewide, national or international). Other benefits and costs could be factored into such an analysis as well. Below we use PVA to analyse the biological benefits of strategies in Table 2; relative valuation of the benefits described with respect to the financial costs (either by formal decision analysis or by subjective ranking) must be left to the local management authorities with responsibility for eastern barred bandicoot recovery in Victoria.

*Simulations of Hamilton Management Strategies*

The next stage of our analysis of management alternatives, therefore, is to predict the impact of the reduced mortality rates and increased carrying capacities on bandicoot population growth and probability of population extinction. To do this, we used a simulation model of eastern barred bandicoot population growth that included: 1) demographic stochasticity (*i.e.* variation in population parameters among individuals in the population); 2) a moderate level of environmental stochasticity, reflecting seasonal variation in birth and death rates due to variation in weather or other environmental conditions; and 3) probabilities of catastrophic events, reflecting what is known about the frequencies and impacts of drought, fire and flood in the Hamilton bandicoot habitat. This model is described in detail in Lacy and Clark (this volume). We assumed an initial population size (as of late 1989) of 150, based on the recent estimates by Dufty (1988) and Minta *et al.* (this volume) with recognition of the probable further decline of the population subsequent to those studies. Birth rates were based on reproductive data from live-trapping studies (see Lacy and Clark this volume). Mortality rates for juveniles, adult males and adult females were set (in the absence of management actions: status quo on Table 2) to produce the age distribution and rate of population decline (about 25% per year in years without a catastrophe of flood, fire, or severe drought; mean of 31% annual reduction if catastrophe years are included) observed in recent population studies (Minta *et al.*, Lacy and Clark, both in this volume).

The results of simulations corresponding to the management strategies in Table 2 are shown in Table 3. The 'status quo' population declines to extinction with virtual certainty within 25 years (alternative 1, Table 3). To reverse this trend and stabilise the population, adult and juvenile mortality rates must be reduced by aggressive management. Neither the fencing underway (alternative 2, Table 2), nor more ambitious programs of

*Table 3.*—Results of 1,000 simulations of the Hamilton eastern barred bandicoot population under various management strategies: $pE_{25}$ = probability of extinction by year 25; TE = mean time to extinction of extinct simulated populations; $N_{25}$ = average population size at year 25 of those populations not extinct; $SD_{25}$ = standard deviation of population size at year 25 of those populations not extinct.

| Recovery strategy[1] | Mean annual growth rate | Probability of extinction $pE_{25}$ | Mean years to extinction TE | Population size $N_{25}$ | $SD_{25}$ |
|---|---|---|---|---|---|
| 1. Status quo | 0.69 | 1.00 | 10.6 | — | — |
| 2. 9 km fencing | 0.81 | 0.93 | 14.6 | 15 | 10 |
| 3. 24 km fencing[2] | 0.82 | 0.92 | 15.1 | 14 | 12 |
| 4. 54 km fencing[2] | 0.82 | 0.90 | 15.2 | 15 | 13 |
| 5. Min. cat control[2] + 9 km fencing | 0.88 | 0.69 | 17.1 | 23 | 17 |
| 6. Max. cat control[2] + 9 km fencing | 0.98 | 0.14 | 19.2 | 104 | 96 |
| 7. Road modifications + 9 km fencing | 0.92 | 0.44 | 18.2 | 38 | 35 |
| 8. 9 km fencing + max. cat control[2] + road modification | 1.10 | 0.00 | — | 808 | 291 |

[1]Management strategies as in Table 2. Midpoints of carrying capacity ranges used for modelling.
[2]Final reduction in mortality and final carrying capacity (years 3+ or 5+) assumed throughout the simulation (from year 1).

fencing (alternatives 3 and 4), nor fencing in conjunction with cat control (alternatives 5 and 6), nor fencing in conjunction with road modifications (alternative 7) are sufficient to protect the bandicoots: In each case the Hamilton population of eastern barred bandicoots would still be in decline and highly vulnerable to extinction within 25 years. Note that the large increase in carrying capacity achieved by strategies 3 and 4 has little impact on probability of extinction if population growth is not positive because bandicoots are not available to expand into the increased habitat.

Although not matching any of the management strategies under consideration, we also examined a scenario which would achieve no net population growth or decline (36% reduction in juvenile mortality, 7% reduction in adult mortality: both slightly better than alternative 6). Even with the population 'stabilised' in the sense of bringing mortality rates down to parity with birth rates, continuing random fluctuations in population numbers would result in a 10 % probability of extinction within 25 years (Table 4). The Hamilton population is not now large enough to be safe from extinction due simply to random events, and a positive growth rate is needed to allow for expansion to fill newly created habitat. Of the strategies we examined, only an aggressive program of cat control in conjunction with fencing and road modifications (alternative 8) appears adequate to achieve the goal of recovery in Hamilton. That management strategy is predicted to result in sufficient population growth (10% per year) to expand into available habitat and to steadily approach the carrying capacity.

*Prospects for Bandicoot Recovery at Hamilton*

It will be difficult to reduce mortality rates in the Hamilton population sufficiently to reverse the population decline, unless actions more drastic than those currently underway can be implemented quickly and successfully. Although many of the actions in Table 2 will take time to accomplish, and even more time to be fully effective, our modelling was based on an assumption of instantaneous benefits (*e.g.* in modelling alternatives 3, 4, 5, 6 and 8 to produce the results in Table 3 we assumed that all fencing and cat control was in place from year 1). Until management actions are completed, the Hamilton population will continue its rapid downward trend, as indicated in the status quo, alternative 1. Delays in implementing management strategies will cause the projected population sizes and probabilities of population survival to be considerably below those indicated in Table 3.

Intensive management of the wild population at Hamilton can yield promising predictions (alternative 8), but an effective adjunct to any strategy in Table 2 would be the establishment of captive breeding colonies. Captive breeding is planned (and partially underway) at Gellibrand Hill Park, near Melbourne, and a fenced population is planned for the Hamilton Community Parklands (Arnold *et al.*; Seebeck *et al.*, both in this volume). The likely benefits and costs of each of these projects should be evaluated with the tools of PVA and decision analysis.

*Hamilton as the Resource for Eastern Barred Bandicoot Recovery*

The establishment of captive breeding colonies or additional wild populations will require the removal of bandicoots from the Hamilton population (until captive facilities begin to produce a surplus of bandicoots that can be used for dispersal to additional sites). This places an additional burden on the Hamilton population that has not been considered in the foregoing analysis. The impact of removal depends on the extent to which it substitutes for other causes of mortality. It seems reasonable to expect that removal of newly-independent animals, as called for by the captive breeding plan at Gellibrand Hill Park (Brown 1989), will be at least partly compensated in that many of those juveniles would likely have fallen prey to cats. If the removals are entirely compensated by reductions in other sources of mortality, they can be made with no impact on the population. More likely, removals will be partially compensated, and management strategies which include removals for captive breeding or reintroductions have more pessimistic outcomes than those suggested in Table 3.

To minimise the probability that young animals removed from Hamilton would be those that otherwise would have survived and reproduced successfully in Hamilton, it might be wise to obtain animals for captive breeding from those areas of Hamilton where cat predation is most severe. This is counter to the recommendation by W.B. Sherwin (in Brown 1989) that animals not be selected from 'those areas where any sampling may seriously deplete the population at that locality.' The *entire* Hamilton area population is presently at extreme risk of extinction (Lacy and Clark, this volume). We therefore recommend that bandicoots be taken from areas where they are least likely to survive (the population 'sinks') (Pulliam 1988), rather than from those areas that have relatively better population growth (the population 'sources'). The only justification for not following this tactic would be if it were believed that the densities of eastern barred bandicoots in the most secure areas of habitat were above the local carrying capacity of the environment (perhaps because of limited food supplies or because breeding was socially inhibited).

Table 4 shows some examples of the impact of 'slow' and 'fast' rates of removal on the Hamilton population. If bandicoots are removed from Hamilton in the absence of aggressive management to reduce predation, the almost assured

*Table 4.*—Impact on the Hamilton eastern barred bandicoot population of removing animals for captive breeding or reintroduction: $pE_{25}$ = probability of extinction by year 25; TE = mean time to extinction of extinct simulated populations; $N_{25}$ = average population size at year 25 of those populations not extinct; $SD_{25}$ = standard deviation of population size at year 25.

| Recovery Strategy[1] | Removal rate[2] | Reduction in mortality Juv/Ad F/Ad M | Mean annual growth rate[3] | Probability of extinction $pE_{25}$ | Mean years to extinction TE | Population size $N_{25}$ | $SD_{25}$ |
|---|---|---|---|---|---|---|---|
| 1. Status quo | None | 0/0/0 | 0.69 | 1.00 | 10.6 | — | — |
|  | Slow | 0/0/0 | 0.69 | 1.00 | 6.4 | — | — |
|  | Fast | 0/0/0 | 0.69 | 1.00 | 4.3 | — | — |
| 8. 9 km fencing | None | 38/14/17 | 1.10 | 0.00 | — | 808 | 291 |
| + cat control | Slow | 38/14/17 | 1.10 | 0.05 | 13.4 | 593 | 356 |
| + road modif. | Fast | 38/14/17 | 1.10 | 0.80 | 7.2 | 164 | 184 |
| Zero population | None | 36/7/7 | 1.00 | 0.10 | 19.0 | 150 | 143 |
| growth | Slow | 36/7/7 | 1.00 | 0.38 | 14.5 | 88 | 86 |
|  | Fast | 36/7/7 | 1.00 | 0.98 | 6.0 | 55 | 61 |

[1] Strategies 1 and 8 are as in Tables 2 and 3. The zero population growth strategy was modelled by assuming a 36% reduction in juvenile mortality, a 7% reduction in adult mortality, and a carrying capacity of 1095.

[2] 'Slow' removals correspond to an annual harvest of 8 juvenile males and 16 juvenile females for five years; 'fast' removals correspond to an annual harvest of 24 juvenile males and 48 juvenile females for five years. Frequently, in declining populations, not enough young are produced in some years to provide the numbers desired for removal.

[3] Mean population growth rate during years subsequent to removals, as calculated from life table analysis.

extinction of the Hamilton population will be accelerated. The Hamilton population, with the present level of mortality and rate of decline, cannot provide sufficient juvenile bandicoots for establishment of additional wild and captive stocks. In most of the simulations of the status quo scenario—lines 2 and 3 of Table 4—the population was, within a few years, so small that the desired numbers of juveniles were not available for removal. If nothing could be done to reduce mortality in Hamilton (almost certainly *not* the case), then the only strategy for achieving recovery of the eastern barred bandicoot in Victoria would be to remove *all* bandicoots from the Hamilton population (quickly, before that population perishes) and to establish captive populations protected by predator-proof fencing. This drastic approach would be an admission of our failure to conserve eastern barred bandicoots in the wild (at present) and should only be implemented as a method of last resort. Recently, wildlife managers in the U.S.A. found it necessary to take such action to preserve the black-footed ferret and the California condor (*Gymnogyps californianus*).

Even if mortality rates were reduced sufficiently to achieve zero population growth (in the absence of removals), removals at the 'slow' rate would put the population at high risk (38%) of extinction and 'fast' removals would likely lead to rapid extinction (Table 4). The most aggressive management strategy examined (strategy 8 in Tables 2 and 3) can provide juveniles for establishment of other populations without markedly damaging prospects for population survival, but only if removal is limited to 24 juveniles per year for 5 years (line 5 of Table 4). With fast removals and (otherwise) rapid population growth (line 6, Table 4), 80% of the simulated populations went extinct quickly (mean time to extinction of 7.2 years). Those simulated populations that survived the early years of removals in sufficient numbers to avoid imminent extinction subsequently expanded rapidly into the available habitat.

Slower rates of removal than modelled above (perhaps 8-12 animals per year) would have less impact on the Hamilton population, and would perhaps be sustainable with slower population growth than achieved with alternative 8, but would likely provide insufficient animals for effective establishment of additional wild or captive populations. The protocol in the Eastern Barred Bandicoot Management Plan (Brown 1989) for establishment of a captive breeding colony at Gellibrand Hill Park recommends transfer of just six bandicoots from Hamilton, breeding two cycles of litters, then return of those six adults to Hamilton and replacement by six more to be captured from the Hamilton population. At that rate of introduction, it would require 5 to 10 years to transfer the 58 bandicoots recommended by W. B. Sherwin (in Brown 1989) for genetic reasons. It is quite possible that the Hamilton population will not persist long enough to provide the needed animals for Gellibrand Hill Park and elsewhere (Table 4), unless animals are moved much more quickly than recommended in the current Management Plan and/or the population decline at Hamilton is reversed (not just slowed).

The number of animals needed to establish a viable population is often underestimated (Griffith *et al.* 1989), and the PVA of Lacy and Clark (this volume) makes it clear that management actions such as captive breeding cannot be spread over a decade or more. Tragically, with each year delay in utilising eastern barred bandicoots from Hamilton to create secure populations elsewhere, the size of the sole source population at Hamilton is markedly reduced. Nevertheless, the difficulty of reversing the population decline at Hamilton, in combination with the remarkable reproductive potential of eastern barred bandicoots, suggests that removals for captive breeding and/or reintroduction may be necessary to accomplish recovery of the species in Victoria.

*Statewide Bandicoot Management*

The last part of our analysis is a qualitative comparison of some of the management options that have been suggested for captive and reintroduced populations of eastern barred bandicoots elsewhere in Victoria. Since bandicoots can be removed from the Hamilton population only at some cost to recovery efforts at Hamilton, it is essential to choose wisely among the possible uses for these animals. Various sites have been suggested for captive breeding programs and for reintroduction in both fenced and unfenced areas. To choose among these, we need to compare the prospects for success in establishing captive or wild bandicoot populations at these sites and the financial costs of doing so. We solicited qualitative information on both constant and sporadic mortality factors at each site that has been proposed for captive breeding or reintroduction from the group listed in Appendix I. These assessments of mortality risks plus 1) estimates of areas of bandicoot habitat, 2) financial costs for establishment and maintenance, 3) sources of funding, 4) potential for genetic management, and 5) availability of special facilities, such as breeding or acclimatisation pens at reintroduction sites, are summarised in Table 5 for captive breeding sites and in Table 6 for reintroduction sites. There is some overlap between what can be considered a captive breeding site and what can be considered a reintroduction site. For example, Gellibrand Hill Park has an outer, fenced area into which bandicoots will be released from the breeding pens; Mooramong and Serendip Wildlife Research Station will have one or a few breeding pens, in addition to the reintroduction area.

Comparing the proposed captive breeding sites (Table 5), there seems to be little to distinguish among them except for size of facility and cost. Since all facilities are to be enclosed with predator-proof fencing, predation risk should be low everywhere (although recent experience at Gellibrand Hill Park with unexpected fox (*Vulpes vulpes*) and/or domestic dog predation shows that

*Table 5.*—Qualitative rating of mortality factors, costs and benefits among three captive breeding options for the eastern barred bandicoot.

| Management consideration | Captive Breeding Site | | |
| --- | --- | --- | --- |
| | Gellibrand Hill Park | Hamilton Community Parklands | Werribee Park |
| **Mortality factors** | | | |
| Constant | | | |
| Predators | low-moderate | low | low |
| Parasites, disease | moderate | moderate | moderate |
| Pesticides | low | low | low |
| Sporadic | | | |
| Epidemic disease | 10%/yr | 10%/yr | 10%/yr |
| Fire frequency | ? | ? | 25 yrs |
| Floods | low | low | low |
| Area (ha) | 325+ | 100+ | 25 |
| Cost[1] | $25,000 for pens | $1,000 | $1,200 |
| Genetic management | moderate | moderate | moderate |
| Main source of funds | CFL[2] | CFL | ZBV[3] |
| No. of breeding pens | 16 | 1 | 4 |

[1]Additional cost, beyond funds allocated as of 9/89, for completion
[2]CFL = Department of Conservation, Forests and Lands, Victoria
[3]ZBV = Zoological Board of Victoria

this should not be taken for granted). Similarly, there is little reason at this point to think that the other constant and sporadic mortality factors would differ among the proposed sites. Gellibrand Hill Park is by far the largest site, with the best potential for sustaining a viable, independent, captive population. However, the smaller sites, such as Werribee Park, could play an important role as insurance against catastrophic disease or other sporadic mortality at Gellibrand Hill Park.

Among sites proposed for reintroduction (Table 6), there may be some differences in mortality risks or at least among mortality sources. Due to the proximity of residential areas, Serendip Wildlife Research Station is more vulnerable to cat predation than the more remote sites. The incidence of foxes at the three sites is uncertain; surveys to assess predator populations would be a wise precaution. Mooramong has the advantage of having some fenced habitat, which will provide refuge from predators over part of the site. At all of the sites, the vegetation is being restored to more natural conditions, but it will be some years before all of the potential bandicoot habitat is available. Mooramong will have one, and Serendip several, small breeding and/or acclimatisation pens that will be useful for holding animals to be reintroduced. Too often, direct release of captive-bred animals results in very high mortality, requiring release of large numbers of animals before successful re-establishment is assured (Griffith *et al.* 1989).

The same process we used to simulate expected population dynamics for the Hamilton management strategies should be repeated for the captive

*Table 6.*—Qualitative rating of mortality factors, costs and benefits among three reintroduction options for the eastern barred bandicoot.

| Management consideration | Reintroduction Site | | |
| --- | --- | --- | --- |
| | Mooramong | Serendip W.R.S. | Cobra Killuc S.W.R. |
| **Mortality factors** | | | |
|   Constant | | | |
|     Cat predation | low | moderate-high | low |
|     Other predation | high? | moderate-high | moderate-high |
|     Road kills | nil | low | low |
|     Parasites, disease | low-moderate? | low-moderate | low-moderate |
|     Pesticides | low? | low? | low? |
|     Habitat destruction | low | low | low |
|   Sporadic | | | |
|     Epidemic disease | <5%/yr? | <5%/yr? | <5%/yr |
|     Fire frequency | ? | ? | ? |
|     Floods | low? | low? | low? |
| Area (ha) | 30+ (1,500)[1] | 250 | 300 (in 10 yrs) |
| Cost per ha | ? | low | low |
| Main source of funds | CFL[2] | CFL | CFL |
| Breeding/acclimatisation pens | 1 | 4 | 0 |

[1] 1500 ha available some time in the future
[2] CFL = Department of Conservation, Forests and Lands, Victoria

breeding and reintroduction sites, in order to give a more quantitative assessment of benefits to be expected from each alternative. Captive populations in breeding pens should be treated separately from the populations in the outer fenced areas at facilities such as Gellibrand Hill. Similarly, the bandicoot population within the fenced area at Mooramong will experience different mortality rates than the unfenced population and should be modelled separately. In addition, these simulations must take account of additions and removals of animals as exchanges are made among captive and wild populations to achieve genetic and demographic goals (Brown 1989).

## Prospects for Bandicoot Recovery Statewide

Success is by no means assured in either the captive breeding or the reintroduction programs that have been proposed. Captive facilities are vulnerable to epidemic disease and parasites, although veterinary care can ameliorate some of these risks. Control of predators is an issue at all sites, particularly those to be used for reintroduction. Controlling rabbits, which is an issue at reintroduction sites as well, may have unexpected adverse effects on bandicoots if predators switch prey when rabbits decline. All of the sites that have been suggested for reintroduction are under public control, so that the use of pesticides and fertilizers can be controlled and native vegetation beneficial to bandicoots can be restored. To make larger areas of private land available for eastern barred bandicoot habitat, private landowners must be convinced of the desirability of undertaking less disruptive forms of land management, such as whole farm planning.

The number of animals that must be released over time to achieve successful establishment of a wild population is often underestimated, leading to discouragement after many captive-bred animals have been released without success. Although care must be taken that unsuitable reintroduction sites do not become an unending drain on the productivity of captive breeding programs, realistic assessment of the number of releases that must be made will allow managers to plan the 'harvest' of animals from the captive program without jeopardising its stability.

Although there are many pitfalls on the way to bandicoot recovery, the reproductive potential of the species augurs well for eventual success. The same success in captive productivity that has been achieved with the black-footed ferret (Clark 1989) should be within reach of the eastern barred bandicoot captive breeding program. Stability of funding and provision for continuing management and maintenance of both captive and reintroduced populations are essential, so that the loss of the eastern barred bandicoot population that was once being established at Serendip Wildlife Research Station is not repeated there or elsewhere.

## Conclusion and Recommendations

Our analyses of management options for recovering the eastern barred bandicoot population at Hamilton suggest that it will be difficult and expensive to reduce mortality rates enough to reverse the decline and restore the population to viable levels. Some of the major causes of mortality at Hamilton, such as cat predation and road kills, will be difficult to control without public support for new regulations and strict enforcement. Efforts to provide habitat and reduce mortality at Hamilton should continue, in order to maximise the probability of survival of the wild population there and in order to serve as a source of bandicoots for captive breeding and eventual reintroduction to other areas. Existing efforts to establish captive populations at Gellibrand Hill Park and other sites provide both insurance against the not unlikely loss of the Hamilton population and a system for producing the large numbers of animals that will be required for successful reintroduction elsewhere.

The simulation studies should be expanded to consider more management strategies, including the statewide management strategies listed in Tables 5 and 6. These predictions will give additional guidance on priorities for management actions at Hamilton and destinations for bandicoots removed from the Hamilton population. Since many eastern barred bandicoot recovery activities are funded by a single organisation, the Department of Conservation, Forests and Lands, making the most effective allocation of resources among actions is essential. Model predictions of population sizes at 5-year intervals should be compared with observed levels as bandicoot management continues, to provide feedback on how expectations compare with experience. Monitoring of all management actions is an essential connection in the loop from action to results (Fig. 1), and should be budgeted for in any programs that are initiated.

Although there is no assurance of success, the rapid reproductive rate of eastern barred bandicoots is a plus that many endangered species do not share. Captive breeding colonies of bandicoots must be established before the Hamilton population declines further. Simultaneously, mortality of bandicoots at Hamilton must be reduced so that this valuable (and, presently, only) population is not lost from the State of Victoria. As soon as captive facilities contain sufficient numbers of bandicoots to assure their persistence while providing surplus animals, bandicoot populations should be established elsewhere in Victoria to restore the species to a secure distribution over more of its former range. The hierarchical strategy of captive breeding, management of the wild population at Hamilton, and establishment of additional populations in fenced and unfenced areas should be a powerful one for achieving recovery.

## Acknowledgments

We thank all those people listed in Appendix I for their thoughtful participation in the assessment of mortality, benefits and costs during the decision analysis workshop. The Chicago Zoological Society supported travel by Lynn Maguire to the workshop. Robert Lacy and Tim Clark were supported by funding from the Chicago Zoological Society and the Zoological Board of Victoria.

## Appendix I

List of participants in a decision analysis workshop, held June 1, 1989, at the Arthur Rylah Institute for Environmental Research, Heidelberg, Victoria.

Lynn Maguire, Leader
School of Forestry and Environmental Studies
Duke University
Durham, North Carolina  U.S.A.

Andrew Arnold
Department of Conservation, Forests and Lands
Portland, Victoria

Robert J. Begg
Department of Conservation, Forests and Lands
Heidelberg, Victoria

Denise E. Casey
Northern Rockies Conservation Cooperative
Jackson, Wyoming  U.S.A.

Tim W. Clark
Chicago Zoological Society &
Northern Rockies Conservation Cooperative
Jackson, Wyoming  U.S.A.

Gary Davey
Department of Conservation, Forests and Lands
Heidelberg, Victoria

Anthony Dufty
Department of Zoology
The University of Melbourne
Parkville, Victoria

Peter Goldstraw
Department of Conservation, Forests and Lands
Warrnambool, Victoria

Cor Lenghaus
Department of Agriculture and Rural Affairs
Hamilton, Victoria

Ian Mansergh
Department of Conservation, Forests and Lands
Heidelberg, Victoria

David Middleton
Sir Colin Mackenzie Sanctuary
Healesville, Victoria

Nick Robinson
Department of Genetics and Human Variation
LaTrobe University
Bundoora, Victoria

Bill Sherwin
Department of Genetics and Human Variation
La Trobe University
Bundoora, Victoria

Bob Warneke
Department of Conservation, Forests and Lands
Heidelberg, Victoria

Frank Wright
Zoological Board of Victoria
Parkville, Victoria

*Appendix II*

Summary of available objective information on mortality of the eastern barred bandicoot at Hamilton, Victoria.

1. *Cat kills*—of 50 dead eastern barred bandicoots examined by Cor Lenghaus, about 30% were predator kills, nearly all cat; of 83 examined by Frank Wright, about 25% were cat kills (note that bandicoot carcasses turned in for examination are a biased sample—likely to be either road kills or domestic cat kills; feral cats probably eat prey; other causes of death are not likely to lead to recovery of carcass); most cat kills are of juveniles (see Brown 1989, as well as Lenghaus *et al.* this volume: 40% adults, 60% juveniles).

2. *Other predators*—2 of 50 carcasses examined by Lenghaus appeared to be dog or fox kills.

3. *Road kills*—about 36% of 50 carcasses examined by Lenghaus were road kills; about 75% of 83 examined by Wright were road kills (see note above about biases); most road kills are adults (see Brown 1989 and Lenghaus *et al.,* this volume: 83% adults and 17% juveniles); observation of number of carcasses on road for one five-week and one three-week period suggest a minimum of one eastern barred bandicoot killed every 5 days.

4. *Parasites and diseases*—based on analysis of carcasses, loads of both internal (roundworms, tapeworms, etc.) and external (ticks, fleas) parasites can be high; sometimes enough external parasites are found to produce perhaps fatal anemia; live-trapped animals sometimes have a huge number of ticks and fleas, particularly at Kennedy Oval and Chatsworth Road areas; toxoplasmosis is frequently found in adults (but with uncertain clinical effect); of 50 bandicoots examined by Lenghaus, 13% of deaths were attributed to parasites and diseases (5% adults, 8% juveniles).

5. *Pesticides*—samples from six carcasses have been analysed for organochlorine residues; five had high levels (1-7 ppm dieldrin).

6. *Flood*—there is anecdotal evidence of increased cat predation when bandicoots are driven to more open areas by flood.

7. *Drought*—bandicoot reproduction apparently ceased during droughts in 1982-83 (Brown 1989).

8. *Habitat destruction*—there is anecdotal evidence of direct mortality from slashing areas of high grass, such as the railway reserve and Kennedy Oval.

9. *Deaths in traps (all of these likely to have been turned in)*—of 50 bandicoots examined by Lenghaus, four were adults dead in traps and 13% were juveniles dead in traps.

*References*


Brown, P. R. 1989. Management Plan for the Conservation of the Eastern Barred Bandicoot, *Perameles gunnii*, in Victoria. National Parks and Wildlife Division, Victoria. *Arthur Rylah Institute for Environmental Research Tech. Rep. Ser.* No. 63. Department of Conservation, Forests and Lands: Melbourne.

Clark, T. W. 1989. *Conservation Biology of the Black-footed Ferret.* Special Scientific Report. Wildlife Preservation Trust International: Philadelphia.

Dufty, A. C. 1988. The distribution, population abundance, status, movements and activities of the Eastern Barred Bandicoot, *Perameles gunnii*, at Hamilton. B. Sc. (Honours) Thesis, La Trobe University, Bundoora, Victoria.

Griffith, B., Scott, J.M., Carpenter, J.W., and Reed, C. 1989. Translocation as a species conservation tool: Status and strategy. *Science* 245:477-480.

Harris, R., Clark, T.W., and Shaffer, M. L. 1989. Estimating extinction probabilities for the black-footed ferret. In *Conservation Biology and the Black-footed Ferret*, eds U. S. Seal, E. T. Thorne, M. A. Bogan and S. H. Anderson. Pp. 69-82. Yale University Press: New Haven, Connecticut.

Heinsohn, G. E. 1966. Ecology and reproduction of the Tasmanian bandicoots (*Perameles gunni* and *Isoodon obesulus*). *Univ. Calif. Publ. Zool.* 80:1-107.

Lacy, R. C., and Clark, T. W. 1989. Genetic variability in black-footed ferret populations: past, present, and future. In *Conservation Biology and the Black-footed Ferret,* eds U. S. Seal, E. T. Thorne, M. A. Bogan and S. H. Anderson. Pp. 83-103. Yale University Press: New Haven, Connecticut.

Maguire, L. A. 1986. Using decision analysis to manage endangered species populations. *J. Environ. Manage.* 22:245-360.

Maguire, L. A. 1989. Managing black footed ferret populations under uncertainty: an analysis of capture and release decision. In *Conservation Biology and the Black-footed Ferret,* eds U. S. Seal, E. T. Thorne, M. A. Bogan and S. H. Anderson. Pp. 268-292. Yale University Press: New Haven, Connecticut.

Maguire, L.A., Seal, U.S., and Brussard, P.F. 1987. Managing critically endangered species: the Sumatran rhino as a case study. In *Viable Populations for Conservation,* ed. M.E. Soulé. Pp. 141-158. Cambridge University Press: Cambridge.

Maguire, L. A., Clark, T. W., Crete, R., Cada, J., Groves, C., Shaffer, M. L., and Seal, U. S. 1988. Black-footed ferret recovery in Montana: a decision analysis. *Wildl. Soc. Bull.* 16:111-120.

Moon, B. R. 1984. Current Distribution of the Eastern Barred Bandicoot, *Perameles gunnii* in Victoria. Fisheries and Wildlife Division, Victoria. *Arthur Rylah Institute for Environmental Research Tech. Rep. Ser.* No. 5. Department of Conservation, Forests and Lands: Melbourne.

Pulliam, H.R. 1988. Sources, sinks, and population regulation. *Am. Nat.* 132, 652-661.

Seebeck, J. H. 1979. Status of the Barred Bandicoot, *Perameles gunnii,* in Victoria: with a note on husbandry of a captive colony. *Aust. Wildl. Res.* 6:225-264.

# Recovery Management of the Eastern Barred Bandicoot in Victoria: Statewide Strategy

*John H. Seebeck[1]*

## Abstract

Recognition of the declining status of the eastern barred bandicoot prompted the preparation of a Management Plan, the revised version of which was published in April 1989. The major thrusts of the Plan are towards the stabilization and enhancement of the remaining wild population at Hamilton, and the re-establishment of the species at other sites within its former range. Implementation of the recommendations is facilitated by an Action Plan supervised by local and State recovery teams. Habitat works and bandicoot conservation at Hamilton include land management on public and private land, cat control, captive breeding, population monitoring, ecological studies and community education. State recovery presently involves the establishment of two satellite colonies, taxonomic research and genetic research and modelling. Management of the satellite colony at Gellibrand Hill Park near Melbourne is described.

## Introduction

Earlier papers (Seebeck *et al.;* George *et al.;* Coulson; Robinson *et al.,* in this volume) have demonstrated the urgent need for a comprehensive conservation strategy for the eastern barred bandicoot (*Perameles gunnii*) in Victoria, and have shown how different biological aspects of the species need to be accounted for when planning such a strategy. In addition, Lacy and Clark (this volume) have provided some numerical bases for planning long-term conservation, and, with those in mind, Maguire *et al.* (this volume) have examined the several options for achieving those population levels. This paper describes the development of the State Conservation Strategy and its achievements so far.

## Development of a Management Plan

Although concern as to the status of *P. gunnii* in Victoria had been expressed as early as 1937 (Harper 1945), it was not until the late 1960s and early 1970s that public concerns were expressed (Wakefield 1967, 1971; Pizzey 1975). Investigations into status commenced in 1972 (Seebeck 1979), but no plans were made to ensure maintenance of the wild population. Brown (1987, 1989) began studies at Hamilton in 1980, one early result of which was a realization that the species' decline was continuing, and that local indifference was placing certain sections of the Hamilton population at threat. A proposal to modify the Municipal Tip extensively, which was providing shelter for a substantial number of bandicoots was widely publicised and was, in part, instrumental in moves by the then Fisheries and Wildlife Division to prepare an interim plan (Seebeck 1982; Seebeck and Chamley 1982), and subsequently to employ P.R. Brown to continue his studies and to prepare a management plan for the species.

This project, which commenced in 1983, was jointly funded by the Department of Conservation, Forests and Lands (CFL), World Wildlife Fund Australia and a private donor. A Draft

---

[1]National Parks and Wildlife Division, Department of Conservation, Forests and Lands, Victoria. Arthur Rylah Institute for Environmental Research, 123 Brown Street, Heidelberg, Victoria 3084, Australia.

Management Plan (Brown 1987) was made available for public comment in February 1987.

This management plan gave details of current status and distribution, examined causes of decline, demonstrated the effects of cats and listed management issues facing *P. gunnii*. Having identified the issues, the plan then explored the possible strategies for conservation, spelt out prescriptions for management and made strategic recommendations in the areas of policy development, habitat management, vermin control, captive breeding and reintroduction, public relations and future research.

Following comment from the public, including municipal and State Government bodies, the draft was revised. Many of the issues raised were incorporated into the revision, which also included reassessments of Departmental priorities, and the provision of new information. The revision (Brown 1989) was released in April 1989.

The major thrusts of the Management Plan are: a) to stabilize and enhance the Hamilton colony; and b) to re-establish the species at other sites within its former range.

The processes by which these two aims are to be achieved have included the preparation of an Action Plan and the establishment of State and Hamilton Recovery Teams to supervise the implementation of the actions as they take place.

The following paper in this volume (Arnold *et al.*) deals in detail with the recovery of the Hamilton population. Briefly, the approaches are to: a) secure and enhance existing habitat; b) expand the area of suitable habitat; c) control predation; and d) reduce road mortality.

## The Action Plan

This document (Conservation, Forests and Lands 1989) identified 15 actions designed to secure eastern barred bandicoots in Victoria. These were as follows.

## Release of Revised Management Plan

As indicated above, the revised Management Plan was duly released in April 1989, at which time an outline of the strategy proposed in this paper was made public.

## Establishment of Hamilton Recovery Team

An essential ingredient in the management process for the recovery of *P. gunnii* at Hamilton is effective and streamlined coordination and communication between the public bodies and community groups which are actively involved.

The establishment of a Hamilton Recovery Team was seen as the best means of achieving this. The Team is chaired by the Assistant Regional Manager (Resource Conservation), Portland Region, CFL with the other members representing the City of Hamilton, the Shire of Dundas, the Hamilton Institute of Rural Learning (HIRL), local landholders and the National Parks and Wildlife Division. The Portland Region (CFL) provides a secretariat.

The broad role of the Hamilton Recovery Team is to assist CFL in the development, implementation and coordination of the management program for *P. gunnii* in the Hamilton area (see Arnold *et al.*, this volume).

## Establishment of State Recovery Team

The recovery strategy involves not only stabilization and recovery at Hamilton but at a number of other sites in western Victoria (see below) at which satellite colonies are to be established. In addition, ecological and genetic research is planned, and there is thus a requirement for an overall strategic planning group for the whole State program.

The State Recovery Team is convened and administered by the Wildlife Management Branch, National Parks and Wildlife Division. It is chaired by the Manager of Research, and consists of representatives from the National Parks and Wild-

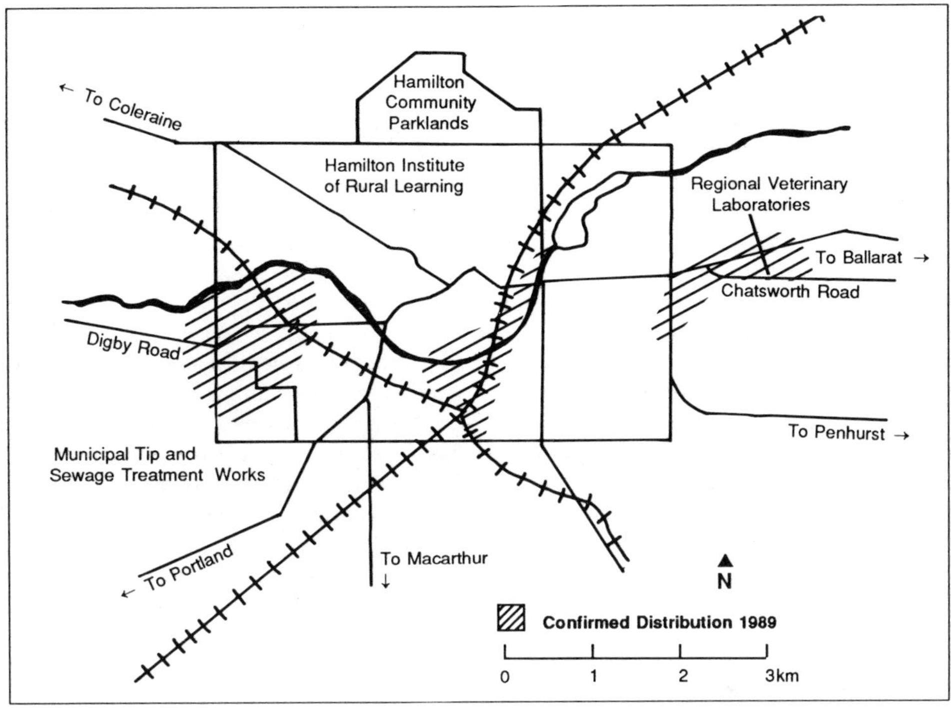



*Figure 1.*—Hamilton, Victoria, location of the wild population of eastern barred bandicoots, 1989, showing places mentioned in the text.

life Division, LaTrobe University Department of Genetics and Human Variation, The University of Melbourne Department of Zoology and other members as agreed, including CFL regional representatives.

*Habitat Management on Public Land at Hamilton*

The requirement for shelter from the elements and predators is a major management issue for *P. gunnii*. Control of habitat on public land (State and Municipal) is relatively easy to accomplish, as it involves minimum expense and activity. The initial works involve fencing, some re-vegetation, shelter construction and protection from clearing. An appropriate burning regime to enhance the rehabilitation and re-establishment of native grasslands is then required.

CFL has identified a number of areas currently controlled by the City of Hamilton which have high priority for habitat management for the bandicoot (Fig. 1). The Department has provided financial incentives in the form of materials to the City so that habitat development works can be undertaken in these areas. The incentives were made available through the Land Protection Incentives Scheme Schedule for the Flora and Fauna Guarantee.

The initial work which has been carried out has been simply the erection of stock-proof fencing to provide areas of cover and shelter for the bandicoots. The cover provided by the growth of grass within the fenced areas will be augmented in future by the planting of a range of attractive and appropriate ornamental shrubs.

Within the Shire of Dundas, the remaining colony of bandicoots is located in the Chatsworth Road area near the Department of Agriculture and Rural Affairs Regional Veterinary Laboratory. The management aim for this colony is to enable animals to expand from their current nucleus by the provision of appropriate habitat along roadsides and on selected private land (see Arnold *et al.*, this volume).

### Purchase of Freehold Land at Hamilton

One of the most important colonies at Hamilton is based in and around the Municipal Tip and the adjacent Sewage Treatment Works. An adjoining property has been purchased, and will enable habitat enhancement at that locality to be consolidated and extended, against the time when the tip is closed.

### Habitat Management on Private Land at Hamilton

A significant proportion of the bandicoot population at Hamilton relies on habitat on private land, both suburban and rural. It is essential that existing habitat on freehold land be retained where possible, and that private landowners be encouraged to retain habitat (primarily shelter) and to enhance habitat when and where possible. These activities should complement the activities on public land in order to consolidate areas of habitat, minimise fragmentation and to provide linkages and corridors.

Two landowner community groups, the Chatsworth Road Bandicoot Action Group and the Digby Road Bandicoot Action Group were established in 1989. Following investigations and discussions, funds have been provided to these groups for habitat enhancement. Arnold *et al.* (this volume) have described this activity in detail.

### Control of Domestic and Feral Cats at Hamilton

A major factor in the decline in numbers of bandicoots at Hamilton is predation by cats (*Felis catus*). Cat numbers have been estimated at over 2,300 (up to 10 times the bandicoot numbers) for the Hamilton area (Brown 1989), although it must be acknowledged that not all of the area supports bandicoots.

It is recognised that the control of domestic and feral cats within the City of Hamilton and in adjacent Shire areas is a contentious issue. However, because of the large number of cats known to occur in and around Hamilton and their active predation on bandicoots (especially juveniles), both the City and the Shire Councils are in a unique position to set an example for other municipalities within Victoria (and for that matter the nation) in the control of cats. The Management Plan suggests a range of control measures for domestic and feral cats. Municipal Councils could take a lead role in implementing these recommendations.

The Parliament of Victoria (Social Development Committee 1989) has recently published the results of an Inquiry into the Role and Welfare of Companion Animals in Society, in which a number of relevant recommendations concerning cats are made. Importantly, it recommends mandatory permanent identification and registration, with differential registration rates for entire and desexed animals. In addition, it recommends

'That municipalities which include areas where companion animals are likely to have a detrimental impact on native fauna be permitted to enact special by-laws to address this problem. Such by-laws could include:

1. Designation of species-specific exclusion zones;
2. Permit systems for the keeping of any type of companion animal; permit to be issued after inspection of premises and assessment of fencing and housing arrangements;
3. Compulsory desexing of specified types of companion animals;
4. Compulsory use of bell collars on cats;
5. Immediate destruction by proper officer of any dog or cat at large; and
6. Immediate destruction by proper officer of any cat wandering at large and not wearing a bell collar.'

Acceptance of these recommendations by the Parliament would enable the Councils to carry out the Management Plan recommendations.

Foxes (*Vulpes vulpes*) and dogs (*Canis familiaris*) are also predators on bandicoots, and should also be controlled. Recent evidence (Kinnear 1989, Kinnear *et al.* 1988) emphasizes the long-held belief among Australian biologists that the fox has been a major causal factor in the decline and subsequent suppression of many small terrestrial marsupials, and highlights the need for urgent research to develop biological control methods for this predator.

It must be stressed that, without a major control program for cats at Hamilton, all our other efforts in the local strategy, and hence the State strategy will be severely compromised.

*Establishment and Monitoring of a Captive Colony at Gellibrand Hill Park*

The Management Plan identified the need to establish satellite colonies of the bandicoots, as insurance against catastrophic loss of the species at Hamilton. The first such colony was to be established at Gellibrand Hill Park, at Tullamarine, northwest of Melbourne (Figs. 2 and 4). This experiment was begun in July 1988, and will be described later in this paper.

*Establishment and Monitoring of a Captive Colony at Hamilton Community Parklands*

*P. gunnii* has become locally extinct in the Hamilton Community Parklands (Fig. 1) area during the past 10-15 years. The habitat is still excellent and has been enhanced by the existing management of part of the Parklands. The Hamilton Institute of Rural Learning, which occupies part of the Parklands, initiated the fencing of ca.100 ha of the grasslands with a predator-proof fence (Fig. 3). A major financial input from CFL allowed completion of the fence in 1989, thus providing a secure site for a small colony of bandicoots. A breeding pen has been incorporated in the fenced area, and animals have been established therein. Arnold *et al.* (this volume) give details of this part of the strategy.

*Monitoring of the Hamilton Population*

Studies in recent years have shown that population numbers at Hamilton have decreased alarmingly (Seebeck *et al.*, this volume, provides a summary). There is no evidence that this decline has been stabilized. Studies by Minta *et al.* (this volume) during the summer 1988-1989 have established baseline population information at the four major population centres at Hamilton, and it is intended that these centres be monitored annually in order to determine population trends. Minta *et al.* (this volume) have devised a protocol to enable this monitoring to be accomplished efficiently (see also Arnold *et al.*, this volume).

In addition to demographic monitoring, it is desirable that veterinary examination of moribund and dead bandicoots, obtained at Hamilton through predators, road-trauma or other causes, should continue. Lenghaus *et al.* (this volume) have described the results of their examinations of some 80 bandicoots from Hamilton, and have established a baseline for further checks on the health of the population. Especially, they have highlighted the potential danger posed by the continuing (illegal) use of organochlorine pesticides, and it is intended that regular monitoring of this factor should occur.

*Establishment and Monitoring of Other Satellite Colonies*

The reintroduction of *P. gunnii* to a number of sites within its former range is desirable for several reasons, but especially to guard against catastrophes at Hamilton or Gellibrand Hill Park. Because of the dramatic changes in habitat over most of the species' mainland range (Seebeck 1979; Seebeck *et al.*, this volume) the options available for a conservation strategy are limited. Several sites have been proposed: Cobra Killuc State Wildlife Reserve near Hexham; Serendip Wildlife Research Station at Lara; Werribee Zoological Park; and 'Mooramong', a National Trust property near Skipton (Fig. 2).

Cobra Killuc State Wildlife Reserve, of about 450 ha, was part native grassland, part eucalypt and wattle plantation and part *Pinus radiata* plantation. A Management Plan for the Reserve, prepared in 1983 (Hastings 1983), proposed the felling of the pines and some of the eucalypt and wattles and conversion of those parts of the Reserve to native grassland. That task was begun in 1986. Regeneration of the grassland (initially mostly *Themeda triandra*) has begun, and is anticipated to take 5-10 years. As the habitat becomes suitable, and predation control can be carried out at a satisfactory level, Cobra Killuc will be used as a satellite colony.

Serendip Wildlife Research Station (ca. 300 ha) has been managed for wildlife since 1960, and during 1972 a small captive colony of *P. gunnii* was established there (Seebeck 1979). Although breeding was successful, and some animals re-

mained until at least 1978, attempts to establish a feral population at Serendip were unsuccessful. Predation and interference by humans during daily station maintenance were partly responsible for this failure. However, the station provides excellent habitat and a future experimental release, given our improved state of knowledge, will have a greater chance of success.

Werribee Zoological Park (ca. 60 ha) is managed by the Zoological Board of Victoria as an open range zoo, with the major emphasis on large grassland species. A section is, however, dedicated to maintaining endangered species and it is hoped that a captive colony of *P. gunnii* can be established there. Depending on the future management of the Park, this could be used either as the nucleus of a free-living population to complement that at nearby Serendip, or as an intensive breeding station to provide stock for re-establishment at other sites or restocking at Hamilton.

Mooramong occupies an area of 1,562 ha. Most of the property is used for grazing, but some 240 ha are set aside as a Nature Reserve (Parr-Smith 1988). Although primarily a wetland reserve, there is an important dry land component. This consists of grassland and stoney barriers with scattered shrubs and trees. The grassland is being managed so as to re-establish the native species, and replanting on and about the wetland margins and the barriers is designed to re-create the former woodland. During 1989, the National Trust (Victoria) and CFL provided funds to construct bandicoot breeding enclosures within the Nature Reserve, and animals were introduced to the enclosures late in that year. As with all satellite colonies, control of predators (particularly foxes) is a major management function. It is envisaged that, in the future, areas of Mooramong outside the Nature Reserve will be managed to enable the spread and survival of the bandicoots over a larger area of the property.

A number of other sites have been suggested, some on private land. Our present strategy is to reserve decisions on these areas until we have demonstrated our capacity to establish free-living

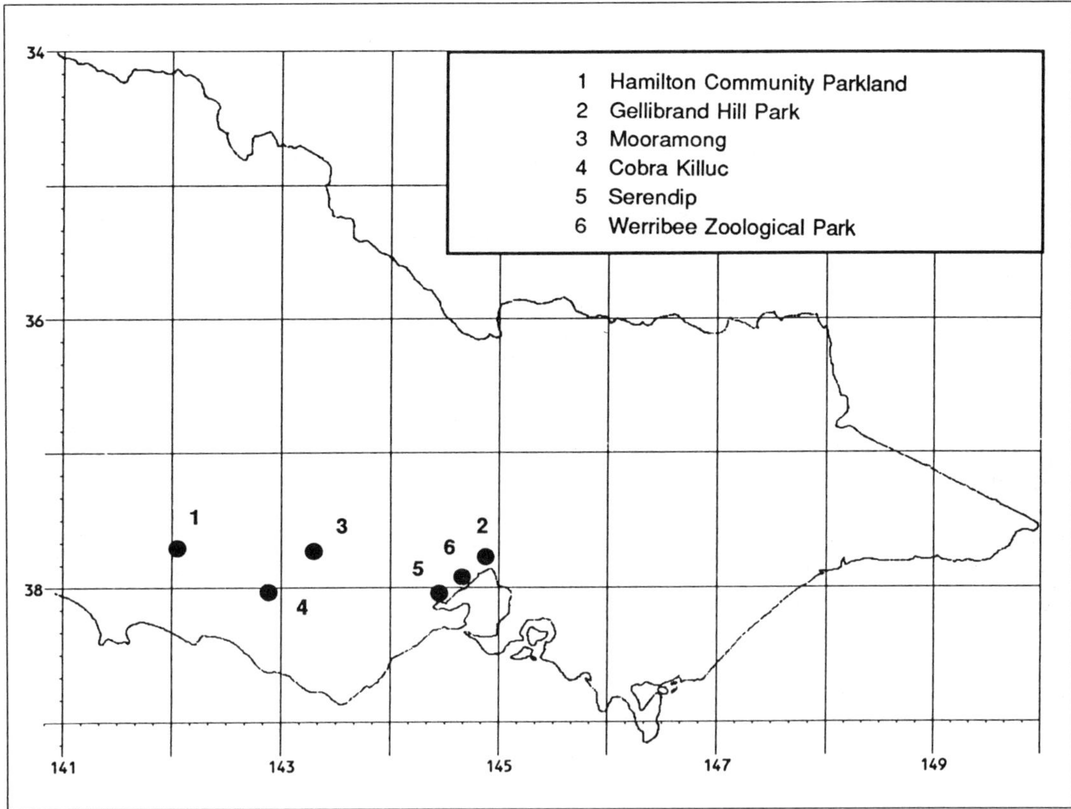


*Figure 2.*—Proposed bandicoot satellite colony locations in western Victoria.

populations on a few specially-selected Government-controlled properties.

*Reduction of Road Kills at Hamilton*

Many bandicoots (estimated 50-60) are killed by motor vehicles in and around Hamilton each year. Most are adult males (Brown 1989; Lenghaus *et al.*, this volume), and this represents a significant impact on the breeding population.

We need to identify and describe the 'hot-spots' for road kills. With that information, decisions on works to alleviate the problem can be made. If the sites are short stretches of roadway abutted by public land it may be possible to provide under-road culverts and directional fences, but if sites are in residential areas, culverts are unlikely to be of much value.

Road warning signs have been in place at selected sites on the outskirts of Hamilton since 1985. Their location needs to be re-assessed and altered if required. One problem site, Chatsworth Road, has already been identified, and relocation of warning signs should be an immediate action. Liaison with the Road Construction Authority, the City of Hamilton and the Shire of Dundas concerning sign placement is necessary. An experiment has begun with headlight reflectors along Chatsworth Road to determine if these may be used to reduce road kills (Arnold *et al.*, this volume).

*Community Education and Extension Programs*

The success of the project will, to a large degree, depend on public approval and support, especially at Hamilton. A properly planned community education and extension package is essential. It can assist by encouraging community support for works on public and private land, the control of cats, and the reduction of road deaths. A grant from the National Estates Program has permitted CFL to employ an officer to help develop such a package.

Materials produced could include printed matter, static displays, videos (especially in the local tourist office), school project material, and a marketing strategy. It could include the encouragement of sensitive bandicoot souvenirs across a fairly wide price range. Arnold *et al.* (this volume) discuss in detail current extension projects in the Hamilton area.

The subsidizing of cat neutering costs and provision of belled collars and ancillary equipment (*e.g.* kitty litter, trays) in the initial phases of a renewed Responsible Pet Ownership Campaign (RPOC) might also be pursued. The recent release of a report on Companion Animals (Social Development Committee 1989) has provided the basis for an effective cat management program at Hamilton. However, legislative change is essential for the program to go ahead.

*Genetic Research*

Genetic studies are essential to the establishment phase of each satellite colony. The value of the captive breeding program depends on establishing and maintaining the broadest possible genetic base. This will be achieved by selecting genetically different founders for introduction into the colonies, and by monitoring individual breeding contributions for each generation.

A knowledge of the genetic structure of the Hamilton population could guide the choice of founders, particularly if the population is highly structured with little gene flow between sub-populations. Having established the broadest possible genetic base for a captive colony, it will be important to prevent loss of variation through over-contribution by certain founders. Since it is difficult to perform controlled crosses for the maintenance of pedigrees in this species, it is imperative that genetic analysis be used to determine the reproductive contributions of different individuals to a colony, until it reaches a large enough size to avoid loss of genetic material (hundreds of individuals). Genetic analysis can be used to guide the timing of returns of founder individuals to the Hamilton population in order to equalise their contributions.

Results of genetic studies on *P. gunnii* will enable us to formulate informed recommendations to ensure the successful management of natural and captive populations. The techniques and analyses will be initially developed at Gellibrand Hill Park.

CFL has provided funds to the Department of Genetics and Human Variation at La Trobe University to assist their development of DNA fingerprinting techniques (see Robinson *et al.*, this volume). The information derived from this work will be used to aid the preparation of genetic management advice.

*Study of Taxonomic Status of Mainland and Tasmanian Populations*

Previous studies (Freedman and Joffe 1967; Sherwin 1987, 1989) were inconclusive in demonstrating the nature of differences between animals from the mainland and from Tasmania. Studies using cranial characters were based on small samples. However, George *et al.* (this volume) have re-examined *P. gunnii* material from museum collections, and concluded that genetic differentiation has occurred, but at a very low level. Studies using electrophoretic analysis

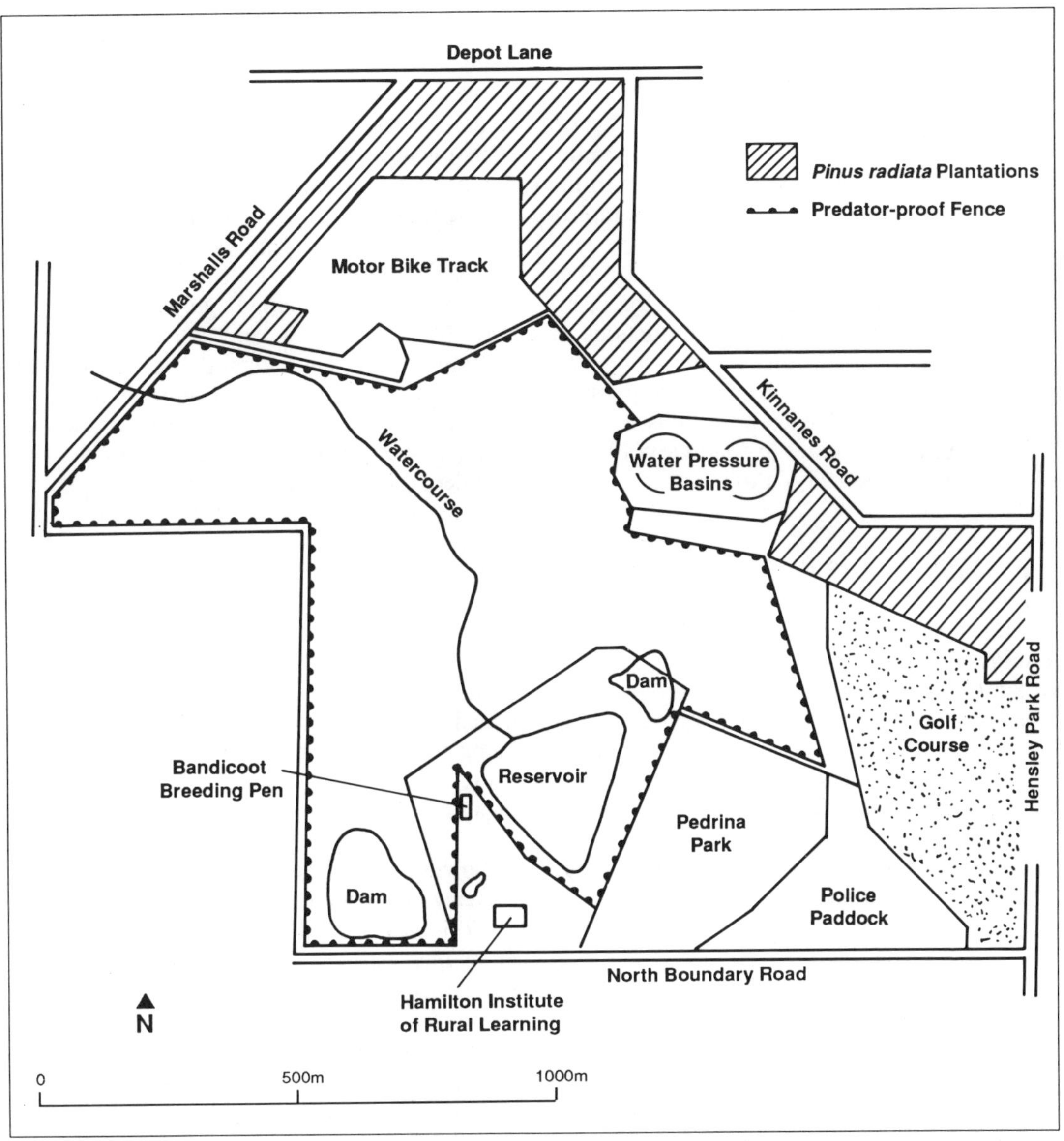


*Figure 3.*—Hamilton Community Parklands, showing location of predator-proof fence, breeding pen for bandicoots and Hamilton Institute of Rural Learning.

of protein polymorphisms have provided little support for separation of the two populations as subspecies.

Comparison of levels of variation in the populations is hampered by a lack of variation in the proteins available for study in blood samples. The evidence that these animals have low variation (in both States) should not be regarded as conclusive until an adequate number of loci (>50) have been analysed. Given the limitations of genetic studies of blood proteins, this requires the study of the DNA itself. Existing programs of genetic research (Robinson *et al.*, this volume) will provide opportunities to continue collection of tissues for DNA analysis.

*The Gellibrand Hill Park Experiment*

The potential of Gellibrand Hill Park as a site for a reintroduction program was recognised by Brown (1987). The large area of native grassland and savannah woodland, which was to be enclosed by a predator-proof fence, would continue to be enhanced by appropriate management, had existing suitably-sized enclosures and permanent management staff seemed to be an ideal solution to the problem of securely establishing a satellite colony. Negotiations were successfully concluded, the necessary modifications to the breeding pens made and the anti-predator fence completed early in 1988 (Fig. 4). A protocol for setting up and managing the colony was written—it appears as Appendix I of the Management Plan (Brown 1989)—and the first pair of animals released into the breeding pens in July 1988. The founders (2 males and 3 females) were in place by October 1988. They had been collected at several sites at Hamilton, individually marked with unique numbers by tattooing in the ears, and standard weights and measurements had been recorded. Weekly trapping and examination followed, and the young were carefully husbanded. Most of the monitoring work was done by A.C. Dufty, as part of a post-graduate study of *P. gunnii*. Thirty-three young (8 males, 19 females, 16 unsexed) are known to have been bred in captivity, and 6 (2

males, 4 females) wild-bred young have been reared. A major husbandry problem still to be overcome is the great difficulty of catching weanling bandicoots. Between the time of relinquishing total dependence on the pouch and independent existence, most young avoid capture, and their fate is thus uncertain. Survival of wild bandicoots at this stage of their life is low. Heinsohn (1966) found a mortality of >75% among post-pouch young *P. gunnii* in Tasmania, and Brown (1987) and Dufty (personal communication) have suggested an even higher percentage loss of *P. gunnii* at Hamilton. However, we were able to rear nine of these total known young (22.5 %) to adulthood. From the first founder group, 9 (56%) of the 16 young produced survived to adulthood. There were, at the time of writing, still nine young present, plus one litter still with their mother.

The agreed protocol has largely been followed, although some founders were prematurely returned to Hamilton. All returnees have re-established at their capture sites, as shown by their being subsequently retrapped and found to be in good condition, and having maintained or increased weight.

Following a re-assessment of the problems and urgency facing the bandicoots in Victoria (Clark 1989) it was decided to revise the breeding program, increase the number of pairs in captivity at Gellibrand Hill Park and thus to raise the rate of production of young significantly. A special allocation of funds enabled additional pens to be constructed during 1989. The appointment of a technical assistant was sought for routine maintenance of the colony. Again, special funding made this possible, and the assistant began duties in June 1989.

Blood samples are collected routinely from each animal brought into the colony or reared within it, and are being used by the Department of Genetics and Human Variation at LaTrobe University for DNA fingerprinting to maintain a genetic profile of the colony (see Robinson *et al.*, this volume).

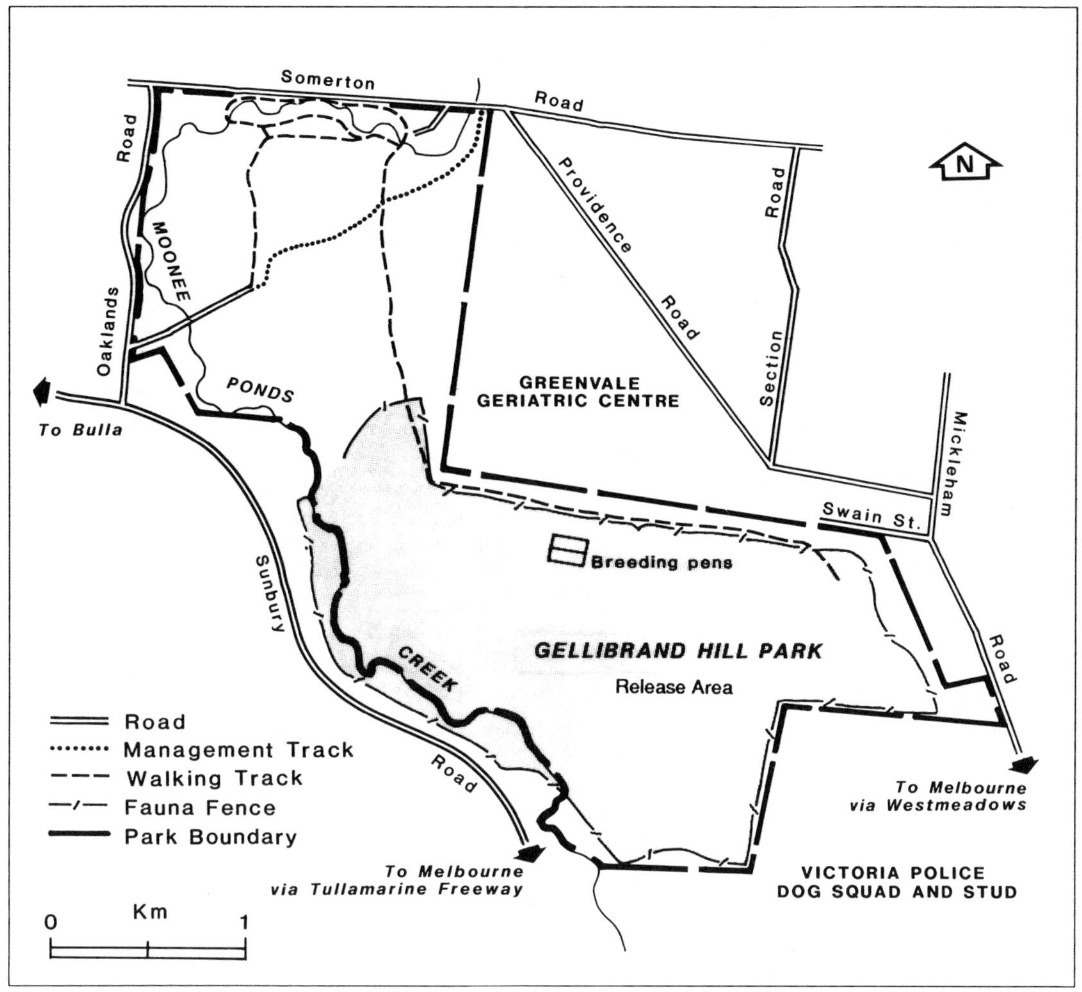


*Figure 4.*—Gellibrand Hill Park, showing location of Nature Reserve, breeding pens for bandicoots and release area.

Predator control within the Nature Reserve fenced area was begun in February 1989, and is a continuing activity. Shooting, poisoning with 1080 on buried meat baits and snare-trapping are the main methods used.

Our assessment that predators had been sufficiently controlled, and the maturation of some of the captive-reared and bred stock prompted a trial release in April 1989. Ten animals (5 males, 5 females), consisting of seven 'captives' and three recently wild-caught were released at the centre of a 27.5 ha grid. The grid of 100 trap stations at 50 m intersects was established by A.C. Dufty, who has since described the vegetation and the vertebrate and invertebrate fauna present.

The release was a 'hard' release (Kleiman 1989), and was followed eight days later by intensive trapping (2 nights/week for 5 weeks) on the grid. Monthly trapping (3 consecutive nights per month) followed, on a grid extended into adjacent areas. Of the 10 released bandicoots, five were subsequently trapped alive, for periods ranging from eight days to 30 weeks following. The other five animals were not encountered during trapping after their release. Nine days after release, one animal was found dead some 600 m northeast of the release site. Another died that night and was found about 150 m south of the first. Both were found on a track, and both appeared to have been killed by a canid. Thirty-nine days later two more dead bandicoots were found in the same area. One of these had clearly been killed by a canid but the other was too decomposed for the cause of death to be determined. The last known survivor (a male) was resident on the grid up to 30 weeks after the initial release.

These events caused an upgrading of predator control measures, and some modifications to Park management to ensure the exclusion of wandering dogs. Despite this initial setback, further releases are planned for late 1989. At least some of the releasees will be fitted with radio transmitters to enable their dispersal to be accurately monitored.

Increase in the size of the captive colony has been dependent on enclosure construction, but at the time of writing (November 1989) there were at least 15 bandicoots in two pens.

Two other satellite colonies have been started. At the Hamilton Community Parklands, two females (captive-bred at Gellibrand Hill Park) were introduced to the breeding pen in April 1989 and joined by a wild-caught male in May. Three litters have since been produced and the male was removed to his capture site in August 1989. The young of the two females will be released into the Parklands.

At Mooramong, Skipton, pens were constructed in May 1989 and the first pair of animals (from Hamilton) was introduced in September 1989. Captive-bred females and wild-caught males were subsequently established in October 1989. To maximize the genetic base, the Mooramong colony is managed as an extension of the Gellibrand Hill Park colony.

## Extension Program

The Management Plan (Brown 1989) recommended the development of extension and advisory services and a community awareness program. At Hamilton, the local officers of CFL continue to be closely involved with extension and advice to the public, especially in the development of bandicoot action groups. The Portland region has sought additional funds to employ a full-time extension officer. The Museum of Victoria and CFL have combined to prepare a static display of eastern barred bandicoots which will be housed at the Hamilton Art Gallery (see Arnold *et al.*, this volume). An interpretive display has been prepared for use at Gellibrand Hill Park, and others will be made for Mooramong and elsewhere.

No conservation strategy can guarantee the 'saving' of an endangered species. However, the processes that have been set in place for the eastern barred bandicoot will address most of the threatening factors facing that species. We have begun the experiment—only time and our collective dedication will reveal if we began the task before it was too late.

## Acknowledgments

This recovery strategy has been developed through the interest and support of many people and organizations. The bandicoots owe a debt to all those who have helped, including: Peter Brown;

Tim Clark, Denise Casey and colleagues; Anthony Dufty; Hamilton Institute of Rural Learning; Bandicoot Action Group landholders at Hamilton; CFL staff from Portland, Melbourne and Ballarat Regions; the Zoological Board of Victoria and the Chicago Zoological Society; LaTrobe University Department of Genetics and Human Variation; World Wildlife Fund Australia; the M.A. Ingram Trust; and the National Trust (Victoria). Anthony Dufty provided records of the Gellibrand Hill Park colony.

My thanks in particular to Rod Gowans (Assistant Director, Wildlife), and Bob Warneke (Research Manager, Wildlife Management Branch), National Parks and Wildlife Division for their support and advice.

*References*


Brown, P.R. 1987. Draft Management Plan for the Conservation of the Eastern Barred Bandicoot, *Perameles gunnii,* in Victoria. National Parks and Wildlife Division, Victoria. *Arthur Rylah Institute for Environmental Research Tech. Rep. Ser.* No. 41. Department of Conservation, Forests and Lands: Melbourne.

Brown, P.R. 1989. Management Plan for the Conservation of the Eastern Barred Bandicoot, *Perameles gunnii,* in Victoria. National Parks and Wildlife Division, Victoria. *Arthur Rylah Institute for Environmental Research Tech. Rep. Ser.* No. 63. Department of Conservation, Forests and Lands: Melbourne.

Clark, T.W. 1989. Recovery of the Eastern Barred Bandicoot and other conservation activities. Unpublished report to Zoological Board of Victoria, Chicago Zoological Society and Department of Conservation, Forests and Lands, Victoria.

Conservation, Forests and Lands. 1989. Action Plan for the Conservation of the Eastern Barred Bandicoot, *Perameles gunnii.* National Parks and Wildlife Division and Portland, Melbourne, Ballarat and Geelong Regions.

Freedman, L. and Joffe, A.D. 1967. Skull and tooth variation in the genus *Perameles.* Part 3: Metrical features of *P. gunnii* and *P. bougainville. Rec. Aust. Mus.* **27**:197-212.

Harper, F. 1945. *Extinct and Vanishing Mammals of the Old World.* The Lord Baltimore Press: Baltimore.

Hastings, I. 1983. Management Plan (1983) for the Cobra Killuc State Wildlife Reserve: with notes on native grassland ecology. Fisheries and Wildlife Service, Victoria. *Resources and Planning Branch Tech. Rep. Ser.* No. 2. Department of Conservation, Forests and Lands: Melbourne.

Heinsohn, G.E. 1966. Ecology and reproduction of the Tasmanian bandicoots (*Perameles gunni* and *Isoodon obesulus*). *Univ. Calif. Publ. Zool.* **80**:1-96.

Kinnear, J.E. 1989. Foxes and wallabies: evidence for multiple population domains. *Abstr. 35th Scien. Mtg. Aust. Mammal Soc.,* Apr. 1989, p. 22.

Kinnear, J.E., Onus, M.L., and Bromilow, R.N. 1988. Fox control and rock-wallaby population dynamics. *Aust. Wildl. Res.* **15**:435-450.

Kleiman, D.G. 1989. Reintroduction of captive mammals for conservation. *BioScience* **39**: 152-161.

Parr-Smith, G. 1988. Preserving native grasslands. *Trust News* **17**(4):19-21.

Pizzey, G. 1975. Have you seen this prowler? *The Herald (Melbourne),* 13 Sept. 1975.

Seebeck, J.H. 1979. Status of the Barred Bandicoot, *Perameles gunnii,* in Victoria: with a note on husbandry of a captive colony. *Aust. Wildl. Res.* **6**:255-264.

Seebeck, J.H. 1982. Interim management guidelines for the management of Barred Bandicoot populations and habitat within and around the City of Hamilton. Fisheries and Wildlife Division, Victoria.

Seebeck, J.H., and Chamley, W. 1982. Conservation measures for the Eastern Barred Bandicoot (*Perameles gunnii*) at Hamilton. Fisheries and Wildlife Division, Victoria.

Social Development Committee. 1989. Report Upon the Inquiry into the Role and Welfare of Companion Animals in Society. Parliament of Victoria: Government Printer.

Wakefield, N.A. 1967. Save the barred bandicoot. *The Age (Melbourne),* 4 Dec. 1967.

Wakefield, N.A. 1971. Mammals of Western Victoria. In *The Natural History of Western Victoria,* eds M.H. Douglas and L. O'Brien. Pp. 37-51. Australian Institute of Agricultural Science: Horsham.

# Recovery Management of the Eastern Barred Bandicoot in Victoria: The Hamilton Conservation Strategy

*Andrew H. Arnold[1], Peter W. Goldstraw[2], A. Greg Hayes[1] and Barry F. Wright[3]*

## Abstract

The eastern barred bandicoot (*Perameles gunnii*) is facing extinction on the Australian mainland. Wildlife managers have adopted an 'adaptive management' approach in dealing with the onsite management of *P. gunnii*. This paper discusses the recently prepared Management Plan and Action Plan which provide the framework for the recovery program at Hamilton. Key elements in the Hamilton Conservation Strategy include (1) population monitoring, (2) habitat management and future habitat development, (3) reduction of road kills, (4) control of introduced predators, (5) establishment of the Hamilton Recovery Team, (6) establishment of a captive breeding colony in the Hamilton Community Parkland and (7) community education and extension programs. At this early stage in the management program, it is not possible to draw any firm conclusions about the success of these methods. The program is to be reviewed on a 6-month basis and the resultant feedback will be fundamental to achieving successful adaptive management.

## Introduction

*Perameles gunnii*, the eastern barred bandicoot, is facing extinction on mainland Australia, and is now confined to one small, fragmented population in and around Hamilton, Victoria (Seebeck *et al.*, this volume). In an attempt to redress this situation, a statewide Recovery Strategy has been developed (Seebeck, this volume) from recommendations contained in a Management Plan (Brown 1989), and implementation of which is facilitated by an Action Plan (Conservation, Forests and Lands 1989). A major component of the Statewide Strategy has been the development of an Hamilton Conservation Strategy. This paper describes the processes and practices which are implemented in this strategy.

The current status of *P. gunnii* at Hamilton is critical, and as a consequence it has been necessary to adopt an 'adaptive management' approach in which we learn and develop our strategy as we go (Holling 1973, 1978). The role of the Hamilton Conservation Strategy is 'onsite management' which focusses on the species and its population *in situ*. The difficulties which have to be faced in developing onsite management strategies are related to the location of the remnant wild population on the outskirts of the Hamilton urban area and along relatively natural corridors within the City on public and private land (Fig. 1). This requires the integration of conservation practices to ameliorate urban development pressures and in particular focusses on the need to harness community support and action.

At Hamilton, *P. gunnii* is under continuing pressure from: (a) continued habitat modification or destruction, (b) direct killing by humans (usually in motor vehicles), (c) the effects of introduced species, and (d) the effects of pollutants. We have attempted to identify these threatening processes clearly and to set in place actions to prevent, reduce or overcome them and to monitor the outcome carefully.

---

[1]Department of Conservation, Forests and Lands, Portland Region, 8-12 Julia Street, Portland, Victoria 3305, Australia.
[2]Department of Conservation, Forests and Lands, Portland Region, 214 Koroit Street, Warrnambool, Victoria 3280 Australia.
[3]Department of Conservation, Forests and Lands, Portland Region, 17 Thompson Street, Hamilton, Victoria 3300 Australia.

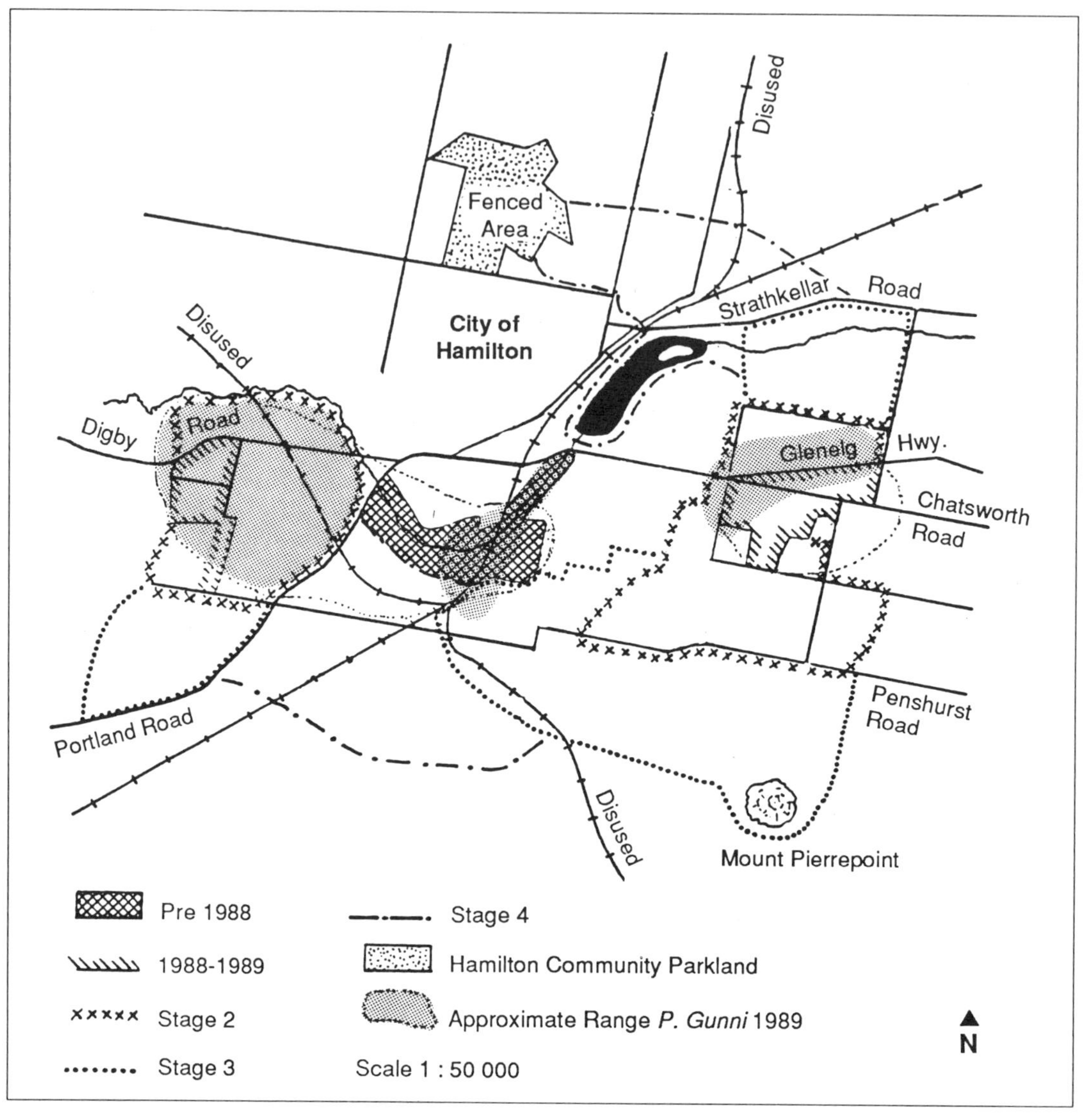


*Figure 1.*—The current range of *Perameles gunnii* at Hamilton and proposed habitat development areas.

### The Hamilton Conservation Strategy

The *Management Plan for the Conservation of the Eastern Barred Bandicoot*, Perameles gunnii, *in Victoria* (Brown 1989) and the *Action Plan for the Conservation of the Eastern Barred Bandicoot*, Perameles gunnii (Conservation, Forests and Lands 1989) give a direction to the needed re-covery process. The Management Plan consolidates recommendations for the conservation of the species in Victoria and is based on current knowledge of the species. However, as Brown (1989) has pointed out, 'The biggest problem is making sure that these management recommendations are put into practice.' The Action Plan addresses this latter issue by describing the necessary actions and management structure to implement these strategies and review achievements regularly.

Specific recommendations in the Management Plan and Action Plan for the Hamilton population are that: 1) 'The population size must be increased by habitat management and predator control. The current population, estimated at about 300, should be increased by about tenfold and the rate of increase should be relatively fast, *e.g.* doubling every few years. This would greatly relieve problems from inbreeding and loss of genetic variation' and 2) 'The fragmented habitat must be consolidated, because fragmentation greatly increases the likelihood that small isolated pockets of the species will be eliminated by ecological or genetic factors. Therefore, a system of corridors of suitable habitat must be planned to connect existing and future sub-populations of bandicoots and to provide radiating fingers and habitat out into surrounding farmland.'

In order to translate these aims into local management practices, the Hamilton Recovery Team was established to coordinate local planning and the community. It is charged with the determination and regular review of priorities and management objectives, and ensuring that set goals are being achieved.

*The Hamilton Recovery Team*

The Hamilton Recovery Team coordinates planning and public involvement at a local level. Its main role is to be a vehicle for communication, concentrating on gathering and exchanging information, providing suggestions for local and State-wide action as well as sponsoring and co-ordinating community support for the recovery program.

Conservation, Forests and Lands (CFL) convened the first meeting in April 1989. Initially, the Recovery Team included a regional representative of CFL as chairperson, representatives of the National Parks and Wildlife Division of CFL, the City of Hamilton, the Shire of Dundas, the Hamilton Institute of Rural Leaning (HIRL) (representing local conservation interests) and a local landholder nominated by the Chatsworth Road and Digby Road Bandicoot Action Groups. The Team meets monthly and is supported by an Executive Officer from the Portland Region of CFL.

Two additional representatives have since been added to the Team. At the initial meeting the desirability of involving local schools in habitat development works was identified, both as a means of carrying out valuable work and as a means of educating a whole new generation of cat owners and landholders. A post-primary Government schoolteacher already involved in a bandicoot program was invited to join the Team. This person's role has since been expanded to include coordinating communication with local schools as well as attempting to develop a range of activities and information for inclusion in school curricula. To aid this process, a separate school coordination team has been developed with every school in Hamilton being represented. Meetings of this group have been organised and serviced jointly by the schools representative from the Recovery Team together with its Executive Officer and the Hamilton School Support Centre. In an attempt to coordinate and monitor veterinary aspects of the recovery of *P. gunnii*, a veterinary adviser has been added to the Team. Often specialists are invited to provide information on a range of issues including habitat management, population monitoring, and the Greening Australia project and its potential for assisting with *P. gunnii* recovery.

Communication is via three routes. Firstly, Team members report directly back to their parent organisations. In some instances, this leads directly into a wider network via newsletters, notably those produced by HIRL and the School Support Centre. Secondly, typed copies of the minutes are available to member groups through their representative and are also sent to a range of groups and individuals from both Hamilton and other parts of the State who have become involved with the Hamilton Recovery Team. Thirdly, a press release is written after every Team meeting for the local press. Figure 2 shows the communication network and areas of involvement of members of the Hamilton Recovery Team in the recovery process.

In the short period of time that the Hamilton Recovery Team has been operating, it has developed an extensive communication network and a school coordination group, produced a planting list for improving *P. gunnii* habitat, carried out an analysis of factors affecting the level of community commitment to cat control, provided information for inclusion in a Museum of Victoria display as well as initiated further investigation into the effect of pesticides on *P. gunnii*. The Team's immediate aims are to coordinate the development of an extension package aimed at the community in general and more specifically for inclusion into the formal education system.

## Habitat Management

The conservation, restoration and creation of suitable habitat for *P. gunnii* in and around Hamilton is the most important component of local management. The loss of suitable habitat for *P. gunnii* can be attributed to a variety of causes. In some instances, there were even legal requirements to make changes which led to a decline in habitat. For example, cover which afforded protection to *P. gunnii* was also seen as an harbour for vermin, particularly rabbits. Cover was also perceived as a fire hazard and required to be removed. When Crown land was made available for purchase under an Improvement Purchase Lease, the occupant was required to remove native vegetation and to improve the pasture. In addition to these legal requirements, more intensive farm management practices and the human desire to have 'tidy' properties have contributed significantly to continued habitat loss.

However, during the late 1980s, greater environmental awareness and concern throughout the community has started to reverse this situation. There is now an increased desire to plant native trees and shrubs for stock shelter and shade, salinity and erosion control, and wildlife habitat.

Recent legislation (*Flora and Fauna Guarantee Act* 1988) incorporates habitat controls as one of five key elements in management.

Of prime importance is cooperation and participation by private landholders in providing habitat on their land because there is not enough local public land to ensure the survival of *P. gunnii*. An attempt to replace some of the lost habitat is being made by the use of hard shelters and double-fenced areas to exclude grazing stock and permit revegetation. Approximately 80% of the *P. gunnii* population at Hamilton relies on private land in suburban areas and the rural fringes. An essential part of the recovery program is the retention of existing habitat on freehold land where possible and the active development of new habitat. Landholders will be encouraged to retain, enhance and develop habitat on their properties. These activities should complement the activities on Public Land in order to consolidate areas of habitat, minimise fragmentation and to provide linkages and corridors.

At present, the cooperation and participation by private landholders is very positive. Two landholder bandicoot action groups have been formed in recognized bandicoot management zones. These groups are participating in the first stage of a four-stage habitat development program. Figure 1 shows the approximate current range of *P. gunnii* around Hamilton, the habitat development works completed prior to 1988 and areas where works have been planned. Stage 1 works were funded in 1988-89. Stages 2, 3 and 4 are areas where works are urgently needed but are as yet unfunded.

Control of habitat on public land is relatively easy to accomplish compared with freehold land, but it does need to involve community participation both in planning and implementing works. Management of public land includes the provision of strategic breaks as a fire protection measure. Many of these breaks are slashed regularly in selected areas to provide foraging areas for bandicoots. This work is being undertaken by the Hamilton City Council and the Department of Conservation, Forests and Lands.

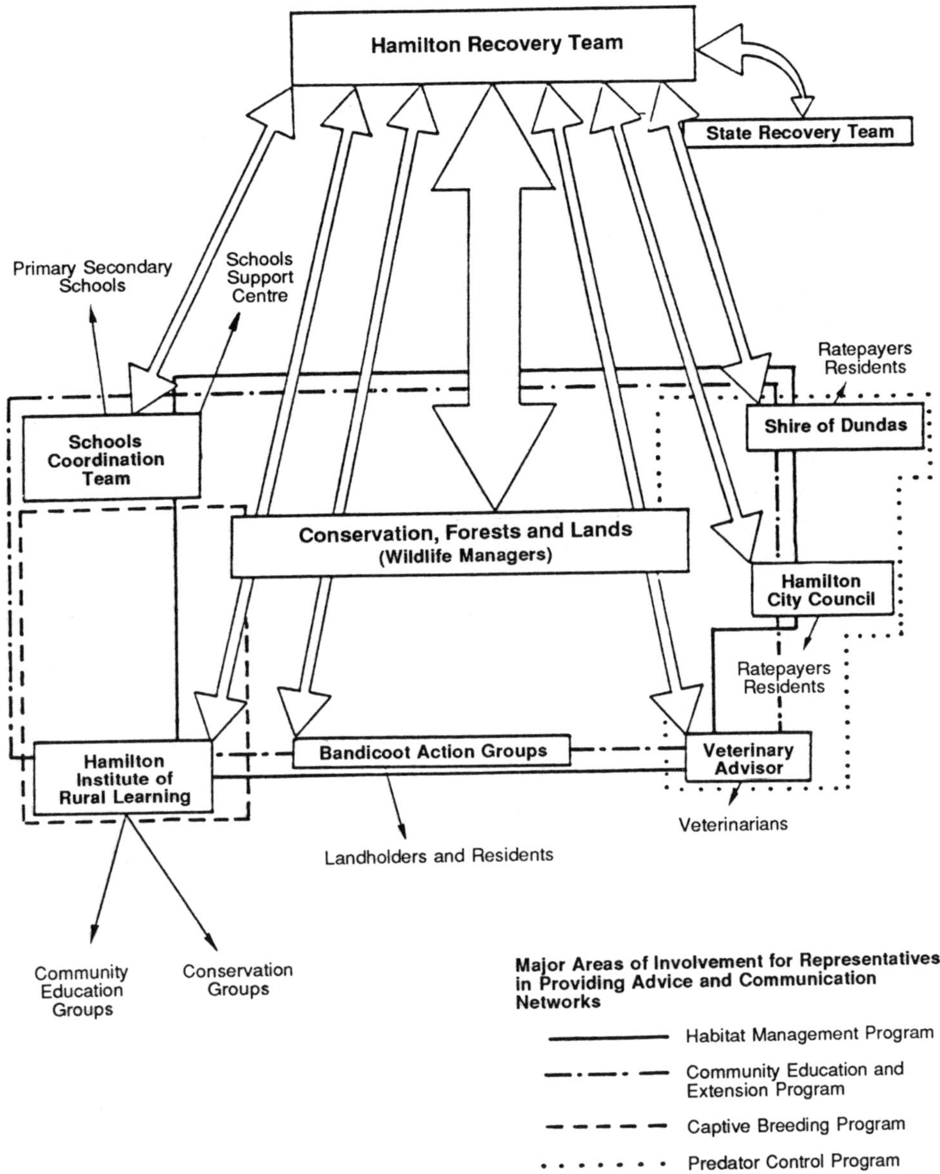


*Figure 2.*—The Hamilton Recovery Team—representation and roles.

## Hard Shelters

Bandicoots use a range of cover provided by man—rubbish tips, log piles, out-buildings and other refuges associated with dwellings. The hard shelters that have been erected are a deliber- ate attempt to provide this type of cover for the bandicoots. They are a 'quick fix' approach to the provision of immediate shelter for *P. gunnii* from predators. Hard shelters are placed strategically within and adjacent to areas occupied by *P. gunnii* to enable independent juvenile animals to disperse with an increased chance of survival. Bandicoots are already using some of the shelters provided.

Hard shelters can be constructed cheaply from a range of second-hand materials, *e.g.* old wooden electricity poles, railway sleepers (ties), roofing iron, concrete culverts, fallen tree limbs and other salvage. These materials can be simply placed in random heaps, or used to build properly-designed, low, weather-proof structures. The latter are less conspicuous and more aesthetically acceptable. They can also be inspected to determine whether there has been occupation by bandicoots, and they can be relocated elsewhere if necessary after appropriate vegetation has been established. If the shelters are not to be relocated, then the vegetation can include attractive native creepers which will cover the shelters and reduce their visual impact.

The shelter design currently in use consists of four 3-m long used railway sleepers which are placed on the ground to form a perimeter support. Two 3-m lengths of 75 mm x 50 mm hardwood are attached to the sleepers to support two sheets of used roofing iron. Before the iron is attached a few used car tyres and a bale of oaten straw are added to the shelter. The tyres provide some partitions within the shelter. The iron is attached with coach screws which can be removed to allow inspection. A gap of no more than 100 mm x 100 mm is provided at each corner of the structure for the passage of bandicoots.

A number of these structures have been built within double-fenced areas near the Hamilton Municipal Tip and on the Sewage Treatment Works. Care has been taken to locate the shelters in areas where they will not become waterlogged. Bandicoots have been observed returning to the shelters after release during the trapping program and have also been seen using them at night.

*Double Fencing*

Double fencing is usually achieved by running a new fence parallel with an existing fence, a minimum of 5 m apart. Advantage is often taken of existing boundary or subdivisional fences on rural properties. In some instances, two new fences may be required. Double fencing provides a linear strip of land which is not subject to grazing by domestic stock and therefore provides long grass for cover and an area where trees and shrubs can eventually be established. A network of interconnecting double-fenced areas together with islands of habitat in grazed pastures has been planned within and adjoining key bandicoot management areas. Figure 3 shows double-fenced habitat areas along boundary and subdivisional fences and habitat islands in the vicinity of the Hamilton Municipal Tip and the Sewage Treatment Works on the western end of known bandicoot range.

To establish a shelter belt for bandicoots, the parallel fences need to be placed at least 11 m apart to provide enough space for trees and shrubs. However, most landholders in the initial stages of the habitat development and management program have small holdings and cannot afford to lose so much productive land. Consequently, most of the double-fenced corridors in the first stage of the program are less than 11 m wide, but they soon provide a good cover of grass which can be utilised by bandicoots while trees and shrubs are being established. Hard shelters may also be constructed within the corridors. In addition to providing cover for the bandicoots, a more diverse food source for the animals appears to develop. As the grasses grow and die off annually, there is a buildup of organic matter which attracts a broader range of invertebrates as the organic material decomposes. This increase in food supply is further enhanced because the soil is not subject to compaction by domestic stock and therefore becomes more friable and well-oxygenated, thus providing better conditions for the growth of decomposer organisms.

All people residing on or owning land within key bandicoot management areas have been approached personally to participate in the habitat development program. Only one of 25 persons approached has declined to be involved in the initial stages of the program.

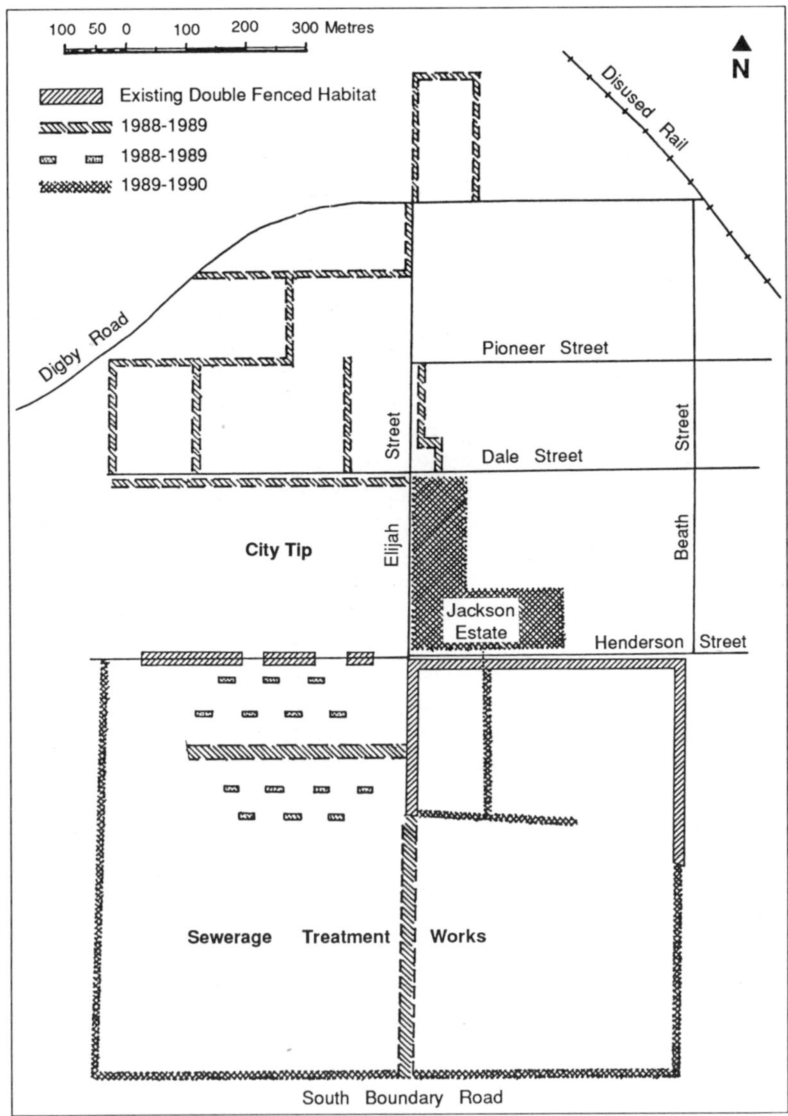


*Figure 3.*—Bandicoot habitat development works planned for western Hamilton.

Fencing materials have been provided by CFL under the Flora and Fauna Incentives Scheme. Materials are provided but the landholder is required to provide the labour for construction. The material value ($2 per m) is based on a standard stock-proof fence consisting of 100 mm-125 mm diameter preservative-treated pine posts at 10 m spacing supporting six-line hinge-joint wire netting and two plain wires. CFL staff members assist with advice on fence design and layout. Landholders are encouraged to participate in the 'Land for Wildlife' program and thus become eligible to receive continuing advice on wildlife management, a 'Land for Wildlife' sign and a bandicoot habitat sign.

During 1988-1989, sufficient funds were made available to construct 9 km of fence, providing a network of corridors in two key bandicoot management areas (Fig. 1). Future monitoring should indicate the effectiveness of these works in providing habitat for the animals. Monitoring in areas where similar works have already taken place (*i.e.* at the Hamilton Municipal Tip and Sewage Treatment Works) have indicated that the habitat established in these areas has been subsequently occupied by *P. gunnii*.

*Revegetation*

Planting appropriate species of plants for bandicoot habitat is in accord with current Government policy, which aims to alleviate land degradation problems (including soil erosion by both wind and water, soil salting and excessive clearing of the original vegetation). This philosophy is now gaining wide acceptance by the rural community, especially as it helps to increase farm productivity. Low shrubby understorey plants in association with tree-planting will provide suitable cover for *P. gunnii*, as well as providing habitat for a wide range of other native animals.

*P. gunnii* has demonstrated a preference for dense, low-growing prickly plants which provide refuge from predators. In the Hamilton urban and semi-rural environment, this protective cover is often provided by invasive exotic species (*e.g. Ulex europaeus*). In the development of areas of new habitat, and in the restoration of existing areas, emphasis is being given to a range of native plants, particularly species indigenous to the Hamilton area. These are highly suited to the range of conditions found at Hamilton, require minimal maintenance, are hardy, and many regenerate following fire, unlike many exotic species. The Hamilton Recovery Team has produced a local planting guide to encourage community and individual planting programs on farms, small holdings and in gardens.

*Future Habitat Development*

Following Stage 1, which has concentrated on providing habitat to stabilize the existing *P. gunnii* population, Stages 2, 3 and 4 will aim at extending habitat away from existing centres of the bandicoot population. An increase in habitat will, it is hoped, lead to an increased population size through an increase in the juvenile survival rate. Double-fenced areas will be designed to draw animals away from the existing key population zones via a network system of corridors to facilitate the safe emigration of animals and to provide new habitat. The corridor network will encourage the spread of *P. gunnii* away from the environs of the City of Hamilton. It is hoped that this will enhance the survival rate of *P. gunnii* for the following reasons. Firstly, outside the boundaries of the City, a broader range of predator control techniques are available, including poisoning, shooting and humane trapping, which are less likely to affect non-target animals. Secondly, it is less likely that intensive agricultural or horticultural practices involving the use of toxic pesticides will be carried out on broad-acre grazing properties. Thirdly, the network will be designed to avoid busy roads where possible and thus reduce the incidence of road kills.

The provision of incentives to landholders to encourage them to provide habitat for *P. gunnii* on private rural land is both more cost-effective and less disruptive to the local community than the purchase of large areas of land by the Government.

Some consolidation of habitat is necessary within the City of Hamilton. This will be carried out on a number of unused roads, roadsides, disused railway lines and other public land. An assessment of these areas for their potential habitat value for *P. gunnii* is underway. Ultimately, the existing key population areas will be linked, thus allowing a better genetic flow in addition to encouraging bandicoot numbers to increase in the rural areas away from the City.

*Purchase of Land to Consolidate Habitat and Provide Corridors*

This process is time consuming, relatively costly and dependent on the availability of funds and suitable land for sale. Whilst it can aid the recovery program, limited resources will likely limit its utility. A 4.25 ha block of land adjacent to the Hamilton Municipal Tip, known as the Jackson Estate, has recently been purchased. This is a strategically important area for bandicoot habitat and will be progressively revegetated to provide habitat in one of the main bandicoot population centres.

*Hamilton Community Parkland Population*

One of the major threats to the survival of *P. gunnii* is predation by introduced carnivores. In an attempt to provide a cat and fox-free environment, CFL has provided a total of $80,000 to the Hamilton Institute for Rural Learning and the City of Hamilton to enclose an area of 100 ha with a predator-proof fence (Fig. 1). The fence is the first step in developing a captive-breeding program capable of supporting about 150 *P. gunnii* (Minta *et al.*, this volume). The area enclosed is part of a section of public land managed by the City of Hamilton as Committee of Management. It is known as the Hamilton Community Parkland and caters to a number of Hamilton's recreational and educational needs as well as providing for flora and fauna conservation. A small breeding enclosure has been constructed inside the larger fenced area, and it is being used to breed some of the animals required to repopulate the Parklands.

Most of the area will be surrounded by a mesh fence 2 m in height topped with an electrified wire; the base netting will be buried horizontally outwards.

The enclosed area contains a considerable amount of reasonably well-preserved native tussock grassland, one of the major constituents of the original habitat of *P. gunnii* (Seebeck 1979). The fenced area also includes a recently-constructed wildlife dam and an old reservoir, thus ensuring a supply of permanent water. Traditionally, the old reservoir has been much used by local anglers and naturalists. Pedestrian access to this area will still be allowed but no dogs will be permitted. Entry will be by means of a double-gated system designed to allow human access but to prevent entry by cats, dogs and foxes. A similar gate will be installed where the fence adjoins the nearby Parklands Golf Course so that golfers may retrieve golf balls. Additional locked gates will be spaced around the perimeter to allow access by the City to maintain their water supply areas and by the Country Fire Authority of Victoria for fire protection purposes. Several extra small reservoirs are planned for the northern part of the enclosure. These have been included to provide extra drought relief for fauna in dry years as well as for public refuge and an additional water supply in case of fire.

The Country Fire Authority of Victoria has also requested that a slashed break be maintained inside the fence. Slashing of this break will be incorporated into a program of slashing and burning required to maintain the grassland communities. Further vegetation management will include planting additional indigenous ground cover in selected areas.

Although the fence is designed to exclude predators totally, it is anticipated that some cats and foxes will find their way in. When the fence is completed, introduced carnivores already present will be eliminated prior to the release of bandicoots.

One of the major benefits of the program, apart from providing a safer habitat for *P. gunnii*, is its value in education. It is hoped that local school and community groups will be involved in a number of activities on the site, including habitat enhancement works, predator monitoring and culling, and bandicoot population monitoring, as well as casual observation of the animals in their natural environment. An additional education program will be required to modify some of the activities of previous users of the area to be fenced. Dog owners in particular have used the Parkland extensively for exercising their animals and must now be directed to other areas.

Building a fence is only the first of several steps towards providing a predator-free environment on the Hamilton Community Parkland. Systems and activities will have to be continually monitored and adjusted based on the experience gained at Hamilton as well as from other similar projects in Victoria at Gellibrand Hill Park and the National Trust (Victoria) property 'Mooramong' near Skipton (Seebeck, this volume).

*Control of Introduced Predators*

Brown (1989) and Seebeck *et al.* (this volume) grouped the causes for the *P. gunnii* decline suggested by Seebeck (1979, 1984) and Menkhorst and Seebeck (in press) into two main categories: habitat alteration and predation by introduced carnivores. Certainly, predation by feral and domestic (pet) cats is a major cause of juvenile mortality in the *P. gunnii* population at Hamilton (Brown 1989; Maguire *et al.*, this volume). In addition to direct predation, cats pose another threat to the Hamilton population through the transmission of disease, in particular the spread of the protozoan parasite *Toxoplasma gondii* (Brown 1989; Lenghaus *et al.*, this volume).

Although control of domestic and feral cats is a contentious issue, it is of such importance that it must be immediately addressed. Local municipal councils have a unique opportunity to set an example nationwide in achieving the control of cats and reducing their impact on wildlife.

As part of a responsible pet ownership campaign carried out in the City of Hamilton in 1984 and 1985, surveys on pet ownership were conducted. Results indicated that in 1985 there were some 2,300 domestic cats in Hamilton, of which about 850 (both females and males) were not neutered. Of the cats acknowledged to be owned, it was considered that up to about 1,800 may have been

preying on local wildlife, including *P. gunnii* (Brown 1989). The surveys also showed that 66% of the residents of Hamilton considered cats to be a problem for one reason or another. Although the 'Responsible Pet Ownership Campaign' appears to have raised the Hamilton community's awareness of the problem of cat predation of *P. gunnii*, it has done little to alter people's long-term practices with regard to controlling their animals.

In July 1989, the Hamilton Recovery Team attempted an analysis of the issues that were limiting the amount of active public support for cat control as a means of assisting in the conservation of *P. gunnii*. They estimated that only about 15% of the residents of Hamilton were aware of the problem and were prepared to take action to reduce the problem. This contrasted with a target level of 80% active support which was suggested as necessary for satisfactory resolution of the problem (Maguire *et al.*, this volume).

The Recovery Team's analysis identified 'driving forces' which were or could be used to shift the level of active awareness (Table 1). Opposing these were 'restraining forces', factors that limited an improvement in the level of community activity aimed at restricting cat predation. Enhancing the driving forces and reducing the restraining forces will be the basis for developing the community education program directed towards this issue.

Brown (1989) suggested a range of measures for the control of domestic and feral cats. For domestic cats, he favoured a strategy that provided some legislative control by local municipalities, coupled with the encouragement of desexing of all cats not required for breeding, backed by a public education program.

In a report to the Hamilton City Council, the Town Clerk (Worland 1989) described a management option to control cats in the urban area. The proposal included registration (with reduced fees for neutered animals), promotion of a desexing

*Table 1.*—Factors affecting changes in the level of Hamilton community activity to reduce cat predation of *P. gunnii*.

| Driving Forces | Restraining Forces |
| --- | --- |
| Many residents regard cats as a nuisance | Cats regarded as 'soft' pets not hunters |
| Responsible pet ownership attitudes | Cats valued as hunters—mice and other vermin |
| Many school students have supportive attitudes | Bandicoots have a poor image with some members of the community (rat-like vermin) |
| Parliamentary inquiry into role and welfare of companion animals | Lack of visual evidence of bandicoot kills |
| Hamilton City Council has proposed 'cat-free' areas, subsidized neutering and cat disposal services | Lack of awareness of bandicoot presence nocturnally |
| | Lack of awareness of cat-borne diseases |
| Improving community awareness of toxoplasmosis | Lack of legislative controls on cats |
| Improved awareness of need to provide more predator-resistant bandicoot habitat | Cat control is unpopular with local government |
| | High cost of cat fertility control using current methods |
| | High cost of cat destruction using current methods |
| | Lack of boarding-out facilities for cats |

program, the provision of 'cat free' areas on land controlled by the Hamilton City Council and the Hamilton Water Board, the approval of a program of cat trapping and elimination on all public land within the City of Hamilton coupled with an extensive public education program. The full recommendations of this report have since been adopted by the Council subject to the availability of resources to implement the various programs.

While the report is reasonably comprehensive concerning domestic cats, (which would hopefully restrict their recruitment), it does not fully address the problem of reducing the existing feral cat population. Clearly, trapping, shooting and poisoning have only limited application for culling feral cats within the City of Hamilton. Biological control techniques need further investigation, particularly the use of reproductive controls.

The effect of foxes on *P. gunnii* should not be underestimated. Foxes are almost certainly preying on the existing urban population, and their impact will increase as suitable habitat is extended further into surrounding rural areas. Fox control needs to be closely linked to habitat works. Control techniques should include poisoning, shooting, cage-trapping and the use of organised drives.

The control of introduced carnivores will require a combination of education and legislative controls coupled with traditional pest animal management methods, and in future, biological control techniques. These methods need to be combined with the systematic introduction of carnivore-resistant habitat.

### Reduction of Road Kills

It is estimated that 50-60+ bandicoots are killed annually, mostly young males. Two sections of road have been identified along which *P. gunnii* are regularly killed by vehicles. A program to reduce road kills along these sections has commenced.

Currently, we are monitoring a 500-m strip of the Chatsworth Road on which CFL (in conjunction with the Shire of Dundas) have erected SWARE-FLEX wildlife reflectors. These reflectors, developed in the northern hemisphere, were designed to minimise vehicle collisions with large mammals, *e.g.* deer. They are being tested in Australia with kangaroos, but it is not yet known whether they will be effective in reducing road deaths of small mammals such as *P. gunnii*. Road signs depicting an eastern barred bandicoot have been erected in a number of locations to create driver-awareness.

CFL is also investigating the feasibility of installing culverts or tunnels and speed humps to assist the safe passage of *P. gunnii* under or over roadways. The main disadvantages of these systems are the higher relative costs (*e.g.* $3,000 for a speed hump) and, in the case of speed humps, restraints on vehicular movement. A local driver education program is also being considered.

*Population Monitoring*

An essential component of recovery management for *P. gunnii* is an effective population monitoring program which will indicate whether or not the strategy that has been adopted for the recovery of the species is working (Minta *et al.*, this volume). At Hamilton we use a live-trapping program carried out at least once annually within the key bandicoot management zones. As the habitat development program is planned and implemented, monitoring will be extended to assess the rate of colonisation of new habitat and its effectiveness in supporting *P. gunnii* populations.

*P. gunnii* are trapped using wire cage traps 360 mm long, 200 mm wide and 160 mm high. Trapping is normally carried out under cool conditions and not when it is dry and hot. The traps are covered with a polythene sleeve so that the animals are protected from the elements. A short length of wood approximately 15 mm in diameter is placed at the entrance of the trap so that the door does not close completely when the trap is sprung. This avoids any injury to the tail of a trapped animal.

The traps are baited with a mixture of peanut butter, honey and rolled oats, set late in the afternoon and checked early the next morning. Trapped animals are transferred to a handling bag for processing (weighing, measuring, sexing and ear tattooing). Only first-capture animals are tattooed before release. Recaptured animals are identified, weighed and released. With females, the pouch is examined to determine breeding condition and the presence of pouch young. The animals are also checked for their general condition and external parasites. On release the animals normally immediately run for cover; the type of cover preferred is identified.

Females carrying advanced pouch young will sometimes eject the young from the pouch into the trap or the handling bag. When this occurs, the female and young are left in the handling bag in a quiet draught-free area for the rest of the day and released at dusk. Processing is carried out as quickly and quietly as possible to minimise stress to the animals.

Although live-trapping is the only reliable method of monitoring the population, general field observations are helpful and are recorded regularly. These include the presence of tracks, scats and diggings where the animals have been foraging for food. At night a spotlight is used to locate *P. gunnii* so that their behaviour may be observed (Coulson, this volume).

The monitoring program will also include examination by veterinary pathologists of moribund road- and cat-killed *P. gunnii* to provide a continuing check on health aspects of the population and pesticide residues (Lenghaus *et al.*, this volume).

*Community Education and Extension*

The nature of the issues influencing the survival of the *P. gunnii* at Hamilton makes it essential that effective community support and action is an integral part of the Hamilton Conservation Strategy. It is becoming increasingly clear that if extinctions of many species are to be prevented, the community must be well informed about the threatening processes and the management issues involved. Very little will be achieved if the community merely espouses a social conscience and concern for such species. The community requires an opportunity to learn about the issues, develop practical options for community action and thoroughly debate the changes in community attitudes which will be necessary to ensure the survival of species.

In this sense, the Hamilton Conservation Strategy for *P. gunnii* is a pilot program. It will challenge wildlife managers to become effective community facilitators and challenge the community to adopt some of the roles of wildlife managers. Such an approach demands a blending of knowledge of ecological management principles with people-management skills, and this is clearly the future direction that effective conservation strategies must take.

The Hamilton Recovery Team is currently developing a number of community education and extension programs both directly and through the schools coordination team. It will organise community information nights to review progress with the Hamilton Conservation Strategy, to obtain feedback on public perceptions of the recovery program and to keep the bandicoot issue alive in the community.

In addition, the Team will concentrate its initial efforts in extension on developing an attitude of responsible pet ownership among residents in and adjacent to key bandicoot population areas. The first target group will be residents living in the neighbourhood of the Kennedy Street Oval in south Hamilton. The program will involve circularising residents through inclusion of leaflets with their annual rate notices and asking for their cooperation and giving some practical advice. This will be followed by a personal visit from CFL field staff who will explain the program and provide residents with an information kit and other items to assist them with better management of their pets. The local school covering this neighbourhood will coordinate its educational program on *P. gunnii* to coincide with the responsible pet ownership campaign.

The results of these preliminary efforts will be assessed, and the experience gained will provide a basis for developing a longer-term strategy aimed at gaining and sustaining whole community support and action. Assessment of the effectiveness of the Responsible Pet Ownership extension program will be achieved by monitoring both *P. gunnii* populations and predator populations (including domestic pets active in the area) and surveys of residents' pet management practices.

*Future Plans*

The Hamilton Recovery Team has identified a number of key issues related to the future management of *P. gunnii* populations at Hamilton. In order of priority, these are:

1. The rapid expansion of potential habitat must continue through the development of corridor networks expanding from existing key population zones. This will require additional funding for incentives for landholders and an expansion of each of the bandicoot action groups. A plan has been drawn up showing the proposed habitat expansion works over three additional stages. Figure 1 shows the completed and planned habitat works around Hamilton. Figure 2 shows a detailed plan of a section of the works near the Hamilton Municipal Tip and Sewage Treatment Works.

2. The implementation of a cat control program in the City of Hamilton and in parts of the adjoining Shire of Dundas will require the cooperation of both municipalities, CFL and the Department of Agriculture and Rural Affairs. The Hamilton Recovery Team has sought the assistance of the State Recovery Team to ensure that high-level support is given to this program and that the need for additional funding is recognized.

3. Examination of only a small number of road- and cat-killed *P. gunnii* individuals makes it impossible to draw any conclusions regarding the impact that the widespread use of organochlorine compounds may have had on *P. gunnii* populations (C. Lenghaus, personal communication). There is also a need to

examine specimens for possible effects of organophosphate compounds, which are in current use as pesticides in agriculture. The Hamilton Recovery Team has requested financial support for a more comprehensive testing program.

## Conclusion

At this stage in the management program it has not been possible to draw firm conclusions from the many methods and approaches being implemented as a result of the recommendations of the Management Plan and the Action Plan. The Hamilton Recovery Team will be putting into place a 6-monthly review process to assess progress with the Hamilton Conservation Strategy for *P. gunnii* and the State Recovery Team will have as one of its principal objectives a regular review of progress in all facets of the recovery process. The feedback mechanism provided by this review process will be fundamental to achieving a successful adaptive management approach.

## Acknowledgments

The Hamilton Conservation Strategy has been developed with the cooperation of the Hamilton Recovery Team; State Recovery Team; Hamilton Bandicoot Action Groups; City of Hamilton; Shire of Dundas; Hamilton Institute of Rural Learning; Environmental Teachers Association, Hamilton Branch; Denis Read, Regional Manager, Portland Region, CFL; John Seebeck and Rod Gowans, Assistant Director Wildlife, National Parks and Wildlife Division, CFL; Dr Tim Clark, Chicago Zoological Society. The authors acknowledge the contribution of Lynn Turner who typed the manuscript and Graeme McDonald who prepared the draughting.

## References


Brown, P.R. 1989. Management Plan for the Conservation of the Eastern Barred Bandicoot, *Perameles gunnii* in Victoria. National Parks and Wildlife Division, Victoria. *Arthur Rylah Institute for Environmental Research Tech. Rep. Ser.* No. 63. Department of Conservation, Forests and Lands: Melbourne.

Conservation, Forests and Lands. 1989. Action Plan for the Conservation of the Eastern Barred Bandicoot, *Perameles gunnii.* National Parks and Wildlife Division and Portland, Melbourne, Ballarat and Geelong Regions.

Holling, C.S. 1973. Resilience and stability of ecological systems. *Ann. Rev. Ecol. Syst.* 4:1-23.

Holling, C.S. 1978. *Adaptive Environmental Assessment and Management.* International Series on Applied Systems Analysis 3, International Institute for Applied Systems Analysis. John Wiley and Sons: Toronto.

International Union for the Conservation of Nature and Natural Resources. 1988. Captive breeding—the IUCN policy statement. *Species* 10:27-28.

McMichael, D.F. 1982. What Species, What Risk? In *Species at Risk,* eds R.H. Groves and W.D.L. Ride. Pp. 3-11. Australian Academy of Science: Canberra.

Menkhorst, P.W., and Seebeck, J.H. In press. The status of bandicoots in Victoria. In *Bandicoots and Bilbies,* eds J. H. Seebeck, P. R. Brown, R. L. Wallis and C. M. Kemper. Surrey Beatty and Sons: Sydney.

Seebeck, J.H. 1979. Status of the Barred Bandicoot, *Perameles gunnii,* in Victoria: with a note on husbandry of a captive colony. *Aust. Wild. Res.* 6:255-264.

Seebeck, J.H. 1984. Mammals of the Plains or, where have all the Wombats gone? In *The Western Plains—A Natural and Social History,* eds D. Conley and C. Denis. Pp. 39-53. Australian Institute of Agricultural Science: Melbourne.

Worland, R. 1989. Report on Cat Control to the Hamilton City Council. Unpublished.

# Other Endangered Species Cases

Seven other cases are presented in this section: southern Australian daisy, giant Gippsland earthworm, Eltham copper butterfly, Australian damselfly, helmeted honeyeater, orange-bellied parrot and Leadbeater's possum. We chose these cases for inclusion in the Conference to emphasise the plight of taxa across the phylogenetic spectrum, both plants and animals. Not all species have the public appeal, the information base, or the biologically 'simple' solutions that appear in the bandicoot case. These cases also represent special conservation challenges because of unique taxonomic status, unique life history adaptations or complex ecological processes—including anticipated global climatic change. The varying scope of the conservation efforts devoted to each species also makes them worthy of scrutiny. All share a common theme, though, in that they illustrate the essential need for habitat and, indeed, ecosystem protection.

All seven instances illustrate the model of the extinction process described previously (Clark *et al.*, this volume); viewing the cases this way reveals the breadth of the problems that endangered species face and it reveals options for solutions. For the vertebrates, the application of population viability assessment procedures, as carried out in the bandicoot case, could significantly strengthen management and conservation efforts. In all cases, decision analysis could draw participants together to share information, explore optimal management strategies, and coordinate their efforts. And lastly, responsible and responsive adaptive management, based on reliable monitoring, could help endangered species recovery programs proceed more smoothly and surely.

# Conservation Biology of the Southern Australian Daisy *Rutidosis leptorrhynchoides*

*Neville H. Scarlett and Robert F. Parsons[1]*

## Abstract

The native daisy, *Rutidosis leptorrhynchoides*, was originally a major species of grassy areas around Canberra and in Victoria from the far west to the Gippsland Plains. It is a slow-growing, preferentially outcrossing species which has become endangered principally by heavy, continuous sheep grazing. In Victoria, it is now found naturally only in eleven tiny refugia—eight rail reserves, two cemeteries and one road reserve. To persist, it requires both protection from stock grazing and regular burning or some other treatment to reduce grass competition. Its numbers are continuing to decline due both to railworks and to increased competition from grasses following cessation of burning-off of rail reserves. It is being reintroduced into secure reserves both by transplanting seedlings and by seed broadcasting. Parallels are drawn with work on conservation of North American prairies. The necessity for continuous, intensive management is stressed and other urgent needs are indicated.

## Introduction

In southern Australia, the natural ecosystems obliterated almost completely by colonial settlement are the lowland grasslands and grassy woodlands. Accordingly, they contain a higher number of threatened plant species than other ecosystems, especially species highly palatable to grazing mammals (Scarlett and Parsons 1982). In this paper we illustrate the main conservation and management problems involved using as an example one such species, *Rutidosis leptorrhynchoides* F. Muell (Asteraceae). Although much more work is needed on this species, it is one of the best-known and most intensively studied threatened plants in Australia. Most of the sites referred to in this paper are scattered over the Volcanic Plains, a region of grassland and grassy woodland carrying about 550 indigenous plant species, of which about 75 are Asteraceae (daisies) as is *R. leptorrhynchoides* (Willis 1964).

## Southern Australian Daisy

### The Species and its Original Range and Habitat

*R. leptorrhynchoides* is a multi-stemmed semi-shrub with upright, linear-lanceolate basal leaves and leafy, ascending stems to 350 mm high (Fig. 1). It is a hemicryptophyte, with buds at the surface of the soil but not below it; it has not been seen to resprout from below the crown of buds. The stems usually die back in the dry conditions of late summer; tender new stems are clearly evident by late winter. Elimination by grazing mammals may well take place mainly at this tender stage (Fig. 2). From our observations of glasshouse plants, it grows more slowly than other native and introduced perennials of similar stature.

Seedlings have a single major root; adventitious roots have never been observed. The depth of the mature root system is unknown, but is thought to be considerable. The rootstock is woody, with secondary thickening present. *R. leptorrhynchoi-*

[1]Botany Department, La Trobe University, Bundoora, Victoria 3083, Australia.

*Figure 1.*—(A) *Rutidosis leptorrhynchoides* in the Canberra area, showing shoots about 15 cm long. Photo J.D. Briggs. (B) Mature achene of *R. leptorrhynchoides* from Manor. Scale bar is 1 mm long. Note scaly pappus which could adhere to some vertebrates. Achene weight ranges from 0.9 to 1.0 mg.

*des* plants do not normally flower until their second year; the normal flowering period is from October to March, when yellow heads of 20 mm diameter are produced. Whenever observed, flowering has been followed by the production of plentiful ripe achenes whose germinability varies from 68 to 92%. The achenes have a pappus of narrow-linear, plumose scales (Willis 1972). Normal achene dispersal distance is very low; seed tends simply to fall to the ground and seedlings have never been seen more than 1 m from parent plants. However, zoochorous dispersal may occur in some circumstances; it is thought that the pappus could adhere to some vertebrates (Fig. 1). We have never seen severe achene losses due to attack by insects or other animals. Seed can remain viable for at least four months in summer-autumn. In trials, maximum germination was at 10-15°C, the lowest temperature used (Australian National Botanic Gardens, unpublished data). This may be related to a normal field germination time of late autumn to early spring. We have found no evidence of innate seed dormancy. Adult plants resprout readily following destruction of all aerial plant parts by fire. While our oldest

plantings are nine years old, the maximum lifespan of the species may well be longer than this.

*R. leptorrhynchoides* is a species of fertile red-brown earths and yellow solodics; in the latter, perched water tables may develop in wet winters. It is never found in areas of severely impeded drainage and/or run-on areas. Mean annual rainfall range is 500 to 635 mm.

Evidence from the remnant sites shows that it was once a major co-dominant species in *Themeda triandra* grassland and in various grassy eucalypt woodlands both in the Canberra-Queanbeyan area and in Victoria (*e.g.* at Dobie's Bridge near Ararat). It is usually found in distinct colonies in the higher parts of the terrain where moisture status is low in summer and where associated herbs and grasses are sparse. The species is not necessarily eliminated by moderate site disturbance; near Queanbeyan, it has been seen colonizing a graded track and part of a former horse yard (M.D. Crisp, personal communication), while in Victoria we have seen it colonizing tyre tracks and bare ground. It is permanently eliminated by severe distur-

*Figure 2.*—(A) *Rutidosis leptorrhynchoides* plant at Rokewood Cemetery, July 1989, showing old stems that died back in late summer 1989 and tender new growth which appeared after the autumn/winter rainfall break of 1989. This plant ungrazed by sheep. (B) As for (A) but showing tender new growth grazed back by sheep.

bance like ploughing, which, by changing the soil structure, allows rapidly-growing alien species to take over and exclude it.

The original range of the species was made up of two areas 500 km apart; one the Canberra-Queanbeyan area and the other from far western Victoria (near Casterton) through to the Gippsland Plains (near Maffra), a distance of 480 km (Fig. 3).

## *Breeding System and Variation*

Studies of three Canberra-Queanbeyan ('northern') populations and five Victorian ('southern') populations showed that all have the same chromosome number (2n=26). Outcross pollinations between plants from the same or different populations were equally successful indicating that genetically determined reproductive isolation has not evolved between geographically distant populations. Although some viable seed is set in the absence of outcross pollen, the species is thought to be preferentially outcrossing (Leeton and Fripp, personal communication). It is assumed that the

flowers are insect-pollinated, but it is not known which insects are involved.

On comparing the reproductive capacity of the large, dense stand at Rokewood with that at Middle Creek (where very small patches of plants occur up to 50 m apart), we found lower apparent live achene yield and lower germinability in the latter (Table 1), samples from which contained many small, undeveloped achenes. One explanation could be a higher incidence of selfing at Middle Creek, recalling studies of *Dianthus* in which population fragmentation reduced pollinator service and hence outcrossing and seed-set (Jennersten 1988).

## *Colonial Settlement and Fragmentation*

Our work on the present conservation status of this species in Victoria began in 1979, when we listed the locations of all Australian herbarium specimens of it and started field searching. As virtually the entire original range is now intensively farmed or urbanized, it was no surprise to find gross range contraction and fragmentation

*Table 1.*—Apparent live achene yield as numbers of full-sized achenes in bulk samples[1] of *Rutidosis leptorrhynchoides* and germinability of full-sized achenes at two sites and two sampling dates.

| Site | Date | Germinability of full-sized achenes (%) | Viable achenes in bulk samples[1] (mean numbers/g) |
| --- | --- | --- | --- |
| Middle Creek | Dec 1987-Jan 1988 | 68 | 266 |
| Middle Creek | Dec 1988-Jan 1989 | Not known | 369 |
| Rokewood | Dec 1987-Jan 1988 | 92 | 497 |
| Rokewood | Dec 1988-Jan 1989 | Not known | 679 |

[1]The bulk samples result from sieving the field samples and include spent flowers and fragments of bracts, stems and leaves.

(Fig. 3; Table 2). In Victoria, the species is now confined to eight rail reserves, two cemeteries and one road reserve.

In this area, railway and cemetery reserves are the refugia which generally afford the best protection from domestic stock grazing (Scarlett and Parsons 1982). Their correlation with *R. leptorrhynchoides* is part of the evidence that the decline of the species is in part a direct consequence of heavy, continuous sheep grazing throughout its former range since about 1835-1850. It must be presumed that feral rabbit grazing was also important, but the evidence from remaining refugia suggests that this factor was not decisive for *R. leptorrhynchoides*. The grazing history for the Wickliffe site is not known but all of the other areas on which it survives have had long-term protection from stock grazing.

Another feature of rail reserves is that, until the late 1970s, they were deliberately burnt in early summer, usually as often as possible (*i.e.* every one to two years). While this can be catastrophic for species with a flowering time starting as late as November or later by preventing seed-set, this does not apply to some species which flower by mid-spring (Scarlett and Parsons 1982), possibly including *R. leptorrhynchoides*. This species has a long flowering period, and, while burns in early

summer may destroy maturing seed, a secondary flowering in March can occur if soil moisture levels remain adequate ('regrowth flowering'). Furthermore, regular burning can have beneficial effects; fire plays an important role in encouraging the regeneration of *Rutidosis* by reducing grass competition and providing an open seedbed. The species does not occur in dense, long unburnt *T. triandra* grassland, and the recent abandonment of the customary 'burning-off' of rail reserves has resulted in a dramatic decline of some railway reserve populations (Table 2) over the last 10 years.

Both roadside stock grazing and sheep droving have declined greatly since the 1950s, except during severe droughts. Most palatable, grazing-sensitive herbs of the grassland flora are rare or absent in most road reserves as a consequence of former grazing regimes, despite the current absence of grazing (*e.g. Senecio macrocarpus*, *Podolepis jaceoides* and *Microseris scapigera*). Presumably *R. leptorrhynchoides* was similarly affected by past grazing.

While frequent fuel reduction burning in January has let *R. leptorrhynchoides* persist in the Wickliffe roadside (Table 2), the many roadsides where this is no longer practised are now too densely grassed to be suitable as refugia for the species.

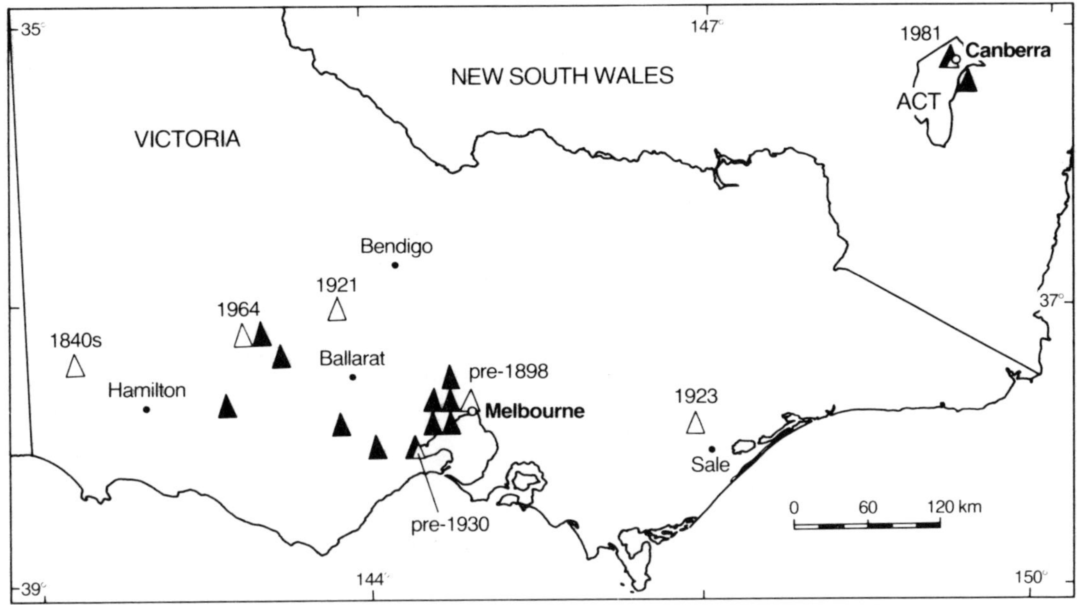


*Figure 3.*—Past and present distribution of *Rutidosis leptorrhynchoides*, showing existing stands (▲), extinct stands (△), and areas where both occur (▲). Date last reported or collected is given for extinct stands. Records are plotted on the usual grid of ten minutes latitude and longitude; the stand shown at longitude 144° also extends slightly into the grid square adjoining it to the east.

Now that regular burning of rail reserves is no longer customary, attempts are made to reduce fuel and construct fire-breaks by using graders, ploughs and weedicides. Damage from these new fire control methods, as well as road construction, line duplication, soil dumping and pipeline excavation has had severe effects on *R. leptorrhynchoides*.

Of the 10 populations on railway sites in Victoria, five have been virtually or totally lost since 1975. Of these five, one has been lost by human disturbance (*e.g.* earthworks and herbicide spraying), one was outcompeted by other plant species in the absence of fire, and three were lost by the combination of both processes (Table 2). At two of the remaining five sites, the populations have been reduced to less than half their original size by the same processes (Table 2). Two of the presumed 'unaffected' sites have been discovered so recently that we have no idea if their populations are declining or not.

In the Canberra-Queanbeyan area, the range of *R. leptorrhynchoides* has also contracted and fragmented, in this case due originally to stock grazing (Briggs and Leigh 1985) and then to urbanization and the filling of Lake Burley Griffin (Gray 1981; Table 2) as well as competition from other species in the absence of fire (Briggs and Leigh 1985). Two minor sites have been omitted from Table 2, at least one of which is unconservable (J.D. Briggs, personal communication).

Of the seven main Canberra-Queanbeyan sites recorded in the period 1980 to 1989, two have been destroyed by building projects. However, one site carrying a large stand has now been formally reserved (Table 2).

*Table 2.*—Site characteristics for the main *Rutidosis leptorrhynchoides* sites seen in the period 1975-1989. ACT=Australian Capital Territory; NSW=New South Wales; Vic=Victoria; pc=personal communication.

| State | Location | Land tenure | Year of record/ size of population[1] | Fate since first recorded[2] | Reference |
|---|---|---|---|---|---|
| ACT | Red Hill (west) | Public land | 1984; 600 plants | Put on National Estate Register and fenced. Woody weed control needed. | Briggs & Leigh 1985 |
| ACT | Red Hill (east) | Public land | 1989; 1,200 plants | Grazed by cattle; will be fenced. | J.D. Briggs pc |
| ACT | Capital Hill | Public land | 1980; 'rare' | Site eliminated by Parliament House construction, but most (150) plants transplanted to nearby areas. | Gray 1981; J.D. Briggs pc |
| ACT | Stirling Park-Attunga Point | Public land | 1980; 'a few thousand' | Put on National Estate Register. | Gray 1981; J.D. Briggs pc |
| NSW | Mount Jerrabomberra | Private land | 1988; 230 plants | Deliberately bulldozed by land developer, April 1988; no longer viable. | Scott 1988 |
| NSW | Queanbeyan | Public rubbish tip | 1981; 1,500-2,000 plants | Area reserved; now called Queanbeyan Nature Reserve. Put on National Estate Register. | M.D. Crisp & J.D. Briggs pc |
| NSW | Queanbeyan | Public land S of rubbish tip | 1988; 450 plants | Negotiations in progress to protect area. | J.D. Briggs pc |
| Vic | Digger's Rest | Rail reserve | About 1980; small stand | 1 plant left; rest killed by pipeline laying or choked out in absence of fire. | Present authors |
| Vic | St Albans | Rail reserve | 1975; 200 plants | All but 86 plants destroyed by pipeline excavations and slashing. | C. Rayner pc & B. Kemp pc |
| Vic | NE of Laverton | Rail reserve | 1979; 217 plants | All plants killed by branch line construction in 1984. | Present authors |
| Vic | SW of Laverton | Rail reserve | 1979; 300 plants | 6 plants left; rest killed by roadmaking and soil dumping or choked out in absence of fire. | Present authors |
| Vic | Truganina | Cemetery | 1982; 600 plants | Unreserved despite requests. | Present authors |
| Vic | Manor | Rail reserve | 1979; 330 plants | All but 64 plants choked out while firing infrequent. | Present authors |
| Vic | Little River | Rail reserve | 1979; 150 plants | All plants choked out in absence of fire. | Present authors |
| Vic | Lara | Rail reserve | 1984; 45 plants | All but 2 plants killed by rail works or choked out in absence of fire. | L. Gilmore pc |
| Vic | Bannockburn | Rail reserve | 1984; 300 plants | | Present authors |
| Vic | Rokewood | Cemetery | 1984; 450 plants | | Present authors |
| Vic | Middle Creek | Rail reserve | 1987; 600 plants | 10% of site lost by firebreak grading in 1989. Site now fenced. | Present authors |
| Vic | Dobie's Bridge | Rail reserve | 1987; 1,000-1,500 plants | Site now signposted. | Present authors |
| Vic | Wickliffe | Road reserve | 1989; 31 plants | | G. Wallace pc |

[1]Some figures are estimates.

[2]Population size much the same in 1989 as when first seen unless otherwise stated.

All remaining stands of *R. leptorrhynchoides* are small and are usually surrounded by vegetation dominated by introduced species. Invasion of *R. leptorrhynchoides* stands by some serious perennial herbaceous weeds (like *Cynara cardunculus* and *Foeniculum vulgare*) has resulted, by *F. vulgare* especially immediately after a September burn. These species occupy the same spaces between the grass tussocks (inter-tussock spaces) as those normally occupied by *R. leptorrhynchoides*. In formerly grazed reintroduction sites (see below), the South African irid *Romulea rosea* may also cause problems by densely occupying the inter-tussock spaces.

Introduced annual grasses, especially *Vulpia* spp., are also a major problem in inter-tussock spaces, their dense surface roots competing vigorously for water in early summer. *Holcus lanatus* (a short-lived perennial) behaves similarly. In the original grassland flora, annual grasses were virtually absent.

In the urban Canberra sites, a further threat is habitat invasion by woody weeds like *Pyracantha* sp., *Acacia baileyana* and *Cotoneaster* sp. (Briggs and Leigh 1985). The other threats recorded are tree-planting and grave construction, both in cemetery reserves.

## Conservation Measures

### Reservation

*R. leptorrhynchoides* is currently listed as endangered Australia-wide (Briggs and Leigh 1988), being one of a number of grassland species now found only on tiny fragments of land, most of which are probably unconservable in the long-term (Scarlett and Parsons 1982). The only Victorian stands with a possible long-term future, those in cemeteries, have areas of 1 to 1.5 ha.

As even degraded examples of the plant communities in which *R. leptorrhynchoides* occurred are grossly under-reserved (Stuwe 1986), the first step in conserving the species has been to seek reservation of areas once very likely to have carried it. Such moves have succeeded in the case of the 40-ha Laverton North Grassland Reserve, a former paddock of public land where horses grazed under lease, resulting in a species-poor grassland with high densities of some introduced species (*e.g. Romulea rosea*) but still dominated by the native grass *T. triandra*. The site would have been grazed by sheep at some earlier time. The other blocks of public land where reservation could occur are of this same type; none have had the long-term absence of stock grazing combined with frequent fire regime that led to the high species-richness of the best rail reserve sites.

### Reintroduction

Having reserved suitable public land, the next step is to reintroduce *R. leptorrhynchoides*. Production of large numbers of readily-germinable seed annually at most sites enables us to raise seedlings in pots for subsequent transplanting into secure reserves in both autumn and spring.

With these methods, we hope to establish 1,000 plants (derived from seed from some western refugia) at the nature reserves of the National Trust property 'Mooramong' near Skipton, and 1,000 plants (derived from seed from some eastern refugia) at the Laverton North Grassland Reserve (LNGR). From plantings since 1980, we now (August 1989) have 711 plants established at LNGR. At Mooramong, there are 20 plants established from the 1985 planting and, of the 1,094 planted from September 1987 to May 1989, 900 are now established. In addition, volunteers at Organ Pipes National Park have established 127 plants (K. McDougall, personal communication; 1989 data).

Site preparation at very weedy sites at Mooramong requires removal of all standing vegetation and 80-100 mm of soil with a grader blade, thus reducing plant competition, soil-stored weed seed and effects of past super-phosphate fertilizer treatments. On semi-natural 'stony-rise' areas at Mooramong we plant among rock outcrops and remove standing vegetation by hand for 400 cm$^2$

around the seedlings. At LNGR, we planted into two former firebreaks created by very light scraping by a grader to about 70 mm depth.

Limited plantings into undisturbed semi-natural areas resulted in high mortality rates both at Mooramong and LNGR; we need to define the minimum necessary level of standing vegetation removal to allow reasonable survival.

Some early plantings on scraped areas were at very close spacing which helped exclude weeds, but within the plots no regeneration of *R. leptorrhynchoides* from seed has occurred. We now use 300 mm regular spacing, which has allowed some sporadic regeneration from seed.

After transplanting, some follow-up weeding is normal, as is supplementary watering in spring and sometimes as late as early summer. After that, the plants are always left unwatered to die back to ground-level in middle and late summer.

Thus, for *R. leptorrhynchoides*, we have reliable propagation methods and understand how to achieve initial re-establishment, *i.e.* using hand-reared plants. The next step on the path to self-maintaining populations is for these plants to produce seed and then establish seedlings un-aided. This has occurred in a limited way at LNGR, where 33 plants have now been established (half of which have flowered and set seed) in gaps between parent plants and up to 500 mm from them.

Further work is needed on the factors determining regeneration from seed, including amount of viable seed set by the transplants, fate of seeds prior to germination, causes and rates of seedling death, etc. Competition from introduced herbaceous weeds like the daisies *Hypochoeris radicata* and *Arctotheca calendula* can be important in the very early seedling stage. There is an obvious need for regular burning or other management process having a similar effect in order to prevent both the transplants and their offspring from being out-competed. This is dealt with more fully below.

As has been done in North American prairie studies (Jordan 1983), reintroduction can choose between the laborious seedling transplant approach or the less predictable but potentially less labor-intensive direct seeding approach. We began the latter at Mooramong in 1988 by broadcasting seed onto grader-scraped ground lightly disturbed to no more than 15 mm deep in both autumn and spring. The high sowing rate (one viable seed/cm$^2$) was to ensure at least some seedlings established. The plots were lightly watered only twice—December 1988 and February 1989, and *A. calendula* seedlings removed in March 1989.

It is clear that *R. leptorrhynchoides* can be established from seed in the field and can persist at high densities through summer during high water-stress (Table 3). Monitoring is continuing, partly to show to what extent the dense, closed-canopy stands of *R. leptorrhynchoides* will exclude invasive weeds.

For the work above to proceed efficiently, garden-bed style seed production plots have been established—the plant equivalent to captive breeding programs.

The work described is what we are able to do with limited resources; what is needed ideally is a major project to attempt to reassemble simultaneously on secure public land the entire plant community of which *R. leptorrhynchoides* is a part, namely, species-rich lowland *Themeda* grassland.

In the Canberra area, other approaches to reintroduction have included propagation from stem cuttings, with a success rate as high as 50-60% for side shoots taken well before or well after flowering. Also, moving mature plants from threatened to secure sites has had a high success rate for at least two years after transplanting (J.D. Briggs, personal communication).

Finally, ease of propagation has meant that a Melbourne community group, Knox Environment Society, has been able to raise 6-to-8-month

*Table 3.*—Results of seed broadcast trials at the rate of one viable seed/cm², assessed on 22 February, 1989.

| Date of broadcast | Date of apparent completion of germination | Seedling density | % establishment |
|---|---|---|---|
| 29 Mar. 1988 | 18 May 1988 | 1 plant/4.1 cm² | 23 |
| 30 Aug. 1988 | 13 Sept. 1988 | 1 plant/7.3 cm² | 14 |

old seedlings in large numbers and sell them to the public for $1 a plant. A private company is planning to do the same thing shortly.

*Management*

As already noted, cessation of burning is causing *R. leptorrhynchoides* to disappear rapidly from rail reserves. Burning every three to four years would be the best way to prevent this. There is a chronic, major problem in persuading under-funded State Government agencies to institute regular burning, so that special pleading by concerned biologists every time burning is necessary is often needed to prevent sites from becoming overgrown and worthless.

In special cases, other methods of keeping *R. leptorrhynchoides* sites open are available. At Truganina Cemetery, annual slashing outside the flowering/fruiting period (with the slasher set well above ground level) with removal of the slashed material does not seem to have reduced the population size. At Rokewood Cemetery, even light sheep grazing each January has allowed persistence of the species, the timing being crucial.

*General Issues*

The case described involves the very rapid contraction and fragmentation of widespread grassland communities as a result of agricultural expansion; it is closely analogous to the case of the North American prairies (Jordan 1983) including the importance of cemeteries (Kerr and White 1981) and rail reserves (White 1986), the parallel extending even to the widespread loss of these due to recent grading and herbicide spraying (Bacone and Harty 1981).

Although the remnant sites are very small, for all we know they may have relevance as refugia for vertebrates, and they almost certainly do have have relevance for invertebrates. Cemeteries, for example, are important refugia for at least two species of flightless grasshoppers threatened Australia-wide (Ride and Wilson 1982), and some taxa from other insect groups like butterflies and moths are dependent on native grasses as food plants, and are apparently confined to lowland native grasslands (T.R. New, personal communication).

The remaining refugia are so small and scattered, and often so unconservable in the long term, that attempts at community restoration on large, secure sites are now a necessity. This necessity for reintroduction of species and restoration of communities is also shared with the prairie case (Jordan 1983) and has strong parallels with the work on creating herb-rich grassy swards in the United Kingdom (Wells, Bell, and Frost 1981). Problems to be faced by such work include (a) those caused by fragmentation itself, such as seed production difficulties caused by fragmentation effects on animal pollinators and (b) those where fragmentation exacerbates another problem, *e.g.* the way it causes the refugia to be surrounded by invasive weeds and infiltrated by their propagules. Much of the restoration effort will have to be directed towards negating the impact of introduced plants on the native vegetation, as in the prairie work (Jordan 1983).

The case also highlights the absolute necessity for continuous intensive management under present conditions; fire or an analogue must be used frequently to control dominance of the native perennial grasses. To simply reserve and fence-off stands of vegetation will rapidly lead to a virtual monoculture, *e.g.* of *T. triandra*. These statements are equally true for prairie conservation (Roberts *et al.* 1977).

Deliberate reintroduction and the sale of plants to the public as in the present case-history can, in some instances, raise objections on the grounds of disrupting natural distribution patterns, especially of local genotypes (Wathern 1986). In the present case, we feel that most refugia are so unconservable in the long-term that reintroduction is often the only alternative, certainly to local extinction and possibly to total extinction. We follow accepted guidelines (Iffrig 1986) by: (a) making every effort to maintain fidelity to original species ranges and habitat conditions, (b) giving strong emphasis to local genotypes or local seed provenances and (c) keeping accurate records of seed provenance and transplanting location for all reintroduction attempts.

For *R. leptorrhynchoides*, as for most plants, we do not yet have the data needed to estimate minimum viable population size (Menges 1986).

The most important needs indicated by the case are: (a) research: work on factors governing successful regeneration from seed in the field, especially around the transplanted stands in secure reserves; (b) management: immediate implementation by government agencies of a regular late summer/autumn burning regime at all Victorian sites to halt the present alarming decline in numbers; and (c) conservation: immediate action by the Victorian Department of Conservation, Forests and Lands both to acquire and reserve cemetery stands and to signpost, protect and monitor all rail and road reserve stands.

## Acknowledgments

We thank J.D. Briggs, M. Bartley and L. Lees for information, help and advice and the National Trust of Australia for permission to work at Mooramong. The work was funded by an Australian Heritage Commission National Estate grant, the Australian Bicentennial Authority and the biological diversity program of World Wildlife Fund Australia.

## References

Bacone, J.A., and Harty, F.M. 1981. An inventory of railroad prairies in Illinois. In *The Prairie Peninsula—in the 'Shadow' of Transeau: Proc. 6th North American Prairie Conference*, eds R.L. Stuckey and K.J. Reese. Pp. 173-76. Ohio Biol. Serv. Biol. Notes No. 15.

Briggs, J.D., and Leigh, J.H. 1985. *Delineation of Important Habitats of Rare and Threatened Plant Species in the Australian Capital Territory*. CSIRO: Canberra.

Briggs, J.D., and Leigh, J.H. 1988. *Rare or threatened Australian plants*. 1988 rev. ed. Aust. Nat. Parks Wildl. Serv. Spec. Publ. No. 14.

Gray, M. 1981. A daisy in danger. *Canberra Times* October 4, p.7.

Iffrig, G.F. 1986. From the editor. *Natural Areas J.* 6:2.

Jennersten, O. 1988. Pollination in *Dianthus deltoides* (Caryophyllaceae): effects of habitat fragmentation on visitation and seed set. *Conserv. Biol.* 2:359-366.

Jordan, W.R. 1983. Looking back: a pioneering restoration project turns fifty. *Restoration & Manage. Notes* 1:4-10.

Kerr, K., and White, J. 1981. A volunteer-supported effort to find and preserve prairie and savannah remnants in Illinois cemeteries. In *The Prairie Peninsula—in the 'Shadow' of Transeau: Proc. 6th North American Prairie Conference,* eds R.L. Stuckey and K.J. Reese. Pp. 181-83. Ohio Biol. Surv. Biol. Notes No. 15.

Menges, E.S. 1986. Predicting the future of rare plant populations: demographic monitoring and modeling. *Natural Areas J.* 6:13-25.

Ride, W.D.L., and Wilson, G.R. 1982. Australian animals at risk. In *Species at Risk: Research in Australia,* eds R.H. Groves and W.D.L. Ride. Pp.191-203. Australian Academy of Science: Canberra.

Roberts, T.M., Robson, T., and Catling, P.M. 1977. Factors maintaining a disjunct community of *Liatris spicata* and other prairie species in Ontario, Canada. *Can. J. Bot.* 55:593-605.

Scarlett, N.H., and Parsons, R.F. 1982. Rare plants of the Victorian plains. In *Species at Risk: Research in Australia,* eds R.H. Groves and W.D.L. Ride. Pp. 89-105. Australian Academy of Science: Canberra.

Scott, K. 1988. Temporary ban on site job considered. *Canberra Times* April 7, p. 3.

Stuwe, J. 1986. An Assessment of the Conservation Status of Native Grasslands on the Western Plains, Victoria and Sites of Botanical Significance. Fisheries and Wildlife Division, Victoria. *Arthur Rylah Institute for Environmental Research Tech. Rep. Ser.* No. 48. Department of Conservation, Forests and Lands: Melbourne.

Wathern, P. 1986. Restoring derelict lands in Great Britain. In *Ecological Knowledge and Environmental Problem Solving.* National Research Council. Pp. 248-71. National Academy Press: Washington.

Wells, T., Bell, S., and Frost, A. 1981. *Creating Attractive Grasslands Using Native Plant Species.* Nature Conservancy Council: Shrewsbury.

White, J. 1986. Why bother to protect prairies along railroads? *In The Prairie: Past, Present and Future. Proc. 9th North American Prairie Conference,* eds G.K. Clambey and R. H. Pemble. Pp. 172-73. Tri-College University Center for Environmental Studies, Fargo: North Dakota.

Willis, J.H. 1964. Vegetation of the basalt plains in western Victoria. *Proc. R. Soc. Victoria* 77:397-418.

Willis, J.H. 1972. *A Handbook to Plants in Victoria.* Vol. II. Melbourne University Press: Melbourne.

# Invertebrate Conservation: Three Case Studies in South-eastern Australia

*Alan L. Yen[1], Timothy R. New[2], Beverley D. Van Praagh[1,2] and Patrick J. Vaughan[1]*

## Abstract

The diversity of invertebrate animals and the lack of detailed information about them limit the development of conservation programs. Species-oriented conservation programs for three contrasting species of invertebrates from southeastern Australia are outlined, the giant Gippsland earthworm (*Megascolides australis* McCoy), the Eltham copper butterfly (*Paralucia pyrodiscus lucida* Crosby) and the *Hemiphlebia* damselfly (*Hemiphlebia mirabilis* Selys). These are exceptional cases and the major need for conservation of these and other invertebrates is protection and management of their habitat.

## Introduction

Invertebrate animals pose problems for conservation which are unfamiliar to most people working solely with vertebrates, and we believe that it is important to demonstrate these problems to an audience that consists predominantly of vertebrate-oriented scientists. Rather than concentrating on a single species, we prefer to consider and compare several taxa because no single invertebrate species can amply reflect the full range of problems that confront us. We have, therefore, selected three taxa, species with contrasting habitats, lifestyles and trophic roles, which are foci of current conservation concern in southeastern Australia. Before detailing these, we make some brief comments about invertebrates and their conservation, to help provide the background against which any given case may be appraised.

## Conceptual Barriers to Invertebrate Conservation

With few exceptions, there is a conceptual barrier to sympathy for conserving invertebrates. Despite the vital and dominating ecological roles of these animals, the public and politicians alike have largely been conditioned to the idea that most 'bugs' and 'creepy-crawlies' should be swatted rather than saved. Allusions to crayfish, prawns, oysters and scallops help to counter this blanket attitude in some way! A recent declaration in Europe—the *Charter for Invertebrates*—adopted by the Council for Europe in 1986 merits very real attention in Australia. Invertebrates constitute the major or sole diet of many vertebrate species, ranging from fish and amphibians to bats and the largest whales. They also play key roles in many essential ecosystem functions such as herbivory, pollination, parasitism, predation and decomposition. It should be remembered that invertebrates constitute at least 95% of the world's animal species (Southwood 1978), but most conservation emphasis is concentrated on the remaining <5%, the vertebrates.

It is no exaggeration to claim that invertebrate conservation, though rarely given a high profile, may hold the major keys to ecosystem conservation, and that understanding of the principles of community ecology and dynamics would be totally deficient if adduced from studies of vertebrates alone.

[1]Invertebrate Survey Department, Museum of Victoria, 71 Victoria Crescent, Abbotsford, Victoria 3067, Australia.
[2]Department of Zoology, La Trobe University, Bundoora, Victoria 3083, Australia.

*Information Barriers to Invertebrate
Conservation*

The amount of sound biological and ecological
data available on any nominated invertebrate
species, be it terrestrial, freshwater, or marine, is
likely to be minimal. This reflects:

a. The enormous number of invertebrate species. Australia alone has well over 100,000
insect species and estimates of the global
diversity of insects reach several tens of millions. Other invertebrate groups, though less
numerous, are commonly several orders of
magnitude more diverse than vertebrate taxa.

b. The fact that many species remain undescribed, and are likely to remain so indefinitely. About half of Australian insect species, for example, do not have names. Many
are recognisable only to a few specialist
workers. Many have not yet even been collected. This state results in:

c. Difficulty of precise species-level identification of many taxa. The level of refinement of
identification needed for communication
about 'names' to decision-makers is often
difficult or impossible to achieve. Many
specialists adopt working codes or 'voucher
numbering systems', which do not have the
same impact on land managers or politicians
as 'real' names, and which are sometimes
taken as symptomatic of disinterest or non-
importance.

d. The existence of divergent life forms, often of
short duration. Immature stages and adults of
the same taxon may appear very different and
be difficult to associate from field samples
(*e.g.* caterpillar and moth, dragonfly larva and
adult). These different stages usually appear
at different times of the year, may have very
different trophic roles, and may live in different habitats, so they do not coincide in either
time or space.

e. The great diversity of taxa present in many
communities, so that the myriad of interacting populations, often without clearly dominant taxa, may obscure the precise resource
needs and ecological role of a given species.

Accurate species recognition underlies the actual
definition of the word 'population', namely, a
group of organisms of one species. If we cannot
accurately define the species, then how can we
accurately define its populations?

*Practical Barriers to Invertebrate
Conservation*

These fundamentals engender a suite of practical
problems for working on invertebrates. They
include:

a. Field identification is difficult for most groups.
Keys for laboratory identification, even to ge-
neric level, may not exist for taxa which are
abundant, let alone many of the lesser groups
or early stages. The only reliable way a field
worker can identify most caterpillars, for
example, is to rear them through to the adult
stage and compare these with authoritatively
identified material in one of our few major
reference collections. This latter step may
also have limitations, as many collections
have not been continuously curated to keep
abreast of recent taxonomic changes and
revisionary work, and actual examination of
the specimens may entail microscopic appraisal and specimen dissection. Presence of
undescribed taxa which may not be appreciated as such by non-specialists adds to the
confusion. There are just not enough taxonomists employed to overcome this very real
impediment to documenting and understanding our natural world. Identification of living
material is commonly very difficult or impossible without capture and close examination.

b. Sampling methods, especially those sufficiently quantitative to estimate population
sizes, may be complex. Most entomological/
invertebrate surveys rely on agglomeration of
dead material for later examination. In rela-

tion to vertebrates, most invertebrates are short-lived and highly seasonal in incidence and apparency. Even diurnal rhythms of activity may render these animals very difficult to detect and, especially, to count, and the opportunities for valid quantitative population/community comparison across a range of different sites may be limited. The prospect of gaining definitive or reliable inventories of invertebrates for a given area, a routine step in conservation assessment of many vertebrates or higher plants, is virtually impossible.

c.   The ecological role of most invertebrates is by no means clear. It may be feasible to classify a given taxon grossly as, for example, a 'predator' or an 'herbivore', but only rarely can accurate details of resource requirements be suggested for any species without considerable further investigation. Many invertebrates have very restricted diets or other resource needs. Many techniques routinely used for vertebrates either are inapplicable or yield only fragmentary information if used for invertebrates.

d.   Documentation of distribution patterns of invertebrates in Australia is in its infancy. Even for common and conspicuous species, such as some of our larger butterflies, distributions can normally only be given in generalised terms, and the suite of environmental influences determining this are likely to be almost entirely unknown. Preliminary distribution maps of butterflies in Victoria (Entomological Society of Victoria 1986) reflecting greater interest in and documentation of this group than any other terrestrial invertebrates, revealed that about half of the State, divided into 10 minute x 10 minute blocks, has **NO** butterflies recorded from it; and Victoria is perhaps the most thoroughly documented State on mainland Australia.

There is thus a major practical problem in quantifying the effects of putative endangering processes except in such general terms as habitat contraction or apparent changes. Data for one invertebrate species may not be extrapolable even to its close relatives. There are invariably subtle but significant differences in their responses to environmental change, but it is important, in practical terms, to assess whatever information may be available on a target species and its relatives.

This conference is about conservation of small populations—a concept that itself is difficult to determine, especially when related to continuing decline. Many invertebrate populations may be locally small and rely on recolonisation from surrounding populations. In these instances the concept of 'metapopulation' is very appropriate. Metapopulations consist of a 'shifting mosaic' of populations; some become extinct, but are recolonised from surrounding populations (Harrison *et al*. 1988). Reduction of habitats that support metapopulations of a particular species increases the distances between populations and reduces the chances of recolonisation after local extinction. This is particularly applicable to many parts of southeastern Australia, where many natural habitats are relatively small remnants of formerly much larger temperate ecosystems. The result is that many species persist in fragments of remnant habitat.

On the practical level, population sizes of any given species of invertebrate may be difficult to assess, as techniques routinely used for large, more conspicuous and more robust animals are not appropriate. Various methods of mark-release-recapture can be used for some robust invertebrates, but even larger butterflies (the invertebrates for which such techniques have most frequently been used) may be mutilated inadvertently, or have their behaviour or vulnerabilty changed, and there is growing feeling that such direct handling techniques should not be used for vulnerable invertebrates. Many taxa, in any case, are not readily visible for application of these methods, and marks on immature stages may be lost with moulting within a relatively short time.

Transect or area counts can be made for easily visible species or their traces (such as galls or leaf miners), but counts of mobile individuals for inter-site comparisons may need to be made at a similar time of day and under similar weather conditions. Short-term activity patterns of many diurnal invertebrates are influenced substantially by such factors as temperature, sunlight, precipitation and cloud cover.

'Rarity' has several different meanings. It may, for example, refer to high dispersion—so that a species occurs over a broad range but in low numbers at a given part of this range—or to occurrence only at a single site or locality where numbers may be high. Any definition of a 'small population' must take such differences into account, as they may lead to very different priorities for conservation management. The working definition most commonly used is of low numbers at one (or few) site(s), with the implication that this may be correlated with vulnerability.

In short, there are commonly substantial conceptual and practical problems (even for committed and knowledgeable conservationists) in dealing with invertebrates. It is emphatically *not* possible merely to transfer *en masse* the accumulated vertebrate-based conservation wisdom to invertebrates and assume it will be effective.

*Management and Conservation of Small Invertebrate Populations*

Addressing some of the specific themes of this conference:

a. Precise estimation of population size and dispersion is often very difficult. For any given taxonomic group of invertebrates found in Australia, the number of people here (or, indeed, elsewhere) experienced in either identification or practical 'hands-on' biology is likely to be extremely small, and there is little or no employment incentive to increase this number. Each invertebrate survey or conservation study which is oriented towards furthering our knowledge of a given taxon is, essentially, a pioneering study in its own right. It may be possible to draw on published work from overseas on related taxa, to a limited extent, but high levels of endemism and the unusual nature of many Australian ecosystems limit the practical application of much of this. Because of seasonal apparency, surveys can only rarely be adequate if restricted to one season, and may need to extend over two or three appearances (that is, probably, two to three years) to provide even approximate data on population size. Short-term fluctuations in population size are common in invertebrates.

b. Population modelling options are very limited. Life-table studies of most invertebrate groups do not exist, and are difficult to construct. Each necessitates several years of intense quantitative appraisal to estimate the effects of the multitude of environmental factors influencing the species' natality and mortality. It may be possible in a single season to detect factors which are *likely* to be important, but we counsel strongly against adopting this as definitive. Many long-term studies (mainly on pest arthropods) have shown that the relative effects of various factors may differ dramatically even between consecutive generations. The prime function of a population model is to have predictive power for future numerical and/or distributional trends: at present, good natural history may be a preferable and more rewarding theme to pursue for most relatively specialised invertebrates.

c. Captive breeding is commonly not a practical option for augmentation of field populations, and has only rarely been adopted in the context of conserving rare invertebrate species. Re-introductions from other populations, if available, are also rarely attempted.

d. Likewise, conservation genetics of invertebrates is in its infancy and is unlikely to be employed as a conservation tool in Victoria for the forseeable future.

Despite these and other limitations, conservation of invertebrates is coming to be recognised as a major issue in ecosystem management. Requests for funding for conservation-related studies on invertebrates are not now seen merely as the products of harmless eccentricity but rather as an important facet of conserving our environments. As with vertebrates, there are two major requirements: a) habitat security, often requiring reservation of lands and waterbodies and their eventual management to conserve precise ecological needs of given taxa, and b) provision for study of the target species, if any, to promote the best possible management options.

Much of the rationale for invertebrate conservation is included in the IUCN Invertebrate Red Data Book (Wells *et al.* 1983), and prospects and priorities for arthropod conservation in Australia were discussed by New (1984) and Majer (1987). An earlier essay by Key (1978) stimulated much of the later work.

The three examples discussed below reflect a range of these concerns and restrictions. The first two are 'charismatic' in the sense that they have rapidly aroused public concern for and interest in their well being—a valuable strength which is difficult to achieve for any invertebrate species. The first and third are species of global interest in being scientifically significant elements of our abundant endemic fauna. Each has broken new ground in the understanding and projection of invertebrate conservation in Victoria, and it is no exaggeration to claim that they have been instrumental in putting Victoria ahead of most other States in recognising the practical need for species-orientated invertebrate conservation programs. They also represent different stages of study and practical management: the first is still being assessed to determine the species' status, and the others have been conservation foci for somewhat longer. Summaries of the comparative biology and ecology and the comparative conservation status of the three species are provided in Tables 1 and 2 respectively.

## The Giant Gippsland Earthworm— A Subterranean Detritivore

### Significance of the Species

The giant Gippsland earthworm, *Megascolides australis* McCoy, is one of the largest known terrestrial invertebrate species in the world. The average size is 1 m x 20 mm, but specimens up to 3.6 m in length have been recorded (Barrett 1931; Quick 1963). However, length may be an inappropriate measurement of size as the worm is able to contract and expand considerably, and fresh weight may be more appropriate (even though much of this weight may be due to soil inside the gut). Adult worms range in weight from 90-380 g, and average around 210 g.

### History

The giant Gippsland earthworm was discovered by surveyors in the Brandy Creek region near Warragul in the 1870s during the settlement of the Gippsland region. Its large size caused debate among its discoverers as to whether it was a snake or a worm. It was sent to Professor F. McCoy at Melbourne University, who described it in 1878 (McCoy 1878). Since then, it has become a folk legend because of its size.

### Taxonomy

So far, it is assumed that there is only one species of *Megascolides* in south Gippsland. It is in the family Megascolecidae, subfamily Megascolecinae, tribe Dichogastrini (Jamieson 1971).

The genus *Megascolides* is found in Australia, New Zealand and North America, and is represented by three species in Australia (Jamieson 1981), although only *M. australis* is a very large species. Giant earthworms have been recorded from Sri Lanka (Jamieson 1965), North America (Wells *et al.* 1983), South America (Jamieson 1965; Johansen and Martin 1965), Africa (Jamieson 1965; Ljungstrøm and Reinecke 1969) and

*Table 1.*—Comparative biology and ecology of the giant Gippsland earthworm, Eltham copper butterfly and *Hemiphlebia* damselfly.

| Characteristic | Giant Gippsland Earthworm | Eltham Copper Butterfly | *Hemiphlebia* Damselfly |
|---|---|---|---|
| Habitat | subterranean | terrestrial | aquatic |
| Trophic level | detritivore | herbivore | predator |
| Life cycle | years | univoltine[1] | univoltine |
| Longevity | 4 years[2] | 1 year | 1 year |
| Reproduction | hermaphrodite | sexual | sexual |
| No. populations | ? | 10 | 3 |
| No. individuals | ? | few thousand | few hundred |
| Est. pop. density | 1590/ha | aggregated | $6/10m^2$ |

[1]In some years there is a second emergence some months after the first emergence.
[2]Estimated minimum term to reach adulthood.


*Table 2.*—Comparative conservation status of the giant Gippsland earthworm, Eltham copper butterfly and *Hemiphlebia* damselfly.

| Characteristic | Giant Gippsland Earthworm | Eltham Copper Butterfly | *Hemiphlebia* Damselfly |
|---|---|---|---|
| Has range declined? | probably | yes | yes |
| Have numbers declined? | probably | yes | yes |
| Threatening process | agriculture | urbanization | pastoralisation |
| Conservation status | vulnerable | vulnerable | vulnerable |
| Protected? | no | no | no |
| In reserves? | no[1] | yes | yes |
| Research | current | yes | yes |
| Management plan | no | yes | yes |
| Monitoring | yes | yes | yes |
| Captive breeding | attempted | no | no |

[1] Only a small population in Mt Worth State Park.

northern New South Wales to southern Queensland (Jamieson 1965; Pope 1955, 1958). Little research has been conducted on these large species. They are apparently unrelated, so that 'largeness' is not a characteristic of any particular taxonomic group.

It is interesting to note that the concept of a 'giant earthworm' is only relative in that most people have only experienced the common garden worm, *Lumbricus* sp., and that anything much larger than that is presumed to be a giant Gippsland earthworm. Over 50% of reports to the Museum of Victoria about the giant Gippsland earthworm are in fact attributable to other species of native earthworms which in all cases are only, at most, the size of a subadult giant Gippsland earthworm.

## Distribution

*M. australis* is restricted to Gippsland in Victoria, while the other two Australian *Megascolides* species are found in south-western Western Australia. Jamieson (1981) suggested that the disjunct geographical distribution of these three closely related species indicates that the genus *Megascolides* has been in Australia for a long period, with a wider original distribution, followed by major extinctions. This contrasts with *Digaster longmani* Boardman, the other large worm in Australia; the genus *Digaster* Perrier consists of 17 similar species with limited geographical distributions in montane coastal forests of eastern Australia. Jamieson (1975) suggested that this results from local origin and considerable speciation; the restricted range is due to ecological preference rather than extinctions.

From a questionnaire survey, Smith and Peterson (1982) concluded that it is distributed over 100,000 ha of the Bass River Valley in an area roughly bounded by Loch, Korumburra and Warragul. Within this area, the distribution is extremely patchy. Most observations of the worm are restricted to blue-gray clay soils. Many local farmers believe that the centre of distribution of the worm is in an area of approximately 5,000 ha

between Loch and Poowong. Until recently, all known worm sites were on private land, but a small population was found in the Mt Worth State Park in 1988 (Fig. 1).

In distributional studies conducted over a 2 km² area north of Loch in the 'centre of distribution', Van Praagh (unpublished data) recorded that over 80% of the worms occupied areas within 40m of the banks of streams or among soaks on south-facing slopes. Systematic sampling revealed that *M. australis* occurred in 6.1% of the study area.

## Basic Biology

Little is known about the basic biology of *M. australis* because it is a difficult organism to study. Much of the published literature extrapolates information gathered from other worms, generally the European species of *Lumbricus*, and this information is often incorrect.

*M. australis* is a sub-soil species. Most sub-soil earthworm species are large, have very extensive burrow systems, rarely, if ever, come to the surface, and feed on organic matter in the soil as they move (Lee 1961). They come close to the surface, but also go very deep into the sub-soil. They never come above ground freely, as they are helpless and unable to move properly on the surface. There are anecdotal reports that they expose their head end out of tunnels in autumn and winter, and they have been found completely on the surface when flooded out (Barrett 1938; Quick 1963; Smith and Peterson 1982); however, this has not been substantiated. The giant Gippsland earthworm appears to use a complex tunnel system which spreads out in many directions. The tunnels do not reach the surface, but come within a few centimetres of it. These tunnels often have running water flowing through them, and are always wet if occupied by a worm. The worms leave their casts in their tunnels, and unlike some other species of worms, do not produce surface casts; many people mistake the mounds of the yabbie (*Engaeus* sp.) to be surface casts of the giant Gippsland earthworm.

Giant Gippsland earthworms are capable of rapid movement by alternatively contracting and expanding the head and tail ends. Rapid movement underground is often indicated by a loud gurgling or sucking noise. They are more active nearer the surface after the autumn rains, and can be found there until early summer (while the soil is still soft and moist). They move deeper into the sub-soil when the soil dries out, although they still can be found in 'damp' patches of soil near the surface in summer. It is not known whether they aestivate.

It is still unknown how long it takes giant Gippsland earthworms to reach reproductive maturity and how long they live. *M. australis* is hermaphroditic, but it is still assumed that external fertilization is required. In the field, there appear to be three size (presumably age) classes based on the appearance of the clitellum: young worms (average weight 33.0 g), subadults (69.1 g) and adults (210.6 g). This suggests that it would take the worm at least three years to reach the adult stage; however, we would also expect a very slow growth rate, and worms could take much longer to mature and may live for a long time.

Egg capsules occur singly at an average density of 1.6 per $m^2$ in optimal habitats. There is no clear pattern as to when eggs are laid or when they hatch. Laboratory rearing suggests that the incubation period is at least 8-12 months and that hatching occurs between August and February. Egg capsules are 40-70 mm x 10-15 mm in size, with an average weight of 9 g, and are hard, leathery, fluid-filled objects. Only one embryo has been found in each egg capsule. They are laid in tunnels, often among grass roots, usually within 400 mm of the surface (average 230 mm).

It has been assumed that the giant Gippsland earthworm consumes soil or decaying organic matter (Eve 1974). Examination of casts has revealed root hairs, root particles, grass blades, leaves of dicotyledonous plants, and seeds, as well as unidentifiable organic and mineral matter.

*Population Status*

As the giant Gippsland earthworm is a purely subterranean animal, it is difficult to determine its population status other than by extensive digging. Clearing of its habitats began in the 1870s, and most had been converted to permanent dairy pastures by the 1930s. Even though practically all of the original extremely dense blue gum, paperbark and tree fern vegetation has been removed, the worm still exists locally in large numbers. This raises the interesting question of how their food source has changed since the land has been cleared.

The work of Van Praagh (unpublished data) in the 'centre of distribution' of *M. australis* indicates that the average density is 1,590 worms per ha.

However, we do not have any estimate of the number of *M. australis* populations, an important factor for conservation if we assume that the dispersal rate of the worm is very slow.

*Causes of Decline*

Whether numbers of the worms are declining, or whether the range is contracting is still debatable. We have to rely on anecdotal evidence from local landowners. Many landowners relate that large numbers of worms were found 'in the early days', but are not so common now. However, there was much more land clearance, dam building, road making, post-hole digging and deep ploughing many years ago. This type of activity has decreased, and the lower number of earthworm sightings may simply reflect changes in land use practices. Many farmers have reported cutting up worms while ploughing; yet during our study, which involved digging up 440 quadrats over 2 $km^2$, we found worms in approximately 6% of quadrats. None was found in pastures unless associated with a soak, which may indicate either that they were never there or have gone. Most worms are presently found on stream banks or hills too steep to plough.

Anecdotal evidence points possible decline to the use of superphosphate and ploughing (Quick 1963). Factors that may influence the worm's numbers are altered drainage patterns, land disturbance (ploughing), altered land use (crops instead of dairying), and addition of chemicals (herbicides, insecticides).

A more recent possible cause of decline is the collection of specimens of *M. australis* for sale by biological supply houses to collectors, educational institutions and museums.

*History of Research*

Most research on the giant Gippsland earthworm has involved anatomical (Bage 1909; McCoy 1878; Spencer 1888a, b; Vejdovsky 1892), taxonomic (Jamieson 1971) or physiological (Weber and Baldwin 1985) studies. Most of the information about its biology and ecology remains in the form of anecdotal information (Van Praagh *et al.* 1989).

*Particular Problems with Research*

The major problem with working on the giant Gippsland earthworm is its subterranean habitat and its relative fragility. Contrary to anecdotal belief that worms cut into pieces will regenerate, we have found that damaged adult worms generally die, although there is evidence that some form of autotomy may occur. We have also found a few younger worms with healed wounds, and it is possible that young worms are able to withstand some damage. The combination of the fragile nature and subterranean habit of the worm have made population estimates through mark-recapture studies impossible up to now. Furthermore, its slow developmental rate and probable high longevity make rearing in the laboratory a difficult procedure.

*The Conservation Program and Aims*

The giant Gippsland earthworm is listed by the International Union for Conservation of Nature as 'vulnerable' along with two smaller American species of *Megascolides, M.americanus* Smith (the Washington giant earthworm), and *M. macelfreshi* Smith (the Oregon giant earthworm) (Wells *et al.* 1983).

While more long-term research is required on the life history and population dynamics of the giant Gippsland earthworm, the most important task would be to establish the habitat factors that determine its distribution in order to map its distribution accurately. The establishment of a worm reserve in the area of its centre of distribution is a high priority, together with the development of stream and river management plans and incentive schemes to persuade farmers to manage their land in ways to assist conservation of the worm. *M. australis* is an important part of the cultural heritage of Korumburra (which has an annual festival named after the worm), and any attempts to enhance the worm's standing would generally be supported by the local community.

*The Eltham Copper Butterfly—
A Terrestrial Herbivore*

*Significance of the Species*

The Eltham copper butterfly is a local subspecies, *Paralucia pyrodiscus lucida* Crosby, described from the Eltham/Greensborough area of outer north-eastern Melbourne, an area subjected to intensive urban expansion during recent decades. This process has already been responsible for decline or disappearance of some populations, and the butterfly was until very recently believed to be extinct near Melbourne. A thriving colony

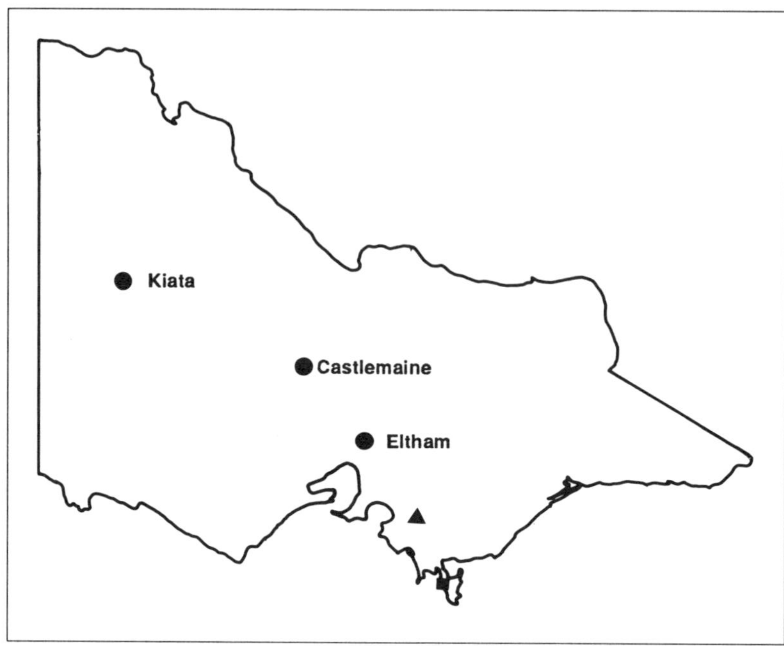



*Figure 1.*—Distribution of the Eltham copper butterfly (●), the *Hemiphlebia* damselfly (■), and the giant Gippsland earthworm (▲) in Victoria (south-eastern Australia).

was discovered at Eltham in early 1987 by Michael Braby on land threatened with immediate subdivision for housing development. Saving the Eltham copper butterfly rapidly became a major issue in the local community, as a symbol of the environmental awareness that Eltham has long sought to foster.

### History

The butterfly was first collected in the Eltham area in the late 1930s and was taken more or less regularly over the ensuing decade or so. It was recognised as a distinctive local form and described as a subspecies of the dull copper butterfly by Crosby (1951). Its present common name dates only from 1987.

### Taxonomy

The distinctiveness of the Eltham form of *P. pyrodiscus* (Rosenstock) is still debatable. It was described because the extent of coppery scaling on the wings differed from *P. pyrodiscus*, but the general validity of this character has not been evaluated fully.

The Lycaenidae (the 'blues', 'coppers', 'hairstreaks' and allied butterflies) is the largest family of the Papilionoidea and contains about 40% of all butterflies. There are approximately 140 species in Australia. *Paralucia* Waterhouse and Lyell is an endemic genus containing three species, two of which are rare and the other local in south-eastern Australia.

216

*Distribution*

*P. pyrodiscus* occurs at intervals around south-eastern Australia from Expedition Range in Queensland to western Victoria. Colonies allocated to the subspecies *lucida* occur in the Eltham/Greensborough area, and colonies at Castlemaine and Kiata also appear to be of this form (Fig. 1). All the colonies are isolated from each other, and there is no practical possibility of natural interchange. They are often confined to open forest areas on drier north to west-facing slopes, although some are on highly degraded situations along roadsides. Intensive searching since 1987 has revealed 10 colonies in the Eltham area, but eight of these are small and unlikely to be viable in the long term (Vaughan 1987, 1988). Only two of these remnant populations therefore appear to have any chance of long-term survival, which depends on security and management of the habitat. These populations occupy only a few hundred square metres of habitat.

*Basic Biology*

*P.p. lucida* apparently has only one major generation each year. Adults are present from late November until February, but their presence in small numbers from early March to April may reflect a partial second generation. Eggs are laid singly or in small groups (six, up to about ten) on or near the larval foodplant, *Bursaria spinosa*, and the life cycle appears to be intricately and obligately limited to a spiny, dwarfed form of this widespread plant. Further, it is restricted to plants which are associated with nests or chambers of the ant genus *Notoncus* (at Eltham, *N. enormis* Szabo). In common with many other lycaenids, the apparently obligate tripartite relationship between caterpillar, plant and ant adds a further restrictive complication to practical conservation. Caterpillars hatch from eggs after about 2 weeks and feed nocturnally on the *Bursaria* foliage. They retreat to ant chambers at the base of the plants during the day. The ants regularly tend the caterpillars, which possess organs that secrete an ant-attractive solution of sugars and amino acids. The caterpillars pupate in the ant chambers just below ground level and the pupal stage for the major generation lasts for about a month. There are five larval instars (Braby, personal communication).

The sex ratio is probably near unity, and adults feed at flowers of *Bursaria* and other plants. They are aggressive to other butterflies, and males actively pursue females when seeking a mate.

*Population Status*

Since the rediscovery of *P. pyrodiscus* in 1987, Vaughan has conducted extensive surveys in the Eltham/Greensborough area to determine population size and distribution. All known colonies are highly circumscribed, and the populations appear to be closed with the adult butterfly (the only likely dispersive stage) not moving far but remaining basically 'territorial'. Counts of butterflies (during their restricted flight season) and caterpillars (nocturnal counts of caterpillars feeding on *Bursaria*) have yielded unusually precise figures for any invertebrate populations. This has been facilitated by the very restricted size and area of the colonies which, however, also emphasises the urgent need for aid if they are to persist.

The major Eltham colony, on the subdivision land, contained an estimated 300-500 larvae. At the other extreme, only six butterflies were observed in a colony on private land. Several of the intermediate colonies had populations estimated at 100-150 individuals each. In contrast, the Kiata colonies contain many hundreds of individuals and there are 100-200 at Castlemaine. It is not yet clear whether these figures represent yearly averages or the peaks or troughs of a natural population fluctuation.

The butterfly was formerly much more widespread around Eltham and Greensborough. Accumulated collector wisdom suggests that it declined markedly from about 1950 onwards, and thereafter became extremely rare. As noted above, it had been feared extinct at the time it was rediscovered.

The ant associated with *P.p. lucida* itself appears to be local, but other species of *Notoncus* occur in Victoria: the attendant ant at Kiata is *N. ectatomoides* (Forel). *Bursaria spinosa* is also widespread in Victoria, but even when both ant and foodplant are present on apparently suitable sites, *P.p. lucida* is found only very rarely. It is clear that the butterfly is now present near Melbourne only as remnant colonies which may be declining and which have undoubtedly been highly vulnerable—indeed, directly threatened with extinction during the last 2 years.

### Causes of Decline

Recent decline in the Greensborough/Eltham area appears to be attributable solely to urbanisation: many former colonies of *P.p. lucida* no longer exist simply because the habitat has been alienated by housing development and removal of native flora.

### History of Research

Virtually all research on the subspecies has been undertaken since early 1987, when the possibility of saving remnant colonies was first raised. Amateur interests have played a major role in contributing to this—as with many Lepidoptera, knowledgeable collectors may contribute the bulk of an initial data base for conservation management.

### Particular Problems with Research

The major problem has been ensuring habitat security.

### The Conservation Program and Aims

A major conservation concern has been to ensure the safety of the habitat of the major Eltham colony, the land planned for subdivision in 1987. As a result of urgent discussions at local and State Government levels and with the developers, a moratorium on development was agreed so that the biology of the species could be studied and the feasibility of site purchase for a butterfly reserve (at a price of $1 million) investigated. A public appeal was launched to raise funds. The State Government contributed $250,000 and the Eltham Shire $125,000. Public donations increased this to over $425,000, by far the largest sum allocated to conservation of an invertebrate species in Australia, and one which seems unlikely to be surpassed.

During the period of the appeal, a management plan was formulated for *P.p. lucida* (Vaughan 1987, 1988) following initial assessment of its conservation status (Crosby 1987). By reorganising and consolidating the areas of public open space in the original plan of subdivision, a substantial area of butterfly habitat was protected from development. A further area of the subdivision has been recently acquired using the funds mentioned above. Another important colony on public (formerly Education Department) land has been protected by designation of the land as a butterfly reserve, and adjacent Council land containing part of the colony will also be managed for the butterfly. With proper management, this habitat should be sufficient to conserve the butterfly for the forseeable future.

The value of the Eltham copper butterfly was as a high-profile species which captured public interest: a general booklet called *Butterfly Conservation* (New 1987) was produced in aid of the appeal, and this also served to increase public awareness of the topic as a whole. It also showed the value of invertebrate taxa as indicator species for subtly different subcommunities which are not apparently identified or delineated for conservation assessment—that is, communities which are not easily distinguished by differences in floral composition. The habitats reserved, although small, may well harbour other unusual invertebrate taxa which are not as conspicuous as the Eltham copper butterfly. It may be possible to expand the effective habitat by promoting natural regeneration of *Bursaria*, and by removal of exotic weeds.

The Entomological Society of Victoria has placed *P.p. lucida* on its list of butterflies for which a Voluntary Restrictive Collecting Code applies. For Lepidoptera, more than any other terrestrial invertebrate group, collecting could contribute a serious threat to species with small and vulnerable populations.


## *The* Hemiphlebia *Damselfly— A Freshwater Predator*

### *Significance of the Species*

The tiny damselfly *Hemiphlebia mirabilis* Selys, only some 22 mm in wingspan, is a 'living fossil'. It has striking primitive structural characters in both adult and larval stages, and these render it extremely isolated in the order Odonata and of unusual scientific interest. Tillyard (1928) commented that *Hemiphlebia* was 'one of the key genera for the right understanding of odonate phylogeny,' and *H. mirabilis* is the only extant member of its superfamily. Adults also have a highly unusual behavioural repertoire.

### *History*

*H. mirabilis* appears once to have been more widespread in Victoria, with records from the Goulburn Valley and Yarra Valley (early records summarised by Davies 1985). Indeed, it was feared to be extinct at the time of its inclusion in the IUCN Invertebrate Red Data Book (Wells *et al.* 1983), in which it is the only Australian odonate to appear. The evolutionary significance of the species had been recognised by the IUCN/ SSC Odonata Specialist Group, which had placed *Hemiphlebia* as its highest priority in world odonate conservation.

*H. mirabilis* was rediscovered in southern Victoria by Davies (1985), an event which aroused excitement in the international community of Odonata specialists. Virtually all detailed knowledge of its biology has accrued since 1987.

### *Taxonomy*

*H. mirabilis* is taxonomically isolated and unmistakeable. It is placed in both a family (Hemiphlebiidae) and superfamily (Hemiphlebioidea) which have no other members.

### *Distribution*

*H. mirabilis* is now known to exist only in a small area in southern Victoria, despite extensive searches over much of the State and its former range in central Victoria (Fig. 1). In central Victoria it was restricted to small reedy lagoons on floodplains, and it seems that deep holes were necessary as reservoir habitats to counter seasonal desiccation.

It is now known from limited and circumscribed swampy areas in the northern parts of Wilson's Promontory National Parks. The habitats are discussed by Sant and New (1988).

### *Basic Biology*

The adult damselfly is present from late November to late February, with few individuals at either end of this period and occasional stragglers in autumn. There is one generation each year. Eggs are presumed to be laid by insertion into aquatic vegetation. The aquatic larvae are predators on a wide range of small invertebrates. They remain small until late winter, and the last four or five instars then undergo a period of rapid growth before adult emergence. The larvae are cryptic in appearance, with legs strongly banded in alternating dark and pale greyish brown annuli. They appear to live openly on aquatic vegetation and not to burrow into the substrate. The fully-grown larva is about 12.5 mm long.

The metallic dark green adults are also cryptic, and spend much of the time resting on vegetation. They do not appear to be strong flyers and have been found only in the immediate vicinity of the larval habitats. Mate-finding is apparently facilitated by an elaborate display. The males, in particular, 'flick' their abdomens and expand their vivid white apical abdominal appendages. Nine distinct postures or display episodes were noted by Sant and New (1988). In contrast, preliminary observations on larval display behaviour suggest that this is considerably less elaborate than in many other damselflies.

*Population Status*

The known populations are both closed and highly localised. The two major colonies are about 4 km apart, but it is highly unlikely that adults fly between them. The adult is the only dispersive stage in the life cycle. It would be feasible to estimate adult numbers by mark-release-recapture methods, as damselflies are much more robust than many other insects.

The species has clearly disappeared from much of its former range, and the known populations are clearly remnants (perhaps the sole remnants) of this broader distribution. Numbers during the last two flight seasons have been very low, and there is strong suggestion of a very recent decline from the more numerous populations witnessed by Davies (1985). The largest known colony occurs in a swamp only some 80 m long, with the water area declining considerably during summer.

*Causes of Decline*

Causes of decline of *Hemiphlebia* are strongly related to changes in land use. The areas in the Goulburn and Yarra Valleys are now unsuitable for *Hemiphlebia* as land clearing and drainage associated with pastoralisation for cattle has radically altered the natural environment. Many of the reedy swamps formerly suitable for the damselfly no longer exist. The remnant habitats at Wilson's Promontory have also suffered from cattle intrusion, and other factors (below) have also caused concern.

*History of Research*

Since the species was described by Selys in 1868, and more fully in 1877, *H. mirabilis* has been recognised as a highly unusual and significant evolutionary unit in the Odonata. There is some controversy over the type locality which was cited as Port Denison (Bowen), Queensland, but it is generally believed that this is an error. It was found near Alexandra (some 160 km north-east of Melbourne) about the turn of the century. Most other references until Wells *et al.* (1983) and Davies (1985) were concerned solely with the unusual morphology of *Hemiphlebia* and speculations on its relationships. Davies' valuable synthesis and rediscovery has provided the basis for further documentation in the hope of conserving the species which may have survived with little change from the Permian period.

*Particular Problems with Research*

It is highly unusual for an invertebrate of such notable conservation interest as *H. mirabilis* to be discovered to exist (as far as is known) solely in a well-established National Park and still to be considered vulnerable. It raises an important theme of the compatability of multiple use for reserved lands and effective management for endangered invertebrates.

The northern part of Wilson's Promontory is still subject to cattle grazing leases, which are due to be phased out over the next few years. The area of the *Hemiphlebia* swamps is in a broader area managed for fuel reduction and preservation of successional stages by rotational low-intensity control burning. Part of the swamp, close to a road, is also mown annually to constitute part of a roadside firebreak to counter sporadic natural fires. The site is therefore subject to a number of potential endangering processes and sporadic reduction of buffering vegetation, but provides an unusual opportunity for considering the effects of some potential management tools on the numbers and wellbeing of the species.

In April 1987, a fire burned through much of the swamp; only the mown area remained green, so that (unusually) mowing could have helped to maintain a reservoir habitat for an aquatic insect. The effects of this fire were serious, as the swamp was thereafter very exposed and cattle trampling increased substantially during the following summer when they were seeking water. Very few adult *Hemiphlebia* were seen in either the 1987-1988 or 1988-1989 flight seasons.

It may eventually be possible to rear *Hemiphlebia* in the laboratory, but this presents some problems. Rowe (1987) has indicated ways of providing artificial substrate for endophytically-laying Odonata in the laboratory, but this would obviously necessitate removal of females from the restricted field population. Rearing of odonatan larvae is labour-intensive because they must be kept separately to avoid cannibalism. Captive rearing is considered unwise for *Hemiphlebia* unless further populations are found, from which local enhancement could be made.

If present apparent population levels persist, the population may be too small for detailed quantitative investigation, and this will be a major problem to refinement of management and formulating a detailed conservation program. Once a species becomes too rare to study, habitat reservation and a policy of non-intervention is the only practical step that can be taken.

### The Conservation Program

The program comprises two parts: (1) reduction or elucidation of the effects of potentially damaging factors and (2) related habitat enhancement, together with continued searching for additional *Hemiphlebia* populations on Wilson's Promontory and elsewhere.

The major site has been fenced to exclude cattle, and mowing has been suspended along the edge whilst the vegetation on the rest of the swamp regenerates from the 1987 fire. With cessation of cattle grazing in the area in the early 1990s, the secondary sites may become more suitable for *Hemiphlebia*.

The species is still highly vulnerable, if not directly threatened, and continued monitoring of the populations is needed. The National Parks and Wildlife Division of the Department of Conservation, Forests and Lands has recognised the importance of this species and is cooperating fully in the conservation program.

### Discussion

In Victoria at present we are witnessing an exciting phase of invertebrate conservation, namely the transition from their being merely passengers in conservation thought and practice to being prime targets of some intricate and expensive management programs. The Victorian *Flora and Fauna Guarantee Act* specifically includes invertebrates—which provides a powerful incentive to concerned biologists to provide information on some of our more notable species, as there is now official recognition and potential practical support for their conservation. Habitat conservation is likely to remain the over-ridingly important issue, but it is now more generally appreciated that the very precise environmental requirements of many terrestrial and freshwater invertebrates which are considered vulnerable may often necessitate precise management for their conservation rather than solely inclusion (fortuitous or otherwise) in areas reserved primarily for other reasons.

The Eltham Copper Butterfly Reserve is itself a landmark, being the first reserve made specifically for an invertebrate in the State. But, however vital such reserves are (together with adequate buffer zones), for safeguarding particular species, they will not be adequate to conserve the bulk of our diverse invertebrate fauna. For these, the only logistically feasible interim measure is large-scale reservation of indigenous communities, to conserve the intricate invertebrate taxa co-evolving with virtually every nuance of vegetation association.

The examples we have outlined are generally atypical of invertebrates, but have demonstrated some of the difficulties inherent in designing effective conservation programs for particular notable and rare taxa. There may well be conflicts of interest, at least on a local scale. It is entirely feasible that conservation management for one invertebrate taxon may adversely affect others—for example, a vulnerable herbivore feeding on a restricted host plant may itself be attacked by unusual and specific insect predators or parasitoids. Our present knowledge does not allow us to predict these situations, but they will undoubtedly occur.

We must reiterate that the key to invertebrate conservation is habitat protection. It is only through this measure that the large numbers of unknown species will be conserved on a long-term basis. The problem then is to decide what habitats to protect and how. Ideally, as most of our natural south-eastern Australian habitats have been seriously depleted, all remnant areas should be conserved. Although this idea is politically difficult, the long-term resilience of these remnant areas in light of future climatic changes (Main 1988) makes their conservation a major priority. Consequently, practical criteria need to be considered for habitat reservation. Should habitats be chosen on the basis of naturalness, representativeness, typicalness, species richness or diversity, levels of endemism, size, threat of disturbance, or any combination of these or other factors? Once these habitats are selected, then how are they to be managed: for climax or successional stages? Do we know what we are managing? In fact, can we define invertebrate habitats? Are physical or botanical definitions of habitats adequate for invertebrates? The belief that reserving botanical communities will conserve their component faunas has been a valuable conservation tool, but it may not always be a sound assumption (Yen 1987).

In the past, conservation need was often taken to be synonymous with taxon or habitat rarity. For many vertebrates, this concept is still workable. However, for many of the myriads of invertebrates, rarity is a fact of life, and although rare species may be the most vulnerable to habitat change, rarity is usually negatively correlated with typicalness, which is determined by the common species. As managing for the conservation of all *rare* invertebrates is an impractical option, White (1987) suggested that conservation management should monitor and maintain the *common* species of a community as a prerequisite for maintaining the rare species. This approach has merit, but changes in abundance of more common species may not always (or even usually) mirror changes in abundance of highly sensitive and specialised rare taxa because common species are sometimes opportunistic generalists.

On a practical level, it is important to define the major invertebrate habitats. In south-eastern Australia, there is need for a major survey to delineate the major invertebrate species assemblages, to ascertain their seasonal occurrences, and to determine their dependence on habitat factors. Although vegetation may not be the best definition of invertebrate habitats (Yen 1987), representatives of the major vegetation communities and other physical habitats (*e.g.* caves) are required to define the major characteristic species assemblages as a baseline for other invertebrate habitats.

It will be difficult to list many invertebrates under the *Flora and Fauna Guarantee Act* because there is inadequate information to determine whether species have undergone demonstrable decline, or are rare or potentially threatened with extinction. It will even be difficult to list invertebrate communities because there is no easily accepted definition of such communities at this stage.

Finally, the differences in our present appreciations of vertebrate and invertebrate conservation are adequately highlighted by this conference. It deals primarily with a single species of mammal, representing a group of animals with wide public and political appeal. It reflects the very substantial amount of attention which such a species can command, and the expertise which may be available for this. We can only speculate that an entire conference on conservation of any invertebrate in Australia, other than some marine or edible freshwater taxa, would be unlikely to attract as many participants or to achieve as much. The spectacular overwintering aggregations of the monarch butterfly, *Danaus plexippus* L. in North America and Mexico have resulted in two international conferences on this species. The second (MONCON II at Los Angeles in 1986) attracted more than 50 researchers (Brower 1986). In contrast, a recent large outbreak of Bogong moths (*Agrptos omfisa* (Boisd.))in the new Parliament House in Canberra only attracted derision of the species by politicians of all political parties.

## Acknowledgments

We wish to acknowledge the assistance of Michael Braby and David Crosby for providing information on the Eltham copper butterfly, Bill Green for assistance with the giant Gippsland earthworm, Peter Lillywhite for technical assistance, and Peter Rawlinson for helpful comments on the manuscript. Financial assistance was provided for research on the giant Gippsland earthworm by World Wildlife Fund (Australia) and the Museum of Victoria. National Parks and Wildlife Division (Department of Conservation, Forests and Lands) provided a permit to work on the *Hemiphlebia* damselfly in Wilson's Promontory National Park and on the giant Gippsland earthworm in Mt Worth State Park.

## References

Bage, F. 1909. Contributions to our knowledge of Australian earthworms. The nephridia. *Proc. R. Soc. Vic.* **22**(N.S.):224-243.

Barrett, C. 1931. Megascolides, the world's biggest earthworm. *Aust. Mus. Mag.* **4**:238-243.

Barrett, C. 1938. Australia's Giant Earthworm. *Bull. New York Zool. Soc.* **41**:66-70.

Brower, A.V.Z. 1986. Update on conservation from MONCON II: notes on the second international conference on the Monarch Butterfly and the preservation of overwintering colonies. *Atala* **14**:12-14.

Crosby, D.F. 1951. A new geographical race of an Australian butterfly. *Victorian Nat.* **67**:225-227.

Crosby, D.F. 1987. The Conservation Status of the Eltham Copper Butterfly (*Paralucia pyrodiscus lucida* Crosby) (Lepidoptera: Lycaenidae). National Parks and Wildlife Division, Victoria. *Arthur Rylah Institute for Environmental Research Tech. Rep. Ser.* No. 81. Department of Conservation, Forests and Lands: Melbourne.

Davies, D.A.L. 1985. *Hemiphlebia mirabilis* Selys: some notes on distribution and conservation status (Zygoptera: Hemiphlebiidae). *Odonatologica* **14**:331-339.

Entomological Society of Victoria. 1986. *Preliminary Distribution Maps of Butterflies in Victoria*. Entomological Society of Victoria: Melbourne.

Eve, J.E. 1974. Gippsland worms. *Victorian Nat.* **91**:36-38.

Harrison, S., Murphy, D.D., and Ehrlich, P.R. 1988. Metapopulation ecology of the checkerspot butterfly *Euphydryas editha bayensis*. *Amer. Nat.* **132**:360-382.

Jamieson, B.G.M. 1965. Recognizing Australian earthworms. *Aust. Nat.Hist.* **15**:39-43.

Jamieson, B.G.M. 1971. A review of the megascolecoid earthworm genera (Oligochaeta) of Australia. Part III—the subfamily Megascolecinae. *Mem. Qld. Mus.* **16**:69-102.

Jamieson, B.G.M. 1975. The genus *Digaster* (Megascolidae: Oligochaeta). *Mem. Qld. Mus.* **17**:267-292.

Jamieson, B.G.M. 1981. Historical biogeography of Australian Oligochaeta. In *Ecological Biogeography of Australia*, ed. A. Keast. Pp. 885-921. Junk: The Hague.

Johansen, K. and Martin, A.W. 1965. Circulation in a giant earthworm, *Glossoscolex giganteus*. I. Contractive processes and pressure gradients in the large blood vessels. *J. Exper. Biol.* **43**:333-347.

Key, K.H.L. 1978. *The Conservation Status of Australia's Insect Fauna*. Australian National Parks and Wildlife Service: Canberra.

Lee, K. 1961. Interactions between native and introduced earthworms. *Proc. New Zeal. Ecol. Soc.* **8**:60-62.

Ljungstrøm, P.O. and Reinecke, A.J. 1969. Studies on influences of earthworms upon the soil and the parasitological questions. Ecology and natural history of the microchaetid earthworm of South Africa. *Pedobiologia* **9**:152-157.

McCoy, F. 1878. *Megascolides australis* (McCoy). The Giant Earth-Worm. In *Prodromus of the Zoology of Victoria*, **1**:21-25, Plate 7.

Main, A.R. 1988. Climatic change and its impact on nature conservation in Australia. In *Greenhouse: Planning for Climatic Change*, ed. G. I. Pearman. Pp. 361-374. CSIRO: Melbourne.

Majer, J.D. (ed.) 1987. *The Role of Invertebrates in Conservation and Biological Survey*. Proceedings of a workshop held during the 18th Scientific Conference of the Australian Entomological Society. Dept. Conserv. Land Manage.: Perth.

New, T.R. 1984. *Insect Conservation—an Australian perspective*. Junk: Dordrecht.

New, T.R. 1987. *Butterfly Conservation*. Entomological Society of Victoria: Melbourne.

Pope, E.C. 1955. Squirter earthworms. *Aust. Mus. Mag.* **11**:384-385.

Pope, E.C. 1958. Giant Earthworms. *Aust. Mus. Mag.* **12**:333-338.

Quick, B. 1963. A giant among worms. *Walkabout* February 1963:14-16.

Rowe, R. J. 1987. *Dragonflies of New Zealand*. Oxford Univ. Press: Auckland.

Sant, G.J., and New, T.R. 1988. The Biology and Conservation of *Hemiphlebia mirabilis* Selys (Odonata, Hemiphlebiidae) in Southern Victoria. National Parks and Wildlife Division, Victoria. *Arthur Rylah Institute for Environmental Research Tech. Rep. Ser. No. 82.* Department of Conservation, Forests and Lands: Melbourne.

Smith, B.J., and Peterson, J.A. 1982. Studies of the Giant Gippsland Earthworm *Megascolides australis* McCoy, 1878. *Victorian Nat.* **99**:164-173.

Southwood, T.R.E. 1978. The components of diversity. In *Diversity of Insect Faunas*, eds L. A. Mound and N. Waloff. Pp. 19-40. *Symposia of the Royal Entomological Society of London* No. **9**.

Spencer, W.B. 1888a. The anatomy of *Megascolides australis. Trans. Proc. Roy. Soc. Vic.* **24**:164-168.

Spencer, W.B. 1888b. On the anatomy of *Megascolides australis*, the Giant Earthworm of Gippsland. *Trans. Roy. Soc. Vic.* **1**:3-60.

Tillyard, R.J. 1928. The evolution of the order Odonata, Pt. 1. Introduction and early history of the order. *Records Indian Mus.* **30**:151-172.

Van Praagh, B.D., Yen, A.L., and Lillywhite, P.K. 1989. Further information on the Giant Gippsland Earthworm, *Megascolides australis* (McCoy 1878). *Victorian Nat.* **106**: 197-201.

Vaughan, P.J. 1987. The Eltham Copper Butterfly Draft Management Plan. National Parks and Wildlife Division, Victoria. *Arthur Rylah Institute for Environmental Research Tech. Rep. Ser.* No. 57. Department of Conservation, Forests and Lands: Melbourne.

Vaughan, P.J. 1988. Management Plan for the Eltham Copper Butterfly (*Paralucia pyrodiscus lucida* Crosby) (Lepidoptera: Lycaenidae). National Parks and Wildlife Division, Victoria. *Arthur Rylah Institute for Environmental Research Tech. Rep. Ser.* No. 79. Department of Conservation, Forests and Lands: Melbourne.

Vejdovsky, F. 1892. Zur Entwicklungsgeschichte des Nephridial-Apparates von *Megascolides australis*. *Archiv für Mikroskop. Anat.* **40**:552-562.

Weber, R.E., and Baldwin, J. 1985. Blood and erythrocruorin of the giant earthworm, *Megascolides australis*: respiratory characteristics and evidence for $CO_2$ facilitation of $O_2$ binding. *Molecular Physiol.* **7**:93-106.

Wells, S.M., Pyke, R.M., and Collins, N.M. 1983. *The IUCN Invertebrate Red Data Book.* Pp. 217-219. IUCN: Gland.

White, E.G. 1987. Ecological time frames and the conservation of grassland insects. *New Zeal. Entom.* **10**:146-152.

Yen, A.L. 1987. A preliminary assessment of the correlation between plant, vertebrate and Coleoptera communities in the Victorian mallee. In *The Role of Invertebrates in Conservation and Biological Survey*, ed. J. D. Majer. Pp. 73-88. Dept. Conserv. Land Manage.: Perth.

# The Helmeted Honeyeater: Decline, Conservation and Recent Initiatives for Recovery

*Ian J. Smales[1], Stephen A. Craig[2], Geoff A. Williams[3] and Roy W. Dunn[4]*

## Abstract

Management of the helmeted honeyeater by reservation and enhancement of existing core habitat has prevented its extinction, but has not arrested decline of the subspecies. The decline of the subspecies is reviewed. Details of the biology of the bird and ecological aspects underlying the continued attrition of the remnant population are provided. A collaborative recovery effort is now underway with the aim of rebuilding the population, which currently numbers fewer than fifty adult individuals. The rationale and methodology of this program are outlined.

## Introduction

The successful recovery of a threatened remnant population, to a condition of security and indefinite viability, requires a multi-disciplinary approach to all available options, techniques and possible contingencies, based upon a thorough understanding of the decline processes, which can be gained only from detailed knowledge of the subject's biology and ecology. Management of the helmeted honeyeater (*Lichenostomus melanops cassidix*) has, until some very recent initiatives, been based upon only one option, with little or no attempt to explore others.

The single expedient of reserving existing core habitat, and even enlarging it through revegetation, may have somewhat slowed the decline of the remaining extant population but has failed to arrest it. Habitat maintenance has been equated, in this case, with population management and conservation. In hindsight it should only have been part of a much broader strategy.

This paper outlines recent moves to adopt an overall strategy aimed at rebuilding the population, which currently numbers fewer than 50 adult individuals. The biology of the bird and the ecological aspects of the population's attrition which underlie the rationale and proposed methods of the program are reviewed.

An important aspect of the new recovery program is that it is a collaborative effort. From its inception, the skills and expertise of wildlife managers, research zoologists, professionals in captive husbandry, geneticists, veterinarians and skilled amateur ornithologists have been pooled, both to design the program and to commence its implementation. The network thus established will, it is hoped, be of lasting benefit to the helmeted honeyeater and perhaps, by the example of its approach, to other endangered taxa as well.

## General Biology

*L. m. cassidix* is the end race of a 'stepped cline' ring species, the yellow-tufted honeyeater (*L. melanops*) (Crome 1973).

[1]Department of Conservation, Forests and Lands, Dandenong Region, 205 Thomas Street, Dandenong 3175, Australia.
[2]Department of Conservation, Forests and Lands, Dandenong Region, P.O. Box 246, Healesville 3777, Australia.
[3]Zoological Board of Victoria, Sir Colin McKenzie Zoological Park, P.O. Box 248, Healesville 3777, Australia.
[4]Zoological Board of Victoria, P.O. Box 74, Parkville 3052, Australia.

With mean total length and weight of mature males in excess of 200 mm and 32 g, it is the largest of the *Lichenostomus* honeyeaters. It has striking black, yellow and olive/grey plumage.

The core habitat upon which the helmeted honeyeater is dependent is the vegetation of streamsides and swamps. *Eucalyptus viminalis* (manna gum) *E. camphora* (mountain swamp gum) and *E. ovata* (swamp gum) are the dominant tree species. The bird occurs only where a dense shrub layer exists, since this provides nest sites.

*L. m. cassidix* is a specialist forager on vegetation, primarily the foliage and outer branches of eucalypts. The bird's diet consists of a variety of arthropods and sugars derived from vegetation. The latter are available to it as manna (phloem exuded from damaged plant tissue), honeydew (the sugary excretions from the nymphal stages of various phytophagous insects) and nectar (Wykes 1982, 1985). When and where available, the berries of *Coprosma quadrifida* are also eaten (Wykes 1982). To protect these food resources, groups of the birds defend well-defined areas of habitat, from which they actively exclude birds of almost all other canopy-foraging species. Occasional foraging outside community sites occurs during the non-breeding period.

Helmeted honeyeater social groups consist of a number of adult pairs occupying adjacent territories, who mutually cooperate in site defence. A pair-bond exists and some pairs have been observed to remain together, occupying the same territory, for successive years.

Nesting activity has been recorded from July to February, with a peak in November and December. Nests are built in understorey shrubs and small trees. Mean clutch size is two. The female undertakes most incubating, brooding and feeding of nestlings. Nests that fail are replaced and adults will continue nesting attempts throughout the season, or until the successful fledging of chicks. Adult pairs may successfully fledge chicks from as many as three nests during a favourable season. Juveniles remain dependant upon adults for food for some weeks after nest evacuation. Rare visits to the nest and to dependant fledglings by birds other than the parents have been noted; in some instances these were by their siblings from earlier clutches. The purpose of such visits is unknown.

No obvious colour differences distinguish the sexes. In a sample of 11 colour-banded, known pairs, a small but consistent degree of size and weight dimorphism differentiated the sexes. Observations of copulation by three of these pairs, along with brood patch size differences, indicate that males are the larger, heavier birds (I. Smales, personal communication). Slight sexual dimorphism of this kind exists in all other *Lichenostomus* species for which data are available (Rogers *et al.* 1986). A number of morphometric and minor colour differences of plumage and soft parts distinguish adults from juveniles during their first year. Successful breeding has been recorded for birds in their second year. Recaptures of banded individuals demonstrate that individuals may live for at least 10 years.

## Historical Decline of the Population

Evidence from literature records and museum specimens indicates that *L. m. cassidix* was formerly distributed within appropriate habitat over some 2,000-3,000 km² of the Upper Yarra basin and northern and eastern catchments of Westernport Bay (Fig.1). Only at Cardinia Creek and in the Woori Yallock system have populations of the bird been known to exist for any length of time. Most of the other locations are represented by one, or only a few specimens, or from observations made during brief visits. Almost all are from before 1910. Nothing is known of the previous population sizes at such sites, only that birds once existed at each. Attrition of the subspecies from its previous wide range to the present single population provides an example of the general extinction process model of Clark *et al.* (this volume).

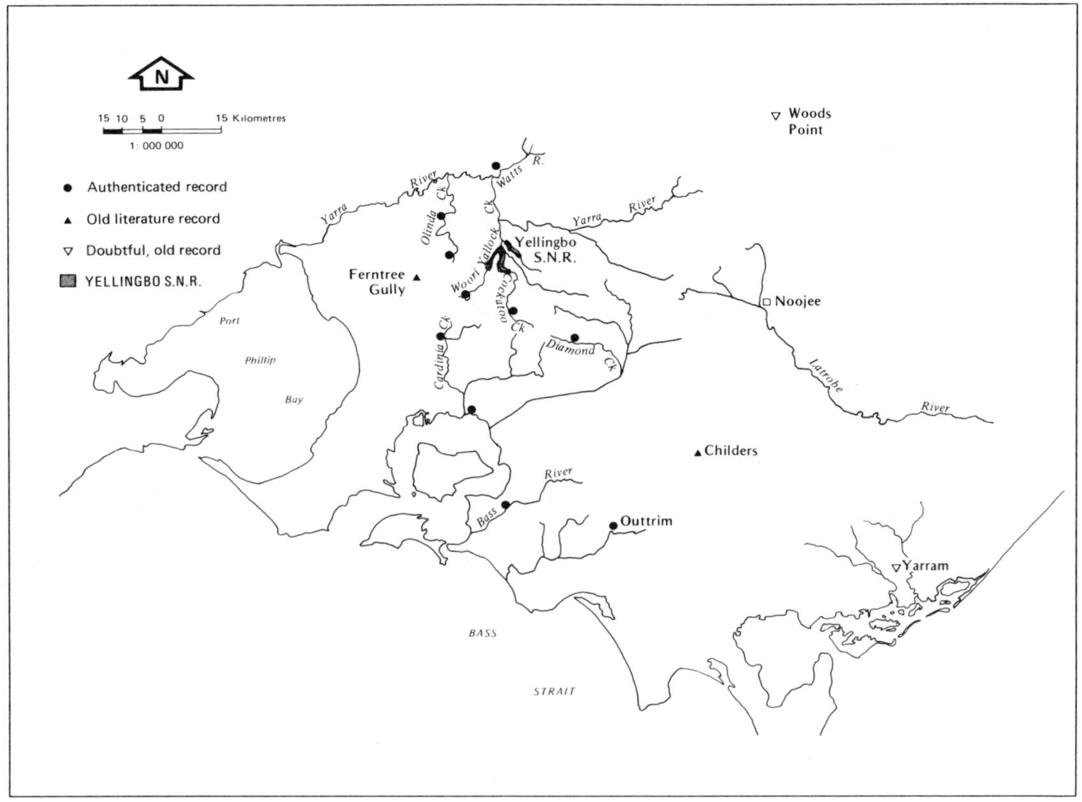



*Figure 1.*—Localities of all helmeted honeyeater records. N.B.-'Authenticated' records are those supported by museum skins, or sightings by competent observers, made in suitable habitat within the accepted former range, since 1960.

Systematic habitat loss, especially from the lower altitude Westernport drainage basins, appears to have led to the total loss of *L. m. cassidix* from that portion of the range prior to 1910. By the late 1970s, continued clearing and fragmentation of natural vegetation communities throughout the more northerly area had resulted in three or four declining and more or less disjunct populations. Random factors have eliminated two of these populations. A relict group of some six to eight birds persisted at Cardinia Creek until at least August 1982 (Smales 1988). Another group near the town of Cockatoo, when observed during January 1983, appeared to be slightly larger. In both cases, their immediate habitat was burnt by the Ash Wednesday wildfires of February 1983. There have been no confirmed sightings at either site since then. The existence of birds in the vicinity of Butterfields Reserve, on the upstream portion of Woori Yallock Creek, reported in 1979 (Wykes 1981), remains unconfirmed. The only population currently known to exist is on the Woori Yallock system, and is essentially confined to the Yellingbo State Nature Reserve (Fig. 2).

Some 40 km east of Yellingbo the Gippsland form of yellow-tufted honeyeater (*L. m. gippslandica*) is known to occur. The intervening area, encompassing the Gembrook and Yarra State

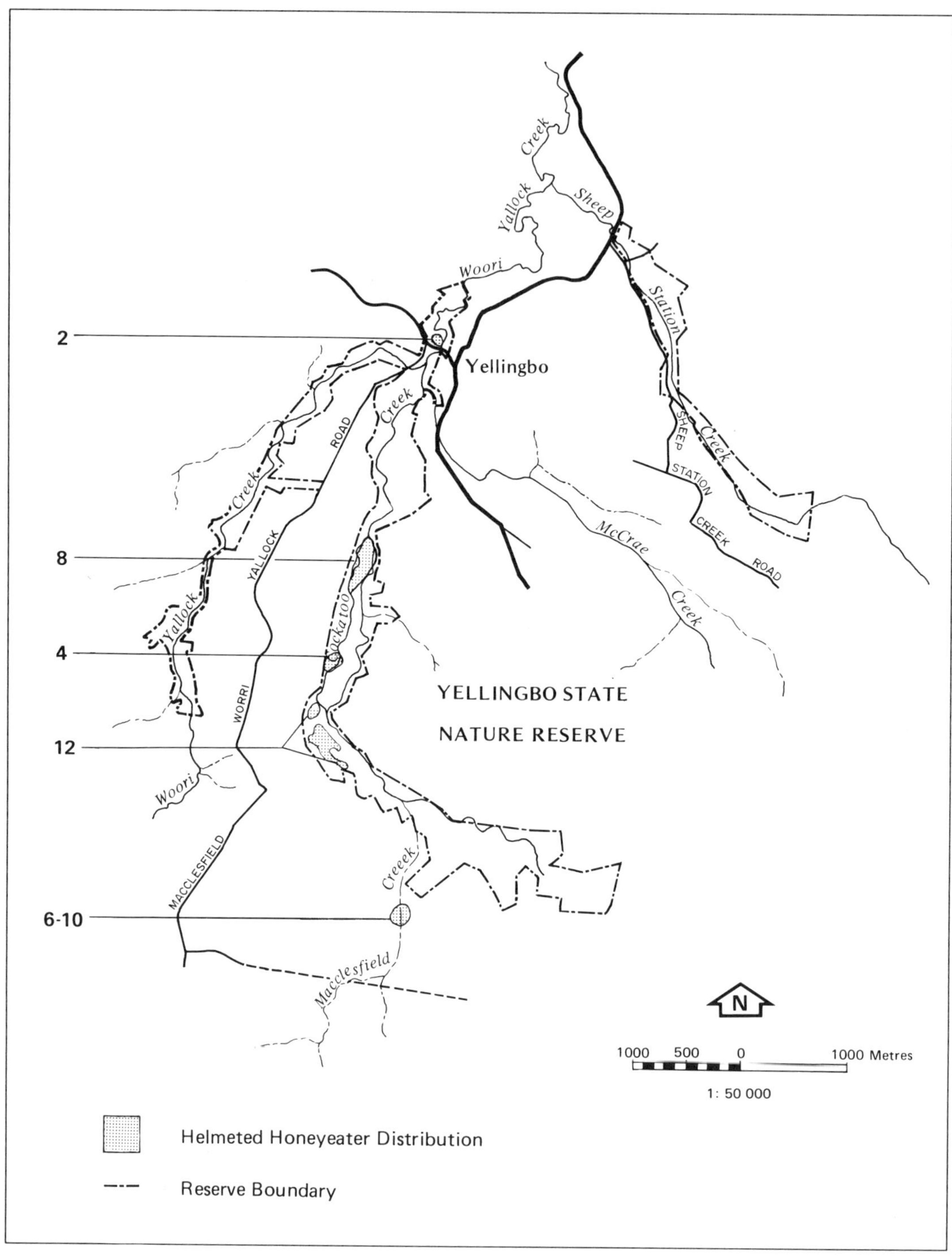


*Figure 2.*—Distribution and numbers of breeding adults per site 1987.

Forests, has never been comprehensively surveyed to determine the presence of *L. m. cassidix* or *L. m. gippslandica*. The possibilities still exist that previously undetected groups of either subspecies inhabit this area or that the two are not genetically isolated. Investigation of these possibilities is essential.

The role of genetic problems in the decline and extinctions of the former populations, once they had become small and isolated, is unknown. However, Crome (1973) discussed some morphologically anomalous museum specimens from such populations and considered that their condition may have been the result of inbreeding depression. Prior to its demise, the Cardinia Creek population may have been affected in this manner. During the breeding season of 1978-1979, when that population consisted of an isolated group of between six and 10 individuals, Woinarski and Wykes (1983) observed birds brooding at a nest for more than 34 days without eggs having been laid. A highly melanistic adult male was also captured there in that season. Wykes (personal communication) considers that these apparent aberrations of behaviour and morphology may have been indicators of inbreeding depression in that population.

## *Processes Affecting the Remnant Population*

The Cardinia Creek and Yellingbo populations provide vivid illustrations of the importance of a sound knowledge of ecology and life history to an understanding of the causes of population failure.

Whilst the final demise of the Cardinia Creek group is directly attributable to fire, it had declined from an estimated 100 individuals in 1947 (Lee and Bryant 1948), to some six to eight in August 1982. The Yellingbo population has also been in continuing decline (Smales 1988). In both instances the bird's habitat of natural riparian vegetation has remained largely uncleared, although it consists of narrow strips surrounded mainly by cleared agricultural land. Clearly, causes more subtle than overt human destruction of riparian vegetation are implicated in the decline of these two populations.

Studies by Crome (1969), Wykes (1981, 1982, 1985), Woinarski (1981) and Woinarski and Wykes (1983) have elucidated many of the ecological factors involved in the decline at these two locations. Some demographic aspects of the Yellingbo population have been investigated (Smales 1988) and this work is continuing in an attempt to determine exactly how the decline in this population is happening.

Wykes (1981) indicated that three factors were limiting the Yellingbo population and that the latter two were directly causing its continuing failure: 1) unsuitability of some former habitat due to lack of shrub-layer nest sites, 2) reduced and declining winter food resources and 3) deleterious interaction with a competitor, the bell miner (*Manorina melanophrys*).

### *Loss of Habitat Within the Reserve*

Some portions of the Yellingbo Reserve support mature *E. viminalis*, *E. camphora* and *E. ovata* but are no longer suitable as habitat for the bird because the shrub understorey required for nesting was removed during earlier agricultural use of the land.

### *Reduced Winter Food Resources*

Helmeted honeyeaters are dependant for most of the year upon *E. viminalis*, *E. camphora* and *E. ovata*, in which they forage for invertebrates, phloem-derived sugars and nectar. Throughout the year, and especially during the breeding season, birds are usually confined to traditional breeding sites where vegetation is dominated by these species. Short movements from these sites to exploit food resources, especially nectar, sometimes occur during the non-breeding period. These movements may be to other riparian locations or to attend blossoms of a variety of

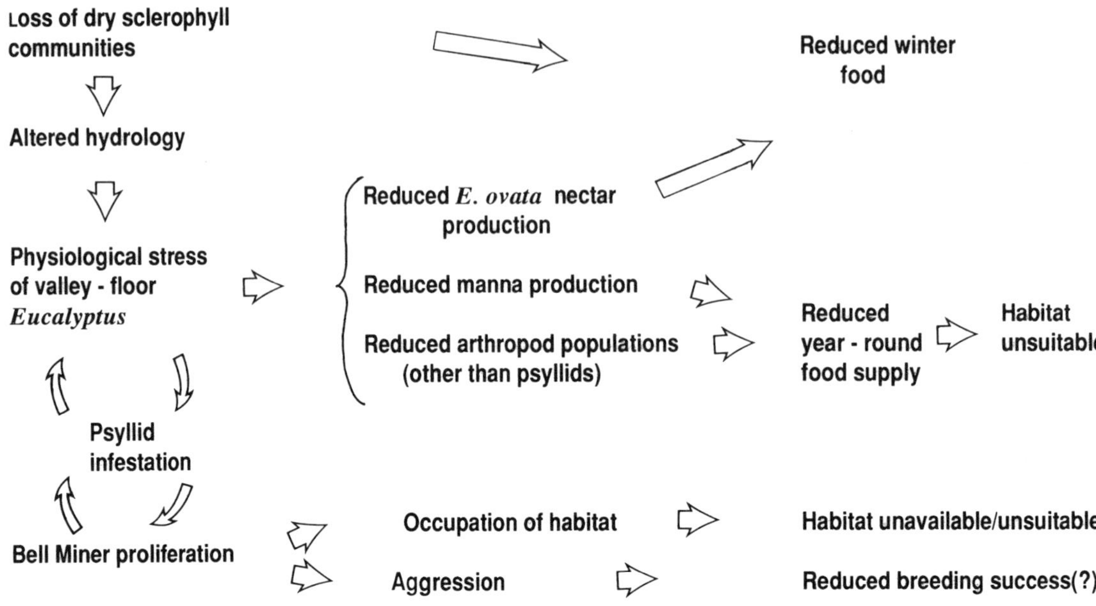


*Figure 3.*—Schematic representation of the processes of ecological degradation believed to be occurring within helmeted honeyeater habitat and their presumed effects upon the population.

species in dry sclerophyll forests (Wykes 1981, 1982, 1985; Smales 1988). Wykes (1981, 1985) studied con-specific Victorian populations of *L. m. meltoni*. He found that a population of that subspecies resident within riparian habitat during the breeding season also dispersed into drier forest communities during the non-breeding period and that other populations are widely dispersed, away from water during the entire year in red iron-bark (*E. sideroxylon*) forest, where nectar is abundant year-round.

Only small remnants of indigenous dry sclerophyll forest now remain adjacent to the Yellingbo State Nature Reserve and none are protected by inclusion within its boundaries. During the past decade, a number of such areas on nearby private land have been cleared, and thus this source of autumn/winter food has continued to be depleted.

For example, Wykes (1981) estimated, from colour-banded individuals, that 65 birds were aggregated at a stand of flowering *E. ovata* growing on private property during the winter of 1978. That site was cleared by the landowner in 1980.

*E. ovata* flowers sporadically between April and November and it is now the most important source of nectar for *L. m. cassidix*. Flowering and nectar production of this species in many stands within the Reserve are being severely reduced as a symptom of a general deterioration of their health, caused by infestations of psyllid insects (Homoptera: Psyllidae).

Another consequence of psyllid infestation is the partial or complete defoliation of eucalypts. Helmeted honeyeaters show a marked preference for unaffected trees (Woinarski and Wykes 1983).

*Competition*

The impact of competition from bell miners was considered by Woinarski and Wykes (1983) to be a fundamental cause of the decline of the helmeted honeyeater at Cardinia Creek. Bell miner communities exist adjacent to each helmeted honeyeater group at Yellingbo and appear to be annexing honeyeater territory. Bell miner populations are far more dense than are those of helmeted honeyeaters. Wykes (1981, 1985) reported mean densities of 64 and 6 per 10 ha, respectively. Smales (personal communication) found that breeding *L. m. cassidix* occupied territories ranging from 0.39 to 0.72 ha per pair at two sites within the Yellingbo State Nature Reserve. One of these at Cockatoo Creek had a maximum of 14 breeding adults in an area of approximately 4.4 ha during a four-year period commencing in 1984. This is less than half the density that Wykes found for bell miners. The area available to helmeted honeyeaters at the Cockatoo Creek site was reduced from 4.4 ha to 3.2 ha by 1988. The lost 1.2 ha was occupied by bell miners who had replaced two pairs of helmeted honeyeaters.

Woinarski and Wykes (1983) believed that when bell miners invade helmeted honeyeater territories 'these incursions may have made the energetic cost of territorial defence prohibitive, or reduced breeding success because of excessive time spent chasing bell miners.'

Proliferation of bell miners in situations like those at Cardinia Creek and Yellingbo is believed to be due to an increase in their food supply, the carbohydrate-rich lerps secreted by psyllids (Campbell and Moore 1956; Loyn *et al.* 1983). Psyllids exploit increased nutrient levels in the phloem in the foliage of eucalypts undergoing physiological stress brought about by altered water table regimes (White 1969, 1971). Changes to the hydrology are considered to be a direct result of the clearing of natural forests from the catchments (Woinarski and Wykes 1983; Wykes 1985). By aggressive exclusion of other canopy-foraging birds, including species which eat psyllids, bell miners permit the psyllid population to increase

and thus provide them with an abundant supply of lerps (Loyn *et al.* 1983). Bell miners appear more readily able to defend territories in remnant strips of habitat, from which surrounding forests have been cleared, than territories within continuous forest (Loyn 1987).

From the foregoing it is evident that the loss of dry sclerophyll forests from the slopes has been a principal underlying cause of the helmeted honeyeater's recent decline. Their removal has led to influences causing systematic ecological degradation of the remaining riparian habitat. The sequences involved are schematically represented in Figure 3. Degradation of this remnant valley floor vegetation is exacerbated by the extremely narrow and extended shape of the Yellingbo State Nature Reserve, which makes it subject to an enormous 'edge effect'. These ecological pressures, combined with the level of resources committed to helmeted honeyeater conservation at the time, led Backhouse (1987) to express doubt about the long-term survival of the bird within the Reserve.

If the presently known groups at Yellingbo do, in fact, represent the entire *L. m. cassidix* population—and only optimism suggests otherwise—then the population has now reached the critical stage at which a single random event, such as wildfire or an epidemic, could wipe it out. If the effects of inbreeding depression are not yet affecting the population's viability, they can be expected to do so if the gene pool is permitted to become much smaller.

*Conservation Management*

The strategy for conservation of the helmeted honeyeater adopted by the Victorian Department of Conservation, Forests and Lands and its predecessor, the Fisheries and Wildlife Division, has been reviewed by Backhouse (1987). In essence, it has centred upon protection, maintenance and enhancement of the remaining riparian vegetation within the Yellingbo State Nature Reserve.

On the basis of censuses of the Yellingbo population conducted in 1978 and 1979 (Wykes 1981, 1982), Woinarski and Wykes (1983) suggested that the population, 'may now be stabilizing at 100-150 birds, after a steady decline over the last two decades.' However, monitoring of the population between 1984 and 1987 demonstrated that the decline was still underway and that fewer than 40 adults could be accounted for in 1987.

Protection of existing core habitat and replanting of cleared areas has nevertheless been of value. Had these protective measures not been taken the population might have already been lost as a victim of total habitat destruction. However, it has failed to reverse the decline process because it has not tackled the ecological problems within the habitat. It has thus proven insufficient as an approach to long-term conservation of the bird, as Backhouse (1987) feared it might.

*Recent Initiatives for Recovery*

Despite the critically small current population, recovery to a level providing long-term viability is possible. It can be achieved only by taking immediate and interventionary measures. Recommendations for some of these actions were made by Smales (1988), and it is noteworthy that these reiterated suggestions made by earlier workers (Crome 1969; Wykes 1981), which had not been implemented. An action plan, based upon Smales' (1988) recommendations and laying the ground work for a comprehensive recovery strategy, was formulated by the Department of Conservation, Forests and Lands in August 1988.

A multi-disciplinary Recovery Team has now been assembled to provide cohesive implementation of the project. It is comprised of representatives of the following organisations and institutions: Department of Conservation, Forests and Lands, Victoria; Zoological Board of Victoria; Friends of the Helmeted Honeyeater Inc.; Royal Australasian Ornithologists Union; Department of Genetics and Human Variation, LaTrobe University; and Bird Observers Club of Australia. Overall, the strategy has two components: 1) a revised management and research program for the wild population and 2) establishment of a captive breeding program.

These components are complementary and will be run simultaneously. The rationale and mechanics of each are discussed below.

*Wild Population Management and Research*

The aim of the recovery project is the attainment of a total population large enough and sufficiently widely distributed to be self-sustaining despite the foreseeable influences of demographic, environmental and genetic variables and natural catastrophes (Shaffer 1981). Further research is necessary in order to determine the population size and distribution requirements for such a minimum viable population. Implementation of the action plan is now underway, however, with the immediate objectives of increasing the population's size and counteracting influences detrimental to it.

Management to conserve the wild helmeted honeyeater population has four elements: 1) continuation of existing management activities at Yellingbo State Nature Reserve, 2) implementation of a program to reverse deleterious ecological trends currently affecting the bird and its environment at Yellingbo, 3) monitoring of the population at Yellingbo and research of biological aspects not yet studied, to determine and maintain an accurate assessment of its viability, and 4) surveys of potentially suitable habitat outside the Yellingbo State Nature Reserve for the existence of further groups of birds and to locate sites suitable for the release of captive-bred birds.

*Habitat Management*

A management plan for Yellingbo State Nature Reserve will be written soon. The plan will provide the framework for a coordinated habitat management program. A number of techniques can be applied to redress deterioration of habitat at Yellingbo and restore its suitability for use by helmeted honeyeaters. One of the initial tasks is a detailed analysis of the vegetation floristics and structure within the Yellingbo State Nature Reserve, with particular emphasis upon sites currently occupied by helmeted honeyeaters.

The revegetation scheme at Yellingbo, in operation since 1978, has planted in excess of 80,000 indigenous trees. It will be revised to provide for the addition of indigenous nest-site, nectar and berry-producing shrub species. Priority will be given to the revegetation of areas adjacent to existing *L. m. cassidix* groups, where such areas have not yet been planted.

Protective measures for remnant patches of dry sclerophyll forest on adjacent private land must be implemented. Perhaps some incentive for private land owners both to retain and to replant appropriate species can be initiated. The recently formed community group, Friends of the Helmeted Honeyeater, has plans underway both to propagate appropriate vegetation and to assist landowners with its planting.

These measures will provide additional sources of food for the bird. In the short term, however, provision of artificial feeders, especially during the winter, may be an option and would be a relatively simple method of supplementing available food. *L. m. cassidix* would not be likely to have difficulty in dominating other bird species for use of the feeders if they were placed within their territories. Care must be taken that feeders do not become a focal point for predators.

The cumulative effects of psyllid infestations, deteriorating eucalypt health and the presence of bell miners must be counteracted. Loyn *et al.* (1983) have experimentally demonstrated that removal of bell miners permitted an influx of other insectivorous canopy birds which rapidly depleted the lerp-producing psyllids. They noted subsequent improvement in eucalypt health.

Removal of bell miners from areas adjacent to selected helmeted honeyeater groups and study of the effects upon breeding success and habitat use commenced during the 1989 breeding season. If it can be shown empirically that this technique has benefits to helmeted honeyeaters and, through reduction of psyllids, results in long-term regeneration of eucalypts, then it will have wider application to helmeted honeyeater management. This study will test a number of hypotheses concerning the interactions between bell miners, helmeted honeyeaters and their habitats (A. Poiani, Zoology Department, La Trobe University, personal communication).

Helmeted honeyeaters can utilize habitat after eucalypts have recovered from psyllid infestation, as demonstrated by one group of birds that currently resides in an area of the Reserve where *E. ovata* has naturally recovered from severe defoliation by psyllids.

The impact of various fire regimes upon psyllid and bell miner populations and upon the riparian vegetation which they inhabit, requires investigation. Experiment and study are needed to evaluate the use of fire as a management tool to restore of existing vegetation to a condition suitable for helmeted honeyeaters and in revegetation works.

*Helmeted Honeyeater Research*

Much has already been learned about ecology, population dynamics and sociality of *L. m. cassidix*. Some studies are continuing and others will commence in order to provide information that is currently lacking, for both the wild and captive management programs.

Smales' demographic studies (1988 and unpubl.) have collected information about mortality and survival of eggs and nestlings; about survival, dispersal and recruitment of fledged juveniles; and about age structure, breeding, life expectancy, mobility and mortality of adult birds. Determination of representative trends has proven difficult because of the small sample sizes. Banding and monitoring of birds at Yellingbo is continuing, with the aim of increasing information about the population dynamics of juvenile and adult age classes and providing surveillance of overall population trends. A new aspect of this work is the location and removal of juveniles to become founders of the captive stock, and monitoring of the response of the wild population.

Specific recommendations for genetic research, and its subsequent application to management, have been made for *L. m. cassidix* by W.B. Sherwin and N. Murray, Department of Genetics and Human Variation, LaTrobe University (unpublished memo to Department of Conservation, Forests and Lands, 1988).

At present nothing is known about the genetics of the subspecies. Studies using DNA fingerprinting and/or mitochondrial DNA will be undertaken and combined with demographic information to determine the genetically effective size of the population as well as relationships among individuals. Knowledge of these aspects will have applications in management of both the wild population and the captive group.

Research into the phylogeny of the entire *L. melanops* complex should be undertaken. The species appears to have split into subspecies around the Great Dividing Range, apparently as a consequence of high site fidelity and habitat specificity (Crome 1973). The degree of differentiation between the named forms and, indeed, the amount of variation which may exist within these forms, has not been determined with certainty. Genetic data from *L. m. cassidix* will have value in study of the phylogeny of the entire species and particularly investigation of the possibility of gene flow between *L. m. cassidix* and *L. m. gippslandica*.

*Surveys of Potential Habitat*

It is highly desirable to know whether more groups of helmeted honeyeaters still exist beyond the confines of the Yellingbo State Nature Reserve. This has clear implications for every facet of their conservation. A systematic approach to surveying potential habitat, by volunteers in conjunction with the Department of Conservation, Forests and Lands, has commenced and will check areas which have not been thoroughly assessed as well as locations of unconfirmed sightings. If any groups of birds are found to inhabit the area between the presently known distributions of *L. m. cassidix* and *L. m. gippslandica*, DNA analysis and comparison of morphologies will be used to determine their race.

*Captive Breeding Program*

The captive breeding program for the helmeted honeyeater is designed to support the recovery of the wild population rather than just to establish a self-sustaining group in captivity.

The captive breeding program will provide: 1) the opportunity to maximise genetic diversity by selective breeding and maintenance of pedigrees, 2) the capacity to increase the total population and distribution of the subspecies by introductions of captive-bred birds both to supplement the existing wild population and to establish new populations in suitable habitat within the former range, 3) insurance against extinction of the taxon which could be caused by some catastrophe overtaking the current single population, and 4) opportunities for learning and research not available with wild birds.

*Program Protocols*

Helmeted honeyeaters will be kept at The Sir Colin McKenzie Zoological Park (Healesville Sanctuary), Healesville, which is within the bird's former range and has a microclimate and vegetation similar to that inhabited by the subspecies elsewhere.

*Experience with Congenerics*

The helmeted honeyeater has never been kept in captivity. However, during the past two decades honeyeaters of a number of other species have been brought into captivity by Australian zoos where some have bred successfully. Experience at The Royal Melbourne Zoological Gardens and Taronga Zoo, Sydney, with the blue-faced honeyeater (*Entomyzon cyanotis*), the white-plumed honeyeater (*Lichenostomus penicillatus*) and especially the yellow-tufted honeyeater (*L. m. melanops*), together with existing knowledge of the biology of *L. m. cassidix,* has been used to develop plans for facilities and husbandry.

Some yellow-tufted honeyeaters (*L. m. gippslandica,* the form most closely related to *L. m. cassidix*), collected in July 1989, will be maintained at Melbourne and Taronga Zoos. Experience gained from management of these birds, especially in selection of compatible breeding pairs, aviary design and dietary preferences, will be vitally important to the successful establishment of the helmeted honeyeaters in captivity. Additionally, some experimental cross-fostering, egg-swapping and double-clutching will be attempted with these groups. If these experiments are successful, breeding pairs of *L. m. gippslandica* could later be used as surrogate parents to *L. m. cassidix* chicks arising from the program. This may enable the breeding rate of the endangered birds to be increased through encouragement of double-clutching behaviour.

*Acquisition and Choice of Founding Stock*

Initial stocks of helmeted honeyeaters for the program will be obtained at fledgling stage, either just prior to fledging or soon thereafter. Juveniles in the wild suffer high mortality. Smales (unpubl.) found that only 22% of banded chicks which successfully fledged attained maturity (8 of 36). Wild adults nest as many as four times during a season following the loss of eggs, nestlings or fledglings. Removal of fledglings into captivity will therefore have little effect upon numbers in the wild population. The maximum number of fledglings possible will be collected for at least two seasons. For the greatest genetic diversity, chicks from as many different wild parents as possible will be included. As DNA analysis of the population progresses, it is hoped that it will provide a more accurate basis for the selection of representative genetic stock. It is anticipated that individuals from the wild occasionally will be added to maintain the genetic viability of the captive group, throughout the duration of the project.

At first, eggs will not be removed from the wild because of the risk of hatchlings imprinting upon humans and therefore decreasing their chances of contributing to the breeding program. This may be revised, if experimentation with *L. m. gippslandica* demonstrates that surrogate parents can successfully incubate eggs or can raise the chicks from artificially incubated eggs.

*Breeding*

It is anticipated that 12 to 15 young helmeted honeyeaters can be collected each year to provide the basis for establishing four or five breeding pairs. After two years there should be at least 10 pairs in captivity, together with some pairs of *L. m. gippslandica* acting as surrogate parents. This should allow an annual production of 20 to 30 helmeted honeyeaters for reintroduction to the wild.

This program requires at least 10 aviaries to be built before the second year to house breeding stock from the first year's intake of fledglings. At the beginning of the third year, additional aviaries will be needed to house the second group of breeders, derived from the combined progeny of the first and second groups of young from the wild. A final bank of aviaries will be required to house birds being prepared for release to the wild.

*Husbandry*

Diets for captive honeyeaters consist of carbohydrate-rich artificial nectar, insectivore cake mixtures high in protein and (usually) a daily supplement of live insects. Captive honeyeaters generally thrive on this diet and may achieve long life spans.

Experience with juvenile white-plumed honeyeaters indicates that fledglings obtained before attaining independence from parental feeding will quickly learn to feed on an artificial nectar mixture and require hand-feeding for a few days at most. Puppy biscuit soaked in nectar mixture and offered in forceps has proven to be a successful diet during the hand-feeding stage. Once the birds have learned to feed independently upon the nectar mixture, they begin to explore other foods such as insectivore cake mixture and housefly pupae and are soon established on the full artificial diet. If several birds are kept together those that are quick to feed will teach the others by example. It is assumed that juvenile helmeted honeyeaters will behave in much the same way as their more common congeners and quickly learn to feed independently.

From knowledge of social behaviour of the wild birds, it is expected that juvenile *L. m. cassidix* raised together in captivity will be compatible, at least until breeding age is reached, and may be maintained as a small flock for much of the first year. This will significantly reduce the amount of aviary space required.

Honeyeaters in captivity are pugnacious and active birds, requiring plenty of space. They are inclined to harass other birds, including conspecifics. They aggressively defend feeding sites, preventing other birds from using them, and may actively destroy the nests of other species. Best results for breeding helmeted honeyeaters are thus expected from provision of aviary space exclusive to pairs. To obtain maximum reproduction from the available stock, sexually mature birds will need to be accurately sexed and separated into pairs. Sex may be determined by laparoscopy, but the trauma associated with operating upon such small birds may pose an unacceptable risk. Alternative sex-determining methods include comparisons of body dimensions and weight, behaviour and faecal steroid analysis.

Based on the behaviour of similar honeyeaters in captivity, the plan is to establish relatively large aviaries, approximately 10 m long x 3.6 m wide x 2.4 m high for each breeding pair. Because virtually nothing is known of the effects of keeping multiple pairs of territorial species of honeyeaters in close proximity, the optimum configuration can only be ascertained by experiment. Accordingly, it is planned to use demountable aviaries so that size and spacing of cages can be varied to achieve the desired degree of separation and interaction between pairs.

Breeding aviaries must be adequately planted with appropriate vegetation in order to encourage nesting. Suitable materials for nest construction must be provided. Materials utilized by the birds in natural habitat are well known and easily obtainable. Once nesting has commenced care will have to be taken to minimise disturbance, particularly of an unfamiliar kind. Provision of adequate quantities of small soft-bodied invertebrates will be essential for the survival of hatchlings. At The Royal Melbourne Zoological Gardens this requirement has been met, for other species, by the captive breeding of houseflies. Flies newly emerged from the pupal stage are ideal and convenient food for small insectivorous birds and can be reliably produced in considerable quantities. Fly pupae at the point of hatching are provided daily and the emerging flies are easily caught by the birds.

Yellow-tufted honeyeaters at The Royal Melbourne Zoological Gardens have been observed to feed their young almost exclusively upon such insect food during the early stage of growth, after which the parents may progressively vary the diet by the inclusion of components of the artificial diets.

*Reintroduction to the Wild*

The release of captive-bred birds into the wild will be the most critical stage of the project, since control of the birds will be largely lost.

A major problem for newly-released birds could be harassment by competing species. Of these, the most aggressive is probably the bell miner, but other honeyeaters, even conspecifics, could prove disastrous to the release program by dispersing newly-released birds before they have a chance to adapt to wild conditions. It will therefore be necessary to select sites which are not occupied by competing species, or to remove such species prior to the release.

Birds to be released must be accommodated in aviaries at the release site where they can be acclimatised for a short period. Some of the birds, perhaps one-third, could then be released and provided with their accustomed food close to their captive conspecifics, the presence of which will probably keep the released birds in the vicinity. When it is clear that the birds at liberty have settled into the area and are feeding satisfactorily, a second group may be released, and so on until all are free.

The provision of artificial feeding should continue until the birds have perfected foraging skills and have demonstrated a loss of interest in the artificial diet. However, it may be that long-term seasonal feeding will be necessary at some sites, at least until the problems of habitat degradation and interspecific competition have been overcome.

Careful selection of release sites will have to be made. All of the measures to manage and enhance the habitat at Yellingbo, outlined above, will be necessary to increase the area of habitat available to helmeted honeyeaters there. If they are successful, then reintroductions to supplement the existing population there will be made. Ultimately, it is desirable to have a wild population distributed over a wide geographical area. Even given the implementation of all of the recent initiatives for the bird's conservation at Yellingbo, the very long-term survival of the helmeted honeyeater cannot be guaranteed within minute remnant strips of habitat such as exist there. Hence, consideration will have to be given, assuming that sufficient birds are produced, to other release sites. Locations within the former range, at which suitable habitat exists as part of the continuum of larger tracts of natural forest, will offer situations free from most of the influences adversely affecting habitat at Yellingbo.

## Conclusion

Conservation of helmeted honeyeater habitat has been underway for more than twenty-five years, but the program outlined in this paper to recover the bird's population has just commenced. Various contingencies will have to be met as the project develops. Hence it will be vitally important to maintain a flexible approach to all options in order to succeed. Problems of both a biological and organizational nature may occur and, indeed, should be anticipated (Clark and Harvey 1988). The organization of the recovery effort must be managed in such a way that it encourages a free flow of information amongst participants, rational decision-making and efficient performance (Clark *et al.* 1989; Clark and Westrum, 1989).

The helmeted honeyeater population is currently at an all-time low. Ironically, and perhaps as an inversely proportional consequence, enthusiasm for its conservation and recovery have reached an all-time high. Some recent examples, like that of the black robin (*Petroica traversi*) of the Chatham Islands (D. Merton, Department of Conservation, New Zealand, personal communication), demonstrate that if such enthusiasm can be channelled into long-term commitment and combined with a sound knowledge of the subject's biology, a willingness to learn, adapt accordingly and become innovative when necessary, exceptional results can be achieved. We believe that a similar outcome can be attained for the helmeted honeyeater and are optimistic for its future.

## Acknowledgments

We would like to thank all those who have contributed to the formulation of the recovery strategy to date, both through formal involvement in the process and through informal discussion. Much of the information about helmeted honeyeater biology and habitat restoration is from the work of Dr. Boyd Wykes, to whom we are also grateful for critical comment on a first draft of the paper. Constructive comments were provided also by John Seebeck and Peter Menkhorst. Greg Horrocks gave valuable administrative support to production of the paper. For word processing and the drawing of figures we are grateful to Fiona Leigh and Alda McManus, respectively. Ian Smales would especially like to thank his wife, Angie, for unstinted encouragement throughout the past eight years of his involvement with helmeted honeyeaters.

## References

Backhouse, G.N. 1987. Management of remnant habitat for conservation of the Helmeted Honeyeater *Lichenostamus melanops cassidix*. In *Nature Conservation: The Role of Remnants of Native Vegetation*, eds D.A. Saunders, G.W. Arnold, A.A. Burbidge and A.J.M. Hopkins. Pp. 287-294. Surrey Beatty and Sons: Sydney.

Campbell, K.G. and Moore, K.M. 1956. An investigation of the food of the Bell Bird *Manorina melanophrys* Latham. *Proc. R. Zool. Soc. N.S.W.* **1955-56**:72-73.

Clark, T.W. and Harvey, A. 1988. Implementing endangered species recovery policy: learning as we go? *Endangered Species Update* **5**(10):35-42.

Clark, T.W., Crete, R., and Cada, J. 1989. Designing and managing successful endangered species recovery programs. *Environ. Manage.* **13**:159-170.

Clark, T.W. and Westrum, R. 1989. High-performance teams in wildlife conservation: a species reintroduction and recovery example. *Environ. Manage.* **13**, 663-670.

Crome, F.H.J. 1969. A preliminary study of the biology of the Helmeted Honeyeater (*Meliphaga cassidix* (Gould)) and its relationships with the Yellow-tufted Honeyeater (*M. melanops* (Latham)). B.Sc. (Honours) Thesis, Monash University, Victoria.

Crome, F.H.J. 1973. The relationship of the Helmeted and Yellow-tufted Honeyeaters. *Emu* **73**:12-18.

Lee, R.D. and Bryant, C.E. 1948. A count of Helmeted Honeyeaters. *Emu* **47**:230-231.

Loyn, R.H. 1987. The bird that farms the dell. *Nat. Hist.* **87**(6):54-60.

Loyn, R.H., Runnalls, R.G., Forward G.Y. and Tyers, J. 1983. Territorial Bell Miners and other birds affecting populations of insect prey. *Science* **221**:1411-1413.

Rogers, K., Rogers, A. and Rogers, D. 1986. *Bander's Aid: a Guide to Ageing and Sexing Bush Birds.* A. Rogers: St. Andrews.

Shaffer, M. 1981. Minimum population sizes for species conservation. *Bioscience* **31**:131-133.

Smales, I.J. 1988. The status of the Helmeted Honeyeater *Lichenostomus melanops cassidix* (Gould) - with recommendations for its continued conservation. Department of Conservation, Forests and Lands, Dandenong.

White, T.C.R. 1969. An index to measure weather-induced stress of trees associated with outbreaks of psyllids in Australia. *Ecology* **50**:905-909.

White, T.C.R. 1971. Lerp insects (*Homoptera: Psyllidae*) on Red Gum *Eucalyptus camaldulensis*, in South Australia. *S. Aust. Nat.* **46**:20-23.

Woinarski, J.C.Z. 1981. The Helmeted Honeyeater at Cardinia Creek; a survey with implications for possible water control activities. Report to Fisheries and Wildlife Division, Victoria (Unpublished).

Woinarski, J.C.Z. and Wykes, B.J. 1983. Decline and extinction of the Helmeted Honeyeater at Cardinia Creek. *Biol. Conserv.* **27**:7-21.

Wykes, B.J. 1981. The ecology of the Helmeted Honeyeater and its relationships with potential competitors. Report to Fisheries and Wildlife Division, Victoria (Unpublished).

Wykes, B.J. 1982. Resource partitioning and the role of competitors in structuring *Lichenostomus* honeyeater (and *Manorina melanophrys*) communities in southern Victoria. Ph.D. Thesis, Monash University, Victoria.

Wykes, B.J. 1985. The Helmeted Honeyeater and related honeyeaters of Victorian woodlands. In *Birds of Eucalypt Forest and Woodlands: Ecology, Conservation, Management*, eds A. Keast, H.F. Recher, H. Ford and D. Saunders. Pp. 205-217. Royal Australasian Ornithologists Union and Surrey Beatty and Sons: Sydney.

# Management of the Orange-bellied Parrot

*Peter W. Menkhorst[1], Richard H. Loyn[1] and Peter B. Brown[2]*

## Abstract

The orange-bellied parrot has undergone a marked population decline and contraction in range during this century. The wild population now numbers fewer than 200 individuals including about 50 breeding pairs. Breeding takes place only in coastal southwestern Tasmania, and the entire population migrates to coastal southern mainland Australia for the winter months.

Reasons for the population decline are not clear, but the destruction or degradation of significant areas of winter habitat was probably critical. Annual counts of birds in the wintering areas show that the population has been fairly stable through the 1980s. Monitoring of nests and flocks of juveniles suggests that recruitment is adequate, yet the population is not increasing. Thus, mortality of immatures or adults may be constraining population growth. A lack of high-quality winter habitat may be contributing to this mortality.

This paper describes the organisation and coordination of a recovery program that began in 1979. Attention is drawn to areas needing greater research and management efforts. The breeding habitat is secure and little changed by European settlement. However, a suitable fire regime must be implemented to promote growth and seeding of food plants. In contrast, a significant proportion of the winter habitat has been destroyed or degraded. Although much of the remaining winter habitat is within conservation reserves, adequate management and rehabilitation of the habitat is hindered by incomplete knowledge of vegetation dynamics. Progress is being made to enhance winter habitat, but more impetus is needed. Attempts to enhance existing habitat involve more serious risks than attempts to create new habitat nearby; the latter process is preferred.

A captive breeding program that began in 1986 has now achieved considerable success after initial setbacks due to a viral disease which killed some immature birds.

## Introduction

The orange-bellied parrot *(Neophema chrysogaster)* has a restricted distribution along the west coast of Tasmania and mainland Australia between south Gippsland, Victoria, and the mouth of the Murray River, South Australia. The total population is less than 200 individuals, including about 50 breeding pairs, making the species one of the most endangered Australian vertebrates. Although always rather limited in distribution and only occasionally numerically abundant, the species has suffered a marked population decline and range contraction during this century. Historical records (Jarman 1965; Loyn and Kinhill Planners 1980; Brown and Wilson 1982, 1984) indicate that in the late 1800s, orange-bellied parrots regularly occurred as far west as Adelaide and north to Sydney, where small numbers may have bred (McGill 1960). Breeding was also recorded in central Tasmania more than 100 km inland from the present known breeding areas (Brown and Wilson 1984). Some reports indicate that at times the species was present in parts of southeastern South Australia in thousands. However, the historical data do not indicate whether the decline was gradual or sudden, nor do they provide many clues about its causes. Several

---

[1]National Parks and Wildlife Division, Department of Conservation, Forests and Lands, Arthur Rylah Institute for Environmental Research, 123 Brown Street, Heidelberg, Victoria 3084, Australia.
[2]Department of Parks, Wildlife and Heritage, GPO Box 44A, Hobart, Tasmania 7001, Australia.

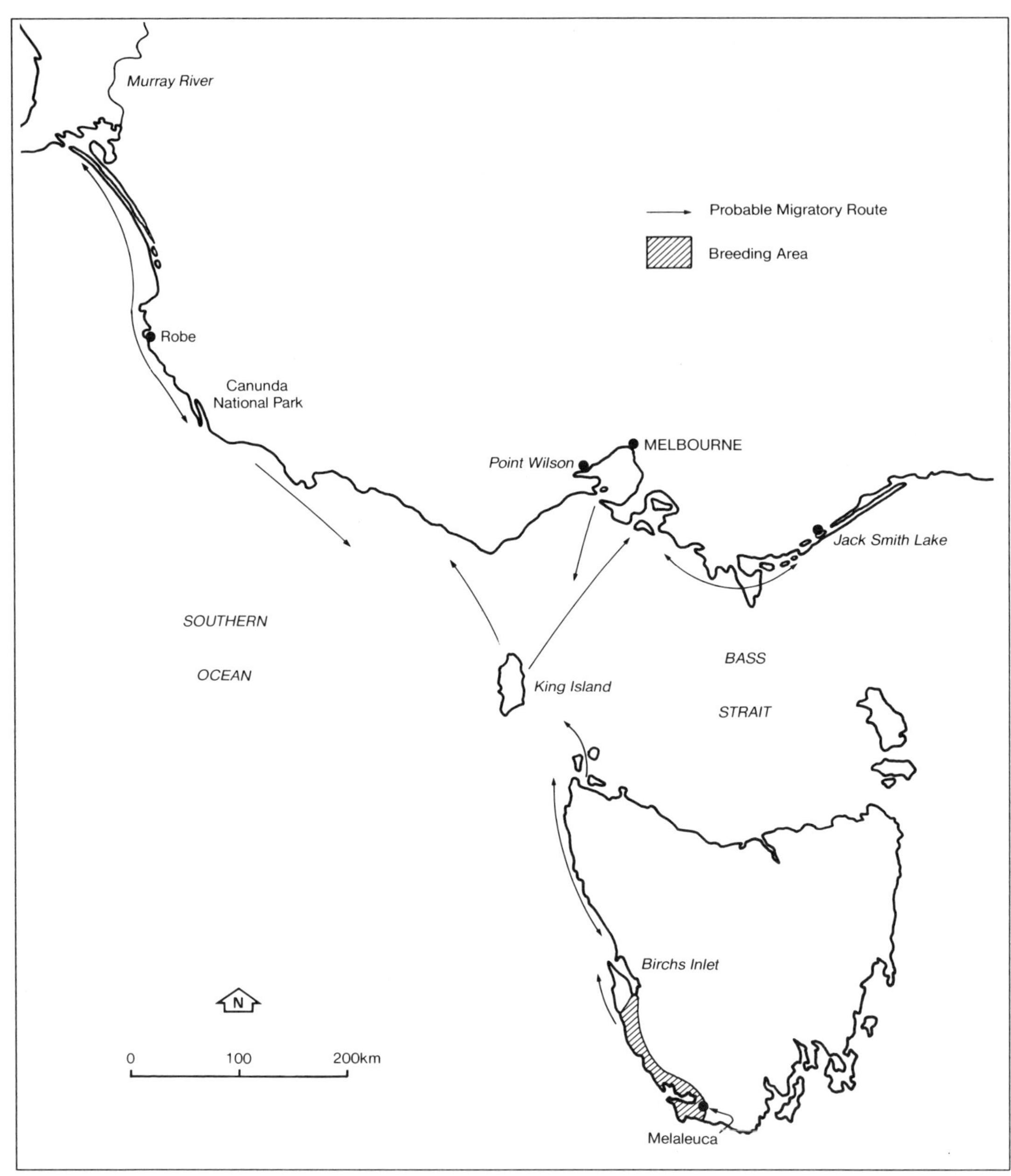


*Figure 1*.—Breeding and non-breeding distribution of the orange-bellied parrot.

systematic extinction processes (Clark *et al.*, this volume) such as destruction or degradation of significant areas of winter habitat were probably critical. Stochastic factors such as trapping for the avicultural trade, epidemics and inbreeding may also have been involved.

The present breeding distribution is restricted to a narrow coastal strip of southwestern Tasmania between Macquarie Harbour and South West Cape. Here, orange-bellied parrots breed in hollows in *Eucalyptus* trees growing in sheltered foothill sites adjacent to extensive coastal sedgelands.

After breeding, small flocks migrate north along the coast during March and April. They pass through the Hunter group of islands to King Island, where some congregate before crossing Bass Strait to mainland Australia. Birds begin arriving on the mainland in mid to late March and disperse along the coast between Jack Smith Lake, south Gippsland, Victoria, and the mouth of the Murray River, South Australia (Fig. 1). A large proportion of the population concentrates in winter around fewer than five over-wintering sites and, at times, 50-70% of the birds congregate at three sites in western Port Phillip Bay, Victoria.

The orange-bellied parrot eats the seeds of a narrow range of plant species: sedgeland and heathland species in the breeding area (Brown and Wilson 1982), and saltmarsh, flooded pasture and strandline species on the mainland (Loyn *et al.* 1986).

While the breeding areas in southwestern Tasmania have remained largely unaffected by Europeans, except for altered fire regimes following the collapse of the Aboriginal population, the wintering habitat has been greatly fragmented and reduced in extent and quality. Fortunately, in recent years most remaining mainland and Tasmanian habitat has been reserved for conservation purposes.

This paper describes the history, organisation and methods of the management effort, including management of breeding and winter habitats, population trends and captive breeding actions.

*History and Organisation of the Recovery Effort*

Until the late 1970s, the orange-bellied parrot remained an enigmatic species, known only to a small group of dedicated bird watchers and aviculturalists. At this time, Imperial Chemical Industries (ICI) announced plans to construct a petrochemical plant at Point Wilson, Port Phillip Bay, Victoria, close to the major over-wintering site. Concerns were raised about the potential threat of this development to the orange-bellied parrot, and highlighted the lack of knowledge about the biology and ecology of the species, as well as its vulnerability to extinction.

To their credit, ICI responded in a positive and constructive manner by funding a series of investigations into the population's status, distribution, habitat selection and feeding ecology at Point Wilson and elsewhere (*e.g.* Loyn and Chandler 1978; Carr and Kinhill Planners 1979; Loyn *et al.* 1986). Plans for the petrochemical plant have since been shelved, but the impetus given to orange-bellied parrot conservation has continued.

In September 1979, a three-year study of the status and ecology of the species throughout its range was initiated by the Tasmanian National Parks and Wildlife Service with funding from World Wildlife Fund Australia (Brown and Wilson 1980, 1981). In 1982, a further year of the study was jointly financed by the wildlife agencies of Tasmania, South Australia and Victoria. Additional winter surveys were initiated by the governments of South Australia in September 1982 (I. May unpublished data) and Victoria in May-June 1983 (C. Silveira unpublished data).

In 1978, Richard Loyn initiated what has become an annual winter population count in Victoria, South Australia and Tasmania. These counts have involved over 100 people in a given year and have now continued unbroken for 12 years (Loyn and Chandler 1978; Menkhorst 1984; Jessop and Reid 1986; Starks 1988) (Fig. 2). Loyn organised the counts from 1978 to 1982, after which the Victorian National Parks and Wildlife Service (NPWS) assumed responsibility for their conduct and funding. Since 1984, NPWS has provided funds for the Royal Australasian Ornithologists Union (RAOU) to organise and conduct the counts throughout the mainland range of the species.

The results of all this research and survey were collated by Peter Brown and Roland Wilson and formed the basis of a comprehensive management plan for the species—the Orange-bellied Parrot Recovery Plan (Brown and Wilson 1984). The plan includes detailed recommendations directed at the wildlife and land management agencies of each State. Recommendations cover land acquisition and reservation, vegetation management (including the planned use of fire), management of people, control of pests (including potentially competing species), population monitoring and captive breeding.

Further research and assessment of habitat has been conducted in South Australia by Gibbons (1984) with funding from South Australian National Parks and Wildlife Service, and in Victoria by Yugovic (1984). The Melbourne and Metropolitan Board of Works (MMBW) has initiated and financed detailed studies of the ecology, seedling establishment and growth of *Chenopodium glaucum*, an important food plant of the orange-bellied parrot on the MMBW sewage farm near Point Wilson. These studies aimed to devise methods of increasing production of orange-bellied parrot food without interfering unduly with the sewage treatment function of the area (Carr 1987; McMahon and Carr 1988).

In recognition of the important faunal values of the Point Wilson area, of which the orange-bellied parrot is a major one, the four main landholders defined the Murtcaim Wildlife Area and formed a committee to advise on wildlife management issues. The committee comprises representatives of ICI, MMBW, Geelong Regional Commission, and Department of Conservation, Forests and Lands. It is responsible for developing a coordinated approach to issues such as public access and education, control of pest plants and animals, facilitation of ecological research, and preparation of a management plan for the area.

A most important feature of the research and management effort for the orange-bellied parrot has been the high level of cooperation between all contributors—government agencies, industry, research consultants, ornithologists, botanists, hydrologists, ornithological organisations, bird observers and the lay public. Of major importance in ensuring cooperation was the establishment in 1983 of a coordinating committee, the Orange-bellied Parrot Recovery Team. The Recovery Team comprises representatives of the wildlife agencies of Tasmania, South Australia, Victoria and the Commonwealth of Australia, as well as the RAOU and International Council for Bird Preservation (ICBP). It meets annually to review progress in implementation of the Recovery Plan, recommend increased efforts where necessary, assess the need for new initiatives and produce educational material about the species and the recovery effort. By inviting relevant field managers to Recovery Team meetings, those responsible for implementation of the plan at the local level can have input and be advised, encouraged and stimulated to greater efforts.

## Management of Breeding Habitat

It is fortunate indeed that the entire known breeding range of the orange-bellied parrot falls within a remote area which is under the direct control of the Department of Parks, Wildlife and Heritage (DPWH) in southwestern Tasmania. Approximately 90% of the parrot population breeds within the Southwest National Park and the remaining 10% in the Southwest Conservation Area. The Conservation Area is administered by DPWH,

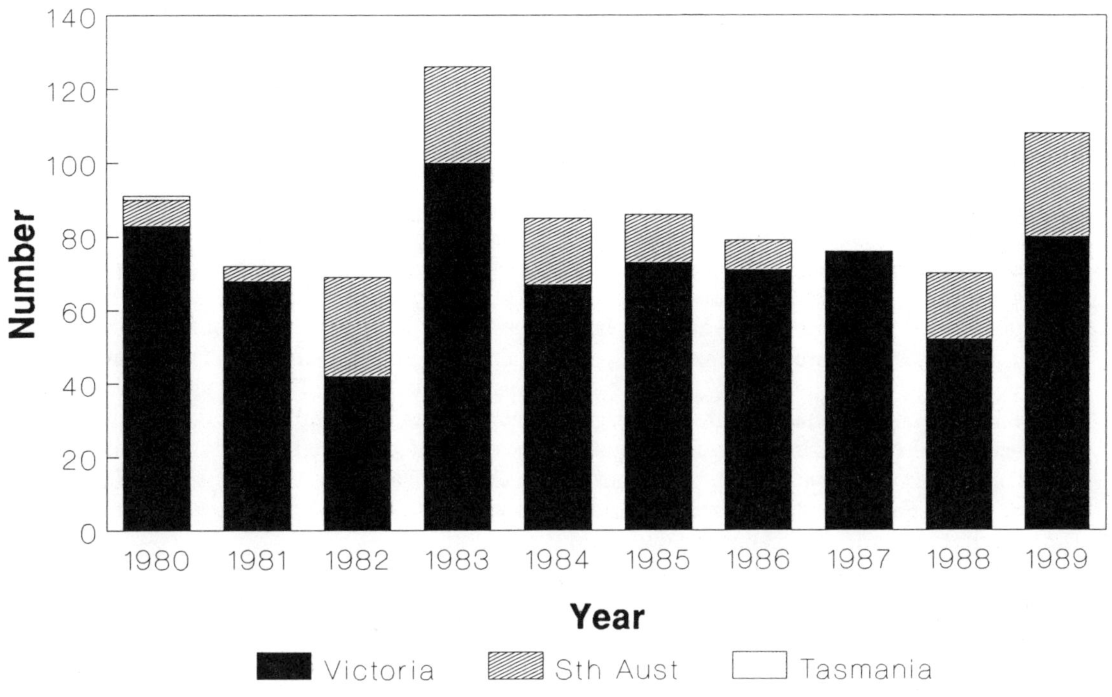

*Figure 2*—Number of orange-bellied parrots counted on the annual July count day, 1980-1989.

but the Forestry Commission and Department of Mines have statutory rights there. Thus, the Conservation Area is not entirely secure from extractive industry or timber harvesting. At Melaleuca a small Conservation Area occurs within the Southwest National Park. Part of this Conservation Area is leased for small-scale tin mining by two miners. Both miners have substantial vegetable gardens which have proved to be a great attraction to orange-bellied parrots. The birds regularly visit these gardens from the time of their first arrival in early October through until the late summer departure for the mainland. During February and March, the majority of juveniles hatched in the surrounding area during the summer congregate in the gardens prior to their northward migration.

The gardens form only part of the attraction for orange-bellied parrots in this area. More importantly, the extensive coastal plains support buttongrass and sedgeland communities of a considerable range of ages since fire. The parrots utilise this diversity in vegetation communities. Early in the breeding season they prefer areas burnt between 7 and 15 years ago, eating seeds of Restionaceae, particularly *Lepyrodia tasmanica* and *Restio complanatus*. During the mid-breeding season they seek out areas burnt between 2 and 5 years before where seeds of *Boronia* spp., *Helichrysum pumilum* and *Actinotus bellidioides* form a major component of the diet. In vegetation more than about 15 years old, the density of shrubs reduces the flowering and seeding capacity of preferred food plants (Brown and Wilson 1984).

The Melaleuca area has been subjected to regular burning over the past 30-40 years, principally as protective measures for the mining operators. This has resulted in a mosaic of different aged stands and provides excellent habitat for orange-bellied parrots throughout the breeding season. It is possible that Aboriginal burning formerly produced similar mosaics over a wider area, though there is little direct evidence. It is imperative that the needs of the orange-bellied parrot are given due consideration in fire management plans throughout coastal southwestern Tasmania.

Melaleuca also boasts an airstrip, the only regularly maintained one in the southwest. Regular flights operate to and from Hobart, taking bushwalkers and sightseers into the area. During summer, as many as 10 flights operate daily into Melaleuca, and its popularity is increasing, especially following the enormous publicity the region has received during debates over world heritage listing. It is of the greatest importance that pressures brought about by increasing visitor numbers and associated infrastructures do not affect the orange-bellied parrot detrimentally. At certain times of year it may be necessary to restrict visitor access to some areas, or restrict use of some types of aircraft, *e.g.* helicopters. Careful thought needs to be given to the location of any new visitor amenities.

*Management of Winter Habitat*

In contrast to the remote breeding habitat in southwestern Tasmania, the winter habitats in coastal Victoria and South Australia have been greatly modified by Europeans. This poses a different set of problems for management. One is that we do not know whether any optimal habitat remains, or how closely it resembled habitats in current use.

Another problem is that many different organisations and private landowners are involved in managing land where the species occurs. This can lead to difficulties in coordination, and can provide varied threats to habitat as well as oppor-

tunities to protect or enhance habitat. The aim of management must be to foster the opportunities and minimise the threats. The Recovery Plan established as first priority the protection of existing habitat, while recognising various opportunities to expand or improve such habitat.

Common features of current over-wintering habitat include coastal saltmarsh or dunes with adjacent supplementary habitats, and an abundant supply of food (small seeds of Chenopodiaceae and other plants including certain introduced grasses and shrubs). The parrots often feed from luxuriant stands of saltmarsh or other plants on the edges of small islands, spits and banks (Loyn *et al.* 1986; Hewish and Starks 1988). They roost in tall shrubs and need fresh water or dew for drinking.

Research has identified mid-winter as the time when habitat is more restricted than at any other time of year (Loyn *et al.* 1986). Population size may be limited by availability of habitat then, at least in some years. This is the period when birds are most concentrated at a few sites, and when widespread plant species used earlier or later in the season do not carry seeds. Some of the plants used at this time have a restricted distribution (Carr and Kinhill Planners 1979; Yugovic 1984; Carr 1987). Diverse saltmarsh communities capable of providing food throughout the winter grow mainly in low-rainfall areas and have been greatly reduced by grazing, construction of salt evaporation pans and shellgrit extraction (Carr and Kinhill Planners 1979; Loyn 1982; Yugovic 1984). But not all is negative, as the parrots also use new food sources on sewage grass-filtration paddocks and golf fairways. There is great scope for making further supplementary feeding areas for use in mid-winter, as recognised by Loyn (1982) and Brown and Wilson (1984). In the case of one food plant, *Chenopodium glaucum*, detailed research has indicated the practicalities of promoting growth and seeding to increase food available to the parrots (McMahon and Carr 1988).

So what has been done? Existing habitat is generally well protected, and various measures have been undertaken to improve the situation further. For example, the Murtcaim Wildlife Area has been established to include the main winter habitat at Point Wilson, with support from four corporate or government land-holders. A management plan is being drawn up for Swan Bay, one of the main winter habitats in the Bellarine Peninsula (Edgar, in preparation). An important new early-winter site for the parrots has been discovered at Lake Connewarre (Hewish and Starks 1988); fortunately, it is already a State Game Reserve. The majority of other areas used in Victoria and some in South Australia are on existing reserves, but others still require basic protection. The most outstanding case is at Carpenters Rocks in South Australia, where blocks of land are regularly offered for subdivision or holiday development.

Expansion and improvement of habitat are more difficult propositions, and less has been done. The safest option is always to expand or add habitat, *i.e.* to make new habitat close to existing areas, with minimal effect on areas currently used. There is a risk that newly-created habitat will not be used, for whatever reason, but this is less serious than the risk of unwittingly ruining a traditional area by misguided attempts to improve it. Unfortunately, it is often easier to obtain institutional support for work on existing areas; hence it is helpful if they can be defined as broadly as possible, so that management can proceed on-site while still avoiding key traditional areas actually used by the birds.

Two examples of active management can be taken from the Murtcaim Wildlife Area, to illustrate different issues which can arise with any species' management. The first action taken (in 1979, in association with the proposed Point Wilson development) was to fence a large area of saltmarsh against grazing by sheep. This resulted in excellent regeneration of saltmarsh on bare areas, and increased use by parrots in the following year (Loyn *et al.* 1986). However, use of this traditional site has declined subsequently (Jessop and Reid 1986; Starks 1988). There is evidence that young regenerating saltmarsh carries more

seed than older stands (G. Carr personal communication), and that luxuriant new growth is favoured by parrots (Loyn *et al.* 1986; Hewish and Starks 1988). Constant heavy grazing obviously reduces the food supply, but it is possible that light or intermittent grazing (or cutting) may be needed to provide optimal conditions in the long term. The saltmarsh is still grazed by rabbits, but these appear not to have the same effect.

This hypothesis needs testing, and there is an urgent need to monitor the saltmarsh vegetation; this is now being addressed. A further test of the successional hypothesis could be made on nearby islands of The Spit State Wildlife Reserve, where small areas are regularly cleared by hand to provide nesting sites for fairy terns (*Sterna nereis*). Orange-bellied parrots have been observed feeding on or near areas cleared in the previous year, but the observations have been casual, not quantified, and the crucial distinction (on or near) has not been made.

In the meantime, a further area of saltmarsh has been fenced, more prudently on an area that was not a key area for parrots. There has been no formal monitoring of the vegetation at this site or its use by parrots, but parrots have not been recorded there in recent years. The lesson from all this is that resources must be allocated for monitoring management actions long after they have been completed.

The second action has involved a more effective integration of research, management and monitoring. With resources from the Melbourne and Metropolitan Board of Works (MMBW), which manages the Werribee Sewage Farm, Geoff Carr and his colleagues have investigated the biology of the main food-plant used by parrots in the sewage grass-filtration paddocks, *Chenopodium glaucum* (Carr 1987; McMahon and Carr 1988). Their experiments outside the Murtcaim Wildlife Area resulted in recommendations on how to favour growth of the species, which had previously been regarded as a weed. The grass-filtration paddocks are grazed seasonally by cattle, and Carr's research identified this as a negative factor. Consequently, a part of the traditional site on Murtcaim Wildlife Area was fenced in January 1986 and good growth of *C. glaucum* resulted; the area was then used extensively by parrots in that year.

Further monitoring is needed to see if this persists as a steady state, or if a regular cycle of alternate grazing and fallow will be needed. Perhaps it was over-optimistic to expect such a marked change to be beneficial in the long term on part of a traditional area that had developed its importance under the old management regime. In general, it is preferable to confine such manipulation to *new* areas close to key sites. Unfortunately, this is sometimes precluded by practical constraints, as in this case. Plans are now being considered to grow more *C. glaucum* on filtration paddocks nearby.

The need for other actions has been identified in several areas. Some opportunities have been lost. For example, certain disused shellgrit extraction areas on the Bellarine Peninsula have been sold for residential subdivision. There may still be similar areas that could be rehabilitated as winter habitat for parrots. Some ideas have changed over time. For example, the expanding population of silver gulls (*Larus novaehollandiae*) on Mud Islands was initially blamed for vegetation changes and reduced use of the islands by parrots. Areas traditionally favoured by the parrots were quite small, and have become overgrown with shrubs, including the uncommon Australian hollyhock *(Lavatera plebeia)*. Gulls may or may not have played a role in these changes, but a simple solution may not be to control gulls but rather to set back the succession through judicious manual cutting of selected areas. This has been planned for several years, but the plan needs to be implemented, and results monitored. It remains possible that gulls will affect regeneration, but it is worth a try.

The pattern of dispersal during winter into small groups spread along almost 1,000 km of coast is also cause for concern. With such a small total population, there is no longer any safety in numbers, and a splintered population may be at greater-than-normal risk of predation. Experience on the breeding grounds and elsewhere suggests that orange-bellied parrots will readily accept artificial sources of food. Therefore, consideration should be given to using supplementary feeding to encourage birds to remain in secure areas during winter. Of course, there *are* potential hazards to be considered. These include: 1) encouragement of non-target species to the food source, *e.g.* other parrots and seedeaters including the house sparrow *(Passer domesticus)*, European goldfinch *(Carduelis carduelis)* and European greenfinch *(Carduelis chloris)*; 2) encouragement of predators to lie in wait; and 3) a requirement for regular human involvement and departmental commitment, which costs time and money.

Such intensive and intrusive management may become increasingly necessary to manage small populations sucessfully.

The main barrier to work of this type has been conflicting demands for time and resources, though it is sensible to be cautious about undertaking actions that could be detrimental (a real danger with attempts to improve existing habitat) or fail to achieve expected goals (a real but less serious danger with attempts to expand habitat). The Recovery Team has provided general impetus, but more could be provided if one person had clear responsibility to facilitate management and monitoring of habitat in the mainland States, and assess the risks involved. Much has been achieved, but efforts in habitat improvement and expansion do not yet match those in habitat protection.

## Population Trends

Attempts to monitor the total population of orange-bellied parrots have been made since 1978. The strategy used is to count birds during mid-winter when they are congregated at relatively few prime sites in coastal Victoria and southeast-

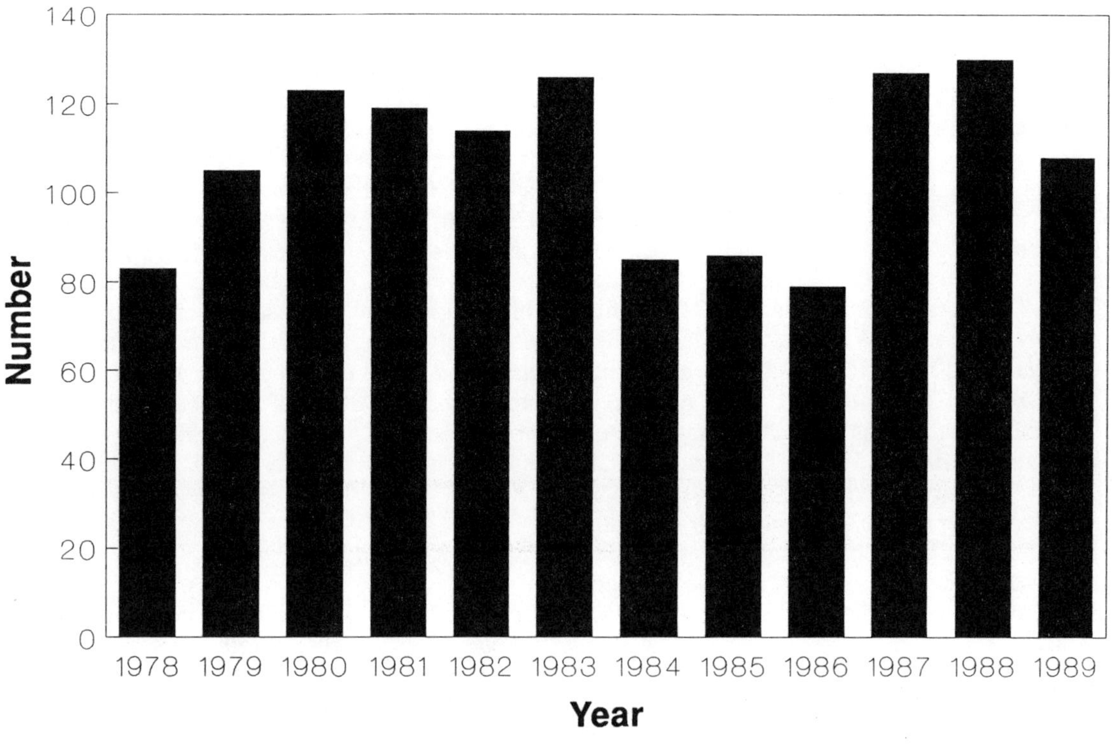



*Figure 3.*—Estimated maximum winter population of the orange-bellied parrot, 1978-1989.

ern South Australia. Volunteer bird watchers are assigned particular areas of habitat to search on the count day. They are asked to record the number of orange-bellied parrots and other *Neophema* species, the time of observation, and to make notes about habitat use and food plants. Where possible the numbers of each sex and age class (immature/adult) are also recorded. Logistic support, in the form of boats or four-wheel-drive vehicles is provided where necessary by the wildlife agencies of Victoria and South Australia.

Figure 2 shows the number of orange-bellied parrots counted in each State during the mid-winter count day between 1980 and 1989. During this period the counts are considered to be reasonably complete and comparable in coverage and effort. However, in some years fewer birds were found on the July count than were seen on other occasions during the winter. These discrepancies are usually caused by inclement weather making birds difficult to find on the count day. Such discrepancies are illustrated by comparing Figures 2 and 3, which show estimates of the maximum population in each winter. The greatest discrepancy occurred in 1988 when only 70 birds could be found in gale conditions on the count day, but previous and subsequent searches indicated that up to 130 individuals were present. The apparent fall in population between 1983 and 1987 (Fig. 3) probably results from a shift in dispersal of many birds to parts of Lake Connewarre State Game Reserve during these years. This shift was not discovered until 1986, and even then an adequate simultaneous count of all major sites was not achieved, resulting in the low count for that year. The increasing estimates between 1978 and 1980 reflect increasing knowledge of how and where to find the birds.

During the summers of 1979-1980 and 1980-1981, nine breeding attempts in south-western Tasmania were closely monitored. Three nests failed to produce young, the other six produced at least 15 fledglings giving a mean of 1.7 fledglings per nest (Brown and Wilson 1984). Unless mortality rates are high, such a fledging rate should allow the population to expand. Yet Figures 2 and 3 indicate that there has been little change in total population during the 1980s. Therefore, mortality away from the breeding grounds may be restraining population growth. Such mortality may be due to a lack of high-quality winter habitat or to stochastic factors such as disease, inbreeding or storms whilst the birds are crossing Bass Strait.

Some circumstantial evidence that the population may be greater than previously thought derives from a colour-marking exercise conducted at Melaleuca over 3 days in late February and early March 1988. During this period, immature orange-bellied parrots were captured in mist nets so that colour-bands and plumage dyes could be applied to allow individual recognition. Twenty-one juveniles were individually marked with colour bands and another 25 were banded with metal bands only. At least four other juveniles were present but were not captured. Thus, at least 50 juvenile orange-bellied parrots were present at Melaleuca at that time, far exceeding expectations and indicative of a high reproductive output. Assuming that the observed fledging rate of 1.7 per nest still applied, then there must have been some 29 breeding pairs in the Melaleuca area to produce 50 young.

Because of the short tarsi of these parrots, it can be extremely difficult to observe the presence or absence of bands. However, flocks of parrots feeding in mown grass on Swan Island allow a good chance of sighting banded birds. On 25 August 1988, a flock of 39 orange-bellied parrots contained 14 first-year birds, at least 13 of which were not banded (J. Starks, personal communication). This indicates that at least 59 young were bred the previous summer (46 banded + 13 unbanded). Resightings of marked birds have since been made at Point Wilson and back at Melaleuca during one week in November 1988 when 12 of 15 first-year birds present were banded birds. This resighting of 12 banded birds (26%) suggests a high rate of survival through the first winter and return to the breeding grounds. Further intensive searches at Melaleuca during the spring return to the breeding grounds will be undertaken to test survival rates.

*Captive Breeding*

A captive breeding program for the orange-bellied parrot was first considered in 1981. Cost was a primary consideration, as it was expected that the program would have to run for 10 years or more. Also, the risks of reducing the wild population had to be weighed against expected benefits (see Maguire *et al.*, this volume). The hardest decision was, and always is, to initiate such a program.

In 1981, an aviary complex was erected by the Tasmanian Government in order to undertake trials using species similar to the orange-bellied parrot—the rock parrot *(Neophema petrophila)* and blue-winged parrot *(Neophema chrysostoma)*. The success of these trials and the subsequent release of the progeny of both species into the wild greatly encouraged the Recovery Team to recommend in 1985 that a captive breeding program begin.

The program is being carried out by the Tasmanian Government and is financially supported by the Victorian, South Australian and Commonwealth Governments. The objectives of the program are threefold: (1) to act as an insurance against the demise of the wild population; (2) to

*Table 1.*—Annual recruitment and mortality in the captive population of orange-bellied parrots. PBFS=parrot beak and feather syndrome. 'Other causes' of mortality include aspergillosis, stress at commencement of breeding, renal failure and accidental death.

| Year | Number taken from wild | Number reared to independence | Mortality | | | Stock prior to breeding in the following year |
| --- | --- | --- | --- | --- | --- | --- |
| | | | PBFS | Other causes | Totals | |
| 1985-1986 | 10 | 0 | 5 | 2 | 7 | 3 |
| 1986-1987 | 6 | 4 | 2 | 2 | 4 | 9 |
| 1987-1988 | 1 | 8 | 3 | 3 | 6 | 12 |
| 1988-1989 | 0 | 22 | 4 | 3 | 7 | 27 |
| Total | 17 | 34 | 14 | 10 | 24 | - |

bolster the wild population with releases of captive-bred birds at appropriate times; and (3) by colour-marking the released birds to establish groups of known-age individuals whose movements and survival could be monitored.

As the wild population totalled only about 150 individuals, it was considered imperative to begin captive breeding. At this population level, the removal of a small number of juvenile birds was not considered to be unduly harmful to the wild population. However, should the population fall further, removal of birds for captivity could have greater repercussions for the wild population.

The first birds were taken from the wild in March 1986, when 10 juveniles where captured in southwestern Tasmania prior to their northwards migration. The juveniles were selected from a trapped sample on the basis of their putative sex, a sex ratio of unity being desired. Juveniles were taken in preference to adults for two reasons: they are generally better able to be established in captivity, and removal of adult birds would have certainly reduced the stock of experienced breeders.

The orange-bellied parrots adapted well to captivity and the first breeding occurred in the summer following first capture when four young were reared in two nests. After three breeding seasons a total of 34 young have been reared to independence from 12 nests, but it was only after the third breeding season (1988-1989) that the total captive population exceeded the number of birds originally taken from the wild (Table 1). Details of captive husbandry are provided by Brown (1988).

The primary cause of mortality in the captive population has been a viral disease known as parrot beak and feather syndrome (PBFS) (Table 1). Symptoms of PBFS are severe distortion and loss of freshly moulted feathers in juveniles undergoing their first moult in April and May, when they are 4 to 5 months old. Some birds also develop distorted bills. This incurable disease has resulted in the death of 14 birds since 1986, including five of the original 10 birds caught in the wild. All remaining deaths were of birds bred in the aviaries.

The virus has been recorded in a range of Australian parrots, both in the wild and in captivity. It is endemic in the captive orange-bellied parrot population, though the occurrence rate has dropped from 50% in the first year to 13% in 1989. It is hoped the disease is being bred out of the group (see Robinson *et al.*, this volume).

At this stage it is not known if the disease occurs in wild orange-bellied parrots. Several wild birds with discoloured feathers have been observed, and this is often a first sign of the infection. However, it is not diagnostic, as some captive birds have developed yellow feathers but have not shown visible evidence of the disease, and have subsequently moulted into perfect plumage.

Disease problems could occur at any time in captive or wild populations (catastrophic stochastic event, see Clark *et al.*, this volume). Ideally, in order to minimise the effects of the disease, infected birds should be held in entirely separate facilities. Unfortunately, budgetary constraints preclude this at present. Veterinarians in Australia, the U.S.A. and West Germany are researching PBFS.

It is extremely encouraging that all seven females which could have bred during the three years of the project have successfully reared young. Previous attempts at captive breeding have had little success, perhaps because birds have been housed as pairs in standard parrot-breeding aviaries. Aviaries used in the present breeding program were designed to allow the birds to be kept in groups of two or more pairs, resulting in greater levels of stimulation and exercise.

In order to maximise annual production, a flock of rock parrots is being maintained to act as foster parents for clutches of orange-bellied parrot eggs. Under normal circumstances orange-bellied parrots are single brooded. By removing the first clutch for incubation by the rock parrots, the females will be encouraged to lay a second clutch and thereby hopefully produce two broods each year.

A future priority must be the use of DNA fingerprinting techniques to measure the degree of genetic variation present in the captive colony and in the wild population (see Robinson *et al.*, this volume). If the addition of genetic material to the captive population is desired, similar techniques may be used on wild birds to select individuals to be added to the captive colony.

The captive breeding program is meeting its first and primary objective (insurance policy), and has raised new questions about the possible role of disease in wild or captive populations. Until these questions are answered, no attempts will be made to release birds back into the wild. Furthermore, the captive breeding program should not be seen as a reason to reduce efforts to improve and increase habitat for the species. It would be futile to release captive-bred birds until habitat restoration has been adequately addressed. The priority for habitat management is clearly evident and needs new impetus.

## Discussion

The orange-bellied parrot was formerly far more abundant and widespread than it is now. Its decline to fewer than 200 individuals with a more restricted range fits the general extinction model outlined by Clark *et al.* (this volume). Several systematic factors are directly implicated in the species' decline, notably habitat loss and degradation; several stochastic factors may also be involved.

Management has focussed on stabilising the species' historic decline by attempting to ameliorate systematic extinction pressures. This has involved identifying, protecting and enhancing breeding and wintering habitat, as well as conducting annual censuses to obtain reliable estimates of the population structure and dynamics. Coordinated action and management planning between Tasmania, South Australia and Victoria, and the assistance of non-government organisations and many individuals has been essential. These actions and arrangements must continue. The captive breeding program aims to insure against unexpected stochastic events, and to maintain the capacity for expansion of the wild population once adequate habitat protection and enhancement is achieved.

These actions may ensure a long-term future for the species, if numbers are indeed limited by habitat and if habitat is successfully increased by management. The next steps are to set goals for increasing the population, and to test the hypothesis that numbers are limited by habitat, and to investigate stochastic factors which may also be involved. Genetic and demographic modelling (described earlier in this volume) may help determine a population size that is highly resistant to extinction, and this could be set as the management goal. All management to achieve this goal will be facilitated by attention to the principles of adaptive management and decision theory described earlier (Maguire *et al.*, this volume). This need is already illustrated from our comments on the need for monitoring and consequent revision of management actions (*e.g.* exclusion of grazing); it is all too easy to neglect these aspects.

If all these issues are addressed, we believe that orange-bellied parrots can be assured a long-term future.


## Acknowledgments

We wish to thank all those people, too numerous to mention, who have taken part in orange-bellied parrot counts since 1978. Without their energy and enthusiasm far less would be known about the ecology and status of the species and sound management would be impossible. We are also indebted to staff of the Victorian, South Australian, Tasmanian and Commonwealth fauna authorities, and of the RAOU, who have readily assisted in many ways. The governments of Tasmania, South Australia, Victoria and the Commonwealth of Australia have all provided financial and administrative support. Several other institutions and corporations have made important contributions including MMBW, Bird Observers Club of Australia, ICI Australia, Kinhill Planners and Ecological Horticulture. Tim Clark and John Seebeck provided helpful comments on an earlier draft.

## References

Brown, P.B. 1988. A captive breeding program for Orange-bellied Parrots. *Aust. Aviculture* 42:165-175.

Brown, P.B., and Wilson, R.I. 1980. A survey of the Orange-bellied Parrot in Tasmania, Victoria and South Australia. A report for World Wildlife Fund Australia. National Parks and Wildlife Service: Hobart.

Brown, P.B., and Wilson, R.I. 1981. A survey of the Orange-bellied Parrot in Tasmania, Victoria and South Australia. A report for World Wildlife Fund Australia. National Parks and Wildlife Service: Hobart.

Brown, P.B., and Wilson, R.I. 1982. The Orange-bellied Parrot. In *Species at Risk: Research in Australia,* eds R.H. Groves and W.D.L. Ride. Pp. 107-115. Australian Academy of Science: Canberra.

Brown, P.B., and Wilson, R.I. 1984. Orange-bellied Parrot Recovery Plan. National Parks and Wildlife Service, Tasmania: Hobart.

Carr, G.W. 1987. Report on the biology, ecology and management of the Orange-bellied Parrot food plant, *Chenopodium glaucum* (Glaucous Goosefoot), at the MMBW Farm, Werribee, Victoria. Ecological Horticulture: Melbourne.

Carr, G.W., and Kinhill Planners. 1979. Survey of Victorian coastal saltmarsh in relation to the habitat of the Orange-bellied Parrot. ICI Australia: Melbourne.

Edgar, B. In prep. Swan Bay Management Plan. Department of Conservation, Forests and Lands: Geelong.

Gibbons, P. 1984. The Orange-bellied Parrot: an assessment of the habitat of the Orange-bellied Parrot (*Neophema chrysogaster*) in the south-east of South Australia. National Parks and Wildlife Service: Adelaide.

Hewish, M., and Starks, J. 1988. Orange-bellied Parrots at Lake Connewarre, Victoria. *Geelong Nat.* 24:100-128.

Jarman, H. 1965. The Orange-bellied Parrot. *Aust. Bird Watcher* 2:155-167.

Jessop, A., and Reid, T. 1986. Winter surveys of the Orange-bellied Parrot *Neophema chrysogaster* in Victoria, 1984 and 1985. *RAOU Rep.* No. **19**.

Loyn, R.H., and Chandler, C. 1978. Avifauna Study, ICI Point Wilson Development. ICI Australia: Melbourne.

Loyn, R.H. 1982. Orange-bellied Parrots, ideas for management of a wild population. In *Rare, Endangered and Limited Gene Pool Species in Australia,* ed. C.B. Banks. Pp.16-21. Australian Society of Zookeepers: Melbourne.

Loyn, R.H., and Kinhill Planners. 1980. Historical records of Orange-bellied Parrots. ICI Australia: Melbourne.

Loyn, R.H., Lane, B.A., Chandler, C., and Carr, G.W. 1986. Ecology of Orange-bellied Parrots *Neophema chrysogaster* at their main remnant wintering site. *Emu* **86**:195-206.

McMahon, A.R.G., and Carr, G.W. 1988. Report on experimental field trials aimed at promoting the standing crop of *Chenopodium glaucum*—food plant of the Orange-bellied Parrot, at the MMBW Farm, Werribee, Victoria. Ecological Horticulture: Melbourne.

McGill, A.R. 1960. Parrots of the genus *Neophema* in New South Wales. *Emu* **60**:40-61.

Menkhorst, P. 1984. Orange-bellied Parrot census 1983—summary of results. *Bird Observer* No. **628** (May):41-42.

Starks, J. 1988. Orange-bellied Parrot *Neophema chrysogaster* winter surveys in southeastern Australia in 1986 and 1987. *RAOU Report* No. **36**.

Yugovic, J.Z. 1984. The Grey Glasswort (*Halosarcia halocnemoides*) in coastal Victoria and some implications for the Orange-bellied Parrot. *Victorian Nat.* **101**:234-239.

# Bioclimatic Modelling and Wildlife Conservation and Management—A Case Study on Leadbeater's Possum, *Gymnobelideus leadbeateri*

*David B. Lindenmayer[1], Henry A. Nix[2], June P. McMahon[2], and Michael F. Hutchinson[2]*

## Abstract

The occurrence of Leadbeater's possum is restricted to a narrow set of climatic conditions which are confined to the Victorian Central Highlands. This area encompasses the entire known range of the species. Bioclimatic analyses were used as a basis for surveys for Leadbeater's possum outside the Victorian Central Highlands. Leadbeater's possum was not detected in those field surveys. The bioclimatic profile occupied by Leadbeater's possum is closely related to the bioclimatic profiles of several key species of plants, including *Eucalyptus regnans, Acacia obliquinervia* and *A. frigescens*. On the basis of its bioclimatic profile, the distribution of Leadbeater's possum is considered likely to undergo a considerable contraction as a result of climatic changes associated with the Greenhouse Effect. The importance of this finding, together with others from the study, are discussed in terms of the value of BIOCLIM and bioclimatic analyses in wildlife conservation and management.

## Introduction

Climate sets broad limits to the distribution of most species (Woodward 1987). Within these limits, other factors such as geology, soils, competition, predation and environmental disturbance will determine the presence or absence and abundance of a species in a given area. Given that climate usually limits the range of a taxon, studies of climatic environments can provide an understanding of why a species exists where it does. Such analyses can, in turn, have important implications for wildlife survey, management and conservation.

If the spatial distribution of a taxon is not fully defined, bioclimatic analyses allow the theoretical probable limits of the distribution to be predicted. These predictions are based on the concept of homoclime matching. Homoclimes are locations that experience similiar climatic conditions. The concept of homoclimes originates from early studies on climate mapping by Koppen (1900, 1923) and Thornthwaite (1931).

Nix and his associates have coupled the homoclime concept with new methods of climate and terrain modelling to develop an integrated system for the analysis of species distributions (Nix 1986a, b; Busby 1986; Booth *et al.* 1987). The climatic variables used to define a taxon's bioclimate are based on the means, range, extremes and seasonality of temperature and precipitation (Nix 1981). Early development of the system took place while Nix, McMahon and Hutchinson were employed in the CSIRO Division of Water and Land Resources and John Busby was seconded from the Bureau of Flora and Fauna to work with this team on the development of a public access version of the package mounted on the nationwide CSIRONET system. This early program, BIOCLIM, has been further developed and refined and remains the computer program underpinning bioclimatic analyses. We outline the steps and procedures used in BIOCLIM and emphasize its value in wildlife conservation and management. This paper has 3 themes: (1) An introduction to BIOCLIM and the steps involved in bioclimatic modelling, (2) the application of bioclimatic analyses in a case study on

[1] Department of Forestry, Australian National University, P.O. Box 4, Canberra, A.C.T. 2600, Australia.
[2] Centre for Resource and Environmental Studies, Australian National University, P.O. Box 4, Canberra, A.C.T. 2600, Australia.

Leadbeater's possum, *Gymnobelideus leadbeateri* McCoy, and, (3) a discussion of the importance of bioclimatic modelling in wildlife conservation and management.

## Methods

### The Distribution of Leadbeater's Possum

Leadbeater's possum was described from two specimens collected near the banks of the Bass River, southeastern Victoria in the mid-19th century (McCoy 1867). In the following 40 years only two additional animals were discovered. One of these was from the edge of Koo-Wee-Rup Swamp, 40 km north of the Bass River. The other specimen came from Mt Wills, approximately 250 km northeast of the other location records. Between 1909 and 1960 there were no new records of Leadbeater's possum, and the species was presumed extinct (Tate 1945; Brazenor 1950; Calaby 1960).

Leadbeater's possum was re-discovered in 1961 at Tommy's Bend in the Central Highlands region of Victoria (Wilkinson 1961), from where the species had not previously been recorded. Since then, Leadbeater's possum has been recorded from more than 160 distinct localities within the Victorian Central Highlands, but the distribution is very restricted, with limits of 37°20' and 37°55'S latitude and 145°30' and 146°20'E longitude (Fig. 1).

Fossil deposits have yielded several records of Leadbeater's possum. Broom (1895a,b) described an extinct arboreal marsupial, *Paleopetaurus elegans*, from limestone breccia in the Wombeyan Caves in New South Wales (34°18'S, 149°50'E). *P. elegans* was later found to be synonymous with Leadbeater's possum (Wakefield 1972). The only other record from New South Wales is from Marble Arch (35°43'S, 149°42'E) (Hall 1974). Fossils of Leadbeater's possum in northeastern Victoria include those from Cloggs Cave (37°31'S, 148°10'E) (Flood 1973, Hope 1973), M27 Cave

(37°26', 148°13') (Wakefield 1967) and Pyramids Cave (37°26'S, 148°13'E) (Wakefield 1960a,b). The age of these fossils cannot be determined accurately, but most seem to date from the Pleistocene (Archer 1984).

These records, together with those from the 19th and early 20th century indicate that Leadbeater's possum was once more widely distributed than it is at present. Many authors have speculated on the possible contemporary (*i.e.* post-1961) occurrence of the species in northeastern Victoria and/ or southeastern New South Wales (Brazenor 1962; Ride 1970; Wakefield 1970; Troughton 1973; Dixon 1978; Broome 1979; Brown 1982). Therefore, the distribution of Leadbeater's possum may be imperfectly known, both within and outside the Victorian Central Highlands.

### Steps in Bioclimatic Analysis

The bioclimatic analysis procedure is based on the development of new techniques for the estimation of climatic variables at any point on the landscape for which latitude, longitude and elevation are specified. The fitting of long-term monthly climatic data for Australia using Laplacian smoothing splines is described by Hutchinson and Bischof (1983), Hutchinson *et al.* (1984) and Hutchinson (1984). BIOCLIM incorporates these mathematical surfaces for estimation of mean monthly maximum temperature and precipitation at any geocoded point in continental Australia and in Tasmania. Geocoded points are those to which latitude, longitude and elevation data have been assigned.

The procedures followed in bioclimatic analyses are:
1. Geocode specimen and/or observation data.
2. Calculate bioclimatic indices from the estimated climatic variables at each geocoded point.
3. Derive a table of statistical values for each individual bioclimatic index from all geocoded points—a bioclimatic profile.

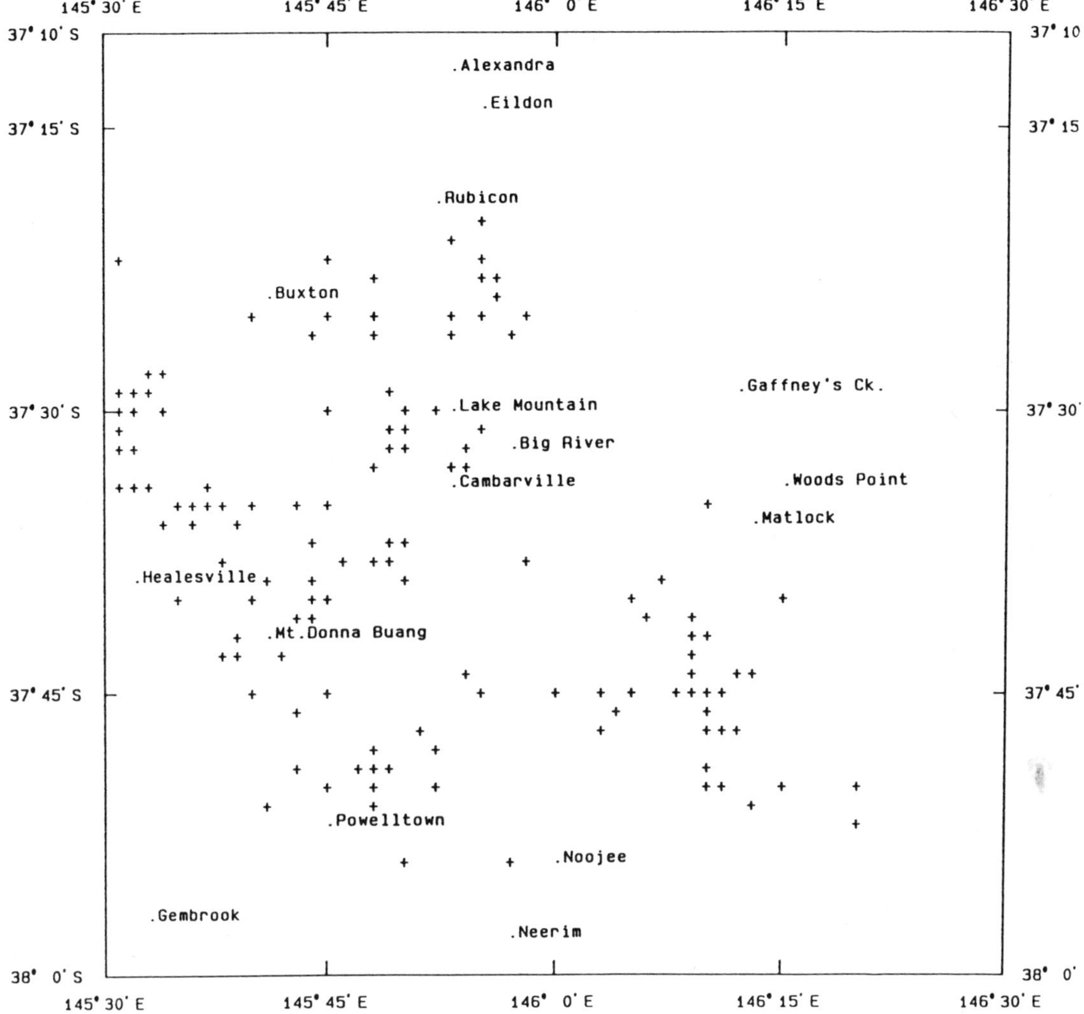


*Figure 1.*—Distribution records of Leadbeater's possum within the Central Highlands of Victoria, collected since the rediscovery of the species in 1961 and used in bioclimatic analyses presented in this study.

4. Calculate a cumulative frequency curve for each bioclimatic index.
5. Check anomalous values for geocoding or other errors.
6. Using corrected geocodes, re-run steps (2-5).
7. Couple the bioclimatic profile to a grid of climate data derived by estimating climate variables at a grid of elevation points.

8. Using limiting and central tendency values for each of the bioclimatic indices, generate a map of the predicted potential distribution of the target taxon.

For the user, the principal interaction is in providing the geocoded data as input to the program. However, it is usual for geocoding errors to occur,

*Table 1.*—Sources of distribution data used in bioclimatic analyses, listed in order of most to least significant contribution.

| Species | Source of data | No. Records |
| --- | --- | --- |
| *G. leadbeateri* | Victorian Mammal Database Lindenmayer *et al*. unpubl. | 165 |
| *E. regnans* | EUCALIST National Herbarium of Victoria | 167 |
| *E. nitens* | EUCALIST National Herbarium of Victoria | 140 |
| *E. fastigata* | EUCALIST | 142 |
| *E. delegatensis* | EUCALIST National Herbarium of Victoria | 348 |
| *E. pauciflora* | EUCALIST | 433 |
| *E. stellulata* | EUCALIST | 196 |
| *E. obliqua* | EUCALIST | 433 |
| *A. dealbata* | National Herbarium of Victoria National Herbarium of Tasmania Gauba Herbaruim (A.N.U.) | 833 |
| *A. obliquinervia* | National Herbarium of Victoria Gauba Herbaruim (A.N.U.). National Botanic Gardens | 407 |
| *A. frigescens* | National Herbarium of Victoria | 294 |

and it is important that users become familiar with, and use, the cumulative frequency analysis as a means of targeting potential anomalies. In this study of Leadbeater's possum, the bioclimatic analyses were extended to include species of trees occurring in montane and sub-alpine communities of southeastern Australia and to examine the potential impact of climate change on the target taxon.

A more detailed account of the methodology associated with each step of the analyses is outlined in the following discussion.

*Geocoding Specimen/Observation Data*

Using best available topographic maps at a scale of 1:100,000 and 1:25,000, the latitude, longitude and elevation of the following groups were determined: (a) current (post-1961) and historical (1867-1909) distribution records of Leadbeater's possum, (b) species of *Eucalyptus* and *Acacia* that are closely associated with, or are marginal to the habitat of Leadbeater's possum.

Since climate estimates are a function of latitude, longitude and elevation, geocoding must be as accurate as possible. Records that are impossible to geocode with an accuracy of greater than ± 5' latitude and longitude and ± 50 m elevation were discarded, as the analyses focussed on highly dissected, mountainous terrains. Geocoded data from the complete known natural range were included so that all the bioclimatic environments inhabited by each species were analysed. Duplicate records and, in the case of plant species, data on cultivated specimens were deleted. Because

*Table 2.*—Climate indices derived from bioclimatic modelling. The number of each index corresponds to that in the bioclimatic profile of Leadbeater's possum (Table 3). These indices describe the range, extremes and seasonality of climatic conditions at each geocoded location.

| Index Number | Index |
| --- | --- |
| 1 | Annual mean temperature (°C) |
| 2 | Annual mean maximum temperature (°C) |
| 3 | Annual mean minimum temperature (°C) |
| 4 | Maximum diurnal temperature range (°C) |
| 5 | Mean temperature of the warmest month (°C) |
| 6 | Mean temperature of the coldest month (°C) |
| 7 | Mean seasonal range (index 5 - index 6) (°C) |
| 8 | Isotherm seasonality (mean diurnal range / mean seasonal range) |
| 9 | Maximum temperature of the hottest month (°C) |
| 10 | Minimum temperature of the coldest month (°C) |
| 11 | Annual temperature range (index 9 - index 10) (°C) |
| 12 | Mean temperature of the wettest quarter (°C) |
| 13 | Mean temperature of the driest quarter (°C) |
| 14 | Mean temperature of the warmest quarter (°C) |
| 15 | Mean temperature of the coldest quarter (°C) |
| 16 | Annual precipitation (mm) |
| 17 | Precipitation of the wettest month (mm) |
| 18 | Precipitation of the driest month (mm) |
| 19 | Annual precipitation range (index 17 - index 18) (mm) |
| 20 | Seasonality index [index 19 / ( index 16 / index 12)] |
| 21 | Precipitation of the wettest quarter (mm) |
| 22 | Precipitation of the driest quarter (mm) |
| 23 | Precipitation of the warmest quarter (mm) |
| 24 | Precipitation of the coldest quarter (mm) |

climate surfaces were calculated from modern meteorological information, fossil records were deleted, as they may represent an historical distribution indicative of past climatic regimes.

The sources of the data are listed in Table 1. The major source of data for *Eucalyptus* spp. was EUCALIST (Chippendale and Wolfe 1984). This was supplemented by additional data from the National Herbarium of Victoria which was also the major source of data for *Acacia* spp.

### Estimating Site-Specific Climatic Attributes

BIOCLIM uses mathematically derived surfaces estimated from a network of meteorological stations in Australia, with most of the primary data supplied by the Commonwealth Bureau of Meteorology. Surfaces of maximum and minimum temperature and rainfall were calculated. These take advantage of the spatial coherence of various climatophysical processes to produce a continent-wide description of monthly climate (Hutchinson 1989a). Estimated mean errors are 0.5-1.0°C for monthly mean maximum and minimum temperature and < 10% for surfaces of monthly precipitation.

### Deriving Bioclimatic Indices

At each geocoded site, the climate surfaces are interrogated by BIOCLIM to derive 36 climatic attributes; 12 for each of monthly maximum and minimum temperature and precipitation. From these, 24 bioclimatic indices are calculated by BIOCLIM. These describe the range, extremes

*Table 3.*—The bioclimatic profile of Leadbeater's possum. See text for key to indices.

**Temperature (°C)**

| | *Index Number | 1 | 2 | 3 | 4 | 5 | 6 | 7 | 8 | 9 | 10 | 11 | 12 | 13 | 14 | 15 |
|---|---|---|---|---|---|---|---|---|---|---|---|---|---|---|---|---|
| MEAN | | 10.27 | 15.00 | 5.54 | 13.05 | 16.77 | 4.34 | 12.44 | 0.60 | 23.16 | 1.27 | 21.89 | 6.41 | 15.80 | 15.94 | 4.94 |
| S.D. | | 1.35 | 1.60 | 1.18 | 1.08 | 1.20 | 1.56 | 0.48 | 0.03 | 1.57 | 1.34 | 0.69 | 1.86 | 1.18 | 1.19 | 1.51 |
| 5% | | 8.38 | 12.92 | 3.93 | 11.85 | 15.03 | 2.02 | 11.75 | 0.56 | 20.87 | -0.91 | 21.05 | 3.45 | 14.02 | 14.16 | 2.64 |
| 10% | | 8.75 | 13.22 | 4.18 | 12.06 | 15.60 | 2.66 | 11.88 | 0.57 | 21.40 | -0.31 | 21.28 | 4.14 | 14.59 | 14.66 | 3.26 |
| 25% | | 9.45 | 13.95 | 4.83 | 12.31 | 16.17 | 3.35 | 12.12 | 0.57 | 22.17 | 0.43 | 21.42 | 5.04 | 15.19 | 15.24 | 3.97 |
| 50% | | 10.20 | 14.71 | 5.63 | 12.54 | 16.72 | 4.41 | 12.57 | 0.58 | 23.15 | 1.36 | 21.65 | 6.25 | 15.74 | 15.95 | 4.95 |
| 75% | | 10.81 | 15.97 | 6.13 | 14.09 | 17.33 | 5.27 | 12.80 | 0.63 | 24.29 | 1.99 | 22.41 | 7.63 | 16.38 | 16.61 | 5.77 |
| 90% | | 11.95 | 17.37 | 6.82 | 14.84 | 18.32 | 6.36 | 12.98 | 0.65 | 25.20 | 2.72 | 23.02 | 8.55 | 17.30 | 17.49 | 6.82 |
| 95% | | 13.02 | 18.10 | 7.52 | 15.07 | 19.22 | 7.12 | 13.05 | 0.65 | 25.80 | 3.41 | 23.21 | 9.59 | 18.10 | 18.21 | 7.56 |
| MIN. | | 5.79 | 10.10 | 1.49 | 11.35 | 12.58 | -0.34 | 10.34 | 0.54 | 18.08 | -3.07 | 19.17 | 1.15 | 11.58 | 11.59 | 0.29 |
| MAX. | | 14.29 | 19.40 | 9.53 | 15.62 | 20.07 | 9.31 | 13.11 | 0.67 | 26.81 | 5.76 | 23.36 | 11.89 | 19.04 | 19.04 | 9.70 |

*(Header row: Index Number* spans columns 1–15)*

**Precipitation (mm)**

| | *Index Number | 16 | 17 | 18 | 19 | 20 | 21 | 22 | 23 | 24 |
|---|---|---|---|---|---|---|---|---|---|---|
| MEAN | | 1517.02 | 167.31 | 76.69 | 90.62 | 0.72 | 479.99 | 246.67 | 260.49 | 461.50 |
| S.D. | | 165.26 | 22.33 | 8.34 | 20.33 | 0.12 | 62.00 | 22.08 | 23.78 | 63.10 |
| 5% | | 1111.36 | 117.43 | 61.68 | 49.97 | 0.54 | 323.66 | 204.43 | 211.80 | 309.50 |
| 10% | | 1343.89 | 142.71 | 68.31 | 70.10 | 0.58 | 420.11 | 225.88 | 237.53 | 391.66 |
| 25% | | 1415.92 | 152.28 | 71.14 | 77.89 | 0.62 | 437.33 | 228.86 | 243.66 | 419.30 |
| 50% | | 1574.16 | 170.53 | 77.15 | 90.00 | 0.69 | 488.56 | 251.41 | 264.19 | 469.50 |
| 75% | | 1643.24 | 185.73 | 81.76 | 106.15 | 0.81 | 530.59 | 263.11 | 278.28 | 512.90 |
| 90% | | 1712.17 | 197.48 | 88.34 | 119.64 | 0.87 | 559.17 | 276.01 | 293.03 | 545.39 |
| 95% | | 1690.21 | 197.67 | 90.51 | 124.08 | 0.94 | 559.23 | 277.47 | 294.23 | 549.80 |
| MIN. | | 1007.74 | 107.98 | 58.08 | 42.37 | 0.50 | 302.72 | 192.95 | 204.41 | 287.80 |
| MAX. | | 1698.50 | 202.39 | 94.11 | 131.18 | 0.98 | 564.47 | 284.82 | 296.75 | 557.95 |

*(Header row: Index Number* spans columns 16–24)*

and seasonality of climatic conditions at each geocoded location and are listed in Table 2.

For each of these indices, a statistical summary of values is produced. Variations in each climatic index are expressed as mean, standard deviation, minimum, 10%, 25%, 50%, 75%, 90% and maximum values. This summary is called a bioclimatic profile (Nix 1986a; Booth *et al.* 1987). The bioclimatic profile of Leadbeater's possum is presented in Table 3.

This summary of the bioclimatic environment of the target taxon has been termed, variously, as a climatic profile (Booth 1985; Busby 1986, 1989; Nix 1986b; Booth *et al.* 1988), a bioclimatic template (Nix and Gillison 1985), a bioclimatic envelope (Nix 1986a; Booth *et al.* 1987), and climatic signature (Nix 1986b). All these terms are equivalent in meaning.

*Developing a Digital Elevation Model*

A key step in bioclimatic analyses involves coupling the bioclimatic profile of a taxon to a grid of climatic indices. This grid is, in turn, derived from estimated climatic variables for a grid of elevation points. The grid of elevation points is a digital representation of the topography of a landscape and is called a Digital Elevation Model (DEM).

In our study, a DEM comprised of a regular grid of elevation points at a resolution of 0.025° latitude and longitude (approximately 2.5 km) was used because the analyses were concentrated in complex mountainous terrain where a grid of a coarser scale would not have provided an adequate sample of the spatial variation in the climate over the landscape. This DEM was the southeast section of an Australia-wide DEM developed by Hutchinson (1989b) and Hutchinson and Dowling (in press) and corresponded to the following 1:250,000 topographic maps: Bairnsdale, Bega, Canberra, Mallacoota, Melbourne, Tallangatta, Wagga Wagga, Wangaratta, Warburton, and Warragul.

To improve the accuracy of the DEM, additional data were digitized from 1:250,000 and 1:100,000 topographic map sheets and added to terrain information already in the database of the model. These additional data were: 1) spot heights and contour labels, 2) streamline data, 3) contour lines, and 4) sinks or locations which did not drain. The contouring and mapping programs GRDCON and MAPROJ (Hutchinson 1981, 1984) were used to plot and check the accuracy of the DEM. Plotting, checking, and adding digitized data were repeated until the DEM accurately modelled key features of the landscape.

*Generating Maps of Potential Distribution*

Homoclime matching was used to identify points on the climate grid where the climatic conditions were within the limits of those summarized in the bioclimatic profile of Leadbeater's possum. Homoclime matching took place at two levels: 1) minimum and maximum values in the bioclimatic profile and 2) the 10-90% level. However, matching can be nominated for any level in the bioclimatic profile.

The scatter of matched points represents the predicted potential distribution of the species. As homoclime matching in our study was undertaken at two distinct levels, the corresponding distributions have two sub-components. The distribution based on the maximum and minimum values in the bioclimatic profile is termed the predicted range of the species. The other, calculated from a narrower set of bioclimatic conditions (10-90% level), is called the core distribution.

Points on the climatic grid where the values of one or more of the 24 indices fell outside the maximum/minimum statistical range were left blank and did not form part of the predicted distribution. It is possible to modify the matching criteria and specify a subset of indices to be matched, but this was not done in our study. Two predictions of the distribution of Leadbeater's possum were generated based on bioclimatic profiles calculated from current and historical records.

*Numerical Taxonomic Analysis*

The relationships between the bioclimatic profile produced for Leadbeater's possum and those for several species of plants occurring in montane and/or alpine areas of southeast Australia were analysed using PATN, a computer-based numerical taxonomy and cluster analysis package (Belbin 1984; Belbin *et al.* 1984). Application of numerical taxonomic analysis was used in an attempt to identify plant species which may have acted as an indicator of the presence of Leadbeater's possum. The bioclimatic profiles of ten plant taxa were analysed: *Eucalyptus regnans, E. delegatensis, E. nitens, E. fastigata, E. obliqua, E. stellulata, E. pauciflora, Acacia dealbata, A. frigescens* and *A. obliquinervia.* From the bioclimatic profile of each species the mean, minimum and maximum values of each climatic index were extracted. A Gower index of similarity (Gower 1971) was used to determine the level of association betwen the subset of climatic attributes of each species. These types of aggregation procedures result in the assignment of taxa into groups, the results of which can be represented as an hierarchical binary tree, or dendrogram. There are numerous strategies for clustering attributes, but in this study, UPGMA (unweighted pair group arithmetic average) (Sokal and Michener in Belbin 1984) was utilized as it is the one recommended by Belbin (1984).

*Table 4.*—The range of climatic scenarios used in predicting the effects of past and future climate changes on the distribution of Leadbeater's possum. Values are shown relative to current climatic conditions. Maximum and minimum temperature are expressed as predicted changes per degree of latitude away from the equator. Precipitation values are precentage changes from current conditions. The area of the distribution of Leadbeater's possum under each scenario were calculated in sq km using the program AREA (see text). Bioclimatic profile 1 is that calculated from post-1961 distribution records of the species. Bioclimatic profile 2 was calculated from the current and historical (1867-1909) records of Leadbeater's possum.

| Time | Max Temp. (°C) | Min. Temp. (°C) | Summer rain (mm) | Winter rain (mm) | Bioclimatic Profile 1 | | Bioclimatic Profile 2 | |
|---|---|---|---|---|---|---|---|---|
| | | | | | Range Area (sq km) | Core Area (sq km) | Range Area (sq km) | Core Area (sq km) |
| 1961 - 1989 | N.A. | N.A. | N.A. | N.A. | 5612 | 624 | N.A. | N.A. |
| 1867 - 1989 | N.A. | N.A. | N.A. | N.A. | 20219 | 1153 | N.A. | N.A. |
| Scenario 1 | +0.04 | +0.06 | +40% | -20% | 29 | 0 | 16001 | 0 |
| Scenario 2 | +0.05 | +0.05 | +50% | -15% | 19 | 0 | 1426 | 0 |
| Scenario 3 | +0.025 | +0.075 | +50% | -25% | 0 | 0 | 77 | 0 |
| Scenario 4 | +0.06 | +0.02 | -15% | +15% | 2795 | 0 | 5158 | 29 |
| Scenario 5 | +0.02 | +0.03 | +20% | -10% | 1012 | 10 | 8641 | 39 |
| Scenario 6 | +0.04 | +0.06 | +30% | -15% | 299 | 0 | 3652 | 0 |
| Scenario 7 | +0.06 | +0.12 | +50% | -30% | 0 | 0 | 0 | 0 |

*Field Surveys for Leadbeater's Possum*

The predicted range distribution of Leadbeater's possum included matched grid cells outside the Central Highlands of Victoria. These were plotted at a scale of 1:100,000 using MAPROJ and transferred to 1:100,000 topograhic maps by overlay. Field surveys for Leadbeater's possum were concentrated in these areas between November 1987 and February 1988. A reconnaissance of each grid cell was made on foot, and the area of forest considered to support habitat most closely resembling that preferred by Leadbeater's possum was surveyed by the stagwatching technique (Smith 1980; Seebeck *et al.* 1983). This technique has been very successful where the animal is known to occur (Smith *et al.* 1985; Smith and Lindenmayer 1988).

*The Impact of Climate Change on Leadbeater's Possum*

An attempt was made to assess the impact of the Greenhouse Effect (global warming) on the distribution of Leadbeater's possum. Climatic conditions predicted to occur by 2030 A.D. were selected because changes associated with the Greenhouse Effect are likely to be established by that time (Pittock and Nix 1986; Pittock 1988, 1989). Estimates of the predicted distribution of Leadbeater's possum were derived with the aim of identifying areas with long-term conservation value for Leadbeater's possum.

As the magnitude of change remains uncertain, a range of climatic scenarios was generated (Table 4) by manipulating four climatic parameters: 1) annual mean maximum temperature, 2) annual mean minimum temperature, 3) winter precipitation, and, 4) summer precipitation. Most of the climatic scenarios are based on estimates of climatic conditions presented by Pittock and Nix (1986). The range of scenarios included those generally considered likely to prevail as well as several extreme cases.

In several scenarios, the absolute increase in °C was greater for mean minimum temperature than mean maximum temperature (Table 4). Atmospheric modifications of the energy balance set limits to the levels of mean maximum temperature but do not exert the same relative effect on mean minimum temperature. For each of the scenarios listed in Table 4, a grid of indices was produced using BIOCLIM and the DEM. The predicted distribution of Leadbeater's possum for each scenario was plotted and the area covered was calculated using the program AREA (McMahon, unpublished).

*Results*

*The Bioclimatic Profile of*
*Leadbeater's Possum*

Initial bioclimatic analyses revealed the existence of considerable discontinuities in the values of all the indices in the bioclimatic profile of the species, as well as unusual cumulative frequency plots (Fig. 2). These results indicated the presence of two bioclimatic sub-envelopes and implied the existence of two distinct populations of Leadbeater's possum, inhabiting areas with different climate. This did not correspond with known information on the species. In addition, preliminary field surveys indicated that the predicted distribution of Leadbeater's possum included areas of dry forest, which was inconsistent with the known habitat requirements of the species. As a result, the geocoded records of Leadbeater's possum were checked. This revealed errors of 1° of latitude in four distribution records.

A revised bioclimatic profile was calculated from the corrected set of data (Table 3), and new predictions of distribution were made (Figs. 3 and 4). The errors in the data had considerable impact on the bioclimatic profile and thus the predictions of distribution (Fig. 5). Subsequent field surveys were based on the revised distribution of Leadbeater's possum. Procedures to avoid these problems experienced in our study include: (a) checking of all geocoded data prior to analysis as the effects of even small errors in sets of distributional data can be significant, (b) examination of the output from BIOCLIM, particularly cumulative frequency plots (Fig. 2) and the bioclimatic

profile, and, (c) determination of the biological meaning of the results and, where possible, accompanying the analyses with field survey.

*The Predicted Distribution of*
*Leadbeater's Possum*

Two predicted distributions of Leadbeater's possum were produced (Figs. 3 and 4). Both consist of two sub-components, which correspond to homoclime matching at the minimum-maximum and 10-90% statistical levels in the bioclimatic profile. The range distribution corresponds to points matched using minimum and maximum values of each index in the bioclimatic profile. Homoclime matching using the narrower set of bioclimatic conditions (10-90% statistical level) has been called the core distribution of the species.

The distribution of Leadbeater's possum based on a combination of the current and historical records was more extensive than that derived from only the current records (Figs. 3 and 4). The four historical records had considerable impact on the values in the bioclimatic profile, and thus the predicted distribution. This was expected, as these records are very different from those of the current distribution and include areas of markedly different elevation (60m-1,500m) and latitude (38°-36°).

The characteristics of the predicted distributions derived from bioclimatic analyses are a function of the scale of resolution of points in the DEM. Climate surfaces generated from a DEM at a coarse scale of resolution will contain grid points with more generalized estimates of climatic conditions than one generated from a DEM of finer scale. Hence, the scatter of matched points corresponding to the predicted distribution of a species will be influenced by the scale of resolution of the climatic grid used. When a climatic grid with a level of resolution of 0.5° latitude and longitude was used, the predicted distribution of Leadbeater's possum (based on a bioclimatic profile calculated from a combination of current and historical records) contained only three matched

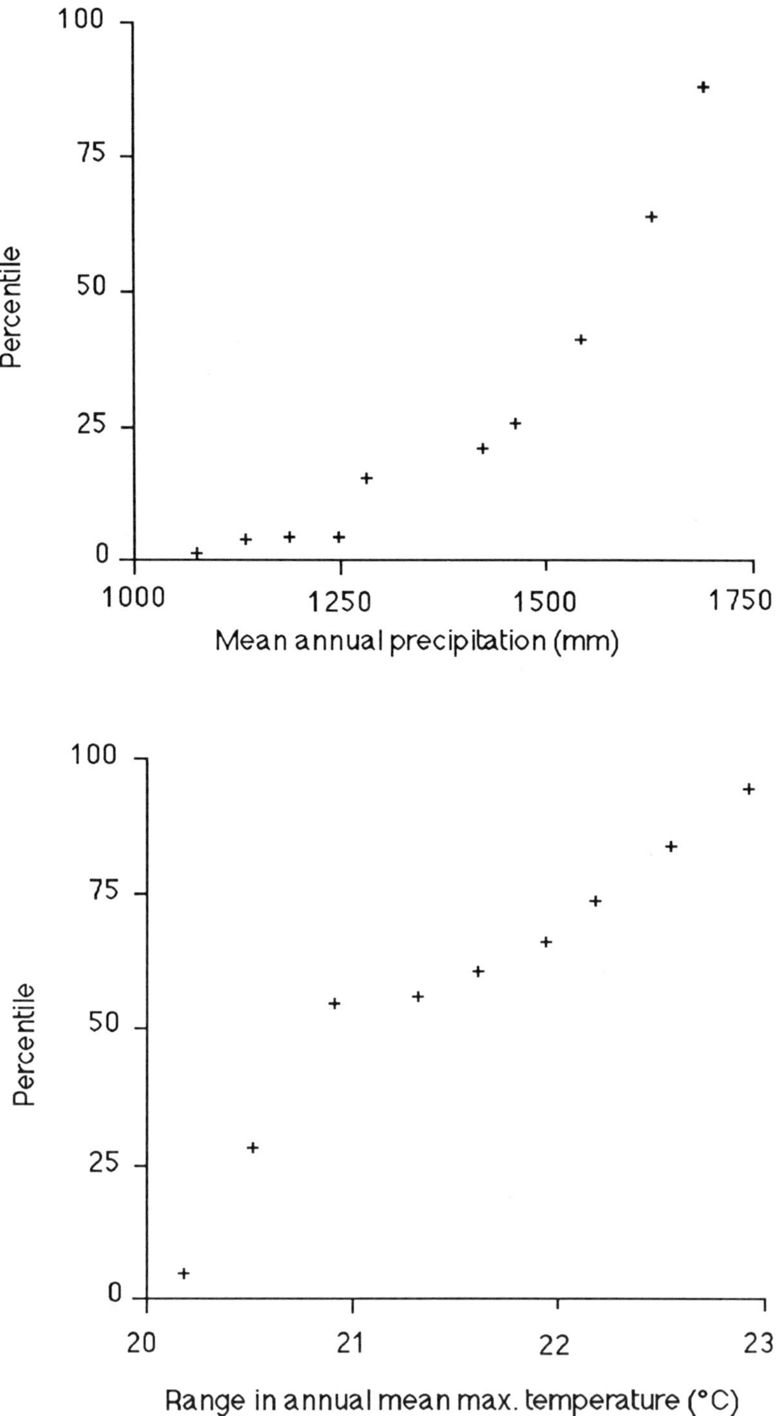

*Figure 2*.—Frequency plots showing major discontinuities, indicating the likelihood of geocoding errors in the distribution data for Leadbeater's possum (see text).

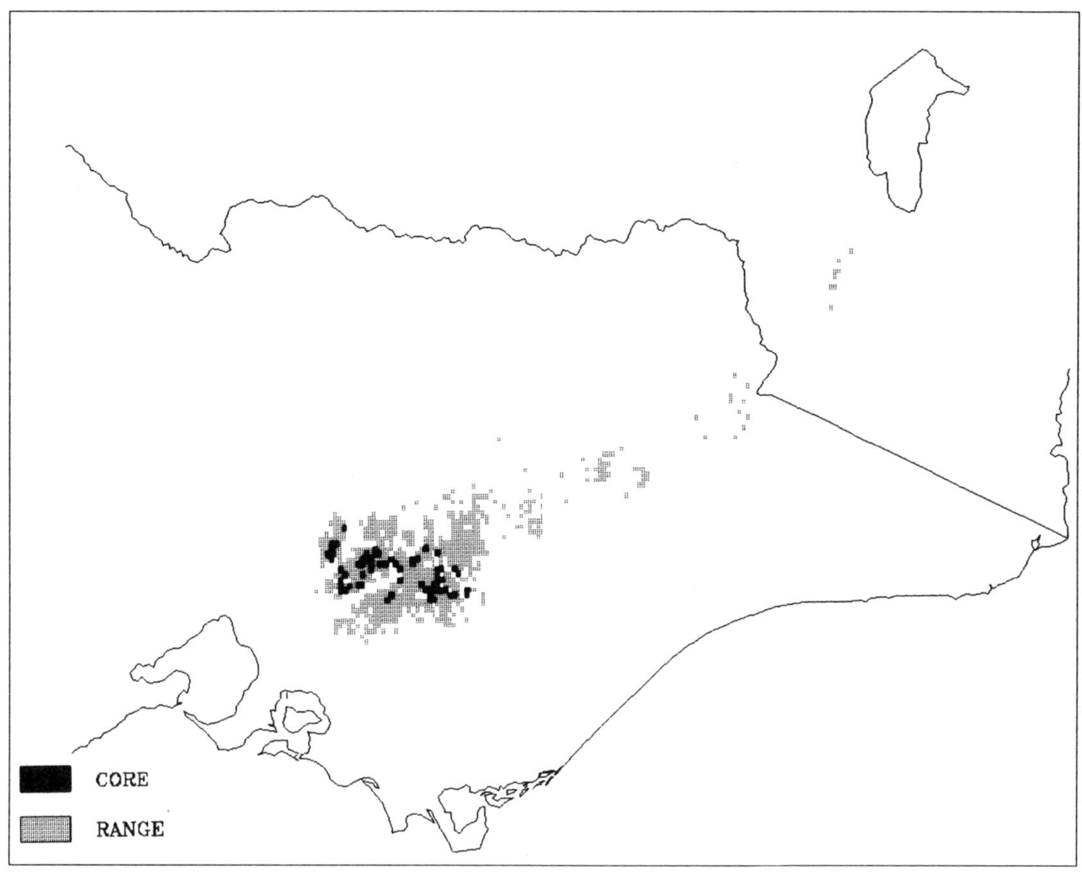


*Figure 3.*—The predicted core and range distribution of Leadbeater's possum derived from a bioclimatic profile calculated from current (post-1961) distribution records of the species.

points. These corresponded to an area in the Central Highlands of Victoria.

*Surveys Outside the Central Highlands of Victoria*

As no areas of core distribution outside the Central Highlands of Victoria were predicted from the bioclimatic analyses, surveys for Leadbeater's possum in these areas were concentrated in the predicted range distribution or sites experiencing only marginally suitable bioclimatic conditions for the species. Some of these areas in the Kosciusko National Park, Errindundra Plateau

and the Berridale Region supported dry sclerophyll forest, which was not expected from analyses of a possum species almost entirely restricted to montane ash forests.

These problems were found to be associated with geocoding errors in the original set of distribution records of Leadbeater's possum. Subsequent surveys for the species were concentrated in areas incorporated in the revised prediction of the potential distribution of the species (Fig. 3).

A total of 64 sites, each of 3 ha, were censused by the stagwatching technique (Smith 1980; Seebeck

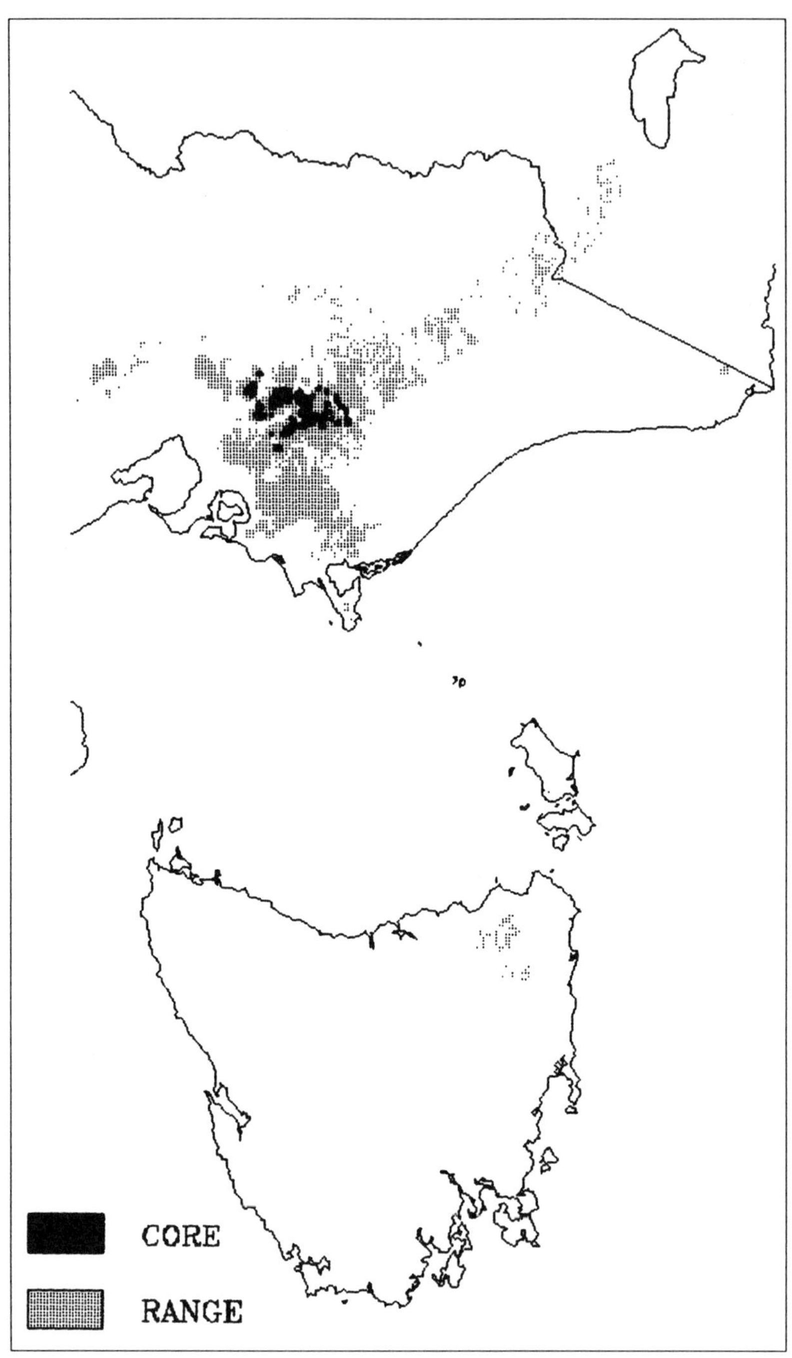



*Figure 4.*—The predicted core and range distribution of Leadbeater's possum derived from a bioclimatic profile calculated from historical (1867-1909) and current (post-1961) distribution records of the species.

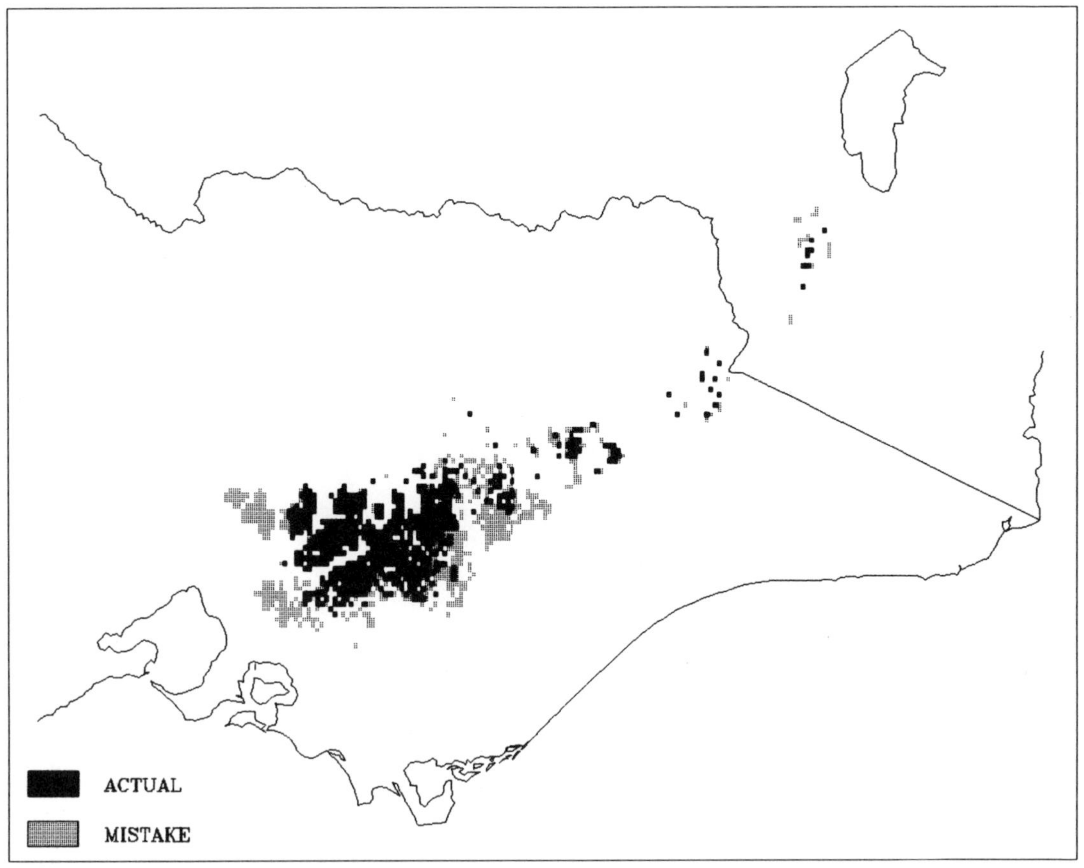



*Figure 5.*—Two predicted distributions of Leadbeater's possum based on (1) the current (post-1961) distribution records of the species and (2) a bioclimatic profile which included four geocoding errors of 1° of latitude.

*et al.* 1983). The dominant species of plant at most of these sites was *E. delegatensis.* Our surveys did not detect the presence of Leadbeater's possum outside the Central Highlands of Victoria. Numerous other faunal surveys in northeastern Victoria have also failed to record Leadbeater's possum. Some of these have been specifically for the species (Robertson *et al.* 1983; Smith *et al.* 1985), whereas others have concentrated on censusing arboreal marsupials *per se* (e.g. Chesterfield *et al.* 1983; Cherry *et al.* 1986, 1987).

The similarity of the core and the known distributions of Leadbeater's possum imply that bioclimatic factors are an important determinant of the distribution of the species. Thus, it appears unlikely that the present distribution of Leadbeater's possum extends much beyond its current known limits.

*Numerical Taxonomic Analysis*

Agglomerative clustering analyses assigned the bioclimatic profiles of the plant taxa and Leadbeater's possum into three groups (Fig. 6): Group 1—*A. frigescens, E. regnans, A. obliquinervia,* and Leadbeater's possum; Group 2—*E. fastigata, E. nitens, A. dealbata, E. pauciflora* and

265

*E. stellulata;* Group 3—*E. delegatensis.* Both of the bioclimatic profiles of Leadbeater's possum were assigned to group 1 by PATN. The mean values of all precipitation indices and most temperature indices in the bioclimatic profile of Leadbeater's possum were higher than for any of the plants or groups of plants examined. In addition, the range of values for each index was smaller for Leadbeater's possum than in other species (Figs 7 and 8). In contrast to the profiles of all other taxa, that calculated for Leadbeater's possum is marked by relatively warm, wet and stable climatic conditions.

Plant species that are key components of habitats occupied by Leadbeater's possum occurred in all three groups of taxa identified by PATN—*A. frigescens, A. obiquinervia* and *E. regnans,* in group 1, *E. nitens* and *A. dealbata* in group 2 and *E. delegatensis* in group 3. Thus, although Leadbeater's possum presently occurs within a relatively narrow subset of bioclimatic conditions within montane ash forests, the distribution of the species cannot be closely linked with the bioclimatic requirements of any particular species of plant or group of plants. Furthermore, the presence of montane ash forest alone cannot be used as an indicator of the presence of Leadbeater's possum because the species inhabits generally warmer and wetter areas within these plant communities. The apparent restriction of Leadbeater's possum to such areas is consistent with its known habitat requirements. Leadbeater's possum nests in very large hollow-bearing trees and forages in dense, luxuriant understory vegetation (Lindenmayer *et al.,* unpublished data). These types of habitat are most likely to occur in areas of high site productivity and thus favourable climatic conditions.

### *The Effects of Climate Change on Leadbeater's Possum.*

The distribution of Leadbeater's possum was much reduced under all the climatic scenarios (Table 4, Fig. 9). The core sub-component of the distribution was eliminated in many scenarios, but where it did remain it was always located in the Central Highlands of Victoria.

However, for the range sub-component of the distribution of Leadbeater's possum, areas supporting suitable bioclimatic conditions for the species were predicted to occur in the Otway Ranges, the Grampians and in Tasmania.

## *Discussion*

### *Bioclimatic Modelling and Wildlife Management*

Bioclimatic analyses add a new and important dimension to wildlife conservation and management. In this study, BIOCLIM has been used as a preliminary step in fauna survey, in an attempt to reduce the cost and increase the effectiveness of what is typically a very expensive aspect of wildlife inventory. This preliminary step has been made with just distribution records, and is important as distribution records may be the only relevant environmental information available for many species. Moreover, such analyses may elucidate factors which govern the distribution of a taxon. This can lead to a better understanding of the biology of the species and assist in the identification of suitable management strategies. Complete biological inventory is clearly impossible, but techniques such as bioclimatic modelling can predict potential distributions of taxa and provide a framework of information from which to make land-use decisions.

When used in conjuction with other packages such as PATN, BIOCLIM may help establish the bioclimatic relationships between taxa such as those between an animal and components of its habitat. This may help to identify other organisms which act as indicators of presence of the target taxon. This can be of substantial value, particularly in surveys.

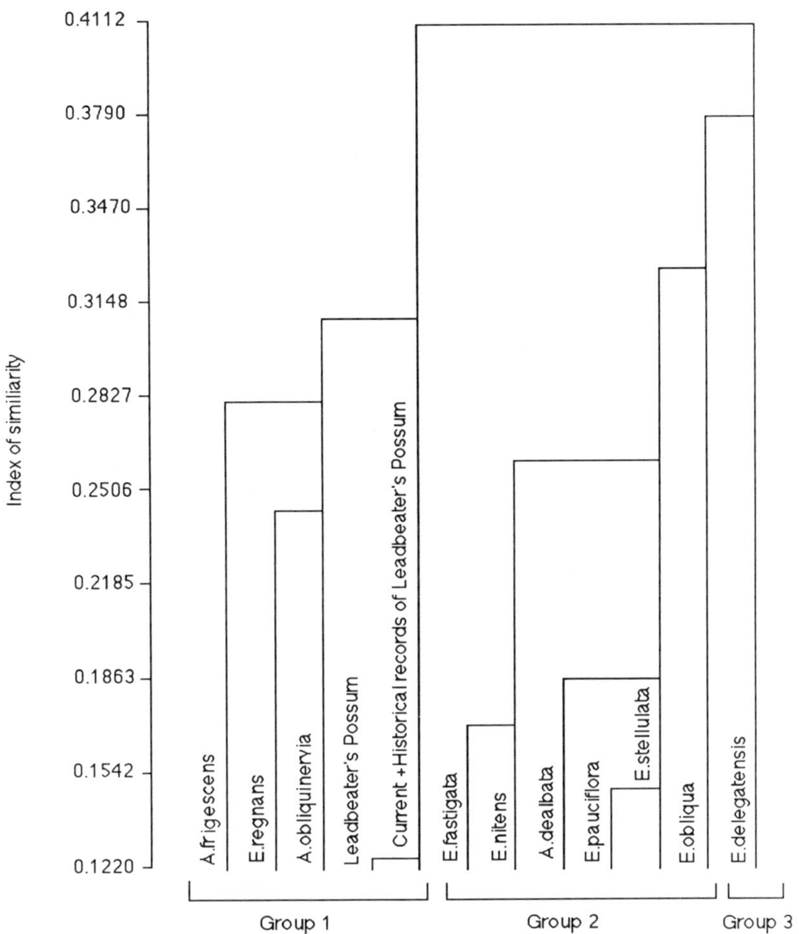


*Figure 6.*—Groups of taxa resulting from cluster analysis on the bioclimatic profiles of several plants and Leadbeater's possum using PATN (Belbin *et al.* 1984). The Gower index was used to show the level of association between taxa (see text).

## The Role of BIOCLIM and the Impact of Climate Change on Leadbeater's Possum

Some of the most important values of bioclimatic analyses using BIOCLIM are highlighted by the results of analyses of the anticipated impact of the GreenhouseEffect on Leadbeater's possum. The potential distribution of Leadbeater's possum was substantially reduced under all the climatic scenarios analysed and indicates the real possibility of the extinction of the species in the near future. This finding was not unexpected given the pre-dicted magnitude of climatic changes associated with the Greenhouse Effect, and the narrow set of bioclimatic conditions described for Leadbeater's possum. These anticipated climatic changes make it clear that conventional, passive and 'hands-off' forms of wildlife management may not be effective in the future. Wildlife management practices will need to be dynamic, flexible, adaptable and highly sophisticated, as areas set aside to conserve a particular species may not achieve such an objective within a relatively short time. Biocli-matic analyses can be used to identify areas with

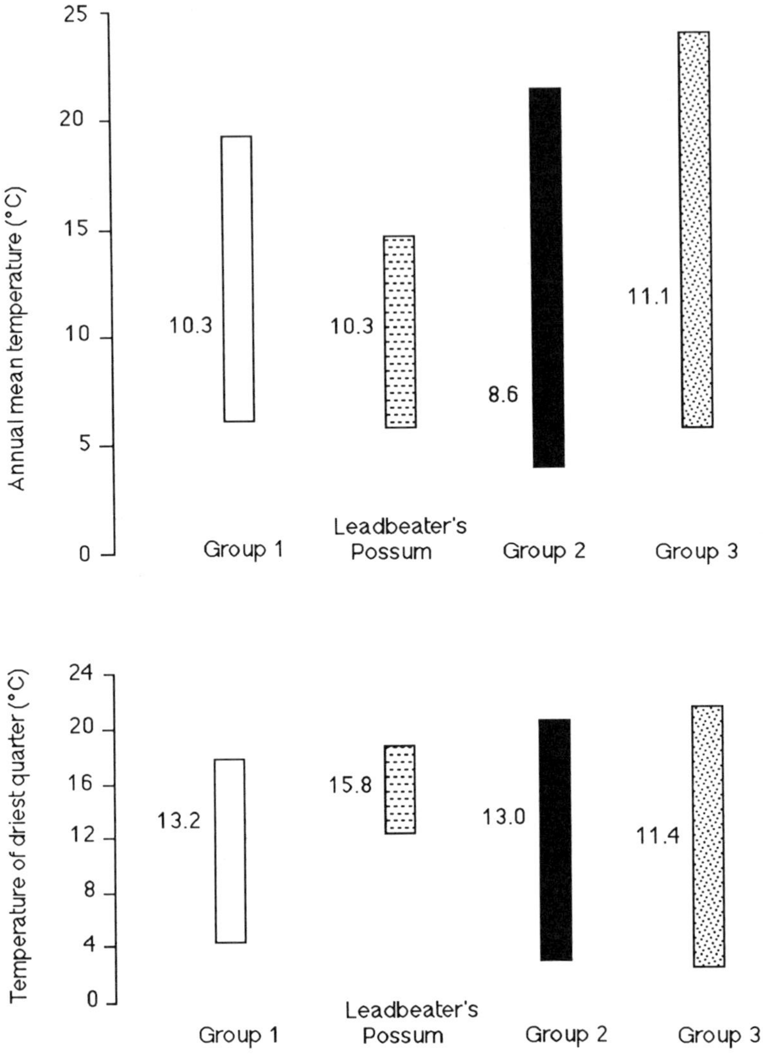



*Figure 7.*—Comparison of the mean and range of 2 indices of temperature from the bioclimatic profile of groups of taxa using PATN. Leadbeater's possum is a member of group 1 but is shown separately. The mean values for each group are listed next to each column. See text for members of each group.

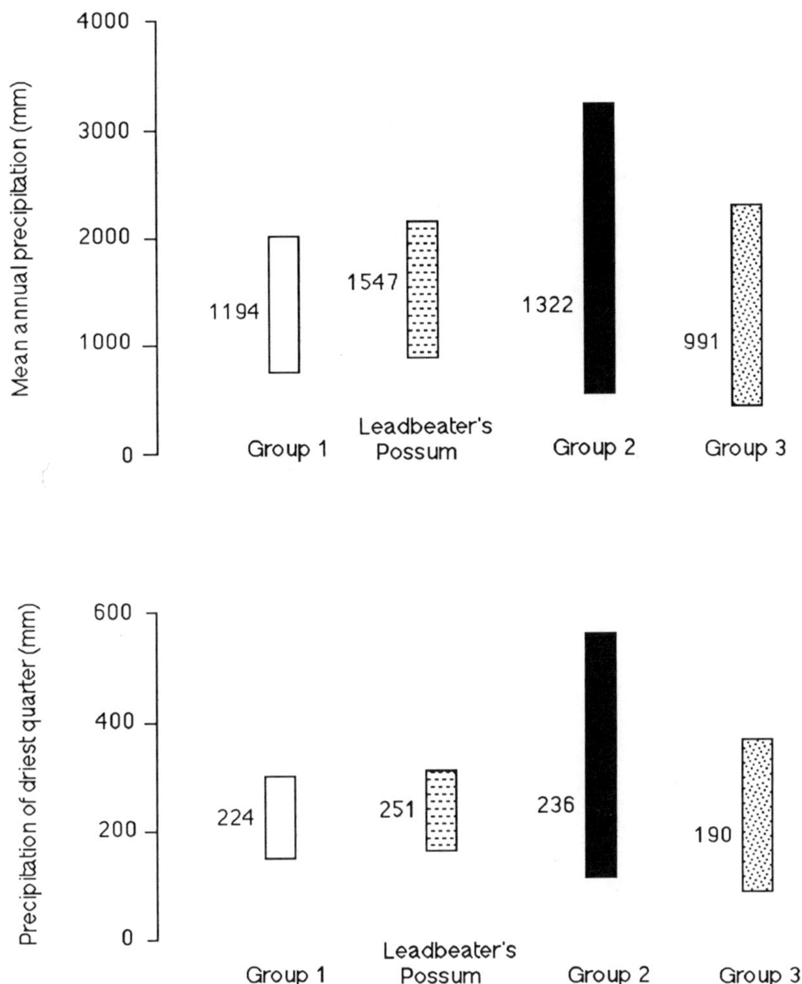


*Figure 8.*—A comparison of the mean and range of values for two indices of precipitation from the bioclimatic profiles of groups of taxa identified using PATN. Leadbeater's possum is a member of group 1 but has been shown separately. See text for members of each group. Mean values are listed next to the column for each group.

*Figure 9.*—The predicted core and range distribution of Leadbeater's possum under the anticipated impact of the Greenhouse Effect (scenario 5, see Table 3).

the greatest conservation value for a species both in the immediate and long term. As the distribution of a species may change in response to changes in climate, the location of reserves may have to be moved. For example, all the scenarios examined in this study indicate that within the next 50 years Snobs Creek Reserve is unlikely to remain climatically favourable for Leadbeater's possum. Thus, in our case study, the application of BIOCLIM has identified populations of Leadbeater's possum occurring at the margins of the distribution of the species that will become vulnerable to extinction in the near future. Thus

bioclimatic analyses indicate the need for a dynamic and flexible reserve system, but this can only be successful if: 1) the spatial distribution and abundance of the resources to be managed are determined; 2) fragmentation and destruction of habitats are minimized to ensure that a) all land in a given area retains the potential to become a reserve at any given time, b) dispersal can take place between areas and c) populations of target species such as Leadbeater's possum are kept as large and as contiguous as possible; 3) management practices are well-planned and their impacts are closely monitored.

The conservation of Leadbeater's possum must be concentrated in areas of predicted core distribution because these are most likely to contain suitable habitat for the species. The results of our study predict that such areas may only occur in the Central Highlands of Victoria. These areas should form the basis of a system of reserves for the species.

If they remain, areas of core environment for Leadbeater's possum are likely to be scattered throughout the Central Highlands of Victoria and will need to be linked by corridors of vegetation to prevent the distribution of Leadbeater's possum from becoming a series of isolated populations. The type, dimensions and spatial distribution of these links can only be determined from knowledge of the dispersal capabilities of the species. Therefore, studies of this aspect of the biology of Leadbeater's possum must become a research priority.

Whilst strategies for the conservation of Leadbeater's possum should be concentrated on reserves within the current and predicted future core distribution of the species, substantial buffer areas must surround each reserve because of the current uncertainity about future climatic changes. A wide range of altitudes and climates must be reserved in these buffers (Busby 1989; Main 1989), to maximize the chance that at least some suitable micro-climates and refugia may remain for the species. Large multiple-use biosphere reserves such as those designated in India (Saharia 1986) may be of a type with the flexibilty needed in future management of Leadbeater's possum.

Bioclimatic analyses indicate the need for a shift toward long-term management planning and the development of new, flexible and dynamic forms for wildlife and resource conservation. This is possibly one of the most important results of the use of BIOCLIM, for such changes in land-use planning will be essential if some species of wildlife are to survive the impacts of the Greenhouse Effect.

## Acknowledgments

We thank Dr P. Gullan and Mr P. Menkhorst of the Department of Conservation, Forests and Lands, Victoria, for providing distribution records of plants and Leadbeater's possum. Records of *Acacia* spp. were provided by the Gauba Museum (Department of Botany A.N.U.) and the National Botanic Gardens, Canberra. Comments from Dr T. Booth, Mr B. Mackey, Ms H.A. Desmond, Dr M. T. Tanton and Mr S.M. Davey improved early drafts of the manuscript.

## References

Archer, M.A. 1984. The Australian mammal radiation. In *Vertebrate Zoogeography and Evolution in Australia*. (Eds M.A Archer and G.C Clayton). Pp. 633-808. Hesperian Press: Carlisle, W.A.

Belbin, L. 1984. FUSE: A Fortran V program for agglomerative fusion for minicomputers. *Computers and Geosciences* **10**:361-384.

Belbin, L, Faith, D.P. and Minchin, P.R. 1984. Some algorithms contained in the Numerical Taxonomy Package, NTP. *C.S.I.R.O. Div. Water and Land Resources, Tech. Memo.* **84/23**.

Booth, T.W. 1985. A new method for assessing species selection. *Commonwealth For. Rev.* **64**: 241-250.

Booth, T.H., Nix, H.A., Hutchinson, M.F and Busby, J.R. 1987. Grid matching: a new method for homoclime analysis. *Agric. and For. Meteorology* **39**:241-255.

Booth, T.H., Nix, H.A., Hutchinson, M.F and Javanovic, T. 1988. Niche analysis and tree species distribution. *For. Ecol. Manage.* **23**:47-59.

Brazenor, C.W. 1932. A re-examination of *Gymnobelideus leadbeateri* McCoy. *Aust. Zool.* **7**:106-109.

Brazenor, C.W. 1950. *The Mammals of Victoria.* Handbook No. 1, National Museum of Victoria. Brown, Prior, Anderson: Melbourne.

Brazenor, C.W. 1962. Rediscovery of a rare Australian possum. *Proc. Zool. Soc. Lond.* **139**:529-531.

Broom, R. 1895a. Report on a bone breccia deposit near the Wombeyan Caves N.S.W., with descriptions of some new species of marsupials. *Proc. Linn. Soc. N.S.W.* **10**:48-61.

Broom, R. 1895b. On a small fossil marsupial with large grooved pre-molars. *Proc. Linn. Soc. N.S.W.* **10**:562-567.

Broome, L. 1979. *The Mammals of New South Wales.* University of New England: Armidale.

Brown, P.R. 1982. The history and status of Leadbeater's possum. In *Rare, endangered and limited gene-pool species in Australasia,* ed. C.B. Banks. Pp. 79-86. Proc. Aust. Soc. Zoo Keepers: Melbourne.

Busby, J.R. 1986. A biogeoclimatic analysis of *Nothofagus cunninghamii* Hook Oesrt in south-eastern Australia. *Aust. J. Ecol.* 11:1-7.

Busby, J.R. 1989. Potential implications of climate change on Australia's flora and fauna. In *Greenhouse: Planning for Climate Change,* ed. G.I. Pearman. Pp. 387-398. E.J. Brill: New York.

Calaby, J. 1960. Australia's threatened animals. *Oryx,* 5:381-386.

Cherry, K.A., Brown, G.W., Carr, G.W, Horrocks, G.F, Opie, A.M and Triggs, B.E. 1986. Flora and Fauna of the Buldah Forest Block, East Gippsland, Victoria. Ecological Survey Report No. 7. Dept. Cons., For. and Lands, Melbourne.

Cherry, K.A, Brown, G.W., Carr, G.W, Horrocks, Menkhorst, K.A., G.F, Opie, A.M and Triggs, B.E. 1987. Flora and Fauna of the Freezeout and Pyke Forest Blocks, East Gippsland, Victoria. Ecological Survey Report No. 13. Dept. Cons., For. and Lands, Melbourne.

Chesterfield, E.A., Macfarlane, M.A., Allen, D., Hutchinson, M.N., Triggs, B. and Barley, R. 1983. Flora and Fauna of the Rodger River Block, East Gippsland, Victoria. For. Comm. Vict., Melbourne.

Chippendale, G.M. and Wolfe, L. 1984. EUCALIST: a computerized data retrieval system for Eucalyptus (Myrtaceae). *Aust. For. Res.* 14:147-152.

Dixon, J.M. 1978. Mammals of the Australian Alps— a brief review of past work, with a view to the future. *Victorian Nat.* 95:216-219.

Flood, J.M. 1973. The Moth Hunters: an investigation toward a pre-history of the south-eastern highlands. Ph.D Thesis. A.N.U, Canberra.

Gower, J.C. 1971. A general coefficient of similiarity and some of its properties. *Biometrics* 27:857-871.

Hall, L.S. 1974. A recent bone deposit at Marble Arch, N.S.W. 10th Bien. Conf. Speleog. Fedn. 35-46.

Hope, J.H. 1973. Analysis of bone from Cloggs Cave, Buchan, north-east Victoria. Appendix XV in J. Flood. The Moth Hunters: an investigation toward a pre-history of the south-eastern highlands. Ph.D Thesis. A.N.U, Canberra.

Hutchinson, M.F. 1981. MAPROJ - a computer map projection system. C.S.I.R.O. Division of Land Use Research. Tech. Pap. No. 39.

Hutchinson, M.F. 1984. A summary of some surface fitting and contouring programs for noisy data. Consulting report A.C.T 84/6. Division of Math. and Div. of Water and Land Resources, C.S.I.R.O., Canberra.

Hutchinson, M.F. 1986. Fitting surfaces to terrain data. Pp. 63-64 in C.S.I.R.O. Div. Water and Land Resources, C.S.I.R.O., Canberra.

Hutchinson, M.F. 1989a. A new objective method for spatial interpolation of meteorological variables from irregular networks applied to the estimation of monthly mean solar radiation, temperature, precipitation and windrun. Proc. U.N.U. Workshop. Need for climatic and hydrologic data in agriculture in south-east Asia. CSIRO Div. Water Resources. Tech. Memo. 89/5, 95 -104.

Hutchinson, M.F. 1989b. A new technique for gridding elevation data and streamline data with automatic removal of spurious pits. *J. Hydrology* 106:211-232.

Hutchinson, M.F. and Bischof, R.J. 1983. A new method for estimating the spatial distribution of mean seasonal and annual rainfall applied to the Hunter Valley, New South Wales. *Aust. Met. Mag.* 31:179-184.

Hutchinson, M.F., Booth, T.H., McMahon, J.P and Nix, H.A. 1984. Estimating monthly mean values of daily solar radiation for Australia. *Solar Energy* 32:277-290.

Hutchinson, M.F. and Dowling, T.I. (in press). A new Digital Elevation Model for Australia. CRES Pap. Australian National University, Canberra.

Koppen, W. 1900. Versuch einer Klassification die Klimate verzugsweise nach ihren Beziehurgen zur Pfanzenwelt. *Geogr. Z.* 6:593-611 and 657-679.

Koppen, W. 1923. *Die Klimate der Erde.* Walter De Gruyter: Berlin.

Main, A.R. 1989. Climate change and its impact on nature conservation in Australia. In *Greenhouse: Planning for Climate Change,* ed. G.I. Pearman. Pp. 361-374. E.J. Brill: New York.

McCoy, F. 1867. On a new genus of phalanger. *Ann. and Mag. Nat. Hist.* 3:387-288.

Nix, H.A. 1981. The environment of Terra Australis. In *Ecological Biogeography of Australia,* ed. A. Keast. Pp. 105-133. Junk: The Hague.

Nix, H.A. 1986a. BIOCLIM - a bioclimatic analysis and prediction system. C.S.I.R.O Division Water and Land Resources Research Annual Report. Pp. 59-60. C.S.I.R.O., Canberra.

Nix, H.A. 1986b. A biogeographic analysis of the Australian elapid snakes. In *Atlas of Elapid Snakes. Australian Flora and Fauna Series No. 7,* ed. R.Longmore. Aust. Govt. Publ. Serv.: Canberra.

Nix, H.A. and Gillison, A.N. 1985. Towards an operational framework for habitat and wildlife management. In *Wildlife Management in the Forests and Forestry-controlled Lands in the Tropics of the Southern Hemisphere*, ed. J. Kikkawa. Pp. 39-55. Uni. Qld. Printery: Brisbane.

Pittock, A.B. 1988. Climatic catastrophes: the local and global effects of Greenhouse effects and nuclear winter. In *Natural and Man-made Hazards*, eds M.I. El-Sabh and T.S Murty. Pp. 621-633. D. Reidel: New York.

Pittock, A.B. 1989. Actual and anticipated changes in Australia's climate. In *Greenhouse: Planning for Climate Change*, ed. G.I. Pearman. Pp. 33-51. E.J. Brill: New York.

Pittock, A.B. and Nix, H.A. 1986. The effect of changing climate on Australian biomass production. *Climate Change* 8:243-255.

Ride, W.D. 1970. *Native Mammals of Australia*. Oxford Uni. Press, Melbourne.

Robertson, P.J., Alexander, J., Lumsden, L. and Silveira, C. 1983. Preliminary report on the Mt. Wills (Apline area) faunal survey. Unpublished report, Arthur Rylah Institute for Environmental Research, Melbourne.

Saharia, V.B. 1986. Strategies and guidelines for sanctuaries and national parks in India. In *The Development of International Principles and Practices of Wildlife Research and Management: Asian and American Approaches*, eds S.H. Berwick and V.B. Saharia. Pp. 31-42. Workshop on techniques in wildlife research and management. Kanha, India.

Seebeck, J.H., Suckling, G.C. and Macfarlane, M.A. 1983. Leadbeater's Possum—survey by stagwatching. *Victorian Nat.* 100:92-97.

Smith, A.P. 1980. The diet and ecology of Leadbeater's Possum and the Sugar Glider. Ph.D. Thesis, Monash University, Melbourne.

Smith, A.P., Lindenmayer, D.B. and Suckling, G.C. 1985. The ecology and management of Leadbeater's Possum. Research Report to World Wildlife Fund, University of New England, Armidale, N.S.W.

Smith, A.P., and Lindenmayer, D.B. 1988. Tree hollow requirements of Leadbeater's Possum and other possums and gliders in timber production forests of the Victorian Central Highlands. *Aust. Wildl. Res.* 15:347-362

Tate, G.H. 1945. Results of the Archbold expeditions. No. 55. Notes on the squirrel-like and mouse-like possums (Marsupialia). *Am. Mus. Novit.* 1305:1-12.

Thornthwaite, C.W. 1931. The climates of North America according to a new classification. *Geogr. Rev.* 21:633-655.

Troughton, E. le G. 1973. *Furred Animals of Australia*. Angus and Robertson: Sydney.

Wakefield, N.A. 1960a. Recent mammal bones in the Buchan district. *Victorian Nat.* 77:164-168.

Wakefield, N.A. 1960b. Recent mammal bones in the Buchan district. *Victorian Nat.* 77:227- 240.

Wakefield, N.A. 1967. Mammal bones in the Buchan district. *Victorian Nat.* 84:211-214.

Wakefield, N.A. 1970. Mammals of east Gippsland. *Walk* 21:14-19.

Wakefield, N.A. 1972. Palaeoecology of fossil mammal assemblages from some Australian caves. *Proc. R. Soc. Victoria* 85:1-26.

Wilkinson, H.E. 1961. The rediscovery of Leadbeater's Possum, *Gymnobelideus leadbeateri* McCoy. *Victorian Nat.* 78:97-102.

Woodward, F.I. 1987. *Climate and Plant Distribution*. Cambridge University Press: Cambridge.

# Workshop Sessions

*Tim W. Clark[1], John H. Seebeck[2] and Denise Casey[3]*

## Introduction

Five workshops offered Conference participants an opportunity to express their views on a range of topics, all directly relevant to the conservation of biodiversity. Participants were asked to examine several major constraints to conservation and to develop some recommendations to improve collective performance. Positive approaches and proactive responses were sought in considering 'what needs to be done?' and 'how might this be achieved?' Both the questions addressed by working groups and their answers are summarized. The editors have inserted background material or additional ideas in some cases and have indicated this.

## Workshop 1. Policies, Legislation and Funding

*Is there need for change in government policy and subsequent legislation? How can private/corporate funding for conservation be improved? How do we encourage a philanthropic attitude in the private sector?*

The group concluded that there is an urgent need for additional policies to conserve biodiversity and to make existing policies consistent with one another.

Before expanding on these two points, the editors will first briefly examine 'policy' and the 'policy process' to help understand what is involved in policy improvements and new policy development. Policy, most simply defined, 'is a broad strategic statement of intent to accomplish aims' (Brewer and deLeon 1983, p. 30). More specifically, policy is that complex set of interactive decisions and actions by which societies and governments establish goals based on their values and establish the means to reach those goals (Ham and Hill 1987). Many policies are codified into law and are supported by additional agency regulations. Policy scientists have identified six phases through which all policies and programs pass over time—initiation, estimation, selection, implementation, evaluation and termination (Brewer and deLeon 1983).

Unfortunately, most people do not understand policy as this lengthy process, but instead consider it to be only the first three phases, commonly called policy formulation. Thus, the critical role of the implementation phase is often underappreciated or overlooked. This is the phase where most biologists work as researchers, managers or conservationists, often in government bureaucracies. They usually see themselves simply as experts, workers or administrators carrying out policies that were formulated earlier, when in fact they are integral parts of the policy process and

[1]Department of Conservation Biology, Chicago Zoological Society, Brookfield, Illinois 60513, U.S.A.
[2]National Parks and Wildlife Division, Department of Conservation, Forests and Lands. Arthur Rylah Institute for Environmental Research, 123 Brown Street, Heidelberg, Victoria 3084, Australia.
[3]Northern Rockies Conservation Cooperative, Box 2705, Jackson, Wyoming 83001, U.S.A.

have broad scope in deciding how to interpret policies and how to carry them out. Indeed, their interpretations and activities *are* the realization of the policies. They are often subject to considerable political influence on both their interpretations and implementation (Clarke and McCool 1985).

It is critical that conservation managers, scientists and administrators understand this. As Clark and Kellert (1988, p. 7) noted, 'if the field of wildlife science is to contribute fully and adequately to the critical societal decisions affecting the future abundance and well-being of our nation's fauna and flora, then it seems essential that young wildlife professionals be sufficiently educated in the complexities, subtleties and techniques of the policy process.'

Returning to the workshop, the group made several specific proposals. New policy is needed to add further protection to Australia's biodiversity. This policy should be comprehensive, focussed on protecting intact ecosystems and restoring those currently damaged. Because many ecosystems and all larger-scale ecological processes (*e.g.* air flows, hydrology, nutrient cycling) can be continental, and in many cases, global in scale, new policy must recognize these ecological realities. The future survival of nations ultimately depends on the welfare of the biodiversity and ecological processes of all nations. The new policy should transcend state boundaries and therefore must be national and international in scope. It must be far-reaching, visionary and offer real strategic guidance to conserve an irreplaceable living natural heritage.

Additionally, much of the existing environmental legislation is in conflict with itself. For example, policy to conserve endangered species is in conflict with policy to cut timber, and there are requirements to remove noxious weeds, which provide habitat for eastern barred bandicoots. Indeed, the Victorian *Flora and Fauna Guarantee Act* (see Freeman, this volume) conflicts with lots of actions—land clearance, pest control, even

service legislation controlling areas such as water, electricity, roads and railways. A comprehensive review of all environmental legislation is needed with a view towards eliminating, or at least reducing, the contradictions. Complementary policy, as well as a policy 'package' that is holistic in its coverage, is needed at several scales—local, state, national and international. The federal government should become very active in these efforts.

Under the Australian Constitution, the various states have legislative autonomy concerning the conservation of natural resources. The Australian Government cannot directly control state conservation issues, only those occurring within federally-administered Territories. State issues can be affected by use of other legislative mechanisms such as the non-issue of Export Licences, *e.g.* for woodchips, Quarantine Acts, Heritage Listing, or Customs Acts.

When it comes to policy implementation, several recommendations were made by the group. Firstly, coordination is needed to enhance policy implementation, especially in cases like the Murray/ Darling river systems and CONCOM (Council of Nature Conservation Ministers), which has a series of working groups concerning Utilization of Wildlife, Endangered Fauna, Endangered Flora, Migratory and Wetland Birds, Rabbit Control, etc. Secondly, the effectiveness of implementation needs to be critically evaluated so we can learn and upgrade our capabilities. Thirdly, there is a need for 'a managerial revolution in government to avoid parochialism,' as the workshop group put it. That is to say, petty jealousies and narrow-minded self-interest may surface when several departments are involved in a conservation issue, as might rigid adherence to bureaucratic rules, roles, and regulations and more concern with procedural correctness than with saving species. Thus, government employees need to be explicitly knowledgeable in how to set up and operate successful programs to ensure that policy is implemented well. Both individuals and organizational systems must learn quickly, correct mistakes, and move ahead in conservation. And fourthly, Environmental Effects Statements need to be consistent and ought to be guided by written Codes of Practice. They can be made more effective by having the user—whoever intends to modify the environment, individuals, corporations, or government—pay for the costs of the original effects assessment, necessary rehabilitation measures and subsequent monitoring and follow-up activities.

Private and corporate funding for conservation in Australia is not generally seen as a valuable or useful activity, although World Wildlife Fund Australia has been relatively successful. Overall, there needs to be a more professional and concerted educational effort focussed on the public and private sectors. They must be made to understand that there is a direct connection between the kind of life they and their children live and the quality of the environment, including the integrity of global biodiversity. Messages must be targeted to potential contributors in an effective way so that they feel they are taking responsibility and action for solution. The group discussed the prospect of an individual levy paid through municipal governments and targeted specifically for the environment. To succeed in conserving biodiversity, much more effective public and private education and fund-raising skills are needed.

Supplemental ideas from the editors include hiring professional fundraisers for conservation organizers; hiring professional advertising firms to 'sell' conservation of biodiversity just like they sell any commercial product; meaningful government publicity campaigns that serve to educate about conservation and convince the public of its values; thinking BIG in terms of international sources for funding and national, global and long-term scales of publicity; convincing big business that it is good business to contribute to conservation; making person-to-person contacts on the basis that people give money to people, not to ideas; and encouraging high-profile individuals to carry the message to their fans or clients—rock stars, movie stars, sports stars, investment bankers, whoever the public listens to (as rock star Peter Garrett has done for the Australian Conservation Foundation).

*References*


Brewer, G. D., and deLeon, P. 1983. *The Foundations of Policy Analysis.* Dorsey Press: Homewood, Ill. 476 pp.

Clark, T. W., and Kellert. S.R. 1988. Toward a policy paradigm of the wildlife sciences. *Renew. Res. J.* Winter:7-16.

Clarke, J. N., and McCool, D. 1985. *Staking Out The Terrain: Power Differentials Among Natural Resource Management Agencies.* State University of New York: Albany. 189 pp.

Ham, C., and Hill, M. 1987. *The Policy Process in the Modern Capitalistic State.* Wheatsheaf Books: Sussex, England. 210 pp.


## Workshop 2. Community Roles

*What extra things can the community do for conservation? Why are they not doing them now? In what ways can conservation be translated to the public?*

One theme underlies all the comments of this workshop, that it is important that details of conservation problems and solutions reach people. Also, many programs and policies are already in place through which people can work. Owing to the diversity of the target groups in communities, a variety of educational and action strategies is needed to ensure that the community is informed and attracted to conservation opportunities.

There are many things that can be done by the community for conservation, but people must know what issues are pressing and relevant to them. It is easier to get the public concerned about conservation of koalas (*Phascolarctos cinereus*) than invertebrates (see Yen *et al.*, this volume) and this will always be a problem. One way around this is to stress the need for ecosystem conservation, whereby not only certain vertebrates—with which the public can identify—are protected, but also the many other species that comprise the ecosystem. Brolgas (*Grus rubicunda*), for example, could be a good selling-point for wetland conservation.

The media could be very helpful in treating conservation issues more thoroughly and seriously, but for a host of reasons currently tend not to. Often the media trivialize important issues, treating them as comic or cute curiosities, or they simplify complex, important issues or distort them into 'green vs. greed' stories of conflict. Wildlife receives more frequent and thorough coverage than other conservation issues, yet the 'story' is too often a melodramatic or sensational look at individual animals, such as the three Alaskan whales 'saved' from the closing ice mass recently. The media themselves must be educated about the importance of the conservation of biodiversity.

Landowners, communities and citizens can get involved in many additional ways. Landowners could be encouraged to be more aware of flora and fauna on their property and report sightings to their neighbours, the community and the agencies. The recent 'Urban Wildlife Watch' programs demonstrate the enthusiasm that can be generated by such activities and the potential for data-gathering. These could certainly be expanded to the rural community. More 'expert' input by scientists, managers and conservationists into community issues and into larger policy initiatives might be helpful. Broad-acre environmental degradation needs more attention, including plantings, wildlife habitat improvements and study of the implications of using introduced grasses, superphosphate and pesticides. The LandCare Groups, set up by Victoria's Department of Conservation, Forests and Lands and concerned with soil conservation, could be expanded with a view of aiding wildlife, too. Landowners should be encouraged to preserve vegetation on 'bush blocks'. 'Land for Wildlife' is a CFL/Bird Observers Club program that encourages rural and semi-rural landowners to become involved in wildlife conservation: after approval, participants receive advice, assistance, signs, and other benefits. The relationship between the conservation of biodiversity and the ultimate requirement for habitat conservation needs more publicity. Communities could develop 'environmental resource centres' to lead public activities and education. Various existing community groups could be enlisted to get the information out, as many individuals may not automatically use the centres. Extensive re-vegtation projects such as 'Tree Victoria' and 'Go Green' are needed on both public and private lands: government could help coordinate many of these activities within and between community groups. New and novel ways to fund these activities are required, such as money from recycling projects. The notion of 'Whole Farm Planning' is excellent and this idea needs to be expanded to whole community management, including lands and habitats for flora and fauna.

The workshop group felt that the major limitation was lack of public awareness and education, both remedial problems. One problem is that some citizens will not get involved in conservation efforts unless the economic benefits can be made clear. The economic benefits of living in a healthy environment seem, all too often, to go unnoticed. Others feel they have nothing to contribute; they need to realize that every little bit helps and that, in complex societies, everyone must do his or her part and assume responsibility for seeing that it gets done. Another barrier is stereotypes: some people view conservationists as 'greenies', a pejorative term. Government should take the lead in breaking down these stereotypes so that individuals working for a clean healthy environment are seen as civic-minded, responsible citizens.

Part of the problem in making the conservation message effective and getting people active is to identify target groups: school children; city dwellers with little or no contact with the land; developers and buyers of both bush blocks and suburban properties; the corporate world; philanthropists; politicians and elected officials; State and Municipal officials involved in land use planning, engineering, covenants, etc. Educating school children is helpful in meeting long-term problems, but unfortunately, many problems are immediate.

A policy of penalties, whereby polluters and others who damage the environment are required to pay fines, have their work curtailed or suffer some other penalties, could be effective in preventing environmental degradation. Environmental 'offenders' ought to be made to undergo a course in conservation ecology: better yet is to target people whose jobs may affect the environment in order to prevent damage rather than punish it. Any and all education that can be organized should be supported and carried out at the earliest possible date. There is a need to use existing groups, such as LandCare Groups, to work for increased community awareness and action.

## Workshop 3. Role of Tertiary Institutions

*Is training for future conservation biologists and managers adequate? Should more emphasis be placed on the concepts discussed at this conference in designing general and/or specific courses? What should be the relationships between government and tertiary institutions as research agencies? How can we develop complementary use of the special skills residing in both areas?*

As background to this workshop's comments, the editors define conservation biology as 'a new stage in the application of science to conservation problems' (Soulé 1985, p. 727) with 'strong roots in wildlife and park management' (Ginsberg 1987, p. 262). The content of this relatively new field is synthetic, eclectic and multidisciplinary, and represents a mix of applied and theoretical concepts and tools. It seeks 'to understand the scientific principles underlying phenomena such as species extinction, the role of genetic variation in species persistence, and the maintenance of habitat diversity. Conservation biology also applies these principles directly to the management of natural areas and endangered species' (Brussard 1985, p. 10). But many of the principles of conservation biology have yet to be adequately refined and articulated because the body of relevant theory behind the concepts is just now beginning to be translated into practical form (Wilcox 1987). Several universities around the world are now teaching courses in conservation biology and more are expected over the next few years.

The workshop group felt that university training for future conservation biologists could be improved with the addition of several courses. The undergraduate level should continue to focus on general biological concepts, but more specialised courses like conservation biology should be taught at the post-graduate level. They felt that the Conference is further evidence that a multidisciplinary approach is the most promising one for species and ecosystem conservation, that the case study approach was invaluable and that the Conference proceedings could be of great value for tertiary training of conservation biologists and managers. The editors, however, felt that at least one semester of conservation biology ought to be integrated into other curricula as well, including technologists, economists, lawyers and humanities students—indeed, all undergraduate students—to sow the seeds of interdisciplinary thought and environmental awareness.

The time is right for greatly expanded communication and cooperation between tertiary institutions and government agencies. Mutual assistance programs could help maintain and upgrade high university standards and provide the quality of graduates needed by agencies to maintain and improve professional standards. Conservation is rapidly becoming increasingly complicated and many technical tools are needed to manage complex systems. This, in turn, requires a high degree of professionalization—both in the narrow specialists' sense, but also in being able to synthesize and integrate vast amounts of information from multiple perspectives into an overall strategy or policy for action. Tertiary institutions around the world are weak in training for this latter type of professionalism.

Tertiary institutions are already providing considerable volunteer time in direct support of many government programs, and governments should begin to budget for this support. Not only would financial support directly aid government projects by ensuring the best and most up-to-date information about a given problem, but it would also serve broader community and professional needs by maintaining a more diverse and responsive body of expertise to assist in solving conservation problems. Many benefits could be expected from more recognition by government of the advantages of such a relationship and the establishment of a special pool of competitive funds for faculty to draw from to do basic and applied research for conservation. State conservation departments may be in an optimal position to obtain funds from Federal environmental projects and redistribute them to tertiary institutions in support of the overall goal of improved management and conservation.

Co-supervision of Honours and post-graduate students should be encouraged. Agency experts should give guest lectures in such courses as conservation biology and demonstrate examples of applied biology. Scholarships to encourage students into conservation studies are essential. Conferences such as this one are particularly effective in bringing together a wide array of professionals interested in a common goal. Publication of the proceedings and of other material describing cooperative projects will be helpful in meeting these concerns.

The editors would like to contribute a few additional ideas. Firstly, universities should increase communication, coordination and collaboration with private conservation organisations, from grassroots levels to national and international groups. The same benefits would accrue to both parties as in increased relationships with government. This coalition—especially if it were a three-way university/government/conservation group coalition—would form a powerful new alliance for conservation. Secondly, high-level strategists from both government and private conservation organisations—those who plan their organisation's or their nation's conservation goals, roles, policies and projects—should be invited to help plan and develop pertinent university curricula. Thirdly, among the possible additional forms of relationship between government and universities are internships, cadetships, work/study programs and exchanges to benefit both students and staff.

## References


Brussard, P. F. 1985. The current status of conservation biology. *Bull. Ecol. Soc. Am.* **66**:9-11.

Ginsberg, J. R. 1987. What is conservation biology? *Trends in Ecol. and Evol.* 2:262-264.

Soulé, M. 1985. What is conservation biology? *BioScience* **35**:727-734.

Wilcox, B. A. 1987. Editorial. *Conserv. Biol.* 1:188-189.


## Workshop 4. Environmental Ethics

*What use is the maintenance of biodiversity? A common question is 'Why bother saving endangered or any species?' Is there a simple way of communicating the answers?*

The values of biodiversity to humankind are well documented (Myers 1979; Ehrlich and Ehrlich 1981; Wilson 1989). Species extinctions result in the loss of new and old food sources, pharmaceutical products, predators for biological control of pests, building materials, fuels, wood products, opportunities to improve genetics (to enhance crop resistance to disease and droughts and to improve domestic animal stock), and the loss of many other benefits. Besides these clearly utilitarian values, flora and fauna and their ecological processes have many other long-term values, including ecological, ethical, educational, scientific and aesthetic. Rolston (1975, p. 94; see also 1981) spoke to the heart of the ethical issue: 'There is...something mostly naive about living in an anthropocentric reference frame in which one species takes itself as absolute and from which one values everything else relative to its utility.' Although the ethical and logical and utilitarian arguments are powerful, they have done little to move public opinion to establish conservation as a high societal goal. As yet, it does not figure prominently in world political, economic or social systems; it does not even rate highly among environmental issues—pollution, air and water quality, climatic change, and ozone depletion all receive more public, political and scientific attention. These are all, of course, essential ecosystem-level or global processes, but the public needs to understand that loss of biodiversity poses equally serious problems. The public at large is simply unaware of the immense value of biodiversity and why we need to protect it.

The workshop group on community education and actions suggested several ways to bring the message to the public through schools, existing and new community groups, and the powerful role of the media. The group on tertiary education suggested new alliances between government agencies and universities and new curricula. This workshop group pointed out that, at a societal level, people need to feel or can be made to feel that they have an investment in the future, and understanding the benefits of biodiversity, which are all around us, should be an important part of the goals of education. With the loss of biodiversity comes the loss of choices in the future, choices about how people want to live, choices for making full use of the value of the land. The environmental movement worldwide is trying to set the conservation agenda, and people need the opportunity to make the right choices.

The editors add, too, that the answers to 'why save species' are not difficult—the principles of the linkages between all life-forms and their functional processes are taught at elementary levels. The key is to convince people to take responsibility, to comprehend the large geographic and time scales involved, to make a connection between their own well-being and the flora and fauna of the world, and to embrace the fact that, as Aldo Leopold put it, 'to keep every cog and wheel is the first precaution of intelligent tinkering.'

*References*

Ehrlich, P. R., and Ehrlich, A. 1981. *Extinction: the Causes and Consequences of the Disappearance of Species*. Random House: New York. 304 pp.
Leopold, A. 1966. *A sand county almanac with essays on conservation from* Round River. Ballantine Books: New York.
Myers, N. 1979. *The Sinking Ark*. Pergamon Press: New York. 307 pp.
Rolston, H. III. 1975. Is there an ecological ethic? *Ethics* **85**:93-109.
Rolston, H. III. 1981. Values in nature. *Envir. Ethics* **3**:113-128.
Wilson, E. O. 1989. Threats to biodiversity. *Sci. Amer.* **261**:60-66.

*Workshop 5. Are We Using the Appropriate Ecological Strategies for Small Population Conservation?*

*Ecosystem management, reserves and corridors are accepted strategies. Are they enough? How is management on private land—an essential component in many cases—best achieved? Can 'supertechnology' help?*

This workshop concluded that we need to shift our conservation strategies to more large-scale ecological management through anticipatory, proactive responses, although this does not mean that we should give up on single-species efforts that currently confront us. These large-scale conservation approaches, sometimes called ecosystem management, should concentrate on ecosystem and community scales. Existing park and reserve systems should be critically evaluated from the point of view of ecosystem management and asked if can they currently sustain viable populations of keystone and other target species—remembering, of course, that species should be represented in several reserves if we are to provide the necessary insurance against extinction. The workshop group noted that many parks and reserves are too small, too few and too widely-spaced to conserve a significant portion of the biodiversity of the region or continent. Obviously, they need to be expanded or managed in concert with surrounding lands in a way that is compatible with the conservation of ecosystems as well as target species. In nearly all cases, connecting parks and preserves with ecologically useful corridors is essential. This will require new ways to think about and manage the land (including cooperative arrangements between public and private lands), and schemes for obtaining adquate funding and for institution building to ensure that the goals are accomplished. The first step is to assemble existing data about parks, reserves and corridors into a database of an appropriate scale to be meaningful. This effort will probably reveal that new and more complete information is needed. Evaluation of databases on existing parks, preserves and connecting corridors should be followed by appropriate policy development, action planning and successful implementation.

One of two sessions that dealt with the question of appropriate ecological strategies discussed corridors in depth. Corridors are a potentially powerful conservation tool. The idea is that isolated patches of habitat can be connected with strips of similar habitat. This would allow formerly isolated, small populations to be made viable through the interchange of individuals living in and dispersing through these corridors. This, of course, theoretically ameliorates extinction risks from inbreeding and genetic drift, for example. For these reasons, the notion of corridors is important and exciting. Corridors or linear reserves, such as rail reserves, have intrinsic value (see Scarlett and Parsons, this volume) beyond their potential value in connecting two or more previously isolated habitat islands. However, two types of information are needed about corridors to help evaluate their utility in conservation: are corridors actually used by dispersing plants and animals, and what is the fate of dispersing organisms? Do they actually contribute genetically to the population in the new home? Of course, corridors themselves can vary in length, width, internal characteristics, ratio of edge to internal area and in many other ways. Species will respond in different ways to all these characteristics. Corridor designs and management may be species-specific. Clearly,

much more research is needed before we understand the contribution of corridors in conservation management.

Although issues concerning private land were addressed in Workshop 2, the suite of techniques available can be reiterated. Without commitment by the landholders, the task of protecting land is much more difficult. In Victoria, if a landholder's actions threaten a species or ecosystem, the Government can intervene by means of an Interim Development Order, a last resort which is limited in duration. Negotiation or land purchase are better resolutions, although not always practical, economical or desirable. State or municipalities can erect covenants over land-use, or they can be voluntary as occurs with Victorian Conservation Trust agreements with landholders. In addition, Victoria has 'Whole Farm Planning', 'Tree Victoria' and 'Land for Wildlife'. Sensitively-handled, 'correct' land management in critical areas can perhaps be achieved in the present climate, but there is a need for an integrated approach—not legislative but organizational, not compulsory but voluntary. We need to take advantage of existing sympathetic concerns felt by many rural people.

Conservation in the modern age is much easier because we can collect, collate and analyse data at a rate not dreamt of a decade ago. Complex planning is thus possible and complex action achievable. Predictive modelling such as that demonstrated at this Conference gives us a powerful glimpse of the future, essential to convince those who hold the purse strings. Organismal study by remote sensing techniques is widely used—refined radio-telemetry, satellite tracking, laptop computers, implantable markers, radioactive dyes, radioimmune assay of reproductive hormones, DNA fingerprinting, tissue culture, and the list goes on. As technology improves, the capacity for this study is widened. Data can now be analysed virtually as it is collected, thus permitting adaptive responses to programs. These are still just tools, however; qualified biologists still need to be in the field.

# Conclusions

*Denise Casey[1], Tim W. Clark[1,2] and John H. Seebeck[3]*

## Introduction

Several conclusions can be drawn from the preceding papers and introductory materials. In this section, the papers and introductory remarks are referred to simply by the authors' names.

## Heavy Losses in Australian Flora and Fauna

Certainly, all the case materials documented the horrifying truth that the loss of biodiversity on the continent has hit taxa at all levels and continues unabated. In their introductory paper, Clark *et al.* cited some of the statistics for the continent: 2,206 species of vascular plants in 150 families and 654 genera are extinct, vulnerable or threatened— 11% of the estimated total vascular flora; 97 taxa of vertebrates are endangered, half of them mammals. Yen *et al.* reported that Australia has over 100,000 insect species alone (not to mention other diverse invertebrates), half of them not named, many not even collected.

None of Australia's major ecosystems has escaped the impacts of human activity. Clark *et al.* reported that the pastoral industry has greatly modified foothill forests, woodlands, mallee, shrublands and tussock grasslands of the semi-arid inland areas. Entire ecosystems in higher rainfall areas have been converted to wheat growing and improved pasture. Vast tracts of dense eucalypt and sub-tropical rain forests of the Great Dividing Range and coastal plains and the jarrah forests of south-western Western Australia have been cleared. Forests have been cut, wetlands drained, rivers dammed. Salinization is widespread. The introduction of rabbits, foxes, pigs, donkeys, horses, camels, cats and other exotic species has greatly modified plant communities across the continent and devastated native animal communities through predation and competition. The contraction and fragmentation of habitats were recounted in each of the case studies—Victoria's western grasslands for the eastern barred bandicoot as well as the southern Australian daisy. And, as Scarlett and Parsons pointed out for the daisy, remaining refugia are usually so small and scattered as to be 'unconservable' in the long term.

The disruption of critical ecological processes has had a serious impact on Australian ecosystems. Scarlett and Parsons described the impacts on grassland communities and Menkhorst *et al.* described the loss of orange-bellied parrot food plants, both because of changed fire regimes. Smales *et al.* determined the complex ecological relationships implicated in the demise of the helmeted honeyeater, beginning with the cutting of dry sclerophyll forests. Seebeck *et al.* documented the demise of the eastern barred bandicoot, largely thought to be the result of both systematic factors and stochastic events.

[1]Northern Rockies Conservation Cooperative, Box 2705, Jackson, Wyoming 83001, U.S.A.
[2]Department of Conservation Biology, Chicago Zoological Society, Brookfield, Illinois 60513, U.S.A.
[3]National Parks and Wildlife Division, Department of Conservation, Forest and Lands, Victoria. Arthur Rylah Institute for Environmental Research, 123 Brown Street, Heidelberg, Victoria 3084, Australia.

*Myths and Misconceptions About the Extinction Process*

There seems to be a need for a better grasp of and, indeed, belief in the 'extinction vortex' which engulfs species and populations. For instance, though the plight of the eastern barred bandicoot has been known for at least 10 years, shock registered in the Conference participants when the grim results of the population viability assessment and the genetic analysis for the bandicoot were presented. The speed at which stochastic events can overtake populations and the inexorability of genetic problems had not been fully appreciated, even by this audience of professional biologists.

There is evidence of lingering skepticism, perhaps even complacency, about the perils of extinctions and the existence of proven techniques to counteract them. 'Extinction is a natural process—why fight it?' 'It's only a subspecies; I'm not sure we should be trying to save it.' 'Species X was down to the last male and female and now the population is over 100.' 'If we lose the species, then we lose it—we did our best.' The arguments against these untenable attitudes have been well attested; here, we can only say that 1) extinction at the current rate is not natural and evolution and speciation is not occurring at a fast enough rate to replace rapidly-lost species; 2) species are made up of subspecies and populations, and therefore, all populations and all taxonomic levels need to be protected; 3) such 'success' stories, though widely bandied about, are actually extremely rare, they are not the rule, and few such species have been restored to total numbers, numbers of populations and adequate habitat to be out of danger; and 4) considering the unthinkable risks and costs of diminishing biodiversity, we simply cannot give up already.

Another misconception, demonstrated in Smales *et al.,* is that habitat protection alone is a panacea. Similarly, Yen *et al.* pointed out that the precise environmental requirements of many invertebrates necessitate specific management rather than the general protection of natural areas. Other as-yet-untested assumptions that were mentioned in the Conference are that protection of plant communities will automatically preserve their faunal associates and that corridors provide adequate interchange of individuals from isolated populations.

*Scientific Gaps*

Clark *et al.* reviewed the kinds of knowledge necessary for the recovery of small populations—key life-history features, population dynamics, genetic and evolutionary concerns, and the use of these data in exploratory, predictive models. Several authors agree on the importance of reliable knowledge, and many of the cases, unfortunately, demonstrate the lack of basic data.

The eastern barred bandicoot case alone demonstrates gaps in the basic knowledge needed for conservation (not to mention the many additional, interesting scientific questions that could be addressed). George *et al.* noted that the taxonomic status of the mainland population is not clear. Coulson called for fundamental behavioral research which could contribute significantly to the species' conservation. The decision analysis by Maguire *et al.* had to proceed with a dearth of hard data about bandicoot ecology, distribution and abundance, mortality factors and the efficacy of habitat improvements. Minta *et al.* attempted to fill some of the gaps in the knowledge of bandicoot population dynamics with reliable and rigorous techniques. Lenghaus *et al.* questioned the assumptions being made about bandicoot deaths in light of the lack of research on the effects of pesticides and other broadacre chemicals. Several times during the Conference, the value of the more secure Tasmanian population was offered for comparative research into bandicoot behavior and ecology and for testing proposed management measures.

The orange-bellied parrot and helmeted honeyeater cases highlighted the risks of implementing management procedures without the data to confirm the value of those procedures—false starts and undefined recovery goals waste precious time, money and public confidence.

Yen *et al.* related the special scientific problems associated with invertebrate conservation—their enormous numbers, the fact that many remain undescribed, the difficulty of identification in both laboratory and field, the existence of divergent life-forms, the wide diversity of taxa in many communities and unclear ecological roles, the complexity of sampling methods, and unknown distribution patterns, to name just a few. Concomitant with these are serious conceptual barriers in getting people and governments to appreciate the critical and immense role of invertebrates (which constitute 95+% of the world's animal species) in ecosystem functioning.

## Program Problems

A number of program problems appeared in the case studies presented in this volume. The discussions of bandicoot management strategies by Seebeck and by Arnold *et al.* revealed the large number of organizations involved in bandicoot recovery. Similar programs are described by Menkhorst *et al.* for the orange-bellied parrot and by Smales *et al.* for the helmeted honeyeater. Participants included one or more state and federal wildlife and land management agencies (including research and regional management branches), City and Shire councils, university research faculties and students, and often several non-government groups with various orientations to the issue and diverse backgrounds. This democratic approach is essential; it shares responsibility and opportunity, fosters a broader range of ideas, skills and perspectives and builds more effective programs. Failure to collaborate, in fact, may consign endangered species programs to a low-profile, slow-moving, unfocussed condition. On the other hand, large coalitions may have difficulty reaching a consensus, their decision-making may be cumbersome, slow and incremental. They may get side-tracked by political considerations rather than staying task-oriented. Often, leadership and roles are not clear, and conflict may become unmanageable. Interests may vary over time. Other problems were noted, delays and failure to use scientific information in decision-making being only two. These organizational problems are often intractable and persistent. Regardless, all these program problems call for professional and explicit management.

Other problems within endangered species programs are limitations on the availability of qualified researchers, managers with heavy workloads, and uneven or minimal funding and organizational commitment. These problems must be redressed, if we are to be successful.

## *Usefulness of Several Powerful Tools*

Although the Conference revealed a number of serious problems facing the conservation of small populations, it countered the problems with several powerful conceptual and technical tools—as it was intended to do. The case study format explained their functioning and permitted some preliminary assessment of their utility.

Foremost among these is population viability assessment (PVA), which constitutes an essential foundation for any endangered species recovery program. As Lacy and Clark described in their application of the procedure to the bandicoot case, the simulation approach projects what is most likely to happen to a small population over time, given the population parameters known or estimated from field data and the kinds and frequency of stochastic events. The benefits are clear: this readily available and 'user friendly' computer model can quantify the cumulative impacts of many forces impinging on a population (when intuition and subjective synthesis fail), identify the risks that most threaten the population and assess the impacts of possible management actions. Although Lacy and Clark identified certain needs for future use of PVAs (including model refinement, more precise data, and monitoring to confirm model predictions), the power of this tool is obvious. The results of PVAs can be used to set target numbers and populations, which can then be used in agency planning, scheduling and funding of endangered species recovery programs, and to garner public and government support for such programs.

Genetic studies are critical for both wild and captive small populations. Robinson *et al.* explained very clearly the genetic problems facing small populations, emphasised the importance of calculating effective population size, outlined their assessment of the bandicoot situation and recommended intensive management actions. Considering the goal of maintaining the wild population as well as establishing one or more captive populations—and such is the case for many recovery programs—genetic management and monitoring demand careful attention.

Decision analysis was used by Maguire *et al.* in the eastern barred bandicoot program to assess the risks and management options with subjective and objective expert advice. Although the analysis was not carried through to its final stages, the initial stages of defining the problem and soliciting information demonstrated the value of this approach. The analysis examined the costs and benefits of various management options for the Hamilton population, and simulation modelling predicted the probability of extinction and the impacts of management procedures on the population's growth. This technique makes explicit how decisions are made and allows for continual, explicit evaluation of the decision process. It helps bring to light all relevant information and possible decision options for consideration and offers team members a sense of responsibility and of participation. All endangered species programs could benefit from this rational approach.

Adaptive management, as illustrated by Arnold *et al.*, is yet another important principle for improved management and conservation of small populations. 'Planning by feedback' maximises the chances of success by responding closely and quickly to changing circumstances, rather than the traditional, rigid 'pre-planning' that has long characterised bureaucracies. Adaptive management of small populations is dependent entirely on regular monitoring of the population's status and the effectiveness of management actions; Minta *et al.* sought to establish sound monitoring procedures that reflected the biology of the bandicoots as well as practical demands. Such an approach promotes critical thinking, self-evaluation and accountability.

Captive husbandry and breeding are necessary techniques in more and more endangered species cases as onsite maintenance of populations becomes more problematic. Captive programs for the eastern barred bandicoot, helmeted honeyeater, orange-bellied parrot and Leadbeater's possum are all mentioned in this volume. Offsite propagation of endangered plants (such as the southern Australian daisy) is also carried out. The benefits include providing insurance against loss of remnant wild populations and building up numbers for release into the wild. As Clark *et al.* point out, zoos are experienced leaders in captive management; they have developed studbook data sets, applied genetic theory, developed regional and international management schemes and investigated new technologies.

Among the important scientific tools to improve management and conservation of small populations, the use of models cannot be overestimated. Lindenmayer *et al.* described the use of BIO-CLIM to model the effects of climate on the distribution of Leadbeater's possum; this model can be tested by comparison with current and projected distributions and can predict the effects of climatic change on species distribution. Other models presented in this Conference were the descriptive model of the extinction process by Clark *et al.*, the population viability assessment by Lacy and Clark, simulation modelling as part of decision analysis by Maguire *et al.* and the modelling of effective population sizes by Robinson *et al.* Modelling forces researchers and managers to think about systems, about what variables are important and how they are related, and about the quality and completeness of their data.

The in-depth coverage of the eastern barred bandicoot case showed the value of a multidisciplinary approach to endangered species recovery. Ten of the papers here pertained directly to bandicoot recovery, and the exclusion of any one field may have jeopardised the program's success. The conference itself served for cross-fertilization of ideas among researchers, and data from diverse sources are being considered by managers at both state and local levels. Smales *et al.* also recognised the necessity of the multidisciplinary approach. The temporal, spatial and complexity scales involved in conservation—*i.e.* achieving the ultimate goal of self-sustaining, evolving, structurally and functionally sound ecosystems— are almost unimaginable. Surely, no one discipline is sufficient to understand and master them.

Another important scientific tool is the compilation of data from all known sources and its synthesis at appropriate scales. Clark *et al.* reported that, although biological research in Australia has increased dramatically in recent decades, field surveys have not been adequately reported, and literature reviews and consolidation of published data are rarely sufficient to prepare sound management guidelines. The Department of Conservation, Forests and Lands' *Atlas of Victorian Wildlife* and the Royal Australasian Ornithologists Union's *Atlas of Australian Birds* are extremely useful models. These databases and others, such as the Entomological Society of Victoria's *Preliminary Distribution Maps of Butterflies in Victoria,* can indicate future research needs.

## The Need for Ecosystem Management on a Global Scale

It is clear from the introductory remarks, all the case histories and the workshop sessions that it is paramount for Australia—and for all nations—to proceed to ecosystem management as the dominant management tool without delay. In order to save endangered species, which evolved in ecologically complex contexts, it is necessary to salvage whole assemblages of flora and fauna, or as Yen *et al.* said, 'large-scale reservations of indigenous communities'. There are so many threatened species that to attempt to save them individually would exceed all human resources and abilities. Many authors recognised habitat protection as the key to conservation, but this must be interpreted in the largest possible sense. Ecosystem preservation is the most economical and efficient way to achieve long-term conservation and prevent future extinctions, but it will necessitate reintroductions and restorations, captive breeding, and many other difficult and expensive means.

Enabling public policy to achieve this end was called for in the workshops. The *Flora and Fauna Guarantee Act,* if broadly interpreted and effectively implemented, will be a milestone and a model for the rest of the world. The *Charter for Invertebrates,* adopted by the Council for Europe in 1986, should receive more attention, as called for by Yen *et al.* Additionally, technical workers must be able to describe the extent of what needs to be protected; expanded and refined models of ecosystem functioning and more sophisticated systems thinking, as described above, are needed. Finally, institutions must develop the capacity to implement these broadscale aims effectively and efficiently.

## The Need to 'Sell' the Conservation of Biodiversity

A final conclusion to be drawn from the Conference Proceedings is the continuing need to build support from the public and from government. Yen *et al.* pointed out special problems in garnering support for invertebrates, but the very fact that all the species described here were permitted to drop to their present low numbers speaks harshly of the failure of conservationists to 'sell' conservation to the public, despite a groundswell of concern and initiative that seems to be growing—from the Hamilton Institute of Rural Learning's long-term efforts in bandicoot conservation and Friends of the Helmeted Honeyeater to the highest levels of government. Freeman's introductory 'game' at the Conference sought to elicit and articulate the values of wildlife, values shared by concerned citizens everywhere. Feilman reinforced the commitment of the zoo world to conservation and described its strong and unique qualifications. The demand, too, is growing for some real goals to be achieved. The Minister for Conservation, Forests and Lands pointed to the accomplishments of her Department—the tremendous promise of the *Flora and Fauna Guarantee Act* and the State Conservation Strategy and the commitment of substantial funds for research and management of numerous species. Saunders contrasted CFL's current strong commitment, increased resources and scientific strengths with some of the gaps in management knowledge of just a few years ago.

There is, nevertheless, as the workshop sessions amply demonstrated, a need for more effective private and corporate funding; greatly expanded and tailored programs for community education, awareness and involvement; more intelligent media coverage; breaking down of barriers and stereotypes; increased communication between government wildlife agencies, universities and non-governmental conservation organizations—in short, increased understanding of the value of biodiversity and the reasons for preserving it.

# Index